THE ROAD TO JONESTOWN

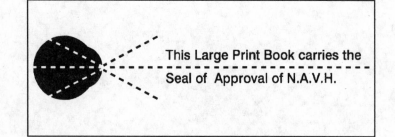

This Large Print Book carries the
Seal of Approval of N.A.V.H.

THE ROAD TO JONESTOWN

JIM JONES AND PEOPLES TEMPLE

JEFF GUINN

THORNDIKE PRESS
A part of Gale, Cengage Learning

GALE
CENGAGE Learning·

Farmington Hills, Mich • San Francisco • New York • Waterville, Maine
Meriden, Conn • Mason, Ohio • Chicago

GALE
CENGAGE Learning®

Copyright © 2017 by 24 Words LLC.
Photo credits: 1: Courtesy of Jim Jones Jr.; 2: Courtesy of Bill Manning; 3: From the Collection of Avelyn Chilcoate; 4, 5, 8, 10: Courtesy of Special Collections & University Archives, San Diego State University Library & Information Access; 6, 9: AP Photo; 7: Photo by Diana Andro/24 Words; 11, 14: Courtesy California Historical Society; 12: AFP/Getty Images; 13, 26, 28, 29, 30, 32: Photo by Ralph Lauer/24 Words; 15, 16: Courtesy of the Ukiah Daily Journal; 17: AP Photo/str; 18: Bettman/Getty Images; 19, 20: The Washington Post/Getty Images; 21, 23, 25: David Hume Kennerly/Getty Images; 22, 24: Courtesy of Gerald Gouveia; 27: New York Times Co./Getty Images; 31: AP Photo/Jeff Chiu

Thorndike Press, a part of Gale, Cengage Learning.

LIBRARY OF CONGRESS CATALOGING-IN-PUBLICATION DATA

Names: Guinn, Jeff, author.
Title: The road to Jonestown : Jim Jones and Peoples Temple / By Jeff Guinn
  Waterville : Thorndike Press, 2017.
Description: Large Print Edition. | Waterville : Thorndike Press, 2017. | Thorndike press large print popular and narrative nonfiction | Series: Includes bibliographical references.
Identifiers: LCCN 2017009011 | ISBN 9781410498656 (hardcover) | ISBN 1410498654 (hardcover)
Subjects: LCSH: Jones, Jim, 1931-1978. | Peoples Temple. | Jonestown Mass Suicide, Jonestown, Guyana, 1978. | Large type books.
Classification: LCC BP605.P46 G85 2017b | DDC 289.9—dc23
LC record available at https://lccn.loc.gov/2017009011

Published in 2017 by arrangement with Simon & Schuster, Inc.

Printed in the United States of America
1 2 3 4 5 6 7 21 20 19 18 17

For Bob Bender and Johanna Li

CONTENTS

7

PROLOGUE:
GUYANA,
NOVEMBER 18–19, 1978

During the late afternoon on Saturday, November 18, 1978, garbled radio messages began reaching Georgetown, the capital city of Guyana on the South American coast. They seemed to be panicky reports of a plane crash, probably in the dense jungle that swept from the outskirts of the city all the way northwest to the Venezuelan border. Operators at Georgetown's Ogle Airport, who received the messages, passed them on to personnel at Guyana Defence Force headquarters; the GDF comprised the country's sparse, underequipped military. The GDF duty officers knew of no scheduled military flights, so the crashed plane, if there was one, wasn't theirs.

About 6 p.m., a Cessna swooped in from the northwest and landed at Ogle, a small, secondary Georgetown airport used mostly by the military. Besides its pilot, it carried two additional passengers — the pilot of another, abandoned plane, and a wounded woman named Monica Bagby. The two pilots, sources of the earlier messages, were almost equally incoherent in person. What they did manage to relate wasn't about a plane crash, but rather an attack at a remote airstrip. Earlier in the afternoon, the Cessna and a second craft, an Otter operated by Guyana Airways, flew to the tiny jungle outpost of Port Kaituma to pick up a large party there, including a U.S. congressman, his staff, and some others. In all, there were thirty-three people waiting at the narrow landing strip, too many to fit in the planes, which had a combined capacity of twenty-four. While the prospective passengers decided who would fly out immediately and who would have to wait for an additional plane, they were attacked by men with rifles and shotguns. The victims in the attack were unarmed, and the result was sheer slaughter. The Otter was so riddled with bullets during the barrage that one of its twin engines was destroyed, its tires were flattened, and it couldn't fly. Its pilot fled to the Cessna, which was still operational. The Cessna pilot, feeling helpless to intervene and wanting to save his own life, taxied from the gunfire and bodies and flew away, taking with him the Otter pilot and a woman who'd been wounded when the attack began as she boarded the Cessna.

Now, at Ogle, they described the gruesome scene at the Port Kaituma airstrip. One of the certain dead there was the congressman, and also some reporters who were with him. Other attack victims were badly wounded. Those who suffered slight injuries or seemed initially unscathed ran into the jungle. The witnesses at Ogle didn't know whether the one-sided firefight ended then or not. There were so many men with guns, lots of fallen bodies, pools of blood.

Their account was immediately relayed to the office of Prime Minister Forbes Burnham. Although the details were sketchy, they were enough to confirm where the slaughter must have been instigated: *Jonestown.*

For more than four years, members of an American group called Peoples Temple had been carving out a 3,000-acre farm community in the heart of the near-impenetrable jungle. The spot was about six miles from Port Kaituma. They'd named the settlement for their leader, Jim Jones. The Guyanese government initially welcomed the newcomers. A colony of Americans in Guyana's North West District provided a welcome barrier to intrusions by Venezuela, which claimed much of that region and sometimes threatened invasion. But Jones and his followers soon proved troublesome. They set up schools and a medical clinic without regard to the regulations of their new home country, and protested when ordered to comply with Guyanese policies. Jones had legal problems back in America that spilled over into Guyanese courts, and, most irritating of all, relatives of some Jonestown residents claimed that their family members were being held there against their will. Leo Ryan, a U.S. congressman from the Bay Area of California, inconvenienced the Guyanese government by insisting that he visit Jonestown to investigate. A few days previously, Ryan had arrived in Guyana with a TV crew and print reporters in tow, along with some of those raising the ruckus — Concerned Relatives, they called their organization. The visit was messy from the beginning. Jones said he wouldn't let Ryan, the media, or the Concerned Relatives into Jonestown. Ryan made it obvious he'd go there anyway and demand entrance, with the press recording it all and making Guyana look foolish and primitive to the whole world. After much negotiation, Jones grudgingly agreed to let Ryan and some others in. They'd flown out of Georgetown on Friday, November 17, in the company of a staffer from the U.S. embassy who'd reported back that night that things were going well. And now, this.

There were difficulties maintaining direct radio communication between Georgetown and Port Kaituma. Besides the near-incoherent initial testimony from the three attack survivors in the Cessna, no one in Georgetown had access to additional information. They had to guess what might be happening, with only one thing certain: the United States government would be furious.

Guyana was a proud, though economically struggling, socialist nation. Still, its geographic proximity as well as reluctant, pragmatic acceptance of American power made it crucial to get along with the United States. If a U.S. congressman was really dead, the American government might very well send in troops, and that violation of Guyanese sovereignty, with its potential for international humiliation, couldn't be risked. About 7 p.m. on Saturday, Prime Minister Burnham convened a meeting in his office with John Burke, the U.S. ambassador. He also included his top ministers, and officers of the GDF and the National Service, Guyana's military training program for teens. The National Service had a jungle camp about forty miles from Jonestown.

Burnham told Burke what little he knew. It was impossible, the prime minister said, to do much immediately. It was virtually impossible to land a plane at Port Kaituma after dark — the narrow airstrip was gouged out of the triple-canopy growth and would have to be illuminated by lanterns. There was no way of knowing how many gunmen had converged on the airstrip earlier, or what their intent might be beyond the murder of Congressman Ryan and his party, which appar-

15

ently included a number of residents who wanted to escape from Jonestown.

Desmond Roberts, one of the Guyanese military men at the meeting, had warned the prime minister and his staff for months that Peoples Temple was probably smuggling guns into Jonestown, but Burnham refused to investigate. Now Roberts pointed out that Jones's followers might have accumulated a considerable arsenal. How many armed men might have control of the Port Kaituma airstrip, or else lurk in the jungle outside Jonestown, awaiting fresh targets? This could be more than a single ambush. Perhaps it was a large-scale insurrection. The Jonestown settlers seemed fanatical in their loyalty to Jones. If he called for an uprising, they would surely obey.

Over the years, Guyanese immigration officials had logged Americans as they arrived to join the Peoples Temple contingent. Now a roster of Jonestown residents was brought in and studied. It seemed that among the nine hundred or so Americans assumed to be living there, perhaps one hundred were men of fighting age, many of them possibly Vietnam veterans who knew how to handle guns in jungle firefights. The GDF couldn't blunder in. Caution was required.

Ambassador Burke demanded that the GDF make every effort to get into the area as soon as possible. He was particularly concerned about those wounded at the Port Kaituma airstrip. They needed immediate protection and medical assistance. And, he insisted, whoever perpetrated this outrage must be brought to justice as soon as possible by the Guyanese government. America expected nothing less.

Burnham promised Burke to do what he could. GDF troops would immediately be flown to an airstrip at Matthews Ridge, a community of 25,000 about thirty miles from tiny Port Kaituma. From there they would take a train partway, then night march through the jungle, reaching Port Kaituma around daylight. Then they would assess the situation and take appropriate action. Burnham asked that the ambassador urgently convey to the American government his deep personal regret regarding this incident. It should be noted, the prime minister said, that the Guyanese government had done all it could to facilitate Congressman Ryan's visit. With that, the meeting broke up. It was about 9 p.m. If any attack survivors remained at the Port Kaituma airstrip, they were still unaided after at least four hours.

Roberts put together a contingent of troops. There weren't many available, perhaps a hundred. They were herded onto transport planes and flown to Matthews Ridge. They disembarked and boarded a train, rumbling into the night toward Port Kaituma. Halfway there they disembarked; to Roberts's great displeasure, he'd been ordered to stop at the National Service camp and gather some of the teenagers there into his force. He thought that was a terrible idea — no one knew what kind of fight the troops might have to make, and kids with guns would only add to the danger. But he obeyed his superiors. Now the group totaled about 120.

They went forward on foot — stealth was required, since gun-wielding Jonestown insurrectionists might be anywhere. Jungle marches were difficult even in daylight, and nearly impossible at night. The northwest Guyanese jungle was among the world's most dense, and infested with poisonous snakes and aggressive, biting insects. There had been a tremendous storm in the area the previous afternoon, and with almost every step the soldiers' boots sank into thick, gooey mud. But they slogged ahead, and reached Port Kaituma around dawn. There was no sign of opposition, armed or otherwise. Some soldiers were left to secure the airstrip and radio Georgetown that planes could fly in to evacuate the wounded and airlift bodies out. Ryan was confirmed among the five dead. There were many wounded, several seriously and in need of urgent medical care if they were to survive. Most of the soldiers cautiously continued down the red dirt road out of Port Kaituma into the wild. After four miles, they reached the narrow cutoff that led to Jonestown. The Peoples Temple farm was now just another two miles away. The soldiers lacked combat experience. They advanced slowly, certain a fight was imminent. Gunmen might be waiting for them anywhere. But no attack came.

As the sun rose, the air grew stifling. Each breath seared the nostrils and lungs. The jungle was soggy from the previous day's violent storm. As the soldiers finally neared Jonestown, clouds of steam wafted up from the ground, making it difficult to see. Around them they heard jungle sounds — birds squawking, monkeys howling, the rustle of unseen animals in the nearby brush — but, as they reached the settlement perimeter, the area in front of them was eerily quiet. That suggested ambush, with a well-armed squadron of Jonestown militia lurking silently in wait until the interlopers came within range. The thick ground fog made it impossible to see more than a few feet ahead. Some of the soldiers couldn't even see their feet; their boots were obscured by steamy morning mist.

In whispers, officers ordered the men to spread out and surround the central area of the settlement. From previous visits by Guyanese military and government officials, it was known that a sizable pavilion dominated there. It was as good a point as any on which to converge.

The ring of soldiers tightened, all of them waiting for the inevitable shots indicating that the Jonestown gunmen were in place and finally firing. But there was no noise at all. The tension heightened, and then the soldiers found themselves stumbling over something, maybe logs placed on the ground by Jonestown rebels to impede them. When the soldiers looked down and waved away what they could of the ground fog, some of them screamed, and a few ran howling into the jungle. Their officers came forward, peered down, and what they saw made them want to scream, too. But they maintained a shaky composure, and did what they could to regroup their men. The pavilion loomed, and they wanted to go there, but the way was blocked by what lay on the ground, in every direction. As the fog lifted and they could see better, they got on the radio and reported back to Georgetown that something terrible had happened in Jonestown, something even worse than armed insurrection and the attack at the Port Kaituma airstrip. They struggled to find the right words. What they had found in Jonestown that morning was almost beyond imagination, let alone description:

Bodies everywhere, seemingly too many to count, innumerable heaps of the dead.

■ ■ ■ ■

PART ONE:
INDIANA

■ ■ ■ ■

CHAPTER ONE:
LYNETTA AND JIM

The way Lynetta Putnam Jones chose to remember it, she began life in privileged circumstances, was married only once to a handicapped veteran of World War I, was terribly mistreated by him and his cruel family, gave birth to a baby boy after a near-death mystic vision, faced down Depression-era bankers and backwoods religious charlatans, reformed a state prison system, unionized mistreated plant workers, and raised the world's greatest man, who was in fact more god than human thanks almost entirely to the constant nurturing of his devoted mother.

None of it was true, beginning with her name.

Lunett Putnam was born to Jesse and Mary Putnam on April 16 in either 1902 or 1904. Her birth records can't be found, and later in life she mentioned both birth years, occasionally throwing in 1908 as well. Even her birthplace is disputed. It's most often assumed to be Princeton in the southwest corner of Indiana, but some researchers believe she was born in Mount Carmel, a small Ohio town outside Cincinnati. Wherever and whenever she entered the world, afterward the girl periodically tinkered with her name, becoming Lunette, then Lynette in various census reports and legal documents, before finally settling on Lynetta.

Reminiscing late in life, Lynetta described her childhood self as "pretty as the first dawn . . . and strong as a tiger, too." Because of her dark coloring, people often mistook her for an Indian — as an adult, Lynetta would frequently claim Indian blood, though there is no record that she had any. Her parents wanted her to act like "a china doll," but she confounded them by constantly tramping in the woods, "investigating the animals." If true, this was an early example of Lynetta's lifelong trait — defying whatever was expected of her.

In a convoluted partial memoir dictated in Jonestown, Lynetta described Lewis Parker, apparently her father's foster father, as a powerful Indiana timber mill owner who helped raise her. Parker, she said, "was practically in control of what happened in southern Indiana." According to Lynetta, Grandpa Parker was renowned for kindness to his many employees, paying fair wages and constantly upgrading work conditions. In particular, he always had jobs for transients.

But he suffered business setbacks, due both to the decline of the timber industry and his insistence on putting the welfare of others before his own.

Though Lynetta's penchant for wild exaggeration makes most of her childhood and Lewis Parker tales questionable, it's certain that in her teen years the girl found herself in tough financial straits. Clearly bright and fanatically ambitious, Lynetta was sustained in these hard times by her firm belief in spirits and reincarnation — she swore she'd been a great woman in previous lives, and would somehow be again in this one. But spiritualism couldn't pay living expenses. Attractive young women in such circumstances had an obvious option, and in 1920 Lynetta took a traditional approach to female survival by marrying Cecil Dickson. She was either sixteen or eighteen years old. The marriage lasted about two years. Lynetta enrolled in Jonesboro Agricultural College in Arkansas, but dropped out after her divorce. Undaunted, she married Elmer Stephens a year later — that union lasted exactly three days, from March 12, 1923, through March 14, though their divorce was finalized only in August. (Nothing is known of either Dickson or Stephens.) Lynetta tried taking classes at a business school, but without a husband providing financial support she had to go to work. Despite being "good in writing, and that sort of thing, and mathematics," the best she could do was a factory job, which in the 1920s Midwest paid perhaps a dollar a day.

Lynetta's father had died; she never elaborated on the specific cause or date of his demise. Her mother, Mary, lived with Lynetta during her marriage to Cecil Dickson. But not long after Lynetta divorced her second husband and struck out on her own, Mary Putnam became ill, probably with tuberculosis, and died in December 1925.

A year later, Lynetta married again. Her approach to this third marriage was pragmatic. Though she yearned to be a great lady, she was currently working for a company in Evansville, Indiana. Typically, Lynetta later bragged that "I started as a secretary and in one year I [became] a top aide," but the reality was that she found herself stuck in another poorly paying, dead-end job. Her health was suffering, too. She later admitted to "some kind of a lung condition." Historian Joyce Overman Bowman has found evidence that Lynetta was treated, probably for tuberculosis, in an Illinois sanitarium. Lynetta wanted security, a life of sufficient ease wherein she could exercise her great intellectual and spiritual gifts and realize her full potential. The obvious solution was marrying well, choosing a man with a family fortune that would allow her to live in a gracious rather than a bare subsistence manner.

Sometime in 1926, Lynetta believed that she'd found him.

John Henry Jones was prominent in Randolph County, Indiana, both for his extensive farmland holdings and his politics. He proudly proclaimed himself a Democrat in a region where virtually everyone else was fervently Republican. John Henry, a devout Quaker, presided over a large family; his two marriages produced thirteen children. Their father expected them to make something of themselves, and most did. The majority, daughters as well as sons, graduated from college — John Henry sold off spare acreage to pay their tuition. As adults, several settled into the same area where they'd grown up. Randolph County was tucked near the Ohio border. Jones offspring worked in managerial capacities for the railroad, farmed, taught school, or else owned and operated local businesses (a filling station and beer garden among them). One ran the county home for orphan children. In only two cases did they fail to flourish. Billy took up with a bad crowd, and fell prey to drinking and gambling. His father mourned such dissolute ways but didn't disown him. And then there was Jim, born in October 1887 and christened James Thurman Jones, who went off to war and returned a physical wreck.

Practically from birth, Jim disappointed his

demanding father. Though a nice enough boy, he had no real ambition. He got a basic grade school education but wasn't interested in higher education. Like his father and brothers, Jim was handy with tools and every kind of machinery, so he ended up working on road crews around the state. Because automobiles were beginning to proliferate, there was always plenty of work. It was steady, if unexciting, employment, which suited easygoing Jim exactly.

It was surprising that Jim didn't marry. Most of his Randolph County contemporaries paired off early, often in high school, and started families. But he didn't, perhaps because he had the same lack of ambition in romance as in the rest of life. Jim was thirty the first time that he ever showed gumption in any form. When America entered World War I, he enlisted in the army and was sent to fight on the front lines in France. There he was caught in a German gas attack; the insidious vapors burned deep in his lungs. Jim was shipped home, a shadow of his former self. It was difficult for him to catch a full breath, and his respiratory system continued deteriorating for the rest of his life. Jim's voice was reduced to a raspy croak. He didn't talk much and was hard to understand when he did.

As a disabled veteran and one of about seventy thousand Americans victimized by gas in World War I, Jim was eligible for a military pension, though it probably amounted to no more than $30 a month. That wasn't enough to live on, so back in civilian life Jim returned to work on road crews. He wasn't able to handle much physical labor anymore, though he did his best. He also developed rheumatism and had to periodically take time off. Single, in constant discomfort, and rapidly approaching middle age, Jim led a lonely life. Then, while working with a road crew around Evansville, he met an outgoing woman named Lynette, though she also called herself Lynetta. She was either fifteen or seventeen years younger than Jim. To the astonishment of the groom's family, who assumed Jim to be a lifelong bachelor, they married on December 20, 1926, almost a year to the day after the death of the bride's mother.

Though she was now saddled with a disabled husband nearly old enough to be her father, Lynetta was still pleased to have married into a prominent family. She expected that she would now assume a more appropriate, even pampered, position in life.

She was mistaken.

The newlyweds needed a place to live, and Lynetta's new father-in-law gave them one, making a down payment on a small farm in Crete, a short distance north of Lynn, where most of the Jones family lived. But John Henry Jones didn't provide anything beyond that, though he had the financial wherewithal to give them the land outright. Thanks to him, his son and daughter-in-law now had property and the opportunity to make something of it. The rest was up to them.

They floundered from the start. There were corn and soybeans to plant and tend, and hogs to raise, slaughter, and sell. Despite her claims of a childhood spent tramping the woods and trapping animals, Lynetta in fact had no experience in any type of animal husbandry, let alone the knowledge of how to plow furrows or care for, then harvest, crops. Her husband, Jim, was more familiar with the daily demands of farming, but he often wasn't on the property. Money was needed for seed and tools and animal feed, so he worked on road crews around the state from time to time. That kept Jim away for days or even weeks at a time, leaving Lynetta on her own. Her work would have been easier with the newfangled farm machinery, but she and Jim couldn't afford any.

When Jim was home and tried pitching in on the endless chores, he tired quickly and had to sit down or even take to his bed. Lynetta couldn't have any extended conversations with her husband. His respiratory problems precluded that. In another location she might have turned to neighbors for socializing, but there weren't many. Crete was a collection of a half dozen farms and a grain elevator. Its population was twenty-eight. Four times a day, trains passed through, two whizzing by nonstop with passengers and the other pair pausing to load grain brought daily to the elevator by area farmers. In local parlance, this made Crete not a village but a "stop place." The cargo trains also hauled coal, and as soon as they pulled away Crete's residents stopped whatever they were doing and hustled to the tracks, picking up any chunks that had fallen off the cars. Even though Lynn, with its shops and grocery stores, was nearby, everyone in Crete did their best to live off the land, raising their own food and supplementing diets by picking the strawberries and raspberries that grew wild near the tracks. They called it "living smart." Jim couldn't pick berries and Lynetta, worn down herself, usually wouldn't. Their meals were sparse and unappealing. Anything beyond basic cooking required energy and commitment she didn't have. The other few families in Crete felt sorry for them — Jim was a disabled war veteran, after all — but they had all they could do fending for themselves. Everybody was wary of Lynetta, who defied local custom for women by smoking in public, instead of privately in her house. She also cursed when she felt like it, no matter who was in earshot. Lynetta enjoyed the resulting stares. If she couldn't be happy, at least she could be different.

At weekend gatherings of the Jones clan in Lynn, instead of enjoying these opportunities to socialize, Lynetta saw women with nice houses and fine things and burned with resentment. She hated her life on the Crete farm, and yearned for "much more lucrative ways to meet the tremendously high goals I [had] set."

Bad as things were in the beginning, over the next few years they grew worse. Jim's health continued deteriorating. He had to give up working on road crews, so the Jones family income dropped accordingly. Jim couldn't do much to assist Lynetta with the farm, and what he did try to do often wasn't helpful. If Lynetta had any previous respect for her husband, she lost it now: "The man [knew] nothing about stock raising or farming." They couldn't afford seed, let alone hired help. Bills piled up. Meeting the mortgage was a monthly challenge. She would have been glad to escape what she thought of as "a type of slavery," but had nowhere to go.

On the farm, at least, there was food, but unless some miracle occurred, Lynetta and Jim would not have the farm much longer. The most obvious source of financial rescue remained John Henry, her father-in-law. He'd suffered his own Depression-related financial reverses and now lived part of the time with a son's family in Lynn, and other times on his remaining acreage in Crete. But he was still reasonably well off, and so were most of the other Joneses. Maybe they'd take in Jim if the farm was lost, but for all Lynetta knew, they'd gladly see her homeless and in a bread line. She felt certain that they disliked her, which wasn't true. Lynetta's quirky personality could be off-putting, but most of her in-laws admired her spunk. Letting Lynetta and Jim struggle to make it on their own was a sign of respect. She didn't see that, and believed something needed to be done to win their sympathy, to make them more inclined to help.

Lynetta had absolutely no natural maternal instincts. She'd never wanted or intended to become a mother. Later, she would weave a tale of becoming ill and falling into a fevered vision of approaching "the Egyptian river of death." As Lynetta was about to cross, perishing in the process, the spirit of her mother appeared and told her that she could not die, because it was her destiny to give birth to a child who would become a great man.

Whether it was due to destiny or desperation, in the fall of 1930 Lynetta announced that she was pregnant. She gave birth in the Crete farmhouse on May 13, 1931, to James Warren Jones. But besides saddling Lynetta with even more responsibility, the arrival of the child changed nothing.

Jim, the baby's father, never articulated the frustration he surely felt from his escalating physical problems to an unhappy wife who was constantly critical of him and the rest of his family. But soon after the child's birth Jim snapped from the stress, suffering a complete breakdown that required months of hospitalization in nearby Oxford, Ohio. An attending physician described Jim as "nervous, emotional, irritable; nervous system & general physical condition below par." Even after being sent home, Jim required periodic return visits and treatment. He couldn't focus on the problems that his wife had no choice but to face, in particular keeping ownership of their property. Lynetta was unsympathetic — what kind of man surrendered to the heebie-jeebies? Later in Jonestown she would scornfully write, "My husband having cried tears of disappointment was resigned to letting the mortgager take the farm."

Lynetta recounted a confrontation in 1934 between herself and a representative of the bank, whom she said was ordered to throw her family out of their house and off their land. In her tale, she refused to leave until guaranteed a house in Lynn: "I intend to have a roof over my child's head come hell or high water. . . . [Tell your boss] I don't know how to play the role of 'worm' and I'm not fixing to learn." The reality was that the other Joneses stepped in. A house, not fancy but

34

perfectly adequate, was found in Lynn for Jim, Lynetta, and Jimmy Warren, as the family called the youngster. It was on Grant Street, where two of Jim's brothers already lived. Jim's army pension would have to be put toward rent, and also whatever occasional wage he might earn should his health permit a return to work. His father and brothers would assume the remaining financial responsibility. That was fine with Lynetta, but then the Joneses set out what they expected of her. While her son was a toddler, she could stay home and raise him. But once the child started school, Lynetta's in-laws would continue helping out financially only if she found a job and earned the bulk of the necessary household income.

She had no choice. Jim, Lynetta, and Jimmy Warren moved to Lynn.

CHAPTER TWO:
LYNN

Lynn, Indiana, was a crossroads town. State roads 27 and 36 intersected there, and the New York Central and Pennsylvania railroads passed through. Most of its 950 or so residents were part of families that had lived in or around Randolph County for generations. Everybody knew everyone else. It was virtually impossible to keep secrets. Living there involved an unspoken but understood obligation to fit in. Conformity was the bedrock of good citizenship. In part, Lynn existed to serve the needs of the farmers whose acreage ringed the town. Country folk came in on Saturdays to trade goods — milk, butter, eggs, fresh beef, and poultry — for things they couldn't grow or make themselves. Lynn offered them the services of a doctor, dentist, and veterinarian, who were often paid in chickens or homemade pies.

There were a few grocery stores in Lynn, as well as a barber shop, a café or two, a drugstore, a daily newspaper, a pool room, and several churches, which reflected the integral role religion played. As in the rest of the traditionally conservative state, evangelical Protestantism reigned. Lynn had small Methodist, Disciples of Christ, Nazarene, and Quaker churches, but not a Catholic one. If any Catholics lived in Lynn, they kept their faith quiet and went to mass somewhere else.

Lynn was a friendly place. People living there worked hard to keep it that way. Those who were better off didn't flaunt it. Everyone dressed the same, clean clothes but nothing fancy. Parents kept an eye on their own kids and everybody else's. No one locked their doors when they went out, secure in the knowledge that nobody from Lynn would steal, and that their neighbors would be on the lookout for any suspicious strangers. There was a comforting sense of shared schedules — on Wednesday nights in nice weather, everyone gathered downtown to watch free movies shown on a sheet tacked up on the side of a building. Westerns, with their inevitable good-guys-whip-the-bad-guys plots, were always most popular.

Saturdays were shopping days. Sundays meant church. Everybody in town went. There were no rivalries between preachers or congregations. Often on major holidays, Lynn ministers would combine their flocks for collaborative services. Every Friday during the last class period, Lynn high schoolers gath-

37

ered in the gym, where town preachers took turns giving hour-long talks on living right and growing up clean.

Men in Lynn had social clubs — the Odd Fellows and the Red Men's lodges were popular, and in the 1930s the Masons were the most prominent, though in the 1910s and 1920s the Ku Klux Klan was foremost. The power base of the Klan had drifted north into Indiana and became the largest organization of any kind in the state. In a single year, from July 1922 to 1923, its registered Indiana membership ballooned from 445 to almost 118,000. Unlike its focus in the South, the Klan in Indiana spent little time promoting racial hatred. There weren't enough black people in Indiana (less than 3 percent of the state population) to make that paramount, though maintaining white supremacy and racial purity was always part of any Klan agenda. Instead, the Indiana Klan stressed better public education and Prohibition, both issues that played well throughout the state, particularly in rural areas. Klan leaders cannily insinuated their group into small towns by sponsoring community picnics and parades, paying for everything and leaving the impression that they, too, were decent people with similar conservative Christian values.

Prohibition in America, mandated by the Eighteenth Amendment in 1920, was repealed in 1933, but that made no difference in Randolph County or Lynn, which re-, mained proudly dry. Lynn preachers thundered against liquor; in such a small, insular place, it was impossible to sneak a drink without everyone else finding out. Even getting that liquor would have involved taking the bus across state lines into Ohio. The few bootleggers in the area knew better than to ply their wares around Lynn. The town pool hall, considered sinful by some because of the "dime bet" card games played there, did not serve alcohol. To this day, locals apologize for liquor stores in nearby towns. They feel tainted even by proximity.

Lynn's public school stood out, in the best way possible. For decades, rural children in Indiana received minimal education in one-room schoolhouses, with students of all ages lumped together and often instructed by teachers who had never graduated from high school themselves. But around 1910, Randolph County hired Dr. Lee Driver to restructure its public school system. Driver was a dynamo who consolidated all the one-room classrooms into full-fledged town schools, including one in Lynn. Transportation was provided. Instead of walking long distances to and from school, farm kids were picked up and brought home by buses — for the first time, they attended regularly. Driver insisted on structured curriculum, and used grant money to hire qualified teachers. High school graduation rates soon skyrocketed by 70 percent, and these kids actually learned enough to qualify for good jobs or even admission to college. Driver was eventually hired away by Pennsylvania to work the same miracles for its public schools; by then, the reputation of Randolph County schools was such that delegations from Canada and China as well as other U.S. states came to study its school system, and adapt its programs to their own. Students in Randolph County were fortunate, especially in Lynn, where courses were available in foreign languages (including Latin), advanced mathematics, and science. For the first time in memory, Lynn Bulldogs had potential career options beyond farming or factory work. Some went on to become architects, doctors, or even educators themselves.

The Depression brought about one major change in Lynn's population. It skewed younger. Previously, the majority of the residents were older, most often married people who had owned farms and raised families. When the parents reached their late fifties or early sixties and no longer could handle the hard physical labor required, they turned the farms over to their kids and moved into town. But by the early 1930s, terrible economic times found many younger couples forced off their farms and moving into Lynn with their children. The town assimilated them easily enough. Most had relatives or friends already living there. Newly arrived husbands took factory work in Winchester or Richmond, the nearest big towns. Young mothers kept house and raised children. These new arrivals automatically fell into all the familiar Lynn ways. Jim, Lynetta, and Jimmy Warren Jones, part of the esteemed Jones clan, were expected to do the same.

They didn't.

The townspeople were ready to embrace Jim and Lynetta Jones and their little boy. Everybody already knew Jim; he'd been raised there and in Crete. He'd always been considered a nice fellow, and there was universal sympathy and respect for his postwar disability. Most Lynn residents had their doubts about the government, but not the country itself. Patriots all, they honored Jim for his service and wanted to do what they could for him now. Some part-time work was found for him in one of the railroad offices, simple clerical tasks since he now couldn't handle any physical labor.

Family and generous neighbors helped the Jones family set up in their new house on Grant Street. As town residences went, it was neither distinguished nor dilapidated, just an ordinary frame structure with a pleasant porch Jim liked to sit out on in the evenings. There was also a garage — Jim and Lynetta had a car, a hand-me-down from some sibling or other but still transportation. Lots of families in Lynn didn't have cars and had to rely on buses when they needed to get anywhere beyond walking distance. Above the garage was a loft, useful for storage. But Jim and Lynetta didn't have a lot to store. The Grant Street house was minimally furnished, with gently used furniture either trucked down from the lost farm in Crete or else donated by members of Jim's extended family. So they had the basics — dining room table, a few chairs, a bed for Jim and Lynetta, and a crib for little Jimmy. A great deal could have been done to make the place more attractive, but that was a wife's responsibility and Lynetta had no knack for or interest in decorating.

The rest of Lynn wasn't automatically condemnatory of such bare-bones housekeeping. In this community of no secrets, everyone knew the other Joneses were subsidizing Jim and Lynetta. The lack of furniture, household amenities, and traditional meals could be chalked up to pride. Jim and Lynetta probably didn't want to take one more cent from his relations than they had to.

But Lynetta dreamed of a finer life. She fancied herself a writer and thought she'd been one in previous lives. She wanted conversation devoted to grand things, reincarnation and progressive, nonconservative politics, not boring chatter about drapery and pie recipes. So she spurned invitations to visit other women in town and never invited them into her home. Even out in public, shopping or attending the Wednesday night community movie, Lynetta rarely spoke to anyone, and when she did kept conversation minimal. Many felt she was taking on airs she didn't deserve — the woman couldn't even keep a decent house. But Lynetta simply didn't have anything to talk to them about and felt there was no basis for friendships.

Lynetta couldn't avoid spending time with the rest of her husband's family. Without them, she and her husband and son would have been insolvent. But she was sensitive to every word they spoke to or about her, always anticipating insults. It was particularly galling that they constantly called her "Lynette" rather than "Lynetta." When they'd first met her, she still called herself Lynette much of the time, and that was how they continued addressing her. They meant no offense, and certainly would have obliged if she'd asked them to call her Lynetta. But she didn't, preferring to assume deliberate insult. Constantly frustrated, unable in any tangible way to fulfill her ambition of being a great lady, Lynetta got through her dreary days by nurturing resentments, and imagining confrontations where she triumphed over enemies through wit and courage. Lynetta later wrote colorful accounts of these fantasies, substituting self-aggrandizing fiction for fact. But during these early years in Lynn, her only audience was her small son. Jimmy's two earliest and most enduring lessons from his mother were these: there was always some *Them* out to get you, and reality was whatever *you* believed.

Even after moving to Lynn, Jim's health continued to fail. He suffered periodic physical and emotional problems. Besides scheduled visits to the hospital in Oxford, Ohio, sometimes one of his brothers would drive him to a Dayton VA hospital for emergency treatment. Jim coughed constantly — his respiratory problems weren't helped by chain-smoking. A cigarette always dangled from his mouth. Jim's posture grew stooped, and he stopped occasionally working for the railroad. In the mornings he dragged himself out on the porch and sometimes sat there all day. People felt sorry for him. They waved when they walked by, and called out greetings. Jim responded as best he could. He could talk better some days than others. He was invariably friendly. Town children liked Jim because, unlike many grown-ups, he always called them by name. Up close, his appearance was startling. Though he was still in his midforties, Jim's face had become a mass of wrinkles and saggy skin. Before, he'd been known around town as "Big Jim" to distinguish him from his son, Jimmy. But now some people in Lynn began calling him "Old Jim" instead.

Lynetta continued keeping to herself. When she did venture into the main part of town, she made a spectacle of herself by smoking and wearing pants instead of dresses. People stared, and she glared back. When she did talk — to grocers or store clerks or to pass-ersby she absolutely had to greet — she pep-pered her conversation with swear words. By Lynn's lights, "damn" and "hell" simply did not pass a lady's lips. Lynetta used them all the time, with an occasional "bullshit" thrown in. She never understood why cursing upset so many people — they were just words. It amused her whenever her swearing bothered someone.

To an extent, everyone else in Lynn could accept even this eccentricity. But there was one thing about Jim and Lynetta Jones that set them apart in a critical way. In a town where everyone else went to church on Sundays, they never did. For this, they might have been ostracized by many devout towns-people. That they weren't was due mostly to respect for the rest of the Jones family, who could be found every Sunday dutifully at-tending Quaker services, and also out of ap-preciation for Old Jim's war service. But it was troubling.

■ ■ ■

The time finally came in the fall of 1936 when Jimmy was old enough to start first grade. Lynetta had to get a job. The area factories were hiring. It was mostly a matter of where she wanted to work. Later, Lynetta spun a tale of persecution by her in-laws. Now, she believed, they resented her for the many prospective employers clamoring to employ her — that, in fact, they really didn't want her to go to work at all: "[My husband's family felt] that one's character if a housewife was dwarfed by working outside the home, especially if she was so skillful and if her services were as much in demand as mine."

Lynetta hired on at a glass factory in Winchester. Every morning she got up and took the bus to work. Before she left, she gave Jimmy a sandwich in a sack and sent him off to school. She left her husband to his own devices. Old Jim mostly filled his time by shuffling downtown to the pool hall. It was that or sitting alone in a dreary house. When he got there, he played cards and drank coffee or soda — the owner of the place abided by Lynn custom and did not serve alcohol.

At night and on weekends when all three Joneses were at home, they had few visitors, mostly family members dropping off food, Lynetta usually being too weary or agitated to cook, or else kids from the immediate neighborhood who came by to play with Jimmy but left soon afterward, spooked by the forbidding atmosphere. Nobody ever seemed to talk at the house but Mrs. Jones, and this always took the form of diatribe rather than conversation. She'd be hollering at Mr. Jones or Jimmy, or else cussing a storm about the mean sons of bitches at work who didn't mind working a woman half to god-damn death. She didn't care who else was there to hear her. No other woman in Lynn took on so; no other husband would have tolerated it.

Still, after two and a half years, people in Lynn were used to Old Jim and Lynetta. The couple was odd, no doubt about it. But now, for the first time, little Jimmy Jones was loose on the town streets, and it soon became apparent that compared to the boy, his parents were almost normal.

CHAPTER THREE:
JIMMY

One weekend morning, twelve-year-old Max Knight and his dad drove toward the central part of Lynn. Mr. Knight operated a small airport just outside town. He always had weekend work to do, and Max liked going with him. Watching the planes, which were mostly crop dusters, take off and land was fun.

As they approached downtown, Max saw a much younger boy — he guessed the kid was maybe six — walking along the side of the road; a beagle trailed after him. The beagle looked a lot like Max's dog, Queenie. Mr. Knight agreed the resemblance was amazing, and pulled the car over so Max could hop out and get a better look. The minute Max did, the smaller boy ran away, the beagle right on his heels. Max didn't want the kid to be scared. He ran after him, yelling for him to stop. The chase lasted about a block and a half before the smaller boy tried to hide behind a tree. Max wasn't fooled. He came up to the kid and was surprised to see that he was trembling. Almost eighty years later, Max described him as "petrified for some reason, just scared to death." Max introduced himself. The other boy said his name was Jimmy. Max said, "I've got a dog that looks like your dog." Jimmy seemed to think he was being accused of pet theft. He said defensively, "It ain't my dog. It belongs to a neighbor and just followed me."

Max felt bad. He hadn't meant to upset anyone, he'd just wanted a better glimpse of the beagle who looked like Queenie. Changing the subject, he mentioned that he was out riding around with his dad, who ran the airport. Jimmy's eyes lit up when he heard that. He said he loved airplanes. Max said Jimmy ought to come to the airport sometime. Then he could see the planes up close.

The next thing Max and his dad knew, Jimmy was out at the airport every weekend, buddying up to Max and telling Mr. Knight that he wanted to be a pilot and fly airplanes himself someday. That pleased Mr. Knight. Lots of local kids liked to hang out at the periphery of the airport and watch the planes, but because Mr. Knight was so impressed with him, Jimmy got special privileges. He was allowed to go right up to the planes and touch them, and to talk with the pilots as they prepared their aircraft for flight. Soon, there was no doubt in Mr. Knight's mind:

Jimmy Jones loved airplanes more than anything else in the world, and the youngster meant it when he said that, thanks to Mr. Knight, he would become a pilot when he grew up. Max Knight started thinking of Jimmy as a little brother. Their age difference kept them from becoming running buddies, but whenever he was in downtown Lynn, Max made a point of looking his little pal up, seeing how he was doing. Jimmy hinted at a bad home life, mostly due to a mean father who scared him. Jimmy was so obviously needy — Max couldn't help liking and wanting to protect him.

Jimmy Jones had already spent considerable time scampering along Lynn's streets before he started grade school. There was nothing unusual about this. From the time they could walk, little boys in town ran all over the place. It was considered part of the natural cycle of growing up. First, they'd stick to a block or two around their homes, then gradually branch out into the neighborhood, and finally, when old enough for first grade, they'd walk to school and back. From there, it was on to the fields and woods surrounding town, always on foot until perhaps a tenth or eleventh birthday when the gift of a bicycle greatly expanded their roaming range. Parents didn't worry about them, because every grown-up in town watched over the boys.

(Girls stayed much closer to home. While boys were encouraged to get out and play, girls from a very early age were expected to stay close and help their mothers with household chores and cooking.) No matter where they went in town, Lynn kids were never unsupervised. The presence of adult strangers was always noted. The children were safe.

The unique thing about preschool Jimmy was that his parents didn't join in general supervision. But from his earliest ramblings, Jimmy still had plenty of adults watching over him. Two sets of aunts and uncles also lived on Grant Street — the aunts mothered him if Lynetta was closed up in her house, which was usually the case. Most days the Jones aunts provided snacks when Jimmy was hungry and first aid when he skinned an elbow or knee. Jimmy's first playmates were cousins. There were dozens of other little Joneses either in Lynn or out on family farms. Age-wise, Jimmy fell about into the middle. He never lacked for company. And, like all the other kids, he was back in his own home by sundown.

But Jimmy's situation changed significantly once he started first grade. His mother was at work all day, and his father still haunted the pool hall. From the day she started at the Winchester glass factory, Lynetta had a rule: Jimmy was not to come into their house until she got home. This edict quickly became known all over town. Nobody understood why, or was friendly enough with Lynetta to ask. But it engendered considerable sympathy for Jimmy, whose relatives' homes were always open to him.

Yet Jimmy seldom ended up there. Instead, he wandered Lynn's streets looking lonely and helpless. The little waif's plight seemed obvious, and around town ladies outside the Jones family did the natural thing and invited him into their homes for snacks, or even full meals when he said he was really hungry. Jimmy swore to each that her food was the most delicious he'd ever tasted. Jimmy was such a polite child, grateful for the slightest kindness. Almost every lady ended up feeling she had a bond with Jimmy — the boy seemed to find something in common with each of them, a shared interest in flowers or animals or handicrafts. This proved especially true for Myrtle Kennedy.

Myrtle was a scarecrow of a woman, six feet two inches tall and self-conscious about it. In a small town where everybody was religious, Myrtle took her faith to extremes. Orville, her husband, pastored Lynn's Nazarene church. Nazarenes were conservative in terms of social behavior — no dancing, drinking, or swearing. Nazarene women never wore sleeveless or short dresses, in fear of inflaming the sinful lust of men. In Lynn nobody tried to woo anyone else from one church to another, but Myrtle was the exception. To her, it was join the Nazarenes or go to hell. Those were the only options. On Sunday afternoons, she was known to buttonhole people on the streets and ask if they'd been to church that day — she sure hadn't seen them in the Nazarene service. Nothing delighted her more than the baptismal dunking of converts in a nearby river.

People forgave Myrtle for her zealotry because in every other way she was a lovely person. No one in Lynn was more generous to the needy. Because the train and a couple of highways ran through Lynn, in the depressed 1930s there were always tramps around town, all carefully monitored by residents. Questionable ones were hustled on their way, but harmless indigents down on their luck were usually fed. No one was more generous to hobos than Myrtle. She was renowned for baking dozens of pies and setting warm slices out on the sill of an open window so passing transients could help themselves. Along with the food came an obligation to listen awhile to Myrtle espousing the Nazarene faith. She claimed that joining her church guaranteed glory in the next life, if not this one. It was a testament to Myrtle's goodness that she kept putting out pies even though none of the tramps was ever converted.

In little Jimmy Jones, though, Myrtle sensed

Nazarene potential. After all, the child had no church. His parents never took him on Sundays, so he was growing up godless. He was an attractive child, too, dark-haired and dark-eyed like his mother, but with none of her standoffishness. The Kennedys lived directly across Grant Street from Old Jim and Lynetta. Every day, Myrtle saw poor Jimmy out wandering. It was natural for her to invite him in and stuff him with pie when he was hungry, which was all the time. Supposedly his mother gave him a sandwich to tide him over during the day, but every time Myrtle asked if he'd had something to eat, Jimmy said no, and this precious little boy would never lie.

Once the pie was consumed, Myrtle took the opportunity to share with Jimmy the Good Word of Jesus, how He wanted everybody to be a Nazarene. Unenlightened people thought Nazarene rules were too restrictive, but all they in fact did was hold everyone to standards set down in the Bible. Myrtle read to Jimmy from the Good Book. He hung on every word and remembered what he heard. Soon he was quoting scripture back to her. It was thrilling.

From there, Myrtle's next step was taking Jimmy to church with her on Sundays. Lynetta didn't care. She was always worn out from her weekday work, and if this busybody neighbor wanted to tote Jimmy off for the morning, well, that was one less thing Lynetta had to worry about on her day off. So every Sunday, Jimmy went to the Nazarene church with Mrs. Kennedy, and listened to Mr. Kennedy talk about the Lord and all the things He didn't want you doing.

After a while, Jimmy started spending occasional nights with the Kennedys. That was all right with his mother, too. Lynetta had only disdain for those who believed in some simple God up in the sky who eventually consigned everyone to heaven or hell, depending. Lynetta's spiritualism was far richer than that, involving reincarnation, one life after another, *destiny*. Sometimes in a life, which was not the only life, a person's grand destiny was thwarted by those unappreciative or jealous of someone else's superiority. That was currently happening to her. But her son in his present incarnation was going to be great. She was certain of it. Greatness wouldn't include falling for Myrtle Kennedy's Nazarene foolishness. Lynetta probably mentioned this to Jimmy now and then, just to be certain that the boy wasn't being duped. Beyond that, let him spend time with old lady Kennedy, go to church with her. It kept Jimmy out of his mother's hair, and, besides, in the grand cosmic scheme of things, Lynetta didn't think it made any difference.

But when Myrtle brought Jimmy to church,

he loved it. The child showed an amazing knack for remembering everything he heard there, the scriptural readings especially. Within weeks, he could repeat lengthy biblical passages verbatim. He couldn't wait for Sundays so he could go to church with Mrs. Kennedy. Privately, he began calling her "Mom." Myrtle was ecstatic. She'd saved a soul for Jesus. Now she'd reap her deserved reward, watching the boy as he grew in God's grace in the biblically mandated Nazarene way.

Then things took an unexpected turn. Jimmy liked the Nazarene service, but was curious about the other town churches, too. He began attending some of the revival meetings that regularly occurred in the area. All the local faiths hosted them, and there were some revivals by nonaffiliated preachers, too. After that, occasional Sundays found Jimmy in Lynn's Methodist church, or with the Quakers or Disciples of Christ. Over the next few years, he joined them all, being baptized by the ones that required it, swearing other forms of allegiance to those that didn't. Jimmy studied everything. There were Sundays when he spent part of the morning in one church service, then scampered out to catch the tail end of a different one. That certainly caught the attention of everyone in Lynn. It turned out that the little Jones boy was just as odd as his parents, though at least in a positive way. Hopefully at some point he'd settle down and pick a church for good. Meanwhile, at least he was going, which was more than could be said for his momma and daddy.

Jimmy learned alienation from his mother. The art of making others feel that they had beliefs and hopes in common was a gift all his own. And even as a small child, he had a talent for explaining away actions that seemingly contradicted his words. This was evident in his relationship with Myrtle Kennedy after he began attending other churches besides the Nazarene. With anyone else, Myrtle would have felt hurt, even betrayed. She'd set the child's feet down on the right path, and he'd wandered off it. But Jimmy somehow managed to retain Myrtle's affection. Whatever he explained to her, perhaps that he just attended other churches to see firsthand how they erred in expressing faith, it worked. Myrtle continued doting on the boy.

Later, it would often be said of Jim Jones that he used others without scruple, coldheartedly conning his way to whatever he wanted and never really caring for anyone, even those who'd helped him the most. In many instances there was ample proof, but not with Myrtle Kennedy. After Jimmy left Lynn and his life took many surprising turns, he never lost contact with the Nazarene woman who once took him in. From the big

57

city of Indianapolis, on to California where he became a famous man, even from the jungles of Guyana, every week or two of his adult life Jim Jones sat down and scribbled a note to Myrtle Kennedy, sharing with her sanitized versions of what he was up to, and expressing hopes that she was well. There was nothing in it for Jim Jones, beyond making certain that Myrtle knew he'd never forgotten her, and he remained grateful for her kindness.

In September 1977, Jim Jones would claim in an interview intended as part of a memoir that he'd never actually believed in God. He'd seen religion as an opportunity to "infiltrate" the church and turn Christians toward socialism. That might have been true. There is no way to look into someone's heart and know the truth about their faith or lack of it. It's also possible to believe fervently as a child, lose belief as an adult, and claim never to have believed at all. But of young Jimmy's early attraction to religion, there can be no doubt. To a child who by Jones's own later admission "sought approval so damn much," the church offered a perfect life's goal.

Max Knight lived in nearby Spartanburg, but whenever he was in Lynn he dropped by Jimmy's house to check on his younger friend. Once he knocked on the door and no one was home. So Max looked for Jimmy across the street at Mrs. Kennedy's house. He thought she was Jimmy's grandmother because his pal was over there so much, and there was obvious affection between them. Mrs. Kennedy said that Jimmy was probably playing in the nearby woods. Max had some time, so he wandered out there, poking around until he finally heard a loud voice off in the trees. He walked in that direction and came upon Jimmy. The little boy didn't notice Max because his back was to him. Jimmy was standing on a stump, hand pressed over his heart, preaching — Max remembered it as "really putting on a show, all about how Jesus loves you and you have to believe in Him if you want to get saved and go to Heaven." Max yelled, "Hey," Jimmy whirled and saw him, nearly fell off the stump and started crying, just like he had when Max first met him walking along with the beagle. Max couldn't understand it — he'd known Jimmy for a while now, it wasn't like he was a stranger. Jimmy probably worried that he was caught in a deception — he'd told Max and Mr. Knight over and over that he wanted to be a pilot when he grew up, and now he'd been caught doing *this*.

But Max wasn't mad. "If you want to preach, okay. Do it, if it makes you feel good." In the next few months, Max "two or three times more found him in the woods doing the same thing." Jimmy confessed that he now wanted to be a preacher, but what if other people made fun of him, or said that he couldn't? Max told him, " 'Do what you want. Don't let people stop you. Be your own man.' Later on, when we met again as adults, Jim mentioned this back to me. He said, 'I was a scared kid,' and thanked me for encouraging him."

CHAPTER FOUR: GROWING UP

As much or even more than their parents, children in Lynn emphasized conformity. They believed in and followed the same rules, respecting parents and teachers above all. This was typical throughout Indiana — according to state historian James H. Madison, "Moderation has been the Indiana way, a moderation firmly anchored in respect for tradition. Among the revolutions that have not occurred in Indiana is a generational revolt."

Lynn kids shared toys and treats. Girls learned cooking and household skills. Boys played sports, roamed the woods and fields, and never shirked chores. Usually, they grew up to be just like their parents, and that was fine with everybody.

To some small extent, Jimmy Jones fit in, at least at first. He ran the streets like everybody else, and loved the Wednesday movies and watermelon. He had a way with animals. Strays followed him everywhere. If he came over to play at your house, afterward your mother probably remarked on what a polite boy he was.

Jimmy often had great toys. Everybody knew his mother had to work because his father couldn't, and that his grandpa and uncles had to help them out financially. But Jimmy still had a lot of things. One was a toy movie projector. He bragged that he could put film in it and show a movie against a wall in his house just like the Wednesday night films in town. Everybody wanted to see it, but Jimmy's mother had a rule that he couldn't go in the house himself if his parents weren't there, let alone bring in friends. Chuck and Johnny Willmore were really interested, so after school one day Jimmy sneaked them into the house — his dad was at the pool hall, as usual — then pulled the blinds to make it all dark and showed the movie on the wall. It was really fun until his mother came home unexpectedly. She pulled off her belt and chased Jimmy around, swatting at him with it. All the time he kept screaming, "I didn't mean to do it, I didn't mean to do it," which made no sense because he obviously had. Johnny and Chuck ran off and told the other boys what had happened. All of them felt sorry for Jimmy.

It was understood, too, that things weren't entirely right between Jimmy and his father. In Lynn, sons and dads didn't bond through long talks and hugs. Instead, boys followed their fathers around, watching and learning as the older men did home repairs, worked on cars, and performed the other routine chores that their sons needed to master to get on in life. Old Jim did none of these things because he couldn't. Jimmy didn't seem to respect Old Jim too much. The only time anyone saw them interacting was when Jimmy ducked into the pool hall and asked his father for spare change. It was sad.

But sympathy went only so far. Jimmy might be forgiven for having a mean mother and sick father, but there were other things about him that set him apart, and not in good ways. Jimmy cried a lot, which boys were never supposed to do, and he cussed all the time. The other boys wondered where he learned the words. Jimmy wouldn't say. He just grinned and enjoyed how his swearing made the rest of the kids uncomfortable. All the other boys were into wrestling around, sometimes getting overzealous and doing some punching or kicking. Everybody got a bloody nose or split lip now and then, except Jimmy. He was scared of fighting and ran away whenever there was any roughhousing.

Then there were the candy bars, rare and prized treats. Jimmy had them all the time, snatching one off store shelves whenever he felt like it. The merchants allowed it because, every Saturday, Lynetta Jones came around and paid for whatever candy bars Jimmy took that week. Any other mother in Lynn would have whacked her son a good one for such behavior, but Lynetta took pride in her boy's audacity. Like her, he found ways to defy convention.

But it was the religious things that set Jimmy apart from his peers the most. All the kids in Lynn believed in God and went dutifully to church on Sundays. It was an accepted part of life. But Jimmy took it to puzzling extremes. Attending all of the town churches instead of sticking to a specific one was the least of it.

The strange religious stuff started with things Jimmy said. One day he and the Willmore brothers were playing in the loft over the Joneses' garage. There was a series of rafters up near the second-story roof; the boys thought it would be fun to try and walk out on them, balancing like tightrope walkers in a circus. The risk was real. It was a straight drop of ten feet or so to the floor beneath. Chuck and Johnny Willmore went first, going single file because the rafters were so narrow. Jimmy was right behind them. After a minute or so, Johnny got nervous and thought he might fall. But when he tried to ease back off the rafter, Jimmy wouldn't move, blocking the way to safety. Johnny yelled, "Move back." Jimmy, with a weird look on his face, blurted, "I can't move — the Angel of Death is holding me!" All three of them teetered precipitously on the rafter until Jimmy finally said the Angel had let him go. Chuck Willmore recalls, "Even at age six or whatever, I thought that was nuts."

A casket manufacturer warehoused its products in Lynn. Jimmy talked a lot about death and its inevitability. The people in charge of the casket company, like everybody else in Lynn, never locked doors. Jimmy led a contingent of kids into the warehouse one night and told everybody to climb into caskets and just lie there; that way they might find out what it felt like to be dead, get some idea of what happened to you after that. The other kids were either scared or, after a while, bored. Jimmy kept going back, but had trouble getting anyone else to come.

Jimmy briefly claimed that special powers were conferred on him by the Almighty. Challenged to prove it, he rigged a cape, probably a towel, climbed on top of the garage roof, and yelled for everybody to watch him fly. The other kids never believed Jimmy would actually jump, but he did. Instead of flying, he hit the ground hard and broke his arm. Afterward Jimmy was unabashed. He apparently still believed in his new powers even if nobody else did, but he didn't mention them again.

Around the same time came the animal funerals.

There were always dead critters of every kind in and around Lynn: roadkill like squirrels and rabbits, mice and rats caught in traps, occasional dogs and cats, always birds. They were accepted as part of the natural environment, like fallen leaves in autumn. They were either left to decay or else scraped up and tossed in the garbage. But now Jimmy Jones started reverently picking the dead things up, calling the other kids together, and performing elaborate funeral services, praying over the animal corpses, sermonizing about how God loved all his creations equally and then burying the things in matchboxes or bigger cardboard boxes, depending on their size. It was entertaining at first, but Jimmy kept on doing it and pretty soon the others his age refused to participate. That didn't discourage Jimmy. He rounded up younger kids, many of whom were flattered that someone older wanted them to play. When they found out reverent obedience was required rather than playing, they wanted to leave, but Jimmy usually scared them into staying. Even when he couldn't muster a congregation, Jimmy conducted animal funeral services on his own, even at recess in the schoolyard, where the other kids had little choice other than to watch, even if they didn't participate.

When Jimmy was ten, America's entry into

World War II provided him with a new obsession. Everyone in Lynn was gripped by war fever. It was a patriotic town. Boys in Lynn played soldier during every waking, non-school, or nonchurch minute, all of them U.S. soldiers or sailors or Marines fighting pitched battles against the Axis and winning every time.

But not Jimmy Jones. From the outset, he was fascinated with the Nazis, enamored of their pageantry, mesmerized by obedient hordes of fighting men goose-stepping in unison. Then there was their charismatic leader — Jimmy studied Adolf Hitler intently, how he stood in front of adoring crowds for hours, claiming all sorts of powers, always keeping audiences engaged with a cunning rhythm of shouting, then hushed tones, then normal conversation building back up to a bombastic finish. American newsreels and newspapers were full of Hitler and his worshipful followers. Jimmy had no shortage of study materials. Hitler was a poor boy who'd emerged to lead a mighty nation thanks to his own determination and charisma. Now the whole world knew Hitler's name, millions followed him, and multitudes trembled before him. He'd gained his power by overcoming powerful foes who looked down on him for his humble upbringing and controversial beliefs. It was inspiring.

Where the other boys pretended to be

American war heroes, Jimmy wanted to emulate Hitler. It would have been impossible to round up some of the other Lynn boys and persuade them to play Nazi storm troopers, so Jimmy turned to other recruits. The gaggle of Jones cousins included several young enough for Jimmy to bully into playing whatever roles he wanted. He herded the little ones into a field and ordered them to goose-step on command. They had trouble figuring out exactly what was required; Jimmy got mad. He cut a switch and began swatting their calves when they didn't march to his satisfaction. Some of them went home with bad bruises, and when their mothers found out who caused it, Jimmy was in big trouble with his aunts. He lost his squad of pretend Nazis, but not his fascination with Hitler. When Hitler committed suicide in April 1945, thwarting enemies who sought to capture and humiliate him, Jimmy was impressed.

Even as Jimmy was obsessed with Hitler and the Nazis, his commitment to religion never flagged. During the summer of 1942, Myrtle Kennedy and her husband lived in Richmond. No one remembers why; they moved right back to Lynn in the fall. But while they were in Richmond and school was out in Lynn, Jimmy lived with them. Lynetta was glad to have him off her hands for a few months. The Kennedys rented part of a big house; other families lived there, too, and there were kids Jimmy's age, ten-year-old Lester Wise in particular. Jimmy and Lester became summer pals, doing everything together before going their separate ways in the fall. The big thing for both of them was religion. There was a Pentecostal church in Richmond, and they went to Bible study there three or four times a week. During every Sunday worship service, the preacher always asked sinners to come up and be saved. The first week, Jimmy went up and got forgiven for his sins. Then the next Sunday, he did it again, and then every Sunday for the rest of the summer. According to Lester, "You usually didn't do that. You got saved once, and it stayed that way. Maybe you went up again sometime if you'd done something especially bad, but Jimmy, he just went every time the preacher asked. He would go up there and kneel. I thought that was a little different, but he never talked about why. He just did it."

Jimmy returned to Lynn that fall with a new quirk. All the youngsters living there were country kids, so they knew the basics of sex from the time they could toddle. Farm animals reproduced, the constant glut of mongrel puppies and kittens provided further elementary evidence of mating, and most Lynn houses were small and less than sound-proof in a time when childbirth was frequent.

Sex was everywhere; it was just that it was never acknowledged by decent people.

As usual, Jimmy Jones became the exception to the rule. He offered explicit facts-of-life lectures to younger cousins until they were sick of it. Other neighbor kids were invited by Jimmy to join him on his porch and hear all about "sexual intercourse." Where he'd learned these things, Jimmy didn't say. His aunts got wind of Jimmy's new favorite topic and warned him to stop. If they asked Lynetta to intervene, she didn't cooperate. Jimmy kept talking about the forbidden subject. But then and later in Lynn, in terms of sex Jimmy was all talk and no action. Peers remember that he never "did anything." If he had, word would have spread instantly throughout the community.

By the time he started high school, Jimmy Jones was marginalized among Lynn teens. But he was not a complete pariah thanks to his talent for compelling conversation. Even those who disliked him found themselves fascinated by whatever Jimmy talked to them about, religion and sex being his main two topics. Jimmy also had retained his knack for eliciting sympathy. For years, Lynn parents had pitied him, and sometimes excused his excesses, because of his obviously dysfunctional home life. Lynetta was initially the parent blamed most — how could a child grow up normally with a mother who smoked and swore and didn't go to church? But as Jimmy reached his early teens, there was a new rumor: Old Jim was a big-time drinker, soused at all hours. In Lynn, even an isolated incident of local drunkenness blighted collective morality. Old Jim had always been the object of pity, what with his awful combat disability and weird wife. But now his habits seemed suspicious. Every day the man staggered down the street, heading toward the pool hall. Everyone had seen him stumble, practically fall — there were days he could barely balance. And sometimes he disappeared for short stretches. Maybe drinking binges were the cause.

Other than his wife, son, and the Jones family, nobody knew about Old Jim's breakdown in 1932, or his trips for treatments. When the tales about drinking started flying, no Jones relative came forward to refute them. In that time and place, mental illness was considered even more disgraceful than alcoholism. It was better for Old Jim to be thought of as a drunk than a lunatic. In fact, he was neither. Old Jim, with his body failing and his scarred lungs convulsing, often had trouble just getting out of bed.

But the rumors proved persistent. For Jimmy truth was never an impediment to his own ambitions. He liked being seen as someone who overcame obstacles, a person espe-

71

cially deserving of sympathy and support.

Jimmy started dressing differently. High school boys in Lynn wore denim jeans and work shirts. On Sundays, white shirts and nice slacks were appropriate attire for church. Jimmy wore Sunday clothes almost every day. He was already striking, with thick, nearly black hair and dark eyes that seemed to stare right through you. Lynetta still sometimes claimed to be part Indian and now Jimmy did, too. His looks and wardrobe made him stick out.

So did the way he acted in school. In hallways between classes, Jimmy developed the odd habit of never replying when someone spoke to him first. He participated in between-class conversations only when he initiated them. Otherwise, he'd lean against a wall near the classroom door until the bell rang, then hustle inside to take his seat, always at the back of the room. It was very dramatic. Sometimes he challenged teachers about some fact or other. In a typical Indiana country school, that might have been cause for immediate expulsion, but Lynn teachers liked evidence that their students were thinking. They'd engage Jimmy in debate. He seemed to enjoy the give-and-take but never admitted being incorrect. Jimmy's grades were good, some As and lots of Bs, but he was not considered an exceptional student.

In school Jimmy was never a leader, but on

weekends and during summers he tried to be. He never liked being part of teams, staying out of pickup basketball games and bike races. The other boys thought it was because he couldn't stand losing. Besides, Jimmy wasn't a good player and often was the last boy picked. Sometimes he'd organize his own team and challenge another one to a game. Jimmy never played in these; he coached whatever squad he'd put together. Most often, Jimmy's players were younger kids who felt proud that somebody older paid attention to them.

Some Lynn old-timers vividly recall the summer of 1945, when fourteen-year-old Jimmy Jones not only formed a town baseball team, but organized and ran an entire league with teams from nearby towns. It would have been a massive undertaking for adults. Jimmy did it all by himself. He got merchants to put up money for bats and balls, then went around finding all the boys who wanted to play and getting them to commit to a formal schedule of games. Nobody was used to that. Jimmy managed the Lynn team. All the boys there and in surrounding towns rooted for the Cincinnati Reds, but only the Lynn team got to call itself the Reds because Jimmy said so.

Even though he was too young to have a license, Jimmy drove his team to games in his family's ancient Model A Ford. It had a rumble seat and most of the guys could squeeze in. The Lynn kids did pretty well, and Jimmy thrilled them by keeping detailed statistics, not just game scores but also individual stats. He did these in long, neat columns, and the other kids loved to pore over them. They'd never imagined anything so elaborate — it was Jimmy's way of demonstrating that they got something special for letting him be the leader.

But things turned sour by the end of the summer. Jimmy's loft was the team gathering place. They'd sit and listen while he lectured about previous games and what their strategies would be in the next ones. There were always lots of pets around. Jimmy took in strays all the time. He seemed to love animals, but one day some of the kids saw him lure a puppy over the open loft trapdoor and deliberately let it fall down to the hard floor below. After that, they didn't want to play on his baseball team anymore. The league fell apart.

The loft incident was a rare instance of animal cruelty on Jimmy's part. He may have abused the puppy because he was upset by something happening at home, a situation that was genuinely traumatic, especially for a teenage boy.

Lynetta Jones grew unhappier with each passing year. It became increasingly apparent that the rest of the world would never recognize how exceptional she was. She'd changed jobs a few times, ending up working in a Richmond plant that manufactured automotive rings. In this shop as in all the others where she'd worked, Lynetta was positive she was smarter than her bosses, entitled to be giving orders instead of taking them. But she remained an ordinary employee, taking the bus to and from work every day while also expected to tolerate a husband who constantly aggravated her with his wheezing, debilitated condition. Her relationship with Old Jim's family remained strained, at least from Lynetta's perspective. She suspected them of encouraging other town residents to criticize how she raised her son. Jimmy — "Jimba" was her nickname for him — was an alternating source of pride and additional frustration to his mother. On the one hand, she still fervently believed that he was selected by the spirits to be special. If Lynetta herself couldn't be famous, at least someday she might shine in her child's reflected glory. But on many days, Jimba was just one more draining responsibility. Lynetta's mothering was sporadic. Sometimes she hovered constantly, espousing her spiritual beliefs, reminding Jimba of his distinguished heritage on her side of the family. More often, she ignored him and was happy to let others assume responsibility for his care. If she talked to him at all, it was to yell about real or perceived disobedience.

Lynetta shouted at Old Jim, too. He was weak and she disdained him. In particular, Old Jim was entirely unable to perform when his long-suffering wife wanted a little pleasure in her marital bed. Sex was important to Lynetta, and about the time Jimba started high school, she took another Lynn man as her lover. The affair lasted several years. The participants were reasonably discreet, but some people in Lynn still found out about it, Old Jim's relations in particular. They were divided on the subject. The Jones men thought Lynetta was acting immorally, but some of the women sympathized. She had a hard life, after all, and her husband was so sick. Though no one directly confronted Lynetta, she understood that they knew. For almost twenty years, Lynetta had always believed that many of her in-laws despised her. Now it was true.

Jimmy also knew that his mother had a boyfriend. He was the kind of teenager who picked up on everything. By this point, it was ingrained in him that, if a side must be chosen, he would sympathize with his mother and not his father. Whatever she did, the old man deserved it.

As Lynetta embarked on her fling, Jimmy also pursued romance. Typically, he went about it differently from the other teenagers in town, and in a manner that he would repeat as an adult. In Lynn, high school dating was serious business. Most teenagers paired off early, married soon after high school or college graduation, raised families and grew old together. Today, many of Jimmy Jones's surviving peers are close to celebrating sixty-fifth or even seventieth wedding anniversaries.

In Jimmy's high school days, the acknowledged belle among the girls was Sara Lou Harlan, the daughter of the town dentist. Sara Lou was sweet as well as pretty. Most of the boys had crushes on her but respected her status as the girlfriend of fellow Bulldog Dick Grubbs. The high school community was as close-knit as Lynn itself. It was simply unacceptable to try winning away somebody else's girl.

One day Jimmy attached himself to Sara Lou. He stayed close to her everywhere at school, and when classes were over he followed her home. It was unwanted attention. Sarah Lou thought Jimmy was a jerk and asked Dick to do something about it. Dick took Jimmy aside and explained that he needed to leave Sara Lou alone, "but he wasn't interested, it had no effect. He felt like if he wanted her, he ought to have her. It was his right, and nobody else's opinion, including Sara Lou's, mattered." When Jimmy persisted, Dick would have been considered well within his rights to take him behind the school and beat him up. But Dick didn't; it was obvious to him that nothing he did would change Jimmy's mind. Maybe Sara Lou's parents could talk to him.

They did, and one day after school Sara Lou was astonished to find Jimmy Jones right there in her house, chatting with her mother and father like an old friend. The Harlans praised Jimmy's good manners to Sara Lou — wasn't he a *nice* boy? They invited him to come to church with the family on Sunday, and he did, staying for the whole service. The fact he'd somehow fooled her parents didn't do Jimmy any good with Sara Lou. She still wouldn't jilt Dick for him. Dick remembers that "it was a long while before he gave up, and then one day he just starts acting like it never happened at all."

When Jimmy finally realized he'd never get Sara, he moved on to Phyllis Willmore. Where Sara Lou was the school pinup, Phyllis was the town's smart girl. Jimmy had more luck with her. The other kids thought Phyllis and Jimmy had a strange relationship because they sat around on her family's porch reading books together. Once in a while, they held hands. Phyllis recalls that it was less a romance than two kids making their first awkward attempts at dating. They went to church togther — Jimmy took her to the Nazarene service, and went with her to the Church of Christ — and once to the movies in Richmond. Phyllis's mother drove them there. The kids sat in the backseat of the car. Mrs. Willmore stayed to see the show. In the theater, Jimmy made a big deal out of getting her settled in a good seat before he joined Phyllis several rows away.

Jimmy and Phyllis never got beyond a mostly platonic relationship. They quickly fizzled as a couple, though they remained on friendly terms. But afterward, Phyllis found very few chances to talk to Jimmy. He had another demand on his time.

A few years earlier, a new faith came to Lynn, a radically different one from the others that had been long established in town. A Mr. Mc-Farland took over an old storefront on Highway 36, just across from a grocery store, and announced the opening of an Apostolic church. He stuck up flyers all over town promising that if people came to the services, there'd be speaking in tongues. The pastors of Lynn's other churches didn't like it. These Apostolics, whom some called Pentecostals, were actively trying to *recruit.* Briefly, it worked. People in Lynn had never seen anything like it, folks actually dropping down on the floor, rolling around, babbling gibberish. It was wonderful entertainment. Townspeople went once or twice, gawked, and returned to their more traditional churches. The congregation that the newly arrived

Apostolics was able to retain was drawn almost exclusively from outside town, usually southerners who'd moved up to Indiana and were used to such services. There was no denying that the Apostolics put on a show, not just on Sundays but also occasional weeknights and Saturdays. On Saturdays, farmers would come in to town to trade at the Highway 36 grocery, then stand outside the storefront across the street and shake their heads in amused wonder at the holy rollers inside making all their crazy noise during Saturday night service.

Often, Jimmy Jones was inside among the Apostolics, watching carefully, soaking everything in. Their pastor had a lot more freedom than the ministers in Lynn's other churches. He didn't stick to some rigid format. Instead, he'd jump and yell or even howl if the spirit moved him. The reactions of the congregation were wonderful, too. They yelled themselves, and sang and danced and turned their gatherings into exuberant celebrations.

Jimmy still spent most Sundays popping in and out of all the Lynn churches. But the holy rollers held a special place with him. He took to attending their weekend revivals out in the country. At some point Lynetta noticed and didn't like it. Even to her, those people were *strange.* She later described a dramatic scene when she confronted the holy roller leader, a woman, and ordered her to leave her son alone because Jimba was having terrible nightmares caused by dreadful things he heard during her services. The awful woman actually had Jimba preach, because when he did awed listeners contributed more than usual to the collection plate. Like most of Lynetta's remembrances, it's not true. Mr. Stump, a pipefitter during the week, conducted the local Apostolic services. Nobody remembers Jimmy delivering sermons in any of them. But he began sermonizing somewhere else, and on the most controversial topic possible.

Randolph County was unique in rural Indiana for another reason besides its exceptional public schools. It was possible for white country people to go years without seeing, let alone interacting with, a single person of color. But there were three black enclaves in Randolph County, clusters of ramshackle homes that were too tiny to achieve official town status. Still, there were collectively several hundred African Americans in the county, mostly farmhands who came in to Winchester and Lynn on weekends to trade and shop. They were not treated as equals. Black children didn't attend the fine Lynn school. White mothers would never dream of inviting "colored" kids over to play with their children. But white people in Lynn saw black people, stood in line with them in town shops, even chatted with them informally outside the grocery store or veterinarian's office.

Like all the other white kids in Lynn, Jimmy Jones grew accustomed to being around black people. Unlike his peers, he demonstrated genuine interest in their lives beyond his hometown's unwritten social boundaries. On trips to Richmond, the nearest "big city" with its population of about thirty thousand, Jimmy noticed and was bothered by African Americans being treated badly by whites — they were called insulting names and ordered around like stray dogs. Quite a few poor blacks lived in Richmond, since it had factory jobs available, and others drifted through on a regular basis. Wayne County, where Richmond was located, had the derogatory statewide nickname of "Little Africa." And so, while he was still in high school, Jimmy would sometimes get up on Saturday mornings, put on his best clothes, and take the bus seventeen miles to Richmond. Then he'd walk from the bus station to the poor part of town by the railroad tracks. Black indigents congregated there. Jimmy would find someplace to stand and then start preaching, always about everyone being equal in God's eyes, how it was wrong to look down on anybody, especially for the color of their skin. The white kid promised black down-and-outers that if they stayed strong, better times were coming. His exact words are lost, but old-timers in Richmond remember hearing about it.

Back home in Lynn, Jimmy went out of his way to emphasize his faith. He took to ostentatiously carrying a Bible everywhere, an affectation that amused rather than impressed the town's other teenagers. They took it for granted that strange Jimmy Jones was destined to be a preacher. That earned him a significant high school accolade. The Bulldogs were about to take on a rival school in some sporting event of particular significance, and Jimmy was asked to conduct a mock funeral service for the other team at a pregame Bulldog pep rally. He enthusiastically complied, astonishing some with how fervently he consigned the opposing team to its mass grave. One classmate recalled, "He had a flair for the dramatic."

That pep rally funeral was teenage Jimmy's last memorable moment in Lynn. In 1948, during the summer between his junior and senior years, he and his mother moved to Richmond.

CHAPTER FIVE: RICHMOND

For twenty-two years, Lynetta endured rather than in any sense enjoyed marriage to Old Jim Jones. All she had for solace was her lover, and when he moved away Lynetta couldn't stand life in Lynn anymore. She worked in Richmond, which had a few cafés and movie houses and a nice big park. Why not at least escape her useless husband and his nasty, carping family and live there instead?

Jimmy was about to become a high school senior, but he was ready to leave, too. He had no close friends in Lynn, and though he could have remained with his father, he disdained Old Jim as much or more than Lynetta did. Recently, he'd started hinting that his dad periodically became violent and beat his wife and son. That didn't gain much traction in Lynn — everybody was willing to believe Old Jim was a drunk, but a man who could barely stagger down the street was unlikely to summon the energy for domestic violence. And if Jimmy's dad beat him, where were the bruises? Childhood pal Max Knight recalls how Jimmy cried when describing Old Jim's alleged brutality.

Old Jim didn't return his wife's and son's contempt. He expressed his sorrow at their abrupt departure with actions rather than words. After Lynetta and Jimmy were gone, Old Jim couldn't bear living alone in the Grant Street house. Lynn had a hotel, and he took a room there. His family provided whatever money he needed beyond his army disability pension. His physical deterioration worsened, and James Thurman Jones died of respiratory disease in May 1951. He was sixty-three and looked ninety. His enduring love for Lynetta is reflected in his burial marker, a double tombstone in Mount Zion Cemetery with Old Jim's name and dates of birth and death carved on one half and her name and date of birth on the other. Underneath their names is a short inscription: "Everyone in the World is my Friend." No one recalls seeing Lynetta and Jimmy at the funeral. Afterward, though, Lynetta filed a widow's claim for Old Jim's army pension.

In the fall of 1948, Jimmy enrolled in a Richmond high school. For a change, his clothes didn't set him apart. Teens in this big town dressed nicer than Randolph County kids, no patched work shirts and pants or clodhopper boots. He retained his old habit of not talking unless he wanted to start a conversation. Surviving Richmond classmates have vague recollections of him at best, generally memories of his thick dark hair and striking eyes. Jimmy's courting technique remained unsophisticated. One girl was greatly offended when Jimmy, a total stranger, came up to her in a hallway and grabbed her hand. Richmond boys were supposed to be polite. She yanked her hand away and complained about it to some other girls.

But Jimmy made a few friends, all of them part of the school Christian Youth Fellowship. They called him Jonesy, and invited him to join them for late-night donuts as they endlessly debated the best way to live righteous Christian lives. The consensus was what they termed "Christian communism," since they believed that "from each according to ability, to each according to need" was the proper church approach. They didn't share this conclusion outside their group. The Richmond High Christian Youth kids weren't advocating communist *government,* where the state owned everything and told you what you had to do. They just wanted their churches to voluntarily adopt a philosophy that mandated compassion and equal treatment for all. But the Cold War was in full flower, and communism in any form was anathema to most Americans. The youngsters kept their beliefs to themselves.

Jimmy wasn't remotely challenged by the school curriculum. His education in Lynn had him so academically advanced that he was allowed to skip some Richmond classes and graduate a semester ahead of all the other twelfth graders. This was a good thing, because while in school Jimmy also held down a full-time night shift job. Lynetta's salary at Perfect Circle, the piston rings manufacturer in Richmond, couldn't cover expenses for herself and her son. Though she would later claim to be a senior employee responsible for unionizing the Perfect Circle shop despite threats from management, she was in fact a simple assembly line worker. Her Jones in-laws had chipped in back in Lynn, but since Lynetta had abandoned Old Jim, there would be no more financial help from them. That left no choice — in Richmond, Jimmy had to go to work. He soon found a job with the city's largest employer.

Reid Memorial Hospital opened in 1905, a gift to his community from industrialist Daniel G. Reid. The philanthropist made certain that the institution named to honor his deceased wife and son had the finest facilities possible. Patients from all over the Midwest enjoyed the best of care at Reid. Its staff was held to high standards. Reid paid well, but supervisors were sparing with praise and quick to weed out undesirables.

Seventeen-year-old Jimmy was hired as a night orderly, the lowest employment rung. It was hard work, often involving disagreeable tasks ranging from cleaning up vomit to helping move the newly deceased or handling disposal of amputated limbs. Working through the night was hard enough, but for a boy trying to handle a full high school class schedule and homework, it was exceptionally onerous. Yet Jimmy thrived.

He immediately demonstrated the ability to function on little sleep, or, some days, none at all. As soon as his final afternoon class was over, Jimmy rushed through homework and reported for duty at Reid. Once at work, he cheerfully tackled all the toughest chores that other orderlies tried to avoid. Above all, these included dealing with cantankerous patients, or else seriously ill unfortunates who literally reeked of decay and despair. Jimmy Jones won them over with warm smiles, sweet-natured jokes, and, always, empathy. Patients of every background and their families felt that this young man *understood.* His memory was prodigious — Jimmy remembered every sick person's name and the names of parents and spouses and children and cousins besides. Some patients required care of especially personal nature — having diapers changed, or being given sponge baths. Jimmy made these potentially embarrassing moments almost fun, with his lively chatter and positive attitude.

Reid management noticed. Orderlies routinely received critical performance reviews. There was nothing to criticize about Jimmy Jones. He was too young to put into a supervisory position over other orderlies, but he could be and was assigned to work with doctors and nurses involved in the most critical forms of care.

By the time Jimmy graduated from Richmond High in December 1948, his choice of future career was in doubt. He'd intended to become a minister. Now he contemplated a career in medicine. Preachers guided lives, but doctors saved them. There was appeal in both. Soon after his graduation, Jimmy took a quick trip back to Lynn and discussed it with a former girlfriend, Phyllis Willmore, who later remembered that Jimmy even mentioned getting into hospital administration, being the one who told the doctors what to do.

Becoming a preacher wouldn't necessarily require going to college, but doctors and hospital administrators needed degrees. Jimmy was ready for that. Of course, he'd have to pay his own way, tuition and living expenses and all, but combining school and work didn't faze him. Much like his mother, Jimmy believed he was destined for, *deserving of,* greatness. Unlike Lynetta, it seemed that he might have the opportunity to reach the heights that he anticipated — especially after meeting a young woman who had ambitions of her own.

CHAPTER SIX:
MARCELINE

Richmond was intended to be more than a drab manufacturing town. It was a point of civic pride to emphasize quality lifestyles beyond job opportunities. Even factory workers and their families had access to decent public schools, a sprawling park, a liberal arts college, downtown shops, theaters and cafés, the many health services of Reid Memorial Hospital, and, of course, a wide selection of churches, virtually all of them Protestant.

The town's African American population, comprising perhaps 15 percent of its citizenry, had value in the finest midwestern tradition. Blacks were needed to fill low-end assembly line jobs, and to serve as maids and gardeners for Richmond's well-to-do whites. Naturally, nice Richmond Negroes kept mostly to themselves outside the workplace. If they did encounter white folks, Richmond blacks were deferential. When white Richmond residents, speaking among themselves, used the word "nigger," they most often considered it descriptive rather than derogatory.

Wealthy Richmond men like Daniel G. Reid were too busy with their thriving businesses to devote the time necessary to hands-on civic leadership — they did their part through philanthropy. For city government and drives for public progress like expanding the local college, Richmond looked to its upper middle class, always finding dedicated individuals glad to contribute toward the common local good. No one epitomized this trait more than Walter Baldwin.

Walter was a fine Christian man who initially tried the ministry. He was gifted musically and brought that gift to Christ's cause, charming congregations with songs and a genuinely kind, loving manner. But spirituality had to eventually be tempered by practicality. Walter met and fell in love with a vibrant lady named Charlotte. When they married, Walter needed better-compensated employment; he ended up in management at International Harvester in Richmond.

The Baldwins settled down in an attractive two-story house — neighbors remember its front yard was larger than most others, and didn't Walter and Charlotte keep it nicely maintained? — and over the years became proud parents of three lovely daughters — Marceline, Eloise, and Sharon. Sharon was a late-life baby, eleven years younger than Marceline and nine younger than Eloise. The Baldwins were active members of Richmond's Trinity Methodist Church. When town Republicans needed a solid, *sound* candidate for city council, they turned to Walter. He served with great distinction, always interested in helping others and never attracting too much attention to himself.

Charlotte Baldwin was Walter's perfect life partner, equally at home on formal public occasions and at down-home gatherings. She was deeply religious, and believed that the Lord sometimes sent her messages in dreams. Charlotte also had a firm sense of propriety — she expected everyone, including her family, to act right at all times. Whenever — in her opinion — someone didn't, Charlotte would sharply correct the miscreant.

For the most part, her daughters were glad to comply. They honored and respected their parents, rarely questioning their rules. Only eldest daughter Marceline, born in 1927, ever rebelled, and then only slightly. One of Charlotte's edicts was that curtains in the Baldwin home must be closed at all times — she didn't want passersby looking in. Marceline sometimes pulled them open, telling her mother that there shouldn't be anything going on that the rest of the world couldn't see. Walter Baldwin frequently hosted political conclaves at his house. He and his friends embraced the Republican Party with nearly the same fervor that they followed Christ. Marceline once shocked them by nonchalantly saying she'd like to vote a straight Democratic ticket.

Otherwise, Marceline was a paragon. Baby sister Sharon had health problems, and Marceline was devoted to her, always concerned for Sharon's comfort even when Marceline's own rheumatoid arthritis periodically prostrated her with backaches. Marceline worked hard in class, where she was an above average student, and after school she always wanted her friends to come over to her house because she believed it was the happiest place anywhere.

Marceline inherited her father's musical talents. She had a sweet singing voice, and often sang solos at church on Sundays. Marceline, her sister Eloise, and church Youth Fellowship chum Janice formed a music ministry, entertaining at Reid Hospital and old folks homes. Eloise and Janice liked to "clown a little" during rehearsals. When they did, Marceline reminded them that it was time for work rather than play. It was everyone's Christian duty to minister to those in need, she stressed. That meant always doing your absolute best, not wasting time with silly behavior. Still, Marceline's faith was never negative. Her cousin Avelyn Chilcoate recalls, "If [Marceline] had to take a good or bad opinion of someone, she would look for the good. I guess you'd call her one of those really positive persons."

Marceline's piety was much admired, but in another critical area she puzzled her friends. While the other teenage girls were obsessed with boys, Marceline showed little interest. It wasn't that she didn't have the opportunity to have as many boyfriends as she wanted — Marceline was very attractive, with a personality to match. But hovering boys distracted from her responsibilities at school and church and her music outreach ministry. Dates would impinge on her time, which she carefully parceled out to fulfill more important obligations.

When high school graduation neared, Marceline had to make decisions about her future. Her grades were good enough to make college possible, but there was another option at home. Marceline was determined to spend her life helping others — what better way than nursing? Even as a little girl, Marceline liked visiting Reid Memorial. She'd bring flowers and little tokens to the sick people there, and was sometimes allowed to follow nurses around. A federally funded program allowed her to enter nursing school at no cost to her parents; housing was right on the Reid campus. As part of her training, Marceline was immediately in daily contact with patients, comforting them, providing services that eased their pain. She loved every moment.

By this time, though, Marceline didn't love Richmond quite as much. Her cousin Avelyn also worked at Reid, and the young women sometimes speculated about what life might be like somewhere else, in particular someplace where it didn't get bitterly cold in winter. Marceline's determination to live a life of Christian service hadn't wavered in the slightest. She still loved her family with all her heart. But it was a wide world, and she and Avelyn had never gotten to see much of it outside of Richmond. Avelyn remembers, "[Marceline] wanted a bigger adventure."

So the cousins studied maps. Atlanta was considered, and Florida, but the two young women kept talking about Kentucky: "It just sounded interesting." They contacted chambers of commerce in the state's biggest cities and requested information about hospitals in them. As always, Marceline was methodical. She wanted every available fact before making a decision. When the time came to tell her father and mother, Marceline was determined to demonstrate to them that moving away was not an impetuous decision, and in no way reflected badly on them.

Around the Christmas holidays in 1948, plans were almost in place. Avelyn and Marceline had narrowed down their relocation choices (Avelyn, now in her nineties, can't remember where in Kentucky); they were determined to go soon. Once her mind was made up, Marceline Mae Baldwin never wavered. That was why, just before Christmas, Avelyn was shocked when Marceline told her that she wouldn't be moving to Kentucky after all.

"She said she'd met a boy and was in love with him," Avelyn says, frowning at the memory. "She'd never said anything about him before, never a hint of it. When she told me it was Jim [Jones], I couldn't believe it, especially since she was so much older than he was. But from that moment, it was like he was all she thought about."

CHAPTER SEVEN:
JIM AND MARCELINE

One night in late 1948 when she was a senior nursing student at Reid, Marceline Baldwin prepared a corpse for pickup by the under-taker. It was a difficult task, and Marceline asked that an orderly assist her. That orderly was seventeen-year-old Jim Jones, who'd earned a considerable reputation around the hospital for perpetual high spirits. Now, wash-ing and dressing the corpse — a young pregnant woman who'd died of trichinosis — Jim was anything but buoyant. He acted solemn and respectful as he helped the pretty nurse, and when they were done Marceline was amazed to see that Jim took a few extra minutes to comfort the dead girl's family. Jim was, she would remember later, "visibly touched by [their] suffering."

After that, Jim always seemed to be around whenever Marceline took work breaks. He liked to talk, and she'd always been a good listener. Jim told heartrending tales of his ter-rible childhood in Lynn, how he'd often gone hungry and constantly suffered at the hands of his alcoholic, physically abusive father. But instead of wearing him down, that mistreatment inspired Jim to become dedicated to raising up other unfortunates in some way that had yet to be determined. He was about to graduate early from high school, and go on to college. After that, he'd accomplish as much as unstinting effort and faith in the Lord allowed. Marceline didn't doubt his sincerity.

For any other young couple, a three-and-a-half-year age difference might have precluded serious romance, but Jim simply overwhelmed Marceline with constant attention. She later joked that she married Jim to get rid of him. Marceline's very proper upbringing, with every young man she encountered following conventional social customs, in no way prepared her for someone who had no interest in traditional courting. As one childhood friend recalls, "Marceline was always very smart, but that's not the same thing as *worldly*." Jim wooed her with words. Every story he told Marceline seemed to place him in a situation where he stood up for the disenfranchised when no one else would. She was especially impressed when Jim revealed he'd once been a highly touted basketball star for the Lynn Bulldogs, only to quit the team when his coach said nasty things about Negroes. Once, he told Marceline, he walked out of a barbershop with his hair cut only on one side because the barber made racist comments. Everyone was equal, Jim insisted. It was the responsibility of all truly caring people to devote their lives to helping others. Didn't she agree?

Marceline did. It seemed natural, even God-ordained, that she should join Jim in that effort. When Jim began discussing marriage, she was agreeable, even though they'd known each other for only a few months. Jim spoke of married life as a grand adventure. They'd go wherever there were others oppressed and in need. It sounded good, and so Marceline took Jim home to meet her family.

Walter and Charlotte Baldwin were kindhearted people. They were certainly prepared to welcome an ambitious young man trying to work his way up in the world. True, his manners were rough, but Marceline explained about his terrible upbringing. Her parents were ready to help Jim learn more genteel ways and were astonished to discover that he expected them to conform to his. Casual conversation about politics set Jim off. His core beliefs were ingrained from childhood, when he listened to constant diatribes from his mother about how the rich exploited the poor, how the powerful didn't want to give anybody else a chance. The Baldwins said they knew from their own experience that just wasn't true. Walter himself had done so much for all sorts of people while on the Richmond City Council. Experience, decades of appropriate community service — these were the things that gave someone the right to offer opinions. But this boy, still a teenager, insisted that he knew better than mature adults. He sounded a great deal like a socialist, and maybe a communist. But Marceline was clearly in love with him, and she was such a responsible girl. This surely meant that Jim's good qualities and potential outweighed his current immature rantings. The Baldwins would have preferred that their cherished oldest daughter choose someone more traditional, but they accepted Jim, rough edges and all, out of love for Marceline.

Marceline's friends were pleased she had finally found someone, though they were surprised that he was so much younger and somewhat crude. Marceline confided that she thought Jim would eventually become a minister, and Janet L. Beach remembers that to most of them, this explained everything: "We thought how perfect it was, that this was the way it should be. Marceline would love being a preacher's wife."

With her own record of early, if failed, marital experience, Lynetta could hardly object to her son's marriage at such a young age. She and Marceline did not immediately become close, but managed to coexist. Jim even took Marceline back to Lynn to meet his Jones relatives there, and she made a predictably good impression, almost too much of one. "My first thought was that she was angelic, just glowing, shining, a will-of-the-wisp and obviously special," recalls Jeanne Jones Luther, who was then sixteen. "I wondered, 'Whatever does she see in *him?*' "

Jim was a young man in a hurry. In January 1949 he resigned from Reid, moved to Bloomington, and enrolled at the University of Indiana. His courses — Elementary Composition, Introduction to Business, Introductory Psychology, Public Speaking, along with Freshman English, PE, and Remedial Methods in Study and Reading — reflected indecision about a future career. Since he was responsible for his own expenses he worked at night, and on weekends took the bus back to Richmond to see Marceline. The hectic schedule seemed to agree with Jim. His first semester grades were all As and Bs, with a low grade of B- in Elementary Composition. Then and always, Jim Jones was more adept with the spoken rather than the written word.

On the afternoon of June 12, 1949, James Warren Jones married Marceline Mae Baldwin at Trinity Methodist Church in Richmond. It was a double wedding — Marceline's sister Eloise married Dale Klingman. The ceremony was strictly traditional, with the brides wearing matching gowns of "dusty rose organza over dusty rose taffeta." Richmond's daily newspaper reported the event in a lengthy article, noting that Mr. and Mrs. Jones would reside in Bloomington. But they couldn't afford that right away. Jim returned to school for the summer, taking classes in Economic History and Advanced Public Speaking. Marceline lived with her parents, working at Reid and saving money to move to Bloomington in the fall. Jim lived with her at the Baldwins' on weekends, and problems soon arose.

Charlotte Baldwin believed she had the right to say what she pleased in her own home. One weekend soon after the wedding, she commented that, in her opinion, it was not Christian for people of different races to intermarry. Twenty-seven years later, participating separately in a series of interviews for a proposed history to be published by Peoples Temple, Jim and Marceline both dictated their memory of what followed. As he recalled it, Charlotte compared black people — whom she called "niggers" — to communists, then berated her new son-in-law for his socialist beliefs. He replied, "I've had enough of your religious hypocrisy, and I'm sick of you. . . . Don't worry, I'll never sit at your table as long as I live and you'll never see me again as long as I live." Then, Jones said, "I whipped out of that goddamn house. I told Marcie,

'You're gonna have to choose between me and that bitch.' "

Marceline's version was less vulgar. "My mother made some remark about it not being Christian to intermarry. Well, Jim started throwing our stuff in bags and suitcases, and we got in the car and . . . [my parents] didn't know where we were for a long time. And when we went back to Richmond, we'd go to [Jim's] mother's place. If my parents walked in [her] front door, [Jim] walked out the back door. And this went on . . . until finally [my parents] had to bend. There was no compromise in him."

That fall in Bloomington, Marceline discovered that Jim didn't believe in marital compromise, either. She'd married him with the understanding that he, like her, believed in the God of the Bible and trusted in His Wisdom. But the newlyweds were barely settled in their tiny off-campus apartment when Jim told Marceline that he didn't believe in *her* God at all, since a just and loving Lord would never permit so much human misery. He would later say in Jonestown that "I started devastating [God], I tore that motherfucker to shreds and laid him out to rest. . . . [Marceline and I would] fight, and she'd cry. We were washing dishes one time and [Marceline] said, 'I love you, but [don't you] say anything about the Lord anymore'. I said, 'Fuck the Lord' . . . we ended up in some goddamn scrap and she threw a glass at me."

Another time, Jim and Marceline argued about God's goodness or lack of it as they drove along a country road; Marceline was behind the wheel. Jim claimed later that she blamed his socialist beliefs for such unwarranted disdain of the Lord: "She said, 'I can't take this anymore. You either change your ideology or get out of this car.' We were in the middle of nowhere. I said, 'Stop the car.' . . . When I stepped out of the car, I said to myself, 'This marriage is broken. I'm not giving up my ideology for [her] or anyone else.' " Jim "walked and walked" for several hours until "she finally came back. She was the one to bend. Because I was determined that I wouldn't."

Afterward, Marceline was less inclined to argue with Jim about matters of faith. She admitted, "He took an awful lot of the starch out of me." Privately, in conversations with her mother, sisters, and cousin Avelyn, she admitted considering divorce. For the first but far from the last time, Charlotte Baldwin advised patience. Marceline was always welcome back home, but her mother suggested that Jim wasn't really that bad. Avelyn thought Charlotte's advice was selfish: "Baldwin women simply did not divorce. It was unthinkable. Charlotte would have been embarrassed." Years later when Marceline's youngest sister, Sharon, divorced, Walter and Charlotte Baldwin gladly took her and her children in, helping Sharon in every way to move on with her life. But now Marceline listened to her mother. Perhaps Jim was just unsettled because he still hadn't decided on a specific career. Things between them would surely get better after he did.

Jim's second year in college was less successful academically. He withdrew from several classes and made indifferent grades in those he completed. Jim still expected to achieve great things, but wasn't sure how to go about it. He started talking about studying law. Marceline, shaken by Jim's statements about God, still coaxed him into attending Methodist services with her on Sundays. Jim's antipathy toward the Lord might yet be replaced with the comfort of unquestioning faith. She also brought Jim back into the Baldwin family circle. Walter and Charlotte tried hard to make him feel welcome. Jim seemed willing. He especially doted on Marceline's grandmother, always making a fuss over the old lady. Everyone agreed it was nice to see such a young man taking an interest in the elderly.

Another of Marceline's relations also appealed to Jim. Her nine-year-old cousin, Ronnie, had a tough life. His father died when the boy was four, his unstable mother moved from one unsuitable man to another, and she frequently sent Ronnie and his two older brothers away to live with relatives or in foster homes. The boys were always separated. Ronnie felt lonely and unloved.

In June 1950, Ronnie was being housed by a foster family when he suffered abdominal pain and had trouble standing straight. The foster family believed Ronnie was faking illness as an excuse to miss school. That weekend there was a Baldwin family gathering at Walter and Charlotte's. Ronnie wasn't there, but his brother Charles was, and he told Marceline about Ronnie's discomfort. Marceline guessed the boy had a ruptured appendix. She and Jim rushed to the foster family's house and took Ronnie to the hospital. His appendix was indeed ruptured. If Marceline hadn't intervened, the boy almost surely would have died.

When he recovered, Ronnie was farmed out to another foster family. But Marceline and Jim stayed in touch, and a year later surprised Ronnie and the rest of the Baldwins by inviting the boy to come live with them. It was a considerable sacrifice on their part. They'd recently moved to Indianapolis so Jim could take pre-law classes at the University of Indiana's campus there. Jim worked part-time to pay for tuition and books. Marceline worked nights as a nurse at a children's hospital. They lived in a small two-bedroom apartment. But they welcomed Ronnie. The now ten-year-old had his own room, and soon a new bicycle.

Burdened as they were with work and studies, Jim and Marceline still took Ronnie to the movies, which Jim in particular loved, and on short weekend trips to Niagara Falls and Canada. They suggested that he call them "Mom" and "Dad," but Ronnie wasn't comfortable with it.

Some nights, Jim would summon Ronnie and launch into long, graphic conversations about sex. He was determined that the boy should know every possible detail. In a 2014 interview, Ronnie joked that, had Marceline been willing, Jim might very well have offered a practical demonstration. The ten-year-old dazzled his pals with his newfound knowledge. They agreed that Ronnie now knew more about sex than any other kid in their elementary school.

Other times, Jim talked about Ronnie's mother. He told the boy that she was a whore because she lived with a man out of wedlock. Jim demanded that Ronnie accept him and Marceline as his new parents. Ronnie wouldn't go along. He hoped that somehow his mother would get her life under control and bring him and his brothers back to live with her. But he didn't tell that to Jim. Ronnie decided Jim was two-faced, all friendly and nice when he was out in public, and much different at home.

■ ■ ■ ■

In Indianapolis, Jim took two University of Indiana courses during 1952, making Bs in both. But completing his college education was no longer a primary concern. He finally knew what he wanted to do in life. It began with a renewed commitment to socialism, even in its more extreme, communist form.

Though the vast majority of Americans viewed communism as a threat, in Indianapolis there were still occasional public gatherings of avowed communists and sympathizers. Jim began attending these meetings, often bringing Marceline and Ronnie along. Much of what Marceline heard was revelatory to her — was it possible that America's system of government was responsible for the problems of the poor? No one she'd known growing up in Richmond had ever said so. It was disturbing.

Jim was in his element. He listened carefully to every speech, studying the speaking cadences and physical mannerisms of the most effective speakers. He made no effort to disguise his enthusiasm, even to the ubiquitous government agents who always stood outside the meeting venues, ostentatiously observing and jotting notes about everyone going in and out. They made many attendees nervous, but Jim would often go right up to these men, formally introduce himself, and walk away grinning. They didn't intimidate him. If anything, he savored their attention.

About the same time, an unexpected source provided Jim with the impetus to pursue his own socialist agenda. Marceline still occasionally dragged Jim to Methodist church services on Sundays. He remained contemptuous of Methodists, and of Christianity in general, all the nonsense about paradise after death, and meanwhile not doing a damned thing to help the needy. But sometime early in 1952, Jim was staggered by a new emphasis in Methodism. The faith's governing body adopted a new, formal social creed, supporting "the alleviation of poverty, the right of collective bargaining, free speech, prison reform, full employment, and racial integration." Jim didn't know, and would not have cared, that this new Methodist platform had been many years in the making. As was true for several other Protestant denominations, Methodist leaders had always encouraged social activism as an expression of faith, particularly during the Depression. Now, in the early 1950s, the plight of black Americans was cause for particular concern. The Bible commanded that all people be loved equally, with those in need clothed and fed. The Methodist church reemphasized its commitment to this stricture. Jim heard sermons urging worshippers to actually practice these beliefs. He informed Marceline and his in-laws that he would become a Methodist minister, since the church now wanted to put *real* socialism into practice. Marceline was ecstatic. This was what she'd hoped for. Jim set about finding a Methodist church that would accept him as a student pastor. What Marceline missed or ignored, as did the other Baldwins, was that this wasn't a matter of Jim admitting he might have been wrong in his previous disdain for traditional Christianity. Jim wasn't returning as a repentant prodigal son to Methodism; from his perspective, the Methodist Church had come to *him.*

As Jim searched for a church, he also explored another approach to expressing faith. On some Sundays and weeknights in Indianapolis, he took Marceline and Ronnie to black churches. Often they were the only white family there. Ronnie was particularly stunned by the participatory nature of these services, so unlike the much more staid behavior of white worship. Here, people jumped up and sang and danced and called out responses to their preachers' sermonizing. Black churches didn't seem to stick to any rigid agenda, or to observe time limits. Their services went on for hours, and nobody minded. People seemed to be having fun, not acting like they were fulfilling an obligation. They *liked* being in church. Marceline enjoyed the music, and Ronnie tried clumsily to join in the clapping and hollering, but Jim loved it all. He whooped and stomped and hugged everybody. He seemed at home at these services in a way that he never did anywhere else. Much of that resulted from the openness of the congregations. Everyone was welcome, whites included. Nobody asked why you were there; they only seemed pleased that you were. Every time they attended a black church, Jim made new friends. The Joneses always liked having company, and now they had as many or more black guests as white ones. Jim was an inquisitive host. He wanted to know everything about his new friends' lives, including their treatment by utility companies and white city officials and shop owners. How did prejudice affect even the most mundane aspects of their lives? Jim stopped lecturing Ronnie so much about sex; now he used every available minute explaining to the boy how blacks were as good as whites.

In the summer of 1952, Jim was hired as student pastor for Somerset Methodist Church, which drew its membership from lower-income white families in Indianapolis. It wasn't a large or distinguished congregation, but that made no difference to Jim. His first sermon extolled "living Christianity" and the virtues of acting on belief. At age twenty-one, he'd apparently found his life's work.

CHAPTER EIGHT:
BEGINNINGS

On March 15, 1953, the *Palladium-Item,* Richmond's daily newspaper, included a lengthy feature story concerning a local boy made good. Reporter William B. Treml gushed about the accomplishments of "a 21-year-old student pastor at Somerset Methodist Church in Indiana." The young minister, respectfully identified as "the Rev. Mr. Jones," had recently launched a campaign to build a recreation center for poor children on Indianapolis's south side. The proposed center was dazzling, "a building costing $20,000, [and] which will include a basketball court, table tennis facilities, volleyball and kitchen equipment." But even more amazing was that the center "will be run by a board of directors composed of all interested neighborhood denominations. . . . The Rev. Mr. Jones has established a church program at Somerset almost unheard of under the strict rules of doctrine [followed] by most religious sects. In [this] program, Jones preaches no doctrine but simply points out moral lessons taken from the Bible."

The article noted that the Reverend Mr. Jones, an honors graduate of Richmond High, currently attended Indiana University and was also taking a correspondence course "to obtain a standing in the Methodist conference." After graduation, "wherever he accepts a parish . . . he hopes to continue his programs of help exclusive of his church to those who need it."

But at the same time the *Palladium-Item* lauded Jim and his promising Methodist future, it was falling apart. Within a year, he'd abandon Methodism altogether.

To Jim Jones, his new position at Somerset Methodist was an opportunity to lead the congregation aggressively forward, with the new attitude of setting aside sectarian divisions and joining forces with anyone equally devoted to helping the unfortunate. To Somerset members, Jones was a student pastor there to assist full-time ministers; boat-rocking was not permitted. Jones could talk all he liked about new ecumenical community centers for neighborhood children, but there is no record beyond the *Palladium-Item*'s mention that such a project existed beyond Jones's own imagination. Jones was volunteer help, not a part of Somerset's official church staff. He had no authority beyond whatever responsibilities someone else allowed him, and these were limited to helping out as required with day-to-day church business and delivering the occasional sermon, which always had to meet the approval of Somerset's *real* minister.

In Jones's view, the services were frustrating. There was always a strict order of worship, with everything decided in advance and conducted within a rigid time frame so worshippers could enjoy Sunday afternoons at home. It was the opposite of the spontaneous, joyful, and open-ended worship that Jones so naturally embraced in African American churches.

Away from Somerset, there were more problems. Despite his claims to the reporter from Richmond, Jones was no longer attending college. Even with Marceline working full-time, more income was needed, and the student pastor position was unpaid. Jones worked at a number of odd jobs, mostly in factories and shops. But it was difficult to make ends meet, and in August 1952 Jones was badly shaken by what he considered a personal betrayal.

Ronnie Baldwin had lived with the Joneses for more than a year. Jones and Marceline doted on the boy, and believed their affection was returned in equal measure. They made plans to formally adopt Ronnie, but didn't consult the youngster until after they had legal documents drawn up and ready for him to accept and his mother to sign. But grateful as he was for the kindness shown by them, Ronnie wouldn't agree. He still wanted, at some point, to be permanently reunited with his mother and brothers.

Marceline was hurt, but Jones was outraged. He ranted at Ronnie for an entire night, warning him that his birth mother was an unrepentant whore — Ronnie would immediately regret giving up the love and security that he and Marceline provided. The boy still refused. Jones seemed to believe that once he did anything for someone, from that moment forward the person *belonged* to him, with no right to disagree about anything or ever leave. While Marceline closed herself in another room, Jones harangued Ronnie until dawn, then petulantly sent the youngster back to his mother in Richmond.

Ronnie thought that was the end of it. His mother was doing better, and enrolled her son in a local elementary school. Soon afterward, Ronnie was summoned from class to the principal's office; there was an urgent phone call for him. It was Jones, calling from Indianapolis to tell Ronnie that his desertion had broken Marceline's heart. Hadn't she and Jim treated Ronnie wonderfully, caring for him when no one else in the world did? *Now* would Ronnie come back and let them adopt him? Ronnie still refused.

At the end of September, the Baldwins held

a family get-together in Richmond. When Ronnie arrived, Jim and Marceline were already there. As soon as Ronnie saw Jones, he turned and ran, certain that Jim would never let him alone. As Ronnie recalls it, "I took off . . . he jumped in his car, he chased me through the west side of Richmond. I went through houses and yards and everything." Jim cornered Ronnie outside the boy's house. But Ronnie's older brother Dean confronted Jones, telling him to go away and leave Ronnie alone. From that moment, Jones never had anything to do with Ronnie.

Perhaps reflexively, Jones and Marceline turned to another child, an eleven-year-old waif they met during Jones's student ministry. Her background is mostly a mystery, but within months of losing Ronnie, the Joneses formally adopted the little girl, who was named Agnes.

Jones's energy and ambition couldn't be contained within his student pastorship. He needed some additional outlet, and found it in the region's evangelical circuit. As a boy in Lynn, Jones often attended revivals where preachers espoused their personal faith. Many preachers had no affiliation with a specific denomination — they felt called to witness to the Word of God as they understood it. Revivals, prayer meetings, and healing ceremonies ranged in scale from itinerants standing on public park benches and shouting at passersby to well-organized gatherings of thousands in big-city venues. Upward mobility depended solely on a preacher's ability to capture and hold attention. Those who could often prospered in ways beyond the joy of spreading the gospel. Collections were taken, and enthralled throngs dug deep in their pockets. The most successful revivalists frequently drove flashy cars and wore tailor-made suits. Most, though, scraped along on donations of spare change and depended on offers of meals and a place to sleep.

Jones still had his duties at Somerset Methodist most of the day on Sundays and whenever else his help was required. But on weekday nights, on Saturdays, and occasional Sundays after meeting his obligations at Somerset, Jones began trying his luck with revivals. Sensibly, he didn't immediately strike out on his own. Instead, he attended prayer meetings and healing services in tents and fields outside small towns in Indiana, Ohio, Illinois, and Michigan, places within reasonable driving distance of Indianapolis. Many of these featured several individuals preaching one after another: Jones paid close attention. What worked and what didn't? Which biblical phrases and references regularly elicited the strongest response? How far did the most effective preachers go in espousing personal beliefs and biblical interpretations? Most of all, he studied healings. Driving out demons, curing cancer or other diseases, making the lame walk and the blind see by the laying on of hands or loudly petitioning the Lord — doing these things successfully and with flair guaranteed not only fame and money, but also allegiance by impressed members of the audience. And so, at first in small, primitive settings, Jones set out to heal. He recalled thinking that "If these sons of bitches can do it, then I can do it too. And I tried my first act of healing. I don't remember how. Didn't work out too well. But I kept watching those healers. . . . I thought that there must be a way that you could do this for good, that you can get the crowd, get some money, and do some good with [the money]."

Jones first successfully amazed revival audiences by relying on memory, not miracles. Before speaking, he began mingling with the crowd, memorizing bits of overheard conversation: "I started taking little notes." Many people attended revivals or healing services in hopes of some miraculous sign that God was aware of and sympathetic to their tribulations. Thanks to his stealthy reconnaissance, Jones provided it. As he preached, he would call out names of some in the audience, speaking about personal things he apparently had no way of knowing, and then assuring them that God would intervene. Listeners were flabbergasted. So was Marceline, who said, "My reaction was one of amazement . . . it was as if I walked on air and I could not feel my feet on the ground and it was difficult for me to even speak."

Word spread about a young preacher with God-given powers to read minds and prophesize. First a few, then gradually more and more people began turning out to witness Jim Jones reading minds. That still wasn't *healing,* but then came a critical moment at a Columbus, Indiana, revival. Jones would claim that "a little old lady" dressed in white called him over and said, "I perceive that you are a prophet. . . . You shall be heard all around the world, and tonight you shall begin your ministry." Jones took his place at the pulpit, "closed my eyes, and all this shit flies through my mind . . . and I'd just call people out and they'd get healed of everything" — or at least they temporarily believed that they were. Even Jones was skeptical: "I don't know how to explain how people got healed of every goddamn thing under the sun, that's for sure. Or apparently got healed. How long [the healings lasted] I don't know."

Jones had always been a showman. His healings were dramatic, and crowds gathered, still not large because Jones stuck to the rural revival circuit. But his confidence grew, and as it did he became more plainspoken about his personal beliefs, using healings as a means of attracting audiences for his real message — "I'm preaching integration, against war, and throwing in some . . . philosophy." Touting integration at revivals to white conservative Christians was particularly risky — Jones always lost some of his audience when he did. He accepted this: "An inclusive congregation, that was [my] first big issue."

Jones's success as a roving revival meeting preacher increased his frustration with Somerset Methodist. There, he had no freedom to say or do the things that were bringing him so much welcome attention elsewhere. If he remained with the Methodist faith, his career path would be rigidly defined — more school, subordinate roles at various churches, and years before finally gaining leadership of a congregation, undoubtedly a small white one. Most Methodist congregations, Somerset included, remained lily-white. Jones was impatient with the philosophy of gradual change — he wanted to make things happen now. The tempting solution was to leave Somerset and go out on his own. But that was a huge step, and for a little while Jones hesitated, uncomfortably balancing his alternate identities of miracle-working country preacher and dutiful student pastor. Then, sometime in early 1954, Somerset made the decision for him. Jones and Marceline would say later that he was dismissed because of his efforts to bring blacks into the congregation. That's unlikely — Jones would have faced a near-impossible task in recruiting African Americans to Somerset because few blacks lived anywhere near the church. A quarter century later, when FBI investigators probed Jones's personal history, they interviewed a former Somerset member who testified that the unpaid student pastor was asked to leave when members "accused him of lying and stealing funds." That aspersion is also dubious. Jones had no access to Somerset's money, and whatever he raised from his outside preaching belonged to him and not the church. But clearly, things had reached a point where both sides were ready to separate, and Jim Jones left Somerset Methodist to establish a church of his own.

CHAPTER NINE:
A CHURCH WHERE YOU GET SOMETHING NOW

One morning in 1954, Ron Haldeman was in his office in a slum area of Indianapolis. Haldeman was director of the Quaker church's inner-city programs, which attempted to provide clothing and other forms of assistance to the city's impoverished black population. All the major denominations made at least some effort on behalf of the Indianapolis poor, and coordinated their individual, limited efforts when they could. Haldeman worked out of a house owned by the Disciples of Christ; they allowed him to turn the tiny kitchen into office space, which Haldeman and a secretary occupied. His responsibility was overseeing his church's services to the inner-city elderly. The assignment was hard, and its rewards few — no matter who Haldeman helped, he realized there were many more desperate old people doing without. Still, he loved his job, and relished the company of other like-minded individuals who weren't offended by his openly acknowledged belief in socialism.

Haldeman's work that morning was interrupted by an unexpected visitor, a young man with striking eyes. He introduced himself as Jim Jones, and launched into a spirited explanation of the church he was trying to found in the area. That in itself wasn't unusual. Self-anointed ministers often opened "storefront churches," unaffiliated and almost always short-lived efforts to establish congregations in the heart of the Indianapolis slums. But Jones bubbled with enthusiasm. He planned to call his new church "Community Unity" because everyone would be welcome. A little space had been found for services. He and his wife were about to go door-to-door handing out flyers. Jones stressed they were focusing on low-income black neighborhoods. It was disgraceful that everyone wasn't treated equally — Jones intended his new church as a way of changing that, at least in Indianapolis. Haldeman was charmed — here was someone who shared his beliefs. Jones asked Haldeman about his own background, and, when Haldeman revealed his Quaker affiliation, Jones exclaimed at the coincidence. Why, he, too, was a lifelong Quaker, had in fact been educated in Quaker schools and wanted nothing more than for Community Unity to soon affiliate with the Quaker faith. That settled it for Haldeman — he had to help. He invited Jones, at no charge, to share his office and the services of his secretary. That would provide him a base for daily operations, and make his efforts seem more official. By the time Jones left that morning, Ron Haldeman badly wanted Community Unity to be successful. But despite his new friend's unshakable belief that it would, Haldeman had doubts. Not that Jim's intentions were wrong or misguided. But this was a city whose system of mostly benign racism had thwarted for decades any efforts at meaningful integration. Without the hostility toward blacks that was openly displayed in the South, Indianapolis whites kept Negroes in their permanent, lesser place.

In 1954, the vast majority of blacks in Indiana lived in its major industrial cities. In Indianapolis, the African American population exploded during and directly after the Depression. The city was relatively close to southern states; its factory jobs and apparent lack of Jim Crow laws were a beacon to African Americans desperate to escape Dixie. Eventually, blacks comprised more than 10 percent of the population; one study estimated 44,000 of them within city limits. This terrified lower-class whites, who felt that their jobs were threatened by employees who would work for less. Middle-class whites anticipated black residential encroachment and plummeting property values as a result.

Backlash followed: it was effective and not particularly overt. Trade unions influenced hiring at major Indianapolis plants, and most of these unions voted not to accept blacks as members. The city established what appeared to be the most democratic of housing ordinances: no one could buy a home in an established neighborhood unless the majority of current residents approved the purchase. The school district sent black teenagers to Crispus Attucks High School, built beside a smelly canal in an area nicknamed Frog Island. Since African Americans were all crammed into homes in the same slum, these students were attending their neighborhood school. For decades, the Crispus Attucks Tigers were not allowed to compete in sports against white city schools. In the 1950s, when national laws mandated integration of high school sports, the Tigers quickly won back-to-back Indiana state basketball championships. Yet even in this, its players were denied a significant honor. Traditionally, white Indianapolis school squads winning state titles were lauded with a parade through downtown. City officials limited the Crispus Attucks parades to streets in the school's immediate vicinity.

Blacks in Indianapolis turned to the leaders of their churches, who in 1943 were instrumental in forming the Indianapolis Citizens Council. The new organization's purpose was to ensure good race relations. African American ministers called the offices of the mayor, senior city staff, school board members, and other influential white leaders, requesting meetings to discuss their grievances. They were gratified at the quick, positive response. Dozens of meetings were held. The white leaders listened intently and promised serious consideration of all they'd heard. Afterward, letters were exchanged. Sometimes committees were formed. Every time the black ministers wanted additional meetings, they were promptly scheduled. If the African American leaders were frustrated by lack of immediate action, they never demanded more from their white counterparts. Confrontation was simply not the Indiana way. Black residents were pleased when their spokesmen reported that there had been another meeting and things looked promising. They mistook access for influence. Nothing changed in Indianapolis.

Trapped in poverty, confined to vermin-ridden slums where their children were educated in crumbling, underequipped schools, African Americans in the city most often found church to be their only source of solace. It was a relief to spend long hours there, listening to sermons reminding them of God's love and His promise of heaven, eternal life in a milk-and-honey Promised Land. Commiseration now and better times after death were the message of the city's black churches. Their ministers did little to help their members overcome the immediate challenges of Indianapolis and its apparently unassailable racism.

It took a white preacher to show them how.

The immediate challenge for Jim Jones was that Community Unity had to offer inner-city blacks something that their present churches didn't. Whatever his personal doubts about a loving "Sky God" and the promise of heaven, these beliefs were ingrained in those he wanted to attract. Attacking what they devoutly believed would get Jones nowhere. In terms of entertainment, of giving congregants a show to take their minds off their troubles, Jones could hardly match the competition: at least in its early stages, Community Unity would have no choir to offer mighty, spirit-raising renditions of hymns. Jones's natural pulpit-pounding flamboyance was matched by many black preachers. Mind-reading and healings would be great attractions, but unlike billowing tents and sprawling fairgrounds of the revival circuit, Community Unity's cramped store-front would have no crowd for Jones to stealthily infiltrate, picking up information from overheard snatches of conversation.

Yet not long after he accepted Haldeman's invitation to share an office, Jones bragged to the Quaker official that neighborhood blacks had begun attending Community Unity — not many, but at least a few. It was a start, and as weeks passed Jones was delighted to report that his congregation had grown to two or three dozen, with new faces every week. Haldeman was pleased, but puzzled: it seemed so unlikely. One Sunday morning he decided to visit Community Unity and see for himself.

Haldeman took his seat on a folding chair. He was surrounded by perhaps twenty-five people, mostly black, elderly women. There were also a few white worshippers — they had followed Jones to Community Unity from Somerset Methodist. Haldeman was prepared for a typical hymn-prayer-sermon-collection-plate service. Marceline Jones wrote the titles of several hymns on a chalkboard. As she seemed about to lead the small congregation in song, Jim Jones barreled into the room and, instead of signaling for the singing to commence, asked a general question of all present: "What's bothering you?" A hand toward the back went up. An old black woman stood and complained about the electric company. There was some problem with her service, and even though she constantly complained, nothing was done to fix it — but the company still sent monthly bills. When she demanded maintenance before she paid, the white people she dealt with threatened to cut off her power. There were murmurs of assent. Almost everyone present, certainly all the blacks, had endured something similar. The woman told Jones that she felt she had no choice other than to pay without getting the requested repairs. Her family, which included grandchildren, couldn't live in the dark. She was ready to give up — she didn't know what else to do.

Jones did. He ordered Marceline to fetch a pen and paper. "Let's write a letter," he told the old woman. Then, with Marceline serving as secretary, Jones dictated a message to the electric company, citing the lady's constant attempts to get her problems resolved, and explaining that all she wanted was the service she paid for. He asked the rest of the congregation for suggestions — what else should be in the letter? They recommended some embellishments, and these were added. Then Jones had the letter passed around and everyone signed it. Jones said that this show of unity proved they were a real family in this church. They worked together to help each other. The next day, Jones promised, he'd personally deliver the letter to the electric company's main office. While he was there, he'd find out who was the right person to discuss the matter with face-to-face, and he'd sit down with him or her and explain how a wonderful lady was being treated unfairly — things had to be, *would be,* made right. Only after making that vow did Jones allow Marceline to lead the singing of a hymn. Then Jones preached a lengthy sermon, heavy on scripture emphasizing tolerance and love.

At the next Sunday service, Jones asked the old woman to stand up and tell everyone what had happened. She joyfully reported that her problem with the electric company was resolved — somebody had come out and things were repaired. She thanked everybody for their help, Pastor Jones most of all. Together they'd stood up to the white people at the electric company, and they'd won. Jones crowed, "See? When you come to this church, you get something *now.*" He urged his small flock to start bringing the rest of their families, and to tell their friends — Community Unity promised heaven someday for the righteous, of course, but it didn't neglect problems encountered during this life, either. That differed from what all the black churches offered, and the message resonated. Some weeks, growth was more than others, but every Sunday brought at least a few new worshippers. Some left after a week or two, but many stayed. This white preacher named Jim Jones didn't just talk about doing things, he did them.

Marceline was pleased with Community Unity's early success, but frustrated with her role. Of course she knew that Jim was going to be the focal point, up there preaching the gospel that his wife loved, and helping people out with their ordinary, day-to-day problems. It was just wonderful how he did that. But Marceline expected to have her own important role, organizing the individual worship services to fit themes. She would ask Jim every week what he planned to talk about in his next sermon; then Marceline would pore over the hymnal, picking just the right songs to get everybody thinking about what specific things Jim and the Bible had to teach them on this particular Sunday. It helped her, too, to know in advance how long Jim planned to preach. Based on her own experience with church back in Richmond, Marceline believed that at a certain point people wanted to get on with the rest of their Sunday. She wanted to pick just the right uplifting hymn to send everybody home with a light step and refreshed spirit.

Jim cooperated, at least during the week. He'd tell her what he was thinking about in terms of a sermon. But no matter how carefully Marceline tried to work out a plan, or how often she went over it with Jim in advance, on Sunday he never stuck to it. He'd ask the people if any of them had problems, and the more of these that he helped solve, the more often he was asked to solve other problems. Some Sundays the letter writing went on for an hour or more. Afterward, Jim was still in no hurry to wrap things up. He might go ahead and stick to the sermon he'd told her about, but usually he'd have read something in the paper that morning, a news story describing an unjust act perpetrated on the powerless, and he'd talk about that instead. It got so there had to be two or three breaks each Sunday, so people could use the bathroom. The service would be over when Jim was too exhausted to talk anymore. Marceline feared everyone else would get so bored that they'd quit coming, but this never seemed to be the case. They appreciated their pastor wearing himself out for them.

Yet most had no idea just how hard he worked on their behalf. It cost money to rent the storefront, and the meager offerings Jones collected on Sundays from his impoverished followers weren't enough. Marceline's salary from her full-time job barely covered essentials for Jones's immediate family. So Jones worked, too, selling spider monkeys door-to-door for $29 each. He imported them from a firm in South America, and in April 1954 the *Indianapolis Star* ran a story about his refusal to accept a shipment of monkeys because they were ill. Beyond that, he held other part-time jobs, anything to bring in a few extra dollars for the Community Unity cause. He slept when he could.

By the standard of what anyone else might have hoped for, Community Unity was a success. It had built a small but enthusiastic congregation, helping its members in critical ways in their everyday lives while still providing the traditional, Bible-based worship that they craved. But Jones wanted much more. Yes, his church was serving needy people without regard for their race or desperate economic straits. In that sense, he was practicing socialism. But any current accomplishments were limited. Already, Community Unity was outgrowing the cramped storefront space it rented on Sundays. Some larger, permanent place was needed — neighborhood fund-raising to buy appropriate property wasn't possible, because no one in this neighborhood had any money. Helping a few people with the electric company or school officials was gratifying, but Jones dreamed of greater things benefiting multitudes. Among his goals was a soup kitchen feeding not only the homeless, as was traditional, but anyone who was hungry and wanted a free meal; a community clothing bank, where everything was available at no cost; free child care for poor working mothers; assistance in helping the unemployed find work. Such services were especially needed among Indianapolis's African American slum dwellers. Jones had no intention of proposing solutions that required participation by outsiders who might threaten his personal control. If the things Jones wanted next were going to happen, it fell to him to bring them about. He believed that he knew how to do it.

CHAPTER TEN:
PEOPLES TEMPLE

Jim Jones returned to the revival/tent meeting circuit with a new agenda. His earlier efforts were, in effect, training, where he learned how to attract audiences of complete strangers and win them over with a mixture of preaching and healings. Now he set out to establish himself as a top-tier traveling preacher. That would position him to bring in badly needed money. To begin with, Jones wanted to own — not rent — a much bigger building for Community Unity, with sufficient space for continued expansion.

His performances were carefully structured; they continued to combine Bible-quoting rhetoric with healings. Jones had a fine sense of just how many miracles were necessary to keep individual crowds enthralled. Most of these still involved eavesdropping in advance, "whatever I could take down." He commanded headaches to vanish, coughs to desist, and, on very rare occasions, the lame to walk. These miracles didn't always come off as Jones would have liked, or as his audiences hoped. He was dealing with strangers and couldn't count on their cooperation, so he was careful not to ask too much. A woman in a wheelchair might be gently instructed to stand and take just a single, shaky step rather than run or dance down the aisle. Then Jones could declare even the slightest hint of progress as the initial moment in a gradual healing process that God had granted through him.

It worked. Many people who came to see Jones for the first time in smaller settings returned to his appearances in larger venues. In expansive tents and midsized auditoriums that held good-sized crowds, Jones preached, healed, had collection plates passed, often taking away hundreds of dollars. Both he and Marceline recognized a September 1954 program as a turning point. Marceline described the scene in a letter to Lynetta Jones back in Richmond:

Dearest Mom,
    I feel that I must write you of the latest developments in the life of your beloved son. Through all our tests and hardships I had faith that Jimmy would be something special. This, however, is beyond our fondest dreams. . . . Saturday night in Cincinnati 200 were turned away. Well over 1000 stayed.

Sunday mornings found Jones back at Community Unity, preaching about helping each other, being a true family. Jones rarely asked the congregation to help compose letters now. He had far less time to personally assist with individual problems, but there was still a sense of excitement among the growing congregation as Jones and Marceline shared stories and news clippings about turned-away crowds at outside programs. Their pastor was a famous man — it gave his followers a pleasant sense of their own improved status. People in other places heard Pastor Jim only every once in a while. Community Unity had him every Sunday. The congregation didn't realize that Jones considered their church to be only the first rung on a very high ladder.

Yet even as his reputation grew, Jones was frustrated. He drew audiences in the thousands, but still couldn't preach the socialist themes that formed the basis of his real philosophy: "I could get the crowds together, but I couldn't get them politicized." The necessity of healings at almost every circuit performance put him under tremendous pressure. Jones certainly knew other healers at least sometimes used plants in the audience, but he didn't have anyone to plant. He traveled without an entourage other than his wife, and Jones was careful, at least for the time being, to let Marceline believe that he had developed the power to read the thoughts of others, rather than simply gaining information by eavesdropping. Jones began showing signs of a stress-related problem of his own, grinding his teeth to the point of developing dental problems. This proved so severe that he had to take a few weeks off for treatment. Jones asked Ron Haldeman to preside over Sunday services at Community Unity in his place. Haldeman was stunned by how the congregation had grown in the few months since his earlier visits. Where there had previously been only two dozen or so, now a hundred people crammed into the storefront.

Soon afterward, Jones asked Haldeman for a favor. The two men had grown close personally as well as professionally. Along with their wives, who were also friends, they often went out for inexpensive dinners. Jones especially liked a place called Acapulco Joe's — he relished spicy food, but this time Jones wanted a private conversation. He told Haldeman that while it was exciting to see Community Unity grow as an independent church, now he yearned for something more. From birth, Jones reiterated, he'd been a committed Quaker. With Community Unity finally established, Jones wanted to formally affiliate his new church with the Quakers. The most critical stage of potential affiliation, Jones knew, was submitting a written request, one that specifically demonstrated how the congregation adhered to, and could help extend, overall Quaker philosophy and goals.

Haldeman was gratified. He said he'd be glad to help his friend with the application. Jones pressed: Would Ron actually *write* the application? After all, Ron knew better than anyone exactly what would convince the Quaker examination board. Of course, Jones could write it himself, but Ron could do it so much better, and wouldn't Community Unity, with its almost entirely Negro membership, move the regional Quaker organization toward complete integration, the very thing that Haldeman himself wanted? Haldeman was flattered and felt that he couldn't refuse. He started immediately.

As later events proved, Jim Jones never intended to surrender control of his church to anyone else, including administrators representing a large denomination. But affiliation would provide him with a powerful tool as he worked to gain social and political influence. It would be harder for elected officials and business leaders to ignore a man theoretically representing tens of thousands of people and a major denomination than an independent ghetto preacher whose church membership totaled a few hundred slum dwellers. There were tax considerations, too. Under Indiana state law, only ministers representing established denominations were entitled to personal tax breaks. Jones was beginning to rake in money on the preaching circuit. He wanted to keep as much of it as possible, though mostly for Community Unity programs rather than for himself.

In very short order, the Quakers declined Community Unity's application. Jones and Haldeman believed that the church, despite its avowed outreach to the impoverished, didn't want blacks. Alternatively, when the Quakers investigated Jim Jones, they may have been put off by his rumored shady financial actions as a student pastor at Somerset Methodist, or suspected him of staging phony healings. He returned to the regional revival circuit, where he was now an established attraction.

By late 1954, other prominent preachers on the circuit took notice of Jones. Some, representing global evangelism programs, offered to hire and send him all over the world to preach. It would have been rewarding financially as well as spiritually — he, his wife, and their adopted daughter, Agnes, could live comfortably. Jones refused. He told Marceline that real social change anywhere could be brought about only if a leader stayed in that place. He'd chosen Indianapolis as his battlefield. Marceline was proud of her husband's principled refusal to move on and up. She believed that Jim didn't need anyone else's worldwide organization to become famous. He could use his God-given gifts to take what Marceline disdainfully termed "the Oral Roberts route" of self-aggrandizing independent ministry, gaining personal wealth as well as evangelical renown. But Jim showed no interest in that, either. It was so admirable. True, some of his private beliefs and actions alarmed her, but look at what he had already accomplished, and all the things that he still intended to do.

Marceline Jones was the first, but far from the last, person to decide that Jim Jones's programs and goals more than compensated for his personal flaws. Taken all in all, Marceline believed, her husband was a great man, though extremely difficult to live with. All right, then: she would remain in her challenging marriage, and do all that she could to help Jim. She stopped mentioning the possibility of divorce to her family.

Jones made a particularly dynamic appearance at a revival in Detroit. Among those in attendance was Russell Winberg, an associate pastor at Laurel Street Tabernacle in Indianapolis. Laurel Street was an Assemblies of God (Pentecostal) church with a white congregation of almost a thousand. Laurel Street's main pastor was John L. Price, an older man. Sunday sermons there were often delivered by guest ministers, and Winberg arranged for Jones to speak. He was an instant success, and, after returning several times, got the impression that he would be asked to replace Price when he retired — which was expected to happen soon. This was a tremendous opportunity. His eventual goal never changed: he intended for his followers to embrace socialism, and exemplify it through their own lives and church outreach programs. To take his next local step, challenging discrimination on a citywide rather than neighborhood basis, he still needed sufficient followers to impress Indianapolis leadership. Some would come from the local ghetto, but there were already black Indianapolis churches with a thousand or more members. What Community Unity required was a racially mixed congregation, blacks and whites united in purpose. Combining Community Unity and Laurel Street Tabernacle under his leadership would give Jones the racial combination he needed.

But when Jones tried to bring his black Community Unity followers with him to Laurel Street, church leaders there were appalled. They wanted Jones, not his congregation. Once that was made clear, Jones cut off all contact with Laurel Street, but not before dozens of white members, equally disgusted by its discriminatory action, walked away with him and joined Community Unity. Among these new white followers were Jack Beam and his wife, Rheaviana, and Edith Cordell, who was convinced that Jones cured her arthritis. Jack Beam was a gruff man, handy at all sorts of equipment maintenance and fiercely loyal to those he trusted. He'd been a board member at Laurel Street and was a good organizer. Both Beams quickly became integral to the public and private aspects of Jones's ministry. Edith Cordell invited other members of her family to hear Jones preach at Community Unity, and some joined the congregation. Jones hadn't left empty-handed.

Though his dalliance with Laurel Street had brought in some white followers, Jones knew they weren't enough. The best place to recruit more was away from Indianapolis, back on the revival circuit. Jones's impassioned sermons would surely win some new white converts, but the chief means of attracting white members for Community Unity would be healings. It didn't matter if newcomers had no initial interest in social reform. Jones was certain that, given sufficient time, he could make good socialists out of anyone, no matter why they originally joined.

How much Jones created the illusion of healing at these revivals, and whether, in some cases, he began using plants in his audience, isn't known. But many people believed the healings to be genuine, particularly if the miraculously cured sufferer was a friend or relative. Joe and Clara Phillips, a white husband and wife, were filled with gratitude when, at an out-of-town healing, Jones proclaimed that he had cured their toddler Danny's serious heart defect. Afterward, the Phillipses took Danny to a heart specialist, who examined the little boy and said that his heart was fine. Joe and Clara dismissed the possibility that earlier doctors might have made a misdiagnosis. They took Jones at his word that he deserved the credit for Danny's survival, and swore to follow him for life. So did dozens of others, almost all of them white, who heard Jones at revivals. Jones's out-of-town recruitment strategy, intended to diversify as well as increase his city congregation, worked. But that wasn't — couldn't — be the end of it.

Once those who believed in his powers joined the Community Unity congregation in Indianapolis, Jones was obligated to perform periodic healings there. Until these newcomers could be fully indoctrinated into socialism, they expected healings, demonstrations of their new pastor's awe-inspiring powers. Jones had to deliver, at risk of losing them. Further, the same style of healing that worked among strangers at revivals would be ineffective among regular congregants. Use of audience plants — someone who'd never attended Community Unity before, and never would again — would tip off longtime followers that Jones's healings weren't genuine.

He had to involve rank-and-file members, familiar faces everyone trusted. That meant letting at least a few people in on his secrets. Who he initially chose isn't certain. The Beams were likely involved. Marceline might have been. But now there were occasional healings during Community Unity services. These were less flamboyant than those Jones performed at revivals. No one lame was commanded to walk. But there was a new type of drama. Jones began miraculously removing cancers. A strict protocol was observed. Jones would name the afflicted person, then designate someone else to escort him or her to the bathroom. Both were in on the act. When they were in the restroom, Jones promised, he'd invoke his power from the pulpit. The afflicted one would "pass" the cancerous mass, which was retrieved by the other person. After a few minutes, they would return to the main room, with the assistant Jones had designated brandishing a bloody, foul-smelling lump clutched in a white cloth or napkin. Jones would declare that here was the cancer — look at it, but not too closely, because it was terribly infectious. The assistant would take away the disgusting mass for disposal as Jones grandly proclaimed the healing accomplished, and the person who was healed shouted praise. Jones's accomplices, then and later, were aware that the cancer was actually chicken offal, allowed to rot a bit before use.

With the Beams and others, Jones was beginning to attract followers who understood and supported a flexible approach to recruitment. If, sometimes, their leader's methods were questionable or even plainly deceptive, that was all right — Jim was doing what he had to in order to build his own mighty church and bring about equality for all. Ron Haldeman, who still attended some services, recalls that "[Jones] was a good psychologist. I was skeptical of faith healing. I was clear about that to him. He never tried to debate me about it. It was like he knew [that] I knew he was doing it for the effect, to draw in his congregation so they'd buy into his social programs."

Not all Jones's healings at Community Unity involved chicken guts passed off as cancer. Jones often engaged in the laying on of hands, commanding aches or tremors or chills to be gone — and, usually but not always, sufferers experienced instant relief. (Jones loudly attributed failure to a lack of belief on the part of the person he attempted to heal.) Not all of them could have colluded in advance with Jones to claim phony cures. Psychosomatic response was likely in most cases — they believed in Jones so much that they essentially willed discomfort away. But a few surviving eyewitnesses agree that he occasionally performed healings that defied rational explanation. His act may have simply been that good — but they believe that Jim Jones did, in fact, have some sort of special healing gift, which perhaps functioned only intermittently.

Word spread that Pastor Jones now practiced healings at Community Unity. Members of other black Indianapolis churches began skipping their regular services to visit, often out of simple curiosity but some, like Christine Cobb, in hopes that Jones would work a miracle on behalf of a loved one. Christine's seven-year-old son, Jim, suffered dizzy spells from an ear ailment. Jones called the boy to the front, touched his ear, and announced that it was healed. Five years later, Jim Cobb required ear surgery, but by then his mother and other members of the extended Cobb family were fully committed followers.

As his flock increased, Jones was able to acquire badly needed space for the congregation. He agreed to purchase a building at 10th and Delaware Streets; it could hold seven hundred worshippers, and was still in the lower-class district of Indianapolis. Community Unity really had its choice of properties in the neighborhood. "White flight," middle-class America's mid-1950s abandonment of the inner cities for suburbs to escape growing numbers of minorities, affected faith-based organizations as it did families and businesses. Several major sects pulled out of downtown Indianapolis; Community Unity bought the property being left by a Jewish congregation. It cost $50,000; Jones promised he would raise the money to pay for it in full within a year, and did, from collections at out-of-town appearances.

Community Unity celebrated its new home with a name change. Briefly, the church was known as Wings of Deliverance. But the word "Temple" was carved in stone outside the building, and so Jones decided that the name of his church would reflect both its philosophy and the carving: Peoples Temple, not People's, because the apostrophe symbolized ownership. After all, one of the key Temple goals was to discourage obsession with material possessions.

CHAPTER ELEVEN:
GAINING INFLUENCE

With his home church now boasting a congregation of impressive size and racial diversity, Jim Jones was ready to assert himself with Indianapolis policymakers. From zoning issues to street repair to upkeep of schools, the city's black community had never had adequate input. Jones intended to change that — but his personal shortcomings threatened to prevent it.

Jim Jones's most effective means of persuasion was empathy. He had an uncanny ability to meet someone, surmise what was important to him or her, and then convince the person that he shared the same interests. They could work together to achieve a common goal. This gift worked well for him in establishing Community Unity. Jones knew all about being poor and powerless, and how much it meant to have someone who could help achieve even little victories. On the revival circuit, Jones could identify with people wanting an uplifting mix of gospel and showmanship.

But nothing in Jones's life so far prepared him to deal at elevated political and business levels. He had no sense of how to effectively gain the attention, then cooperation, of important individuals whose time and influence were in constant demand. Sheer force of personality worked for Jones at lower administrative levels. He'd lobbied successfully on behalf of impoverished Indianapolis followers with utility company clerks and public school secretaries. Now he wanted to deal directly with the highest public officials and business executives. Jones realized that in itself access meant nothing. Indianapolis's black ministers had participated in supposedly high-level meetings for years without any tangible results to show for it. Jones wanted to persuade important people to *do* things, but had no idea how.

Fortunately for Jones, he was married to someone who did.

Marceline Jones chafed at her role in Jones's early ministry. But she had the critical background and skills that he did not. Marceline was the daughter of a former city councilman, the child of parents involved in all manner of important civic issues. She understood that you didn't develop working relationships with important people through demands and bluster. You did your homework, learned about every aspect of an issue, and then suggested plans that in some way benefited all sides involved. Essentially, whenever you could, you offered solutions. Then, when you did point out a problem, people who could do something about it listened and were ready to help.

Marceline began attending public meetings, at city hall and the school administration building and in private homes all over Indianapolis where neighborhood associations gathered. Jim Jones had no patience with any meeting where he was not the featured speaker. Marceline always listened and rarely spoke, beyond introducing herself and complimenting others on their remarks. Afterward she jotted extensive notes about which people she'd just met seemed to be the most capable, the best-connected. She made a point of cultivating them. Marceline brought home information packets about proposed city and school bond programs and read every line. She coached Jones on critical aspects, some of them obscure to anyone unfamiliar with the intricate details legally required in public projects. Then, at important public hearings, Jones came with Marceline, and he was the one who stood up to make surprising, relevant points, impressing panels who assumed no one other than staff read all the fine print. Often, he made helpful, pragmatic suggestions — wouldn't it make sense if this item was added to the budget, or that program expanded? Jones rapidly gained a reputation as one of the few community-based leaders, and probably the only minister, who really understood how these things worked. Jones just as quickly learned how this game was played. Publicly, he acted as though he'd known all along. When, for the first time, some black neighborhood streets were included in bond improvement packages, or some of the poorest schools in Indianapolis got bond-funded playground equipment, Jim Jones of Peoples Temple received much of the credit and his wife got none. Marceline didn't mind. What mattered to her was that, finally, the Joneses were a *team.*

Marceline also took the lead in establishing the next source of income for Peoples Temple. Inevitably, some of the church's older members, often black women, physically deteriorated to the point where they could no longer care for themselves and were placed in publicly funded nursing homes. Jones made regular visits and was in his element, telling jokes and offering uplifting prayers. But at home, he complained to Marceline about substandard conditions. She investigated licensing requirements, and soon the Joneses' own home was renovated to meet standards for state certification. With the help of fifty-five-year-old Esther Mueller, a white woman hired as an assistant, they accepted several elderly live-in patients, receiving government payment for their care. It wasn't a scam. Inspectors from the Marion County Welfare Department made regular visits and came away impressed, especially with Marceline, who was complimented in one report as "very competent and kind." Based on this initial success, she and Jones formed a corporation and, during the next few years, took over management of several nursing homes. These provided jobs for Peoples Temple congregants, and the money needed not only to pay for outreach programs, but to promote them. Jones was able to purchase daily time on a local radio station, fifteen minutes at 4:45 p.m. on weekdays. It was enough time to offer a taped prayer, short sermon, Jones's thoughts on some relevant issue or to announce a Temple-sponsored event.

The most important of these took place in June 1955, when Jones co-headlined an Indianapolis religious gathering with Rev. William Branham, one of the most famous evangelists in the country. Jones wasn't nearly as well known, but he drew a significant portion of the audience, mostly blacks. One who came away impressed after hearing Jones was Archie Ijames, a self-educated, independent-minded man in his midforties. Ijames had despaired of any church being able to effectively challenge racism. But he found Jones's all-inclusive message inspiring, and afterward visited Peoples Temple with his wife and children. The whole family enjoyed the experience and became members. Ijames was a natural leader, smart, energetic, and dedicated. Jones recognized his potential. He noticed some weaknesses, too — Ijames tended to talk so rapidly that one word blended into the next, sometimes rendering his speech incomprehensible. Jones also felt his new Temple member was a player, someone constantly looking to turn situations to personal advantage. He named Ijames an associate pastor, giving him a title but limited authority. It looked good for Jones to have a black man as his primary public assistant, and he found plenty for Archie to do. In particular, Ijames was involved in daily management of the Temple's public programs.

Thanks again to income from the nursing home operations, the church opened a café that was grandly named "The Free Restaurant." Anyone who had no money and was hungry could come there and eat. On its first day of operation, eighteen people were served; the second day, nearly a hundred. Soon, about 2,800 were fed weekly. All day, lines stretched outside. After their appetites were satisfied, particularly ragged diners were invited to choose clothes from a selection of mostly secondhand items. These were sometimes patched, but always clean. Jones solicited clothing donations on the radio and in his public appearances. The Bible commanded followers of Christ to feed the hungry and clothe the naked. Peoples Temple did both, and in a manner that demonstrated respect for everyone served.

For the first time, Jones presided over a congregation that included dozens of children. He wanted them to think coming to church was fun, not something adults made them do. Sometimes during services, Jones would stop preaching and tell the kids to get up and stretch. Once, he interrupted his own Easter service to ask the youngsters what song they wanted to sing next. When they screamed for "Here Comes Peter Cottontail," that's what the whole congregation sang, Jones's pleasant voice booming out loudest of all. Marceline loved organizing anything that involved children. Under her guidance, Peoples Temple soon had youth choirs and dance troupes. Sometimes these groups were invited to perform on local television shows. Jones began touting Temple youth programs to prospective members with children: Didn't they think their kids would be better off in wholesome church activities instead of dangerous slum streets? For some parents, especially single mothers, that was reason enough to join Peoples Temple.

At Jones's invitation, candidates for city or county offices began dropping in to Sunday services. Peoples Temple now represented a sizable voting bloc — it had hundreds of adult members, and Jones urged everyone to register to vote and go to the polls in every election. He stopped short of openly telling his congregation how to vote, but wasn't shy about declaring his own preferences. Even in a big city like Indianapolis, three or four hundred votes could swing a close election. Jones wasn't hesitant to remind anyone of that. He and his followers enjoyed hearing candidates, most often white men who'd never set foot in the slums before, asking for votes and promising support of Peoples Temple programs in return.

In Indianapolis, Jim Jones now had the influence he craved. Peoples Temple, which welcomed everyone, freely distributed food and clothing to those in need of them most — the truest form of socialism. More money was always needed, but income from Jones's outside appearances and the nursing homes subsidized the good works. Jones, and Peoples Temple, weren't beholden to anyone else.

But it wasn't enough. Jones had learned of someone else doing everything he was, only bigger and better. At this stage in his ministry, Jones still didn't mind playing the part of student. Here was someone with much to teach him, and so Jim Jones reached out to this other preacher, who claimed that he was the Lord — and whose followers believed it. In their worship services they sang, "God is here on earth today, Father Divine is his name."

CHAPTER TWELVE: FATHER DIVINE

The mysteries about the man who convinced many that he was God begin with his birth. Most historians and biographers estimate that he was born to a former slave around 1879 or 1880 in Rockville, Maryland. His original name was probably George Baker. As a young man, Baker worked as a gardener, but his fascination with Christianity led him to follow a series of evangelists, each of whom claimed to offer the only true path to salvation. Some claimed God-given powers in their roles as holy prophets.

Baker studied each of his mentors, cherry-picking the aspects of their preaching that suited him best. He would recall, "I find that there is something good with all of them. I endeavor to be as a honeybee to get the good out of every seed or flower." Around 1912 he renamed himself the Messenger, and set out on his own to prove that "the Gospel can be preached without money and without price." Everywhere he traveled, the gist of the Messenger's teaching was that heaven can be found only on earth, not some undefinable place in the sky. Hymns composed by whites were really "death songs," intended to trick Negroes into thinking they should suffer now in exchange for future admission to heaven. The Messenger promised that God would provide immediately in the welcome forms of social, economic, and political progress if people would only be kind and generous to each other. He revealed himself as God on earth, claimed the power to heal, and began acquiring loyal followers, at first mostly African American women.

The Messenger initially based his ministry in the South, but after several brushes with white law enforcement he relocated to Harlem in New York. There he began housing his followers together in apartments. He forbade smoking, swearing, drinking, and sex — men and women could be together only for worship and other nonromantic interaction. Newcomers were welcome to join, but only if they accepted and followed these rigid rules. Even the leader conformed. He married a woman named Penniniah, but swore it was a spiritual union and never physically consummated.

Next, the Messenger organized his followers into a work collective. He placed them in jobs; salaries were pooled to cover group expenses. Shelter, clothing, and food were all provided through him. The ranks swelled. Many came to him physically or emotionally unable to cope. He expanded his program to include physical therapy for those who needed it, and instituted job training programs so that when he found people work, they would be successful. With reason, most swore that he'd completely changed their lives for the better. They were a family, encouraged to address the Messenger as Father and his wife as Mother. Then their leader took another name: Reverend Major Jealous Divine — "Major" to indicate high rank, "Jealous" to reflect the scripture passage citing a jealous God. He was Father Divine to his flock, and to the media that increasingly wrote about such a colorful character.

In the late 1910s, Harlem experienced a rebirth of community-generated art and music. Father Divine didn't want his followers tainted by such worldliness, so he moved his flock to the Long Island village of Sayville. He had thousands of followers now, and some of them were white. His philosophy of enjoying life now by sharing and working together resonated beyond race.

Father Divine expanded his communal control in Sayville. Everyone lived together, and worked in jobs where he placed them. Divine himself began studying books about building economic empires. His ambition reached beyond a single isolated colony and the pooling of blue-collar wages. As his welcome in Sayville wore out — residents were bothered by so many whites living with blacks — Father Divine returned to the revival circuit and was absent much of the time. Even as his popularity with locals dwindled, he drew sellout crowds around the rest of the country. In 1932, these were estimated to average twelve thousand, and he crowed that, in all, more than three million people were now "believing in me and calling on me." Some formed offshoots of the Sayville commune. These settlements were known as Peace Missions. Divine began publicly commenting on politics and social issues — to combat racism, he insisted that his followers be completely integrated, to the point of blacks and whites being alternately seated at meals and in cars.

Inevitably, some disillusioned followers left Peace Missions and complained to authorities about mistreatment. Father Divine was attacked from pulpits by other ministers who were offended by his claim to be God. There were raids on gatherings of his followers. Though he insisted that the charges were manufactured by his enemies, in 1932 Father Divine was sentenced to one year in prison for various forms of fraud. He entered prison defiantly, proclaiming that "Every knock is a boost, every criticism is a praise." Divine served only a few weeks before being released on bail. Afterward, the Peace Movement flourished; its leader now focused mostly on secular issues. Divine presided over the opening of dozens of Movement-owned businesses, including hotels and restaurants. Many of his followers lived in the hotels; empty rooms were rented to the public for a dollar a night. In Movement restaurants, diners paid whatever they thought the meals that they'd eaten were worth. Profits from other businesses funded further expansion. In the 1930s, the Movement acquired extensive farmland in Ulster County, New York, and named it Promised Land. Most produce grown there fed those living in Peace Mission communes — Father Divine meant for his people to be self-sufficient.

There was more trouble in the late 1930s. Some of his most trusted associates left the Movement and accused Father Divine of keeping his followers in a state of virtual slavery. They also claimed that, despite his prohibition against sex, Divine and Movement members sometimes indulged in orgies. A highly publicized lawsuit alleging fraud was brought against Divine by a former adherent claiming he'd cheated her of money and property. When, after years of courtroom haggling, a judge in New York City finally ruled against Divine, he responded, "I have long since declared I will shake creation," and in

1942 moved his headquarters to Philadelphia.

He remained controversial. Penniniah became ill, and, despite her husband's promise to cure her, died in 1943. Three years later, Divine married a twenty-one-year-old white woman, proclaiming that Penniniah's spirit had simply chosen to leave an old body for this new one. Thus, his promise to cure his wife hadn't failed at all. Afterward, for the first time, Divine's sermons began touting reincarnation. The second Mother Divine was far more active in his ministry than the first.

In 1953, Father and Mother Divine occupied a spacious mansion in the upscale Philadelphia suburb of Woodmont. Its seventy-two-acre grounds included tennis courts and a swimming pool. The elderly Peace Mission leader was worshipped as God by hundreds of thousands, controlled virtually every aspect of his followers' lives, and reveled in controversy. Accusations, by outsiders or disgruntled former followers, only made his true believers more loyal to him. Now, in the sumptuous surroundings of his home or adjacent woods and gardens, he occasionally met and counseled young preachers who aspired to bring about social equality through their own ministries.

In late 1956 or early 1957, Jim Jones requested a meeting with Father Divine at Woodmont. With a large mixed-race church in a major U.S. city, Jones's credentials were sufficiently impressive for Divine to agree. His initial visit to Woodmont was a revelation for Jones. He was particularly struck by the staff of worshipful women in the mansion who were eager to act on their leader's behalf. Here was a leader who was *appreciated*. Jones undoubtedly told Divine about Peoples Temple programs, free food and clothing and well-maintained nursing homes. But he'd come to learn rather than brag. Like many older, accomplished men, Father Divine enjoyed describing his achievements to an up-and-comer who clearly hung on every word. Jones wanted to know how this communal housing worked, and how Movement businesses provided jobs for followers. There was also the Promised Land farm project — the concept of a social ministry feeding itself was fascinating. Divine was flattered; Jones's visit extended for an entire day.

It was the first of many. During the next few years, Jones would frequently slip out of Indianapolis and fly to Pennsylvania. He'd spend the day with Father Divine and fly home that night. He adopted some of his new mentor's affectations. Peoples Temple members were encouraged to address him as Father and Marceline as Mother. Father Divine always dressed in fine suits; he stressed that the appearance of success was critical. As a boy in Lynn, Jones always dressed a little better than the others. He'd stopped being as concerned about fashion in Indianapolis, but now he upgraded his wardrobe. Jones's old friend Max Knight, who'd become a reporter for Richmond's daily newspaper, bumped into Jones on a sidewalk in town and was struck by his appearance: "He had his hair combed straight back, so much so that it stuck out behind his ears, and he was wearing fancy clothes. . . . He had a pair of dark glasses pushed up on his head, real affected-like. This was not the Jim that I knew, and I said, 'Jim, I don't understand. Why are you wearing a suit like that, and why are you wearing those glasses on the top of your head?' He leaned in to me and said, 'Max, if you want to reach the top, you've got to play the part.' "

Over coffee and lunches, Jones discussed Father Divine with Ron Haldeman, focusing not so much on what Divine had done as how he did it. The key, Jones believed, was reaching the kind of people who also composed the bulk of Divine's most devoted followers — these were "the impoverished and the alienated." Jones constantly described the control Divine held over every aspect of his followers' lives. At communal dinners in the Woodmont mansion, countless pots of steaming food were brought to banquet tables, but no one, no matter how hungry, took a bite until Divine, taking his time, completed blessing each individual pot. Such ceremonies were critical, Jones believed. They reinforced the leader's authority.

Haldeman gradually realized that Jones intended not only to emulate Divine's ministry, but also to inherit his followers after the old man died. That would be tricky — Divine preached about his own immortality. But, according to Divine himself, the spirit of the first Mother Divine willingly transferred to the body of a younger woman. Perhaps Jones could use that scenario and one day present himself to Peace Mission members as Father Divine reappearing in new flesh.

To prepare his own Peoples Temple followers for potential merger with the Peace Mission, Jones published and distributed a fanciful pamphlet titled "Pastor Jones Meets Rev. M. J. Divine." Its subtitle was "How a pastor of a large full gospel assembly was more consecrated to Jesus Christ by his contact with the Rev. M. J. Divine Peace Mission movement." Declaring that "I owe it to my many Christian associates to give an authentic, unbiased, and objective statement of my experiences with this group over the past three years," Jones claimed he was originally reluctant even to visit Divine's church. He'd heard "it was supposed to be a harem run by a demonically possessed immoral person." But once there, "the spirit of truth stimulated me." Though Jones stressed that he did not agree with Divine's claim to be God, "but merely an instrument who had done a good work," and said so to Divine and his followers, they still made him welcome and shared their superb, scripture-based philosophy: "From each according to his ability [and] to each according to his need." Thanks to income from their own businesses, they did not have to rely on collections at services. Jones vowed to do the same. He even embraced — mostly — Divine's exhortations against sex. Thanks to Divine's example, Jones wrote, "I can say that I am free from the sexual thoughts for many days at a time."

The last few pages had nothing to do with Divine, but everything to do with one of his teachings that Jones would observe for the remainder of his own ministry. Divine openly challenged his critics. Now Jones did too:

My avid opponents prophesied months ago that the glory of the Lord had departed from us because of our work, but I inform everyone, not in spite but for clarification, that God is moving in greater manner than ever before since I founded Peoples Temple. Hundreds attend the services regularly each week in all our assemblies and never a service passes without someone being miraculously healed, converted, or filled with the Holy Ghost. Our files are filled with the names and addresses of persons who have been completely healed in the last few days. We will gladly furnish these testimonies to friend or foe alike upon request. . . . Observe the future with a pure mind and you will see the mystery of our ministry unfold before your eyes; then you will say along with every honest Christian, "surely this is the Lord's work."

At this point, Jones couldn't name specific "opponents" because as yet he had none besides America's capitalist economy and general social system. No organizations in Indianapolis or anywhere else had attacked Jones and Peoples Temple. They weren't yet prominent enough. But while he waited for Father Divine to die, Jim Jones changed that, taking steps to raise his public profile in ways that were bound to attract strenuous opposition. He'd learned well from Father Divine that having enemies, real or imagined, was invaluable in recruiting and retaining followers.

CHAPTER THIRTEEN: "ALL RACES TOGETHER"

In 1950s America, blacks didn't have to imagine enemies. They were all too real. Lynchings and cross burnings had left their horrific mark even before 1954, when a Supreme Court decision initiated a new wave of racial turmoil. *Brown v. Board of Education* was understood to have wider implications than ruling that "separate but equal" schools for white and black children were unconstitutional. The court's unanimous vote set aside *Plessy v. Ferguson,* an 1896 court ruling establishing "separate but equal" as a legal basis for all forms of segregation. Clearly, the Supreme Court was now prepared to support other legal challenges on behalf of African Americans. Racists were outraged, and some responded violently.

On December 1, 1955, in Alabama, Rosa Parks refused to relinquish her seat on a Montgomery bus and was arrested. This precipitated the Montgomery Bus Boycott; the city relented and desegregated its bus system in 1956. The issue propelled black preacher Martin Luther King Jr. to the civil rights forefront. Across the nation, particularly in the Deep South, great marches began taking place, with violence often erupting. Communities balking at court-mandated school integration sometimes refused to comply and dared the federal government to do something about it. In the fall of 1957, President Dwight D. Eisenhower ordered National Guard troops to protect integration at Central High School in Little Rock, Arkansas. Tension ratcheted higher across the nation.

But the Supreme Court's *Brown* ruling didn't change anything in Indianapolis. Black teens went to Crispus Attucks, their neighborhood school. If they'd lived in other neighborhoods they could have gone to schools there, but the city housing regulations still legally in place prevented African Americans from living anywhere else. Most city businesses were segregated. Nobody marched in protest — that wasn't the Indiana way. White leaders continued agreeing to meet whenever black ministers asked, and afterward nothing changed — except when Jim Jones was involved. If he wasn't moving racist mountains, he at least flattened some bumps. White officials came to Peoples Temple and followed through on promises made there, about minor issues like pothole repair or more up-to-date school textbooks, perhaps, but such things were significant compared to the complete failure of black ministers to get anything at all for their congregants. Black folks around the city took notice; the January 4, 1957, edition of the *Indianapolis Reporter,* a prominent black newspaper, included Jones on its "human relations honor roll."

That guaranteed Jones the unwavering loyalty of black Temple members. Far from mistrusting him because of his race, they considered it an advantage. He preached like a black man and got things done like a white one. It was a unique combination. These black congregants never doubted that the white majority, in Indianapolis and elsewhere, was implacably determined to deny them even the most basic rights. Pastor Jones, now Father Jones to many, was unquestionably on their side against white oppressors. He made their lives better in tangible ways. He gave them hope. This meant that his enemies were their enemies.

But thanks to the arrival of many former Laurel Street Tabernacle members and Jones's own skill at recruitment on the revival circuit, the Peoples Temple congregation now skewed white. These members were drawn not through commitment to integration or socialism, but because they admired Jones's healing gifts and Bible-based preaching. Most Peoples Temple whites came from the same working class that opposed the civil rights movement. Some, like Jack and Rheaviana Beam, genuinely embraced Jones's emphasis on civil rights, but until he could bring his other white followers around to the same viewpoint, Jones had to bind them to him by pulpit showmanship and his own personal example.

He started with the Bible, and its warnings that Satan was present everywhere, trying to undo the Lord's good works. Regardless of race, all members of the congregation believed that. And if Satan was the common enemy Jones preached, then everyone in Peoples Temple was united in this critical way. All right, then: they must fight the devil on every front. Satan rejoiced when people disdained others because of the way they dressed or talked or the color of their skin. Want to defy him? Then accept everyone in this church as part of your family, regardless of any differences between you. Rick Cordell, a white teenager, recalled, "His message was always very stark . . . brotherhood, all races together. You were accepted just as you were, you were not judged by the way you looked, or how much education you had, or how much money you had."

Outside of church, Jones organized activities for everyone, picnics and talent shows and outings to zoos all over the region, and carpooling without regard to race. Everyone in the congregation was welcome in his home. The Joneses lived unpretentiously. Their furniture was a hodgepodge of Baldwin family hand-me-downs and acquisitions from rummage sales. The only item of note was a gargantuan dining room table. There had to be room for at least a dozen people to eat at a time because Jones invited virtually everyone he encountered home for meals. Her husband's habit of unexpectedly showing up at all hours with guests caused Marceline considerable stress. She'd been taught by her mother that no visitor should ever find a lady's home anything other than spick-and-span. A slumber party for the Temple kids resulted in an infestation of bedbugs. Marceline begged Jim to stop inviting people over until she was certain that the pests were eradicated. At the next Sunday service, Jones announced, "I want all of you to feel welcome to come visit us anytime, because now we've rid ourselves of the bedbugs." After that, Marceline remembered, "I got over worrying about what people thought."

Around 1957, Lynetta moved to Indianapolis from Richmond. Her son, Jimba, was becoming a celebrity of sorts, and she wasn't going to miss it. Lynetta moved in with him and Marceline; since money was tight, she had to find a job and contribute toward household expenses. She was hired as a guard in a nearby women's prison. Typically, Lynetta would later claim that she was an administrator who eventually ran afoul of higherups by insisting on reforms. Having such an opinionated mother-in-law as a permanent houseguest wasn't easy on Marceline, but she soon was distracted from Lynetta's constant carping in the best of ways.

Agnes had not proven to be the ideal child for the Joneses. The little girl was able to overcome a problem with stuttering, but nothing could alter her balky, unpredictable personality. A happy, smiling family was critical to Jones's public image, and Agnes didn't fit. He and Marceline didn't consider giving Agnes up, but they did decide to add more children to their family. Both doted on kids. Marceline's health problems meant she would have complicated pregnancies even if she could carry a baby to term, so they decided to try adopting again.

It was Marceline who first proposed a "rainbow family." Why not adopt multiple children of different races? She and Jim would love the children, of course, and try to be the best possible parents, but there would be the added benefit of the Jones family being a constant, unmistakable example of racial harmony. Her husband was enthusiastic. A black baby was the obvious choice, but never in Indiana history had a white couple adopted an African American infant. The Joneses would investigate that, but decided to begin with an Asian child. Since there were none available in their home state, the Joneses traveled to California, where they met and adopted two Korean orphans, a four-year-old girl they named Stephanie and a two-year-old boy renamed Lew. The children fit perfectly into their new home. Their adoptive parents adored them, and so did the congregation of Peoples Temple. Their new grandmother was less welcoming. Lynetta still didn't care for kids.

Almost at the same time Stephanie and Lew arrived, Marceline learned that she was pregnant. Marceline loved children, and the thought of giving birth to one of her own was thrilling. The pregnancy was uncomfortable from the start, but Marceline was a trained nurse and knew how to take care of herself. As she came closer to term, she cut back on outside activities and had lots of bed rest. Temple women were glad to pitch in and help with Agnes, Stephanie, and Lew. The church continued involving its children in all sorts of wholesome activities, and in May 1959 there was a weekend outing to the zoo in Cincinnati. Jones led the group, which included his children but not their mother, who was in her final weeks of pregnancy and stayed home to rest.

It was a rainy weekend. Thunderstorms lashed the region, but the Temple trip to Cincinnati went on as planned. They car-pooled in a variety of vehicles. Everyone had a fine, if wet, time, and on the way home Stephanie Jones rode with one of the congregants. On the way, they were hit squarely by a drunk driver — Stephanie died instantly.

Further pain was inflicted on the little girl's grief-stricken parents when they prepared to bury her. Stephanie was Korean, and no Indianapolis cemetery would allow her body to be interred next to whites. Only a black mortician would prepare the dead girl for burial. The Joneses were directed to "Negro cemetery sections," which were in the worst areas. It was still storming when Stephanie was laid to rest. The hole dug for her coffin was half full of water. Jones sobbed as Stephanie was lowered into the muck. He would recall later, "Oh, shit, it was cruel, cruel." Three weeks later, Marceline gave birth to a baby boy. His parents named him Stephan, spelling it with "an" rather than the traditional "en" to honor his dead sister. But that wasn't the end of it. Marceline Jones was never given to claiming prophetic visions. She left that to her husband. Only once did Marceline claim to have received a mysterious message, and, according to her, it happened on the night that little Stephanie died.

While her husband and children were away on the Cincinnati trip, Marceline rested in bed. On the rainy night of the accident, she was too tired to wait for them. She fell asleep, only to be awakened by Stephanie outside on the porch, calling, "Mommy, let me in." Marceline got up, brought the girl inside, and asked, "Where's your father?" Stephanie replied, "Oh-boke needs a mommy and daddy." Marceline didn't understand, and, too weary to pursue the conversation, put the child to bed and went back to sleep herself.

Jim Jones spent that terrible night identifying his daughter's body and arranging for her remains to be transported back to Indianapolis. He dreaded breaking the news to Marceline. When he arrived home at dawn, he woke his wife and gently explained that Stephanie had died in a car crash. Marceline insisted that couldn't be true. Stephanie had come home in the middle of the night — she was asleep in her room. When Jones took her to look there, the bed was still made and there was no sign of Stephanie. Marceline described her vision, including Stephanie's comment about "Oh-boke."

After the heartbreaking funeral, and after Stephan was born, the Joneses couldn't forget about "Oh-boke." They contacted the adoption agency in California, and learned that Stephanie had a six-year-old sister named Oboki. The child was still in a Korean orphanage. Jones and Marceline both accepted her vision as a sign, and adopted the girl. They renamed her Suzanne.

The nature of Marceline's vision can be

debated — an actual prophetic dream, a later response to tragedy that she honestly believed to have been a vision, or a lie told so many times that Marceline eventually convinced herself that it was true. But, for the rest of her life, it was a story she told repeatedly, with great conviction.

The Joneses didn't complete their rainbow family with Suzanne. In 1961, they defied Indiana tradition and adopted a black infant. Tellingly, they named the child James Warren Jones Jr.

During the late 1950s, Temple recruits included several individuals who would, over time, become some of Jones's most trusted lieutenants. First was Russell Winberg, the associate pastor of Laurel Street Tabernacle, who'd initially brought Jones to the attention of that church. Winberg had been passed over to lead the tabernacle. He left afterward to join Jones's staff at Peoples Temple. This was a coup for Jones. It proved that an educated, ordained individual was willing to leave a more established church to join his ministry.

Even as Peoples Temple grew, Jones continued making appearances in the revival circuit. He developed a schedule, speaking regularly in Indiana, Michigan, and Ohio. Always anxious to curtail expenses — every cent was needed for Temple programs — he began naming "state coordinators," regular attendees at his programs who were responsible for finding donors who would feed Jones and his entourage, then house them overnight, always at no cost. In South Charleston, Ohio, Jones came upon Patty Cartmell, an obese white woman obsessed with the possibility of a world-ending apocalypse. Often dragging her husband and children along, she attended all manner of religious gatherings until deciding that Jim Jones, with his combination of religiosity and socialism, was the prophet she sought. Cartmell considered it a great honor to be selected as one of his coordinators, and periodically went with her family to stay with the Joneses in Indianapolis. Her addition provided Jones with a worshipful accomplice who enthusiastically obeyed all of his instructions, no matter how questionable. In particular, Cartmell became Jones's eyes and ears at out-of-town gatherings. He no longer had to mingle with crowds before his appearances to gather information for healings and revelations.

A young minister named Ross Case was determined to integrate his Disciples of Christ Christian church in Mason City, Illinois. Case heard about Jim Jones and Peoples Temple while attending a religious gathering in Indiana. Just as Jones had sought out Father Divine, Case was anxious to meet with someone who appeared to have achieved goals similar to his own. Jones agreed to see

Case in Indianapolis, and the two men hit it off. When Jones asked Case to join Peoples Temple, he agreed to consider it. But Case had a suggestion for Jones — why not affiliate his church with the Disciples of Christ? The denomination, one of the largest in the Midwest with about two million members, advocated more community outreach by individual congregations — doing God's work and not just talking about it on Sunday. Peoples Temple seemed an ideal match. To leadership in the Disciples denomination, Jones and his church would provide a constant example of what all their member churches should be doing. Jones and Peoples Temple would benefit from the association, too. Affiliation with Disciples would convey more legitimacy to outsiders than was possible for an independent church, and, of course, there would be welcome tax exemptions. Best of all, from Jones's perspective, the Disciples granted virtual autonomy to their individual congregations. There wasn't even a process in place for dismissing errant churches from the denomination.

Jones remembered very well how his earlier, impulsive effort to affiliate with the Quakers had failed. He took careful steps this time, discussing potential Disciples affiliation on several Sundays with his Peoples Temple flock before calling for a congregational vote on the matter. Jones made it clear that he hoped

181

the verdict would be overwhelming approval, and it was. From there, Jones, with Case's help, made formal application to the Disciples. The record of Peoples Temple in providing food, clothing, and geriatric care for the needy was persuasive. So was the church's substantial black membership. The Disciples supported integration. Peoples Temple was accepted for membership. The one caveat was that Jones had to earn a college degree before he could be fully certified as a pastor within the denomination. Jones enrolled at Butler University in Indianapolis, transferring what credits he could from the University of Indiana and going to class at night to earn the rest required for graduation. He was allowed to remain in the Peoples Temple pulpit in the interim, and Ross Case left his Mason City church to serve as an assistant pastor to Jones.

Jim Jones had come a long way since 1952, when reading the new Methodist Church social creed convinced him that a career in the ministry could help bring about socialism in America. He had his own integrated church, newly affiliated with a prestigious denomination and considerable political and cultural influence in Indiana's biggest city. If he never accomplished anything else, Jim Jones could rightly have been judged a man of considerable achievement. Then a new opportunity emerged.

Indianapolis had a Human Rights Commission. Its directorship, which paid $7,000 annually, came open. A selection committee was named, and applications were invited. It was all right for the director to have outside employment. The commission job was essentially honorary. A director wasn't expected to do much besides preside over occasional meetings where much was discussed and nothing done. The position was considered so nonprestigious that there was only one applicant.

In 1961, the mayor introduced Jim Jones as director of the Indianapolis Human Relations Commission. Immediately afterward, to the surprise of everyone but the new director, things in the placid, go-along-to-get-along city began changing, rapidly and radically.

CHAPTER FOURTEEN:
A MAN TO BE RECKONED
WITH

In 1961, Indianapolis wasn't considered a
hotbed of racial unrest. It was never the site
of dramatic Freedom Marches, with national
media on hand to record fire hoses and snarling police dogs turned on courageous black
protesters. But less overt hostility existed.
Like everywhere else in America, blue-collar
whites in Indianapolis enjoyed relative comforts that were new to their generation —
houses in nice neighborhoods, jobs that paid
more than a bare subsistence wage, good
schools for kids who might one day go to college and then on to the kind of white-collar
careers that were beyond the reach of their
parents. Many believed that integration,
especially when mandated by the government, was a threat. Once *they* were in white
Indianapolis neighborhoods, factories, and
schools, it was easy to imagine new national
laws giving black people further advantages
at the expense of their white counterparts.
For more than a decade, there had been

increasingly widespread claims that the federal government was falling under the control of communist sympathizers. Many believed that communists orchestrated the civil rights movement in an attempt to undermine America's core of white citizens. When Robert Welch founded the ultraconservative John Birch Society in December 1958, he made the announcement in Indianapolis.

So in addition to the inherent lack of authority in his new office, new city Human Rights Commission director Jim Jones had an additional handicap. His goal was the integration of blacks into every aspect of Indianapolis, and he firmly espoused socialist policies that, to most of the politically conservative white people he had to convince, were the same thing as communism. As he set out on this apparently hopeless quest, there was one source of encouragement. At the same time Jones was named commission director, the Indiana General Assembly passed legislation mandating equal opportunity in state employment and equal access to public accommodations. It was progressivism in a state never previously known for it. However, the new laws had no effect on privately owned businesses.

Jones, at this stage in his life, was both visionary and pragmatic. Economic segregation was deep-seated in Indianapolis and would have to be challenged from the bottom up. Most corporate owners would be impervious to any requests. He couldn't bring sufficient political or economic pressure to bear on them, and his talent for empathy wouldn't work because they had nothing in common. But small businessmen, operators of mom-and-pop companies, were different. Jones understood their fierce pride in achieving ownership, and fear of losing what they'd worked so hard to attain.

So he began his crusade with white-owned neighborhood cafés and restaurants. Most routinely turned away prospective black diners, though in passive-aggressive fashion rather than openly denying service based on race. Blacks who arrived and asked to be seated, even in places with many empty tables, were informed that advance reservations were required. If reservations were then requested, the blacks were told that every table at that time was already spoken for.

Jones and Marceline went to medium-priced restaurants where they regularly dined as a couple or together with the white Haldemans, but this time they brought African American friends. When informed that reservations were required, they replied politely but firmly that this was never the case before. If no table was currently available, they'd wait to be seated. Occasionally, they finally were, though the service provided and food served was always deplorable. Most often, they were left standing until the restaurant closed. Either result suited Jones. The next day, he'd be back by himself, asking to speak to the owner. If the owner wasn't on hand, Jones kept returning, as often as necessary until he was granted a meeting. Then, in a reasonable tone, Jones would ask that the restaurant begin accepting African American guests, and provide the same quality of food and service to them that was enjoyed by whites. At first he was always refused and told to mind his own business. Jones would politely ask that the owner reconsider; he'd be back to talk again. During a second conversation, Jones worked to establish common ground. He'd grown up poor, he understood how hard it was to even start a business, let alone keep one going. Jones wasn't pressing integration to cause trouble; he was suggesting something that would actually boost revenue by bringing in new customers. Everyone would benefit. Of course, continued refusal to integrate would result in a third visit, and this time Jones would bring a crowd of blacks and whites with him not to dine but to protest. He'd regret the necessity of it, and of course it would be picketing of a peaceful nature. Still, the restaurant's white customers would have to maneuver through polite protesters asking them to withhold their business until this restaurant served diners of all races. It would be embarrassing; income would be lost.

Jones's sincerity was obvious. No one dared call his bluff. When the first few restaurant owners capitulated, Jones rewarded them by appearing with lots of new customers, most of them Temple members. He was shrewd, usually arriving at off-hours rather than busy ones, providing the restaurants with additional traffic without inconveniencing or driving away their regulars. Bills for these meals were paid out of the Temple general treasury, so cash-strapped members of the church enjoyed dining out for free.

And he did more. The Temple regularly distributed flyers and newsletters announcing various church programs and outings. Now, whenever a mom-and-pop restaurant integrated at Jones's request, Peoples Temple would distribute flyers announcing the latest progress in integrating Indianapolis. These might praise a specific establishment and urge everyone to dine there. Often, grammar and spelling were atrocious — Jones thought it was more important to give his members a sense of unfettered trust than to provide even the most cursory editing. But even with such poorly written flyers, these white restaurant owners benefited from the free advertising. Word spread — if you cooperated with Jim Jones, he and his church people became some of the best friends a small businessman could have. Soon, when Jones asked for initial meetings with café or restaurant owners, more were agreeable. Only a few failed to comply. Jones's success was so widespread that he didn't order any picketing. The possibility was enough to serve his purpose. Besides, Jones understood that establishing actual picket lines would violate the nonconfrontational preferences of city leaders who were otherwise willing to let him pursue integration as he pleased.

From there, Jones moved on to other types of businesses, using the same tactic. He never shouted, never became unpleasant even when those he was meeting with did. Jones presented himself as the voice of reason. He could refer recalcitrant business owners to others who had changed their segregationist policies. These people had more customers than ever. Most were glad that they'd cooperated with Jim Jones — just ask them. Again, his success rate wasn't perfect. But it was still impressive.

There were committed segregationists higher on the Indianapolis economic ladder than individual shop owners. When they noted Jones's success at street-level business integration, they tried derailing his efforts by buying him off. Surely the man needed money. His salary as commission director was only $7,000, and from the look of them, the members of his church couldn't afford to pay their pastor much. Jones was offered a job at $25,000 a year to quit the Human Relations Commission. Marceline remembered later that it was with the Indianapolis Chamber of Commerce.

Jones did need money. He and Marceline were now raising four children on a shoestring budget. Jones received 55 percent of all collections taken at Peoples Temple services, but that wasn't much. Income from outside appearances went directly to church programs, not to him. With the full support of his wife, Jones turned down the offer. Principle mattered more to them than money.

As more businesses integrated in terms of customers, Jones began pushing them to integrate their workforce as well. Through Peoples Temple he formed an employment service, modeled on those operated by Father Divine and the Peace Movement. Members of the Temple, and some impoverished, desperate outsiders, too, were placed in entry-level positions with companies that would never have considered employing them before Jones became Human Relations Commission director. It was not Jones's intent to burden employers with incompetent workers as a regretful but necessary concession to integration. Just the opposite — he expected the people he placed to become outstanding employees. Before they began their new jobs, Jones told them that he'd put his reputation on the line for them. If they messed up, he'd be blamed, and afterward be that much less effective leading the fight for integration. So it was on them as much as on him. Most responded as Jones hoped, by doing good work. They were grateful to Jones, and so were their employers. His prestige, and his confidence, grew.

Jones also took steps to reassure the Indianapolis power elite that he was not a dangerous radical, that, in fact, he represented a reasonable approach to change. The so-called Black Muslims of the Nation of Islam were headquartered in nearby Chicago, and considered menacing even by most liberal whites. Jones called on them there, offering an opportunity to work together to achieve integration. The offer was rejected; Jones made that widely known because it exactly suited his purposes. Here was proof that Jim Jones wasn't in league with dangerous blacks who spurned him. He championed the safe ones.

Jones also positioned himself as a buffer against the radical white fringe. The American Nazi Party constantly opposed integration, claiming it would result in miscegenation that fouled the purity of the white race. Jones wrote to the party leadership in Arlington, Virginia, requesting a meeting to discuss the issue — after all, God loved everyone. Surely the Nazis agreed. He expected to be rebuffed, and was. A letter he received from Nazi Party lieutenant Dan Burros declared, "It does not surprise me that an integrationist would attempt to annihilate his opponents with love. The trouble with all your beliefs is that they are unnatural. Natural laws require, nay demand, struggle. Your doctrines of weakness cannot possibly prevail. . . . Our natures are so divergent that we could never understand each other. Heil Hitler!" Copies of the letter were circulated at Indianapolis City Hall. In contrast to the unnerving divisiveness of the Nazis and Black Muslims, Jim Jones's positive efforts to bring about integration seemed appropriate, even reassuring.

For all his work as commission director, Jones didn't neglect Peoples Temple. As had Father Divine, Jones demanded that his congregation be fully integrated in everything, including seating during services. The edict extended to his family. Marceline and their children were often separated after entering the building. Anxious as any mother to ensure her kids behaved in church, Marceline used chewing gum as bribes. Before the service, she allocated a stick per child, and tore the sticks in two. Each was given a half stick before church started and got the other half only for exhibiting good behavior.

Jones even used personal illness to further the cause. In the early fall of 1961, he was rushed to an Indianapolis hospital with severe abdominal discomfort. Jones was assigned a room in the hospital wing reserved for whites and insisted he would stay only if there was immediate integration. Things were further complicated with the arrival of Jones's personal physician, who was black. Administrators were aware of Jones's reputation as director of the city Human Relations Commission. They promised to open building wings to all races. That wasn't enough for Jones. In terrible pain — he would be diagnosed with bleeding ulcers — Jones refused to be treated until he saw for himself that integration was being carried out. Several black patients had to assure Jones that they had been moved to rooms in previously all-white wings before he finally allowed himself to be cared for.

By the end of 1961, Indianapolis was a significantly more integrated city than it had been twelve months earlier, and Jim Jones was almost entirely responsible. He'd managed it without alienating the local white officials whose support he needed to do more. Jones was revered in the black community. Even those who didn't belong to Peoples Temple knew what he'd done on their behalf. And, despite all the other demands on him, Jones had just earned his undergraduate degree at Butler and was finally eligible for ordination in the influential Disciples of Christ denomination. It had been a glorious year for him, with many achievements and the apparent inevitability of greater things to come. The poor country boy who'd wanted so badly to be important had grown into a big-city leader: in Midwest parlance, a man to be reckoned with. Jones had drawn on the best of himself — his unyielding commitment to social justice, his boundless energy, his indomitable will. But although Jones was a man of immense gifts, his flaws were equally great. Now they threatened to overwhelm his talents and undo all that he had accomplished.

CHAPTER FIFTEEN: BREAKDOWN

In 1961, at the height of his success in Indianapolis, Jim Jones met his childhood friend Max Knight for lunch. Jones talked about how many businesses in the city he'd managed to integrate and reminded Knight that, back in Lynn, Max had encouraged him to become a minister. Knight congratulated Jones on all he'd achieved and asked what was next, expecting to hear about more plans for integration in Indianapolis. He was stunned when Jones replied that he wanted to move his ministry out of that city — Indianapolis, with its nonconfrontational, everybody-get-along ways, "wasn't wide open." Jones said he could accomplish only so much there. The West Coast was "where real social church ministries are needed. In California, there would be no limits." Being in Indianapolis, trying to get things done, was frustrating and took a physical and psychological toll. Throughout 1961, Jones rose before sunup and worked all day and most of the night. Sometimes he'd ask Ron Haldeman to come with him to lunch because he needed to get away from all of the pressure, and then, over the spicy food he loved, Jones would talk incessantly about something in Indianapolis that needed to be changed and how he was going to change it. So far as Haldeman could tell, Jones never took even an afternoon off.

There was too much for one man to do, but Jones wouldn't delegate. Marceline remained his trusted behind-the-scenes partner in Temple outreach programs, and Walter and Charlotte Baldwin came from Richmond to help with the nursing homes. Jones still came by these facilities on a daily basis, talking one-on-one with clients there, promising he'd personally look into any problems they had. He had a handpicked team of associate pastors — Russell Winberg, Ross Case, Archie Ijames — but didn't trust them to lead Temple services in his absence. When Jones absolutely had to be away on a Sunday, he always asked Ron Haldeman to preside in his place. Haldeman said that "Jim suspected they might be a lot like he was with Father Divine, waiting for the leader to die or be gone so they could take over."

Jones's paranoia extended to the Temple congregation. In any growing church with an outspoken, controversial leader, there were bound to be some who joined for a while and then chose to leave. Other ministers accepted this inevitable attrition, but not Jones. He made a point of knowing every member and tried to forge a personal bond with each. Anyone could call on Father Jim for help or counsel, anytime. But much was also asked of those belonging to Peoples Temple. They were expected to attend every Sunday service without fail, and to participate in all extracurricular activities as well as put in volunteer hours at church social service programs. In these, and also in every aspect of their personal lives, members had to follow socialist principles as espoused by Jones — no superior airs, no obsession with material possessions. They were instructed to watch each other and report transgressions. Jones held regular "corrective fellowship" sessions, where individual members stood before their peers and were criticized for any wrongdoing. There was always something each person needed to do better.

For some, it was too much and they stopped coming, thinking that was the end of it until Jones inundated them with letters and phone calls beseeching them to return. It wasn't just what he wanted, Jones stressed — it was God's Will that they remain part of the congregation. If there was something about Jones's demands on his followers that they didn't understand, it shouldn't be questioned — God didn't want them doing that, either.

To challenge Jim Jones was to challenge the Lord, and God would respond accordingly.

In an undated, handwritten letter to Earl Jackson on "Peoples Nursing Home" stationery, Jones declared,

My beloved brother in Christ, concern for you kept me up praying the entire night! I'm going to speak sincerely and frankly! God sent you to Peoples Temple and you must not release yourself. I know that there are things about the Message that you may not see but it is God. As long as we love Christ we have unity and understanding to compensate for all the little things you & I might disagree on. Earl you will be making a serious mistake if you leave our Temple that God has ordained and declared you to be part of. Don't go out to see the proof of what I just said. Hear me as a voice crying to you from the depths of love & fondness for you. "Stand still and see the salvation of the Lord." Don't go back on the light! I know you wouldn't [do that] intentionally but if you leave the place that Christ has set you in much sorrow and heartache will be the result. God impressed my mind strongly in every prayer in the early hours before dawn that you would be making a terrible mistake to leave. Please hear my counsel which I give with a heart full of love for you! Yours in Him, Pastor James Jones.

P.S. I called last night but you were asleep. I'll be in contact by person or phone with you soon! My prayers and love go all out for you!

Even as he obsessed about the loyalty of individual Temple members, Jones also had to reckon with oversight and criticism from his affiliate denomination. For Jones, the Disciples of Christ had two specific attractions: commitment to racial and economic equality, and a general hands-off attitude toward individual member churches. But there was still oversight. Observers from the Disciples regional office attended some Sunday services at the Temple, and afterward informed Jones that he talked too much about current social issues and "didn't preach Jesus enough." Jones was furious. He retorted that "Jesus preached whatever needed to be said." Temple members, Jones said, felt powerless. These downtrodden people were exactly who he wanted in his congregation, and he knew what they needed to hear. Bible stories about the life of Christ paled compared to His command that there should be love and fairness toward all. Jones would emphasize "the words of Jesus" in terms of modern-day oppression that Temple members could relate to in their own lives.

Jones's response curtailed denominational criticism of his sermons, but he had another, more serious concern. All affiliate churches were required to submit annual reports citing membership, income, and the percentage of that income contributed to denominational programs. Then and afterward, Jones wanted control of every cent raised by Peoples Temple, whether from contributions by members or gifts from outside organizations and benefactors. The idea of sharing any of it with the Disciples distressed him. So the reports submitted by Peoples Temple routinely misrepresented church membership and income. As many as seven hundred people regularly attended Sunday services. Annual Temple membership was reported at 264 in 1960, and at 233 in 1961. Fewer reported members meant less reported income. Other member churches routinely contributed a minimum of 10 or 15 percent to the Disciples, some sent as much as half. Peoples Temple gave 3 percent, totaling no more than a few hundred dollars, and Jones begrudged even that.

The Disciples regional office had the authority to audit Temple books. Its observers could have demonstrated that Temple membership far exceeded what its annual report indicated. But the continued participation of Peoples Temple was vital to the denomination: its social outreach programs exemplified what Disciples wanted its other churches to do. The appropriateness of sermons and veracity of annual reports were secondary.

To Jones, it was critical that his followers believe he worked tirelessly to improve their lives at great risk to his own. That was the best assurance of their loyalty. It was a given, particularly in the Deep South, that white integration activists were always in physical peril. No integrationist in Indianapolis had ever been attacked, until Jim Jones began calling police to report attempted assaults. The earliest of these were minor, rocks thrown at his house, and in one instance the perpetrators were even caught. They turned out to be black teenagers breaking windows at random — Jones hadn't been selected as a specific target. He was still offended and told them that he was the last one they should be harassing, since he was trying to do so much for their people.

As Jones's reputation grew, the nature of the attacks he reported also escalated. There were anonymous threats of armed violence against him and his family, he told police — he bought guns of his own so he could defend his loved ones. Not much later, a shot was heard outside his house in the middle of the night. Jones was in the kitchen. Everyone else had been asleep. Jones told his family that it was an assassination attempt. Someone fired at him, but missed; the bullet hadn't come through the window. He insisted they go outside and see where the shot had hit, and, sure enough, there was a bullet hole in a porch pillar. The police were summoned. The Jones family had three dogs; investigating officers thought it odd that none of the dogs barked when the perpetrator approached the house and opened fire. The angle of the bullet hole in the pillar was curious, too. The shot appeared to be fired away from, rather than toward, the house. In his next sermon and for several Sundays after that, Jones told the story to his congregation. People wanted to kill him because of what he was trying to do for Peoples Temple and the oppressed everywhere. He was alive only because God was protecting him.

Jones told family and a few friends that the pressure was becoming too much. Besides being in constant danger, everyone he met wanted something from him. For the first time, though only in private, he began incrementally revealing the considerable divide between the Bible-based religion he still preached and his true beliefs. Jones talked about reincarnation — not only his faith in it, but his conviction that "Jim Jones" was simply the latest physical manifestation of a spirit previously occupying the earthly bodies of other great men, all of them dedicated to equality and justice. Those closest to him, Jones declared, had been his helpers and confidants in previous lives. They were together again to move humanity forward. Jones's love of history came in handy when he offered specifics. Joe Phillips, who had become a devoted follower after Jones apparently cured his young son of heart disease, was told that he was the current incarnation of Ashoka, a distinguished emperor in India and a devout disciple of the Buddha. Jones, of course, had been the Buddha in that previous life. Now Phillips was back to serve Jones once again. Phillips believed it, just as he believed in Jones's powers as a healer. Whatever Jim said must be true.

Near the end of October 1961, Jones began telling Temple associate pastors about a terrible prophetic vision. Jones claimed to his subordinates that it had been revealed to him America would soon be under nuclear attack, and Indianapolis and everyone living there would be obliterated.

In 1961, many Americans lived in fear of nuclear holocaust, and had since November 1955 when Russia successfully tested a thermonuclear bomb. Jim Jones was one of them. As the Cold War escalated, advances in science resulted in nuclear weaponry as much as 750 times more lethal than the atomic bombs America dropped on Japan to end World War II. Bomb paranoia swept the United States. After his election in November 1960, President John F. Kennedy suggested that public school basements would be the best shelter option in the event of nuclear war. In a June 1961 nationally televised address in response to recent Soviet threats, Kennedy said Americans should be prepared: "In the event of [a nuclear] attack, the lives of those families which are not hit in a nuclear blast can still be saved if they can be warned to take shelter, and if that shelter is available."

Jones's Temple staff was prepared to accept the validity of any Jones prophecy, but because of the widespread obsession with nuclear war, this one especially struck home. Jones offered details: the attack, presumably by the Soviets, would target several major American cities, including Chicago. Indianapolis would be leveled by fallout from the Chicago blast. It would come on the sixteenth of some month, which Jones believed but could not be certain was September. He also didn't know what year, but the time would be 3:09, either a.m. or p.m. — the vision hadn't specified. But the upshot was that for the safety of its members, Peoples Temple must relocate somewhere far from potential nuclear targets. Jones would use his physician-mandated sabbatical to find the right place. Since his absence would now be quite extended, he formally named Russell Winberg to take charge of the Temple until his return. Ross Case, Archie Ijames, and Jack

Beam would serve as Winberg's assistants.

Then Jones left Indianapolis. His only previous foreign trip had been to Cuba following the 1959 revolution led by Fidel Castro, going before the American government forbade its citizens to travel there. He believed that he would find many potential Cuban recruits for the Temple, socialist-leaning Hispanics eager to join his Indianapolis whites and blacks. But Jones was disappointed by the apparent lack of interest from the new revolutionary government.

Now he visited British Guiana on the northeast coast of South America. He found the country, currently moving toward formal separation from the British Empire, to be interesting. The majority of its people were based along the gradually eroding coast; only Amerindians lived in the wild, dense jungle that covered much of the rest of the country. British Guiana's population seemed primarily black, and English was the national language. Once it was an independent nation with a stable, hopefully socialist government, it might prove worthy of consideration. But not yet.

Jones's next stop was Hawaii. The rest of his family joined him, with the exception of Lynetta. Jones wanted his mother back in Indianapolis, keeping an eye on the nursing homes. He and Marceline loved the lush islands, so much so that in December 1961

Jones applied for an unspecified job at Honolulu's Church of the Crossroads, renowned in evangelistic circles for its large mixed-race congregation and social outreach programs. It was undoubtedly Jones's hope to bring his Temple followers into Crossroads membership, then eventually take personal leadership of the combined churches. Rev. Katharine Kent of Crossroads was sufficiently impressed with the applicant to send queries back to Jones's references in Indianapolis. Audrey E. Howard, secretary of the Human Rights Commission, responded with a flowery testimonial:

> [Jim Jones] is one of the most dedicated persons I have ever known and his broad experience with ethnic groups would certainly provide the skills required by any service agency. In addition, his devotion to every cause beneficial to mankind is the most unselfish I have ever observed. His morals, executive ability — as exemplified in the two nursing homes, the interdenominational church, first local church to integrate — would compare favorably in any type of inquiry. . . . I am certain that the trust we place in him would be exemplified wherever he goes.

Despite the glowing recommendation, Jones wasn't hired. He and his family returned to

Indianapolis, where he insisted that the threat of imminent nuclear annihilation still loomed. Jones's assistant pastors expected him to do something about it. So did those rank-and-file Temple members who'd heard rumors that their leader had predicted something catastrophic was going to happen. New relocation possibilities were suggested by an unexpected source: *Esquire* magazine, written for Americans seeking informed, sophisticated information on world affairs, politics, sports, literature, and fashion. Jim Jones was a dedicated *Esquire* reader, and for him its January 1962 issue (which reached newsstands in December 1961) could not have been timelier. One lead story, touted on the cover, was titled "9 Places in the World to Hide," the cities and/or regions where inhabitants had the best odds of survival following nuclear war. Reporter Caroline Bird dramatically declared, "Now a shift has come about in some of the world's thinking: war will destroy *much* of the life on this planet, but not all. And what this means, if it is true, is that your security depends not so much on who you are or what you believe or even what kind of fallout shelter you build, but where you live." Based on projections of wind, weather, and geographic quirks, Bird identified nine places where post-nuclear survival was considered by many expert scientists and military leaders to be most likely. These included Eureka, California; Cork, Ireland; Guadalajara, Mexico; Chile's Central Valley; Mendoza, Argentina; Belo Horizonte, Brazil; Tananarive, Madagascar; Melbourne, Australia; and Christchurch, New Zealand.

Jones was still attracted to California, but governments outside the United States seemed more likely to support relocation and growth of a socialism-based church. Relocating to a foreign land would also increase Jones's daily control of his followers, since they would be isolated from relatives and nonmember friends who might lure them away from Temple attendance and activities. South America seemed likeliest, and of the options listed there by *Esquire,* Brazil appeared to have the most potential, based on a government that seemed less dictatorial than Argentina's and more commodious than the Central Valley of Chile. Most Temple members were American city folk. Belo Horizonte was a center of agriculture and mining in the eastern Brazilian state of Minas Gerais. American missionaries based there found great numbers of potential converts from among Brazil's indigenous population, as well as the poor who thronged the city. Jones had complained to Max Knight that Indianapolis wasn't sufficiently "wide open." Even its ghetto population was limited. Belo Horizonte was the opposite. In that city, there seemed to be no discernible limits for someone with the energy and vision to pursue socialist dreams. How could he not succeed?

Jones made hurried arrangements. Russell Winberg would continue as acting pastor of Peoples Temple. Lynetta Jones and the Baldwins would manage the Temple nursing homes. Money from Temple accounts would regularly be sent to finance new programs initiated by Jones in Belo Horizonte. When Jones was sufficiently established, church members would begin emigrating and a new Peoples Temple would be founded there. Finally, Jones resigned as director of the Human Relations Commission. With high hopes, he took his wife and children to Brazil.

CHAPTER SIXTEEN: BRAZIL

Jones's journey began inauspiciously. Instead of rushing to Belo Horizonte, he stopped off in Mexico on the way. Archie Ijames met him there, and reported that Russell Winberg was already changing the nature of services at Peoples Temple. In his sermons, Jones had emphasized social issues. Winberg presented traditional Bible-based preaching. He'd invited other evangelists to offer guest sermons, when Jones had always wanted to restrict outside influence as much as possible. Ijames said that Winberg might be plotting to take control of the Temple for himself — Jones should return to Indianapolis right away.

The slightest hint of potential treachery was always enough to trigger Jones's paranoia. Ijames's report alarmed him in the extreme. But thanks to his own prophecy of a looming nuclear apocalypse, Jones could hardly make an immediate return to the Temple pulpit. His followers had to believe that his priority was saving them, not reclaiming them from a potential usurper. All he could do was ask Ijames to continue monitoring Winberg and report any further concerns.

He put on a brave front with his family. After landing at an airport in Brazil, Marceline was taken aback by the relative primitiveness and wide-spread poverty. Sensing her dejection, Jones embraced her, and together they sang, "I'll be loving you always."

Using the limited amount of money they'd brought from the United States, the Joneses rented a sparsely furnished, three-bedroom house in Belo Horizonte. With a population of about a million, their sprawling new home city was intimidating. Everyone spoke Portuguese. Much of the surrounding scenery was lush, even breathtaking — Belo Horizonte translates in English as "Beautiful Horizon" — but its streets teemed with beggars, many of them children on the verge of starvation. Local orphanages could support only a small percentage. In Indianapolis, the black ghetto was an obvious place for Jones to base a ministry. In Belo Horizonte, there were almost too many choices. It was hard for Jones and Marceline to learn to function for themselves — even the seemingly simple task of mailing letters back home proved perplexing, since none of the post office clerks understood English.

It was in a Belo Horizonte post office that

Jones made his first significant new acquaintance in Brazil. A short man was summoned by a staffer to help translate. He introduced himself to Jones as Ed Malmin, an evangelist who had been in Brazil for three years. Malmin spoke Portuguese like a native. A friendly sort, he invited Jones to bring his family over for a meal. The Joneses were charming dinner guests. Jones talked about his vision, and how he had come to Belo Horizonte for its relative safety from nuclear fallout, and to study it as a possible relocation site for Peoples Temple. Malmin, who'd attended the Los Angeles seminary of famed evangelist Aimee Semple McPherson, was sympathetic. He offered to introduce Jones to local officials, and to do what he could to assist his family in assimilating.

By the time dinner was through, Jones and Marceline had made another new friend. Malmin's sixteen-year-old daughter, Bonnie, had quarreled with her parents about her Brazilian boyfriend. The elder Malmins thought dating a boy of another race was inappropriate. The Joneses, with their rainbow family, didn't see anything wrong with it. Bonnie was soon a constant presence at the Jones's home, helping Marceline with chores and serving as a translator. Soon, with her parents' permission, she moved in with them. Bonnie found life there much more congenial. Following Marceline's example, the teenager began wearing less makeup and keeping her hair in a simple ponytail instead of the more elaborate styles she'd previously favored. Bonnie loved the Jones children, Jim Jr. especially. Jones struck her as genuinely compassionate for all living things. When someone gave the Joneses a live duck for their evening meal, Jones couldn't bear to kill it and insisted that they keep the fowl as a pet. He also graphically advised Bonnie about sex, including the use of condoms. Jones gave her one, and insisted that she carry it in her purse when she and her boyfriend went out on dates. He also taught Bonnie the technique of driving a knee to the groin of any overaggressive male. Jones's sex advice didn't make Bonnie uncomfortable — his demeanor was always paternal — but other things caused her some concern. Jim Jones was in Belo Horizonte as a missionary, but there was no copy of the Bible in his house. No grace was offered at meals. When Bonnie asked if she could say it, Jones and Marceline were agreeable. They apparently had nothing against prayer. They just didn't use it themselves in their private lives.

Jones soon became frustrated in Belo Horizonte. He met various officials, but had no means of influencing them. He was just one among many American missionaries. Perhaps Jones could have distinguished himself by initiating free food and clothing programs for the city poor as he had in Indianapolis, but he had no money to pay for them. He had counted on receiving regular stipends from Peoples Temple, but never received any. Back in Indianapolis, the Temple was in trouble.

Peoples Temple was no longer a strictly neighborhood church, attended by nearby residents because it was convenient. Almost all its members joined and stayed for one of two reasons. Either they were attracted to Peoples Temple because of its socialist principles and outreach efforts, or else they believed in Jim Jones and his great powers, and wanted to be part of a church that he personally led. With Jones absent in Brazil, and with Russell Winberg reverting to old-school, Bible-based worship, neither reason remained valid. People were leaving, in far greater numbers than the one or two a month that had so distressed Jones when he was still in charge. That meant Sunday offerings were drastically reduced, at the same time when there was no longer income from Jones's appearances on the revival circuit. Profits from the Temple-operated nursing homes weren't sufficient. Resident-patients were accepted there based on need, and paid only what they could afford. So Archie Ijames, acting as Temple treasurer, had no money to send to Belo Horizonte. Jones and his family had to subsist on whatever he could earn at part-time jobs and occasional small donations from Brazilian Christians impressed with his visionary zeal. Jones and Marceline still did what they could. Their family dinners were spare, usually consisting of the cheapest possible staples — rice, bread, vegetables. Marceline boiled the rice in a five-quart pot. After serving her family, she would set anything left over out in small bowls on the veranda for hungry street children.

Much of Jones's time was spent trying to hold Peoples Temple together from long distance. He barraged his associate pastors with letters of encouragement. They'd had his example in recruiting and retaining members — surely they could put a stop to the current erosion. The situation was particularly touchy with Winberg. Too much criticism might cause him to openly rebel and claim the remaining congregation as his own. All Jones could do was encourage continuation of his own policies. And, always, he pleaded for money. To make a new home for Peoples Temple in Belo Horizonte, Jones had to first establish the same progressive example there that he had in Indianapolis, as someone working effectively toward equality for all, a man once again to be reckoned with. Then when Temple followers arrived in their new home, they'd immediately become part of a prominent church, shining examples of what socialism should be.

Jones also stayed in constant communication with rank-and-file Temple followers. All of them were encouraged to write their true pastor, asking whatever questions they liked. Some, like Patty Cartmell, wrote almost daily. They asked what he wanted them to do back in Indiana, and when he planned to summon them to their new, fallout-safe home. Jones encouraged them to continue believing in him and to keep supporting the Indianapolis programs he'd established. He described not only the wonders of Brazil, but also its great need for the kind of vision and compassion that only Jim Jones and Peoples Temple could provide. And, always, whether from assistant pastors or rank-and-file members of his flock, Jones requested reports. Who was straying from Jones's directives? Who did they suspect was acting out of selfish, rather than altruistic, reasons?

Events in America and around the world worked to Jones's advantage as he tried to retain the loyalty of his Temple followers. Freedom marches by black and white civil rights activists in the Deep South often erupted in violence. In October 1962, photographs taken by American spy planes indicated that the Soviets were building a missile site in Cuba that, if completed, would give them unprecedented proximity to U.S. targets in the event of nuclear war. President Kennedy demanded that the site be dismantled, and put a shipping embargo in place around the island. Soviet freighters steamed forward. For thirteen days, the world trembled on the brink of catastrophe. Then the Russians agreed to abandon the Cuban site in return for the removal of American missiles in Turkey. It had been a near thing, and made Jones's apocalyptic prophecy appear all the more valid to members of the Temple back in Indianapolis. They wondered if their pastor was about to send for them in Belo Horizonte. Instead, he prepared to leave.

Jones could make no headway in Belo Horizonte. Without sufficient funds, he could not initiate the kinds of social programs that would impress local officials and pave the way for the relocation of Peoples Temple there. For a while, Jack and Rheaviana Beam joined the Joneses in Belo Horizonte. They provided firsthand reports about Temple problems. Next to Marceline, Jack Beam had become perhaps Jones's most trusted associate. His hearty sense of humor leavened Jones's obsessiveness, but Beam was every bit as committed to socialism as his leader. Belo Horizonte frustrated him as much as it did Jones. Even though Beam was a talented jack-of-all-trades who could quickly master any mechanical skill, he couldn't find a full-time job in the city. In early 1963, the Beams returned to Indianapolis.

Jones didn't give up on Brazil yet. Instead,

he moved his family to Rio de Janeiro, and was hired to teach English at an American school. With a steady income finally assured, Jones and Marceline spent his off-duty hours ministering to the city poor. In particular, they volunteered in Rio's orphanages. Jones attempted to raise money for the orphanages without much success. As in Belo Horizonte, he was only one of many Christian missionaries, and some of the others represented well-financed organizations that provided ample funds. Once, Jones had spurned offers to join groups doing worldwide missionary work. Now he wanted such employment, with its access to money. At his request, in May 1963 Ed Malmin wrote a generic "To Whom It May Concern" letter recommending Jones to any such organization willing to employ him. It read in part,

Rev. Jones and I have cooperated in meetings together and have prayed together. I have the utmost confidence in Mr. Jones and believe him to be a man of outstanding character. I would trust his word of honor implicitly and can recommend him for any position of trust.

The letter didn't help. No missionary group hired Jones, who continued teaching at the American school.

It was while he was in Rio that Jones later

claimed he engaged in a surprising act to raise money for a particularly impoverished orphanage. As Jones told the story to his followers — and he repeated it many times over the ensuing years — he caught the eye of the wife of a prominent diplomat, who offered to donate $5,000 to the orphanage if Jones would have sex with her. Jones claimed that many women, captivated by his attractiveness and charisma, had approached him before, and he'd always declined. But this time was different — the money would help feed and clothe children in desperate need. Jones was perplexed. Trading sex for money was the equivalent of prostitution. Yet refusal would be selfish, placing more value on his personal moral code than on the orphans. After much thought, he approached Marceline and asked for her permission to sleep with the woman. Marceline put aside a natural sense of possessiveness and agreed that he should. As Jones told the story, because he was an exceptional lover, the diplomat's wife enjoyed considerable physical ecstasy. She then honored her part of the bargain, and the orphanage received the money. Jones declared that his sacrifice exemplified true dedication to socialism. The lesson for Jones's followers was that an honorable end justified whatever morally questionable means were necessary to achieve it.

Unfortunately for the orphans, no similar

offers from other rich women were apparently forthcoming. He accomplished as little in Rio de Janeiro as he had in Belo Horizonte. Temple news from Indiana continued to be bad: Russell Winberg was solidifying his old-fashioned control of the church, and its remaining members were split between Winberg supporters and stubborn Jones adherents. Jones felt he had to act, but didn't trust Ross Case or Archie Ijames enough to dismiss Winberg and raise one of them to the acting pastorship in his stead. Ed Malmin provided a solution. He decided to take a break from his Brazilian ministry and spend some time back in the United States. Jones asked him to take over Peoples Temple and Malmin agreed. It was understood that Malmin's pastorship there would be temporary and give Jones time to think of something else.

When Malmin arrived in Indianapolis and went to the Temple to take charge, he discovered that Jones hadn't told anyone there that he was coming. Winberg was outraged, and left soon afterward, taking with him several dozen members who'd come to prefer his more traditional ways. Malmin presided over perhaps two hundred remaining congregants, but it soon became clear that he, too, was Jones's opposite in the Temple pulpit. Like Winberg, Malmin was a traditionalist who believed every word in the Bible to be immutable truth. When word reached Jones back in Brazil, he realized that instead of buying himself time by substituting Malmin for Winberg, he'd only made things worse. But he couldn't arbitrarily remove Malmin, too, because he suspected Ijames and Case as potential usurpers. If Peoples Temple was to survive as the principal instrument of Jim Jones's ministry, he could trust only himself to properly lead it.

Jones came to Brazil with the announced intent of preparing the way for a full-fledged Peoples Temple exodus there. After two years, it was apparent that wouldn't happen. In Belo Horizonte and Rio de Janeiro, Brazil took no notice of Jim Jones. Its vastness, and the extent of its impoverished class, defied his best efforts to become someone of consequence. Even if he brought the loyal remnants of his once impressive congregation there, they'd no longer see Jones as a great man who brought about significant social change because, in Brazil, he wasn't. Instead, he was a pastoral nonentity, no different from the black ministers in Indianapolis he'd mocked for having occasional meetings with important people but never making the slightest difference. Peoples Temple thrived on accomplishments orchestrated by Jim Jones. He couldn't deliver anything less.

He needed plausible reasons for coming home and offered his remaining Indianapolis followers some. The November 1963 assassination of John F. Kennedy was further proof that America was coming apart; his faithful flock in Indianapolis needed their *real* pastor's strong, comforting presence. The Brazilian government hadn't proven as liberal as he'd hoped. Although the country, and Belo Horizonte in particular, might be a geographic refuge from nuclear fallout, its political leaders were evil and would never tolerate a socially committed church that demanded equality for all. Jones had never committed to bringing Peoples Temple to Brazil. His two-year sojourn there had been for purposes of fact-finding, and what he'd found indicated the necessity of looking elsewhere for a fallout-free haven.

But that was for the future. Jones's immediate concern was saving what was left of the Temple in Indianapolis. He was certain that when he returned, he'd quickly reestablish himself as a powerful man and rebuild his congregation. What had worked once would surely work again.

It didn't.

CHAPTER SEVENTEEN: LOOKING WEST

Some three dozen members of Peoples Temple gathered at the Indianapolis airport to welcome the Jones family home. But there weren't enough of them to allay Jones's concerns. Prior to his departure for Brazil, he'd been able to regularly turn out several hundred congregants to the most insignificant events. Clearly, Temple enthusiasm as well as membership had dwindled. Something had to be done right away.

The first, most pressing problem was in the church pulpit. In Brazil, Ed Malmin had been Jim Jones's mentor. But Jones wanted to reestablish himself immediately as Peoples Temple's sole leader. Malmin found himself reduced during Sunday services to virtual flunky status as Jones dominated the proceedings. At meetings, Jones presided and Malmin's opinions weren't requested. The older man, no stranger to pulpit politics, knew what was happening and didn't offer any resistance. Soon enough his sabbatical in the

United States would be over, and he'd return to missionary work in Brazil. Meanwhile, he'd help Jones as best he could within the new limits set by his former protégé.

Jones had plenty of time to focus on Temple issues. During the two years he was away, state and local government had taken huge strides toward near-universal integration. The Indiana General Assembly created its own Civil Rights Commission and, for a change, drafted legislation with teeth. In education, in employment opportunities, and in access and use of public facilities, discrimination within state borders was absolutely forbidden. Officials were required to first seek cooperation by meeting with transgressors, but if negotiation failed, courts would force compliance. Civil rights activists chastised state legislators for not including open housing in their new laws, but the Indianapolis City Council didn't wait for the state to act on that. The 1963 council, which now included two black members, crafted an ordinance that outlawed discrimination in sales or rental of housing in the city. Indianapolis's Human Rights Commission was given the authority to issue subpoenas and turn evidence against violators over to city attorneys for prosecution. Jim Jones's yeoman service as commission director had certainly paved the way for this eye-popping progress, but he'd resigned that office two years previously and things had moved forward without him. Jones could no longer tout himself as irreplaceable in Indianapolis's integration process.

There was still not complete equality in Indianapolis. It was one thing to give blacks the right to live where they pleased, and another for housing to be made available to them at affordable prices. Even the finest stores and restaurants now had to serve customers of all races — but few nonwhites in the city had much, if any, disposable income. Equal opportunity employment was designed to relieve racial economic disparity, but even if it succeeded the process would still take years, perhaps generations. In other parts of America, blacks refused to wait. Civil rights marches continued. Soon, full-fledged race riots regularly erupted in the ghettos of major cities. Had such simmering tension existed in Indianapolis, Jones might have reemerged as the city's foremost civil rights spokesman by leading marches, or by appearing in burning streets to demand justice for the still unfairly oppressed.

But such things would never happen there. Indianapolis blacks were, at core, *Hoosiers,* inherently nonconfrontational. Compared to African Americans in most other large American cities, they were now ahead in matters of civil rights. An unprecedented number of liberal politicians recently elected to state and city office was responsible. In just a few more years, more traditional conservatism among Indiana's vast white voting majority would reassert itself, and most of the 1962–1963 civil rights advances would be negated. For now, current progress denied any opportunity for Jim Jones to assume his former position of city influence and leadership. It hurt, and not only because Indianapolis had moved on with integration without him. Previously, his most effective means of recruiting new church members from among Negro citizens was that the Temple could help them get something in life as well as after death. Pastor Jones would intercede for members with city officials, utility companies, banks, and shop owners. Now Jones was no longer the only or even the most convenient conduit. Human Rights Commission staff had all the legal clout necessary to help. Jones wasn't potential Temple members' only option.

Then came additional humiliation. Jones had to move the Temple to a smaller building after the old one suddenly seemed cavernous — now there were sometimes fewer than a hundred congregants on Sundays. Dwindling attendance reflected poorly on Jones's reputation, his *power*. People had to be reminded of how important he was. His fury and frustration manifested themselves in several ways.

Jones retained his radio program, 4:45–5:00

p.m. on Indianapolis station WIBC. Archie Ijames had substituted as host while Jones was in Brazil. Jones reclaimed the microphone. Where he'd earlier quoted scripture and urged loving brotherhood, now he spat out angry diatribes dismissing the Bible as propaganda and suggesting himself as a modern-day prophet. This was hardly the sort of soothing message expected by the station and its listeners. Jones was warned to change his tone, and when he didn't, WIBC removed him from the airwaves.

Still determined to have an audience beyond Temple membership, Jones returned to the regional revival circuit. His message was changed there, too. Ably abetted by Patty Cartmell, he still amazed audiences with miraculous mind-readings and prophecies. But now his sermons bypassed biblical references almost entirely. Instead, he talked socialism, though he was careful not to specifically identify his subject as such. Jones's message was clear: only full equality for all was acceptable. For the ever-swelling ranks of the oppressed, anyone disagreeing was the enemy. Change was coming. Better to welcome it than stand against it.

In Sunday services, in meetings with associate pastors and other Temple loyalists, Jones went further. The less he felt recognized and appreciated by the outside world, the grander he proclaimed himself to the followers remaining to him. He unnerved some by denigrating the Bible. He declared that it was "the root of all our problems today. Racism is taught in it. Oppression is taught in it."

There was more. Previously, Jones had shared his belief in reincarnation with only a few discreet confidants. Though he'd identified himself as a great man in previous lives, he'd never claimed the ultimate identity. Now, he did. Upon his return to the Temple pulpit, Jones curtly dismissed the concept of a "Sky God" who promised eternal life in exchange for belief but ignored the sick and suffering. The real Christ or God, Jones preached, existed as a mind or spirit that could choose a host body, becoming an Earth God capable of bestowing immediate blessings on the living.

Jones usually stopped just short of declaring himself to be God. But from that time forward, he led his congregation toward that conclusion. A sermon he delivered in 1975 offers the best example: "The mind that was in Christ Jesus is in me now. As a man thinketh in his heart, so is he. If you think you see a man, a man I am. But if you think you see God, God is here. What matters is, 'Who do you say I am?' "

It is impossible to know whether Jones gradually came to think that he was God's earthly vessel, or whether he came to that convenient conclusion precisely at this low point in his career. Either way, if Jones already believed he'd previously lived as the Buddha and other extraordinary incarnations, it was an almost inevitable progression for such an ambitious man to eventually place his current self on the highest possible level. Encouraged as a child by his mother, who believed in reincarnation and the transmigration of souls, Jones had felt certain all of his life that he was special, marked for great things even before birth. As an adult, he had the example of Father Divine, who claimed to be God in human form and was worshipped by thousands of followers as such. Father Divine, in Jones's opinion, was misguided — Jones said as much in the pamphlet he wrote about the Peace Movement, noting that "Rev. Divine [is] merely an instrument who [has] done good work." But Jones, too, wanted to be worshipped, and that desire meshed perfectly with the concept of reincarnation and his newly announced divinity in human form. Where Father Divine was mistakenly presumptuous, Jones was simply acknowledging fact. Jim Jones was God or Christ on Earth, meaning that whatever he wanted was right and must be done. Jones still believed in the virtues of socialism and was dedicated to lifting up the oppressed. But he would no longer have the capacity to learn from mistakes, because he didn't believe that, as a superior incarnation, he could make any. In the future, anything that didn't work exactly according to Jones's desires would be the fault of flawed followers or implacable enemies — and, with each passing day, Jones became more convinced that he had enemies everywhere.

Jones picked his spots, avoiding outright declarations of actual divinity in non-Temple settings. But he expected his closest associates to acknowledge him as godlike and this troubled some of them, Ross Case and Archie ames especially. It took Ijames some time to ne around. Case never did. But other s followers either believed immediately they were certain they'd seen him dem- istrate otherwise inexplicable powers — or, ke Jack Beam, didn't care what outrageous ms Jones made about being God. The list principles that he shared with them hat mattered. Whatever Marceline ght, she kept to herself. If she ve in her husband's divinity, she as a man of special, God-driven pur , and never wavered in her public support.

It was a critical turning point. Jones's time in Indianapolis was almost up. He recognized that. Father Divine took his flock from New York to Philadelphia and grew stronger because of it. Peoples Temple had to relocate somewhere Jones could regain social and political influence while retaining those loyal followers he had left. There were perhaps a hundred in all. Where he chose to take them was influenced by something other than thwarted ambition in Indiana, or Jones's belief that, as God, his people would thrive wherever he chose to lead them.

In later years, most who had been associated with Jones and survived speculated on his honesty about anything. He exaggerated and lied so much — perhaps he never told the truth. Jones's ultimate choice of destination proves that, at least occasionally, he did. His fear of nuclear holocaust was genuine. The Earth God did not believe himself immune to death by nuclear explosion or fallout. Had Jones's only intention been to move the Temple to a place where he could attain increased fame and power, there were obvious choices. Because of his appearances on the regional revival circuit, Jones was already established as a potential force in several major Midwest cities seething with racial unrest, Detroit and Chicago prominent among them. It would have been relatively easy to relocate there. Jones knew how to insert himself in controversy, how to exploit black frustration and confront white opposition. He'd been relatively restrained in Indianapolis. In Chicago or Detroit, he could indulge in full-throated advocacy.

Instead, he returned to the list of ostensibly fallout-free possibilities in *Esquire*. Belo

Horizonte had discouraged Jones, at least for a time, from the prospect of foreign escape. Of the nine cities and regions listed, only one was in America:

"The safest place in the United States is Eureka, California, a landlocked port of nearly 30,000 people 283 miles north of San Francisco and more than 100 miles north of the nearest [nuclear attack] target. Eureka is the principal city along the lightly settled, dry stretch of California's coast. It generally escapes damage in the war-game attacks because it is west of the Sierras and upwind from every target in the United States. . . . Eureka is on the safest stretch of the continent's West Coast."

Jones's best chance to build a massive following and achieve national rather than local fame could be found in a major city. If he wanted one in California that offered plenty of opportunities to plunge into the vanguard of nationally reported racial conflict, Los Angeles was the perfect choice. It would soon explode in riots in its Watts ghetto. San Francisco was a less obvious, but still ripe, possibility to acquire and exert civil rights leadership. Its minority neighborhoods were being gradually eradicated in deliberate fashion by city planners. Eureka, with a population of thirty thousand that included few minorities, didn't offer the same option. But it was supposed to be safe from fallout, and it was in California.

Jones sent scouts ahead. Jack and Rheaviana Beam relocated to Hayward, an Oakland suburb. Jones didn't completely discount the allure of San Francisco and its surrounding communities. Ross Case settled 150 miles north of Hayward in Ukiah, the Mendocino County seat. Ukiah was about halfway between Eureka and San Francisco, but still beyond the hypothetical Bay Area fallout zone.

While he waited for their reports, Jones tied up a professional loose end. Though Peoples Temple had been affiliated with the Disciples of Christ since 1959, Jones was still not ordained as a denominational pastor. He'd earned the college degree required, but left for Brazil immediately afterward. Now, Jones wanted that Disciples certification, a credential that would help establish him in a new California location. So he made formal application, and a Disciples vetting process followed.

The critical aspect of the Disciples' investigation into Jones's worthiness was an eight-member Ordination Council appointed to look into his background. Four members were associated with the Disciples. Four more would represent the secular perspective. Despite his irregular approach to Christian ministry, the Disciples wanted Jones confirmed as a candidate just as much as he did.

Under his leadership, Peoples Temple was a shining example of a service-based church that the denomination wanted all of its congregations to emulate. Rejecting Jones would have been paramount to rejecting the worthy accomplishments achieved by Peoples Temple under his guidance. So the eight-member council was stacked from the start. Its four nondenominational members included Archie Ijames, Jones's associate pastor at the Temple (the church was a Disciples affiliate, but Ijames was not ordained in the denomination); Walter Baldwin, Jones's father-in-law; Harold Cordell Jr., a member of one of the Temple's most loyal families; and Ed Malmin, the veteran missionary who had befriended and mentored Jones in Brazil. The council vote in Jones's favor was a formality, and in an 8 p.m. Temple service on February 16, 1964, he was formally ordained as a Disciples minister. In Temple services during the weeks immediately afterward, Jones technically followed Disciples guidelines but gave them his own twist. When communion was required, Temple congregants were offered coffee and donuts rather than wine and wafers. The newly certified Reverend Jones then reminded them that coming together was the real communion, not the snacks. If denominational administrators in the Disciples regional office were informed, they chose to ignore it.

Jones began taking inspection visits to California himself, sometimes with other Temple confidants and at least once bringing along his family. Everyone loved San Francisco, but Jones couldn't suppress his fears that it would soon disappear in a mushroom cloud. Ukiah looked more promising. It was some distance inland from Mendocino County's scenic coast, with surrounding hills and mountains that blocked even a trace of ocean breeze. But Joe Phillips, who'd spent part of his life farming, pointed out that crops grew well in the area. If the Temple could get access to land, its members could grow enough food to be nearly self-sufficient. That appealed to Jones, who'd been impressed by the Promised Land farms of Father Divine's Peace Movement.

A propitious meeting in the restaurant of Ukiah's Palace Hotel sealed the deal. Jones, Phillips, and Jack Beam overheard a conversation between a half dozen men and women at a nearby table. They were board members of Christ's Church of the Golden Rule, a Ukiah-based social gospel group that had broken away from a larger organization and eventually settled on sixteen thousand rolling acres in the hills just above Ukiah. Jones and the other two Temple members introduced themselves. After some conversation, the Golden Rule elders invited their new acquaintances to visit their community. The trio was greatly impressed — here were people who lived their faith as they pleased, essentially self-supporting and not subordinate to any larger, overseeing organization. To Jones, this was undoubtedly a predestined opportunity. He proposed to the Golden Rule leaders that they consider allowing Peoples Temple to join them. Most members of the Ukiah group were older. Due to age and other attrition, they now numbered about two hundred. Adding young, enthusiastic newcomers from Indianapolis would provide new energy for continued growth of the service-oriented faith that members of the Temple and Golden Rule shared. An understanding was reached: if Jones brought his followers out to Ukiah, they could immediately begin worshipping in the Golden Rule settlement as a separate faith-based group. If, over a period of time, Temple members proved compatible, a merger might be considered. But Temple members couldn't move onto Golden Rule property immediately upon arrival. They'd have to live in Ukiah or other surrounding towns, and find jobs in the community.

Jones pronounced himself not only satisfied, but thrilled. He promised the Golden Rule elders that he and his followers would stay in contact and relocate soon. Jones didn't mention that it was his intention to eventually become the sole leader of the new, consolidated group. At this first negotiation and many times in the months ahead, Jones insisted to his new friends that he would gladly serve as their humblest member. But he made his true intentions clear to Temple associates. Of course, he would become leader. It was his destiny; it was his right.

Ross Case was deeply troubled by how the others deferred not only to Jones's ambition, but to his sense of himself as godlike. In March 1965, after Jones returned to Indiana to prepare for California relocation, Case wrote to him, explaining why he could no longer be his follower. As a Christian, he couldn't in good conscience "submit my mind completely to the mind of Jimmy." He would continue to support Peoples Temple projects as a friend but also as a nonmember: "I will not work on a religious basis under any circumstances where I cannot work in the name of Jesus for his glory." Case anticipated a clean, friendly break. He'd continue living and working in Ukiah, enjoying an ongoing relationship with Temple members there. Jones saw Case's decision as betrayal, and made other plans for him.

But those had to wait. Jones's current problem was convincing all remaining Temple members to come with him to a backwater outpost in California. Many had never traveled beyond the Midwest or even Indiana. To them, Ukiah was the equivalent of a small town in a foreign country. While several dozen Temple followers were eager to go — they believed their leader when he said it was best for them — others were reluctant. Jones had promised Golden Rule a substantial influx of potential new members. He meant to deliver one, and that required all his considerable persuasive powers.

Even when Temple membership had been at its height, Jones made a point of having a personal relationship with each follower. Jones remembered everything that was shared, every secret fear, every confessed longing or sin. In fall 1964, those remaining were either longtime members or else joined after seeing Jones perform miracle healings at revivals. These were the followers he knew best, and he exploited that knowledge. Most had benefited personally from something Jones had done on their behalf. Perhaps it was intercession with a utility company, or placing an elderly, penniless relative in one of the Temple nursing homes and not charging them. Originally, these acts of kindness had been presented as simple obedience to Christian principles. But Jones kept careful track of every favor done. Now he reminded those he'd assisted that it was selfish to belong to a church only to get something. Giving back was required, too. Jim Jones and Peoples Temple had been there in their times of need. They must step forward and make what might initially seem to be a sacrifice, moving to a place they didn't know and didn't want to go to. Jones promised that their lives would be better in California, that everyone would work together to achieve the kind of equality that would inspire the rest of the world. Meanwhile, it was time to repay what Peoples Temple and Jim Jones had unselfishly done for them.

In other instances, Jones skillfully calculated what individual enticement would be most effective. Elderly members who suffered greatly from Indiana's freezing winters and blast furnace summers were told of Ukiah's Eden-like climate. Advocates of social change were reminded of the stultifying "get along, go along" attitude embedded in Indianapolis tradition. In California, there was greater opportunity to make progressive things happen. Women trying to free themselves and their children from abusive relationships were told that it was easier at greater distance. Tired of cramped ghetto life with escape impossible thanks to prohibitive housing costs anywhere else in Indianapolis? Here was a chance to enjoy living in the bucolic countryside. However someone wanted to change his or her life, Jones promised that Mendocino County in California offered the perfect opportunity.

Jones's overriding means of persuasion remained the same. Nuclear war was coming. The destruction of Indianapolis was assured.

Those who didn't get out would perish horribly there. In 1961, Jones claimed to have experienced a vision that the attack would come on the sixteenth of some month — he couldn't be certain of a specific year and date. Now, he was: Russia would launch its nuclear attack in July 1967. Come with Jones to Northern California and live, or stay in Indianapolis and die.

About ninety of the remaining Temple members were persuaded. In the early summer of 1965, Jones preached a final Peoples Temple service, saying he and his people were leaving Indianapolis for California to escape persecution. One day, they would go even farther than California, to a place where everyone could be happy. Most assumed that he meant heaven. Imminent nuclear holocaust was not mentioned.

As soon as the service was over, Jones and his followers embarked on a car caravan to their new California home. It was a jolly journey. They stopped at supermarkets in towns along the way, buying loaves of bread, packs of lunch meat, and then enjoying picnics in shady roadside spots. There were long delays at gas stations as people took turns using the restrooms. Everyone was excited; their leader's enthusiasm was contagious.

Then they arrived in Ukiah, and the newcomers' collective good mood quickly faded.

Jones had planned for everything but a place that didn't want them.

■ ■ ■ ■

PART TWO:
CALIFORNIA

■ ■ ■ ■

CHAPTER EIGHTEEN:
REDNECK VALLEY

Ukiah and Redwood Valley initially seemed as much of a haven as Jones had promised. It was a quiet, relatively remote area, far enough removed from the spectacular Mendocino County coast that tourists rarely ventured there. But this interior region still had its geographic charms, including rolling hills and a few lakes.

Peoples Temple didn't arrive as indigents. Marceline Jones stunned a local banker with a deposit of $100,000. But with the church back in Indianapolis essentially closed down, careful husbanding of funds was necessary. After finding work, members were expected to donate every spare dollar. Jones himself took employment as a junior high and high school teacher — civics and American history were his subjects. Marceline was hired by the state of California as an inspector of hospitals and nursing homes. Lynetta Jones got a job with the Red Cross.

In July 1965, Jones filed articles of incorporation with the state of California on behalf of "Peoples Temple of the Disciples of Christ," emphasizing the denominational affiliation. The stated purpose of the organization was "to further the Kingdom of God by Spreading the Word." A few months later, the state's Franchise Tax Board formally recognized the Temple as nonprofit: "Contributions made to you are deductible by the donors" who followed proper reporting procedures. Temple directors were identified as Jones, Marceline, and Archie Ijames.

Messages went back to Temple members in Indiana who'd so far refused to make the trip west: *Come out here. It's paradise, just as Father described.* Fifty or sixty more were persuaded. They received effusive greetings upon arrival, and were congratulated on saving themselves from the coming nuclear conflagration. It was impossible not to be impressed by Father's services in a building on the Golden Rule grounds. During Jones's last months in an Indianapolis pulpit, his messages had been menacing. Now in rural California he seemed more positive again, affirmative rather than alarming. Life was going to be *good.*

Then came a glimmer of potential concern. Dan McKee, city editor of the *Ukiah Daily Journal,* instructed reporters to look into this new church and its members. Was there anything about them that might prove troublesome in their conservative community? *Journal* reporters began asking questions, and soon Jones was alerted. Within days of his staff's first inquiries, McKee remembers, Jones "swept into" the newspaper office and had a long, closed-door meeting with the publisher and executive editor. Afterward, McKee was told by his bosses that there would be no further investigation of Peoples Temple or Jim Jones. Instead, Temple officials would begin submitting articles to the *Journal* about their church and its activities. These were to be published promptly, unedited. In Indianapolis, Jones had learned to deal with big-city newspapers. Charming the bosses at a small town paper was no real challenge.

But small-town racism couldn't be so easily overcome. The population of Ukiah and its surrounding hill country communities was about fifteen thousand, almost universally working-class whites who lived far away from urban areas on purpose. In summer 1965, many major American cities were in turmoil because of civil rights protests or growing numbers of protesters against the Vietnam War. Though most residents of Ukiah and Redwood Valley were suspicious of the federal government, they were fervently patriotic in a more general sense. To them, antiwar demonstrators were traitors and communists — the terms were interchangeable. Outraged blacks were ungrateful Negroes who didn't appreciate what they had, and whose genetically programmed propensity for violence represented a terrible threat to law-abiding whites. The Church of the Golden Rule didn't alarm locals. Its members were white and they mostly stayed out of sight up in the hills. Peoples Temple was different. They shoved their way into what had previously been nice, quiet neighborhoods, and some of these interlopers were *black*.

When the first Peoples Temple car caravan arrived, this wasn't the case. Only a few blacks, notably Archie Ijames and his family, came in the first Temple wave. But another dozen or so blacks were among those coaxed into following them, and they stood out starkly in Ukiah — "like flies in a bowl of milk" was a common description. White Ukiahans knew what the arrival of Negroes meant. Even if they weren't violent, no decent white family in town wanted to live anywhere near them. A Negro presence instantly lowered property values. Yet Jim Jones, the leader of this Peoples Temple bunch, rented houses around town and stuck his followers in them, black folks included, without regard for or permission from people already living on the same street. Once this second wave of Temple settlers arrived, local hostility toward all its members commenced. Temple children were ignored by classmates. No one invited them home to play, or to birthday or teen dance parties. Their parents were served in local shops and cafés with stony, minimal courtesy. Temple members soon nicknamed their new home "Redneck Valley." There was real danger that many would decide to return to Indiana.

So Jones resumed his message of imminent nuclear war. Based on the vision he'd originally reported, it was less than two years away. Anyone going back to Indianapolis was likely to die there under hellish circumstances. He'd led them to Mendocino County to save them from that fate, and now Jones announced that he'd done even more. He and several other Temple leaders had explored the hills north of town and discovered, thanks to Father's powers, an amazing cave, one sufficiently deep to provide protection from nuclear fallout and vast enough to accommodate every Temple member plus the supplies necessary to sustain them until the danger was past. Then they would emerge not only to survive, but thrive, in the post-nuclear world. This plan required some alteration of Jones's previous assurance that Ukiah was well outside any danger zone, that simply moving there would be protection enough. Now, Russian bombs intended for San Francisco might fall too far north, or winds counted on to protect Mendocino County might change. When nuclear war came, taking shelter in the cave would guarantee complete safety. There were no caves back in Indianapolis.

Jones described the local cave in detail, but never took rank-and-file followers to see it for themselves. They were told that it was too isolated to be easily reached. When the time came, Father and Archie Ijames and the few others who knew its location would lead them there. Meanwhile, it was being stocked with provisions.

Later, some former Temple members decided that Jones lied about there being a cave. But there was one, much too small to accommodate more than perhaps a few dozen people at once, yet still there deep in the hills north of town. Jones, Ijames, Joe Phillips, Jack Beam, Mike Cartmell (Patty Cartmell's teenage son), and a few others found and explored it. In this instance, as he often did, Jones exaggerated actual fact. It was unlikely any followers would call his bluff, but had that happened, he could have taken a few skeptics out to see the entrance. It was possible to get into the cave only by dangling descent via rope, and it would have been easy for Jones to find some excuse not to subject the doubters to that.

But the cave and threat of looming nuclear war were only stopgaps. Jones had prophesied that Russian missiles would strike America in July 1967. If that didn't happen, disgruntled followers would have no reason for remaining in Ukiah or Redwood Valley. It was not Jones's way to plan too far ahead. In a talk at Bucknell University in 2013, Jones's son Stephan said, "[It was ascribed] to my father a level of planning and forethought and diabolical intent and orchestration" that he did not deserve. Jones frequently spoke and acted on impulse, trusting himself to concoct some persuasive justification afterward.

Whether Jones himself believed in most or even any of his publicly proclaimed visions and prophecies, he made them frequently and many did not come true. But Jones's ability to improvise, to divert followers when necessary toward a different social mission or outside threat, kept most believing that their leader was infallible. Jones himself quickly realized that moving the Temple to Redwood Valley was a mistake. Quietly, among his inner circle he began discussing moving yet again — Vancouver, Canada, and Guadalajara, Mexico, were considered prime possibilities, Vancouver for its perceived liberal civic attitudes and Guadalajara because it, like Eureka in Northern California, was mentioned as a safe fallout zone in *Esquire*. Jones said that he and Joe Phillips would personally make scouting trips to both cities. Other Temple members weren't immediately told of another potential exodus so soon after arriving at their supposedly permanent new home in Northern California. Instead, Jones stressed safety from fallout, describing in Sunday sermons the horrors of radiation poisoning and the safety of the nearby cave.

At the same time, Jones sought to ingratiate the Temple with locals. If their enmity couldn't be entirely overcome, perhaps it could be mitigated. As a first step, donations were made to local charities, and Jones aggressively sought meetings with elected officials. Whenever these were granted, Jones stressed his church's intention of contributing in every possible way to its new community. The Temple was comprised of honest, hardworking people. All they wanted was to be accepted.

In Indianapolis, with its sprawling city and county government offices and hundreds of officials, lack of contact or poor relationships with some didn't matter, so long as Jones and the Temple were on good terms with a majority. In sparsely populated Mendocino County, each official was critical. When none appeared to be immediately won over, Jones and his followers attempted to wear them down with gestures of appreciation. Lists of prominent area leaders were compiled, including all available information about them, plus whatever gossip Jones's followers picked up around courthouses or city halls. Soon, some Temple members were assigned writing duties. Anytime a school board member cut a ribbon, whenever a county lawman made a public talk or presentation, he or she would receive a letter of thanks — at least one or two, sometimes a dozen or more, depending on Jones's evaluation of their importance. Even a general reputation for almost any political or social stance warranted a handwritten letter, in which the recipient was first praised, then informed that Peoples Temple and its pastor were of like mind:

Dear Judge Broaddus:

I am writing to express my appreciation for the work you are doing to deal with the drug problem.

As a member of Peoples Temple Christian Church, Disciples of Christ, Redwood Valley, California, Rev. James W. Jones, Pastor, I have heard many good things about efforts you are making in this field. Our own program, which provides financial aid to the families of slain police officers and which tries to improve community understanding, is enhanced by leaders such as you who are concerned about the needs of our community.

Thank you for taking the time out of your busy schedule to search for solutions to the problems that cause criminal behavior.

Each letter was reviewed by Jones or another Temple leader before being mailed. After the initial letter came follow-up notes, and then, perhaps on the official's birthday or some other celebratory occasion, a cake, accompanied by a card expressing the admiration of "the Ladies' Aid Society of Peoples Temple Christian Church." It eventually became a source of competition — one local judge might brag to another that in the past six months he'd received two cakes from Peoples Temple, while his fellow jurist got only one. Jones and Temple leadership termed it "cake diplomacy," and reveled in responses like a note from the wife of Ukiah city councilman Sterling Norgard, thanking the Temple "for the gracious letter to my husband. It is gratifying to hear that one's efforts, whatever they may be, are appreciated. We also thank you so much for the most delicious cake. . . . I surely hope to have the pleasure of meeting your Pastor and his wife and family — and perhaps attend one of your services in the near future."

Once informal, cordial connections were established, Jones would personally call the individual, building a relationship, discussing some shared critical concern — better local school curriculums, the need for cleanup around a local lake — and offering the Temple's help if ever the church's new friend required it. After hanging up from one such conversation, Jones beamed and boasted to the associates around him, "I never played chess, but to me, all of this is like chess. You move pieces around."

The Temple also kept local mailmen busy delivering letters to ordinary citizens. Congratulatory notes went out for births, marriages, and graduations. Sympathy was expressed when appropriate. Even those who openly opposed the Temple and its members were contacted. Colleen Rickabaugh, a lifelong area resident, remembers, "It's hard to admit, but my father did not want to live with blacks. We lived on a dead-end street [in Ukiah] and Jones got an old house on it. Black people moved in. We had nothing to do with them or their Temple. Then my mother passed away, and we got letters of condolence from [Jones's] church members. They said that they would help with anything in our time of loss. All we had to do was let them know what we wanted."

Jones knew the minds of most locals couldn't be changed. But it was important at least to blunt as much animosity as possible while he sought out a more hospitable place for the Temple. After these first few discomforting months in Northern California, it was time to start expanding the Temple membership. Congregational stagnation, let alone attrition, wasn't acceptable. Peoples Temple had become a power back in Indiana; its purpose was bringing about socialist progress. More members meant more influence and, of course, more income, which was vital to establishing outreach programs. The methods of recruiting new members — the right kind of people, everyone committed sufficiently to the cause, and to Jones himself — weren't as obvious as back in Indianapolis. Ukiah and Redwood Valley had no ghettos filled with downtrodden black people prime for recruitment. Politically conservative white residents seemed unlikely converts. With a full-time teaching job as well as Temple obligations during off-hours and on weekends, Jones couldn't preach on the West Coast revival circuit and attract new members from outside Mendocino County with prophecy and miracles.

Still, there were ways, and Jim Jones was resourceful.

CHAPTER NINETEEN: DEAD END

Garry Lambrev was typical of many white, idealistic young Americans in the mid-1960s. Raised by liberal parents, he was appalled by what he believed was inherent national racism and warmongering. Lambrev also had a wide spiritual streak and believed he had visions. One involved "Jesus coming back as an ordinary person. Then I had a dream of a nuclear war, and a leader saying. 'We're going down in the cave.' " He began participating in antiwar protests; wanting to help lift up the disenfranchised, he became a social worker, drifting awhile before taking a job as a welfare counselor in Ukiah. He considered his new home to be "a cow town. I knew I was going to feel isolated there."

One Wednesday morning in March 1966, Lambrev was on his way to the Ukiah courthouse when "a huge woman in a passing car" dropped a package of leaflets on the street, apparently by accident. Lambrev picked them up and returned them. The woman identified herself as Patty Cartmell, and told Lambrev that she and her church group were new to the area. She'd lost the leaflets while taking her California driver's test. Her pastor had prophesized she'd pass the test — she did — but that something would happen in the middle of it. That accounted for the leaflets. After chatting a little longer, Cartmell said that she and some friends were getting together that Friday night — would he like to join them? Lambrev didn't think it sounded very promising; he was dubious of most churches. But since he had no other Friday night social options, he agreed to drop by.

It was a small gathering, just Lambrev, Cartmell, her teenage son Mike, nineteen-year-old Joyce Beam, Archie Ijames, and Joe Phillips. Lambrev was told that their church came to Ukiah to escape persecution in Indiana, "a corn belt culture of fundamentalists." He was urged to talk about himself and his beliefs; only later would Lambrev realize that he was being carefully screened. He thought that it was amazing how like-minded he and these people were, similarly concerned with racism and unjustified war. After a while, someone suggested they move on to a larger party with more members of their church — Peoples Temple, it was called. Lambrev was told this was a party for church teens. Kids danced while adults chaperoned. Lambrev found himself chatting with another

258

man; within minutes, he felt he was having "the most extraordinary conversation of my life. I'd express a thought, and *wham,* he'd respond to it perfectly, like he knew me completely and agreed with everything I believed. I finally said to him, 'I missed your name,' and he replied, 'Jim.' He was the pastor."

Jim invited Lambrev to the Peoples Temple Sunday service, and provided directions to the schoolhouse where they met on the hill property of the Church of the Golden Rule. He added modestly, "We're a very backward group of simple-minded people. You have everything to offer us, and we have nothing to offer you." Lambrev went. He counted eighty-two there, almost all white except for the Ijames family, several children of Jim and Marceline Jones, and a few others. All were welcoming. Lambrev was amazed at how everyone shared his values. He returned every Sunday after that. Temple services took up the entire day, with the morning program lasting three or four hours, and then a Sunday service beginning at 7 p.m. and extending until 10:30 or 11. Jones always spoke movingly of equality for all, and denounced the evils of racism and war. Lambrev recalls, "He was dynamic, totally dedicated to social change. Energy radiated from him. I felt that I had entered a new world. [Jones] seemed to have powers and an almost unfathomable understanding of the evils in the world and the need to set an example so that everyone could see how to rise above them. In my experience, there was no one else like him, nothing else like Peoples Temple."

It was common in the mid-1960s for many disillusioned young Americans to leave big cities for rural communities, where, presumably, there was less corruption and racism: "Getting back to the land" was the popular phrase. These seekers wanted to find some means of positive participation to turn America into the right kind of country, one dedicated to racial and economic equality and avoidance of war. Mendocino County, far enough away from San Francisco to provide a sense of geographic distance, attracted more than its share of them. They found work in county factories and hospitals, but most immediately felt the same sense of ideological isolation as Garry Lambrev. Jones and his followers identified and reached out to them, picking the most idealistic. The more frustrated they felt with local closed-mindedness, the better. Once these newcomers were recruited, they in turn helped attract the few like-minded locals to the Temple, in particular co-workers at hospitals and social service agencies.

Linda Amos from the county welfare office became one of the most enthusiastic new members. So did Larry Layton, a conscientious objector who worked in the county mental hospital in lieu of military service. Layton's wife, Carolyn, a high school teacher, also joined. No chance meeting was ignored as a recruitment opportunity. The Jones family, out for a weekend drive, had met the Laytons when they passed them walking along a back road and offered a lift.

Jones also recruited among his students. In addition to his regular teaching job, he began instructing night classes in Ukiah's adult education program. Many of those enrolled were also in their teens, struggling with family or drug problems and unenthusiastic about education. But unlike other night class instructors who relied on dull textbooks and uninspired lectures, Jones created a lively atmosphere, encouraging discussion and making a point to engage personally with each student. Some, estranged or otherwise separated from their parents, were encouraged to move in temporarily with Temple families. Teenage Christine Lucientes's life was torn apart when her father was caught selling marijuana to an undercover agent. Afterward, the entire Lucientes family was shunned by almost everyone in Ukiah. Jones was sympathetic. He took time to encourage Christine, but never pushed too hard. At one point, he told her they wouldn't talk about the situation any longer because he could tell that discussing it caused her too much pain. Christine was moved by his sensitivity. Soon, she joined Peoples Temple — and talked her friend Janice Wilsey into joining with her.

Once teens became members, Jones monopolized their lives. During the week, their new pastor expected them to be exemplary in school — their behavior now reflected on Peoples Temple. Outside class, they weren't encouraged to mix with other local youngsters. Instead, they shared church-sponsored fun with their Temple friends. On Friday and Saturday nights there were dances and other social activities. No drugs or alcohol were allowed. Nonmember parents who'd despaired for their children couldn't help but be impressed, even if they disdained the Temple itself.

The teens were also given responsibilities, foremost among them an obligation to care for older church members in the event of nuclear catastrophe. Mike Cartmell was placed in charge of a proto-military youth battalion. The church was antiwar but committed to self-defense. Twenty Temple youngsters were selected for special training. They were taught to read compasses and issued crossbows; if bombs fell, the teens would lead Temple seniors into the hills and protect them if necessary on the way to the cave and safety. It was far-fetched, but fun. The teens felt empowered. Issuing crossbows to them ran little risk of causing local outcry. Mendocino County was popular with hunters. Lots of locals owned bows and guns.

By late spring 1966, Temple membership had risen to about 150. Jones announced that the church would stage a march in Ukiah to protest America's increasing military involvement in Vietnam. The procession would make its way along the town's main streets to the county courthouse. The protest would undoubtedly alienate many area residents. Some of Jones's followers asked if it was worth it. They'd worked hard to become accepted — why risk undoing that effort? Jones shrugged and said, "We're here, so they've got to know who we are." He appointed recent members Garry Lambrev and Bonnie Hildebrand to organize and lead a Friday demonstration. Then Jones announced he'd be out of town that day with Joe Phillips, on a trip to Guadalajara. His deliberate absence during the march troubled some, Lambrev and Hildebrand especially. Father was the church's leader, its shield against an antagonistic outside world. They didn't question his decision to be somewhere else — Jim Jones was never wrong. Still, they were concerned about trying to pull off the march without him.

Jones and Phillips left on Thursday. Shortly after they departed, Jones called Marceline and asked that she pass along a message: While driving south to Mexico, Jones said, he'd had a vision that someone might try to hurt Lambrev during the protest. Garry should be very careful. After that, Lambrev and Hildebrand were both convinced that the march would be sabotaged, and that they might even die while leading it. But their antiwar beliefs and devotion to Jones were such that they carried on anyway.

On Friday, Temple members staged their public protest. All along the short route, townspeople stared. Some jeered. When the procession reached the courthouse, Lambrev stood on the steps and nervously began to speak. As he did, he noticed a man coming up the steps toward him. Lambrev decided that this was who Jones had warned him about; sure enough, he was going to be attacked. At the same moment, Lambrev also saw Jim Jones striding purposefully toward the courthouse. "I felt as though there were suddenly glass walls around me, that Jim was completely protecting me from this man," Lambrev remembers. "And the man took one look at Jim, turned away, headed back down the steps, and I never saw him again." Afterward, Jones told Lambrev that his vision had been so vivid that he'd insisted to Joe Phillips that they turn around and rush back to Ukiah — this was how Jones had arrived just in time to save Garry's life. The rescue confirmed Lambrev's belief in his leader as something more than human: "This was God here, the human embodiment of the Divinity."

Lambrev wasn't the only one impressed. Judge Robert Winslow, justice of the Mendocino County Superior Court, watched the proceedings outside the courthouse, and was struck by this preacher and his followers risking public wrath with their demonstration. Winslow, who'd been elected to county office despite his liberal leanings, met with Jones afterward and appointed him foreman of the county grand jury. Jones valued the title less for the limited scope of authority it granted than for the impression it gave his followers of newly gained political influence. They'd done what Father had asked, and something positive and important resulted.

In subsequent Sunday sermons, Jones began stressing his visions. He kept them both catastrophic and vague. In August 1966, he announced that Peoples Temple was about to enter "an accident cycle." This dangerous phase would run through September 16. If everyone was careful, if they believed in Jim Jones, it was possible for Temple membership to emerge from the crisis without a fatality. In particular, everyone was to drive carefully. Jones repeated this warning for several weeks. As mid-September approached, it seemed that his followers would escape unscathed.

The road leading from Ukiah to the Church of the Golden Rule property twisted up and down steep embankments for several miles.

There were potential drop-offs of more than a hundred feet. The drive was particularly difficult in the dark.

On Sunday, September 11, Marion "Whitey" Freestone had had a tough time at the Temple services. Jones would regularly "call out" members who had in some way offended Temple precepts. Freestone was a frequent target, criticized for lack of commitment to socialism or acting superior to other members. Nobody else noticed these transgressions — Whitey generally seemed like a nice guy — but if Father said he did these things, it had to be so. As usual, Freestone apologized for his mistakes and promised to do better. Well after dark, when the evening meeting was over, he and his wife, Opal, and their two children got in the family car and left for Ukiah. Other Temple members followed, Jones among them in a car driven by Patty Cartmell. Just before reaching the most precipitous turn in the narrow road, they were flagged down by members, who told them Whitey Freestone's car had careened off the road and down into a near-vertical ravine. Jones walked to the precipice. The night was so dark and the drop-off so abrupt that it was impossible to see what had happened to the Freestones. Still, Jones cried, "My place is down there," and, grabbing a flashlight, climbed down the side of the ravine. He skidded and tumbled, bruising himself badly. Teenage Mike Cartmell followed right behind. They directed the flashlight beam around the brush, but couldn't find the Freestones or their automobile.

Help was summoned, and firetrucks arrived from Ukiah. Firemen were lowered down the ravine by cable. Eventually they found the car, which was partially crushed. Three of the Freestones were trapped inside, too badly hurt to move or even make a sound. The oldest child had managed to crawl free. Jones watched as the parents and their younger daughter were pulled by cable up to the road, and followed the ambulances to the emergency room in town. Jones was in poor condition himself, but insisted on staying by his critically injured followers. Other Temple members waited nearby, catching occasional glimpses of the three crash victims, who appeared to be "just butchered." Jones came out once and said there was no hope for the little girl, but promised that Whitey and Opal were going to make it. When they survived, most Temple members credited the miraculous healing powers of Jim Jones. Jones accepted the praise — and also, on behalf of the Temple, $1,300 that the Freestones collected from their insurance company for the wrecked car.

In addition to constant mention of visions — granted to him by mysterious "messengers" that he, though not his yearning followers, could see and hear — Jones also changed the focus of his rambling sermons. In Indianapolis, he spoke not only of, but directly to, victims of social and governmental repression: poor blacks denied basic rights. Jones's emphasis then was on laws that had to be changed; he frequently cited biblical passages as justification. In Mendocino County, most Temple members were white. They sympathized with victims of racism, but had not experienced it themselves. So Jones began criticizing the government; unfair laws reflected the racist beliefs of arrogant legislators determined to retain wealth and power at the expense of the downtrodden. There were two American governments, Jones insisted. One was public and relatively powerless. The real U.S. government was run in secret by white men dedicated to the eradication of socialism and who used the FBI and CIA to carry out illegal attacks on organizations such as the Temple. A significant portion of Temple membership was now comprised of younger whites who'd grown up in comfortable circumstances and felt guilty about it. Jones played to that, insisting it was their responsibility to compensate now for the unfair advantages that they had enjoyed as children.

A significant difference between Temple meetings in Indianapolis and Mendocino County was the near-lack of healings in

Ukiah. Jones's mostly well-educated young California recruits, who were not steeped in flamboyant evangelistic tradition, were likely to be skeptical of chicken guts displayed as miraculously excised cancers. Those who'd been won over by Jones on the Indiana evangelist circuit and come west with him already believed in his healing gifts. For now in Mendocino County, prophecy was the most effective way for Jones to maintain a sense of awe in his followers — it required a deft psychological touch, but Jones's real gift was always an instinctive understanding of what worked best for specific audiences and adapting his approach as necessary.

For the most part, Jones also stopped predicting nuclear doom. He still mentioned the cave from time to time, but now as an example of how he was always prepared to protect his people. Russia was no longer portrayed as about to use its nuclear arsenal to kill as many Americans as possible. Now Jones described it as a socialist paradise whose leaders were sometimes forced into an understandably threatening posture by unwarranted U.S. economic and military aggression. He began occasionally claiming that he'd been Lenin in a previous life. Perhaps as a reward to young Mike Cartmell for rushing into the ravine with him after the Freestone car crash, Jones informed the teenager that he was the reincarnated spirit of Trotsky.

Jones frequently cited the Bible when he preached, but now he sometimes pointed out its despicable declarations. The Bible said women were inferior, that slavery was permissible. In fact, Jones said, it was the Bible's endorsement of the hateful practice that made slavery possible, which in turn led to modern-day racial injustice. Jones still recognized Jesus as more than human. It was just that imperfect men had written an equally flawed book about him.

By 1967, Jones felt confident that he had once again assembled enough of a loyal core following to establish him as a local force. But he still didn't consider Mendocino County to be the Temple's ultimate home. In October, Jones interrupted his own Sunday afternoon sermon to announce that the spiritual messengers only he could see and hear instructed him to call an immediate emergency meeting. Archie Ijames, Jack Beam, Joe Phillips, Mike Cartmell, Garry Lambrev, and a few others followed Jones into a small side room. Jones insisted that the room be searched for hidden microphones — government spies might be listening. After none were found, Jones said that fascism was "closing in." He claimed to hear the sound of jackboots: "How are we going to get out of this death trap before it's too late?" They should all think about what he'd said, and meet again "to look at alternatives."

In subsequent meetings, Jones said that the Temple should move to Russia and asked for comments. Everyone but Joe Phillips agreed. Phillips wondered why a decision had to be made in a hurry. Shouldn't they learn more about where they would go in Russia? What would they do when they got there? It seemed unlikely that the Soviet government would allow the Temple to continue operating autonomously. What did Jones have to say about that? And how could they move to Russia when no one in the Temple even spoke the language? Surely there were many things to investigate before an informed decision could be made.

Jones was furious. Though only Phillips had objected openly — several others acknowledged private doubts — Jones cursed at the entire group, then dismissed them. For the time being, a potential Russian relocation was dropped, though Lynetta Jones decided to get her first passport, just in case. When she was turned down because she couldn't find her birth certificate, Lynetta contacted the Bureau of Vital Statistics in Washington, D.C., asking for another copy. In her typically grouchy, irreverent way Lynetta wrote, "I have just about had it when it comes to being unborn and non-existent. Dammit!"

There was nothing humorous about Jones's retaliation against Joe Phillips for questioning his plan. Soon after the meeting where he incurred Jones's wrath, Phillips was tempted to begin an extramarital affair with another Temple member. He discussed it with Jones, who granted Phillips permission to be unfaithful to his wife, Clara. Then, in a January 1968 meeting, Jones called Phillips out and accused him of infidelity. Phillips replied that the relationship "had been authorized," and was astonished when both Clara and his girlfriend, apparently coached in advance, joined Jones in denouncing him. Humiliated, Joe Phillips left Peoples Temple and moved away from Ukiah, effectively purged by Jim Jones for the sin of disagreement.

Another disagreement in 1968 ended the relationship between Peoples Temple and the Church of the Golden Rule. The Golden Rule organization did not allow its members to attend the services of any other religious organization. But with the Temple holding its meetings at the Golden Rule settlement in the hills north of Ukiah, it was inevitable some Golden Rule members would go. One was Carol Stahl, a young woman whose talent for administration had already gained her a place on the Golden Rule Board of Elders. Stahl's father and stepmother were also Golden Rule members; she had no intention of leaving that church's fold. But Stahl became friendly with some of Jim Jones's followers, and fell in love with one of them. She and the young man wanted to be married and, at least initially, retain full membership in their individual churches. There was still some talk of Golden Rule and Peoples Temple merging. Stahl thought that her marriage to a Temple member might "help bring this about." Jones was in favor of the wedding, but the Golden Rule's senior elders forbade it. Some Golden Rule leaders already harbored well-founded suspicions that Jones wanted to bring their church under his personal control. This proposed wedding might be part of a plot. So if the young people married, they would have to choose one church or the other. Carol Stahl was told either to accept this edict or leave Golden Rule.

Jones asked for a formal meeting with Golden Rule's elders, where he pleaded on the engaged couple's behalf. Peoples Temple had no reservations about an interorganizational couple, Jones said. If anything, the marriage would reinforce the friendship between the groups. The Golden Rule elders remained adamant, and Jones lost his temper. He'd brought several Temple members with him to the meeting. Declaring that he wanted nothing more to do with such closed-minded people, Jones dramatically led his followers away. Carol Stahl left Golden Rule that night, joined Peoples Temple, and was married by Jones to her fiancé soon afterward.

Peoples Temple was left without a location for services. Jones was no longer willing to borrow or rent meeting space. For a while, members gathered at individual homes, while construction of a permanent church structure began adjacent to the two-story house where Jones lived in Redwood Valley. It wasn't the first Temple building project on the property. After many members complained of hostile treatment by locals at area lakes, Jones ordered a swimming pool for the Temple's private use to be built a few hundred yards from his home. Now an entire edifice was built in the same place, with the pool retained as part of a larger indoor facility. Temple members did most of the construction work themselves. The finished building and parking lot were close to a well-paved country road; traveling to and from meetings was easy, no matter where in Mendocino County members lived. There was a meeting room that could hold five hundred or more, and grassy acreage perfect for congregational picnics. The only drawback was that the same road making access easy for members was also convenient for those who despised the Temple. Members became accustomed to catcalls from detractors speeding by in trucks or cars. Sometimes they tossed garbage as well as epithets. Local police were of little help. As Jones constantly stressed, it was the Temple against a mostly unfriendly world. It wouldn't always be that way, he promised. The example being set by Peoples Temple would eventually inspire the rest of the country. Perhaps there weren't that many members now, two hundred or so, but more were coming. In the meantime, his current flock should enjoy him in a more intimate setting while it could: "You're getting the best of me. In four or five years, when there are masses around me, I'll be talking more simply. I'll have to dumb it down for the larger audience."

But during 1968, no masses appeared. A few former members of the Church of the Golden Rule followed Carol Stahl to Peoples Temple. The opening of the new Temple building was a festive occasion, and some curious locals who heard about the gala service and attended were intrigued enough to join, including Don and Neva Sly and Sylvia and Tom Grubbs. These two couples were impressed by Jones's initial sermon in the new location — he focused on the nurturing of children, and the importance of becoming personally involved in the creation of an egalitarian culture. County social service agencies, now staffed with multiple Temple members, sometimes helped entice area newcomers into the fold — there were always a few recent arrivals to the area who didn't fit in anywhere else. Jones's night classes still yielded occasional followers. But, in general, there weren't enough potential Mendocino County members for any significant Temple growth.

Outside news was equally discouraging. America was becoming increasingly embroiled in Vietnam. War protesters crammed streets in major cities. Racial unrest escalated, especially after the April assassination of Martin Luther King Jr. And then on June 4 — only two months later — Robert Kennedy, brother of the assassinated president, was himself assassinated shortly after winning California's presidential primary. Making matters worse locally, Judge Robert Winslow finished last in a three-candidate primary. Whoever voters chose in November to succeed Winslow as justice of the Mendocino County Supreme Court would be more politically conservative and would undoubtedly remove Jones as foreman of the grand jury. "Everyone felt discouraged," remembers Garry Lambrev. "We'd tried so hard, and now it seemed like the end."

Jones took stock. For Peoples Temple, there seemed only limited possibilities. They could move somewhere else and try to start again, or else stay where they were and remain a small backcountry outpost of socialists and antiwar protesters, surrounded by hostile neighbors and disdained by antagonistic local government. Even beyond location, there was a greater, if yet unspoken, dilemma. What, exactly, was the reason for Peoples Temple to continue existing? Only Jones could answer that. He had personal options. He could dissolve Peoples Temple and go off somewhere else with his family to start a whole new mission from the ground up — a church based in some racially charged big-city slum, or another tour of the evangelism circuit, building first a local, then a regional following. Jones had done both before, and could again. His powers as a manipulator and orator remained intact. He could even bring a small group of core supporters with him — the Beams, the Cordells, Archie Ijames, Patty Cartmell. They would surely remain loyal under any circumstances.

But starting over would indicate that Jones had been wrong — about leaving Indianapolis for Brazil and then Mendocino County, and for promising that Peoples Temple would flourish in Redwood Valley. Then and afterward, Jones never admitted personal error. Sometimes outsiders lied to him, or else someone he trusted betrayed him. It was always someone else's fault. At the same time, Jones retained faith in his ability to bend any circumstances to his will. Though no one else might see how, Jones still expected to make great things happen. His overall goal was as grand as ever: taking the lead in an American embrace of socialism, as defined and practiced by Jim Jones and his Peoples Temple.

He was the Earth God, able to bestow the kind of here-and-now blessings that the biblical Sky God couldn't. Jones felt certain that somehow, opportunity would present itself. When it did, he would take full advantage.

God or not, he was right.

CHAPTER TWENTY: RESURRECTION

Jim Jones still spent some of each day reading newspapers and magazines, searching out articles describing the plight of oppressed people, seeking material that could form the basis for Sunday sermons. The *New York Times* remained a favorite publication, but in Redwood Valley he also subscribed to both major San Francisco newspapers and also Bay Area periodicals from black publishers. Stories about an upcoming event in San Francisco caught Jones's eye. Macedonia Baptist, one of the city's major black churches, announced a memorial service honoring Martin Luther King Jr. Several other black churches were participating. The public was invited to attend.

Jones ordered every Peoples Temple member, regardless of any personal or job obligation, to go with him to San Francisco and attend the King service. On the morning of the program, a colorful car caravan made the one-hundred-mile trip south from Mendocino County. Because Jones railed against pride of possession, the procession was mostly comprised of battered station wagons, old jalopies, and some trucks. The directions Jones provided to the church were vague. When the caravan reached San Francisco, many drivers got lost in the winding city streets, and it was a near thing for everyone to gather in time in the parking lot so that Temple members, about 150 of them, could make a dramatic first impression by entering together. The members of the host churches were astonished when so many white people came inside looking for seats. What had been a reasonably large crowd instantly expanded to standing room only. The Temple members mingled with Bay Area blacks, offering murmured words of sympathy and a shared sense of loss. The sentiments came across as genuine because they were. Those who'd stuck with the Temple in its current hard times truly did believe in racial equality, and the nobility of King, who'd first dedicated, then sacrificed, his life for the same social principles that they embraced.

The African American ministers leading the memorial service were equally surprised and impressed, especially when they learned how far Temple members had come to attend. It was only natural during the program for the ministers to recognize Reverend Jones, who'd brought these fine people, and to invite him to say a few words to the entire audience. At first, Jones spoke humbly. He praised King's life and work, and declared, "We have to come together. We have to follow his example." The blacks in the audience responded warmly. The hall echoed with shouted "Amens." This was the kind of preaching they knew and loved — and it was coming from a white man. Jones's few words grew into extended remarks, though not so much so that he dominated the remainder of the program. He knew better than to ostentatiously overshadow his hosts. But he spoke about the programs Peoples Temple wanted to initiate in Redwood Valley, how they were already making efforts there to promote racial harmony and social equality. Jones declared that the spirit of Martin Luther King was being honored, kept alive, *extended,* up in Mendocino County, right in the heart of racist country. Would everyone from San Francisco like to see for themselves? (*"Yes!"*) Well, Jones said, as it happened, Peoples Temple planned a grand community service in just a few weeks, one where they would be proud for their newly acquainted brothers and sisters to come north and attend. Would everyone come? What an honor for Peoples Temple, blessed by the presence of new friends, and playing its own small part in spreading the Word of God and the example of Martin Luther King Jr. Hallelujah.

The Temple members were as surprised as the rest of the San Francisco audience. They knew nothing about any special community-wide service being planned in Mendocino County. Jones probably came up with the concept on the spot, but immediately afterward planning commenced under his direction. The Temple still had some money stashed in Ukiah bank accounts, set aside for emergencies. This was treated as one. Funds were withdrawn to rent the Mendocino County fairgrounds for an entire weekend — the arena there was the only structure large enough to hold the several thousand people Jones expected to fill it. Jones stayed in touch with the black ministers in San Francisco, promising a memorable program for their congregations if only they would come. Surely Martin Luther King Jr. would want them to make this special effort, whites and blacks joining together in common, positive cause. If they didn't come, the members of Peoples Temple might lose heart, and how would that reflect on the San Francisco churches and Dr. King's sacred memory?

The program itself was designed to appeal to the black visitors on two levels. First was an emphatic call for social justice, as exemplified by King's life and career. But religion itself had to be integral, and not the relatively sterile worship common to white, Protestant churches. The presence of God must be felt in entertaining form, and Jones knew the most dramatic approach. It was time again for healings, done on a visual scale far beyond the occasional laying on of hands or prophesizing that Jones had limited himself to since the Temple relocation to Redwood Valley. To this end, he relied on the old hands, Patty Cartmell especially, and a few other Indianapolis veterans who understood what had to be done. Yes, there would be trickery. But these accomplices believed that Jim was simply doing what was necessary for the continued survival of Peoples Temple.

So, not once or twice, but throughout the extended service, he would not only remove cancers, but have them displayed to the crowd. The subterfuge involved was simple. Plants in the audience would call out for Father Jim to heal them of the dread disease. They would be escorted to bathrooms by other Temple members in on the act. There, they'd unwrap smuggled packages of rotting chicken innards and return claiming that the sufferer had "passed" the tumor at Jones's command. To heighten the effect, Temple members not in on the plan would be handed the foul-looking, smelly trophies, and ordered to march up and down the aisles, presenting the ghastly lumps as proof of the healing. Only the most gullible were selected for this responsibility. Jones instructed these followers not to let any visitors look too closely at, let alone touch, the supposed tumors. If someone tried to examine one too closely, Jones said, its bearer should swallow it immediately, since the cancers were so contagious that contact would likely cause instant infection. The selected tumor bearers blanched. Wouldn't they get cancer by touching the tumors, too? Jones promised that he'd use his powers to prevent it.

On the big day, Temple members waited at the fairgrounds, uncertain if anyone from San Francisco would come. The morning hours passed, and then a bus chugged into the fairgrounds parking lot, then another and another, until it seemed to the relieved Temple members waiting to greet them that the line of buses might go on forever. Everyone pouring out of the buses was greeted with warm hugs. Light refreshments were offered — Temple women had baked until dawn — and then everyone was ushered inside for the service. Of course, the visiting pastors were invited to offer remarks, and, caught up in the joyous atmosphere of this special occasion, they were moved to oratory. No one rushed them or tried to cut them off. There were no time limits. No one shouted "Amen" louder than the white Peoples Temple members. And when Jim Jones finally took his turn, he completely mastered the moment. Though his usual Redwood Valley sermons rarely cited the Bible except to denigrate it, this time he quoted the Good Book positively and at length. Temple members understood the need for this blatant contradiction. Father, a gracious host, was making their visitors feel at home.

The gospel having been properly praised, Jones moved on to the healings, roaming the arena, making selections apparently at random. All the theatrical bells and whistles worked to perfection. The squeamish expressions on the faces of those brandishing the bloody "tumors" added to the effect. Perhaps a few doubted, but afterward Jones was swarmed by admirers in awe of his powers.

When the service was finally over, everyone limp from sustained excitement, there was social time. Quite a few of Jones's followers wanted to stay in touch with their new pals, and requested mailing addresses and phone numbers. Jones himself spent several hours huddled with the San Francisco ministers, discussing possible joint efforts, and thanking them profusely for honoring his humble little church with their visit. Garry Lambrev recalls, "Little did those black ministers know that their undoing was right there in their midst, in the person of Jim Jones."

The tone of the calls and letters from Temple members to their new friends was always warm without being too presumptuous. If the black ministers were aware of messages, they felt no threat. Jim Jones and

Peoples Temple were a hundred miles away. And, at first, only a few of the San Francisco visitors accepted invitations for a return trip. The Temple provided round-trip transportation. These repeat guests basked in all the friendly attention before and after the service. Everyone was so interested in anything they had to say. The services themselves — Peoples Temple called them meetings, but they were worship services, sure enough — were lively, lots of singing and always some healing, and Pastor Jones talking about how things could be fixed right here, right now on earth, if enough people wanted it. And during the services and after, Temple members would testify, telling how their church helped them get this Social Security problem straightened out, or that son away from street gangs, or a daughter off drugs.

As had been the case in 1950s Indianapolis, members of black San Francisco churches in the late 1960s were constantly frustrated as they tried to go about everyday life. Laws permitting segregation had been struck down, but in the opinion of many whites the government continued to give blacks unfair advantages, everything from college and hiring quotas to a welfare system that leached away even the most marginal financial security from hardworking, law-abiding white folks. These beliefs were at complete variance from the daily experience of African Americans trapped in crushing poverty and inadequate housing. Far from effortlessly benefiting from federal largesse and rioting at the slightest perceived provocation, they struggled with bureaucratic red tape in the social service and legal systems. Applying for welfare, Social Security, and disability payments was a complex, often tortuous process. Gangs and drugs were rampant in slums and public housing. A disproportionate percentage of poor black males were either in prison or at risk of it. In too many instances, black women had to raise extended families without an adult male presence or financial support. And, always, there was the despairing sense that things were never going to get much better. The civil rights movement of the 1950s had segued into the civil rights legislation of the 1960s, and still their lives had not changed.

Neither had the approach of pastors in many black churches. They urged patience in Sunday services, recommending a Christian acceptance of unfairness in life in return for the glory of the Promised Land afterward. This was particularly true in San Francisco, where there was little black participation in critical civic decision making. For those in the city's black churches, forbearance seemed the only option until the first few visitors returned from Sunday meetings at Peoples Temple in Redwood Valley and spoke about their experiences there. They'd poured out their hearts, related their troubles, and the congregation of Peoples Temple did more than just listen. Temple members volunteered to help them fill out complicated government paperwork for welfare or work disability, or explained how to get a doddering family member into a decent nursing home. And it wasn't just a few minutes of assistance after Sunday services. These Temple folks, who seemed to know how to cut through every snarl of government red tape, offered to write letters on their behalf, or make phone calls for them, or even drive a hundred miles and come along on appointments — and they did all these things cheerfully, as if it was as much a blessing for them to help you as it was for you to be helped. All you had to do was share your problems with them, and things got done.

More black San Francisco Christians began making the trip up to Redwood Valley, dozens every Sunday, and though a few were put off by the Temple pastor's occasional put-downs of the Bible, most were enthralled by a church where you also got secular help. Some chose to move to Mendocino County and join Peoples Temple. Those who did were assisted in finding jobs and housing. The Temple made the transition easy, warmly welcoming the newcomers into the church family. Peoples Temple's congregants included county social service employees, professionals trained to provide the kind of practical help that black San Francisco churches didn't. Jones hadn't planned it that way, but he was quick to take advantage.

This new influx of blacks into their conservative white community upset many in Ukiah, but Jones made use of that, too. Outside resentment bound Temple members closer together. For many younger white members, who'd joined in part from feelings of guilt about privileged upbringings, this was their first chance to interact with lots of black people on a daily basis. It reinforced their own dedication to the Temple — this was the egalitarian, interracial culture that they'd yearned for.

Jones emphasized the "us against them" attitude, accusing locals of even more aggressive racism than they actually exhibited. One day Jimmy Jr. came home looking puzzled. He said that someone at his elementary school called him a nigger and asked his father what the word meant. The youngster wasn't upset, just curious, but Jones exaggerated the moment in a particularly raging Sunday sermon.

They [sent Jimmy] home crying when they'd spit on him [and used] that word "nigger." . . . "Niggardly" means to be treated cheatedly. You've been heated. And we know Indians and blacks and poor whites have been cheated, don't we? But [Jimmy] said that word hurt, so I turned it around in my home, and I made it the proudest word for the chosen people. I said, "Yes, we're niggers, and we're proud." And now we say the word and our children don't get worried. The [next] time little Jim was called a nigger, he said, "Sticks and stones may break my bones, but you're sure not going to hurt me with that word, because that's the best word in the world."

When Jones declared, "Anyone in America who's poor — white, brown, yellow, or black — and does not admit that he's a nigger is a damn fool," everyone stood and cheered.

New black membership offered the Temple a welcome source of fresh income. Many arriving families included older members. There were also individual seniors who wanted to move to Mendocino County but required daily care. Marceline Jones was currently employed as a state inspector of nursing homes; in Indianapolis, she and her husband had owned and operated facilities. Now, using some of the money brought from Indiana, Peoples Temple acquired residential properties in Ukiah and converted them into church-owned nursing homes. As in Indianapolis, Temple members served as administrators and staff. The care provided to Temple nursing home residents met and exceeded state requirements. Marceline Jones saw to that. Client disability income and Social Security checks more than covered expenses; all profits went to the church. This money was used to fund outreach programs, which in turn attracted more new members to the Temple.

As African Americans moving north from the Bay Area began to swell Temple membership and coffers, Jones looked for other sources of recruitment. In Indiana, he had never bothered attending annual conventions and other gatherings of Disciples of Christ administrators and ministers. Now in California, he went to all that he could, and even made presentations about Peoples Temple and some of the new programs it was establishing in Mendocino County. These included encouraging teens to stay away from drugs and marriage counseling. Jones invited ministers from other Disciples churches to come and visit. When they did, they were amazed by the Temple's mixed-race congregation and struck by Jones's emphasis on community service. His sermons when such visitors were present always focused on outreach rather than racial resentment. Many Disciples ministers were impressed enough to refer their own troubled congregants to Peoples Temple and its programs. Those that came enjoyed a carefully orchestrated reception, usually at a Sunday morning service. As soon as their cars pulled into the Redwood Valley church parking lot, visitors were individually greeted by Temple members, who began testifying about the powers and good works of Jim Jones. Their descriptions were vivid — cancers removed, dead people revived, near-fatal drug addictions miraculously cured. Then the newcomers were ushered inside and directed to reserved seats in the front rows. Temple members walked over to chat, asking apparently innocuous questions, often giving hugs before stepping aside so that others could briefly visit. There was singing from an adult choir, and more songs from Temple children, black and white youngsters walking hand in hand, all of them smiling.

When Jones finally appeared, there were testimonials to his grace and power. Each person was gently asked to limit remarks to three minutes, because so many wanted to praise Father Jim. After that, Jones might announce a miracle or two, generally something that couldn't be disproven: someone had been fated to die in a car wreck the next morning, but because he'd come to Peoples Temple that day and believed all he'd heard there, he'd be spared. This was a plant, who'd rise up in tears to thank Jones for saving his life. Visitors taking that kind of pronouncement for hokum were often astonished when

Jones next directly addressed *them,* by name and often describing something in their lives — an ill, elderly relative, a car that kept breaking down — that seemed impossible for him to know anything about. Few realized that the chatty Temple members visiting with them prior to the service, usually Patty Cartmell and others experienced in assisting Jones's public performances, scrawled notes with information they'd learned and passed these along to him before he came out to preach. Jones would assure them that Granny's bladder problems were about to get better, or that the family car was going to start running perfectly. If that didn't turn out to be the case, come and tell him, because he and everybody in the Temple cared about these problems and wanted to help.

Jones's lengthy sermons surprised many guests, particularly white visitors accustomed to short Sunday messages. By the time the Sunday morning service was over, it would always be well into the afternoon and everyone was hungry. Jones sent them to tables set up behind the church building, where Temple women served a hearty meal. Members sat with guests, talking more, asking what they thought of the service, seeming especially sympathetic and attentive if anyone mentioned something bothersome — maybe a problem with Jones criticizing the Bible, or the impression that the pastor sounded like a communist, the way he insisted that everybody should share everything equally.

After plates were cleared, visitors were thanked for coming, and invited to stay for the evening meeting if they liked. Few did — they were exhausted from the earlier marathon. Jones would make some farewell remarks, emphasizing that they were welcome to come back whenever they liked. There was minimal vetting. Only a year earlier, Temple membership had almost dwindled away, and had to be built back up. For now, Jones cared more about numbers than compatible philosophy.

Some of the visitors had no further contact with the Temple. They made it clear to their hosts that it wasn't for them. But those who'd shown even a glimmer of interest received calls and letters asking them to return. There were packages, too — homemade cookies or other treats, tokens of the Temple membership's regard, and indicative of their hopes to welcome recipients into their loving church.

Those who made a second visit usually had some private conversation with Jones. Thoroughly briefed by confederates before the meeting, he would know exactly what to say to each, speaking directly to any concerns they might have. His powers of persuasion remained exceptional. By the end of 1969, about five hundred people regularly attended Peoples Temple, more than three times the membership of a year earlier.

For a time, Jones felt secure enough to allow a few disillusioned current members to leave. Through intermediaries, he even encouraged their departure. Garry Lambrev had joined Peoples Temple in the belief that Jones was something more than human, and that the Temple would exemplify the right way for America to function. Some of Jones's machinations troubled him, and it showed. Jim Pugh, one of Jones's most ardent supporters, told Lambrev, "Garry, we know you're not comfortable. We need people who can really make a commitment." Lambrev left for a while, but stayed in touch with Temple friends. After a few months he was back, beginning a series of departures and returns that went on for several years. The lure of good Temple works in spite of its leader's flaws kept drawing Lambrev back.

For the present, those flaws didn't endanger Peoples Temple, or lessen most members' certainty that their pastor was above reproach. A few loyalists knew that the miracle healings were faked. Some also doubted Jones's insistence that he was, in some way or another, godlike. Anyone even remotely close to Jones realized he was obsessed with control, and could not bear to delegate any real authority. But to them, what mattered more was all the good that was being accomplished through Jones's leadership. It was his vision and apparently limitless energy that drove the Temple forward, in a time and place where its shining example was so unlikely, and so badly needed.

But if 1969 was the year of the Temple's rebirth, it was also the year when Jim Jones's personal failings and delusions, previously peripheral to his good works, began manifesting themselves in more overt ways that escalated for almost a decade until he brought himself down, and Peoples Temple along with him. Eventually Jones betrayed everyone who followed him. He began during the summer of 1969 by betraying his wife.

CHAPTER TWENTY-ONE: CAROLYN

In the summer of 1969, Jim and Marceline Jones had been married for twenty years. Partners inevitably grow and change in two decades of marriage, but for the Joneses, those changes were extreme. At twenty-two, Marceline was eager to experience life outside her Indiana hometown, and the ambitious goals of eighteen-year-old Jim Jones appealed to her own religious beliefs, which were rooted in a hands-on approach. Marceline had no patience with passive Christianity. Her niece Janet L. Jackson remembers, "One time when she and Stephan were visiting here [in Richmond], there was a revival meeting and we went. Whoever was leading [the revival] was talking all about, 'Praise Jesus,' and Aunt Marceline comes up and says, 'Give me the microphone.' And she takes the microphone and says, 'You know, all this is good, praising God and everything, but you also have to get out there and do things. You can't just sit on the sidelines and praise Jesus.'

Then she handed the microphone back."

Gradually, Jones won his wife over to what she once would have considered radical ideals. Marceline would never have believed herself to be a racist, but she came to her marriage with little real understanding of the plight of American blacks. Through her husband's ministry, Marceline became committed to racial equality. She also accepted some of his other beliefs, in particular the possibility of reincarnation and the inconsistencies of the Bible. Marceline knew Jim Jones too well ever to think of him as God or the returned Christ, but she did agree that he had powers which transcended normal human limits. At some point Marceline discovered that most, if not all, of his healings and prophecies were stage-managed. She accepted the deception, to the point where she would eventually claim that her husband miraculously cured her of cancer.

Away from the public eye, Jones was frequently coarse and self-centered, often as thoughtless with his wife as he was thoughtful to the oppressed he sought to serve. But Marceline was firmly convinced that her husband was still in most respects a godly man, and one whose great gifts were desperately needed by the rest of the world. She, more than anyone else, could help him most because she understood him best. Any difficulty Marceline had living with the emotionally erratic Jones was more than compensated for by the good things they accomplished together. He needed her; they really were a team. Marceline took satisfaction in her own contributions to the cause. Avelyn Chilcoate remembers, "All of Marceline's family felt like she and Jim had made good, and Marceline was proud and happy, too."

There was one hiccup, an intimate problem. From childhood, Marceline dealt with chronic back pain, which doctors occasionally treated with traction. Sometimes, too much physical activity confined her to bed. She tried not to let it limit her, bearing discomfort stoically. But carrying and then delivering Stephan took its toll, and, as Marceline delicately phrased it to her mother, for some time afterward she and Jones were not able to "live as husband and wife." The Joneses regretted, but accepted, that there could never be another pregnancy. Eventually they resumed their sex life, but apparently on a careful, limited basis.

In Indianapolis, Marceline had been Jim's chief conduit with public officials. She knew how to approach them, how to make the Temple seem like a welcome partner rather than a demanding, impractical adversary, and Jim didn't. But he was always a quick learner, able to absorb anything useful. Jones had little interest in anything that didn't advance his ministry. In California, using what he'd learned from his wife in Indiana, Jones no longer relied on her for political advice. He went by himself to meet with mayors, judges, and city council members, or else took along other Temple members but not her.

As Marceline's role as a political advisor to her husband diminished, she compensated by having even more interaction with Temple members. Jones's pronouncements from the pulpit often upset some listeners, and his rants about antagonistic locals deliberately added to a collective sense of paranoia. Marceline didn't openly disagree with her husband; in many instances, she thought that what he said was right, if tactlessly expressed. Her new, crucial Temple role was as a buffer, taking responsibility for soothing the concerns or ruffled feelings that Jones frequently caused. Where he expected obedience, Marceline thanked members for the ways in which they participated. If it came to his attention that some assigned task hadn't been done right, Jones was critical. Though she also expected the best of everyone, Marceline preferred explaining how to correct mistakes rather than reprimanding members.

For all his egotism, Jones recognized Marceline's value to his ministry. Many Temple members called him "Father," but they also addressed Marceline as "Mother." In the dark days after Robert Kennedy's assassination and Judge Winslow's defeat, Jones decreed in a handwritten document that in the event of his own demise, Marceline Jones would "be my successor as pastor, president of Peoples Temple Nonprofit Inc., and spiritual leader of Peoples Temple in all matters." Secular Temple matters, fund-raising, and property acquisitions, and establishing outreach programs would be directed by the Temple's Board of Elders. But Jones instructed that "Marceline Jones is to be consulted in all church decisions for in her their [*sic*] is absolute integrity." All this meant very little — Jim Jones had no intention of going anywhere, let alone dying, and even in that unlikely scenario he'd made it clear she was not to enjoy the same autonomy that he did.

Marceline found solace in her children. As in all families, things didn't always run smoothly. Agnes, whom the Joneses adopted at age eleven in Indianapolis, was a restless spirit. As a teenager, she caused her parents considerable anguish by taking up with a series of unsuitable men. When the rest of the family moved to Brazil, Agnes stayed behind in Indiana. She eventually made her own way out to California, where she stayed in touch with her parents while entering into additional bad relationships. Those familiar with the situation thought Agnes wanted to please her parents but never could — her balky, independent personality didn't allow her to conform to their expectations. When the Rainbow Family was featured in appearances, interviews, and photographs, Agnes was not included.

Suzanne, who in 1969 was seventeen, had a touchy relationship with her mother. Since Marceline was away on job-related trips so much, Suzanne was expected to help keep her younger siblings in line. She did so effectively — among the Jones kids, it was accepted that their big sister was the boss — but often resented the responsibility. Thirteen-year-old Lew was an exceptional athlete, friendly but always more of a follower than a leader. Stephan, ten, felt considerable pressure as the only biological son of Jim Jones. It was widely assumed by Temple membership that Stephan was Jones's real heir apparent — if the Joneses were the royal family of Peoples Temple, then Stephan was crown prince. Intelligent and intuitive, he understood his position and sometimes abused it with bad behavior. Jimmy, nine, was outgoing and funny, everybody's favorite. He was also the child most often shown off to outsiders by Jones as proof of his adoptive father's solidarity with blacks.

Marceline tried diligently to offer her children affection and attention. She would go to great lengths to make them feel not only loved, but also special to her in individual ways. Jim Jones Jr. remembers that once in

Redwood Valley "I tried to play the race card on my parents. We argued about something and I said they didn't love me because I was black and they were white. There was a tree outside our house and I ran outside and climbed up into the tree. My mother came out to the tree; she was crying and she had smeared soot all over her face. She called up, 'Now am I black enough for you to love me?'"

During the summer of 1969, Marceline's back gave out completely. Sometimes she was confined to bed and kept in traction. Pain and boredom left her fretful and uncharacteristically snappish with her husband. There was nothing Jones could do about his wife's physical discomfort, but he could have been more attentive than usual to make Marceline's convalescence less aggravating. Instead, he concerned himself with his own gratification. Jones was obsessed with sex, and had been since childhood. As a teenager, he'd seen his mother — by far the most dominant adult influence in his life — openly enter into a long-term love affair when her ailing husband was no longer able to engage in sex with her. By 1969, Marceline's physical frailties had already curtailed Jones's marital sex life for a decade, and now his wife was unavailable for an extended period, perhaps permanently. No evidence has been found that Jones previously strayed, but now, surrounded by a growing number of adoring female followers, many of whom believed he was in some sense God on Earth, he took a mistress. Virtually any female in the Temple could have been his for the asking, but Jones selected perhaps the most unlikely woman of all.

Twenty-four-year-old Carolyn Moore Layton was physically unprepossessing, very lean, almost always taciturn, her long dark hair usually caught up in a tight bun. To most, her attitude seemed as forbidding as her looks. Former Temple member Laura Johnston Kohl wrote later, "Carolyn reminded me of the woman in the *American Gothic* painting by Grant Wood . . . that grim Pentecostal essence." But in many ways, Carolyn's background perfectly prepared her for membership in Peoples Temple. John V. Moore, her father, was a pastor and district superintendent in the Methodist church who gained prominence for his liberal preaching. Reverend Moore, like Marceline Jones, believed in participative rather than passive Christianity. He and his wife, Barbara, raised their daughters, Carolyn, Rebecca, and Annie, to be socially conscious and to act on their beliefs. The Moores participated in antiwar demonstrations, civil rights marches, and boycotts supporting the rights of farmworkers, taking pains to keep their children involved with, rather than separate from, the oppressed people his ministry strived to serve. When Reverend Moore pastored a church in Youngstown, Ohio, Carolyn was placed in a nursery school where she was the only white child. Eventually, Moore's assignments brought him and his family to California.

The three Moore daughters developed distinctive personalities. Middle child Rebecca was intellectual. Youngest girl Annie was sweet-spirited. Carolyn, the oldest, was organized and independent. Boyfriends didn't interest her. While still in high school, Carolyn announced to her parents that "I'm going to be a bachelor girl," and they expected it would be true. But in college, where Carolyn studied to become a teacher, she met Larry Layton, a soft-spoken young man who came from a troubled family background. His convictions matched hers, and they married in 1967. Larry opposed the Vietnam War and was classified as a conscientious objector, which required him to find public service employment as an alternative to military service. Larry found work in a Mendocino County mental hospital. Carolyn taught in a local high school. From the outset, Reverend Moore remembers, "Theirs was not a marriage of equals. Carolyn was dominant."

Carolyn took the lead in choosing a church in their new home. The Laytons attended several different services — Mendocino

County didn't lack for Sunday alternatives. Carolyn and Larry church-shopped until, out on an afternoon walk, they were offered a ride by the Jones family. It was natural to attend a service conducted by the friendly fellow at the wheel, and, when the Laytons did, Carolyn was stunned by everything she saw and heard. With its avowed purpose of "caring for the least among us," Peoples Temple fit exactly the beliefs imbued in Carolyn from childhood. Sometime in 1968 she and Larry became members and, from the outset, believed passionately in Jim Jones. Neither of the Laytons seemed destined for a prominent place among their new fellowship. To those who took any particular notice of him, Larry appeared almost puppylike in his eagerness to please. Carolyn's serious demeanor discouraged familiarity. But away from Peoples Temple, Carolyn in particular expressed considerable enthusiasm for the group, or, more specifically, its leader. When she called or visited her parents in the immediate aftermath of joining the Temple, Reverend Moore says, "[She] told us all about her new pastor. That was the only subject that seemed to matter to her." Carolyn was convinced that Jim Jones was a great man and the incomparable embodiment of genuine, loving social commitment. John and Barbara Moore were pleased that their daughter had found her new church, but also concerned because such effusion was so uncharacteristic of Carolyn.

Then, for several weeks, the Moores heard nothing from Carolyn at all. Concerned, they drove to Mendocino County. It wasn't a long trip; Moore currently pastored in Davis, California, about seventy miles away. Carolyn told her parents that she and Larry, who wasn't present, were finished. He was away in Nevada arranging a quickie divorce. Meanwhile, she wanted them to meet her new pastor. Carolyn called Jones, who came over immediately. He put on a full-blown performance, proclaiming his dedication to social justice. The Moores weren't impressed. Jones put them in mind of the fictional Elmer Gantry, a flamboyant con man masquerading as an evangelist. Then, to her parents' horror, "Carolyn said she was with him." They quickly took their leave; Barbara Moore cried during the ride home. After much discussion, the Moores decided not to criticize or question Carolyn's decision — that would only drive their daughter away. Instead, they hoped that she would eventually come to her senses, the sooner the better. The hardest thing to understand was how quickly Jim Jones had seduced their daughter. Why was it so easy for him?

In fact, it wasn't.

Jones did not home in on Carolyn Layton because she was easily manipulated prey. There were many Temple women who would

307

have instantly tumbled into bed with Father. But Jones wanted more than that. Others in the Temple believed Carolyn was cold and emotionally distant. Jones, with his insight into personality, realized that Carolyn had the potential to bring to a relationship many of Marceline's qualities. Jones needed someone who could make sense of his often convoluted instructions and, by force of will or personality, make others obey. Like Marceline, Carolyn was whip-smart and, if she believed in a person or a cause, absolutely dedicated. Unlike his wife, Carolyn was healthy with no sexual limitations. She could satisfy his needs in both of these crucial ways. Once Carolyn was won over, Jones would have a new partner as well as a lover.

But it wasn't a given that she could be convinced. Jones sensed that Carolyn's relationship with her husband was shaky, but she'd been raised in a minister's home and was unlikely to commit immediate adultery at Jones's request. Making the initial approach himself was risky. What if she was offended, what if the rest of Jones's followers, the ones who believed him to be morally pure, a god above human carnality, learned that Father was trying to cheat on Mother? So Jones chose an intermediary. Patty Cartmell took Carolyn aside and explained that Jim had a serious personal problem. Marceline was crippled, psychologically as well as physically. She really belonged in an institution, but Jim was too soft-hearted. Yet, to maintain his amazing spiritual gifts, Jim had to have critical emotional support and physical release, which Marceline was unable to provide. Through his great insight, Jim realized that only Carolyn could provide these with the quality and devotion required. One former member who was aware of the situation remembers Cartmell, outside the Temple after a Redwood Valley Sunday service, whispering to Carolyn, "Jim *needs* this," and Carolyn looking doubtful and shaking her head. But within days she was persuaded to discuss it confidentially with him, and Jones's powers of persuasion did the rest.

Jones informed Marceline that he wasn't leaving her. To almost everyone in the Temple, and to the outside world, he and Marceline would continue appearing as loving, monogamous husband and wife. Marceline would retain her role in the church. She should not make any fuss. Jones's new relationship with Carolyn was the result of Marceline no longer being capable of physically satisfying him. He still loved her, but he needed something more.

This was perhaps the most significant risk on Jones's part — if Marceline made the affair public knowledge, if she left him and stormed back to Indiana, it would certainly be a blow to the Temple and might even irreparably split its membership — Marceline was that beloved by so many. But Jones understood his wife, too. Her ultimate acquiescence stemmed from several facets of her character. Jones was a complex man, but Marceline was complicated, too. Primarily, once Marceline committed to something or someone, her loyalty was unwavering. After so many years dedicated to her husband and Peoples Temple, it was not in her nature to turn away from them even under such devastating circumstances. She believed in the Temple's mission, and in her husband as the leader of the Temple, and as an unequaled force for necessary social change. There was also something old-fashioned in Marceline's attitude toward marriage, stemming from her upbringing in a small, socially conservative Indiana town. You married for life. Husbands, being men, were fallible by nature. It was the wife's responsibility to be perfect in all things, keeping her husband so satisfied that he would not surrender to base urges. If a husband strayed, at some level it was the wife's fault. And, like the Moores, she entertained the hope that the affair would run its course — maybe Jim would soon tire of this strange girl. Meanwhile, Marceline had to help the children through this terrible, confusing time — Jones, always open with youngsters about physical matters, informed them that he was now involved with Carolyn because their mother no longer sexually satisfied him. He told the kids that they were to think of Carolyn as a special friend. Stephan and Suzanne were resentful but generally complied, at least in their father's presence. Lew and Jimmy, easygoing and adoring of their dad, didn't question his decision. Agnes, as usual, wasn't consulted.

Even Larry Layton went along. After divorcing his wife in Nevada, he returned to Redwood Valley and resumed his place among Temple members. Soon he married another member named Karen Tow — the new Mrs. Layton was much more physically attractive and vivacious than her predecessor. Despite losing Carolyn to Jones, Layton, if anything, grew more devoted to his leader, more determined to prove to Jones at every opportunity that he was a loyal, obedient follower.

Months later, Carolyn Layton wrote joyfully to her parents about her new romantic arrangement. She lived in her own small house, and Jones alternated nights between her and his "old" family:

I can't express how completely [my] every need for companionship and romance is fulfilled by [Jim]. He only sleeps 2 or 3 hours a night and thus sees that he is always present when I need him. He gives me so much time. And he does also, in spite of such a heavy load, to his children by having

311

time with them regularly each day to do special things that they want and need. Then to think that he patiently holds up to meet the needs of Marcie who . . . can be very kind when lucid but when she's out of it she would drain any other man of his life in a few short days, but he always manages to be so kind and patient. Then to give me at least four nights a week. . . . She maintains her balance as long as she has three evenings and nights a week.

In June 1970, Marceline wrote a note to Jones. After he began his relationship with Carolyn and spent less time with his wife, Marceline often communicated with her husband in this way.

As the time approaches for our 21st wedding anniversary, it seems appropriate to take inventory of our lives together. In one more year, I will have spent half my life with you. It is the only part of my life that counts. . . . At times I don't know what is best for you. But — I do know you care. Regardless of who else you might care for, thank you for including me. I'm sorry for the times that I made you feel unloved. In my frustration as I tried to measure up but never quite doing it. . . . Thank you for your kindness and understanding. I don't know about tomorrow but today I give thanks for each moment I share with you.

Everything worked out as Jones hoped. He had Carolyn without losing Marceline, and as far as most of his followers were concerned, Father and Mother were together as always. His success heightened Jones's opinion of himself as uniquely entitled: of course his personal desires had been met. That was how, despite constant demands, he could retain the energy, the power, necessary to lead the Temple forward.

Even more ominously, this was the second time that Jones and a few insiders deliberately deceived the rank-and-file Temple membership. The first was when he had enlisted confederates to help stage healings. They were told by him that the fakery was something necessary for effective, widespread recruiting — though on the surface it might seem wrong, they must not only accept, but support the deception because it was committed for the overall greater good. Now, they had helped Jones break up the Layton marriage and betray his own loyal wife because, as Patty Cartmell told Carolyn Layton, Jim needed it. For them, their leader and their cause — the greater good — had become the same thing.

Chapter Twenty-Two:
A Socialist Example

In years to come, Jim Jones would frequently be compared to murderous demagogues such as Adolf Hitler and Charles Manson. These comparisons completely misinterpret, and historically misrepresent, the initial appeal of Jim Jones to members of Peoples Temple. Jones attracted followers by appealing to their better instincts. The purpose of Peoples Temple was to offer such a compelling example of living in racial and economic equality that everyone else would be won over and want to live the same way. Government would be altered, not overthrown. Temple members might march to protest racism or unjust wars, but would never resort to violence as a tool to bringing about a better society. No one joined Peoples Temple with the intent of doing harm or achieving subjugation. Instead, they felt better about themselves by doing good things for others.

An integral element of the Temple cause was a political agenda that, in Redwood Valley, was kept secret from outsiders because the term for it was so misunderstood. To many Americans, socialism and communism were the same thing, and, since the conclusion of World War II, communism and communists were widely considered the archenemies of democracy, especially in conservative communities like Redwood Valley and most of Mendocino County. In fact, in its most basic form, socialism was a belief in more equitable distribution of wealth, with everyone afforded the opportunity to thrive in accordance with personal achievement regardless of race or social position. A nation could *choose* to observe socialist tenets. Communism meant rigid government control — people had no choice other than to comply, and government mandate rather than personal accomplishment determined the course of their lives. Peoples Temple socialism was intended to change hearts through example, not coercion.

When most members joined in Redwood Valley in the late 1960s, they initially had no idea that they were committing themselves to any form of socialism. All they knew was that they were becoming part of a church dedicated to lifting up the oppressed — Jones frequently described them as "the least among us." For many blacks and whites, attending Temple services and social events was their first opportunity for extended racial mingling, and it was thrilling to learn, in practice as well as in principle, that people really were the same, no matter the color of their skin. The money you did or didn't have, the clothes you wore, the car you drove — none of these things mattered in Peoples Temple. For newcomers, the sense of joyful, nonjudgmental fellowship was overwhelming. If you were out of work, you were helped to find a job — Jones had apparent ins with many local employers. If you were disabled or otherwise in need, Temple members employed at the county welfare department were eager to assist. Help was available at any hour for any reason. When Elmer and Deanna Mertle joined the Temple and moved their family to Mendocino County, they noticed a bad smell coming from the front lawn of their new house. A sewer inspector informed the Mertles that their leach lines were clogged. New ones had to be dug immediately — it would cost $500, which the Mertles didn't have. When they mentioned their dilemma to Temple members, they were told not to worry. The next day, fifteen Temple men arrived at dawn and spent the day excavating the old lines, laying new ones, and then replacing the grass that had been torn up. When the Mertles asked how much the work would cost, they were told that Temple members were glad to help each other.

Jones himself was a constant, positive presence in every member's life. He had a remark-able memory for names — everyone was ad-dressed in some personal way, and made to feel special. If, sometimes, he railed a little too long or too ferociously at meetings, as members were taught to call services, Jones was kindness itself in individual conversa-tions. He addressed most women as "dar-ling," and younger men as "son." There was no doubt he took his leadership role seriously. Jones made a point of telling everyone that he hardly slept. Followers were encouraged to call him in the middle of the night, if necessary, and whenever anyone did Jim always seemed to be up and about.

This amazing all-for-one, one-for-all atmo-sphere was formally categorized by Jones in a Wednesday night meeting sometime in 1970. Saturday and Sunday morning and afternoon meetings were open to anyone, but Wednes-day nights were "closed," reserved only for Temple members. Jones often spoke more politically in these. On this night, Neva Sly Hargrave recalls, "Jim brought [our dreams] together." After describing the egalitarian society that would eventually exist thanks to the example of Peoples Temple, Jones dra-matically announced, "We are all socialist!" The congregation stood as one, she says, "and rocked with thunderous applause."

As socialists, Jones instructed, they would live such shining, equality-based lives that anyone who observed or interacted with them would want the same sense of fellowship and satisfaction. But it wouldn't do, at least yet, to proudly proclaim themselves as socialist, because that would alienate many whom they wanted to convert. As much as possible, Jones said, Temple business should not be discussed with outsiders. Entice by example; let them come to us.

Subsequently, "open" meetings no longer were. Greeters, mostly women, waited in front of the Redwood Valley Temple and intercepted outsiders planning to attend the service. Laura Johnston Kohl remembers that "[We] would tell them about the service and find out how they got there, and what they were expecting." Then the greeters jotted brief notes about their impressions of each visitor; these were taken back to Jones. He personally decided which would be allowed inside, and which told sorry, they couldn't attend this meeting, perhaps another time. These turndowns were tactful. Jones wanted members to believe the surrounding community was relatively hostile — "us against them" mind-sets were helpful in keeping members loyal — but he didn't want active widespread antipathy, either. It was critical to maintain a balance.

To a large extent, Jones's efforts at manipulating community opinion succeeded. Constant positive coverage from the *Ukiah Daily*

Journal helped. Management there continued observing the rule of printing Temple-provided stories without fact-checking or editing. No activity or pronouncement by Jones was too trivial for publication. After Jones fetched some strays out of a busy Ukiah street, the paper's headline read, "Pastor Risks Life to Save Dogs."

Jones had a well-deserved reputation as a wonderful teacher, mostly for his work in adult night classes. The Temple itself offered community programs, and social service agencies, schools, and county offices could count on enthusiastic Temple volunteers for community construction or repair projects. Families facing health crises or deaths continued receiving offers of Temple help with chores. Cakes were still delivered to local officials. In 1969, Jones was even asked to deliver the commencement address at an area high school.

There was one misstep, though. As Temple membership grew, Jones saw the opportunity to have more influence in town and county elections. Temple members began packing halls at campaign debates, unsubtly cheering every utterance by their candidate of choice and sitting silently otherwise. When the Ukiah adult school program hosted a debate in the spring of 1970, Jones arrived with a substantial number of followers who applauded one candidate and ignored the rest. Such blatantly partisan tactics were not usually practiced in Mendocino County. Supporters of the other candidates complained on the spot to adult school principal Billy Tatum, who had been designated program chairman. Tatum, angry and embarrassed, stalked to the podium and accused Jones of "rigging the debate." Jones, stung at being verbally attacked in front of his followers, responded by threatening to resign his teaching position. Soon Jones was gone from the adult school faculty. Tatum said he fired Jones; Jones said he resigned, and also gave up his high school teaching position. In the next election cycle, Temple members again swarmed to debates and, if anything, were even more loudly supportive of their candidates and dismissive of the opposition. It wasn't the best approach for a church trying to set a positive, secretly socialist, example, but Jones didn't want to appear intimidated. No members objected; any outsiders finding fault with Father were at fault themselves.

There were other, ample opportunities for the Temple to shine through community service. In particular, it opposed the use of illegal drugs, and in this the Temple was aligned with most local parents. Peoples Temple initiated a drug rehabilitation program that focused almost exclusively on teens. The majority of clients, whose families usually did not pay for their participation, were drawn from black churches and ghettos in San Francisco, but some came from Mendocino County.

The Temple process for breaking addiction to drugs was simple. When clients first arrived, they were quarantined in a special house designated for that purpose. There were no doses of methadone to gradually wean them free. Instead, they immediately went without drugs — "cold turkey." Temple counselors were present at all times, and when the shrieking, vomiting, cramping, and other immediate aspects of the rigorously enforced cleansing process were complete, individuals would move to homes of Temple members. They remained part of those households while they continued rehabilitating. Eventually convalescents either returned to their own homes or else were absorbed into the Temple community — those who did were helped to find jobs and become self-supporting. Among the youthful addicts who entered the Temple program, only a few dropped out. Everyone successfully completing the process and emerging drug-free was evidence of the Temple's commitment to productive community involvement that benefited everyone. This was the sort of example that the Temple wanted to offer.

But Jones's ambitions ranged far beyond Mendocino County. He envisioned a revival of his traveling ministry, this time far more wide-ranging and impressive than his previous road evangelism in the Midwest. He also wanted a permanent Temple presence in San Francisco, where there was potential for broader social and political influence. Raising the Temple's socialist example from a local to a state or even a national level required vision, charisma, and energy, all of which Jones had in abundance, and vast amounts of money, which he didn't. And so, while his Mendocino County followers rejoiced in their present-day fellowship and sense of exalted socialist vision, Jones concerned himself with paying for what would come next.

He began by gaining complete control of the funds he already had. At least theoretically, a Peoples Temple Board of Elders considered all expenditures. But in a handwritten document dated April 6, 1969, the membership signed a statement instructing Temple treasurer Eva Pugh "to transfer all funds from the church treasury to a missionary account to be used by our Pastor James Jones at his discretion." Now, not a cent could be disbursed by others without Jones's approval, yet he had the authority to use Temple money as he personally saw fit.

But that authority wasn't the same as the knowledge of how to accumulate, invest, and report income to the Temple's best possible advantage while still operating, if barely, within the law. Any prominent religious entity overtly involved in social reform and politics was certain to attract scrutiny from state government and tax entities, and would have to be properly defended in any investigation. There were ways to do it, but Jim Jones didn't know them. Neither did anyone else in his inner circle or among current Temple membership. What Jones desperately needed now was someone with comprehensive legal expertise, and who was also committed to the same socialist goals as the church.

He found him.

In 1967, Mendocino and neighboring Lake County opened a joint Legal Services Foundation to help lower-income residents who needed help and either couldn't afford or else had no idea how to find it. Its director was twenty-nine-year old Tim Stoen, who joined the Mendocino County district attorney's office after graduating from Stanford Law School. Ferociously intelligent and equally ambitious, Stoen described himself as "a theological conservative and a social radical." He wanted to act on his beliefs, not just talk about them.

The offices assigned to the new service entity were dilapidated, and Stoen needed every penny of its limited budget for legal assistance, not redecoration. He contacted other local agencies, asking for donated materials and volunteer labor. Nobody stepped up. Then someone suggested Stoen contact a Redwood Valley church called Peoples Temple — its members were supposed to be community-minded and willing to pitch in for a good cause. When Stoen called the Temple office, explained his problem and requested help, he was asked to name a time and place. Stoen suggested Tuesday morning. When he arrived that day, Stoen told a reporter in 2003, he found "20 to 30" Temple members, "black and white," already at the building, "carrying paint and Tide and hammers and nails. What I think is going to take two weeks they do in one day. They come back the next day, put in some Masonite paneling and disappear. They don't ask for a word of thanks. . . . That was my introduction to Peoples Temple."

Stoen remembered that the pastor of Peoples Temple also served on the Legal Services Foundation board of directors. He'd met Jim Jones while interviewing as a candidate to run the agency. During that brief meeting, Jones shrewdly took Stoen's measure — here was someone who could be a great asset to the Temple. Before the Temple contingent went out to spruce up the agency office, Jones informed them that they were undertaking a critical assignment. Garry Lambrev remembers, "It was like Jim was courting [Tim]."

The courtship went on for several months.

When impoverished clients came to the agency for help with marital or teen problems, it was natural for Stoen to refer them to the free marriage and drug counseling programs available at Peoples Temple. Through contact with Temple members, Stoen learned more about the Temple's avowed goal of reaching out to the lowest in society, of setting the kind of generous-spirited example that Tim Stoen believed in so strongly himself. Though he customarily drove down to Berkeley on Sundays to attend a Presbyterian church, Stoen developed great admiration for Peoples Temple and its pastor.

Still, Stoen moved back to the Bay Area for a while. He was interested in running for office, and the political prospects were better there. He did some work at a legal aid office in Oakland, where his clients were mostly poor and black. It was a reasonably fulfilling life. Stoen had enjoyed a financially comfortable upbringing, and his private law practice left him well compensated. He rented a nice apartment, wore expensive clothes, and bought a Porsche. Besides his work in Oakland, Stoen assuaged his social conscience by attending rallies in support of environmental concerns and social justice. Peoples Temple remained in his thoughts.

One Sunday in September 1969, Stoen drove north and attended his first Temple service. He was impressed by the spirit of the meeting that stretched into late afternoon, and stunned to learn that there was an evening meeting yet to come. He skipped that one, but returned on subsequent Sundays. Each time Stoen was expected, Garry Lambrev says, "Jim would say something like, 'Next week Tim Stoen is coming, and we have to be prepared.'" With Stoen in the congregation, Jones's sermons stressed reaching out and raising up. Political rants were kept to a minimum, as were healings. As Jones anticipated, apparent miracles didn't impress Stoen as much as the Temple's social mission. At a Temple New Year's Eve gathering, Stoen told Jones that he was going to join his church. In March 1970, he left the Bay Area and returned to Ukiah, where he rejoined the county DA's office. They were thrilled to have him back on staff — Stoen's ability was such that he automatically was a standout wherever he was employed. Jones took no chances that Stoen might change his mind at the last minute — he sent Temple members down to San Francisco to help Stoen move.

After returning to Ukiah, Stoen also worked for Peoples Temple, though as an unpaid advisor rather than a salaried employee. It benefited Jones to have a member who served in the highest rank of the county legal system. There was no need for Stoen to stress his

Temple affiliation to supervisors or co-workers, though he occasionally mentioned it. But frequently, after weekday work and on weekends, Stoen immersed himself in Temple business, often in grueling one-on-one sessions with Jones, who rambled about grandiose plans and schemes and expected Stoen to find legal means to implement them. Stoen didn't think Jones was divine himself, but rather in some way chosen to carry out divine acts. What the man lacked in sophistication, he more than made up for in charisma and genuine commitment. Being associated with him was uniquely empowering — Jones had such vision, such energy, and Stoen was quickly caught up in it. Jim Jones Jr. says, "Tim Stoen *believed*, as much or more than anybody. He loved my dad."

The feeling was apparently mutual. Jones's most veteran followers recognized that the young lawyer and their leader had a relationship that differed from those between Jones and any other Temple member. Father constantly looked to Stoen for advice. Jones always made at least token efforts to give the appearance that he valued the opinions of his inner circle; that closeness was their reward for dedicating themselves to his service. But it was different between Jones and Stoen — they always seemed deep in conversation, with Father, for once, listening just as much as he talked. Some jealousy was inevitable, but what other Temple members didn't realize was that there was no real personal relationship between the two men — Jones and Stoen talked business rather than shared confidences. Before formally joining the Temple, Stoen had concluded that God was too slow in moving mankind toward better behavior. That made Jones's unwavering commitment to action especially appealing. Temple good work was never complete; its demands on members were constant, and Stoen gladly accepted the challenge.

When Stoen made his return to Ukiah and joined the Temple, he brought a fiancée with him. Grace Grech was much younger, just nineteen, the very pretty working-class daughter of a San Francisco butcher and a seamstress. Grace was distinguished by naturally high spirits. After high school graduation, she went to work as a secretary while attending City College at night. Despite their age difference, Tim and Grace got along well. Though she'd been raised as a Catholic, one Sunday when her boyfriend asked her to drive up to Redwood Valley with him for another type of church service, Grace agreed. Her initial impression of Jim Jones wasn't positive, but in 1970 when Tim told her that he wanted to return to Mendocino County, work in the district attorney's office there, and also join the Temple, she agreed, thinking it would be for only a little while. On June

27 of that year, Grace and Tim were married in the Temple, with Jones officiating. Soon afterward, she shocked her husband by saying, "I don't want to go back to Peoples Temple anymore." She didn't like Jim Jones. But Marceline talked to her, and Grace was persuaded to stay.

The newlyweds' lives were almost completely consumed by the Temple, Grace's as well as her husband's. Of course, Tim had a lot to offer Jones and the church, but Jones also seemed vastly impressed by Grace. He insisted that she, too, had valuable services to render the Temple. Though the rest of the membership liked her well enough — while many had trouble feeling comfortable with Stoen, who was so intellectually intimidating, Grace was charming — everyone, Grace included, was astonished when Jones eventually announced she was to be a Temple counselor, one of a select group responsible for offering advice and direction to any other members experiencing personal problems. Grace felt overwhelmed, but proved successful in her new role, mostly due to genuine sweetness: "She didn't sometimes have a kind of hard edge like a lot of the rest of the leaders," Alan Swanson remembers. "She was nice, like Marceline. Grace seemed like she really cared about you."

Seven years later, when they had become enemies, Jim Jones filed a deposition that emphasized how much influence Tim Stoen had in Peoples Temple, and in Jones's own life:

> When [he] joined my church . . . I was thrilled. Besides the addition of another sincere, committed member I was overjoyed to have his help because in my rapidly growing church I needed a concerned, dedicated lawyer badly. . . . I trusted him fully and entrusted him with more responsibility than any other single member of the organization. . . .
> He was my chief legal advisor and I did nothing either with respect to the church or with respect to my own personal legal affairs without first consulting him and getting his legal approval.

When Stoen joined in March 1970, Peoples Temple was a backcountry church with modest membership and some local influence. Inspired by its fiery, messianic pastor, the Temple had ambitious goals, but neither the funds nor the legal expertise necessary to achieve them. But now Jim Jones had Tim Stoen as his right hand, and, very quickly, everything changed.

CHAPTER TWENTY-THREE: MONEY

Since resettling in Mendocino County, Peoples Temple had looked mostly to its membership for contributions. Collection plates passed at Redwood Valley meetings added contributions from visitors and prospective members, but bedrock income was derived from active members' tithes. Ten percent of personal income was the required minimum. Fifteen percent was encouraged, and 20 percent preferred. Eventually 25 percent became the norm. Some members voluntarily tithed 30 percent or even more. No one felt unfairly dunned; many churches required tithing.

But virtually all employed Temple members held low-salaried jobs — hospital orderlies, office clerks, public school teachers. Alan Swanson had a paper route. Everyone could have tithed half their paychecks, and still Peoples Temple would have been relatively poor. Collections at meetings yielded little extra, even though Jones constantly hectored everyone to give generously. A running joke among members was that it wasn't wise to wear penny loafers to services, because Jim would insist on getting those pennies, too. Even in 1969 and 1970, as the congregation expanded, most new members were relatively low-income. Jones envisioned a Temple business empire modeled after the Peace Movement of Father Divine, but start-up costs for care facilities and children's homes and other quasi-charitable ventures were prohibitive. Since tithing wasn't sufficient, Jones looked beyond it. Members had more to contribute than portions of their working-class salaries. Since the avowed purpose of the Temple was equal opportunity and a corresponding lack of obsession with personal possessions, a document was eventually circulated for members to complete and sign:

I [name] am a member of Peoples Temple Christian Church, also known as Peoples Temple of the Disciples of Christ. I am fully aware of, and I fully believe in the ideals and standards of this church, and of its pastor, Jim Jones. Because of this belief, and my faith in its humanitarian works, I have donated and given, and will in the future donate and give, certain items and monies to this church to be used as this said church or said pastor sees fit. I have given these items and monies freely and willingly, without any pressure of any kind. I have no intention of ever asking for or receiving them back again.

In the event that I should resign my membership in this church, or that my membership should be terminated in any way whatsoever, I hereby promise and affirm that I will never ask for nor expect to receive any of these items or monies back again. They have been given as a gift, and they are no longer my property or the property of my heirs.

There were lines for the signatures of the member and of two witnesses.

Members were now expected to reduce their personal property to a minimum. Donated clothing had an obvious use — extra coats, sweaters, shirts, dresses, and shoes were all passed on free of charge to the needy in Temple giveaways. But members gave up other things, too — furniture, televisions, jewelry, anything Jones or Temple leaders might deem an extravagance. No one was forced to comply, but everyone did — this was a way to demonstrate commitment to the cause. Jones emphasized his own compliance. In his early ministry, he had dressed in natty attire to offer a successful appearance. But in Redwood Valley he wore only second-hand clothes, and belittled "celebrity preachers" who wore expensive suits and drove fancy cars. Jones was among the first to sign the new donations release, and praised the noble sacrifices of his followers when they did, too.

The resulting inventory of donated property was examined, priced, and put up for sale in Temple-operated secondhand stores. The income generated, usually several hundred dollars each week, was then used for additional Temple ventures, in particular acquiring houses around the county that could be converted into care facilities. These were frequently leased to and operated by Temple members, who would then pay the Temple annual rents — $15,000 was a typical sum. Additionally, the facility would be staffed by Temple members, who tithed substantial portions of their salaries. Clients usually paid from disability insurance or Social Security checks. The care provided always met or exceeded state requirements. Everyone benefited.

In 1970, Jones took the next step toward the Temple's financial growth. In the months since he'd made his first San Francisco inroads at the Martin Luther King memorial, Jones had offered occasional guest sermons at Macedonia Missionary Church on Sutter Street. Macedonia did its best to publicize these visits, including buying ads in the *San Francisco Chronicle*. One of these, besides touting Jones's appearance, urged white read-

ers to "Worship with the Negro Community."
Macedonia's goal of integrated attendance
seemed to perfectly match the aspirations of
Peoples Temple.

But a Jones appearance at a Macedonia
service did more for the San Francisco
church than his own, and now that sufficient
funds were available he began periodically
leasing space for Peoples Temple programs at
a local school in the same section of town. In
these, Jones was at his charismatic best,
denouncing prejudice, leading energetic
renditions of hymns and performing countless healings. It all resonated, and as Jones's
Bay Area reputation spread, his audiences
gradually changed from virtually all low-
income and African American to racially
mixed. The school venue comfortably held
perhaps five hundred. After a few monthly
appearances, Jones enjoyed standing room
attendance, and some of these people wanted
to move up to Mendocino County and become full-fledged Temple members.

Besides the generous offerings collected at
these San Francisco services — $3,500
wasn't an unknown take — the Temple's
newest members relocating from the Bay
Area expanded the possibilities for tithing
and property donation. For the first time,
Jones regularly attracted professionals whose
salaries were, by previous Temple standards,
astronomic — college professors, successful

attorneys, business owners or managers as well as line workers and minimum wage employees. The turbulent times had much to do with it — at every social and economic level, Americans were discontented with escalating racial strife and the increasingly unpopular Vietnam War. Jones challenged visitors to stop talking about problems and actually do something to make America better — Peoples Temple was the way. And when eager, relatively well-heeled applicants arrived in Redwood Valley, they were offered the opportunity to immerse themselves in the effort, often by producing the pink slips for their very nice cars, or the diamond necklace and earrings bequeathed by a beloved grandmother. Some balked, but enough complied so that the Temple enjoyed substantial economic benefits. Best of all were those who owned property and were willing to turn over the deeds. Jones and his close advisors quickly became expert in flipping real estate.

Temple-operated businesses began proliferating in Mendocino County. Soon, besides nursing homes, these included a ranch for troubled children, a laundry, and a print shop. Each new operation also offered employment for the swelling ranks of members. The California legislature lent an inadvertent hand when it closed down state-operated mental health facilities, anticipating that private business would step into the service breach. Peoples Temple immediately did. Marceline Jones had the professional medical background to organize the new businesses, and Tim Stoen brought the necessary legal expertise.

Jones stretched his ministry further afield with occasional services in Los Angeles and Seattle. When these drew encouraging crowds, he began scheduling the programs on a regular basis — once a month in Seattle, twice monthly in San Francisco and L.A. Before and after these services, Temple members mingled with the audiences, turning apparently random, innocuous conversations into shrewd interrogations, as they had so often done. Immediately after the Temple contingent returned to Redwood Valley, letters would be sent to those they'd met, all of them citing something unique about the recipient, and almost always including assurance that Pastor Jones was keeping him or her in his prayers. Just before the next visit to Seattle or Los Angeles or San Francisco, there would be follow-up letters urging the person to attend the upcoming sermon. Each individual was made to feel valued.

As these road audiences increased — Jones always urged attendees to bring family and friends the next time he preached in town — the Temple found additional means of raking in money. Temple ladies offered snacks for sale — cookies, cakes, even healthy treats like collard greens — at temporary booths set up inside or just outside the venue. Jones interrupted his own sermons to hawk photos of himself for $5 each. Having such a photo — the picture blessed, of course, by Jones — guaranteed the owner immunity from disasters such as assault, fire, or cancer. Since each photo was good for protection from only one potential catastrophe, it was sensible to buy several. Jones was so mesmerizing at the pulpit, so convincing in his claim, that many people did just that. Often, photo sales at a single service totaled $2,000 to $3,000.

The Temple turned its burgeoning mailing list into a constant sales tool. Its letters began offering additional personal protections. Membership in the "Apostolic Blessing Plan" required whatever donation an individual could afford. In return, donors received a certificate stating they were now included in the daily meditations of Pastor Jones: "Expect the promise of God to be fulfilled and the blessings to begin to flow." Because Pastor Jones loved all true believers equally, even if they couldn't afford to send just a few dollars to support the Temple, there was still the "Blessed Penny." Upon request, Pastor Jones would hold a penny in his left hand, bless it, and then send it to the person who'd requested one. Though any possible donation was always appreciated, recipients were assured, "There is no charge for Pastor Jones's meditations. He will meditate on your needs whether you are able to send an offering or not." Business was brisk. The Temple had to open a special letters office to handle the flood of mail.

Jones's new travel schedule kept him away from the Temple's Redwood Valley church on many weekends. He usually managed to preside over at least one Sunday night service there, and at others either Marceline Jones or Archie Ijames led the meetings. Even then, it was still the Jim Jones show. A large photograph of Jones or a robe he often wore would be prominently displayed on the stage, and tapes of his previous sermons played. He frequently phoned in during meetings, and sometimes even rushed in toward the end, assuring Redwood Valley members that he'd risked life and limb racing over to share even a few precious moments with them.

The Redwood Valley congregation included members who hung on Jones's every word, and who bought into every theatrical aspect. Others, loyal to the mission as much or more as they were to the Temple leader, certainly entertained occasional doubts about their church's apparent descent into hucksterism. It was one thing to espouse socialism, and another to peddle photos and mail out pennies. But even the most dubious couldn't deny another fact: the money pouring in from these questionable practices made possible exceptional outreach to those in need. Peoples Temple now had abundant clothing to distribute and food to serve at free meals in low-income areas. Its care facilities accepted clients even if they couldn't pay a cent toward their treatment. Always, it seemed, Peoples Temple devised new, effective ways to help raise up the oppressed. One of the most impressive programs sent worthy teens to college, kids who otherwise could never have afforded an hour of education after high school. The Temple not only covered books and tuition, it purchased houses and remodeled them into serviceable dormitories — the students had free housing and meals. Most of them were the children of Temple members, but some came from the outside, often after successfully completing drug rehabilitation through that Temple program. The school they were sent to was a community college in nearby Santa Rosa, but still, none of this was cheap — members admired Jones's absolute commitment. The man would do *anything* for the cause. Having seen the results, how could they do less?

Prospective members now appeared by the dozens each week, some arriving in Mendocino County because of what the Temple could do for them (housing, professional training, jobs), and many because of what membership in the Temple would allow them to do for others. Anxious to emphasize its denominational affiliation to state and federal tax authorities, the Temple kept in close contact with the regional office of the Disciples of Christ. Many veteran Temple members realized that the affiliation was a sham, just one more distasteful thing Jones had to do for the socialist cause — "We all knew that the Disciples of Christ thing was just for the tax write-off, nobody took it seriously, Jim least of all," former follower Alan Swanson recalls — but the Temple filed annual membership and income reports to the denomination office. These had to be reasonably accurate — the Disciples of Christ office could always send examiners to check. By 1973, Peoples Temple of Redwood Valley claimed 2,570 members, with only thirty listed as regularly "non-participating" in services and church programs. Its annual income was estimated at $300,000 (the equivalent of approximately $1.7 million today), with so much expended on its own outreach efforts that only $1,080 remained to be forwarded to the Disciples of Christ in support of denominational operating costs and activities.

Peoples Temple was finally on sound financial footing. As church operations expanded, so did Jones's demands on its members. Jones had their money and personal possessions, but he also wanted their *time.*

CHAPTER TWENTY-FOUR:
WORKER BEES

In 1971, nineteen-year-old Terri Buford fled her home in Pennsylvania after her schizophrenic mother tried strangling her with the family dog's leash. It wasn't the first time Buford's mother had assaulted her, but the teenager was determined it would be the last.

Buford cadged a ride with a friend who was driving his van cross-country to San Francisco. Once they arrived, Buford had nowhere to go. She bummed around the southern part of the state, then reconnected with the friend who'd driven her west. He talked about an amazing preacher he'd encountered up north in Redwood Valley: "I found God. We raise our hands in the air to feel his energy." He claimed that Jim Jones, his new idol, had such supernatural power, he could even raise the dead. Buford was skeptical, but with nothing to keep her in L.A. she decided to hitchhike up to Redwood Valley and see for herself. Near Ukiah, she got a ride with a chatty man who claimed to know all about Jim Jones and his church, which was called Peoples Temple. He asked Buford if she had anywhere to sleep, and offered to drop her off at the home of some Temple members who would be glad to help out. Elmer and Deanna Mertle greeted her warmly, and said she was welcome to stay with them awhile.

After a few days, the Mertles began telling Buford about Peoples Temple and its mission to "feed the hungry, clothe the naked," and, by its socialist example, inspire the rest of America to do the same. That resonated with the teenager, who considered herself "a compassionate socialist." When the Mertles brought Buford to a Temple meeting, the people she met there were all she could have hoped for — friendly, entirely accepting of a ragged, homeless newcomer — but Buford wasn't impressed with Jim Jones. When he appeared at the Redwood Valley pulpit wearing a dark robe and sunglasses, he reminded her of a cockroach. Jones seemed to spend most of his pulpit time either bragging about his great healing powers or else dunning everyone present for money during frequent pauses when collection plates were passed. Buford had about $20 when she arrived. By the end of the service, feeling worn down and intimidated by Jones, she'd given it all.

Even though she was put off by Jones, Buford was grateful to the Mertles for their hospitality and accepted when they invited her to stay longer. Feeling welcome and safe, she even wrote to her family back in Pennsylvania, providing them with the Mertles' address and inviting them to write to her there. She was disappointed when she didn't receive any replies.

Buford kept attending Temple meetings, mostly to enjoy the fellowship of its members and out of obligation to the Mertles. Her opinion of Jim Jones changed after she spoke to him several times. Buford thought Jones must really have special powers — he was able to read her mind, telling her all kinds of personal things about herself and her very dysfunctional Pennsylvania family that Jones could not possibly have known. These weren't things she'd told the Mertles, or anyone else at the Temple or in Redwood Valley.

"Only much later," she says, "did I learn that the Mertles were stealing letters to me from my family when they got to their mailbox. That's how Jones got all that information, but since I didn't know it then it gave him his first hold over me. He could read my mind, he had these powers, and the Temple was working toward the things that I believed in. So I joined."

Jones enthusiastically welcomed Buford into the fold. She was so special, so talented — the Temple badly needed her. Jones promised that she'd no longer be homeless — the Temple would provide accommodations for her in a house that they'd purchased; she'd room with some other bright young adult members. Everything would be provided there — meals, clothes, every necessity. All she had to do each week was fill out a form, listing what she needed. Because everyone enjoyed the occasional soda or candy bar as a treat, Buford would also receive a weekly allowance of $2. She could even return to college part-time until she completed her degree — the Temple would pay her tuition. Naturally, Buford would want to earn what she was getting, so in return she would work full-time for the church. Tim Stoen, one of its most important members, needed a secretary. So she could do that, and also help out in whatever other ways she might be asked.

Buford moved into a house near the Redwood Valley church and the home where Jones lived with his family. It was crowded — sometimes a dozen people slept in space that could comfortably accommodate half that number. But everybody was friendly and excited about being part of the Temple. There always seemed to be one or two extra chores every day that Jim or somebody else needed to be done right away, and these had to be attended to after regular work hours, so there were plenty of nights with little or no sleep. But as Father frequently pointed out, it was an honor to work yourself into near-exhaustion for the cause.

■ ■ ■ ■

Terri Buford's experience as a new member of the Temple was unique only in her assignment to work for Tim Stoen. Almost everyone else was, at least initially, given less important drudge work, but there was plenty of that. A plan was in place to make certain that neophytes were rapidly absorbed into the consistently frantic Temple pace. Every aspect of their lives was monitored and controlled, even manipulated when necessary. Experienced members like the Mertles didn't consider it wrong to steal mail. Deanna Mertle would recall, "We were learning a new set of ethics from Jim: 'The ends justify the means.' He also called it 'situational ethics.' The way it was translated to [Temple] members was, 'You do whatever Jim says because he knows what is needed for the Cause.' Whenever he suggested something that sounded a little dishonest, he would lovingly remind [us] of the Cause and tell us not to worry."

In Redwood Valley, and soon in San Francisco and Los Angeles after Peoples Temple established permanent churches there, a few particularly promising newcomers were occasionally singled out for full-time employment. On weekdays, there was always something that needed to be done — driving elderly members to doctors' appointments, ferrying indigents to meetings with social service agencies, monitoring recovering drug addicts, and visiting sick members in the hospital. Most members' day jobs limited their availability for these mundane, but important, chores. The approach to potential full-time Temple workers, given usually by Jones but occasionally by a subordinate, was always the same: "There'll be no salary, but we'll meet all your financial needs" — and they did. Even car payments and automotive insurance were paid for, though it was assumed that in these instances the vehicles would always be available for Temple use.

The Temple acquired a long, narrow building just down the road from the church itself. One end was turned into a laundry, and the rest renovated into office space for Temple business. These offices were open twenty-four hours a day, seven days a week, and most church business and outreach operations were conducted from there. There was also an all-important phone line, whose operator followed rigid guidelines. On each call, the phone must be allowed to ring exactly four times, indicating that there were too many other calls to take this one immediately, but not such a long delay that the caller would grow impatient and hang up. Information about Redwood Valley service dates and times was freely provided, as well as when and where the next services were planned in San Francisco, Los Angeles, and other cities. If callers asked to be put through to Pastor Jones, they were told he was away — could someone else help? Usually they were then referred to one of the Temple social service programs. Those insisting on talking specifically to Jones — it was an emergency, something only he could help with, usually a healing — were assured that if they provided information, it would be passed along to him — "[You] do not have to tell him directly what the problem is." Above all, Temple operators were reminded in a prominently posted notice that it was necessary to be polite and patient, no matter how insistent a caller might be: "REMEMBER in answering [Father's] phone, you are representing the highest office in our church. Be KIND and LOVING, even as Pastor would be!" Sometimes at two or three in the morning, it was hard to be patient with near-incoherent callers, but that was what Jones expected.

The Temple acquired houses in Mendocino County, including several immediately adjacent to the main church building, and gradually converted a few into communal dwellings. As space permitted, members were urged to "go communal." In Redwood Valley, perhaps 15 percent of all members did. As with Terri Buford, all of the communals' material needs were met — if they had salaries, child support, or any other outside income, all these funds were turned over to the Temple. The church, in turn, made a profit by purchasing food, clothing, and personal supplies in bulk, everything in the most basic, inexpensive form. This meant many communals dressed in discount store attire or hand-me-downs from other members. Those with "professional jobs," who worked in banks or law offices or schools, were permitted to wear nicer attire. Jones was always concerned with public image — it would have been detrimental to the Temple's local reputation if members working in formal public jobs looked like ragamuffins.

Communal diets consisted of inexpensive, simple fare — oatmeal for breakfast, peanut butter sandwiches for lunch. Those lucky enough to live with inventive cooks benefited. Communal member Laurie Efrein was renowned for her ability to turn bread, a few vegetables, and some cheese into delicious toasted sandwiches. To some, who'd survived ghetto life or stretches of living hand-to-mouth on the street, the food provided was better than any they'd previously had. At night, communals crammed three or four to a room, sleeping on narrow cots or in sleeping bags. Private bathroom time was at a premium, if enjoyed at all — modesty was a bourgeois affectation. Bodily functions were natural, not something to be ashamed of.

True socialists understood this.

Some members were tapped for nighttime security duty, guarding the Temple's Redwood Valley property against attack by the violent, racist locals Jones assured his followers were lurking everywhere. There were occasional incidents of harassment, trash tossed or epithets screamed from cars speeding along the road adjacent to the Temple and the entrance of its parking lot. No actual physical encroachment had yet taken place; no Temple members had been assaulted either on church property or out in the community. But Jones assured them it was always possible and, at some point, inevitable, so every night there were guards all around the perimeter, unarmed but alert. Even though some also had day jobs, they stayed on duty until dawn, sneaking naps in the church hallways whenever they could, taking turns so there was always someone standing watch.

Security concerns spilled over into the Redwood Valley meetings on Saturdays, Sundays, and on Wednesday nights. At Jones's direction, everyone was issued a membership card, which had to be produced to enter the building. The cards served a twofold purpose — they minimized the risk of infiltrators (Jones constantly warned that government agencies might dispatch spies, the better to learn about and undermine the Temple's socialist mission), and emphasized a sense of exclusivity that Jones wanted to nurture. It was, he repeated in virtually every sermon, a matter of *us* against *them,* and the mission was to change the country, the *world,* through example rather than intermingling with outsiders on *their* unacceptable terms. Since everyone who joined the Temple was alienated in some way from a perceived racist, class-controlled mainstream America, that message resonated. Stephan Jones would recall decades later that "it was about . . . if you don't agree with us, we're going to convince you. If we can't convince you, you're the enemy."

Jones begrudged even an hour of a member's time spent on anything not directly related to the Temple. Going to a movie or to dinner at a café or restaurant was prohibited; the time and money involved was better invested in furthering the cause. Social interaction with outsiders was frowned upon. Chatting with neighbors, having after-work drinks with day job co-workers, might result in members inadvertently revealing something that could be used against the Temple. Better to devote every possible minute to whatever tasks Jones or his lieutenants assigned. Other common comforts were denied. Use of alcohol, tobacco, and drugs was forbidden. A single beer, a quick smoke, a toke on a joint — all these things, Jones insisted, weakened the will as well as the body. He also discouraged romantic relationships; devotion to a lover might outweigh commitment to the Temple. Couples who joined the church were allowed to remain that way, but time together was severely limited by Temple chores and duties.

Even for Jones's most devoted followers, his demands sometimes seemed too much. Ragged from lack of sleep, resentful of not being able to see the hit film that everybody else at work was raving about, they occasionally grumbled among themselves. But almost without exception, they did whatever was asked of them. Part of the reason was belief in the Temple and its purposes, but there was also the example of Jim Jones himself, who seemed to work harder and longer than anyone. A few nights each week he was absent from Temple property or the Jones family home adjacent to the church, but wherever it was that Jones went, undoubtedly attending to some critical task, he usually returned the same night, and continued working. Members exhausted after laboring over index cards until two in the morning would see lights still on in the window of Jones's Temple office. Guards ending their shifts at dawn routinely saw him racing past them in the parking lot, hurrying to an early-morning breakfast meeting. Sometimes his absences were extended, two weeks or even more, but it was assumed that he was away on some critical, secret mission. At least to outward appearances, Jones also took the same minimalist approach toward possessions. He wore hand-me-down clothes, and Marceline used the battered Jones family station wagon for her own transportation. If Jones needed a car, he usually borrowed one from various Temple members. Even the robes he wore during services were patched and faded.

Jones routinely popped into the index card or letter offices at all hours, urging everyone there to keep at it just a little longer, reminding them that the Temple needed their help so much. Anyone idle was sharply informed, "If you don't have anything to do, come see me. I'll find something for you." It shamed the slackers. No one, day or night, ever saw Father taking a break.

Jones didn't always chide. Because the Temple had grown so much, rank-and-file Mendocino County members no longer had much individual time with him. But Jones seemed to have a sense of when someone was especially worn down. He'd appear in the letters office or the card stacks, take the aggrieved member aside, and talk awhile. It wasn't generic chitchat; Jones invariably established an emotional connection. He had something in common with every member — enduring the indignities of poverty, struggling with an isolating, lifelong sense of being different from most others, the frustrations of

354

trying to bring about change instead of meekly accepting social injustice. Jones could even connect with the gradual influx of young, well-educated white members who'd previously lived in comfortable circumstances. He was just as informed as they were. Because he voraciously read newspapers and magazines, Jones was conversant on a wide variety of topics. But mostly he challenged those who had been well educated and financially well off before joining the Temple, especially when they seemed resentful of the demands placed on them. They'd been spoiled by the privileges they'd enjoyed at the expense of the working poor, Jones said. Now they thought they were too good to work hard. Did they really believe in socialism, in the equality of all? Then prove it. Take on the toughest tasks, and do them cheerfully and well.

Usually, they did, but the best-educated among his followers posed an additional challenge for Jones. His sermons often misrepresented facts or ignored inconvenient ones, especially regarding the Soviet Union. Most Temple members accepted what they heard; if Father said it, it must be true. But a few who knew their history or at least kept up with current events squirmed when Jones insisted that everyone in the Temple should honor the memory of Stalin, whose ruthless purges cost countless innocent lives. In one

San Francisco meeting when Jones praised "the Soviet government maintaining the wildlife and tribes and ethnic groups in Siberia," Garry Lambrev couldn't help himself. He stood up and asked, "Jim, what about the gulags, about the millions of people murdered?" Jones's face turned bright red. He shouted, "You arrogant brat, you think you know everything," and ranted at Lambrev for several minutes, condemning him and any other self-important intellectual who claimed to know everything. "He was screaming so hard that saliva was spraying out of his mouth," Lambrev recalls. "I was humiliated."

When Jones felt that his point was made, not just to Lambrev but to anyone else who might ever consider correcting him in midsermon, he went on with the meeting. When it was finally over, Lambrev bolted, only to find Jones waiting for him in the hallway. Jones pulled his cowed follower aside and said quietly, "Garry, I want to apologize for what I just subjected you to. You have to understand — most of my people are simple people. The only things they can really understand are in blacks and whites. Gray doesn't exist for them. So I have to make definite statements and not present anything at all complicated. If you tell them that something I say isn't true, you make them doubt me, and that means they may also doubt the cause."

Jones reminded Lambrev that he worked harder than anyone else in the Temple: "I don't have time to read every book and know every fact. I authorize you to come to me privately whenever I make a mistake in public and let me know about it. I want you to do that, but never in front of my people. They can't be allowed to think that I'm ever wrong." Lambrev felt honored that Jones had taken him into his confidence and resolved not to challenge him in public again. Nothing was more important than the cause, facts included.

All members were constantly kept busy, but in the process many discovered talents they had no idea they possessed. This not only gave them increased self-esteem, but usually assured their ongoing devotion to the Temple. Jones took particular pride in his knack for placing individuals in just the right jobs: "My greatest ability is to know [their] talents and use them for the cause." As the Temple membership swelled, as its outreach programs thrived, Jones reminded members collectively in sermons and individually in conversations that their work, exhausting as it was, made a difference. Many, like Terri Buford, had the Temple to thank for rescue from a miserable existence. Everyone, in some sense, had felt like an outsider. Praise from Jones was a drug in itself. Members often competed to see who could sleep less. If someone bragged, "I worked so long last night, I only slept three hours," someone else was likely to retort, "I only slept two."

Highly educated members begged to be assigned the most menial tasks. High school dropouts who'd previously held menial, dead-end jobs found themselves supervising the same kind of people who'd been their bosses. Everyone was worn out — and most, at some point, found themselves simultaneously exhilarated. Predictably, the atmosphere of mandatory humility fostered in many a simultaneous sense of moral superiority. The less they slept, the more they sacrificed material possessions and bourgeois pride, the more worthy they were. These Temple members felt that they were exhibiting the proper socialist attitude, living the way everyone else should — and someday *would,* thanks to them. They were better than anyone else because they proved that everyone was equal. None had either the leisure time or the inclination to consider the contradiction. Observing with satisfaction what had literally become his kingdom, Jones observed to Terri Buford, "Keep them poor and keep them tired, and they'll never leave." How well he understood his people.

CHAPTER TWENTY-FIVE:
ON THE ROAD

Not all the money coming into Peoples Temple was spent purchasing property and subsidizing communal housing. The greatest potential for substantial income lay beyond Mendocino County and even the West Coast. Fifteen years earlier, Jim Jones established significant financial footing for his ministry by plunging into the Midwest revival circuit. Now he planned to make his new evangelical mark not in drafty tents outside small country towns, but in venues in the heart of major cities, returning to Mendocino County after each excursion with considerable sums of money and legions of new followers. It all began with transportation.

For his earliest programs in San Francisco, Los Angeles, and Seattle, Jones brought along followers to set up the sound system, interview and record personal information from attendees, take up collections, and assist with staged healings — at least a few dozen on every trip, all of them part of a car caravan, jalopies and trucks traveling north and south of Mendocino County in an informal procession. Some drivers inevitably lagged behind because they'd forgotten to fill up with gas before leaving, or needed emergency bathroom stops, or got lost in confusing downtown city traffic. The more attendance Jones attracted in his out-of-town appearances, the more Mendocino County followers he required to support these performances, and the more inefficient the car caravan system became.

So Peoples Temple began investing in buses, the better to load equipment and efficiently convey great numbers of members on the road with their pastor. These buses were purchased from Greyhound, older models that the company planned to replace, and so would sell to the church at reasonable prices. Most were manufactured in the early to mid-1950s, built to hold perhaps forty passengers. The Temple acquired a dozen, as well as a smaller yellow bus that was used to haul sound equipment — Jones's road show included live musical accompaniment by a full band, and he refused to risk distorted amplification of its performances or his sermons with potentially faulty local sound systems.

The new Temple fleet needed parking space in Redwood Valley, and because of their age and mileage, each bus required constant maintenance. The Temple built an extensive garage near its administrative offices, and members with mechanics backgrounds were assigned to work there. One bus, Number Seven, was designated for Jones's personal use. Seats were removed to make room for a private area, just in case Father needed a place for quiet reflection or conversation. A bed was installed, in case he wanted to nap, and also a small sink and a cooler for drinks and snacks.

Once all the buses were in good running order, Temple members were trained to drive them. The training program was the equivalent of teaching someone to swim by pushing them into the deep end of the pool. Trainees were taken in the buses to newly opened Interstate 5, put behind the wheel, and instructed to start driving. When they were sufficiently adept, they took tests to qualify for state licenses to operate commercial vehicles. The Temple instructors were exacting, and everyone passed.

The buses were first used on test runs to San Francisco and Los Angeles. Because Jones was determined to have standing room only at these services, and could never be certain that enough locals would come, he instructed that each bus be filled to capacity — Temple capacity as opposed to that suggested by the manufacturer. Forty-seat buses were filled with a minimum of sixty passengers. Often each carried a load of seventy or more. Older people had first call on the seats. Other adults sat and slept in the aisles. Children nestled in overhead luggage racks. Two drivers were assigned to each bus, and alternated four-hour shifts. The off-duty driver slept on a mattress in the bus's underneath luggage compartment.

The trips were planned with the precision of military maneuvers. The buses maintained uniform speed. Rest stops were planned in advance — it took some time for five or six hundred people to take turns at gas station bathrooms. The buses were stocked with fruit and sandwiches, and each bus had someone designated to hand these out, along with other necessities like diapers and Band-Aids and aspirins. It all worked very well. Nobody complained about cramped quarters, or soggy sandwiches, or being bothered by someone else's snoring or flatulence — this would have been interpreted as bourgeois selfishness. Upon arrival, everyone had tasks. Many mingled anonymously with the crowds, positioning themselves to cheer or utter amazed gasps at appropriate moments.

Afterward came the long trip home — San Francisco was only a few hours south of Mendocino County, but Los Angeles was an eight-hour drive and the return trip from Seattle was even longer. Because Jones's West Coast appearances came almost exclusively on weekends, the followers who accompanied him on trips had to go to work on Monday morning even if they'd only gotten home a few hours earlier. It was hard, but it was worth it, seeing Father thrill whole auditoriums of strangers, each exhausted member having helped in some small way to bring the example of Peoples Temple socialism to a large new audience. On Bus Seven, Jones was joined by a few of his inner circle; Jack Beam and Patty Cartmell were nearly always present. Jones's traveling companions counted the donations — sometimes there would be $10,000 or more in bills and change.

Most traveling in 1971 was confined to the West Coast. But as the road routine was refined, the itinerary changed. Jones still made weekend trips south to Los Angeles and San Francisco and north to Seattle, but gradually he began planning longer excursions into the Midwest and South, to cities like Houston and Chicago and Detroit. Each prospective stop had substantial populations of poor blacks, still Jones's target audience. As yet, few knew of Jim Jones or Peoples Temple — it wouldn't be enough to rent an auditorium, arrive with some busloads of supporters, and expect a large turnout of disenfranchised locals to fill the rest of the venue. Peoples Temple would gain no money or new members with Jones preaching to empty seats. So he took steps to prevent it.

■ ■ ■ ■

Jones initially used his contacts with San Francisco African American churches, querying their leaders about friends who pastored similar congregations elsewhere. When specific names and churches were suggested, they were sent packets of information about Peoples Temple and its leader, including press clippings (most from the ever-friendly *Ukiah Daily Journal*) and pamphlets produced by the Temple's printing operation. Would these churches be willing to host a contingent of Temple members if Jones came to their cities for programs? In return, Jones would usually offer guest sermon at the church in addition to his own public events. Many churches weren't interested, but when some responded favorably, Jones dispatched scouts to glean further information. Was there an auditorium or another gathering place that could be rented for a reasonable fee? Did area newspapers seem interested in writing advance stories that would help publicize the event? Were enough members of the host church willing to house some Temple visitors for a night or two? What about relatives of current Temple members? Did any live in the city who might be willing to accept overnight guests? Only when these essential elements were in place would a trip be scheduled.

Several weeks before the event, a Temple advance crew was dispatched to the city, perhaps a half dozen members traveling in a car or van. Jones insisted that they constantly represent the Temple's policy of racial diversity — even in the vehicle there was to be complete integration.

The crews traveled light in terms of personal possessions — a change or two of clothes and toiletries. The bulk of vehicle storage space was reserved for flyers printed by the Temple. These touted Jones and the scheduled programs in glowing terms. One for a Chicago event, besides noting the time, date, and location, promised "The Most Miraculous Spiritual Healing Ministry in the Land Today! Rev. Jones often calls scores of people from the audience who are healed of all manner of diseases! THE BLIND SEE! THE DEAF HEAR! THE CRIPPLES WALK!" Beyond the healings, there would also be a sermon by Reverend Jones: "HEAR HIS URGENT LIBERATION MESSAGE FOR THESE TROUBLED TIMES!" Finally, there was the promise of being in the presence of divinity: "SEE THE MIRACLES, SIGNS & WONDERS That God Is Manifesting Through REV. JIM JONES!" A flattering photograph of Jones dominated the upper portion of the flyer. In smaller print, physicians testified that Jones's cures "are genuine and permanent." Peoples Temple was always presented as a national rather than West Coast church. Its advance materials routinely claimed congregations in seventeen cities, including "missionary outposts in Mexico and Africa." Admission to its events was free, but there would be an opportunity to purchase "miracle" photographs of Reverend Jones for $5 each.

Once the advance crew arrived, its members stayed with local supporters or guest church hosts. They spent each day passing out flyers in minority areas, often public housing projects and ghettos — ten thousand flyers might be handed out in a single day. Local media was contacted, too, including newspapers and radio stations specifically serving the black community. Reverend Jones was always available for a phone interview in advance of a public program.

When the venue opened an hour or so in advance of Jones's appearance at the pulpit, a Temple band and choir were already in place, expertly performing uplifting hymns. Audiences skewed toward black and poor, but there were white attendees, too.

The healings were always a high point. By now they were presented in particularly compelling fashion. Besides utilizing his own accomplices, Jones now would sometimes call out a name from an index card, announcing that this person was perhaps unaware of a cancer in his or her system. A Temple "nurse" would be dispatched into the crowd to swab out the person's throat in preparation for Jones's healing effort. In the process, utilizing sleight of hand, a bit of chicken offal would be dropped into the mouth, and the natural gag reflex resulted in it being coughed back up. The nurse would brandish "the cancer" — Reverend Jones had caused it to be spit right out! A life had been saved! The Temple band played a fanfare, and Jones spoke eloquently of how the divine power flowed through him. *Anything* was possible for those who believed.

After more songs, Jones cited scripture — away from Temple members-only meetings, he still quoted the Bible — and then moved on to his ultimate message. Unlike the selection of hymns and the number of healings, this rarely varied. Jones cited current events — there was always a recent race riot, another military atrocity in Vietnam, social or antiwar protesters being tear-gassed or beaten by police. An ominous sense of growing menace was palpable throughout the nation, and Jones took full advantage. He wasn't the only one offering an extremist view of widespread, justifiable despair. Jones could, if he wished, quote Maine senator Edmund Muskie, who had emerged as a leading candidate for the Democratic Party's next presidential nomination: "We have reached the point where men would rather die than live another day in

America." Jones reminded his mostly poor, predominantly minority audiences of the obvious threats to their well-being, particularly inherent racism that manifested itself in new, even more ominous ways: the election of Richard Nixon on a thinly veiled racist campaign theme of "law and order" (veteran political reporter Jules Witcover described it as "the politics of oppression, under the guise of patriotism"), the emergence of former Alabama governor George Wallace as a political force among angry whites. Black Americans were in danger from their own country as never before — and they weren't the only ones. On May 4, 1970, four white students participating in a student antiwar demonstration at Kent State University in Ohio were shot and killed by members of the National Guard. Even white people of good conscience were at immediate risk if they refused to kowtow to warmongering, racist policies. Jones suggested that worse was coming. Concentration camps loomed in the near future for blacks and anyone else who attracted negative government notice. Beyond that, there was nothing to prevent government agencies from turning other forms of lethal attention toward anyone even suspected of opposition. Did anyone in the audience doubt it?

Yet, there was a way out. In this nation full of violence and hatred and greed, Jones preached, the poor of all races and backgrounds must care for and help each other because no one else, especially the government, would. God helps those who help themselves. Singly, we are nothing. Together, with divine guidance and grace, all things are possible. Jones spoke to this for an hour or more, sometimes as long as two or three hours if he sensed the audience was amenable. He regaled listeners with tales of individuals who'd salvaged lost lives and found first refuge then complete fulfillment in Peoples Temple — why, some were present and gladly testified.

Collections were taken at intervals. Everyone was urged to give what they could, and though Jones stressed it was no disgrace to be empty-handed, he also emphasized the responsibility for all to contribute whatever they could, from a penny to hundreds of dollars. All proceeds would be used to defray the cost of bringing the Peoples Temple spirit all the way here. Did everyone want him to come again soon? Generous donations would make that possible.

Each program concluded with promises by Jones to pray for all present. They should contact Peoples Temple regarding any problem or personal emergency — their new friends *cared*. Special prayers would be offered — even long distance, the powers of Reverend Jones were potent. Everyone in the crowd was urged to hug all those around them — fellowship had been established, a union of the like-minded, everyone believing in, and now committed to, complete social and economic justice. Despite all the terrors of the outside world, they had each other, and Peoples Temple, and Jim Jones.

Soon afterward the bus caravans were back on the highway, heading home to Redwood Valley. Often, an advance crew was already hundreds of miles away in some other direction, preparing for the next event. In Bus Number Seven, Jones and his entourage sipped chilled soft drinks and counted the day's recent proceeds. They were succeeding on a scale that would have seemed impossible only a few years before.

CHAPTER TWENTY-SIX:
FAILURES

Despite the gains realized by Peoples Temple — increased membership, growing coffers, a reputation extending beyond Mendocino County and even the West Coast — the years immediately following 1968 were not an uninterrupted series of triumphs. There were stumbles, some of them critical. Jones attempted so much that a significant percentage of failures was inevitable.

It began with recruitment. As Temple departments and programs expanded, Jones needed an ever-larger pool of members. But they had to be the right kind of people — given the demands made on them, they needed to buy in completely to the idea of the Temple cause and the infallibility of its pastor. So the vetting process was extensive. Very few aspiring members were accepted on first visits, no matter how effusively they promised complete belief. Beyond their professed personal allegiance, Jones wanted to know more: What property or material possessions did they have to contribute to the cause, what skills that would lend themselves well to Temple efforts? Did they exhibit the potential for long-term commitment? First exposure to a Jones sermon or a Temple program might result in initial infatuation that soon dissipated. The idea was to welcome only those who could be counted on to stay.

That meant that most visitors to the Temple in Redwood Valley or Jones's road services didn't become members. The percentage was perhaps one in ten. A great deal of time was spent weeding out undesirables, and even then there were always some who passed rigorous inspection and still didn't live up to expectations. If they didn't leave of their own accord, Jones dismissed them, declaring them lacking in true socialist faith, never suggesting that perhaps the Temple had failed in some way to meet their needs.

Jones expected current members to proselytize with the rest of their relations — Temple fellowship included three generations of some families. Larry Layton was joined in Temple membership by his mother, Lisa, and younger sister Debbie, who brought with her a British friend named Phil Blakey. Phil, too, joined the Temple, and soon, with Jones's encouragement, he and Debbie married — a marriage of convenience, so Blakey could get his green card and remain in the United States. Carolyn Moore Layton wanted her parents and two younger sisters to join — Jones would particularly have relished adding a prominent Methodist minister like Rev. John Moore to the Temple fold — but Moore and his wife, Barbara, were greatly put off by what they perceived as worship of Jones himself rather than God. Carolyn's sister Rebecca rejected Temple membership, too. She came to Redwood Valley, was given an extensive tour of Temple operations there, and was granted personal time with Jones. In contrast to his extroverted public persona, she found the private Jim Jones to be "low-key, a kind of depressing guy. For some reason, he decided he wouldn't be 'on' for me." Rebecca never attended a Temple service — she'd heard about Jones's tendency to sermonize for hours. At the end of the visit, Rebecca made it clear she wasn't interested in joining: "[Jones] claimed to be working to eliminate racism, but I thought it was odd that there was only one black [Archie Ijames] in the Temple leadership. I was already politically active, and I had no time for [Jones's] bullshit." But Annie, the youngest Moore daughter, was absolutely entranced. After graduating from high school, she joined the Temple and enrolled in nursing school.

Jones also couldn't prevent occasional tragedies involving members, even if one of the tenets of Peoples Temple was that a benefit of joining was coming under Father's protection. He regularly announced "danger cycles" during which everyone should be especially cautious. If anything bad happened to a member during one of these, it only fulfilled Jones's prophecy. If nothing did, then he was responsible due to his timely warning. Sometimes he announced specific acts everyone must undertake to avoid potential problems. Car wrecks would not happen to members who walked around their vehicles two times before getting in and starting the engine. Jones would press a photo of himself into the hand of a follower, and inform him or her that something awful had been going to happen — crippling or even death in an accident of some sort — but by possessing the picture, the follower was saved.

Still, there were events that seemed to contradict Jones's claims of protection. After a long night of Temple-related meetings, Joyce Swinney left Redwood Valley near dawn to drive to her job in Ukiah. She fell asleep at the wheel, ran into another car, and was killed. When Jones announced her death to a shocked congregation, he explained that it was Swinney's own fault. He'd stopped her on her way out of the Redwood Valley church and told her that she needed to meditate for two full minutes before driving off. Swinney didn't, and so she died. The glib spin control worked, but Jones had to be constantly on guard. Any incident beyond his control involving a member threatened his support within the Temple congregation.

Not all Jones's road expeditions worked out as planned, either. He received an invitation from an African American Baptist church in Houston to preach to its members. The reputation of Peoples Temple had spread almost two thousand miles to the South, and the Houston congregation wanted to hear what Jones had to say. When the Temple buses arrived, they were warmly welcomed, so much so that Jones failed to take his usual accurate reading of what would move a specific audience most. Assuming that he was addressing a crowd ready to buy into his most extreme pronouncements, Jones skipped his usual biblical references and launched into a diatribe against the U.S. government and a Sky God who was worshipped by deluded fools. When he declared that only socialism could prevent secular and spiritual disaster, church leaders stepped up to the pulpit and asked him to leave, taking his people with him. Jones went quietly, professing only deep respect for all involved. The Temple bus fleet headed back west, but at the first rest stop Jones gathered his followers together and told them that the black Houston Baptists had fallen under the control of the Ku Klux Klan. Since Father said so, they accepted it as fact.

In October 1971, Jones and the Temple Greyhounds set out for Indiana. A visit to

Indianapolis was irresistible. He was returning in triumph to the city where his ministry began, where he personally led the fight for integration and brought down racist traditions. Jones had never completely severed the Temple's Indianapolis roots. Even after Peoples Temple moved to California, the church continued operating nursing homes in the city, and he had retained some followers there.

Before Indianapolis came a stop in Lynn. Temple members gawked at the sight of Father's old childhood haunts; he'd often regaled them with tales of his life there, mostly emphasizing his suffering at the hands of a tyrannical father and the pain of being part of the extended, racist Jones clan. None of these other Joneses came out to greet him, though several aunts, uncles, and cousins still lived in the area. If they'd heard he was coming, they had no interest in seeing him, and the disdain was mutual. Instead, Jones stopped the buses outside the home of Myrtle Kennedy, whom he introduced to his followers as his second mother. Jones's first mother, Lynetta, would have bridled at the notion of any woman other than herself getting maternal credit, but she was back in California. Some of Jones's old acquaintances came over to say hello. They were surprised when the buses moved along to a town gas station and Jones personally passed out rolls of toilet paper to followers who went inside to use the bathroom. One local, impressed by Jones and the procession, asked a Temple member how she could join their fellowship. The reply, repeated around Lynn for weeks, was "Come along now, and bring the deed to your house." She didn't.

Jones left Lynn satisfied that he'd made the impression that he'd wanted, but things turned sour in Indianapolis. He expected his appearances there to be hailed as the return of a conquering hero, and when sizable crowds showed up for afternoon and evening programs, Jones couldn't resist bragging that he had the power to raise the dead, and, because he wanted all the healings to go off spectacularly, he involved only Temple members who'd been trained to participate. The healings at the afternoon event went well, but an *Indianapolis Star* reporter attended both of the day's programs. Though he stopped short of calling Jones a fraud, his article noted that "the people who were called upon [to be healed] in the evening [service] had a striking resemblance to some who were called upon earlier in the day."

Jones, accustomed to fawning coverage in the *Ukiah Daily Journal,* was stung by the obvious implication — the article's headline read "Church Filled to See 'Cures' by Self-Proclaimed 'Prophet of God' " — and further upset when, on the basis of the story, the

Indiana State Psychology Board announced it would investigate Jones's claim that he had the power to heal. This was hardly the kind of publicity that benefited the Temple, so Jones returned to Indianapolis in December and gave a sermon about the Temple's fine social outreach and other good works. After criticizing other healers who worked their miracles for personal profit, Jones performed another healing of his own, apparently causing a woman in the audience to "pass" a cancer, which was then held up to be viewed by the audience. Then he cautioned everyone not to "give up on the medical profession."

His Indianapolis critics weren't appeased. Jones was challenged to submit the "cancer" to an independent laboratory for tests. He responded that he could not risk enemies somehow rigging the results. Jones retreated to California, and afterward the Temple divested itself of all its remaining businesses and property in Indianapolis. Tim Stoen subsequently convinced the psychology board to drop its investigation. It was a disaster for Jones, but still not equal to the blow to his ego he suffered around the same time, when he tried to claim the legacy — and the followers, and the money and properties — of Father Divine.

In the years since he'd visited Father Divine and the Peace Mission in Pennsylvania, Jones had kept careful track of his mentor's ministry. In late 1963, while Jones struggled to keep Peoples Temple afloat after returning from Brazil, Father Divine retired from public appearances. A Peace Mission spokesman claimed that age-related infirmities weren't the reason: "[Father Divine] has said everything there is to say about everything." Two years later, on September 10, came another announcement: Though he didn't actually die, Father Divine had chosen to "lay his body down." He remained "spiritually present" and would eventually resurrect himself in new human form. Meanwhile, his beloved wife, Mother Divine, would lead the Peace Mission. She retained the movement's headquarters on the luxurious Woodmont estate outside Philadelphia. Peace Mission businesses, including its chains of hotels and restaurants, and its farm community in New York State, continued operating as before.

In the fall of 1965, Jim Jones was too preoccupied with establishing Peoples Temple in Mendocino County to rush across the country and lay claim to the empire of Father Divine. For the next half dozen years, his focus remained on expanding his own ministry. Until Peoples Temple had its own successful operations, and until Jones established his own reputation as a divinely inspired, perhaps divine, prophet himself, he realized it was unlikely that Father Divine's followers, let alone the great man's widow, would accept him as their original leader somehow returned in Jim Jones's corporal body. But Jones stayed in regular touch with Mother Divine and Peace Mission members, sending them Temple newsletters that updated Jones's latest triumphs, first in Mendocino County, then along the West Coast, and finally across much of America. Jones was not a patient man. It was hard to wait. If he could claim the Peace Mission, absorb it into his own control, then his influence would effectively bookend America — Peoples Temple on the West Coast, Peace Mission on the East. Mother Divine would clearly take some persuading; she was still a relatively young woman in her early forties, and undoubtedly enjoyed wielding absolute power from Woodmont. But she was, after all, only a woman, and an attractive one at that. Jones believed his personal charm would overwhelm her.

In the late spring of 1971, having achieved new heights in Temple business expansion and gratifying personal success as a traveling evangelist, Jones contacted Mother Divine and asked to visit her at Woodmont. She was amenable; in her new role as head of the Peace Mission, Mother Divine regularly received visitors.

Jones chose about two hundred of his most dedicated, energetic followers to accompany him, and prepped them rigorously before departure. He explained that Father Divine had failed — he'd died before completing his life's work. Jones had come to understand that it was now his responsibility to lead Divine's people down the same socialist path followed by Peoples Temple. The goals of both movements were the same — achievement of economic and social equality. Father Divine hadn't persisted until this was achieved, but Jim Jones would. Meanwhile, it was critical to make the right impression on Mother Divine and the Peace Mission members, who lagged behind Peoples Temple in socialist achievement. Unlike Jones, Mother Divine lived extravagantly. This shouldn't be criticized to her followers. The Temple women must wear dresses and skirts on this visit — Mission women never wore pants. Say "thank you" for even the smallest courtesy. These people still observed such bourgeois amenities. The purpose of the trip was to persuade them to join the Temple. Once they did, they would learn to adopt more appropriate socialist attitudes.

Temple buses took almost three days to make the trip. Stops were made only for gas and bathroom breaks. For a change, there was lots of room on the individual vehicles, empty seats to hold all the Peace Mission members who'd want to return with them to California. When they arrived in Philadelphia, Temple members were housed in Peace Mission apartments, which they found to be clean and comfortable. They liked their hosts, who seemed genuinely pleased to meet them. The Temple members asked for everyone's name and the best addresses at which to contact them — this was standard Temple procedure. Jones himself stayed at Woodmont, and all the guests were taken on a tour of the property, which included a lengthy stop at a bronze-doored chamber enclosing the body of Father Divine. Afterward there was an elaborate banquet, with much fancier place settings and food than the Temple members were used to back in California. Dessert was ice cream shaped like flower petals. Mother Divine invited Jones to make some postprandial remarks; he praised the ministry of Father Divine and pointed out the similar good works he and the members of Peoples Temple were accomplishing in Mendocino County. It was a pleasant, positive evening.

The Temple visitors stayed a second day, during which Jones spent time talking with Mother Divine and apparently was dissatisfied. That night there was another gathering for dinner, a barbecue this time, and Jones spoke again. This time his tone was critical. There were things about the Peace Mission that were wrong, all its luxurious trappings in particular. Father Divine had "conferred his mantle" on Jim Jones. "His spirit has come to rest in my body," and now all Peace Mission members must follow him. Mother Divine took offense and ordered Jones and his people to leave at once. They did, stopping first at the Peace Mission apartments to collect their personal belongings. Perhaps a dozen Peace Mission members who'd spent time talking with the visitors from Peoples Temple left with them. A Temple event in Washington, D.C., was already on the schedule, so they stopped there and Jones put on his usual performance.

The drive back to Mendocino County was tense. When they arrived, Jones gathered the followers who'd made the trip and explained that what had happened at Woodmont was not his fault. Mother Divine had been enthusiastic about merging their ministries under Jones's leadership, so much so that, after maneuvering so they were alone, she tore open her blouse and insisted that they have sex. Jones refused — "She flaunted her sagging breasts in my face but I wasn't tempted." This was why she had ordered him and his followers to leave Woodmont. Everyone was urged to help the defecting Peace Mission members, who were mostly old women, to assimilate to the Temple. Jones asked for contact information provided by others back at the Peace Mission apartments, and for a while nothing more was said about Mother Divine and the Peace Mission ministry.

But Jones hadn't given up. The Temple letters office began sending messages to Peace Mission members back in Pennsylvania, describing the latest miracles worked by Jim Jones, who had absorbed the blessed spirit of Father Divine. Simon Peter, one of the former Peace Mission members, sent a scathing missive directly to Mother Divine, testifying that "Pastor Jones" in every way was "manifesting the works of Christ," which was only possible because he was, indeed, Father Divine's spiritual heir. Simon Peter cited physical ailments that he suffered while a Peace Mission member. He hadn't been healed then, but Pastor Jones was in the process of healing him now. Why did Mother Divine deny Pastor Jones his proper due?

Mother Divine sent back a lengthy letter. Simon Peter's sufferings at the Peace Mission were his own fault: "you could have made a change under [our] jurisdiction . . . if you had the mind and desire to do so." As for his new spiritual leader, "If Pastor Jones is manifesting the works of Christ as you say he is, I say, GLORY TO GOD! If he is, he is doing no more than each one who is born of God should do." But Simon Peter shouldn't believe any claims that Father Divine had returned in the person of Jim Jones, "one born in sin and shaped up in iniquity." She concluded, "I am completely satisfied with FATHER DIVINE and . . . I stand steadfast on My Conviction that HE alone is GOD."

In the summer of 1972, when he felt that enough Peace Mission members might be wavering, Jones sent them a new, lengthy letter, with the headline "THIS MAY BE YOUR LAST CHANCE FOR LIFE!" Ostensibly written by Temple members rather than their leader, the letter announced that the "spirit that was operative in the body called Father Divine is now calling his Children . . . to come share with Him the abundance of what His great love has provided for all the Children here in Redwood Valley. . . . Father has returned in the hundred-fold degree. His work and his mission [are] being continued in the ministry of Jim Jones." Peoples Temple's "modern, air-conditioned Greyhound-type buses" would be ready to make pickups at Franklin High in Philadelphia at 6 p.m. on July 16. Everyone wishing to move to Redwood Valley should contact the Temple at one of two numbers provided to make reservations. Those who lacked personal transportation to the high school could be picked up at their homes.

The rest of the letter reiterated Jones's great gifts, and enumerated the latest miracles he'd performed: he'd caused a storm to stop in Canada, raised thirty people from the dead, and "as in the days of Jesus . . . walked on the waters of the Pacific."

On the appointed day and time, the Temple

buses were at Franklin High in Philadelphia. Only a few Peace Mission defectors showed up. Most were old, and, despite the immortality they had been promised, passed away in California at a rapid rate. About a half dozen long-term members were all Jones had to show for his attempt to usurp Father Divine's ministry. The Peace Mission continued; Mother Divine, at least, defied death. Decades later she was still leading a much reduced ministry from Woodmont, and in 2014 sent a message through a spokesman that Jim Jones "used charisma to hide his human weakness, violating the laws of God and misleading . . . innocent people. Without the mind of God it is destructive and misleading to follow spiritual illusions."

Jones occasionally mentioned Father Divine, mostly citing the absolute faith Peace Mission followers had in their leader, and grumbling that not enough Temple members felt the same way about him. "It was like he was jealous," Temple survivor Juanell Smart remembers.

CHAPTER TWENTY-SEVEN: DRUGS

Jim Jones always had to worry that the next stumble might be the one that he couldn't explain sufficiently. He understood that once any significant erosion of belief in him occurred, it would only escalate. The obvious way to avoid failure was to stop trying to do more. Peoples Temple was already an unqualified success. Its membership was impressive, its mission admirable, its outreach programs effective. A substantial number of needy people had been and were being helped to have better lives. Though members were taught that personal pride was wrong, they could still feel justly proud of their church and its accomplishments, and grateful enough to the man who made it possible that they could overlook an occasional, infrequent stumble on his part. All Jones needed to do was settle for what he and the Temple already had.

But Jones never accepted limits. It stemmed from his mother, Lynetta, who, in her sporadic attempts at parenting, regaled him with tales of visions and reincarnation and how it was preordained that her son should do great things. Even when Jones was an adult, Lynetta hammered home that he was special from birth. If her son was "Father," then she gloried in her self-assumed role as Temple "Grandmother." To any who were willing to listen and, often, to those who weren't, Lynetta repeated the tale of her initial vision that she would give birth to a godlike son, and related wildly fanciful stories about how everyone back in Lynn, Indiana, came to little Jimba for comfort and counseling. To hear Lynetta tell it, her child's emergence as a unique spiritual leader was only possible through the careful nurturing of his mother. She took to writing and reciting poems about it. A favorite was "The Molder":

I took a bit of plastic clay
And idly fashioned it one day.
And as my finger pressed it still,
It molded, yielding to my will.

I came again when days were past,
The bit of clay was firm at last.
The form I gave it, still it wore,
And I could change that form no more.

A far more precious thing than clay,
I gently shaped from day to day,

And molded with my fumbling art,
A young child's soft and yielding heart.

I came again when years were gone,
And it was a man I looked upon,
Who such godlike nature bore
That men could change it —
    NEVERMORE.

It's impossible to be certain whether Jim Jones truly believed that he was God, or that he was the spirit of Jesus that reappeared once in every generation. What's inarguable is that he felt himself to be something beyond an ordinary man, that there was a special divinity in him. Much of his healing stagecraft was manufactured, but sometimes he would muse that perhaps occasional cripples did walk or cancers were cured because the afflicted believed in Jim Jones, and so he did wield a form of healing power after all. When Jones alternated descriptions of his godliness from sermon to sermon — sometimes in the same sermon — it was at least in part because even he felt hard-pressed to define something so powerful and vast. And God, or someone who believed himself to be at least partially God, did not *settle.* Every day, the ambition of Jim Jones ratcheted up, and so, inevitably, did the pressure he felt.

Because of Jones's leadership style, he could not share this burden with others. From his

first days of storefront preaching in Indianapolis, Jones was determined to control
every aspect of his ministry. He sometimes
appointed committees and advisory boards,
always giving the impression of wanting
congregational input, but these invariably
went along with whatever Jones wanted. As
Peoples Temple grew, a few members gradually formed a small, ever-evolving inner circle,
but Jones didn't confide completely in anyone. Survivors agree he led on a "need to
know" basis, and Jones was determined to be
the only one who knew everything. For a
while, Marceline came close, and she alone
had any sense of Jones prior to his ministry,
some familiarity with his quirks and the most
effective ways to counter his very human failings. But Jones never considered Marceline a
coequal in the Temple, and once he began
his relationship with Carolyn Layton, his wife
was relegated to the same compartmentalized
role as Jack Beam or Archie Ijames, someone
to do Jones's bidding rather than share in any
significant decision making. Even Carolyn
didn't share Jones's most innermost thoughts.
Besides sex, her value to him lay in supervisory skills to see Jones's edicts carried out.
There wasn't anyone associated with Jones in
Peoples Temple to tell him no and make it
stick.

Because only Jones understood and oversaw
everything, he had to be involved in every

detail of each Temple activity. Nothing was insignificant enough to completely delegate. Someone else might script the responses of Temple phone operators, but Jones had to read and approve each line before it was put into effect. Another member might attend a public meeting to represent the Temple, but Jones required a full report afterward — which key officials had been there? What attitudes did they seem to have toward the Temple and its programs? If a member wanted to get married or divorced or even bring an outsider to a Temple meeting, Jones had to be consulted first. Not a penny could be spent without his permission. Members sometimes chafed at the length of meetings, but he was there for every minute, too, even to the point of discreetly relieving himself in a basin behind the pulpit rather than take a bathroom break.

On surviving tapes, his sermons sound interminable and frequently incoherent, but careful examination suggests they were less stream-of-consciousness than they seemed. Jones realized his appeal differed among followers. Some, usually the newest, thought he was God, and other recent members wanted affirmation of their belief that some spark of divinity was possible in anyone. Those who'd followed him from Indiana remembered when Jones had never claimed divinity, only dedication to social causes, and loved him for that. Many more followed him because of his apparent powers — most meetings had to include at least a healing or two. Older members, the pensioners whose Social Security and disability checks formed the bedrock of Temple finances, frequently retained at least some attachment to the Bible. There were agnostics and atheists in the Temple, attracted by its socialist goals and Jones's frequent dismissal of the Bible as racist propaganda. He had to please them all. And so, his sermons deliberately rambled. Like a great composer crafting a multi-movement symphony, Jones varied his rhythm and tone. He ran the gamut from fire-and-brimstone preacher to acerbic social commentator. At one point Jones might throw down a Bible, even stomp on it, and yet a little later cite scripture to reinforce some socialist point. He'd refer to himself as God, the reincarnation of Christ, or Lenin in a single turn at the pulpit. No one listening, even those who were the most devoted to him, could take it all in. But at some point each follower heard something that reaffirmed his or her personal reason for belonging to Peoples Temple, and for believing in Jim Jones. As Jonestown historian Fielding McGehee observes, "What you thought Jim said depended on who you were."

It was exhausting to sit through a single three- or four-hour Saturday service, and on

Sundays in Redwood Valley there were two, plus additional meetings during the week that frequently lasted far into the night. But it was even more exhausting to conduct the marathons. Hearing a Jones sermon on tape doesn't sufficiently convey the energy he expended in delivering them. Jones was constantly in motion, gesturing broadly from behind the pulpit, marching dramatically around the stage, jumping down onto the main floor to roam the aisles, patting heads, squeezing hands, offering embraces. Before, between, and after services he mingled and tried to make as many as possible feel individually noticed by Father. While everyone else enjoyed Sunday's group potluck meals, Jones usually talked some more on a portable sound system, reminding them to revel in the fellowship, and afterward prepare for another week of "feeding the hungry, clothing the naked." Aside from the Temple services, when Jones wasn't on constant call in Redwood Valley, he was often in Bus Number Seven on his way to or from a program where he'd put on a dazzling show for thousands of outsiders. During each drive he would deal with dozens or even hundreds of separate issues, ranging from which city the advance crews should visit next to how many hand towels should be purchased for the Redwood Valley church bathrooms.

There was an additional strain, one never

acknowledged by those who think Jones's only motivation was acquiring and wielding power. Even as a child, Jones was genuinely moved by poverty and by race-related suffering. At every stage in its existence, Peoples Temple outreach programs really did practice what Jones preached. Needy people were served. Outcasts from every corner of the community were warmly welcomed. Yet no matter how many people were fed, clothed, helped to find jobs, or rescued from drug addiction by Temple programs, Jim Jones ached for all those who still were not. He identified with individuals as well as multitudes. Once, just before the Temple's Greyhound convoy left the Redwood Valley parking lot for an out-of-town trip, Jones convened a meeting of a few divisional supervisors in Bus Seven. Outside, several hundred members stowed luggage and climbed aboard other buses. Jones's meeting was important — he was giving instructions for some program to be implemented while he was away. The trip ahead was a long one, and they needed to get on the road as soon as possible. But as Jones talked, he frequently glanced out the window, and all at once pointed to an elderly woman struggling with a bulky suitcase. Jones barked, "Some of you get out there — that sister needs help!" He refused to continue the meeting until the old lady's bag was securely stowed and she had been escorted to a seat on her bus.

Because he genuinely did want to lift up the oppressed, Jones's pace couldn't slacken. Wherever he went, he saw human suffering. Sometimes his twin motivations — power and ministry — coexisted comfortably. What served one, served the other. More often, as Peoples Temple expanded, the admirable motive was sublimated in favor of Jones's baser objective. Ultimately, personal ambition completely won out. But in 1971, he still struggled to satisfy both. In doing so, Jones drove his followers relentlessly and drove himself harder.

This took its inevitable toll. Jones was as physically exhausted as his members, and the emotional strain on him was much greater. God or not, he became more worn down with each passing day. By his own design, Jones had made the Temple's well-being entirely dependent on his own. This justified his evolving belief that anything he did for himself benefited those who believed in and followed him, as well as all those in desperate need of Temple assistance. No matter how apparently selfish some of his personal actions might appear, nothing was ever really for him, but for them.

By 1971, Jones already permitted himself a few personal indulgences that were concealed from most Temple followers. Movies were frowned on for the rank-and-file, but in spare weekend hours between meetings, especially when they were held in San Francisco or Los Angeles, Jones headed for the cinema. He loved mysteries and action films — over the years, he identified his favorites as *Chinatown* and *M*A*S*H.* Jones told the truth when he claimed to only wear hand-me-downs and clothes purchased at discount stores, but he had a fondness for a specific style of black lace-up shoes with thick soles. These were the only shoes he wore — but he had six pairs. Above all, though he swore in sermons that he spent every available minute on Temple business, he took vacations with his family, often for one or two weeks at a time. Members were told that Father was away on important business. These trips cost money, and Jones received no salary from the Temple — ostensibly the Joneses lived on Marceline's earnings as a state employee. But Jones controlled the Temple bank accounts, and on at least two occasions he withdrew a few thousand dollars for personal expenses. It wasn't embezzlement; the transaction records were logged in Temple files. Still, only Jones and a few discreet associates had access to these files, and he certainly preferred for the general Temple membership not to know.

Eventually such minor pleasures weren't sufficient to offset growing pressures, and, probably sometime in early 1971, Jones began turning regularly to a source of greater relief. He was influenced this time not by his mother, but his father.

After being gassed in World War I, James Thurman Jones, "Big Jim," never passed a comfortable day, and deflected his physical and mental distress with pills supplied to him during treatments at regional VA hospitals. Almost forty years later, Jim Jones emulated his dad. As far back as 1965, Garry Lambrev remembers Jones occasionally pausing in mid-sermon to complain about his need to use pain medication. Jones said that he didn't like doing it, but sometimes needed the pills to alleviate discomfort from various unspecified ailments. Temple membership was then less than a hundred and most had come west from Indiana with Jones. They knew him well and harbored no belief that he was a god above the human need for occasional self-medication. As the Temple grew, Jones's references to personal use of pain pills stopped. Whether he'd actually discontinued them or not, his expanding ranks of more worshipful members couldn't be allowed to think that Father needed drugs to function, especially since he forbade them to his followers. It would have been a contradiction that even Jones couldn't explain away.

But sometime around 1971 he began abusing drugs on a regular basis — amphetamines and tranquilizers, pills and liquids to provide significant boosts of energy, or else slow down his racing imagination and allow him to rest. The more Jones used one, the more he needed the other. Access to these drugs wasn't a problem. There were physicians sympathetic to the Temple cause who provided prescriptions, to Jones or else to followers sworn to secrecy as they passed the medications along to Father. Jones didn't have to depend entirely on prescriptions, either. Temple members worked as nurses and aides in any number of hospitals and care facilities. In an era when records were kept by hand, it was relatively simple to smuggle out whatever Jones wanted. He stressed to these suppliers that they were serving Peoples Temple in a very special, private way.

To a great extent, Jones was able to disguise the resulting mood swings from the general congregation. Out on the road, he could self-medicate in his private quarters aboard Bus Seven, acquiring chemically enhanced stamina for bravura public appearances, then drugging himself to sleep as the Temple caravan headed back to Redwood Valley and all the demands that awaited him there. The abuse to his system was evident in certain ways, but some, like a frequent sharp temper, weren't readily identifiable as drug-related — Father had always been impatient. A more obvious side effect was red, watery eyes, and Jones, who had sometimes worn dark glasses, now began wearing them everywhere. He claimed this was because his inner powers were so great that holy energy often glowed from his eyes — followers looking directly into them might be scorched.

The most harmful side effect was Jones's heightened sense of paranoia, a typical side effect of amphetamine abuse. Jones already assumed there were individuals and entities out to get him, and taught his followers to believe the same. An integral aspect of Jones's hold on his followers was their belief, constantly reinforced by their leader's citing of the latest headlines, that their own government was a danger to them. Increasingly on edge as his drug use escalated, Jones began offering specifics: He had learned, he said, that the FBI and CIA were tapping Temple phones. The U.S. government, led by notorious witch-hunters such as President Richard Nixon and FBI director J. Edgar Hoover, thought Peoples Temple was dangerous because it helped so many people and in every way exemplified how generous-spirited socialism was far superior to blood-drenched capitalism. The FBI planned to infiltrate the Temple with undercover spies, if it already hadn't. Members had to be constantly alert, and suspicious of everyone, even each other. Everyone was to be on the lookout for questionable behavior, and report it immediately. An obvious example would be someone speaking against Jones, criticizing him in any way. That's what an FBI infiltrator would do, try to shake belief in Father.

Jones had previously posted guards on the Redwood Valley church grounds. Now he warned of a new threat. The U.S. government had tried to kill Fidel Castro and might have been involved in the assassinations of Martin Luther King and John F. Kennedy; in fact, the murders of anyone trying to lead Americans to a better, more egalitarian way of life. Obviously, Jones would be on such a hit list. The government hated and feared Peoples Temple, and its leader most of all. So Jones assembled a squad of personal bodyguards, mostly menacing-looking young black men. Prominent among them was hulking Chris Lewis, a San Francisco street thug who'd come through the Temple drug program, and who afterward balanced gratitude and loyalty toward Jones with a continuing attitude of barely suppressed violence. Jones went out of his way to support him, eventually using Temple funds to pay for Lewis's successful defense in San Francisco against murder charges unrelated to Temple business. The murder case was an example of the government pursuing its vendetta against proud black men, Jones insisted. Some Temple members wondered — Lewis scared them. But they didn't protest, to Jones or among themselves, because then they might be accused of being FBI infiltrators bent on causing internal Temple dissension.

Some of Jones's bodyguards were armed. Everyone carrying a gun was first required to qualify for the appropriate permits — Jones was not about to have members charged with unlawful possession or use of a firearm. Now, when the Temple Greyhound convoy was on the road, a few guns were stored on Bus Seven, just in case. On some occasions the bodyguards also wore uniforms — matching shirts, pants, ties, and berets. Their appearance was intended to impress the rest of the Temple fellowship as much as to intimidate potential outside attackers — their presence was proof that Father was determined to protect them. These guards, and the less militaristic security teams prowling the Redwood Valley church and local Temple-owned buildings at night, noticed but did not mention to others a significant change in Jim Jones's personal behavior. Before, unless he was out of town, Jones could routinely be found working in his office well past midnight, and sometimes all night, occasionally emerging to offer encouraging words to members who were also up late attending to Temple tasks, or else to chide perceived malingerers, and shame them with his own self-sacrificing example. Now, most nights, sentries posted outside his closed office door heard loud, wet snores. Father, after bursting with superhuman energy all through the day, was now sleeping soundly, if noisily, for much of the night. They didn't realize why.

CHAPTER TWENTY-EIGHT: SEX

Jones had always been frank and open about sex — up to a point.

With teens like Mike Cartmell and Bonnie Malmin, Jones matter-of-factly discussed masturbation and intercourse, making it clear that these were natural rather than obscene subjects. Even Marceline's ten-year-old cousin Ronnie Baldwin received detailed facts-of-life lectures from Uncle Jim when he lived for a while with the Joneses, and wowed his elementary school pals with his new knowledge. When Marceline could no longer engage in sex, Jones told his children that was why he took Carolyn Layton as a lover. As pastor of Peoples Temple, Jones insisted on being familiar with all aspects of his followers' sex lives, and telling them who they should and shouldn't sleep with. He generally stopped short of forbidding anyone to have sex. "He couldn't completely regulate it," former Temple member Tim Carter recalls. "People [were] going to do it. But he tried to at least make it as difficult as possible. It was one more way for him to control us."

Still, among some members of Peoples Temple, there was a certain reticence, even prissiness, about sex. In 1972 and 1973, the pornographic film *Deep Throat* became a national sensation, and its star, Linda Lovelace, was for a time one of the most famous women in America. Linda Amos, one of Jones's most devoted followers, was so humiliated by the X-rated notoriety of the actress that she insisted on being called Sharon, her middle name, rather than share a first name with Lovelace. Jones himself, for all his frequent references in sermons to the human sex drive, sometimes including his own, rarely engaged in public displays of affection with Marceline, and one reason most members never guessed of his relationship with Carolyn Layton was because he never touched her in public, either. Except for his oft-told tale of having intercourse with an ambassador's wife in Brazil in return for her generous donation to an orphanage, so far as most Temple followers were concerned, the only evidence of Father's actual sex life was his son Stephan.

But about the same time he started abusing drugs, Jones began sexually indulging himself beyond Carolyn Layton. In many ways, his relationship with Carolyn took on aspects of

404

marriage, including a gradual lessening of intimacy. Jones considered himself above reproach; the only restraint on him was his own sense of self-control, and with every passing day it diminished. Two years earlier, because of Marceline's physical problems, he'd needed a different source of sexual gratification and limited himself to a single new partner. This time, Jones didn't replace Carolyn Layton. He began having sex with others — essentially, Carolyn became the senior concubine in an ever-evolving harem. For her, and for those followers who formed Jones's inner Temple circle, there was nothing discreet about it. Jones picked out whom he wanted among members, took them, and afterward bragged about it locker-room style with pals like Beam and Ijames. Carolyn was hurt, and furious, but Jones didn't consider her feelings to be critical. He believed that he needed more sex with a variety of partners. It would be good for him, and therefore good for the Temple. As he had with Marceline, Jones correctly guessed that Carolyn would reluctantly acquiesce. She still had her turns in Jones's bed, and an important place in Temple operations. If Carolyn resented Jones's infidelity, that was her problem, not his.

Jones's quandary was whom to pursue first. He confined himself to Temple members — since Father discouraged even passing friend-

405

ships with outsiders, Jones could hardly risk consummations beyond the church. But, having never tested these impulsive sexual waters, Jones wasn't prepared to force himself indiscriminately on female followers; he would have been hard-pressed to explain away complaints about unwanted advances. He began with a safe target.

Besides total belief in and devotion to Jim Jones, Karen Tow Layton, Larry Layton's second wife, had the additional advantage of being one of the most attractive young women in the Temple. When he took Carolyn away from Layton, Jones helped persuade Karen to take Carolyn's place as Layton's spouse — she was an attractive consolation prize. It helped bolster Layton's bruised ego that so many other men in the Temple envied him his new, much prettier wife. But Karen's primary allegiance was to Jones. Taking her as a lover in 1971 was both a satisfying and safe move on Jones's part. Beyond Karen's own devotion to him — she gladly gave herself to Father, so there was no risk of repercussion there — Jones also knew that there would be no protest, at least overtly, from her husband. Larry Layton was completely under his control. Carolyn initially found some solace in believing that the attraction was one-sided on Karen's part, and wrote to her parents that "[Karen] has stated repeatedly . . . that she is very much in love with Jim," but Jones made it absolutely clear to the lovestruck young woman "that nothing will ever be reciprocated by [him] at this level." (Carolyn also wrote that Larry Layton had a homosexual crush on Jones, which was one reason she divorced him. There is no evidence that this was true.) By the time Carolyn realized that Jones was equally attracted to Karen, it was too late.

While her brief affair with Jones lasted, Karen took pride in the relationship — Father wanted, needed, *her.* Ijames tried tactfully warning Jones to keep his sex life private: "Brother Jones, I think you trust people too much."

Once his desire for Karen was satiated, Jones moved on to other Temple women. His sexual self-image bloomed to a point where he believed that all women, regardless of age and whether they would admit it or not, were attracted to him. The result was a subtle, but significant, change in the way he asked females to take on particularly difficult Temple tasks. His encouragement of men remained the same: "You've got qualities we need to get this accomplished." But now he told women, "You can do this because you love me."

Jones began engaging in episodic sex typified by whim rather than even short-term seduction. Consciously or not, Jones restricted himself to young women either securely in his personal thrall or else so uncertain of themselves that they would feel overwhelmed and submit. Eventually, almost all the women in Jones's inner circle became his occasional conquests. They either considered it part of their duties to him and the cause, or else an honor bestowed on them for distinguished service. Jones always insisted he was doing it for them as well as himself — they *needed* sex with Father; it was good for their self-esteem.

In almost every case, Jones's advances took them by surprise. Terri Buford was working in an adjacent office during a Temple service. Jones came into the room during a lull while the collection plate was being passed and asked her, "Who are you attracted to?" Buford, caught off guard, mentioned a few Temple men. Jones, sounding offended, said, "You're not attracted to me?" Buford said that she'd never thought about Jones that way. He pressed her, and they soon had sex. Reflecting decades later, she said that it wasn't anything special, besides the fact that it involved Jones. It didn't occur to her to resist — this was Father, after all.

Debbie Layton's account in her memoir, *Seductive Poison*, indicates that, at least with her, Jones crossed the line into rape. Layton, then about nineteen, was invited by Jones to ride with him in his private bus compartment on a drive back to Redwood Valley from San

Francisco. She was shocked when he told her to unbutton her shirt, and mumbled, "I am doing this for you . . . to help you." Still clothed, "pants opened just enough," Jones pushed her on the bed, clambered on top of her, satisfied himself, and got up. Layton, confused, somehow felt obligated to tell Jones that she was sorry. He replied, "Don't worry, my child. You needed it." Then Jones instructed her to stay where she was; he'd order everyone else to get off the bus at the next rest stop, and she could make her way out and to another bus unnoticed.

Jones had sex with Debbie Layton a few more times, once in a Peoples Temple men's room, never in any situation where Jones asked permission or Layton had time to think about it. Jones eventually promoted her to positions of greater Temple responsibility; she felt honored to be part of an inner circle that included Carolyn Layton, Karen Tow Layton, Terri Buford, Sharon Amos, Tim Stoen, and one or two others.

Because Jones had managed to keep his long-term affair with Carolyn Layton so closely guarded, for a while some of the women with whom he had liaisons believed that they had replaced Marceline as Father's new mate — in Terri Buford's words, "God's chick." They were soon disabused of the notion. Once they'd been taken by Jones, he no longer bothered to disguise his additional

409

sexual activities. Buford learned she wasn't Jones's only lover when she heard him loudly having sex with another woman in the next room. But neither Buford nor any of the others ever caused a scene, or accused Jones to his face of sexual abuse or deception. They never made public complaints about his actions to the wider Temple membership. For some, it was because Jones's constant preaching about bourgeois attitudes and selfishness made them feel guilty for even contemplating airing a personal grievance. Others realized that the bulk of Jones's followers would always align themselves with Father in any dispute. Leaving Jones, and the church, was rarely considered an option. Jones always found some means to make his sex partners feel even more committed to the cause, often, as with Debbie Layton, by assigning them new, critical roles. His manipulative gifts were never more evident. Jones himself never formed an emotional attachment to any of the women. They'd served his pleasure, and that was their reward.

Jones even found a way to make his sex life rewarding to a devoted female follower that he didn't want. No one adored Jim Jones more than Patty Cartmell; she was always ready to unquestioningly obey him, and would have felt honored to serve Jones sexually. But she was grossly obese, and Jones's professed motivation to help raise up women by having sex with them didn't apply to one so physically unattractive. When Jones's serial sexualizing reached near-frantic proportions — there always seemed to be one more Temple woman that he just had to have — he included Cartmell by putting her in charge of his "fuck schedule," a notebook listing who Jones was scheduled to sleep with, and when.

Most, though not all, of the time Jones confined himself to adults. There were winsome underage girls in the Temple, and Jones had sex with at least one of them, a fourteen-year-old whose family found out and left the Temple, though without making the reason public out of respect for the cause. Jones sent emissaries to persuade them to return, but without success.

Jones also crossed another sexual line. A young man recently recruited to the Temple, and immediately raised to a position of considerable responsibility due to Jones's recognition of his organizational skills, was stunned after one service when his new leader mentioned casually, "I'll fuck you in the ass if you want." When he stammered, "No, thanks," Jones grinned and said, "Well, if you ever want to, I can."

Jones had occasional sex with male followers. Never as often as he did with women, but on a regular enough basis that younger men leaders were warned by some of Jones's previous male partners, "If you ask Father to fuck you in the ass, take a douche." Whenever he discussed same-sex coupling with his inner Temple circle, Jones insisted that "I have to be all things to all people," and some male followers either needed to be sexually humbled or else encouraged to become even more dedicated to the cause, and intercourse with Jones produced those results. Jones was clearly bisexual, though he chose not to openly admit it. For a long time, he discouraged gay relationships among his followers. Garry Lambrev, who made several abortive breaks with the Temple, left for good after Jones refused to allow him even the possibility of having a long-term male partner. "He said that if I had to have [gay] sex, I should go to some bar in San Francisco and have a one-night stand," Lambrev said. "I wanted something more than that, and Jim wouldn't allow it." As with women followers, Jones showed some restraint in the men he approached, and, in those rare cases when he was turned down, didn't insist.

Most of his followers had no idea that Jim Jones had numerous sex partners among Temple members. But it was impossible for Jones to keep his activities entirely secret from a growing number of Temple leaders. He was openly challenged only once. Juanell Smart, a black woman married to David Wise, a white assistant Temple minister, noticed a constant among Jones's conquests and confronted him: "Jim, why do you only sleep with whites and never with blacks?" Jones snapped back that whites needed to be more dedicated to the Temple's cause, and to its rejection of bourgeois attitudes; sex with Jones helped them retain an appropriate, socialist attitude. Blacks didn't have that problem, so there was no reason for him to have sex with them.

Sometime in early 1971, probably in March, Jones chose an unlikely new sex partner. In her first contact with him, Grace Stoen disliked Jones as a person, though she strongly believed in the social missions he espoused. Tim Stoen in some ways was the most important member of Peoples Temple after Jones himself. Whatever Jones planned — sometimes *plotted* would be a more accurate term — Stoen was responsible for keeping it within the law. He was someone Jones couldn't afford to alienate, let alone lose. Yet Jim Jones made his way into Grace's bed.

Around the end of 1970, it became common knowledge within Temple membership that all was not well between the Stoens. Survivors remember Grace complaining about her husband's ego, and his penchant for leaving her alone at home while he counseled Jones at any hour. At some point, she mentioned that she and Tim had not

413

been intimate for months. Jones made it his business to know every bit of personal gossip about his followers. Information cards on prospective members were constantly updated, and so were cards about current members. As soon as Grace Stoen began grumbling about her husband, Jones knew.

Jim Jones Jr. thinks his father always lusted after Grace, who, like Karen Layton, was very attractive: "He wanted to get in her pants. It's that simple." Even so, Jones had to recognize the risk involved. Tim Stoen was no meek Larry Layton. It would be bad enough if the man he relied on for expert legal advice left the Temple, and worse because, next to Jones himself, Tim Stoen knew all the Temple secrets. Jones, his natural paranoia exaggerated by drug use, was haunted by the belief that the FBI and CIA were eager for any potentially incriminating information about the Temple and its leader. Tim Stoen, seeking revenge on Jones for cuckolding him, would have plenty of dirt to dish.

But Jones felt that he had the measure of the man. Tim Stoen was a passionate believer, if not in Jim Jones as God Himself, then at least in the Temple cause. Stoen could have made a fortune in private practice or as a partner in some venerable San Francisco law firm. He gave up not only personal wealth but professional prestige to hold down a staff job in the district attorney's office of an isolated California county. His marriage was in trouble at least in part because of his devotion to his Temple obligations. Yet Stoen obviously believed that helping Jim Jones lead the way to a better world was worth these sacrifices.

Another Jones trait was also in play. It was important to Jones that everyone else in Temple leadership demonstrate subservience to him. A special few were allowed more leeway than others. Jack Beam sometimes told less than worshipful stories about Father in the old days, and on occasion gently mocked Jones to his face. Archie Ijames cautioned Jones when he thought the Temple leader talked too much or too bluntly. Marceline was allowed to question some of Jones's decisions, and Carolyn Layton had personal expectations of him that he allowed, though these were not always met. Still, they all acknowledged his supremacy. They might make suggestions, plead, or even argue, but they ultimately obeyed him. Jones's relationship with Tim Stoen was different. Because of the legal acumen he possessed and Jones didn't, Jones needed to treat Stoen almost as an equal. Ever since Stoen had joined Peoples Temple, Jones had no means of reminding him of his proper place in the Temple hierarchy, which might be above all other members, but still beneath Jim Jones. Then came an opportunity with Grace, who was unhappy with her husband — and had his permission to engage in sex with someone else. Stoen wrote in his memoir, *Marked for Death,* that he adopted an "open marriage" policy with Grace and took advantage of it himself with "a single lonely woman with five children." If, at some point, Grace also wanted to stray, "I did not want to be a hypocrite." Sometime during late March or April 1971, Grace Stoen became pregnant.

CHAPTER TWENTY-NINE: FAMILY

So far as almost anyone was aware, things were fine with Jones's immediate family. Marceline Jones played an integral role in the Temple, helping to organize outreach programs, leading services in place of her husband when he was away from Redwood Valley, standing nearby when Jones was in the pulpit, coming forward sometimes to assist him in some way. Her public posture toward her husband never varied. Laura Johnston Kohl remembers, "Marceline seemed like she was just mesmerized by Jim. She would give him that adoring Nancy Reagan look."

The Jones children appeared to be thriving. Agnes remained frequently estranged, but Suzanne had grown into an attractive, self-assured young woman. Stephan, Lew, and Jimmy were generally boisterous, typical teen boys, and a fourth son had been added — Tim Tupper, the child of a Temple member, who was about Stephan's age and had attached himself to the family. Though Jones and Marceline wouldn't formally adopt Tim for a few more years, he'd already been accepted by them as a full-fledged family member.

There were perks that all of them enjoyed. Though he kept the excursions from most of the Temple membership, Jones believed in family vacations. He took his brood to every World's Fair, and they also made trips to Hawaii. A couple of sons accompanied their dad on a jaunt to Germany. These getaways were always great times, awkward only in the sense that if any lasted two weeks, Jones had Marceline along for one week and Carolyn for the other.

The Jones kids had horses and a variety of pets. Besides dogs, there was a chimpanzee named Mr. Muggs, who occupied a cage just outside their house in Redwood Valley. Temple members were told that Jones had saved Mr. Muggs from death in laboratory experiments, though some later came to believe the chimp was purchased by Jones from a pet store. Jim Jones Jr. remembers, "I think Stephan somehow saw [Muggs] tested and we got him instead of the ocelot I was supposed to get for my birthday." The chimp became the unofficial Temple mascot.

Other Temple youngsters learned that it was a good idea to be friends with the Jones boys — then you got to do more. The Jones gang of brothers and their pals were allowed to go to movies and wore spiffy sports gear. Some resentment grew among the general Temple membership about such favoritism, when the rest of the Temple kids and teens were expected to live as abstemiously as their parents. Carolyn Layton felt compelled to issue a statement: The Jones offspring needed extra privileges due to the constant pressure they felt because of outside threats to their father. And it was true that the Jones daughter and sons were under constant, sometimes emotionally crippling, pressure — not from outside threats against Jim Jones, but from their father's own aberrant behavior.

Forcing Carolyn on his children was one of the main issues. Jones insisted that they treat her with the same respect as Marceline, but it didn't take. Although Carolyn wrote a rapturous note to her parents claiming "the children love me like a second mother," Stephan felt no warmth. Carolyn's relationship with Stephan couldn't have been as close as she claimed; she didn't spell his name correctly, identifying him as "Steven" in her letter to the Moores. Lew and Jimmy, both in many ways closer to their father than to Marceline, tolerated Carolyn. But all the children sympathized to some degree with their mother, and never considered Carolyn as a maternal replacement. Tension caused by what Stephan termed "a forced family" was constant.

Jones's additional sexual activities didn't affect his children because, for a long time, they didn't know about them. But his drug use had a particularly profound effect on the young Joneses, who soon realized that rather than lying down "meditating," their father was passed out from self-medicating. There were pill bottles in medicine cabinets and trays of white liquid in the refrigerator. Once they found him facedown in the front hall. After Marceline revived him, Jones said to Stephan, "I'm sorry for the little scare, honey. There's so much on me . . . I just can't give any more."

The other children mostly compartmentalized — Jim Jr. says he had no idea of the extent of his father's drug use until years later in Guyana — but Stephan was more sensitive to it. He'd suffered for some time from his own illness, congenital narrowing of the urethra that required surgery and catheterization. Jones explained that he couldn't use his own healing powers to banish the ailment because suffering through the affliction would help Stephan grow as a leader. The youngster was pleased that Jones and Marceline both spent time with him at the hospital — "[It] looked like we were a family again, like everything might be okay."

But it wasn't.

Stephan Jones was twelve when he swallowed fourteen Quaaludes from a bottle on his father's dresser, hoping to seem sick enough afterward to be allowed to skip at least some of a Wednesday night Temple meeting. Marceline, a trained nurse, saved his life, rushing Stephan to Ukiah General Hospital where he received emergency treatment. She and Jones had to subsequently endure a hospital meeting with psychiatric staff that was a condition of Stephan's release. The boy deliberately took heavy Quaalude doses twice more, leaving suicide notes both times. In an essay written decades later, he mused that he didn't intend to actually kill himself, just get more attention. Once he had to be taken to the hospital again, this time to one in San Francisco since Jones didn't want to risk any more local gossip. Stephan remembers that on this drive, his brothers took turns slapping him "with a little too much verve" to keep him awake. After the first incident, and even after the second and third, Jim Jones still left his pills and liquid drugs in places where they were easy for anyone to find. Marceline always thought that in spite of his flaws as a husband, Jones was at least a good father. Now he was willing to endanger his children because he wanted his drug stash handy.

Two years after her husband had taken up with Carolyn Moore, Marceline might still have held some hope that he would tire of the other woman. Meanwhile, Marceline had her children, her rewarding job with the state, and a continuing role in Peoples Temple, if no longer as her husband's primary advisor. It was hard, but she bore up. When Marceline's younger sister Sharon divorced, Marceline invited her to move with her kids to Redwood Valley — it would have been a comfort for Marceline to have a sister so near. Sharon made a visit, but after hearing her brother-in-law preach about his godly powers had no desire to be around him. Marceline stayed in her own difficult marriage, perhaps thinking that after Carolyn Moore and drugs, things couldn't get worse. But they did.

For a short time, Marceline may not have been aware of Jones's increased sexual activities with other Temple members besides Carolyn. Everyone in the Temple loved her, even the women sleeping with her husband. No one dropped cruel hints, hoping to enjoy her dismay. Certainly in the two years since Carolyn began sharing Jones's bed, Marceline had learned to ignore clues that might cause her additional pain. She had enough problems already.

Then on January 25, 1972, John Victor Stoen was born in Santa Rosa Hospital. The healthy infant's birth certificate listed his mother as twenty-one-year-old Grace Lucy Grech Stoen and thirty-four-year-old Timothy Oliver Stoen as his father. Under California law, that established the two as John

Victor's legal parents. But on February 6, 1972, Tim Stoen signed a statement addressed "TO WHOM IT MAY CONCERN":

I, Timothy Oliver Stoen, hereby acknowledge that in April, 1971, I entreated my beloved pastor, James W. Jones, to sire a child by my wife, Grace Lucy (Grech) Stoen, who had previously, at my insistence, reluctantly but graciously consented thereto. James W. Jones agreed to do so, reluctantly, after I explained that I very much wished to raise a child but was unable, after extensive attempts, to sire one myself. My reason for requesting James W. Jones to do this is that I wanted my child to be fathered, if not by me, by the most compassionate, honest and courageous human being the world contains.

The child, John Victor Stoen, was born on January 25, 1972. I am privileged beyond words to have the responsibility for caring for him, and I undertake this task humbly with the steadfast hope that the child will become a devoted follower of Jesus Christ and be instrumental in bringing God's kingdom here on earth, as has been his wonderful natural father.

I declare under penalty of perjury that the foregoing is true and correct.

In his memoir, Stoen said that as a lawyer

he believed the statement, which was not an official affidavit, "had no legal effect, could not constitute perjury, and could never be used in court. . . . Everything about the declaration was untrue," except that Stoen had chosen to believe that Jones was, in fact, John Victor's father. If he had any doubt — or any hope — it wasn't true, in 1972 there was no scientific means to prove or disprove paternity. The human leukocyte antigen test (HLA) compared HLA levels in a child's blood to its putative father, but it did not rule out paternity. There was also a blood type matching test — a child with blood type O could not have been sired by a father with type AB blood. But DNA testing was still a decade away.

Jones, Stoen wrote, came to him a week before the child's birth to inform the stunned attorney that he was John Victor's biological father. By Stoen's account, his belief in Jones was so strong that "I could not fathom a good person saying such a thing if it were not true." So, to reassure Jones that he would never "seek to take" the child from him, Stoen signed the "inordinately eulogistic" statement whose "only possible purpose [was to cause] me maximum embarrassment in the highly unlikely event of my ever trying to deprive Jones of John Victor."

Jones didn't demand that the child be turned over to him immediately — John

Victor would remain in Stoen and Grace's care. But he now had the signed statement from Stoen, with all its humiliating overtones. Even if requesting it was substantially motivated by Jones's own love for the baby and fear that he might somehow be denied contact with him, another factor was certainly in play. Tim Stoen was acknowledging that Jim Jones slept with his wife and got her pregnant. The humiliation was deliberate — the statement could certainly have been worded in a kinder way toward Stoen. But Jones intended the document to humble not only Stoen, but also someone else. There was a line at the bottom of the statement for the signature of a witness. There were plenty of available Jones loyalists who would have gladly served in the role. But Jones had someone else specifically in mind, another person besides Stoen he believed needed reminding of her proper, subservient place. On the witness line, written in painfully neat cursive, appeared the signature "Marceline M. Jones."

Marceline's mood when she signed can't be determined, but her actions in the months immediately afterward prove that she had reached the end of her patience with Jones. She told someone that if she could be any animal, it would be a turtle, so that she could crawl back into her shell. Marceline found herself a new shell of sorts when she rented an apartment in Santa Rosa, about sixty miles south of Redwood Valley. Previously, she'd often spent a few weeknights away from home; her state job inspecting health care facilities required some travel. But now she was home only on weekends, when she obediently carried out her Temple duties, standing in for Jones when he was out of town and playing supporting roles during services if he wasn't. During those public moments, her demeanor remained substantially the same, respectful of her husband, supportive of the Temple and its existing programs. Still, there was a sense that she had become emotionally withdrawn; new members felt Marceline was hard to get to know. Veteran Temple members noticed she was less active in developing new outreach efforts.

Marceline's children, already used to both parents' frequent absences — a full-time housekeeper named Esther prepared meals and kept a watchful eye on the Jones brood — didn't notice that much difference. "We lived in a bubble, and it was usually good," Jim Jones Jr. remembers. So far as they knew, the Mom-Dad-Carolyn combination was still in effect. If for a time they were seeing their mother less, she was still a strong presence in their lives. But Marceline was using the space she'd created away from Redwood Valley to look at the possibility of a future for herself and her children without him. She remained an attractive woman, intelligent and capable in her own right. Jim Jones boasted to his male Temple friends of his sexual magnetism, how women found him irresistible. He forgot that Marceline had her own appeal. Then came a reminder.

Sometime after the birth of John Victor Stoen, Marceline Jones returned to her home near the Temple church in Redwood Valley and informed her husband that she was leaving him. She had fallen in love with a psychologist she'd met through her work for the state. Marceline planned to divorce Jones, marry the new man in her life, who lived in Fort Benning, Georgia, and take the children with her.

Perhaps she hoped that Jones would beg her to stay, or at least admit that his own selfish actions had irreconcilably ruined their marriage. Instead, Jones summoned the children to join him and Marceline immediately in a family meeting. Jones took the offensive, saying, "Mom wants to break up the family." He declared that she was being selfish, putting her own desires ahead of what was best for everyone. This man, this doctor or whoever he was, wanted to take Mom — and *them* — to Fort Benning, away from all the things they had in Redwood Valley, the horses and the pets and their friends and all the fun. Revealing his parental sense of chauvinism — Suzanne was a girl, so her opinion didn't matter — Jones demanded of

Lew, Stephan, and Jimmy, "Do you want to go with your mother?" All three said, "We want to stay with you, Dad" — choosing the familiar over the unknown. Jones felt that he'd won. Then Marceline said she would leave, marry the psychologist, and take the children anyway.

In front of their children, Jones thundered that if Marceline tried to take them, "You will be met by the avengers of death." Marceline Jones knew her husband well, including how he fabricated demonstrations of superpowers. A threat to summon "avengers of death" might have caused gullible Temple members to quail; she knew better. But then Jones switched to more basic terms: "If you ever take my boys away, you'll be dead." He now had armed bodyguards who were fanatical in their worship of him, and undoubtedly willing to kill on his command. Marceline took this threat seriously. She backed down. Jones dismissed the family meeting.

Marceline resumed her secondary place in the Temple, and, as it expanded, was required to stand in for Jones much more often. Added to the ongoing demands of her state job, there was no time or opportunity left to continue one outside romance, or to pursue another. Stephan said decades later that "I think my Mom did the best that she could do with what she had because it was all that she could do . . . there were a lot of things that kept her there." Love of her children was foremost, as well as a sense of responsibility to all of Jones's followers, who she believed were good people, genuinely trying to change the world for the better. But after the family meeting there was also the possibility that Marceline's own life was at stake. Better than anyone, she understood Jones's ruthlessness. So she stayed, and it cost her. Jim Jr. recalls, "Of course Mom wasn't happy after that. More than ever, she became a sad woman."

For the Jones sons, life mostly went on as it had before. It was different for Suzanne. A few years earlier, she'd dated Mike Cartmell, the teenage son of Patty Cartmell, and who helped run the Temple youth activities. Cartmell, to Jones's mind, was the perfect husband for Suzanne. He was the child of perhaps Jones's ultimate loyalist, he'd demonstrated his own dedication for years, and he was strikingly intelligent, apparently heading for a career in law. At one point Jones told Mike, "I'd love to adopt you, and would, but for Suzanne. Then you couldn't marry her." So far as Jones was concerned, Suzanne would marry whomever her father wanted.

But Suzanne was strong-minded. She dated Cartmell for a while when they both were in high school. He was a senior and she was a freshman, but it was the younger one who broke things off. Cartmell despaired — he was enthralled with Suzanne's assertive personality and blossoming good looks — but Jones didn't give up. He spent the next few years constantly telling his daughter about the latest great things Mike Cartmell had done. Jones went so far as to tell Cartmell that he was Jones's "chosen successor," making it logical that Cartmell and Suzanne would marry to keep the next generation of Temple leadership entirely within the Jones family. It was a ploy; privately, Jones had already designated that in the event of his death Marceline would lead the church until such time as Stephan was ready to assume the helm. But Jones never let facts interfere with convenient promises. Suzanne relented and began dating Cartmell again. They eventually married in June 1973. Afterward, Cartmell noticed a change in Marceline's attitude toward him. Previously, she'd been friendly. Now she snapped at him almost every time they were together, finding fault with whatever Cartmell said or did. He complained to Jones, who replied, "Son, you've just got Marceline on your ass and I don't envy you." For a long time, Cartmell couldn't figure it out, but finally felt that he understood. Marceline Jones, swept into marriage with the leader of Peoples Temple and then betrayed by him, was furious that Jones had maneuvered their daughter into the same potential fate.

CHAPTER THIRTY:
THE PLANNING COMMISSION

Though ultimately it was his opinions alone that counted, Jones always maintained the illusion that he led Peoples Temple based at least in part on the counsel of members serving on advisory boards. When the Temple relocated to Redwood Valley, its Board of Elders consisted of loyalists who'd held the same positions back in Indiana. The group was known simply as the Board, chaired by Cleve Swinney. Its membership included one black person, Archie Ijames, and consisted only of men, though women had significant roles within the Temple — Marceline, Carolyn Layton, Patty Cartmell, and Eva Pugh, the organization's treasurer.

Soon after the Temple relocation, Board membership was expanded. A few selected newcomers were asked to serve, including Garry Lambrev and Sharon Amos. Amos, a trained psychiatric social worker, caused a sensation during one of her first meetings. Eager to impress Jones, who was also in attendance, Amos said that to prove her gratitude to the Temple and its leader, she would feed her three children only birdseed so that the money she saved on more traditional food could be donated to Temple programs. For once, even Jones was at a loss for words. Jack Beam eventually broke the stunned silence by saying, "That won't be necessary, sweetheart, but I know Jim sure appreciates your commitment to the cause."

Whether making foolish statements or genuinely discussing substantial issues, the Board had no authority. Jones was always present, though he usually listened rather than talked. It was a way for him to get a better sense of the general Temple atmosphere and goings-on.

Another Temple board had legal authority, but still no influence. California state registration and operating regulations required a board of directors and some record of its meetings. Membership on the formal Board of Directors of the Peoples Temple of the Disciples of Christ was restricted to seven — Jones, Marceline, Tim Stoen, Ijames, Carolyn Layton, Mike Cartmell, and Amos. Every recorded discussion and vote of the seven-member Board of Directors always reflected the will of Jim Jones.

But Jones wanted some additional system that let him keep better track of and control all the diverse aspects of Temple activity, from the public programs to the closely held trickery that allowed him to perform healings and read minds. The result was a new group called the Planning Commission, soon known as "the P.C." among Temple membership. Around 1972, it replaced the Board of Elders as Jones's ostensible internal advisory group. Like its earlier iteration, it existed to do Jones's bidding.

No one other than Jones understood how P.C. members were selected. The acknowledged Temple leaders were included: Jones wanted both Stoens, Jack and Rheaviana Beam, Carolyn Layton, Terri Buford, and Patty Cartmell on hand. Grace was always present, but Tim Stoen was frequently occupied with other Temple business. The Mertles were P.C. members, and Laura Johnston. Marceline occasionally attended; her husband did not feel a need for her constant presence. But Jones also selected some members whose contributions to the Temple seemed less significant. He viewed the P.C. as his best means of keeping a closer eye on followers whose loyalty he doubted, to impress women he intended to take as lovers, and to reward his most unwavering followers, the ones who would do anything for him.

From the outset, P.C. members were viewed by everyone else in the Temple as the followers that Father valued most. Some who weren't selected by him were hurt, and vowed to work for the cause even harder to prove their commitment — just as he knew who it would benefit him to appoint to the P.C., Jones also had a sense of who would work even harder to impress him if they weren't selected. Initial P.C. membership totaled about fifty. The number eventually grew to more than one hundred. Where the earlier, smaller Board of Elders had routinely met in members' homes, the P.C. was too large for that, so its meetings were often held at the Temple offices in Redwood Valley, with everyone crammed into a workspace above the Temple laundry. Other meetings took place in the Temple church, before or after services.

No matter where they occurred, P.C. meetings were multihour marathons. Many of its members had day jobs, but Jones sometimes kept the group working until sunrise. He rarely presided. Jones named Grace Stoen as "head counselor," and while the P.C. debated new Temple business — consideration of establishing permanent churches in San Francisco and Los Angeles was part of early P.C. agendas — Jones encouraged lengthy expression of opinions, always listening for any hints that someone wasn't completely committed to whatever he wanted, and constantly watching for gestures or careless words indicating potential disloyalty. No matter how long the meetings dragged on, P.C. members remained engaged, probably from physical discomfort. The lucky ones had chairs; the rest sat on the floor. Bathroom breaks were generally forbidden. Jones himself lounged on a couch that was cushioned with extra pillows. Food was provided; Jones ate a lot, and drank most of the fruit juices and soft drinks that were on hand. During many P.C. meetings, he had an oxygen tank placed by his couch and frequently held a mask to his face for reviving draughts. Jones also relieved himself whenever he wished. Everyone agreed that Father needed to conserve his strength because the burdens on him were so great.

It was originally understood that the purpose of the Planning Commission was to help develop, then direct, the activities and overall mission of Peoples Temple. But almost immediately the topic of sex was introduced. At one of the first P.C. conclaves, Jones repeated the story of having sex with an ambassador's wife in exchange for her generous donation to a Brazilian orphanage. When Marceline asked why he wanted to share something so personal, Jones said he wanted everyone in the room to realize how much he trusted them, and also the extent of the sacrifices he made for the cause.

Marceline asked if she could respond. When Jones granted permission, she told the others that in the past she had been reluctant "to share my husband" for the cause, and that her intransigence forced him to demand a divorce. But she loved and believed in Jim Jones and didn't want to lose him, "so I agreed that I would share him with people who needed to relate to the cause on a more personal level." She admitted, "This has been a very difficult thing for me to live with, and it's caused me a lot of heartaches." But after listening to her husband in the P.C. meeting, "I realized that I have been very selfish. I want to make a public statement tonight that I am willing to share my husband for the cause, and I won't resent it any longer." With that, Marceline left the room.

As soon as his wife was gone, Jones bragged, "I hope Marcie's unexpected offer doesn't cause a lot of you to begin making demands on me. I'm already overworked in this area."

Sex became a recurring P.C. meeting topic. Jones described his own carnal activity and challenged members to reveal their own secret desires. As new members were appointed to the P.C., they were soon disabused of their vision of focusing solely on critical Temple business. Hue Fortson remembers, "It was supposed to be an honor to be [appointed]. And at [my] first meeting, everyone was businesslike and cordial. Then at the next meeting, all they talked about was who fucked who."

Besides discussing legitimate Temple business and fixating on sex, the Planning Commission took on an additional role — meting out discipline.

"Catharsis meetings" had been part of the Temple tradition from its earliest days. Members who acted inappropriately were called out in front of their peers, confronted with their perceived misdeeds, and offered the opportunity to correct their behavior. It was, initially, a fairly gentle procedure, more of a controlled discussion than a kangaroo court, with Jones admonishing where necessary and eliciting promises to do better. The philosophy was that nobody, with the exception of Jones and Marceline, could be expected to act perfectly at all times. Catharsis meetings, always closed to outsiders, offered Temple members the opportunity to benefit from constructive criticism.

In Redwood Valley, these were usually held on Wednesday nights. As time passed, the criticism offered took on a harsher tone, mostly from Jones himself. He was under great stress, first from the Temple's near-disintegration in 1968 and then when it began its explosive growth and the pressures on him increased exponentially. Screaming at an errant member, delivering verbal abuse that touched on character flaws as well as specific slips in behavior, seemed to help. Whitey Freestone, both before and after his family's horrific car wreck, was a regular target — Whitey was told repeatedly by Jones that he was stupid. Larry Layton was convenient, too. No matter what or how hard he tried, Jones always found some way that Layton had failed the Temple and its leader. Freestone eventually left the Temple, but Layton never did.

As the Temple grew, the influx of new members included many whose backgrounds included all manner of crimes, from drug dealers to alcoholics, and from street thugs to pedophiles. When relatives of Temple members faced prison time, Jones sometimes personally appealed to judges to release the accused into Temple custody instead. It was the avowed Temple custom to accept all those the rest of society cast out. This was admirable in theory, but risky in practice. New members were supposedly reformed for good thanks to the Temple's influence, but a certain percentage of backsliding was inevitable.

Jones preached, and his followers believed, that the U.S. criminal justice system was corrupt, as well as rife with racism. Local police were untrustworthy, too, and undoubtedly eager to have Temple members fall into their clutches. So Jones instituted a rule: "Don't ever go to the authorities. . . . Don't call police on a member, [especially] if they're black. They may spend their lives in jail." To discourage the kind of activities that would otherwise involve outside authorities — buying or selling drugs, stealing, committing assaults — whenever possible, the Planning Commission doled out private Temple punishment. Sentences were passed by the P.C., always with the approval of Jones. These often involved beatings, sometimes with a board, other times with a rubber hose. The belief was that it was better for the Temple to deal harshly but fairly with its own rather than abandon members to the malignant control of cops and judges.

Consequences weren't as severe for lesser transgressions, which usually involved violations of internal Temple strictures. Sneaking to a movie, taking a drink, smoking a joint or even a cigarette, and above all, being disrespectful in any way of Father, were against Temple rules. Violations were reported to the P.C. by other Temple members. If the accused was found guilty by Jones and the committee, the penalty assessed might be a swat or two, or else extra hours of night work, usually unpleasant chores like cleaning toilets or policing Temple grounds.

To a great extent, the system worked. Temple members seemed, and usually were, law-abiding to the extreme. Their children were exemplary, both in and out of school; when some area parents wouldn't let their offspring associate with Temple kids, it was because of doubt about the Temple itself.

Most locals eventually considered Temple members to be good neighbors, or at least grew accustomed enough to the Temple's presence to tolerate them. Jones's followers were embedded in the district attorney's office, county and town welfare offices, hospitals, care facilities, and almost every other agency and business of consequence.

Yet by 1972, seven years after he brought Peoples Temple west, Mendocino County and Redwood Valley were no longer sufficient to Jones's ambitions. There was no more room to grow, not enough jobs and housing to sustain the multitude of additional followers he intended to attract. He had, for the present, no intention of abandoning Redwood Valley as his headquarters, but Jones wanted additional, permanent bases of operations. Though he'd extended his reach deep into the Midwest and Southwest, preaching in the largest metropolises there, Jones had his eye on two California cities. Each, with its very specific cultural identity, offered unique opportunities for Jim Jones and Peoples Temple. He was eager to take full advantage of both.

CHAPTER THIRTY-ONE: LOS ANGELES

In Los Angeles, the economic and social divide between whites and blacks was as stark as in any major American city. Los Angeles ghettos were desperate places; there, an estimated six in every ten families survived on welfare payments. Impoverished blacks were virtually landlocked into their slums. The city's vast sprawl — about five hundred square miles — and freeway system, along with limited public transportation in poor areas, made it virtually impossible to get from one place to another without automobiles, which many blacks didn't own. Ghetto kids couldn't escape their horrific surroundings with outings to the beach or the green hills outside town. Unemployed adults — in some years, three out of four adult African American men in Los Angeles slums had no jobs — couldn't look for work in districts where business was booming. Even if they got jobs, commuting could prove insurmountable. Constant discomfort was present even overhead: flight paths for the busy Los Angeles International Airport passed directly over the slum known as Watts. In 1972, most Americans were familiar with that name. The Watts riots of the 1960s still resonated. White Angelenos expected black rioters to come streaming into their genteel residential areas, but in reality, by and large young black males took out their frustration and rage on each other. Los Angeles ghettos were battlegrounds for gangs, teens, and twentysomethings who gave up hope for better lives outside the slums and fought each other instead for control of every blighted block. If beaches and decent schools weren't readily available to them, drugs and liquor were. Parents despaired for their children, and were desperate for virtually any source of safety for them.

Another sizable segment of Los Angeles's black slum population was the elderly, often widows, survivors of the wave who came to the city for defense industry jobs during World War II. They lived, for the most part, on Social Security checks, which barely financed even the most basic subsistence living. These old folks lived in constant fear. Violence was all around them. Their few dollars and personal possessions were constantly at risk — lurking addicts in desperate need of a fix were always eager to prey on the old and weak. Understandably, the old people yearned for protection — the LAPD was notoriously slow to respond to calls from Watts — and the opportunity to live out their last years in some degree of comfort.

This made the Los Angeles ghettos a perfect recruiting ground for Peoples Temple. Jones had a built-in potential audience that already had good reason to believe the government was out to get them, that white cops were the enemy, and that it was only right that America should distribute its wealth more equally. For the young, Temple programs offered an alternative to the gangs. Old people could join the Temple, go communal if they chose, and enjoy a lifestyle where everything they needed was provided. From Jones's first occasional expeditions to Los Angeles, he drew large crowds which responded enthusiastically to what he said. Sometimes, seating in rented school auditoriums was insufficient; folding chairs had to be placed in the aisles, and still people were left outside, clamoring to come in and hear Jones preach.

Though these crowds were predominantly black, there were also whites among them, some of them poor and disenfranchised, too, but others well-to-do and hoping to assuage their racial and financial guilt. Racial equality in the form of fairness in employment and housing and justice was becoming a rallying cry among celebrity Los Angelenos. Jane Fonda came to a Peoples Temple service, along with her husband Tom Hayden, the political activist who'd helped found Students for a Democratic Society (SDS). Afterward, she sent Jones a letter enthusiastically praising the Temple. It gave instant cachet to Jones among Los Angeles's liberal glitterati.

In the summer of 1972, Peoples Temple purchased a church and adjacent apartment building at 1336 South Alvarado Street. The property perfectly suited Temple purposes — the church itself, originally built sixty years earlier for another denomination, featured an elegant, columned entrance and enchanting tower. Inside was seating for about 1,200, with capacity for perhaps 1,400 if extra chairs were added. There was a substantial parking lot behind the church. The Temple paid $129,000 for the property, and Jones bragged that "if race wars and concentration camps don't come by 1980," it would eventually be worth $1 million. The lovely Temple building easily outshone the battered church structures that were much more familiar to residents of Watts and South Central. Just by its attractive appearance in a nice setting, Peoples Temple gave the impression of being something more, something special.

Jones wanted the new Los Angeles temple full for weekend services — his Greyhound fleet virtually assured that. On the weekends that he came to preach in Los Angeles, Jones loaded a half dozen buses with Redwood Valley followers and made the drive south, usually on a Saturday afternoon so he could hold Saturday evening and Sunday morning services before returning to Mendocino County. Jones and some of his entourage spent Saturday night in the South Alvarado Street apartments. Others were farmed out to homes of Los Angeles followers.

Once the Greyhounds unloaded Redwood Valley riders at the Los Angeles temple, they set out to pick up ghetto passengers. Though South Alvarado Street was reasonably close to the slums — in other cities, only a quick bus ride or short walk — the distance was still daunting. So the Temple provided transportation, sending the buses to designated pickup points. Attending Peoples Temple became not only safe, but convenient for people who otherwise feared for their lives while walking even a block or two.

Besides Jones's lengthy sermons, there was music and healings, quite dramatic ones involving multiple participants, and even an occasional raising of the dead. Those resurrected were usually longtime members who'd recently offended Jones in some way. Jack Beam would inform the latest soon-to-be corpse that he or she must topple over when confronted by Jones during the service, and lie still until Jones called for them to rise and live again.

And the Temple offered more than entertaining meetings. At the back of the main room, nurses provided tests for hypertension and diabetes. Trained social workers helped with welfare and other government-agency-related issues. Legal advice was available; many Los Angeles members either had relatives in trouble with the law or else had problems themselves. Youngsters with drug problems were brought back to Redwood Valley and placed in the Temple addiction program there. "There was practical help, whatever people needed," says Laura Johnston Kohl.

After services, there were meals out in the parking lot, and lots of friendly social interaction. "What nobody understands now is, we did a lot of things as a church group, and we very often had fun," recalls Juanell Smart. "There were times when it was like a carnival, laughing and having a good time. It was not grim in any way. And we knew then, and you have to realize now, that if not for Jim, all of these people would not have come together."

At first, Smart was reluctant to attend even a single Temple meeting. A federal government worker, Smart was twice divorced and had four children. Her life in Los Angeles was stressful — there were so many dangers for her kids, and her job sometimes required her to travel as part of emergency teams working with victims of natural disasters like floods. In 1971, Kay Nelson, Smart's mother, and Jim McElvane, her uncle, began attending whenever Jones's traveling ministry made a Los Angeles stop. Nelson cared for Smart's children when their mother was away, and she took them to some of Jones's services. Smart, though, resisted Nelson's requests to come along: "Even though my mother and uncle said that this was *it,* I wasn't looking for any kind of enlightenment. I was in another relationship that was going bad, and I was thinking about that."

One Sunday, Nelson took Teri, Smart's youngest daughter, to a Temple service. The service dragged, and Smart needed to pick up her daughter and go somewhere else, so she went inside for the first time. The child was seated in the balcony; Smart had to go up to get her. As she did, she couldn't help listening to Jones preaching down on the stage. "He wasn't talking about God or salvation or anything like that," Smart remembers. "He was talking about real life, and how it hurts women when they make bad choices in men, and it felt like he was talking directly to me . . . everything that man said made sense."

Smart became what she termed "every-other-weekend faithful," coming to the new Los Angeles temple on those Saturday nights and Sunday mornings that Jones preached there. She began dating associate Temple pastor David Wise. But shortly after the permanent Los Angeles temple was established on South Alvarado Street, Smart went out drinking and driving following an argument with Wise. She got into an accident and was arrested. When Kay Nelson arrived to bail Smart out, she brought several Temple counselors with her. They harangued Smart about the evils of alcohol, and on the next Sunday that Jones was in town, he chastised her, too. She didn't like it — "I [was] not a child and [didn't] deserve to be treated like one." After she married Wise, her new husband revealed some Temple secrets to her, including how Jones staged healings: "David took me to this little back room upstairs in the church where they had all these pieces of cut-up chicken that Jim would use. During his healing sessions Jim would tell us all to close our eyes, but after that I never did, and I could see him sometimes taking a chicken part and claiming it was a tumor he'd just removed." After about a year of membership, Smart felt sufficiently disillusioned with Jones to think about quitting Peoples Temple. But all four of her children loved it there, and participated enthusiastically in church youth groups and activities. Smart weighed her personal dissatisfaction against the welfare of her kids and decided, "They're into it 100 percent, and it'll disappoint them if I leave. I thought, 'It's good for my kids to have a church, it's better for them than what's out on the [Los Angeles] streets.' I stayed for my kids and in spite of Jim, and I know I wasn't the only one who did that."

Even on the weekends when Jones wasn't there and Marceline substituted, people still came for the music, health and legal services, and fellowship in a safe environment. Every weekend, Los Angeles contributed considerable sums to Temple coffers, often $25,000 or more — the Temple was popular there, and lucrative. Yet Los Angeles wasn't the ideal Temple location. Its church brought in money, and the conditions of city slums and their desperate residents were such that Jones could always count on a solid base of followers. But city politics and the geography of Los Angeles itself thwarted any ambition he might have had to acquire wider influence in the city. African American Tom Bradley, a former LAPD lieutenant, had already been elected to the city council, and shortly after Peoples Temple founded its South Alvarado Street church, Bradley was elected mayor — he was only the second black man ever elected to head a major U.S. city. The slums still stagnated, providing Jones with plenty of sermon fodder, but Bradley hadn't needed Jim Jones and Peoples Temple to become mayor, and he just as clearly didn't require their support to stay there. (Bradley's tenure extended through 1993.) The new mayor occasionally attended Temple programs, and

Jones maintained a cordial relationship with him, but not in any prominent advisory capacity. Further, though Peoples Temple did considerable good for the poorest ghetto residents, Watts and South Central were so isolated from the rest of the massive city that their programs could never extend to every area.

But Jones had never intended Los Angeles to be his ultimate showcase, a major city where elected officials kowtowed to him and no critical public programs were undertaken without Temple involvement and Jones's approval. Los Angeles had its advantages, from the ripe recruiting grounds of its slums to the wealthy who wanted to ease their social conscience with donations. But Jones had greater ambitions for the Temple, and for himself. It was no longer enough for power brokers to acknowledge the Temple and consult with Jim Jones. He wanted to be a power broker himself. To achieve the stature that he craved, Jones had another city in mind. Los Angeles had *money;* San Francisco offered *influence.*

CHAPTER THIRTY-TWO:
SAN FRANCISCO

San Francisco had long been renowned for attracting colorful eccentrics — the Beats of the 1950s, the hippies of 1967's Summer of Love. Its cultural delights abounded, and the city's hills, winding streets, and location made it arguably the most attractive metropolis in America.

But San Francisco's considerable visual charms and glitzy, liberal reputation were at considerable odds with the makeup and philosophy of its power structure. Historian David Talbot describes 1960s San Francisco as "a city of tribal villages," but only one tribe, the conservative whites, had real power. They decided that tourism would drive San Francisco's economy, and the tourists must see exactly what they expected — a compact, charming place offering lots of irresistible ways to spend money. To that end, certain neighborhoods and ethnic groups were accepted. Chinatown lent itself to the image that city leaders wanted, so it must be maintained. Working-class Irish provided construction muscle, and Italians caught the fish that stocked Fisherman's Wharf markets and the kitchens of upscale restaurants. Gays contributed to San Francisco culture.

Blacks, however, particularly poor ones — and the vast majority of blacks who in 1972 made up 13 percent of San Francisco's 715,000 total population were poor — had no critical role in attracting tourists. If anything, they were considered a detriment — cash-laden visitors to San Francisco wanted to see pretty places, not ghettos. San Francisco's substantial black ghetto, known as the Fillmore for one of its border streets, couldn't be hidden or disguised. So city leaders conspired to eliminate the Fillmore District eyesore altogether. They spent years trying to accomplish their goal. But Fillmore residents tried to fight back. A group of ministers formed the Western Addition Community Organization (WACO) to rally opposition, but the WACO organizers were mostly white and were soon forced out by blacks. This was appropriate in terms of reflecting the district's racial population, but ineffective in making an impression on elected city officials, who had little regard for the demands of those with dark skin.

In general, black ministers whose churches were based in the Fillmore didn't take leading roles in WACO or other efforts to save what remained of the district. J. Alfred Smith, pastor of a politically active black church in Oakland, wrote, "[It was] a dark age for the black church in San Francisco. Most . . . had become little more than social clubs, where chicken dinners and raffle tickets were the only activities on the agenda. After the Sunday morning service was finished, the [San Francisco] church fathers would seal the buildings up tighter than Pharaoh Ramses' tomb."

The city had very few eloquent, energetic black spokesmen. Foremost among them were state assemblyman Willie Brown and Dr. Carlton Goodlett, a general practitioner who also owned a string of newspapers published in black communities including the *Sun-Reporter,* the most influential black newspaper in the Bay area.

By 1972, there was clearly opportunity for some church leader to step forward on behalf of the city's disenfranchised, not only to rally opposition to oppressive city government but also to instill a new sense of community pride. Jim Jones sensed that the time was right, though to lay groundwork rather than pursue a course of immediate confrontation. He demonstrated considerable restraint, inserting himself and his followers incrementally into the city's social and political wars.

It began with the black churches. Beginning in 1970, Jones conducted San Francisco services that were no longer directly affiliated with Macedonia Baptist. His preferred venue was the auditorium at Franklin Junior High on Geary Boulevard and Scott Street in the Fillmore District. The Temple proceedings often didn't directly conflict with Sunday services at Macedonia and other black churches. Saturday afternoons or nights, or Sunday nights, worked fine. Churchgoers who'd enjoyed Jones's sermonizing at Macedonia often came to hear him preach again. They were joined by substantial numbers of those Fillmore residents remaining amid ongoing redevelopment — prior to each Franklin Junior High event, Jones had his followers inundate the district with flyers promising "revelations [by Jones] that no man could possibly know," and "an opportunity to learn the beautiful concepts of apostolic social justice." If that didn't persuade people to come, Jones appealed to their bellies. One flyer promised in capital letters, "FREE BANQUET after services!"

A little before Peoples Temple purchased its Los Angeles property, it also acquired an old multistory building at 1859 Geary Boulevard in San Francisco, a yellow-brick structure in the Fillmore District. The building had a large auditorium with a seating capacity of about 1,800, as well as space for a reception area, and warrens of first floor and upstairs rooms suitable for apartments and offices.

The Temple paid $122,500, and renovation cost an additional $50,000 to $60,000. Until the property fix-up was finished, the Temple continued holding meetings at Franklin Junior High. The Geary Boulevard temple wasn't nearly as imposing as its Los Angeles counterpart, but it was in the right location. Jones set up for business there, alternating his weekend service presence between Los Angeles and San Francisco and spending weekdays in Redwood Valley.

It had always been Jones's habit to poach Temple members from other churches — Laurel Street Tabernacle in Indianapolis, the Church of the Golden Rule in Mendocino County. Now he wanted to lure new members from Macedonia Baptist and other black churches where he had established a reputation and, apparently, cooperative relationships. But this time he was somewhat more subtle. Once Jones was in San Francisco to stay, he didn't make direct appeals for members of these now rival churches to abandon their old congregations and join the Temple. Instead, Jones's sermons emphasized that Temple members enjoyed more of everything — quality preaching, music, fellowship, and healings, and many visitors from other congregations agreed. Pastors of neighboring black churches found themselves losing members. Several took outraged exception, Macedonia's Rev. George Bedford especially.

The black pastors banded together and called on Carlton Goodlett, apparently hoping that the physician-publisher would label Jones and Peoples Temple as rapacious intruders on the pages of the influential *Sun-Reporter*. Instead, they were dismayed to discover that Goodlett was already on board the Temple bandwagon.

Lynetta Jones had become one of Goodlett's patients, and through her, he became acquainted with her son. Goodlett was pleasantly surprised to learn that he and Jones had a great deal in common, particularly a thirst for racial and economic equality. The doctor had long believed that the city's black churches had to become more socially active. When the pastors demanded that Goodlett oppose Jones and the Temple, Goodlett's response was a rewording of Abraham Lincoln's reply to Union generals jealous of General Ulysses S. Grant's unexpected rise to prominence: "This man looks to me like he's pretty successful in interpreting the functional gospel. I don't know what brand of whiskey he drinks, but if he drinks a special brand of whiskey, you better drink it [yourselves]."

Though Jones actively built a faithful San Francisco Temple congregation from new followers lured from other churches, he refrained from similar aggression in city politics. Providing adequate housing for low-income residents wasn't a controversy limited to the

Fillmore District. Though the effort was most extensive in the Western Addition, all over San Francisco houses, apartments, and hotels considered eyesores were being bulldozed in the name of urban renewal and in the service of tourism. In its early days in Mendocino County, Peoples Temple staged a controversial antiwar march down the main streets of Ukiah. Jones said then, "We're here, so they've got to know who we are." He wasn't ready for his new city to know yet. In these first months in San Francisco, not a single Temple member joined WACO sit-ins in front of Redevelopment Agency bulldozers. San Francisco mayor Joseph Alioto faced constant, if essentially futile, criticism from blacks, gays, and other city disenfranchised, but Peoples Temple members sent him gifts of homemade candy and bought a bloc of seats at an Alioto fund-raiser.

Jones maintained a public attitude of pious modesty. He and his people were pleased to be in San Francisco doing good works inspired by the example of Jesus Christ. They aspired to nothing beyond loving service. Privately, Jones reveled in his initial San Francisco foothold and took frequent advantage of new proximity to big-city movie theaters and fine restaurants. Carolyn Layton was his constant companion on these outings. Sometimes they brought Lew, Stephan, Jimmy, and Tim along, but just as often they left the teens in the care of Mike and Suzanne Cartmell, who had an apartment conveniently nearby. The young married couple didn't enjoy being babysitters on demand — the Jones brothers tended to be rowdy and were always ravenous, emptying the Cartmells' refrigerator. But Jones and Carolyn never asked if they'd mind watching the boys or offered to restock their groceries.

Whether enjoying a night out as a couple or else bringing along the children, Jones and Carolyn made no pretense of feeling guilty about enjoying leisure time away from Temple pressures. Once, Planning Commission members were left waiting at a meeting called by Jones while he and Carolyn and the boys lingered over dinner. Jim Jones Jr. remembers that when one of the brothers reminded the adults that the P.C. was supposed to already be in session "Carolyn just laughed, and I guess my dad did, too."

Myrtle Kennedy (*center, standing*) participates in a Nazarene Church baptism in a river near Lynn, Indiana. Jim Jones often referred to her as his "second mother."

Marceline Baldwin, shortly before she became a student nurse and met Jim Jones.

The "Rainbow Family," posing at an Indiana airport. Clockwise they are Jim Jones, Marceline Jones, Suzanne, Jim Jr., Stephan, and Lew. Oldest child Agnes—as usual—is not included.

4

Jim Jones leading a Peoples Temple service, with Marceline standing behind him. Jones kept a vessel on a shelf behind his podium so he could discreetly relieve himself during the hours-long Temple services.

5

All Temple services featured lively musical performances by an orchestra and several choirs. Exceptional music was part of the Temple's appeal to potential members.

Father Divine, whose Peace Mission inspired Jim Jones's plans for Peoples Temple. After Divine's death, Jones tried unsuccessfully to assume leadership of his ministry.

Peoples Temple in Redwood Valley, California. Because of the hostile attitudes of many locals toward the mixed-race congregation, Temple members nicknamed the area "Redneck Valley."

Jim Jones, in a rare photograph without his sunglasses. This photo was taken during his Peoples Temple pastorship in Redwood Valley, California.

9

San Francisco mayor George Moscone shakes Jones's hand at the ceremony naming him to the city housing commission.

10

Temple members traveled the country in their church's fleet of used Greyhound buses, sometimes sleeping outside along the way and, more often, sleeping in cramped seats, luggage racks, and even cargo compartments.

11

*Jim and Marceline Jones
send heartfelt wishes
for a joyous Holiday Season
and a Happy and Blessed New Year*

Marceline and Jim Jones pictured on a family holiday greeting card. Their pleasant expressions disguise the fact that Jones was living with another woman four days a week.

12

GREETINGS
Peoples Temple
Agricultural Project

The sign at the front gate to Jonestown. The wording on the sign changed according to Jones's attitude toward individual visitors.

The massive jungle between Jonestown and the Guyanese capital city of Georgetown on the coast is virtually impenetrable. Yet a few dozen Temple "pioneers" successfully carved out a nearly self-sustaining agricultural mission in this jungle.

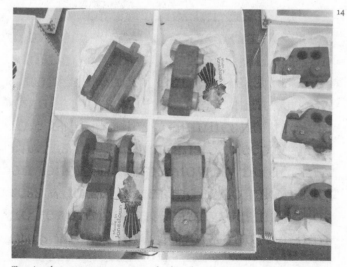

To raise the money necessary to subsidize the Jonestown settlement, residents there crafted wooden toys and cloth dolls to be sold in the stores and open-air markets of Georgetown.

15

Jones's lover and confidante Maria Katsaris's expression demonstrates her disdain for her brother Stephen during his fatal visit to Jonestown in November 1978.

16

On the night of November 17, 1978, Jim Jones introduced John Victor Stoen to the American newsmen who had been allowed into Jonestown. The next day, the child would die by Jones's order.

Congressman Leo Ryan in Jonestown. He survived an initial assassination attempt in the settlement, but died in a hail of gunfire at the airstrip in Port Kaituma.

The scene at the Port Kaituma airstrip following the November 18 attack. Guyanese soldiers who were present at the time refused to intervene because "it was whites killing whites."

Jonestown infants and children had poison squirted into their mouths with syringes. Most of the other settlers drank cups of poison from a vat. Those who resisted were held down by guards and forcibly injected.

Bodies lay scattered around Jim Jones's personal chair that was always in place on the pavilion stage. His followers would sit crammed on long wooden benches as he preached or ranted well into most nights.

21

The body of Jim Jones, found on the stage of the Jonestown pavilion. Instead of ingesting poison, he died from a gunshot wound to the head.

Jonestown seen from the air following the tragedy. The dots around the settlement's pavilion in the center of the photo are the bodies of the victims.

Jonestown after the suicides/murder. Some corpses were so decomposed that U.S. military crews had to use snow shovels to scrape them into body bags.

24

When the first Guyanese military responders reached Port Kaituma on November 19, they were shocked by the carnage at the airstrip.

25

Larry Layton was taken into custody in Port Kaituma on November 18, but a Guyanese court eventually ruled him not guilty of murder. Layton was extradited to the United States, where he was convicted of participating in the murder of a congressman, and served a long sentence before eventual parole.

In the wake of the November 18 suicides and murders, it took several days to learn the total number of Jonestown dead. Guyanese officials were especially anxious to charge someone still living with at least some of the murders, and loyal Jones disciple Chuck Beikman was an obvious candidate.

Along with the other bodies, the body of Jim Jones is prepared for shipment to the United States. Despite the best efforts of medical personnel, hundreds of bodies went unidentified.

Gerald Gouveia, who flew the first plane into Port Kaituma on November 19, 1978, points out where most bodies were found in Jonestown by the Guyanese military on the same morning.

29

Former Guyanese official Kit Nascimento was assigned by Prime Minister Burnham to be Guyana's public spokesman in the wake of the Jonestown tragedy.

30

Except for a few square yards, the jungle has completely overgrown the old Jonestown site. The rusted skeletons of a few trucks and part of the cassava mill are all that remain of the original settlement.

Stephan Jones and Jim Jones Jr. today. Their adult lives have sometimes been difficult, but they remain close to each other and their brother Tim.

The monument to
Peoples Temple dead at
the Jonestown site.

CHAPTER THIRTY-THREE:
NARROW ESCAPES

In San Francisco and Los Angeles, Jones continued the Temple tradition of open and closed meetings. Only in closed meetings did he rant for hours about outside enemies, and how everyone in the Temple was in constant danger, himself most of all. The threats Jones most commonly cited were nuclear war, the U.S. government in general, and the CIA and the FBI in particular. Sometimes he warned of other dangers, first asking the organist to play soft music while he shared alerts with Temple members through his gift of prophecy. These were much more basic than government plots and usually involved relatively mundane, daily activities. No one was to ride a motorcycle for a month — Jones had a vision of spinning wheels, bent handlebars, broken bodies. Jones once urged followers not to use Crest toothpaste: "The only toothpaste that will make your gums resistant to atomic radiation is Phillips toothpaste."

But warnings went only so far in assuring

that followers remained devoted, that they believed unreservedly that only Jim Jones and his powers stood between them and annihilation by Temple enemies. Healings and resurrections during services weren't quite enough. There were only so many variations; though they continued to astound newcomers, to a certain extent those who'd followed Jones for a few years or all the way back to Indiana had already seen these apparent miracles countless times before. Something new for the longtime loyalists, something unforgettably dramatic, was necessary.

During the summer of 1972, when so much of his time and attention were devoted to opening temples in Los Angeles and San Francisco, Jones still conducted some weekend services and weekday catharsis sessions back in Redwood Valley. That was where many veteran followers still lived, dutifully attending the temple there if Jones didn't require them to fill seats in the newly established pair of churches. The Redwood Valley meetings were often led by Archie Ijames and Jack Beam and occasionally Marceline, though more and more she was required to lead weekend services in either Los Angeles or San Francisco while Jones presided in the other city.

On a pleasant day when Jones was present, Redwood Valley members enjoyed a late-afternoon potluck meal in the temple parking lot during the break between morning and evening services. It was a smaller congregation than those in the big cities, perhaps a few hundred followers. Jones, clad in a mustard-colored shirt, mingled with his followers, seemingly in a fine mood. Almost everyone had the opportunity to shake Father's hand or share a warm hug with him. As evening approached and the sky began to darken slightly, the chatter and laughter were drowned out by loud *booms,* one or two or three of them — witnesses could never agree. Someone shouted that these were rifle shots; people screamed and scattered.

Jim Jones slumped on the parking lot pavement, his yellow shirt suddenly splotched with red. He appeared to be limp, almost certainly dead based on the amount of gore, but when Stephan Jones's pet dog went charging into the vineyard on one side of the lot, Jones somehow raised himself to sitting position, pointed to the opposite end, and wheezed, "It's over there, it's over this way," before collapsing again. Temple members racing after the dog reversed direction. Jones had pointed in the general vicinity of a hill, beyond which was a house owned by a Redwood Valley local known to be hostile toward the Temple. But no movement could be discerned at the hill's crest, so everyone returned to the side of their stricken leader. Marceline Jones crouched over her husband;

Jack Beam helped lift him to his feet. As the rest of the Temple members stared, many of them sobbing, Marceline and Beam, along with a few others, helped Jones back into his house adjacent to the church and parking lot. The door closed behind them. Outside, followers stood in anguished vigil, awaiting the inevitable news that Father had died.

Half an hour later, someone announced that the evening service was beginning as scheduled. People filed sorrowfully into the church — perhaps this was when Father's death would be formally announced. Instead, Jones himself came striding to the front, followed by Beam and Marceline and the others who'd carried him off after the shooting. "Tell them," he demanded, and they took turns rhapsodizing about the miracle that had just taken place — Father healed himself! Jack Beam brandished the gory yellow shirt. Jones invited everyone to examine his chest. There was no wound, just a spot, something like a small indentation, where Jones said the bullet had torn through. He declared that this assassination attempt, which would have been successful but for his amazing healing power, proved that enemies with murder on their minds lurked everywhere. Constant vigilance was mandatory. Security at the Redwood Valley temple, and in San Francisco and Los Angeles, would be stepped up — surely everyone now understood the danger

462

that they all were in.

Jones also explained the gesture he'd made immediately after being shot, when he redirected those racing toward the vineyard. Stephan's dog had been right. The shooter really was in the vineyard, Jones said, but in his infinite mercy he hadn't wanted his followers to tear the would-be assassin to pieces with their bare hands, which, in their rage and sorrow, they certainly would have done. So he sent them off in the opposite direction, allowing the shooter to escape with his life. Everyone was so relieved that Father was alive, and so thrilled by this demonstration of his power, that no one suggested calling the police to report the incident. The Redwood Valley temple was sufficiently set apart from the rest of town so that no one else apparently heard the gunfire and contacted the authorities to investigate. This would never have been the case at the San Francisco or Los Angeles temples. Someone would have summoned the police or called for an ambulance. Jones's supposed fatal wound would have been examined on the spot by outsiders. But in Redwood Valley the incident was kept in-house by the Temple — a private, unforgettable manifestation of Jones's healing gift that amazed those who'd been following him longest. Afterward, more of the Temple security guards were armed; some carried rifles in addition to handguns.

463

■ ■ ■ ■

Another assault on Jones came in September 1972, this one in print and very real rather than staged. Jones could orchestrate his own apparent shooting and resurrection, but prominent *San Francisco Examiner* columnist Lester Kinsolving was beyond his control.

In the early 1970s, San Francisco's two major daily newspapers were engaged in a philosophical slugfest. The *Chronicle* embraced the colorful, sometimes whimsical, nature of the city, with the intention of appealing to the widest possible readership. The paper covered all the so-called hard news, but almost every day there was something *fun* to read in the *Chronicle.* Some of the city's most famous rock bands like Jefferson Airplane credited *Chronicle* music critic Ralph Gleason's coverage with helping them build an audience. Columnist Herb Caen entertained subscribers with daily doses of show business rumor, political gossip, and other tidbits that allowed his readers to feel that they were insiders, too. The *Chronicle* didn't shy away from investigative journalism, but one of its most exhaustive series probed why the quality of coffee in San Francisco restaurants and cafés was so uniformly poor. The overall approach was a gamble that worked. *Chronicle* circulation had lagged behind that of the rival *Examiner,* but by the late 1960s and early 1970s, thanks to a deliberately lighthearted approach, it had pulled well ahead.

The *Examiner* took a sterner approach. Coverage of a major city was serious business; frivolity was for lesser publications. San Francisco business and political leaders much preferred the *Examiner* to the *Chronicle,* with good reason: its editorial tone reflected their own conservative beliefs. The *Chronicle* had Caen, blabbing on about who was seen drinking after hours and where in the city he'd nicknamed "Baghdad by the Bay." By contrast, the *Examiner* offered religion reporter and columnist Kinsolving, by background a fourth-generation Episcopal priest who turned to journalism after years spent working in the church hierarchy.

Jones had already made friendly connections at the *Chronicle,* and felt confident that he could essentially control coverage in both major San Francisco dailies just as he did with the much smaller newspaper in Ukiah. Jones had no sense that when two daily newspapers competed for primacy in a major city, each was constantly on the lookout for sensational stories that would one-up the other. In the late summer of 1972, Kinsolving apparently found one.

Cindy Pickering, a reporter for the *Indianapolis Star,* wanted to keep tabs on Jones and the Temple after the *Star*'s sensational stories about Jones's claim in Indiana a year earlier of successfully raising the dead. Learning that the Temple was establishing a new San Francisco church, she wrote to the *Examiner* news department asking for details. Kinsolving's editors forwarded the letter to him. He'd already heard rumors about Peoples Temple, and the *Star*'s stories intrigued him enough to contact the *Ukiah Daily Journal* and ask what they knew about this church and self-proclaimed healer. Kinsolving's suspicions were aroused when dozens of letters praising Jones and the Temple began arriving at the *Examiner,* and when he learned that management at the *Daily Journal* had contacted a Temple official to warn him that a San Francisco reporter was snooping around. That official was Tim Stoen, whom Kinsolving discovered worked in the Mendocino County district attorney's office.

His investigative instincts now thoroughly aroused, Kinsolving got to work. He went with a photographer to a Redwood Valley service. The photographer wasn't allowed inside, but he and Kinsolving saw several armed bodyguards in the parking lot. At a second service Kinsolving attended in San Francisco, Jones, who obviously knew the reporter was present, put on a show, which included two resuscitations of followers who apparently died, as well as other healings.

But he also took great pains in responding after a "healed" follower cried out that Jones was Jesus: "What do you mean by that? If you believe that I am the Son of God in that I am filled with love, I can accept that. I won't knock what works for you — but I don't want to be interpreted as the creator of the universe. If you say, 'He is God,' some people will think you are nuts. They can't relate. I'm glad that you were healed, but I'm really only a messenger of God. I have a paranormal ability in healing."

Kinsolving began looking for sources who didn't idolize Jones, and besides the same ministers of black San Francisco churches who'd previously complained to Carlton Goodlett, he also found a few former Temple members who were willing to talk. Tim Stoen didn't help the situation when, acting on Jones's behalf, he sent Kinsolving a letter explaining why the reporter shouldn't write an article about Jones: "Whenever there is publicity, the extremists seem to show themselves." In the same letter, Stoen swore that "Jim has been the means by which forty persons have literally been brought back from the dead this year," and offered a graphic account of resurrections by Jones that he had personally witnessed.

Negative press coverage, especially in the conservative *Examiner,* was exactly what Jones didn't want as he attempted the tricky task of building a base congregation of San Francisco's disenfranchised without alienating its white power structure. But beginning on Sunday, September 17, 1972, he got that and more, the first in what was advertised to be a series of eight articles, each exposing apparent fraud and even violence on the part of Jones and the Temple. Sunday morning's headline was "The Prophet Who Raises the Dead." In short, dramatic paragraphs, Kinsolving presented an image bound to startle, and almost certainly repulse, any reader:

REDWOOD VALLEY — A man they call The Prophet is attracting extraordinary crowds from extraordinary distances to his People's [*sic*] Temple Christian (Disciples) Church in this Mendocino County hamlet.

His followers say he can raise the dead.

. . . And one director claims that the Prophet has returned life to "more than 40 persons . . . people stiff as a board, tongues hanging out, eyes set, skin graying, and all vital signs absent."

There was more, including descriptions of "impressively armed guards . . . attendants at services [wearing] pistols in their gun belts." Kinsolving related how the Ukiah newspaper was apparently under Temple control, and emphasized that Mendocino County "assistant prosecuting attorney" Timothy O.

468

Stoen doubled as "assistant to The Prophet." Kinsolving's description of other Temple works besides Jones's "claim[ed] . . . resurrections" was confined to two sentences: "A 40-acre children's home, 3 convalescent centers, and 3 college dormitories. Other operations: A heroin rehabilitation center and, in the words of one of the Temple's three attorneys, 'our own welfare system.' "

Even these were presented in terms of income rather than people served: " 'Grand total income' is said to have been $396,000 for the year ending June 30, 1972.' " And, after extensively quoting from Stoen's letter about Jones's excessive personal modesty, Kinsolving neatly skewered the Temple leader's obvious ego: "Stoen's written affirmation of the self-effacement of The Prophet did not include any explanation for the three tables just outside the main entrance of the People's [*sic*] Temple. These tables are loaded with either photographs, or neck pieces and lockets — all bearing the image of the Rev. Mr. Jones, and on sale at prices running from $1.50 to $6.00."

Kinsolving closed out his Sunday installment with a description of the Temple's frantic efforts to persuade the *Examiner* not to run any story and that Stoen swears his leader " 'wears only used clothing and takes in abandoned animals.' Meanwhile, [Jones's] sturdy bodyguards lend the temporal assur-

469

ance that the Temple of The Prophet is the best-armed house of God in the land."

The Sunday article was a blow to Jones and the Temple, but there were errors in Kinsolving's reporting, from adding an extraneous apostrophe in "People's" to stating that Jones's followers routinely referred to him as "The Prophet." Though Jones frequently claimed to be a prophet, among other things, he was always called "Jim" or "Father." Other information in the story was incorrect — Kinsolving identified eleven Greyhounds when there were a dozen, and claimed "no less than 165 Indianapolis Temple-ites" followed Jones from Indianapolis to Redwood Valley when it was slightly more than half that number. Though reportorial balance was expected from established, big-city daily newspapers, even in the hardest-hitting investigative stories, Kinsolving wrote nothing about those genuinely served by Temple outreach programs. Almost one-third of the article was based on a single letter from Tim Stoen. Jones would have been justified in making a controlled complaint to the *Examiner,* contacting its newsroom that same day and formally requesting corrections, though not a complete retraction since some of what Kinsolving wrote was based on his first-person observations, and also on a letter

Jones could not deny that Tim Stoen had written.

Instead, Jones panicked, and rather than acting immediately, waited with a mounting sense of horror to see what the *Examiner* would print the next day. The promise of an eight-day series, and the tone of the first installment, indicated that the reporter must have accumulated a considerable amount of additional, damaging research material. To a far greater extent than even his closest intimate among Temple followers, Jones realized all the questionable things he'd done — what had Kinsolving discovered?

Monday's article — " 'Healing' Prophet Hailed as God at S.F. Revival" — reemphasized Jones's healing displays during Temple services, touched on the claim by a healed follower that Jones was God and his response, and described the armed guards in the Temple parking lot. A Marceline Jones musical solo was described: the "trim blonde" sang "My Black Baby" while Jimmy Jones ("a handsome boy of 14") stood nearby. Marceline's performance of that song was a Temple standby. Temple music directors had rewritten a few lyrics to "Brown Baby," a tune popularized by Nina Simone. Temple songs were often revamped versions of popular hits.

This second story was also worrisome, and now Jones decided to act. On Tuesday morning, his Redwood Valley followers received

471

orders to gather in the Temple parking lot. Even Temple kids were kept out of school so they could join their parents on the buses waiting in the lot. Only after they had boarded and were heading south was an explanation offered: the *Examiner* had printed something bad about Father and the Temple. Temple members hadn't marched or protested in San Francisco against the Fillmore District's deliberate demolition or in support of any other public cause, but they were summoned into action for this. Jones's followers were dropped off in front of the *Examiner*'s building; some were given signs to wave ("This Paper Has Lied"), and everyone was instructed, "Keep marching, and don't talk to anyone." The protest garnered considerable coverage. Kinsolving, delighted at the response, came out to personally greet the protesters, who walked and waved their signs for several hours.

On Tuesday they were back again, bolstered by a busload of the Temple's students from Santa Rosa Community College. Kinsolving's third installment, "D.A. Aide Officiates for Minor Bride," focused on Stoen marrying teen Mildred Johnson to another Temple member. Kinsolving questioned whether Stoen was properly certified to do so — Stoen "contended, 'I meet all the requirements of the State Civil Code,' " but the reporter didn't agree. Kinsolving quoted "Mr. and

472

Mrs. Cecil Johnson" of Indianapolis, Mildred's parents, former Temple members who'd relocated to Mendocino County with Jones, became disenchanted with him, and returned to Indiana. The Johnsons told of how Jones predicted nuclear catastrophe in July 1967, and promised followers they'd survive only by moving west with him. Much worse was Kinsolving's paraphrasing of the Johnsons' description of how Jones tricked followers into believing he could read minds: "[He] uses people to visit potential church members, noting anything personal in the house, like addresses on letters, types of medicine in the medicine cabinet, or pictures of relatives. Then, when [the prospective members] show up in church, he tells them things about their ailments and the kinds of pills they take."

Stoen responded in the article for Jones and the Temple: "I don't remember anything like this. I believe Jim's gift is authentic."

There were still five installments scheduled, and the Temple protesters had no intention of giving up. Their numbers increased daily, and so did coverage of the protest by other Bay Area media. On Wednesday, when the *Examiner* ran Kinsolving's "Probe Asked of People's [*sic*] Temple," John Todd, one of the paper's editors, came outside to meet with Jones. That day's installment was by far the weakest. Its gist was that Rev. Richard G.

Taylor, a former pastor of Ukiah's First Baptist Church and now a denominational regional official, had asked the Mendocino County district attorney and sheriff to investigate alleged Temple misconduct, including any possible involvement in the suicide of a local woman. Jones told Todd that Kinsolving must have some personal grudge against him. Stoen suggested ominously that what the *Examiner* had printed so far was "morally reprehensible and legally libelous." Jones and Todd agreed that the Temple leader would meet with *Examiner* reporters, and Kinsolving would be excluded. But Todd would not agree that certain elements Jones considered objectionable — for instance, identifying him as "The Prophet" — would be eliminated from subsequent installments.

Jones need not have worried. *Examiner* senior editors and the newspaper's attorneys made the decision to cancel the four final articles. These were increasingly accusatory, alleging that the Temple stole from Maxine Hawpe's estate and threatened "Mrs. Cecil Johnson" by phone for her family's cooperation with Kinsolving. The reporter had tracked down Whitey Freestone, one of Jones's favorite targets for verbal abuse before he quit the Temple, and Whitey and his wife, Opal, had lots of nasty, but unsubstantiated, things to say. Rev. George Bedford, pastor of San Francisco's Macedonia Missionary Baptist Church, told about Jones and other Temple members abusing his congregation's trust, and Rev. L. S. Jones of the city's Olivet Baptist Church, who'd lost members to the Temple, called Jones a "sheep stealer." Bedford claimed that he'd recently buried "three [members] who became involved with Jones and the People's [sic] Temple." Kinsolving also wrote that 4,700 among Ukiah's total population of 10,300 were Temple members, when in fact only a few hundred Jones followers remained in town.

"The People's [sic] Temple and Maxine Hawpe," "The Reincarnation of Jesus Christ — in Ukiah," "Jim Jones Defames a Black Pastor," and "Sex, Socialism and Child Torture with Rev. Jim Jones" were never published in the *Examiner,* even though subsequent events proved some of Kinsolving's allegations in the stories to be true, particularly that Temple members were punished in cruel and unusual ways for minor transgressions.

Jones guessed that Kinsolving wouldn't let the matter rest. To eliminate the *Examiner* reporter as a threat, Jones turned to one of the newest Temple members. In Brazil, evangelist Ed Malmin's teenage daughter, Bonnie, had lived for a while with the Jones family. They lost contact for several years, but in 1971 Bonnie, now married to a former Bible student and living in California, reconnected with the Joneses. She attended some Temple services and eventually joined. She resumed a warm friendship with Marceline, and Jones appointed Bonnie to the Planning Commission. She was shocked to hear other members talking about Jones's serial infidelity to Marceline, but wrote later that Jones "never tried anything illicit with me."

After Kinsolving's first articles appeared in the *Examiner,* Jones asked Bonnie, who was very attractive, "Do you think you could seduce Kinsolving and get him off our back?"

She felt an obligation to protect the church in any way necessary and told Jones that she would try. But she never had to follow through because Jones found a better way to stymie the reporter.

To counter the four negative *Examiner* articles that had been published, Jones instructed that packets of positive newspaper stories be gathered and sent to various publications, including church magazines. Some material appeared under the letterhead of Rev. John V. Moore, Carolyn's father and a distinguished leader in the regional Methodist Church. Though there was no actual message from Reverend Moore, the clear implication was that he had collected and sent the glowing stories rather than Jones and his followers. Moore learned about it only when he was contacted by the editor of *Christianity Today,* who wanted to know why he was endorsing Peoples Temple. Moore was furious, and became more so when Lester Kinsolving found out about the packets and demanded an interview with him. Grudgingly, Moore granted the interview at his house across the bay from San Francisco. It didn't go well. Kinsolving was hard at work on the follow-up to the Temple stories, and knew that two of Moore's daughters were members. Moore recalls, "It was not a friendly conversation. He seemed to want facts and if not that, then innuendo. I asked him to leave and he did, but after he did I discovered that he had left his briefcase behind."

Moore decided he would send Kinsolving's briefcase back to him, but spoke to his daughters Carolyn and Annie before he did. When Moore mentioned the briefcase, they asked him and their mother, Barbara, to come to the Temple at once to discuss the matter. The Moores went, but as a precaution left the briefcase at their house. At the San Francisco temple, Jones and a few other Temple leaders demanded to be given the briefcase. Moore refused. Finally, Jones and the others seemed to give up.

"They kept pleading and pleading and then, all at once, stopped," Reverend Moore remembers. "My wife and I went home, and I sent the briefcase back to the reporter. Only later did we learn that while we were kept occupied at the Temple, someone, I suspect our daughter Annie, went to our house and copied everything that was in the briefcase. So after that, Jim Jones knew exactly who [Kinsolving] had been talking to, and what facts he had or didn't have about Peoples Temple."

After perusing copies of the briefcase contents, Jones felt reasonably certain that Kinsolving didn't have enough new information to write more Temple exposés — or, at least, that there wasn't enough solid evidence for the *Examiner*'s management to agree to publish them. Still, he didn't intend to be surprised by the print media again. Jones established a new Temple department called Diversions, and told Terri Buford that she would run it.

" 'Diversions' meant that we would divert the press's attention from Jim," Terri Buford later explained.

Buford and several assistants began searching out information about other controversial preachers with large followings — Reverend Ike and Rev. Sun Myung Moon in particular. "We went through newspapers and magazines, police records, getting anything that looked bad, and sent copies on ahead to the media in whichever towns Jim would be preaching in next. We'd write letters to the editors of the city papers about it, and call the TV stations. We had one woman who'd call the TV people and say this or that preacher tried to have sex with her, or else had an illegitimate baby. We also started going through the trash at local magazines and newspapers, trying to see what the writers there were up to."

Jones bragged during Planning Commission meetings that Buford and the rest of the Diversions team was so good at sniffing out scandal, they could provide him the means to destroy anyone he pleased. "He made it sound like we were terrorists or something, that no one was safe from us if we wanted to get them," Buford says. "It got so that lots of people on the Planning Commission were afraid of me. They thought if they did even the slightest thing that Jim didn't like, [Diversions] might come after them next."

CHAPTER THIRTY-FOUR: REACHING OUT

Despite what Jones and his followers had feared, Lester Kinsolving's published stories did no damage. Even Mayor Alioto was sympathetic to Jones and his church. Alioto never attended a Temple service, but Joe Johnson, one of his assistants, did. When Jones invited Johnson to say a few words, the city official effusively praised the Temple for its good works. A few months later, when Jones prepared to lead Temple members on a cross-country trip that would culminate in Washington, D.C., Alioto sent a "To Whom It May Concern" letter ahead on his personal stationery, urging police and government officials in Houston, Chicago, Philadelphia, and the nation's capital to extend "every courtesy and consideration" to Jim Jones and his people, whose social service programs "are extremely supportive of local law enforcement."

Kinsolving's stories helped with Temple recruitment, too. He'd intended to expose

Jones as a fraud for claiming he could raise the dead. Instead, the Temple was contacted by people all over the country, some of them terminally ill and hoping for a miracle, others just willing to follow anyone with the power to revive the deceased.

One of the prospective members who'd read the *Examiner* stories without being put off was Tim Carter, a white, sometimes homeless Vietnam veteran who had been emotionally scarred by his experiences there, and by a painful childhood where his mother died and his alcoholic father provided corporal punishment rather than nurturing. Following his discharge from the military, Carter wandered around the West for several years, seeking out various spiritual leaders. Then Carter heard about Jones and his church, and in January 1973, along with his sister, Terry, pooled what little money they had and traveled to the Geary Boulevard temple. A black Temple member, Lee Ingram, intercepted the Carters at the entrance — Carter learned later that Jones considered white males to be the most likely government spies. He and his sister were escorted "to a good-sized room and interrogated, though it felt like more of a conversation because they were so good at it." For several hours, Carter told about himself, how during the worst of his war experiences he experienced a spiritual epiphany that left him certain there were great powers at work, and great possibilities for humanity.

That convinced his interrogators to let the Carters attend the meeting. They climbed to seats in the balcony; as they seated themselves, Jones launched into a sermon that, to Carter, "was the synthesis of everything I believed spiritually and politically." Mesmerized, Carter was eager to contribute when a collection plate was passed, but he only had some pocket change. "I whispered to Terry, 'I hope you've got money for cigarettes, because I've just given my last sixty-eight cents.' " After the collection, Jones pointed dramatically up to the balcony, finger jabbing directly at Tim Carter, and announced, "You gave your last sixty-eight cents, and that means more than people who can afford to give a hundred dollars." Carter was stunned. "I thought, 'This guy has psychic ability.' What I didn't realize was that they had a guy planted in the row right behind Terry and me. He wrote what I'd said on a card and passed it to somebody who passed it to Jones. By the time that meeting was over, I felt that I'd come home."

After the service, Carter was stunned by how naturally blacks and whites interacted in the temple lobby. There was food for sale, and it all smelled and looked wonderful. Since Jones had announced to everyone that Carter had no more money, someone treated the former GI to a plate of collard greens. Then Jones himself came up, held out his hand, and said, "Hi, I'm Jim." As they left Peoples Temple, Carter and his sister debated who Jim Jones must have been in previous lives — Jesus? An apostle?

Carter attended another meeting in Los Angeles, and was told, "Father wants to know if you want to move up with us in Redwood Valley." When he replied that he had no money to get there, Carter was assured he didn't need any. Carter joined the Temple. So did Terry and their brother Mike.

In Redwood Valley, Carter worked in the Temple letters office all day and then filed index cards for most of the night. He lived in East House, one of the Temple communes, along with eleven others and loved it. Soon, Jones gave Carter the responsibility of organizing Temple bus trips. The details involved were staggering, and when Carter confessed he didn't think he had the experience or talent to do the job well, he was assured that Father believed in him. So Carter tried, and, to his amazement, discovered he had a talent for organization and planning. Jim Jones apparently knew him better than he knew himself. It reinforced his belief in and loyalty to Jim Jones, who clearly was something more than human.

Temple recruitment efforts didn't always go as smoothly. About the same time Tim

Carter first visited the Geary Boulevard temple, Merrill Collett did, too. He and his wife lived in the Western Addition, about a dozen blocks away from the church. Collett, who is white, was intrigued by his black neighbor's description of what a Temple service was like and wanted to see for himself. Like Carter and his sister, the Colletts were stopped in the lobby and required to speak with Temple members. As they were escorted to a small room, Collett noticed a table in the hall stacked with copies of an article in a recent issue of *Psychology Today:* in "Violence and Political Power — The Meek Don't Make it," sociologist William Gibson concluded that "in the U.S. experience, a group that wants political clout and recognition is likely to do better when it is large, centrally organized, and ready to fight if push comes to shove."

Their questioning by Temple members was periodically drowned out by the tune being loudly performed in the adjacent auditorium as part of the service — Collett was surprised that it sounded like "a rhythm-and-blues ensemble, not a gospel choir." Eventually the Colletts were allowed to go sit "in one of the very upper rows" of the auditorium balcony. One of their interrogators, a young white man, went with them, and immediately offended the couple by informing them that they were about "to be niggerized." He gestured down at the main body of congregants on the floor, many of them older, most of them standing up and dancing to the pulsating music, and explained that "What we really have is two churches," one comprised of politically astute members working to bring about social change, and the other made up mostly of pensioners "[who] won't take a shit unless they're read[ing] the Bible, but they're the backbone of the church."

Collett felt violently repelled by Jim Jones, who "was in dark glasses . . . swaggering around on the stage in full paranoia mode, violently denouncing this and that cabal who were out to get him and the church. He scared the bejeezus out of me." When the service finally ended, Collett says, "I was thrilled to get back into sunlight and fresh air." The Colletts did not join.

But many did, and in some of these recruits Jones found exceptional qualities that he and his church badly needed. One of his strengths was not casting his congregational net toward a single type of individual or personality. It was as though Jones could almost effortlessly reach out into the communities around him and pluck those individuals whose talents and experience perfectly qualified them to serve him and the Temple in different, critical ways.

Prior to joining the Temple, Jean Brown was a Republican committeewoman from Mendocino County, making her a natural conduit to that party's politicians. Brown became one of the Temple's most effective public relations operatives, often dealing with the staffs of elected officials and various other government entities. In Brown, Jones had an advisor who understood the best methods of communicating the Temple's socialist goals without unduly alarming conservatives. Sandy Bradshaw was a probation officer in Ukiah. Bradshaw's expertise was invaluable as the Temple attempted to rehabilitate young offenders separately from the justice system. Bob Houston was a teacher at the same Mendocino County public school as Carolyn Layton. A gifted musician, writer, and an innovative educator, Houston was a perfect father figure for troubled teens who became legal wards of the Temple. Gene Chaikin, a deputy counsel for Shasta County in California, attended some services in Redwood Valley and volunteered to work with Tim Stoen on the Temple's legal affairs. He soon quit his county job and joined the Temple, working for Jones full-time. Chaikin's wife, Phyllis, was equally driven to contribute to the Temple cause. At Jones's request, she earned a nursing degree so that she could help manage the church's extensive senior care operations. Dick Tropp was a former college professor whose insightful intellect and exceptional communication skills were assets to Jones from the first day Tropp joined the Temple. Tropp brought with him his sister

Harriet, an especially articulate former law student with a gift for sorting out organizational problems and a knack for solving them. For Jones, her only drawback was her fearlessness: Tropp became the Temple member most likely to tell Jones the truth, even if he didn't want to hear it.

Michael Prokes was a television newscaster in Modesto, California. In the fall of 1972, he read Lester Kinsolving's stories about Jones and Peoples Temple, and decided to do his own investigation, either for a television segment or as the basis for a book. But when Prokes met Jones and other Temple members, he was struck to such an extent by their commitment to social equality that he joined the Temple himself. Perhaps Prokes, among all of Jones's followers, identified most with the church's political aspects. One day in San Francisco, Tim Carter mentioned something to him about faith, and Prokes replied, "Cut out that Jesus shit. We're socialists." Prokes became a Temple spokesman, issuing statements and dealing with the media whenever Jones didn't want to appear or go on the record himself. Edith Roller earned a graduate degree in creative writing and, prior to joining the Temple, served both the United Nations and U.S. Office of Strategic Services overseas. She was assigned by Jones to keep a daily history of life as a Temple member. He intended Roller's journal to be used as part of an eventual Temple history to be published through the church printing operations.

All these individuals played significant roles in Temple history, but two more became especially prominent.

Johnny Moss Brown, a native of the Fillmore District, was a tough, street-smart black man in his twenties who was exactly the person Jim Jones needed to reach out to disaffected young members of the Western Addition. Brown had credibility with the gangs and a personal passion for justice that made him a natural leader in any setting. Pragmatic and articulate, he was loyal to the Temple and to Jones without descending to a level of unquestioning devotion. Some members were afraid of Brown, but they all respected him. Even Jones was reasonably straightforward with Brown; to be anything else would have risked losing him for the Temple cause.

Maria Katsaris loved children and animals. Her father, Steven, was a former Greek Orthodox priest who became headmaster at Trinity School in Ukiah. He was divorced; Maria and her brother, Anthony, lived with their father and his second wife. Maria took a job as a teacher's aide at her father's school, where she became friends with Liz Foreman, another staffer. Foreman was also a member of Peoples Temple, and, like all of Jones's followers, actively proselytized for him and the church. Steven and Anthony Katsaris weren't impressed with Jones and the Temple, but Maria joined. Her first church assignment was in the letters office, where fellow worker Tim Carter remembers her as "maybe nineteen or twenty, [and] the shyest person I'd ever met. Maria was very sweet, but she had trouble looking people in the eye, she was so bashful." Still, Maria's devotion to the Temple and its leader was complete. Steven Katsaris soon noticed that his daughter no longer had much time for him, her brother, and her stepmother. She was always occupied with Temple chores.

Late 1972 and early 1973 were fine times for Jim Jones. Amphetamines put a spring in his step and other drugs helped him sleep at night, but for the moment there were few outward signs of physical or mental deterioration. He had all of the sex that he wanted with multiple partners. Marceline remained his supportive public partner. Recruitment was at an all-time high, and the Temple was getting just the right mix of new members — seniors with their monthly Social Security checks, young whites with money and professional skills to put at the Temple's disposal, and, always, the genuinely needy, abused or shunned by the rest of the world but warmly welcomed into Temple fellowship. Money poured in, too; Jones used some of it to demonstrate that, despite the Temple's recent wrangle with the *Examiner,* he and his church not only believed in, but actively supported freedom of the press. The Temple made regular, substantial contributions to various journalism-related causes, and backed up the donations with action. When four reporters from the *Fresno Bee* were briefly incarcerated for refusing to reveal names of story sources, Jones packed Temple buses and went with five hundred followers to join a protest march on the jailed journalists' behalf.

At times, a sense of playfulness lightened Jones's usual grim sermons during members-only Temple services. Preaching exclusively to his followers, Jones habitually peppered his pronouncements with obscenities. Temple members loved it — Father was talking like a real person, not acting prissy like so many pastors. At one Geary Boulevard service, Jones launched into a tangent about how cursing allowed people to blow off steam, and helped cope with painful situations and emotions. He knew it, he believed everyone in the congregation knew it, and he wanted the rest of the world to realize it, too. Jones ordered the auditorium windows opened, and then commanded everyone to shout "Fuck!" in unison. They did, and Jones insisted that they do it again and they did, finally bellowing the same culturally forbidden epithet over and over for a full minute, with passersby on the sidewalks outside certainly puzzled and probably alarmed by what they heard. Inside the temple, everyone shook with laughter. Sometimes, apostolic socialism was *fun.*

Perhaps Jones felt too cocky. It had been a pattern in his life that when things were going best, Jones acted as his own worst enemy. In January 1973 he did it again, making a misstep that, at the time, didn't seem especially consequential.

Jones taught his followers that they should behave a certain way if confronted by police: "Stand there calm, and make eye contact. Don't act guilty or afraid, or threatening, either. Look them in the eye, and be the one in charge." Followers braced by cops were to keep their arms crossed — that reassured the officers, who had to be alert for potential attack. Jones followed his own advice. Many followers remembered a particular incident during a road trip through Chicago, where bullying city police tried hassling Temple members and Father cooled things down, looking the cops in the eye, talking quietly but firmly, keeping his arms crossed — the cops backed off.

But outside the Los Angeles temple on January 7, 1973, things were different. During Jones's Saturday evening sermon, an elderly female member fainted. It wasn't a planned, fake collapse so that Jones could apparently revive her. Marceline Jones, a trained nurse, examined the old woman and had someone call an ambulance.

Whatever concern Jones felt for his fallen follower was mitigated by this affront to his healing powers. Father didn't need medics to cure whatever was wrong with the lady. But within minutes a city ambulance, sirens wailing, roared up outside the temple. Medical personnel rushed inside, gathered up the old woman, who was still woozy, and helped her out. A crowd of Temple members followed, many concerned for their friend, some infuriated that one of their own was being taken away by outsiders.

Johnny Brown was serving that Saturday as one of the temple security guards. He was armed, and had a license to carry his weapon. When Brown snapped at the attendants not to put the befuddled lady in the ambulance, one of them used a radio to summon police. Squad cars raced to the scene. Police tried to move Brown and Clay Jackson, another armed Temple guard, away, and they resisted. Many Temple members at the scene lived in the nearby ghetto, where residents considered themselves in a virtual state of war with white city police. They shouted support for Brown and Jackson, and for a few moments a full-scale riot seemed possible. Then Jones appeared, calling out for everyone to stand back. Police arrested Brown and Jackson, who were cuffed, placed in patrol cars, and taken to jail. Jones told his followers to go back into the temple and continue the service without him. Then he left with the police, too. It wasn't clear whether he'd also been arrested, or was just going along to help sort out the mess.

Soon Jones was back, with Brown and Jackson following later. The Temple guards were charged with disturbing the peace and later convicted. Jones was never cited. There is apparently no record of what became of the stricken woman. Though Jones was never formally cited for any offense that night, he bragged in subsequent sermons that he'd been tossed in a cell with men who the cops believed were the worst, most dangerous thugs in city custody, and not only won over his fellow inmates, but refused to leave the jail until all of the others were released, too.

But Los Angeles police had long memories. Though all the armed Temple guards had permits for their weapons, the sight that night of well-armed black men circling in front of a menacing mob alarmed the cops, and their superiors felt the same concern when they read reports about the incident. That the black troublemakers were led — incited? — by a white preacher made it worse. And so Jim Jones became known to the L.A. cops as an antagonist and someone to watch carefully. City government might think Jones was all right, but the police were an entirely separate entity. Before, Jones and Peoples Temple hadn't been blips on the LAPD radar. But now, all Jones had to do was to take one additional wrong step. They'd be waiting.

For the time being, Jones had no idea. But he'd learn.

CHAPTER THIRTY-FIVE: THE GANG OF EIGHT

Black people were integral to Jim Jones's ambitions. Without black followers, and black causes to encourage and support, Jones might have ended up pastoring a tiny Methodist congregation in backwater Indiana, largely frustrated and entirely unknown. Racial injustice was a common theme in his sermons. Most whites might think themselves superior, he preached, but in fact it was better, more *righteous,* to be black: "Black is a disposition, to act against evil, to do good." Yet despite this incessantly professed love and admiration for blacks, few held positions of actual authority in the Temple. As years passed, Archie Ijames's position became more ceremonial. When he presided over services in Jones's absence, Jones usually arranged for a tape of one of his previous sermons to be played rather than allow Ijames to preach extensively himself. Johnny Brown gradually assumed a secondary leadership role, but when he joined the Temple in San Francisco he was initially relegated to security duty. For years, no followers challenged the racial disparity among Temple leaders. But when it finally happened, the consequences were potentially dire.

Peoples Temple provided an array of worthwhile social services, all intended to improve lives. Arguably the most unusual, and one frequently pointed to with pride, was providing free college education to deserving young followers. The opportunity wasn't automatic. At any time, only three or four dozen students might be involved, most of them from families with multigenerational Temple membership. Their parents and perhaps grandparents, sisters and brothers and cousins, all followed Jones. The institution they attended on the Temple's dime was Santa Rosa Community College. Mike Cartmell, Patty Cartmell's son and now Jones's son-in-law, had graduated and was going on to law school. Several of the Temple's young women took courses at Santa Rosa CC in preparation to serve their church as nurses.

The Temple purchased three apartments in Santa Rosa and converted them into dormitories. Though students received free room and board as well as tuition, they were expected to live communally with the other Temple students. No one was allowed to live alone in his or her own apartment. This saved money, which allowed more students to be subsidized, and also let Jones, more in theory than in practice, keep a closer eye on everyone. He appointed a "college committee" of adult Temple members who were charged with visiting the students every Tuesday night to offer advice concerning any problems, and, not coincidentally, to check on their grades. Those not maintaining decent class averages could give the outside world a bad impression of Peoples Temple, and might, at Jones's discretion, be removed from school anytime.

Besides faithfully attending classes and studying late into the night, the students were also expected to attend Temple services and constantly be on call. The only thing that trumped school obligations was serving the Temple in whatever way Jones wanted. When Jones ordered followers to picket the *San Francisco Examiner,* a bus stopped in Santa Rosa for the college kids. On weekends, the students were also expected to participate in weapons training — it remained the younger followers' obligation to defend senior members in the event of world war or any other life-threatening scenario. Jones expected a lot of the college students, including their gratitude. In his view, no one owed the church more.

Occasionally, one of the Temple's Santa Rosa students rebelled and left both the school and the Temple. One young woman fled after Jones took her to task for practicing vegetarianism. All the other students ate meat; by being different, she was effectively raising herself above them, acting elite. When Jones forced her to eat a few bites of chicken, she ran away. There was no attempt to persuade her to return. She'd proven herself unworthy.

Jim Cobb was a different matter. The young black man was unhappy with the makeup of Jones's inner circle, all of them white. For months, he stayed in school but boycotted services in Redwood Valley to protest the racism he perceived. The Cobb family was Temple bedrock — they'd been followers since Indianapolis. Cobb's mother eventually wore him down; he came back to services and made a public apology. But the leadership inequity continued to trouble him, and he learned that a few other students felt the same way. They reinforced one another's misgivings, and in the fall of 1973 eight Santa Rosa students — Cobb, Mickey Touchette, John Biddulph, Vera Biddulph, Lena Flowers, Tom Podgorski, Wayne Pietila, and Terri Cobb Pietila, four white, four black — packed and abruptly left the area, certain that Jones would send followers to track them down.

They left behind a letter for him, explaining what they'd done: "To put it in one word — staff. The fact is, the eight of us have seen a grotesque amount of sickness displayed by staff. The ridiculous double standard and

498

dishonesty that's practiced does not agree with us."

They stressed that their quarrel wasn't with Jones himself ("To us, you are the finest socialist and leader this earth has ever seen"), but with those he allowed to influence him: "You said that the revolutionary focal point at present is in the black people. There is no potential in the white population, according to you. Yet, where is the black leadership, where is the black staff and black attitude? . . . Black people are being tapped [in the Temple] for money and nothing else."

The letter also reminded Jones that, although he preached that sexual activity should be limited, he constantly engaged in it himself — they blamed the other selfish Temple leaders for that: "STAFF . . . has to be fucked in order to be loyal. . . . The thought of demanding your sensitivity and dedication in such a manner is grossly sick."

The students promised that at some point "we will contact you and wish to talk to you and if you see fit work with you," but their missive's conclusion emphasized that socialism was the only aspect of Jones's preaching that they accepted.

Their abrupt desertions, and the contents of the letter they left behind for him, presented Jones with any number of problems. Because members of prominent Temple families —

the Cobbs, the Touchettes, and the Biddulphs especially — were involved, the student defections could hardly be kept secret or treated as a minor matter. Everyone in the Temple was going to know that they were gone, and want to know why. Jones's normal response — that the eight had revealed themselves as intrinsically evil and were to be considered enemies — might not work this time. What if their family members remaining in the fellowship were offended and left themselves? Jones believed them to be loyal, but he'd thought that of the Santa Rosa students, too. Ranting, condemning the young defectors, only increased the risk of losing additional followers.

There were also things in the letter that threatened Jones personally. What the students had put in writing, they might also have discussed with other students who still remained in Santa Rosa, or with members of their families. Jones had felt certain that his extramarital sexual activity was a closely held secret among members of the Planning Commission and his partners themselves. But these students knew, and they'd named names, including Carolyn Layton, Karen Tow Layton, and Grace Stoen. Clearly, some of his trusted confidants had talked out of turn.

Jones was left with the challenge of acknowledging the defections, deciding how to respond to the accusations in the letter, and making it clear how he expected his followers to react, without alienating the families of the students and, most of all, not acknowledging error in the makeup of Temple leadership. That would be admitting he had allowed himself to be misled, and a critical aspect of Jones's hold over his people was that so many of them considered him to be infallible.

A few days after the students — identified later by writers as the "Gang of Eight" or "the Eight Revolutionaries" — departed, Jones walked purposefully onto the stage at a closed Temple meeting and, for the better part of two hours, demonstrated his un-matched oratorical and psychological skills. Much of what he said was extemporized. All of it proved that Jones understood his follow-ers far better than they did him.

Jones began by wishing peace on all of his "precious hearts." Just as Jesus once taught, he reminded them, it was important to always do what was right without expectation of thanks. That's what Jim Jones personally did: "I don't expect anything from people. And," Jones said with heavy emphasis, "don't *you.*"

Everyone expected him to talk immediately about the eight student defectors, but Jones instead segued into a tale of how, just a few days earlier, "our enemies" tried to take away "Sister Jones's job," for once identifying Mar-celine as "Sister" rather than "Mother," mak-ing her, and himself by inference, one among, as well as above, the rest of them. As Jones told it, Marceline's bosses believed she was "befriending the poor" too often in her work with state hospitals and care facilities, and so they fired her, claiming "conflict of interest." But Jones stepped in, he set them straight, and Sister Jones not only got her job back, she was promoted. Standing up for Marceline, doing what was right, almost killed Jones: "[Those] people brought my strokes up, blood pressure up . . . my heart wasn't worth two cents." Yet he persevered.

Marceline, onstage beside her husband, asked his permission to speak: "One of the things I wanted to say is, you know we can sit and we can praise our leader for what he is, but the time's come when we've got to become what he is . . . the only difference between him and us is that we're not willing to live the selfless life to become what he has become."

Then Jones finally mentioned the eight students, and spoke sorrowfully. These young people now found themselves out in the cruel world: "It's not going to be much fun out there." Panicky, confused, they were certain to contact family members or other Temple friends, "so if they call any one of your phones, you tell them, 'Father loves you, Father cares for you, Father says come home.'"

If any or all of the students did return,

Jones wanted everyone to welcome them warmly, citing a famous New Testament change of heart: "Let's remember that Sauls become Pauls. . . . We can still make something of them, if they'll let us. Have you got that message in your mind and in your heart? . . . If they call, let them know we love them."

Jones didn't mention any of the accusations against Temple staff in the students' letter, or the references to his sex life, gambling that the few family members the young people might have privately shared these concerns with hadn't mentioned them to anyone else. Instead, Jones gave the wayward young people some credit. They had access to funds in a Temple college account and left the money where it was. "They could have drawn it out without any trouble." He was making certain that everyone knew this, Jones said, because some of his followers might have erroneously concluded that these traitors were entirely bad, and it was important "to always tell all sides of the story."

Jones predicted that these errant young people would eventually be overcome by guilt, especially when they realized how much pain and suffering they had caused Jones, their families, and the rest of the Temple membership. "If any of those children call, do not tell them any pain that we've had, any suffering we've had. I think it might be in their minds sometime that they might try to restore themselves [to the Temple] by trying to, you know, act out against our enemies. . . . They're going to want to make it up to us. And we don't want them to do anything wrong."

The message was effectively delivered and its theme clear — no grudges, no new enemies, love the wayward children, forgive them, welcome them if they came back — and, although there were occasional communications between them and their families, and a few fruitless conversations with Jones himself, they didn't return. A few among the eight would eventually become active enemies of Jones and the Temple.

Toward the end of the meeting, while engaging in call-and-response with his audience, Jones broached another subject, interjecting it smoothly, planting a seed without undue emphasis. What would become first a gradually recurring, then a dominant, topic in Peoples Temple was mentioned obliquely, but publicly, for perhaps the first time.

Jones said, "I'll tell you, each of you'll [count] for a thousand [instead of] one, 'cause you are people who upon the ends of the world have come, wherever you are at, you're going to make history. . . . It's destined to be. Now you may not like the kind of history we make, we may be swinging through the sky on a rope . . . but I would rather go down as [abolitionist] John Brown [hanged for leading a pre–Civil War insurrection against slavery] than, who was that fella that sold out? Nathan Hale?"

Someone shouted, "Benedict Arnold."

"Benedict Arnold. Now, of course, if the British had won, *he'd* have been a hero. . . . [There's] a quote I had here. It's important. It's very good, from John Brown: 'Now, if it is deemed necessary that I should forfeit my life for the furtherance of the ends of justice, and mingle my blood further with the blood of millions in this slave country, whose rights are disregarded by wicked, cruel, and unjust enactments, I say, let it be done.' John Brown, [speaking] as he was on the scaffold, ready to be hung after the raid on Harper's Ferry, the federal arsenal, Virginia . . . October sixteenth, 1859. . . . His demeanor prompted one conservative New Yorker to confide in his . . . journal, 'One's faith in anything is terribly shaken by anybody who is ready to go to the gallows condemning and denouncing it.' And we can do that. We can shake people's faith in the love of money and racism. We can shake their faith in it, dramatically and tremendously, if we will be willing to go to the gallows for what we believe. I don't think we're going to the gallows, but I'm ready. Aren't you?"

His people stood and cheered.

Chapter Thirty-Six: Consequences

Jones's soft public words aside, the Gang of Eight defections left him determined to exert even more control over his followers. That kind of betrayal wouldn't happen again.

The new, tougher era started with the same inner circle that had been criticized as too white and too influential. Jones made his expectations of Carolyn Layton, Terri Buford, Jack Beam, Tim Stoen, and some other key members of the Planning Commission clear. They must be more observant and crack down on anyone displaying even the slightest sign of straying. To prevent any Planning Commission members from acting on traitorous thoughts themselves, Jones devised an effective method of ensuring their loyalty. Blank pieces of paper were distributed — some remember Carolyn Layton handing them out — and the P.C. members were instructed to sign their names at the bottom. If any of them angered Jones, he was free to fill in whatever "confession" he liked over their signatures, then display it to the rest of the Temple membership or even the police. Everyone complied. Tim Carter remembers, "It was like a loyalty test. That was the way we looked at it." The signed pages were kept carefully filed, ready for use if Jones deemed it necessary.

Previously, Jones mostly observed at P.C. meetings. Now he did much of the talking, most of it on some nights, though seldom about Temple programs and goals. Instead, Jones moaned about all the responsibilities placed on him, or else boasted about his sexual prowess, particularly how the women he favored with his attentions enjoyed unequaled carnal bliss. For Jones, this bragging was an effective way to remind everyone of his complete mastery. They were sometimes required to report on their own sex lives and sexual fantasies, occasionally in writing. Most understood that Father wanted these verbal and written responses to take the form of personal tribute. Sandy Bradshaw wrote, "The only person I have had sex with for the last eight years has been J." This was the kind of kowtowing Jones especially enjoyed — of course, Bradshaw wouldn't sleep with anyone else. She'd had him, and who else could compare? It was no coincidence that Bradshaw became one of his most trusted lieutenants.

The changes were more incremental for the

general members, who had no idea of what took place at P.C. sessions, only that they were rumored to be interminable. There was still considerable fellowship, good times with good friends, and opportunities to help the downtrodden, to offer a socialist example that would encourage others to make the world a better, fairer place, and even the opportunity to travel, the kind of cross-country excursions that were far beyond the means of most ghetto dwellers. Better-heeled members might find crammed buses, bland box lunches, and gas station restroom stops to be annoying, but for many of Jones's followers, just the opportunity to get out on the road and see sights beyond the burned-out Watts Street and rat-infested Western Addition tenements seemed miraculous.

In August 1973, the Temple bus fleet, jammed from aisles to luggage racks with excited adults and kids, most of them black, set out from California for Washington, D.C., making stops in Houston, Chicago, and Philadelphia. Advance crews blanketed the poorest areas of the cities with leaflets, and auditoriums were filled — it was always thrilling to see strangers' responses to Father. The nation's capital, though, was the highlight. Temple old folks and kids wandered wide-eyed around the Capitol Building and National Mall, and then, to the absolute astonishment of onlookers, began picking up trash, doing this chore cheerfully, leaving the area spick-and-span — but not before a reporter from the *Washington Post* arrived. On August 18, a small item with the headline "The Welcome Tourists" appeared in the newspaper:

The hands-down winners of anybody's tourists-of-the-year have got to be the 680 wonderful members of the People's [sic] Temple Christian Church of Redwood Valley, Calif. — who bend over backwards to leave every place they visit more attractive than when they arrived. Like thousands of other tourists, they went calling on the U.S. Capitol the other day, but unlike others who tramp through our town spreading litter helter-skelter, this spirited group of travelers fanned out from their 13 buses and spent about an hour cleaning up the grounds.

One 82-year-old woman who was policing the area at the foot of the Capitol explained to reporter Frank Jones that the members take pleasure in sweeping across the country this way. The church, which has black, white and American Indian members, has already won friends in dozens of cities since its tour left Redwood Valley Aug. 8, and still more areas will benefit by the members' stop offs on their return trip.

Jones orchestrated the whole thing, having

a Temple member posing as a D.C. resident call the *Post* newsroom and report this amazing act taking place at the Capitol. Reporter Frank Jones was steered to the eighty-two-year-old member who had been prepped in advance to say just the right things. Once the brief mention was published the Temple promptly announced that its members in the caravan had been declared "Tourists of the Year" in the nation's capital by the prestigious *Washington Post.*

Eventually, the Temple newsletter was expanded into a full-fledged, professional-looking publication named *The Peoples Forum.* Until the Temple bought its own, Carlton Goodlett allowed the church to use his newspaper presses; the *Peoples Forum* editorial staff bickered constantly about each issue's content, only to find at deadline time that every story had to be approved in advance by Jones himself. He always wanted last-minute changes. Many copies were distributed door-to-door for free. Members with day jobs in the San Francisco and Los Angeles business districts were expected to spend their lunch hours selling copies on the street.

As Jones's determination to thwart potential betrayal increased, so did the Temple's commitment to disciplining its members. The Planning Commission sometimes decreed corporal punishment as a last resort for members who'd committed acts that otherwise would qualify for correction by outside law enforcement. It was one more aspect of the Temple taking care of its own. Occasionally, some P.C. members felt moral lines were being crossed, even with the worst offenders.

Peter Wotherspoon was a pedophile, accepted into Temple membership despite his openly admitted failing. He was informed from the beginning that even the slightest further illicit act with a child would be unacceptable, but he couldn't resist. A ten-year-old Temple boy reported that Wotherspoon had engaged him in a sex act, and Wotherspoon was brought before the Planning Commission to answer for it. An obvious solution would have been to turn Wotherspoon over to the police, but that ran counter to Temple tradition. Instead, Wotherspoon was taken to a back room and ordered to strip and lay his genitals flat on a table. Then Jack Beam, wielding a length of rubber hose, pounded Wotherspoon's penis and scrotum until they were swollen several times over. Wotherspoon had to be catheterized and lay in bed for days afterward, unable to move. But he was allowed to remain in the Temple, with the understanding that any additional transgression would result in something even worse. Though no commission member questioned the seriousness of Wotherspoon's statutory rape or that a substantial disciplinary act was required, some were shaken by the barbarity of his punishment.

Even more troubling to several P.C. members was Jones's brutal treatment of longtime Temple member Laurie Efrein. Unlike Wotherspoon, she committed no crime beyond adoring Jim Jones, and at one P.C. meeting he chose to humiliate her for it.

During a commission meeting, Jones griped that the sexual demands being made on him were just too wearying. He called on some of the P.C. members who'd been with him. Efrein hadn't. Quite a few Temple members felt that she had a crush on Jones, and hoped at some point he'd have sex with her. Now Jones turned his attention to Efrein. He told her to stand, and demanded that she explain to the rest of the group what she thought she had to offer Jones sexually. Then he ordered her to take off her clothes.

Efrein complied — disobeying could have been interpreted as a traitorous act. When she was naked, Jones said that she'd "been coming on to [me]. . . . If I had a list of the people I didn't want to fuck, you'd be on top of the list." He demanded that Efrein admit she wanted him to die. After Jones verbally abused her some more, Efrein was required to remain naked for the remainder of the meeting, which lasted another few hours. A few weeks later, Sharon Amos called Efrein aside and explained that Jones was sorry for what had happened — it had been an attempt to provide her with "personal therapy." Efrein replied, "It's all right," and remained a loyal follower.

None of the Planning Commission members who were upset by Jones's treatment of Efrein criticized him for it, either directly or in private conversation with each other. Letting Jones blow off steam, even in such questionable ways, was preferable to the risk of him becoming overwhelmed by constant stress and breaking down. So they praised him for everything he did, and agreed with all he said. Jones fed off that; almost forty years later in a speech at Bucknell University, Stephan Jones said, "My father's image of himself resided completely in his perception of other people's perception of him . . . if you're surrounded by a lot of people, who . . . regardless of what they're thinking, are showing you that you're okay and not only are you okay, but you're the cat's meow, you're not going to get better." And Jones didn't.

His new, sterner approach extended to the rest of the Temple members. Public meetings with their emphasis on social justice remained the same, but some of the discipline doled out at Planning Committee sessions spilled over into the private meetings. Father called members "on the floor" to answer for relatively minor transgressions — smoking, misbehavior in school, exhibiting bourgeois behavior — and announced a penalty. These might entail staying up all night cleaning Temple bathrooms, or a few extra hours of other church chores. Some were inventive — a youngster caught with cigarettes had to smoke a cigar in front of the whole congregation, and his resulting nausea amused everyone. But now there were, occasionally, "licks" administered, a whack or two on the ass with a board. Most of Jones's followers were white working class or black lower class, and they were already familiar with corporal punishment. "To me, a swat on the rear really wasn't much," Alan Swanson remembers. "I thought, so what?"

But it escalated. Swanson wasn't put off by licks, but he was appalled when, in a private Redwood Valley meeting, Jones ordered a woman who'd allegedly broken some rule to have her hands tied and then tossed into the swimming pool. She was left to gasp and struggle for a few moments, then pulled out. "I started wondering, 'What if he does that to me sometime?' " Swanson recalls.

Yet some former members, repulsed by much of what Jones did, caution that physical punishment was only used as a last resort.

"At least 80 percent of all problems in the Temple were not even brought up (in public meetings)," Tim Carter says. "Step one, if somebody screwed up, was counseling. Step two was more counseling. Step three, you were called up on the carpet. Sometimes being called up in front of everybody, that humiliation, worked where counseling didn't. I remember one boy, eleven or twelve, had watched his father murder his mother. This kid was very antisocial, in fact he was a bully. He got one-on-one counseling in the Temple for years, just everything the Temple knew how to do, and he was never brought up until 1976 in San Francisco when he got a spanking, five whacks. And after that, he changed. The discipline worked where love hadn't. That kid only responded to fear."

Jones was careful not to become legally liable for physical punishment of children. When youngsters under eighteen were disciplined, their parents (or Temple legal guardians) signed releases that permitted the kids to be beaten.

Eventually, Jones began ordering occasional boxing matches during private services. A transgressor would be instructed to put on boxing gloves, then fight another, usually tougher, member of the congregation. Sometimes, the person being punished would have to box several others in succession, until, in Jones's estimation, he or she had absorbed enough punishment. Many onlookers cheered — Father's justice was being administered. Those who felt differently questioned their own reactions.

"We individual Temple members had no real authority, but we weren't mindless robots," Tim Carter says. "We willingly gave up some freedom for the greater goal. If you got upset with something, with Jones, you still felt respect for others in the Temple and you'd think, 'If this is wrong, these other very intelligent, very decent people wouldn't be here, so, therefore, I must be wrong.' " The boxing matches and the beatings with a board or rubber hose went on, not in every private meeting, but frequently enough that they were not an uncommon occurrence.

Some members, put off by the harsh discipline or by other Jones edicts (posted notices sometimes concluded, "Nothing is to be said in public or private in opposition to this policy as it was put into effect by Father"), tried to leave. Most found it difficult to get away. The problems involved in defecting began with money. Most dissatisfied members were destitute. If they lived communally, they'd turned over all that they owned, including paychecks if they had outside employment. Everyone was reduced to minimal personal possessions, and bank accounts were discouraged. Moving away from Redwood Valley or to some other neighborhood in San Francisco or Los Angeles required deposits on rent and start-up utility costs. Turning to relatives for money or a place to stay was often impossible. Jones actively discouraged contact with outsiders, especially kin who had not chosen to join the Temple. Many members had already been estranged from parents or siblings even before they decided to follow Jones.

Especially in Redwood Valley and to some extent in Los Angeles and San Francisco, members with outside jobs got them through Temple connections, often reporting to supervisors who were also in the Temple. To quit the church was to risk being fired. Adult members employed full-time by the Temple itself often had no conception of how to look for work in the outside world. Terri Buford recalls that at her first post-Temple job interview, she showed up barefoot and eating an ice-cream cone: "I had no idea of how I was supposed to look or act."

When someone did leave, Jones had varying reactions, depending on the person and the level of threat he believed that he or she potentially represented. Those who joined only briefly, leaving after a few weeks or months, were sometimes allowed to go. Bonnie Burnham, frustrated by contradictions in Jones's preaching and actions, left with minimal resistance from Jones. He warned Burnham that if she quit the Temple, she was likely to die. When that didn't dissuade her, Jones sent Marceline to plead the Temple's case. Marceline offered rote objections — Jim loved Bonnie and was sincerely worried for her safety outside the Temple — and left it at that. Afterward, Marceline stayed overnight with Burnham "fifteen or twenty times." The women would laugh and chat about inconsequential things, giving Marceline a much-needed break from her obligations as "Mother" in the Temple. Sometimes, Burnham wrote in her memoir, "I would hear Marceline sobbing in her room. . . . I would go in and try to comfort her, but there wasn't a lot that could be said. It was helpful for her just to cry." Unhappy as Marceline was, Burnham wrote, "She would not criticize her husband," which is undoubtedly why Jones permitted the friendship and even allowed Burnham to visit the Jones family at their home after her defection.

In almost every other instance, Jones didn't want former members anywhere near his other followers. He announced that anyone leaving the Temple must move at least one hundred miles away, and soon increased the distance to five hundred miles. Defectors would violate these boundaries at their peril — accidents would surely befall them.

Those who left the Temple, but remained inside Jones's arbitrary boundary, were harassed by Temple security. The squads Jones sent out to intimidate former members almost always included Jim McElvane and Chris Lewis, both big, dangerous-looking black men. Tim Carter, the Vietnam veteran, once went with them. When Jones learned that David Wise, who briefly served as a Temple associate minister, was still living in Los Angeles, Carter recalls that "me, McElvane and two other guys were sent to scare him away. We went to his house and told him, 'You better not talk about the Temple.' We didn't rough him up. He stayed inside his house and we were outside the door. The visit was to show him that Jones knew where he was, that we could find him any time Jones wanted. I felt uncomfortable doing it, and I never went out on something like that again. But [Jones] had other people to send."

Juanell Smart, present at the Planning Commission meeting where Jones humiliated Laurie Efrein, was disgusted by the incident, and further offended when, at another meeting, someone alleged that her husband, David Wise, had tapped Jones's phone with Smart's full knowledge, if not cooperation. "I started crying, and I told Jim that I wanted out. He said to me, 'Then you'll have to move a hundred miles away.' I told him I wouldn't, that I'd lived in L.A. for most of my life. So then he comes up with these other conditions."

Jones told Smart that before she left, "I'd have to sign my four kids over to the church. Well, I realized that signing something like that wouldn't mean anything in court. So I did it. Then he has somebody bring out this gun, and they make me put my hand on it, hold it, and after they had my fingerprints on it they put it in a bag and took it away. The threat was, if I went out and said or did something against Jones or the Temple, the gun could be used in some criminal way and I'd be [implicated]."

For a while, Smart's three youngest children lived with their father, and her nineteen-year-old daughter, Tanitra, lived with her grandmother Kay. All four remained active in the Temple. Smart believed that "at least there, they still were away from the streets and the drugs. Tanitra found a boyfriend in the Temple named Poncho, and of course she always wanted to be with him. So I stayed out and they stayed in."

Jones sometimes used emissaries to try talking defectors into returning, particularly former members who'd been of particular use to the Temple. Garry Lambrev was the first Californian to join the Temple and afterward ran a church antique shop and worked on the staff of *The Peoples Forum*. Lambrev had an ongoing disagreement with Jones about Lambrev's desire for a long-term, loving gay relationship, and had left and rejoined the Temple several times. But in 1974, his latest defection seemed that it might last. Lambrev still kept in touch with Temple friends, and at one point he spoke on the telephone with Karen Layton. In their conversation, Lambrev told Layton that he was considering suicide. His romantic, non-Temple relationship was floundering, and "it's like the sky is caving in." Layton reminded Lambrev of Jones's teaching about reincarnation — everyone experiences many lives, trying in each to become truly enlightened, until, finally, success allows the individual to "graduate" to a higher, happier spiritual plane. If Lambrev killed himself, Layton said, "Just think, you'd have to regress all that way back and start it all over again . . . go through that same shit again. It's just not worth it."

In his next reincarnation, Layton warned, Jones "won't be here to help, you know. It'll be a horrible place. Think of living through this hell again." But if Lambrev was truly intent on killing himself, he should consider an alternative: "If you're gonna die, you might as well die for the cause. I mean, you might as well die a noble death than die a coward's death, really . . . do something to make it a better world for other people, you know. If we can just hold on for a few more years [in the Temple] . . . then everybody graduates."

Lambrev didn't kill himself, and he didn't go back to Peoples Temple. But a few years later, he would have a horrifying reason to recall Karen Layton's words.

■ ■ ■ ■

Sometime in 1973, Jones brought another element into play.

Even before the Gang of Eight defections, Jones constantly kept his followers in what former Temple member Hue Fortson terms "crisis mode," warning that no matter how bad things in America had been, they were about to get worse. In 1973 and most of 1974, the Watergate scandal was Jones's favorite point of reference.

In his sermons, Jones began predicting that despite talk of impeachment Nixon wouldn't go quietly — wouldn't, in fact, go at all. This evil man, who represented all that Peoples Temple stood against, was capable of any awful act. Jones compared Nixon's power to that of Hitler. Nixon and his modern-day Nazis hated poor people, blacks especially — concentration camps were coming, and it required very little imagination to guess who would be sent there. Of course, when they came for Jim Jones's people, Father would lead the resistance. Anyone threatening Temple members, especially the children, would face one hell of a fight. But there was another option, and during a few of his early and mid-1973 sermons, Jones began alluding to it.

That April, Jones reminded everyone that

nuclear war was inevitable — but there was a more immediate, equally terrible, threat: "Between now and that [nuclear] prophecy, a [Nixon] dictatorship could come which would mean that we have to take a short journey out of this land to save our lives." But the Temple had an escape plan. "Now, what we have in mind when [the martial law] comes . . . we're going to serve people abroad. We'll quietly take our little trip through the wilderness and leave Pharaoh's Egypt, Pharaoh's Washington, Pharaoh's America, we'll leave it quietly and we will go along humming our songs, riding in our buses 'til we get to the border . . . and we're gonna build a clinic and then we're gonna get some land where we can raise food, that's our hope, and some animals."

In a subsequent sermon, he described, but didn't name, the destination: "I know a place where I can take you, where there'll be no more racism, where there'll be no more division, where there'll be no more class exploitation. I know just the place. Oh, yes, I do."

And that, at least, was no exaggeration. Though it would be almost six more months before Jones specified the location, he frequently identified it by another name that struck an especially deep chord with his older African American members:

The Promised Land.

CHAPTER THIRTY-SEVEN: THE PROMISED LAND

Jim Jones had keenly studied traditional black religion in America, and eventually his own preaching assimilated one of its recurring themes: sometime, somehow, true believers would throw off their shackles — formerly the real, jangling chains of slavery, afterward poverty and racism — and be guided to a place where true equality and brotherhood exist. The Promised Land was an important motif in the African American church.

Elderly African Americans, mostly recruited in San Francisco and Los Angeles but originally hailing from the South, comprised perhaps one-third of the Peoples Temple fellowship. They remembered well black visionary Marcus Garvey and his heralded Back-to-Africa movement of the 1920s, where Garvey envisioned a black society blessed with modern-day industry and economics. Garvey failed in the face of vigorous opposition from colonial powers, but at least the concept had been widely discussed. For many black Americans, what Garvey described was the Promised Land.

Father Divine, Jones's former role model and mentor, incorporated the Promised Land theme into his ministry. Divine's Peace Mission established Promised Land farming communities in Ulster County, New York, and used the crops grown there to feed members of the Mission's communes. Jones knew all about the Promised Land farms; he'd studied them, as he'd scrutinized every aspect of Divine's operations, cherry-picking programs for Peoples Temple.

There was another critical reason that the Promised Land theme appealed to Jones. Outside influence was pernicious. The Gang of Eight spent more time on campus and in classrooms than they did surrounded by Temple membership. They got *ideas* that way. If potential traitors were isolated on some farming community far away from anywhere else, allegiance to the Temple — to Jim Jones — would be their only realistic option.

By the time Jones raised the Promised Land with the Planning Commission and Temple membership as a whole, he already knew where it should be. It was necessary to give the impression that a global search might be required — that would make the ultimate choice a group decision rather than one dictated by Jones, an important distinction if he wanted everyone to have a sense of ownership. In the tradition of Marcus Garvey, somewhere in Africa seemed like a logical choice, a country with a majority black population. South America had possibilities, too — Jones had attempted a personal ministry in Brazil. Elmer and Deanna Mertle were instructed to prepare for scouting trips to Kenya and Peru. Tim Stoen presented them with a "To Whom It May Concern" letter requesting aid and assistance anywhere the Mertles attempted "locating and investigating a permanent missionary location to be developed and supported by this church." The Mertles were one of the few couples in the Temple still to have extensive outside property, much of it rental units. As they prepared to leave, they were persuaded to temporarily sign over control so that Temple leadership could manage the properties in their absence. Then, at the last minute, the Mertles were told not to go: there were worrisome political problems in Kenya, and the illness of Peru's leader made that government too unreliable. But the Temple would retain control of the Mertles' property — they were too valuable as members to be distracted by such petty business concerns.

On September 10, 1973, the seven-member Temple board of directors (Tim Stoen, chairman, and Sharon Amos, secretary) formally authorized investigation of "developmental sites and locations for an agricultural mission." It was a formality. At the next meeting, on October 8, the board voted unanimously that "Guyana, South America, was the most suitable place," and authorized "James W. Jones, pastor and president . . . and all persons designated by said pastor, to take any and all actions necessary or convenient to the establishing of a branch church and of an agricultural and rural development mission in the Cooperative Republic of Guyana."

Twelve years earlier, on an extended trip where Jones visited possible places to relocate his family, and, perhaps, his church from Indianapolis, he had visited British Guiana. Approximately the size of Kansas or Idaho, bounded by Venezuela, Brazil, Surinam (now Suriname), and the Atlantic Ocean, the country was then in the process of separating itself from the British Empire. Though Britain still had ultimate control, it allowed Guyana's first general election in 1953. Much to British consternation, the Guyanese elected avowed Marxist Cheddi Jagan as prime minister. Both British and American intelligence services believed that communist nations — Russia, Cuba — were providing secret financial support to Jagan and his People's Progressive Party (PPP). Jagan remained in office until 1964, when he was defeated by Forbes Burnham, whose allegiance to socialism was considered by British and American powers a lesser evil than Jagan's Marxism. England and the United States covertly underwrote much of Burnham's campaign. The money came in handy for bribing ballot box officials — rigged elections were already standard in Guyana. Only after Burnham's election did Britain finally grant Guyana complete independence, even though with his People's National Congress (PNC) party controlling the country's parliament, Burnham's election effectively made Guyana an official socialist state, which made Guyana attractive to Jim Jones.

Jones also liked Guyana's ethnic makeup. Its population of 850,000 was roughly equivalent to San Francisco's, but 40 percent of the Guyanese were black, and 50 percent East Indian, the result of Britain's importing workers from another colony. A Peoples Temple colony would be a good match. And, besides, Guyana was the only country in South America where the national language was English. Its location was convenient, too — boats could make a relatively easy trip from Miami to Guyana's capital of Georgetown, a port city.

Jones wanted isolation for his new agricultural mission, and Guyana lent itself perfectly to that. Virtually the entire population lived along the Atlantic coast. The vast majority of Guyana was covered with dense jungle. There were no connecting roads in the interior. It was necessary to fly, traverse winding rivers, or else cut your way through the jungle. With the exception of some hardy denizens of manganese mining camps, the jungle's only human inhabitants were Amerindian tribes. Peoples Temple could clear enough acres for use as reasonably fertile farmland. How hard could that be? A small but significant portion of church membership was made up of rough-and-tumble former Indiana farmers. The Guyanese jungle could be an ideal setting for Peoples Temple.

Though Jones described the proposed Promised Land mission site as a place where everyone in the Temple would flee to avoid American martial law and concentration camps (Marceline referred to it as an "exodus"), Jones, at least initially, had no intention of moving all his followers to Guyana. For one thing, he realized that many of them wouldn't be willing to go. Tim Carter remembers, "In Planning Commission meetings, we talked about how lots of people wouldn't want to live in primitive [jungle] conditions. What we finally figured was that there'd be maybe five hundred or six hundred who'd go. We got that number from about how many people we had [in the Temple] who were currently living communally. We thought they were probably the ones who'd be most willing to try it. The main [church] would still be in California."

For the time being, Jones avoided publicly announcing Guyana as the promised paradise. Though the Temple board had decided on Guyana, the Guyanese had yet to be consulted. In early December 1973, Tim Stoen led a five-person advance team to Georgetown. They were joined about ten days later by Jones himself, along with another dozen Temple members, including Marceline, Carolyn Layton, Archie Ijames, Dick Tropp, and Johnny Brown.

The Temple delegation visited the Guyanese parliament in Georgetown, and was granted interviews with Burnham and several of his administration's top officials. The Americans made their case for establishing a mission — they, too, were socialists, and would support the Burnham government; they would contribute to the national economy, buying goods in local markets; they were solid, law-abiding citizens who'd cause no trouble. They were pleased to find Burnham and his people receptive. The Guyanese even had a prospective location to suggest, and within days arrangements were made to fly Jones and his people there to see it for themselves. It seemed almost too easy. The Temple contingent had no idea that the timing of their request exactly matched a critical need that had been identified by the Guyanese government.

In December 1973, Guyana was in economic distress. Prices in international markets for its sugar-related crops were down, and the recent Arab oil embargo drove up prices for goods the fledgling country desperately needed. With money so scarce, Burnham's government couldn't afford much of a military. Guyana's few thousand soldiers were mostly young, untrained, and poorly equipped. That, in turn, attracted the attention of neighboring Venezuela with its large, vastly superior armed forces. For decades, the exact location of the border separating southeast Venezuela and northwest Guyana had been in dispute. Venezuela claimed its border extended hundreds of miles into territory claimed by the Guyanese. While Guyana was under British protection, there wasn't much the Venezuelans could do. But with Guyana now an independent nation, and one with only a meager defense, Venezuela's leaders began rattling sabers. Guyanese leaders reluctantly realized that if Venezuela invaded, it could take as much land as it wanted with minimal opposition. However, Venezuelan leaders feared American military might. If a settlement of U.S. citizens was established in Guyana's northwest, precisely in the middle of the region under dispute, then the Venezuelans would have to reconsider military encroachment. Burnham and the other Guyanese officials welcomed Jones and his people to their country as fellow socialists, but what really mattered to them was that these people were *Americans.*

The Guyanese saw another potential benefit in Peoples Temple establishing its mission deep in the jungle. Every substantial Guyanese town was located on the Atlantic coastline — and the coast was eroding. The capital city and every other Guyanese town was barricaded by jungle. The government had used its limited resources to establish inland communities, but none lasted long. The jungle was a hard place. The people on the coast had no interest in relocating there. In desperation, the government had hacked out a National Service settlement in the North West District, close to Matthews Ridge and about thirty miles from where it hoped the American church would build its mission. The National Service was Burnham's brainchild. Teenage boys were recruited and trained for military duty. Because many young Guyanese lived in abject poverty, the boys signed up less out of patriotic zeal than for guaranteed meals and a covered place to sleep. There were about 1,100 National Service cadets at the North West District camp, not enough to give pause to the Venezuelan army, or to inspire other Guyanese to join them as jungle dwellers. But perhaps these American church people could do both.

On December 21, the Americans were

flown 190 miles over the jungle to Matthews Ridge, a mining town in the North West District. Matthews Ridge had a rail line that ran another thirty-five miles, close to the much smaller village of Port Kaituma, which had a small airstrip and also a dock — the Kaituma River connected the town to the Atlantic Ocean, so it was possible to sail there along the coast from Georgetown. But that took a full day; flying was a matter of hours, and the Guyanese wanted their American friends — hopefully, soon their neighbors — to see the proposed mission site immediately.

What they saw seemed ideal to Jones. While Port Kaituma itself wasn't much — it existed as a shipping port for the Matthews Ridge manganese mines, which were currently shut down, and consisted mostly of four or five dozen battered huts and a few bars — its dock and airstrip offered access. The suggested mission site was several miles removed from the town. There was a small, partial clearing left from previous attempts to establish a settlement, barely a few square yards, but enough to convince Jones that clearing the jungle would be difficult but not impossible. There was considerable concern on the part of Guyanese officials, who feared the isolation of the site might put off their American visitors, but the isolation was exactly what Jones wanted. He announced on the spot that this was it: Peoples Temple would build its mission here in the North West District. On the way back to the capital, someone asked what the new settlement would be named. There was some discussion, but the choice was obvious: Jonestown.

Back in Georgetown, there were business details to work out. Peoples Temple asked to lease 25,000 acres; Guyanese officials thought that was too much. They reached an agreement for an initial lease of 3,000 acres, with an option for the Temple to expand its holdings if the settlement was successful. The lease was for five years; an extension could be negotiated after that if both parties were agreeable. The Temple's annual rent would be 25 cents per acre, with that price reviewed and, if appropriate, adjusted in five-year increments. The Temple promised to invest a minimum of $400,000 in building and maintaining the mission during the first two years of the project. During the first five years, Temple members would be required to cultivate and occupy at least half of the leased land. These official negotiations took time, and weren't concluded until 1977.

But lease details were less important to the Guyanese than getting Americans into the North West District, and Jones was anxious for work on the Promised Land settlement to begin at once. So in March 1974, Jones dispatched a half dozen followers to Guyana, where they began surveying the mission site.

Within a few months, another few dozen Temple members would join them, and the clearing and building, led by Jones loyalist Charlie Touchette and his son Mike, would begin. Jones hoped to send the first settlers by August. The Guyanese promised to assist with temporary housing for the workers, and friendly Amerindians were recruited as guides. The Temple bought a boat named the *Cudjoe* to bring members back and forth from Georgetown, and also to make supply runs between Port Kaituma and Miami. The arrangements were flawless, except in one regard: they'd underestimated the jungle.

The Guyanese jungle is triple canopy — as one flies over it, its towering trees resemble sprawling, tightly massed stalks of broccoli with claustrophic square miles of unbroken, impenetrable dark green bisected not by roads but a few meandering, muddy rivers. On the ground, the trees' thick trunks stand together like barely separated slats in a giant picket fence, and winding between the trees is underbrush bristling with thorns. Sunlight barely penetrates, but rain does, particularly during the wet seasons, dripping down through the layers of the tree leaves and limbs, turning the jungle's dirt floor to mud. The air is thick with humidity and the stink of rotting vegetation. Birds and animals abound, often unseen in the gloom, though their rustling is constant. There is a cacophony of coos and caws from the birds and yelps from monkeys. There is also the constant buzzing of insects, many of which bite or sting. The ground is frequently crisscrossed by marching columns of ants, some as large as thumb joints. Everywhere in the brush are snakes, many poisonous, some instantly lethal. Lurking, but seldom seen, are jungle cats.

The overall effect is simultaneously ominous and awe-inspiring, nature at its most primitive — and lovely. In clearings, and where there are gaps in the trees, bright bird plumage flashes in contrast with often azure sky. But the first small wave of Temple workers — dubbed "the Pioneers" by their church — were there to build, not sightsee. At least initially, they were frustrated rather than impressed by the jungle. Even with the Amerindian guides helping them thread their way several miles from Port Kaituma to the Jonestown mission site, the newcomers were in constant danger of getting lost: Mike Touchette told playwright and author Leigh Fondakowski, "When you walk through that jungle, you could turn 360 degrees and have no clue where you're at." But the Pioneers had to master the jungle, and quickly, because the first full-time settlers were expected soon.

The first challenge was clearing acreage. The Pioneers expected to fell the mighty trees with chainsaws, but when they tried, the chainsaw blades shattered — the wood was harder than the metal. If the trees couldn't be cleared, then nothing else could be done. The Amerindians came to the rescue, demonstrating how to rig a pulley system with ropes tied to several trees, and then one tree at a time could be leveraged out of the ground. It was backbreaking work, and very slow. The Americans hired more natives; Amerindian labor was the basis for initial Temple progress in the jungle. After some space was cleared and a narrow path from Port Kaituma to Jonestown was cut, heavy equipment could finally be brought in, all of it initially rented from the Guyanese government, then gradually supplemented and eventually replaced by machinery purchased in the United States by the Temple and shipped to Guyana. Because conditions in the jungle were so brutal, the equipment kept breaking down. Replacement parts were costly. There were months, even weeks, when repair bills totaled thousands of dollars. Often parts had to be ordered while broken-down machines stood idle.

But the Pioneers were never idle. Even when they weren't working in the jungle, they were kept busy in the huts they rented in Port Kaituma. Jones demanded detailed records of all daily expenditures, from $963.00 for metal rods and buckets to $6.50 for tea bags and cheese. The Pioneers also suffered ailments they expected — sunburn, bug bites, pulled muscles, cuts from tools — and some they hadn't, especially damage to their feet. Worm larvae permeated the jungle soil, and the pests thrived upon transfer to human flesh. Foot fungus and other skin ulcers were also constant problems. The heat was prostrating even on the coolest days, and the jungle humidity compounded the effect. Sometimes the Pioneers generated additional heat, lighting deliberate "burns" to rid partially cleared land of tree roots and ground growth. The workers lost pounds each day in sweat.

Yet the Pioneers persevered. They believed in the work they were doing. The Jonestown mission would further contribute to the great socialist example Peoples Temple set for the world. Once they had sufficient land cleared to begin farming, they were certain that fertile jungle soil, properly maintained, would bear immense amounts of produce, enough to feed four hundred or five hundred Jonestown settlers with sufficient excess to load on the Temple boat and distribute to hungry communities along the South American coast.

Back in America, Jones promised that and much more. After returning from Guyana, he first teased followers by announcing, "In the next few days we're going to get some land south of the equator." (Guyana is slightly north of the equator.) Soon afterward, he revealed that the property — the Promised Land — was in Guyana, a country he described as a wondrous tropical paradise. He was certain everyone would want to move there, but before any relocation was possible, Jonestown still had to be built, and that would cost money. Members had previously been dunned for excess personal possessions. Now Jones demanded that all those with life insurance policies cash them in and turn the money over for use in the Jonestown project. At every service, members were expected to hand Jones "commitment envelopes" with a minimum 25 percent of their weekly earnings — and they had to write their salaries on the outside of the envelope, so it could be verified that they were contributing the appropriate amount. The massive Temple mailing list was utilized, too — the church printing operation turned out a snappy "Operation Breadbasket" pamphlet and copies were sent to hundreds of thousands of supporters. After being informed of the Temple's new overseas agricultural mission intended to feed "hungry people of the world," recipients were urged to donate suggested amounts for specific uses, anywhere from $2 for a drill bit to $5,000 for a secondhand generator. Every cent, Jones emphasized in his sermons and in print, helped make the difference between Jonestown lasting or failing.

In retrospect, it all happened very fast, the

wearying struggles of the Pioneers notwithstanding. Jones first broached the Promised Land in the spring of 1973, visited Guyana that December, had tentative lease agreements in place and work crews onsite by March. From the Temple perspective, the whole process took only about a year.

It seemed even faster to the Guyanese. They were approached by the Temple in late 1973, and loaned heavy equipment to the first wave of workers the following March. More than forty years later, former official Christopher "Kit" Nascimento admitted that he, Prime Minister Burnham, and other national officials were "too quick to close the deal. But we felt it would be a matter of using America for our national purposes, as opposed to what Americans always wanted to do, use other countries for theirs. Frustrate Venezuela — wonderful. Jones and his people fit our government's plans to populate the interior. It's obvious now that we didn't do due diligence on Jonestown, on Jones and his followers. We just didn't, because they seemed such a perfect fit."

That was a relief to Jones. There was a recent incident that he especially did not want the Guyanese to know about.

Jim Jones had been satisfying his sexual urges with different partners from among Temple membership, most often women and occasionally men serving on the Planning Committee. Occasionally, he took lovers from the general membership, at least once committing statutory rape with a girl in her early teens. When pregnancies resulted, Jones expected the women to get abortions. Grace Stoen had been the exception.

In December 1973, Jones had reason to feel especially triumphant. The *Examiner*'s investigative series was not only quashed, but apparently forgotten. San Francisco's political leaders were highly complimentary of Peoples Temple's good works. The danger posed by the Gang of Eight's defection had been avoided. The students' families still in the Temple remained loyal. The Gang's departing criticism of Temple leadership's racial makeup and Jones's sex life had come to nothing. Jones himself was about to leave for Guyana, where he was certain he would begin the process of successfully establishing a Peoples Temple agricultural mission. Godlike or simply a superior human, Jim Jones was on a roll. At such moments, he habitually overstepped, and now was no exception.

Los Angeles police had received numerous complaints about gay men soliciting prospective partners in MacArthur Park, and especially in the nearby Westlake movie theater. Both were about a mile and a half from the Peoples Temple church in the city. Vice squad officers began plainclothes stakeouts in the park and theater. At the Westlake, they took seats in empty sections of the balcony, or else loitered in the men's room, and waited to be approached.

On the afternoon of December 13, an officer sitting in the balcony watching Clint Eastwood in *Dirty Harry* saw a man motioning for him to come over. The officer left the balcony and went into the nearest bathroom. The other man followed him. When the man began masturbating in front of the policeman he was arrested and taken to Ramparts police station, and there James Warren Jones was charged with lewd conduct. On the way to the station, Jones identified himself as a minister, apparently hoping to be set free, but to no avail. On station paperwork, Jones identified his employer as "Disciples of Christ," not "Peoples Temple." His bond was set at $500. Jones promptly made bail and found a doctor who provided a possible medical explanation for his action in the men's room: Jones had an enlarged prostate, and had been advised to run or jump in place to ease discomfort. He'd been doing that, not masturbating. It was all a misunderstanding.

One week later, a municipal court judge agreed to dismiss the charge, but only if Jones first signed a "stipulation [for] probable cause," meaning the arrest had been appropriate. That got Jones off the legal hook but left him otherwise dangling. There was now a public record of what he'd done, prime material for investigative journalists or representatives from a foreign government doing a comprehensive background check. Tim Stoen was called in to help; he was initially informed that only minors could have their arrest and court records sealed. Stoen kept trying, and in February 1974 the same municipal court judge who originally ruled on the case ordered that Jones's records regarding the incident be destroyed. It seemed that Jones was in the clear, but the arresting officer was so incensed that he filed an internal complaint about the judge's action. A drawn-out process ensued; the judge was eventually asked to reconsider but refused.

Jones wasn't certain if his arrest remained on public record or not. Other matters demanded his immediate attention, foremost among them the details involved in building Jonestown. He prepared an explanation if arrest details ever emerged. The LAPD had been out to get him since the ambulance-related riot outside the Los Angeles temple back in January. He'd stood up to them then, and this setup, the false charge and arrest, was their revenge. Jones maintained his complete innocence — and, certainly, everyone knew of the LAPD's well-deserved reputation for framing its enemies. If nothing else, that story would likely resonate with the Temple's black members who hailed from

Los Angeles. No one understood better than they did about LAPD corruption. Whether it would work as well on Guyanese investigators was another matter, but Jones never had to find out. Guyana's prime minister and his advisors wanted an agreement in place just as quickly as he did, and early construction work on Jonestown continued.

CHAPTER THIRTY-EIGHT: KIMO

Following his arrest, Jones began emphasizing a theme in his sermons and in Planning Commission meetings: everyone is homosexual. He'd occasionally made the statement before, but now it became constant. Those engaging in heterosexual intercourse were compensating for their real carnal desires. Anyone Jones wanted to take down a peg was required to stand and admit his or her homosexuality. Those who initially refused were browbeaten until they complied. Stephan Jones thought that his father "was just trying to feel okay about himself . . . for him to deal with [his bisexuality], every other guy had to have the same sexual feelings."

Tim Stoen was the exception who refused to confess when confronted by Jones, telling him, "No, Jim, I am not [homosexual]." Jones couldn't afford an open clash with his attorney, so he said, "Well, we'll let Tim think about it," and Stoen did. He concluded that "when the opportunity presented itself, I would move elsewhere and exit anonymously." For the time being, he stayed, both out of continued belief in the Temple's goals and programs, and his attachment to young John Victor Stoen. For the first two years of the child's life, he lived with Tim and Grace Stoen. After the little boy's second birthday, he was raised communally in Redwood Valley, living with Temple member Barbara Cordell — she had custody of several youngsters. The Stoens saw John Victor, often called John-John, every day. The Temple's purpose in raising children communally was to instill in them the essence of socialism, with everyone brought up under equal circumstances.

Potential fallout from the arrest wasn't Jones's only pressing concern. Months earlier, the Geary Boulevard temple in San Francisco had burned. Terri Buford believes that the fire was deliberately set, reinforcing members' belief that outside enemies continually plotted their destruction. "Just before the fire, Jack Beam came up to all of us working [at Geary Boulevard] and said we had to leave for Redwood Valley immediately for an important meeting there," she says. "All of us went, except for Jack Beam. That night the Temple burned, and Jim made it sound like it was arson. From then on, security was tighter and everyone coming in was searched." The actual incineration didn't cause Jones distress. What upset him was

546

discovering that insurance wouldn't pay for rebuilding the temple — church administrator Tish Leroy had forgotten to make monthly payments. That meant hundreds of thousands in unexpected costs. To defray reconstruction expenses, Jones asked all able-bodied members to come in on weeknights and weekends to help with construction. But it took months, and meanwhile San Francisco meetings had to be held again at nearby Benjamin Franklin Junior High.

Jones also had to maintain a delicate balance in keeping his followers opposed to the political and cultural status quo while maintaining positive relations with San Francisco's mainstream leadership and press. When Patty Hearst was kidnapped in early 1974 by the revolutionary Symbionese Liberation Army (SLA), the heiress's captors demanded that her father, Randolph Hearst, fund a multimillion-dollar food giveaway to the poor in exchange for his daughter's safe return.

In sermons during private Temple meetings, Jones expressed sympathy toward SLA members who'd been driven to extreme actions by racist oppressors. In public, he first offered to exchange himself for Patty Hearst as the SLA's hostage, and then on the Temple's behalf donated $2,000 to help defray the cost of the food giveaway. It was a pragmatic gesture — Hearst owned and operated the *San Francisco Examiner;* Jones simultaneously indicated that he bore no ill will regarding the Kinsolving series. He hoped that he had earned future editorial goodwill. (The food giveaway was a fiasco, and Patty Hearst famously went on to participate as an SLA member before the firefight destruction of most of the group and her own subsequent capture and prison term.)

The mission in Guyana was constantly on Jones's mind. He kept extolling its wonders to his followers, and often during services would ask for a show of hands — who wanted to go and live in the Promised Land? There were lots of aspirants, enough to assure Jones that he'd have no trouble populating Jonestown with its anticipated five hundred to six hundred residents. But spring 1974 stretched into summer and then fall, and Jonestown still wasn't ready for the first contingent. Construction was expensive and slow. Jones sent some additional workers to join the original Pioneers. They lived in huts on the site and fought back the jungle yard by yard. There were disappointments — there was only about an inch of natural topsoil, and even that wasn't compatible for some plants; Jonestown residents would have to learn to live without tomatoes, for example. Crops would have to be rotated. The Amerindians taught the Temple Pioneers how to get nutrients into the topsoil by burning trees to create potash. These efforts took time that

Jones hadn't factored in.

Part of the lease agreement required periodic inspections of the Jonestown site by Guyanese officials. These, at least, went as well as Jones might have hoped. One inspector enthusiastically reported, "The Settlement is, by its very existence, profound evidence of the application and triumph of human will, ingenuity and determination over the forces of nature." The Guyanese government was every bit as eager as Jones for settlers to begin moving in.

Jones had to see for himself. In December 1974, he and an entourage flew to Georgetown, planning both a tour of the settlement and meetings and public events in the Guyanese capital city that would firmly establish the presence of Peoples Temple. A few Temple members had opened a small church headquarters in Georgetown. Prominent among them was Paula Adams, a vivacious young woman whom Jones intended to be the Temple's chief representative to the Guyanese government. He soon discovered that she had succeeded far too well, beginning an affair with Laurence "Bonny" Mann, Guyana's ambassador to the United States. Besides violating Jones's edict of avoiding relationships with outsiders, the affair was doubly dangerous because Mann was married. What if a scandal ensued? Adams and the first few Temple women in Georgetown were expected to act flirtatiously — they hosted dance parties and paid special attention to older Guyanese ministers and officials — but actual sex was forbidden. Laura Johnston Kohl and Terri Buford believe that Jones's ego wouldn't allow him to share Temple women with anyone. Tim Carter recalls Jones ordering him not to have complete intercourse with a woman who'd previously been Jones's lover: "When we were in bed, I had to stop short of actual penetration. That was supposed to be Jim's privilege."

But Jones had sufficient self-control to look beyond his immediate instinct to order Adams out of Georgetown, or to at least terminate her affair with the ambassador. It was well known in the Guyanese capital that Mann had an especially warm relationship with Prime Minister Forbes Burnham — "a sort of favorite son," recalls Kit Nascimento. "Burnham had no actual son, and so Bonny could get away with anything. Bonny was completely self-centered and often took advantage of [Burnham's] affection." Angering Mann by arbitrarily ending his affair with Adams might also annoy Burnham. Besides, the closer Adams drew to Mann, the more access she would have through him to Burnham and his inner circle. Jones was already dismayed by his lack of direct, extended access to the Guyanese prime minister. Most often, Jones was directed to Deputy Prime

Minister Ptolemy Reid, who also served as Guyana's minister of agriculture and economic development as well as overseer of the military. So Adams was allowed to continue the affair, with the understanding that her real — only — allegiance was to Jones and the Temple. She was to report anything Mann said that touched on or even indirectly involved the Temple, and, whenever opportunity occurred, go through his briefcase and private papers. That made it Adams's turn to attempt a private balancing act. She believed in Jones and the Temple, but was genuinely in love with the ambassador. Jones eventually hedged his bet, bringing in Sharon Amos to serve as his primary contact with Guyanese officials in case Adams's loyalty wavered.

Beginning with this visit, Jones identified himself in Guyana as a bishop; the title was self-bestowed rather than awarded by the Disciples of Christ. Jones made a major misstep when he attempted to insinuate himself among Georgetown's established religious entities. The country was roughly 40 percent Christian and 50 percent Muslim; in Georgetown there was a church council with representatives of several Christian denominations. Jones quickly identified Father Andrew Morrison of Georgetown's Sacred Heart Catholic Church as perhaps the dominant cleric. He asked and received permission to conduct a guest service at Sacred Heart on December 30.

The service was packed. Jones began by praising brotherhood among all faiths. He joked about wearing a suit, and asked for a robe to cover it: "I never wear [the suit], and I feel most ridiculous in it. . . . I only own one pair of shoes and I find that's most convenient for me [because] I only have two feet." He said he based his personal and ministerial modesty on a philosophy of "apostolic cooperative living." In a prayer, he asked God to provide "a movement of the Holy Spirit in our midst today that will cause people to believe that there's hope. . . . We ask it in the name of Christ." Then Jones began calling out individuals, describing their various ailments and promising to cure them. One person complaining of arthritic knees was commanded to "jump up and down, just like a little child," did as instructed, and claimed to be healed. Jones cautioned that "we believe in doctors, we believe in medicine, but we also believe that when man cannot reach you, God can reach you." He told another person describing chest discomfort, "You lift up your hands now. The pain will go away." He went on for some time, finally giving the Temple's mailing address in Redwood Valley and assuring his audience that "healing is available to anyone, no matter what their religion, no matter what their creed."

Father Morrison had expected a traditional prayer-based service. Afterward, he learned that everyone healed in the Sacred Heart service was a member of Peoples Temple. He made an official complaint about Jones's sham healing to Kit Nascimento, who functioned as Prime Minister Burnham's chief of staff. "I told [Father Morrison] the truth," Nascimento says. "The Prime Minister wanted this man and his mission in our country to succeed, so there was no use complaining." But Jones's reputation among other Christian leaders in Georgetown was permanently damaged. There would be no further collaborations or guest services.

Jones's visit to the North West District mission was also disappointing. Significant progress had been made — within a few months, Guyanese officials would note that over one hundred acres of jungle had been cleared and planted — but Jones had described vast fields of vegetables and fruit to his followers back home. Elmer Mertle, serving as trip photographer, was given the unenviable task of taking pictures that would back up Jones's descriptions. Finally, Jones and Mertle purchased fruit in Port Kaituma, transported it to Jonestown, and Jones posed in a field, proudly gesturing at the gorgeous produce. No one back in California knew the difference, and those along with Jones on the trip weren't telling.

Jones's December 1974 trip to Guyana was significant in another way. Besides his usual array of intimates and Planning Commission members, he brought along Maria Katsaris. There was some question among the others about why Maria was included. She was a dutiful follower, and worked hard in the letters office, but remained painfully shy. She was also extremely self-conscious about her appearance. Her father, Steven, had been a Greek Orthodox priest, and there was some sense that he and Jones disliked each other.

But on this trip Jones and Maria became lovers, and not for the usual few weeks that defined Jones's other affairs except for his ongoing relationship with Carolyn Moore. The change in Maria was startling. Almost overnight, her shyness morphed into self-confidence. She demonstrated not only considerable intelligence, but abilities as a leader. "Jim always claimed that he had sex with women to lift them up, to help them become stronger and better," Tim Carter says. "With Maria, that really happened. Jones started having sex with her, and she blossomed." Back in America, the relationship continued. Maria became very protective of Jones. She assumed a leadership position in the Temple, and Planning Commission members who'd previously known a meek, somewhat immature girl now found themselves dealing with a self-assured woman who made it clear that she knew what Father wanted, and who intended to see things done exactly that way. It was soon accepted by the rest of Temple leadership that now Maria Katsaris often spoke for Jones, just as Carolyn Moore frequently did.

There was also a great change regarding Carolyn. By mid-1974, she had been intimate with Jones for five years. She still considered him to be a great leader, but knew Jones too well to believe he was in any way godlike. Her attachment was to the man, and, through him, to the Temple and its mission. It was impossible for her to separate one from the other. In public, she served as Jones's un-official chief of staff. That would have been burden enough for anyone, but Carolyn also had to deal with Jones in private, seeing him sometimes comatose from drugs, nursing him through frequent episodes of hypochondria, mothering his unruly children, and standing by while he indulged in sex with multiple partners. Perhaps most painful of all, when Jones had another biological child, it was with Grace Stoen rather than Carolyn.

For a while, Carolyn may have hoped that her sacrifices would someday be rewarded with marriage. If nothing else, becoming Jones's wife would have been recognition of her value to him, and to the Temple. But she eventually realized that would never happen. After her thwarted attempt to break away from Jones in the early 1970s, Marceline evidently resigned herself to her own frustrating lot and made no further attempt to leave. Jones made it obvious, even putting it in writing, that in the event of his death he wanted Marceline rather than Carolyn to lead the Temple. (Jones specified that Marceline would immediately succeed him, and that Stephan would be next in line "if he is willing." He added that Carolyn could serve as chairman of the Planning Commission.) And Marceline made it equally clear that she was now willing to serve Jones in whatever capacity he wished. In February 1974, she sent her husband a handwritten note:

Dearest Jim:
   I wanted to send you a Valentine but searched in vain for one I could relate to. I thought of writing my deep sentimental feelings I have for you but decided that was selfish since you might feel it required some response from you. So, I decided that the things I most wanted you to know was:

1. How much I appreciate what I've learned about life by knowing you.
2. Even though I have a strong personal attachment to you, if some fate

should separate us forever, I will lend what strength I have to defend the defenseless and oppressed.

3. You have been my only lover and there shall never be another. I enjoyed our intimate times together and face the rest of my life, happily, just remembering those moments I loved you before you were "God" and will always be sentimental about those years when I thought us lovers.

4. My love for you, today, wishes for you peace, rest and the fulfillment of your dream of a better world.

Happy Valentine's Day,
Marceline

Jones did not entirely take Carolyn for granted. She had to have something, a special gesture that proved how much he valued her. And so, in the summer of 1974, Carolyn Moore Layton disappeared from Peoples Temple. Jones made it known that he'd sent her away on a crucial, secret mission — she'd be gone for some time. He didn't elaborate. A few months later, Jones revealed dreadful news. Carolyn's mission had taken her to Mexico, where she'd been arrested and jailed. Now she was being tortured by her captors, and bravely refusing to reveal Temple secrets. "The impression given was that if Carolyn could make that kind of sacrifice, then if the rest of us thought we were working hard and felt exhausted, we should remember what she was willing to do," Tim Carter says. Jones embellished the story, telling Planning Commission members that Carolyn had gone to Mexico to purchase the components of an atomic bomb for the Temple — once the church had the bomb, then the government would have no choice but to respect them. Before her arrest, Jones said, Carolyn had acquired all the necessary components but a detonator, which Temple secret agents assigned by Jones would continue trying to locate and purchase. The P.C. members believed him — anything was possible with Father.

Then, in the spring of 1975, Carolyn returned — and she had a baby with her.

Rev. John V. Moore remembers, "In, I believe, August of 1974, Carolyn contacted her mother and me and said she was pregnant. She asked to come live with us in Berkeley until the baby was born. We knew, of course, that Jim Jones was the father. Whatever our feelings were about the matter, Carolyn was our daughter, and so we invited her to come."

During the next six months, Jones would occasionally stay overnight with Carolyn and the Moores. He conducted himself like a son-in-law, except when Barbara Moore asked, "When are you going to divorce Marceline and marry our daughter?" Reverend Moore remembers, "[Jones mumbled] something about Marceline not being well, and that she couldn't deal with a divorce. And Carolyn had always told us that [Marceline] was emotionally unstable, and that [Jones] remained married to her out of pity. So although Barbara and I distrusted Jim Jones, we kind of had a truce with him. He was going to be the father of our grandchild."

On January 31, 1975, Carolyn gave birth to a son named Jim Jon. Immediately afterward, she stunned her father with a new request: he must perform a marriage ceremony between her and Michael Prokes, the former newsman who'd joined the Temple and become one of its principal spokesmen. "When I asked why, she said it was what she and Jim wanted," Moore says. "I thought it was what he wanted rather than her, but she continued to insist, so I reluctantly performed the ceremony." The child's birth record recorded his full name as Jim Jon Prokes.

But when Carolyn returned to Peoples Temple with her infant son, she didn't identify Prokes as the father. Instead, conflicting reports emerged that Jim Jon, soon nicknamed Kimo, was the unwanted child of one of Carolyn's cousins, or that the baby was the result of Carolyn's having been raped in the Mexican prison. Carolyn was as reserved as ever. The circumstances of the child's conception remained unconfirmed. The Temple welcomed Kimo into its fold, and a significant exception was made for the child — once beyond infancy, all Temple offspring were raised communally, but Kimo remained with his mother. This was Jones's private recognition of Carolyn's special place in his heart.

But Carolyn returned to find that Maria Katsaris had assumed a nearly equal place, sharing not only Jones's bed but a considerable amount of Temple responsibility. In certain physical and personal respects, Maria resembled both Marceline and Carolyn. All three women were slender, intelligent, and exceptionally good at attending to details and seeing that things got done, the latter skill compensating for Jones's own administrative weaknesses. The difference between them was that Marceline had status as Jones's wife, Carolyn now had his child, and Maria had neither, only what she considered the honor of being Jones's lover and trusted confidante. For her, then and later, that was enough.

Kimo's birth did ease some of the tension between Carolyn and Jones's other children. Suzanne remained aloof, but Stephan warmed to her a little more. Jimmy found a practical reason to like Carolyn: "She and my dad would go out, and I was old enough to watch the little ones, John-John [Stoen] and Kimo. They'd get back and my dad would give me $20, but Carolyn would sneak me forty."

Money was also on the minds of Jones and Marceline. In July, they signed last will and testaments. These listed Johnny Brown among their children — they stressed that they now considered him their son, though he was never formally adopted. Agnes, still a disappointment — Marceline had recently become legal guardian of Agnes's daughter, Stephanie (the child was then communally raised) — was to receive a single lump sum of $5,000, with everything else divided equally among the others. Carolyn Layton was named executor, with Michael Prokes and Carolyn's sister Annie as alternates.

Jones spent much of summer 1975 touting the Promised Land to followers, encouraging them to ask to go there. Those who'd accompanied him on trips to Guyana vied to offer the most enthusiastic descriptions. Sandy Ingram gushed that the ragged patch gouged out of the jungle so far by the Pioneers resembled nothing so much as "a magnificent estate." Jones continually emphasized how Temple members in America lived under the threat of confinement in CIA or FBI concentration camps. According to Edith Roller's journal, by mid-July when Jones asked how many at a Geary Boulevard service were ready to move to Guyana, "only a scattered few" failed to raise their hands.

Most Temple members thought Jones really did want everyone to go. Privately, he was more practical. The plan, always, was to restrict the Jonestown population to five hundred or six hundred. That was maximum capacity for the projected housing to be built there, and a sustainable number for the food that could be produced on-site, at least during early years as they experimented with various crops and livestock. But he hoped that half of the Temple's 4,000 to 5,000 members would want to go. The competition would better ensure that those chosen would stick it out under living conditions that were far rougher than Jones led followers to believe.

Jones, Carolyn, Maria, and a few others began making "priority lists" of members who would ideally go first — some rugged young men and women who could physically handle grueling jungle labor, teens who couldn't stay out of trouble in San Francisco and Los Angeles, teachers to conduct classes, and, most critically, older members whose pensions could be used to help defray the costs of maintaining the Guyanese mission. Leola Clark, who received monthly checks of $223.10 in disability payments and $130.10 from Social Security, was deemed "very desirable." Simon Elsey, with a $935 monthly pension, was even better, but he was reluctant to go. Though Melvin Murphy's monthly pension was $500, he had pending "legal problems." Jones didn't want requests for assistance from U.S. law enforcement bringing the Temple to the attention of Guyanese courts. Guyana had no official extradition agreement with the United States, but it still wasn't worth the risk.

Whether they were included on the priority list or not, all members were urged to give even more to the Temple in support of Jonestown. No keepsake was too precious to be sacrificed. Every possible penny was wrung out of current Temple operations. Members living communally had been allowed to make many of their own meals. Now all communals in San Francisco were required to come to the Geary Boulevard temple to eat what was served there. Rheaviana Beam took charge of food purchasing and preparation. Buying in bulk, soliciting donations of day-old goods from bakeries, she soon bragged that meals for each communal cost the Temple only 16 cents per day. The resulting menus were unexciting — cereal moistened with non-fat powdered milk, peanut butter and bologna sandwiches, dinners with lots of starches and very little meat — but at every meeting Jones emphasized that each bland bite choked down was in service to the greater good.

He occasionally mentioned another potential sacrifice. Not everyone might get to the

Promised Land, since so many malign forces were dedicated to preventing Peoples Temple from setting its persuasive socialist example. If the Temple couldn't be discouraged by constant harassment, then the U.S. government would order the CIA and FBI to consider more violent means. Jones preached that the message to these enemy agencies must be, "If you come for one of us, you're coming for all of us." In a September sermon he added, "I love socialism, and I'd die to bring it about. But if I did, I'd take a thousand with me." His followers surely assumed that he meant a thousand of the Temple's enemies, but a few weeks later Jones sternly noted, "A good socialist does not fear death. It would be the greatest reward he could receive." Loyal Temple members must not only be willing to dedicate their lives, but also their deaths, to the cause. Several times Jones specifically mentioned Masada, the mountaintop fortress in Israel where almost one thousand Jewish revolutionaries, women, and children committed suicide rather than surrender to a Roman army about to breach the walls. More than nineteen centuries later, their courage and sacrifice still resonated with all who refused to accept subjugation. Individual suicide was wasteful, but mass suicide that sent a message of defiance, and that encouraged future generations to fight oppression to the death, was admirable.

That same September, Jones reemphasized that point to the Planning Commission in an especially terrifying way. It began with an apparent treat. The Temple grew grapes on ranch property it owned in Mendocino County, never a big crop, but enough sometimes to make some wine. Jones generally forbade drinking alcohol, but on this night at the Geary Boulevard temple he told the P.C. members that it was all right for once. Each of them drank some, and after their cups were emptied Jones informed them that their wine had been laced with poison — all of them would die within forty-five minutes to an hour. There was no antidote. They were doomed.

Jones had prepped two committee members about what he was going to do. When the deadly announcement was made, Patty Cartmell screeched, jerked up from her chair, and tried to run from the meeting room. Michael Prokes, using a pistol loaded with blanks, fired several shots. Cartmell collapsed and lay moaning on the floor.

Jones watched as everyone else sat around, some staring into space, some talking about dying, a few lamenting that they would no longer be around to protect the Temple children from the FBI and CIA and the rest of the evil outside world. After three-quarters of an hour, several said they were beginning to feel faint. Jones let them describe their symptoms for a few minutes, then announced that there was no poison in the wine. It had been a test of their loyalty; now they knew that they had it in them to face death unflinchingly. Cartmell got up and rejoined the group. No one criticized Jones for tricking them. Decades later, several of those present claimed that they knew all along that it was a hoax, exactly the kind of dramatic thing Jones liked to do to make a point. Terri Buford said that, in retrospect, she and the others missed the most important message: "Yes, we proved that we were willing to die, but what that night really proved was that [Jones] already had the intention or at least was considering the possibility that, at some point, he would kill us all."

During fall 1975, Temple business continued mostly as usual. Jones touted the Promised Land in Guyana, preached against racism — in one service, he demanded that all white Temple members fast for five days so that they could understand the hunger endured by generations of oppressed blacks — and kept the Temple a constant presence at public meetings and government hearings, never favoring one political side over another, but making sure that the Temple and its good work was never far from the thoughts of city leaders.

In October there was a startling defection

— Elmer and Deanna Mertle and their children fled the church. The Mertles had been valued members; their canny marketing sense had been instrumental in helping develop the Temple's outreach through letters and pamphlets, and they'd been exemplary parents to communal kids. But constant demands by Jones for even more time and contributions wore them down, and when their daughter was badly beaten after being called on the floor, they had had enough. Fearing retribution by Jones — they'd seen his previous antagonism toward defectors firsthand — they went to court and legally changed their names to Al and Jeannie Mills. They also decided, once they felt certain they'd slipped any Temple pursuers, to contact government officials and offer testimony regarding all the wrongs being done by Jones and his staff: the beatings, the harassments, and, especially, the bilking of members' property in the name of Peoples Temple and the socialist cause. The newly minted Millses hadn't forgotten losing some of their own property to Temple legal shenanigans after being asked to travel to Peru and Kenya on Promised Land scouting trips.

Elmer and Deanna, now Al and Jeannie, were clever, determined people, armed with inside Temple knowledge — potentially the worst sort of enemies that Jones could have imagined. At almost any other time, under almost any other circumstances, he would have been obsessed with either bringing them back into the Temple fold or else finding some means of guaranteeing their silence. But less than three weeks after the Mertles left, Jones's attention was claimed by another even more pressing matter, this one not an emergency but an opportunity that offered Jim Jones and Peoples Temple the chance to become much more influential, even, for the first time, politically powerful.

On November 5, State Assemblyman Willie Brown called on Tim Stoen and asked the Temple attorney to arrange a meeting between Jim Jones and George Moscone, who was embroiled in a runoff election for mayor of San Francisco.

CHAPTER THIRTY-NINE:
CITY POLITICS

George Moscone's background was classic poor-boy-makes-good. Born in 1929, Moscone was the product of a single-parent San Francisco family; his mother, Lee, threw out her drunken husband, George Sr., when the boy was nine, and raised her only child on a meager secretarial salary, working a second job on weekends to make ends meet. Young George's greatest asset was personal charm. This, combined with striking good looks, made him instantly likable.

Moscone paid his own way through the College of the Pacific, working on staff at public parks, and then went on to Hastings College of the Law in San Francisco, defraying tuition costs by working as a school janitor. Another poor, ambitious Hastings student was doing the same; co-workers Willie Brown and George Moscone became fast friends. Moscone was also pals with John Burton, whose brother Phil established himself as a leader among Democrats in the

U.S. House of Representatives. That connection, along with his friendship with Brown as the latter swiftly rose in California state politics, left Moscone well positioned to fulfill political ambitions of his own. He understood and quickly mastered the mechanics of politics — gladhanding, fund-raising, creating the right image to impress voters (Moscone and his lovely wife, Gina, had four photogenic children) — but Moscone also burned with genuine social commitment.

San Francisco was almost unique among American metropolises in that it had hybrid government, combining county and city offices. Its mayor was also chief county executive. The county Board of Supervisors was also the city council. San Francisco elections were always hard-fought; the Board of Supervisors was elected at-large, meaning the top few vote getters gained office without regard to where in the city they lived. Candidates representing black, working-class, or gay districts rarely had enough campaign money to compete with conservative whites representing the established business leadership. But Moscone, who earned his first political stripes in a losing campaign for State Assembly in 1960, put so much effort into walking San Francisco streets and making personal appeals to voters that he was elected to the Board of Supervisors in 1963. A year later, he gave up his place on the board to run successfully for a seat in the California State Senate. Soon afterward, Moscone was voted majority leader by his Democratic colleagues.

Willie Brown was Democratic whip in the State Assembly. The friends made a formidable team as they regularly opposed policies proposed by Republican governor Ronald Reagan, and often won the day for their own proposals. These included a free lunch program for impoverished public school children and decriminalization of sex between consenting adults.

By the early 1970s, when Reagan set his sights on the presidency, Moscone was considered a strong gubernatorial candidate among Democrats. But California secretary of state Jerry Brown, the son of a former governor, had the political muscle to take that nomination, so Moscone turned his attention back to his hometown. Joseph Alioto was stepping down as mayor. No one knew San Francisco better than Willie Brown, and the wily state assemblyman counseled Moscone to run. The city's gay population was undergoing explosive growth — these men and women would enthusiastically support a candidate willing to grant them real political influence. Blacks would certainly back Moscone. If sufficient additional support could be found among middle- and working-class whites, the overall coalition might be —

should be — enough to elect him. So in December 1974 Moscone announced he would run on a platform of more fairly redistributing power among city residents. He'd already demonstrated his personal skills as a campaigner. There was considerable basis for confidence.

But Moscone wasn't the only strong candidate vying to succeed Alioto. Democrat Dianne Feinstein and Republican John Barbagelata, both current city supervisors, put together their own well-structured campaigns. Feinstein was a centrist who promised more equitable representation in city government, but not the kind of radical shake-up that would result if Moscone was elected. Barbagelata ran on a conservative platform. On November 4, 1975, Moscone received a plurality but would have to face Barbagelata in a runoff. In the December 11 runoff, Moscone was favored to win. In any previous San Francisco election, it would have been virtually automatic.

But not in 1975. Barbagelata's give-us-our-city-back message resonated with voters beyond the city's conservative Republicans. Many white, straight middle-class taxpayers who traditionally voted Democratic were concerned that their hard-earned quality of life was in danger of disruption from the demands of blacks and gays. Feinstein's supporters in particular considered themselves pragmatic liberals; Moscone was too radical for their taste. If they chose to sit out the runoff, then Moscone would lose. He had to have black votes, plenty of them, to win, and Willie Brown knew who could deliver them. That's why Brown asked Tim Stoen for help getting Moscone and Jim Jones together, the sooner the better.

Moscone and Jones already knew each other. As two men who were both intensely committed to raising up those in San Francisco's poorest communities, their paths occasionally crossed. Tim Carter remembers Moscone and Harvey Milk, who owned a camera store and was perhaps the city's most prominent gay activist, attending various Temple programs. Willie Brown knew Jones, too. But prior to the 1975 mayoral race, Moscone and Brown considered Jones to be the pastor of another black — or mostly black — church who was, thankfully, more actively involved himself in pressing city social issues than leaders of other San Francisco black churches. Peoples Temple also appeared to be the *right* kind of black church, one with the sort of law-abiding members whose support for Moscone wouldn't alienate white voters leery of the Black Panthers and ghetto rioters. Moscone and Brown certainly realized Jones's desire for more influence; this was what they had to offer in exchange for his help. Jones would want a quid pro quo.

He put them off for a while, giving them more time to grow anxious. On November 13, Jones and Moscone sat down together at Moscone's campaign headquarters. In his memoir, Tim Stoen writes, "Moscone did not offer [Jones] any deal," but that is disingenuous. Moscone already knew that Jones would expect not only access, but actual influence in the form of a place for himself on some prominent city board, and additional appointments for his followers, in return for help in the runoff campaign.

What form that help took is a matter of ongoing debate. A spokesman for the Moscone campaign later told the *San Francisco Examiner* that Jones and the Temple "provided about 150 [runoff] election day workers for Moscone." There has been considerable speculation that Moscone didn't want campaign workers so much as he wanted Jones to ensure that his 1,500 or so San Francisco followers went to the polls on December 11 and voted for him. But as Moscone and Brown both must have known even before requesting the meeting, only a handful of the city's Temple members were even registered voters. What Moscone wanted, and Jones supplied, were people, many more than 150, getting out into the Western Addition and urging all the registered voters there to vote in the runoff. The Temple's letter-writing office was pressed into Moscone's service, too: Jones bragged that his followers produced three thousand letters a day to potential voters. These services were valuable, but Jones had an additional asset that served Moscone even better — the Temple fleet of Greyhound buses. On December 11, Western Addition voters were picked up at designated stops, or even at their individual homes if that was what they wanted, taken in the Temple vehicles to polling places, and dropped back in their neighborhoods or residences afterward.

Jim Jones Jr. remembers some of the Temple bus fleet doing even more: "I sat in on a meeting with Moscone and my dad where they worked on finding people in L.A. who were eligible to vote in San Francisco. Then they actually sent our buses down there and brought them north to vote on that election day. There were a lot of them, and it was a planned-out thing. If my dad committed to something, he followed through."

On December 11, Moscone nipped Barbagelata by 51 percent to 49, winning by the razor-thin margin of about 4,400 votes out of 198,741. That total almost matched the 207,647 total from the original election on May 4, meaning Barbagelata had picked up a far greater percentage of votes from the other original candidates than did Moscone. Jones and Peoples Temple tilted the balance in favor of Moscone; both the mayor-elect and his defeated opponent knew it. Barbagelata demanded a recount, which only gained him a few dozen more votes. Afterward, Barbagelata charged that members of Peoples Temple, among other unregistered voters, had cast fraudulent ballots for Moscone, and called for a thorough investigation. Jones and the Temple had not only worked on behalf of Moscone but for the successful election of liberal Joseph Freitas as district attorney, too. Freitas and his staff — which soon included new hire Tim Stoen — duly investigated and reported no wrongdoing. Stoen, in his memoir, writes that there was no investigation specifically targeting the Temple.

When Moscone called Jones five days after the runoff, Jones had the conversation taped. A Temple secretary noted, "Moscone acknowledges in essence that we won him the election promises J an appt." That, in Jones's mind, would be only the beginning. The Temple also produced a list of members Jones deemed qualified both for "salaried job appointments" and "commission appointments," with capsule descriptions of each.

Neither Jones nor any of his followers received immediate appointments, beyond Michael Prokes being named to a forty-eight-member committee to screen applicants for jobs in Moscone's administration. The lack of Temple picks soon became a source of behind-the-scenes friction between the

Temple and city hall. But Moscone made it clear that Jim Jones of Peoples Temple was now a man of considerable influence and a confidant. When Moscone attended public Temple meetings now it was treated as a state occasion, and Freitas and reelected liberal sheriff Richard Hongisto came to services, too, standing and singing along with the rest of the congregation, even when the tunes were overt socialist anthems. They didn't realize, as they swayed and sang, that Jones was secretly filming their enthusiastic participation — the day might come when one or all of these officials forgot their obligations to the Temple, and then discreet reminders would be in order.

Other local leaders also began attending the services. Harvey Milk was most prominent among them. Milk had lost an earlier attempt for a place on the board of supervisors, but a priority of the Moscone administration was to institute district rather than at-large elections, so the makeup of the board would more equitably reflect all city constituencies. That would apparently be the case in the next election, and Milk was positioning himself for another run. Jones was sufficiently enthusiastic about Milk's chances to assign Tim Carter and a few others as Milk's special contacts at the Temple, so that any request by him — the printing of campaign flyers, door-to-door volunteers — could be acted on. Carter, like almost everyone else in the Temple who got to know Milk, grew to like him immensely: "Before him, all I knew about gays were that some of them were bears and others were queens. But Harvey became a friend of mine, and I went to his house and spent time with him and his partner and realized that a gay couple was just that, a couple. See, that was something good about the Temple — if you were part of it, you always had the opportunity to grow as a person, to be around and learn to accept, to appreciate, all different kinds of people."

Jones's influence extended to the state capitol in Sacramento. Lieutenant Governor Mervyn Dymally, a transplanted native of Trinidad and one of the first men of color elected to California statewide office since Reconstruction, was so impressed by Jones and the Temple that he even accompanied Jones on a trip to Guyana, where Dymally emphasized to national leaders that Jim Jones was a *very* important man. Governor Jerry Brown acknowledged Jones, too. Once, when Brown missed speaking at a Temple service due to a schedule mix-up, he called while the service was in progress to apologize. Jones took the call offstage, taping it so Brown's apology could immediately be replayed to the congregation, who heard the governor of California asking their forgiveness.

It was always exciting for San Francisco

Temple members to see Lieutenant Governor Dymally, Willie Brown, Mayor Moscone, elected officials who were in positions to bring about the kinds of political and social change Jones and his followers sought. Even better for members with radical sympathies were the visits and guest sermons by Angela Davis, linked with the Communist Party and Black Panthers, Dennis Banks of the American Indian Movement, and Laura Allende, whose Marxist brother, Chilean president Salvador Allende, had been deposed and killed in a military coup rumored to have been underwritten by the United States It created a sense that the Temple members stood shoulder-to-shoulder with the most prominent activists. Jones encouraged that belief. Temple members weren't just reading in the newspapers about these inspirational people they admired so much, or watching them on television — now, they actually *knew* them. Jones had promised that the Temple would make history. Troubling aspects of his ministry aside — the rantings, the beatings, the histrionics — what Jones had pledged was really happening. The members of Peoples Temple were helping to bring about a new, better world. For those Jones followers who needed it, here was confirmation.

CHAPTER FORTY: MORE MONEY

Tim Stoen wasn't in San Francisco on the day of the mayoral runoff election.

Although Peoples Temple struggled financially in its early days, by 1975 the church had some significant money. Much of it, though not all, was dutifully recorded in Temple ledgers. The church had been granted tax-exempt status, but Jones always wanted financial records ready for audits by state or federal authorities. Jones also had a few private accounts. Though he proudly proclaimed that he never took a salary as Temple pastor, with his family living on Marceline's state pay, Jones needed additional funds available for personal expenses, like the Jones family vacations that most Temple members knew nothing about. Jones also hid money in savings accounts under the names of various family members. Marceline had personal accounts of as much as $200,000 (almost $800,000 in today's dollars). At one point, his mother, Lynetta, had accounts totaling

$89,584 ($380,000 in current value) in eight different California banks. Whether in terms of its public records or Jones's private accounts, the Temple was flush.

Yet this brought Jones no comfort — if anything, the Temple's wealth added to his ever-burgeoning sense of paranoia. His schemes to ensure that no one other than he knew how much money there was, and where, owed as much to uncontrollable compulsion as to deliberate design.

Throughout his life, Jones was never able to accept any form of shared possession — it was always *his* children, *his* Temple, *his* followers, and *his* money, everything to be controlled by him as he pleased without regard for others. Even back in Indianapolis, Jones blatantly fudged annual reports to the Disciples of Christ regional office, vastly underestimating congregational size and yearly income and even then sending along a much smaller contribution than other churches. In California, Jones no longer concealed the Temple's ever-growing membership, but still sent very little money for denominational support. Decades later Rev. Scott Seay, studying dusty records at a Disciples seminary in Indianapolis, commented, "It was like [Jones] was saying, 'This is all I'm going to give you,' and almost daring them to challenge him about it, and they didn't."

Jones was equally resentful of having to apply for state tax-exempt status. As Peoples Temple began to thrive in California, Jones worried about audits, and as his paranoia grew he feared that the government might freeze Temple bank accounts, claiming that Peoples Temple was using the money for subversive purposes. For some time, Jones had relied on Terri Buford to maximize Temple income. "He always wanted me to set up CDs, with maybe a million to turn over in six months, another million in a year, another million the year after that," she recalls. "At that time, interest rates were in the teens, and [Jones] wanted a rolling cascade of income." But that income, recorded and reported by the financial institutions involved, could always be scrutinized by the American government. Jim Jones wanted his money out of reach, so in 1975 he assigned Tim Stoen to research means of transferring Temple money somewhere beyond the jurisdiction of U.S. authorities. Stoen did as Jones asked and ultimately recommended opening accounts in Panama. The Temple would organize Panamanian corporations and funnel money through them into Panama banks, as well as establishing safe-deposit-box accounts in a few other countries, "with different trusted Temple members having the respective keys."

Jones approved. In early December, he sent

Stoen to Panama to do the initial legal legwork. After that, on Jones's orders other Temple members began an intricate series of trips there to deposit money in the new accounts. With the possible exception of Carolyn Layton, no one but Jones knew about every transaction. Terri Buford says, "Carolyn would come in with these financial documents and cover most of the pages up, just showing me where to sign at the bottom. So it was my name on a lot of them; if there was any trouble, I'd be the one legally responsible. At the time I thought I knew about all the money [going out of the United States], but it turned out that I didn't."

Led variously by Carolyn and Maria Katsaris, small squads of Temple members began bringing large amounts of cash from the United States to banks in Panama. The use of cashier's checks or bank transfers would have left a paper trail; though he allowed some traditional transactions, Jones limited that. More often, his followers taped packs of bills to their legs and wore money belts under their clothes. They arrived in Panama by plane, bringing with them on the same flights cases of goods they swore to customs officials were supplies for missionaries, which some were. But there were always cases that ostensibly contained boxes of Kotex. Customs inspectors in Panama were almost exclusively male, and they squeamishly peeked into the boxes if they looked at all, always ignoring those containers emptied of female sanitary products and crammed instead with cash.

Soon, Jones began depositing money in Swiss banks, too, dressing his female couriers in I. Magnin suits to throw off the U.S. government agents he felt certain would attempt to trail them. Marceline also went on overseas banking trips, and the money she deposited went into accounts in her name, her husband's, or even her children's. Carolyn apparently knew about these accounts — at least one authorized her, along with Stephan and Marceline, to make withdrawals.

Money also had to be deposited in Guyanese banks, but this was done openly, so that the country's officials would be constantly reminded of just how much Peoples Temple was investing in their nation. One to two hundred thousand dollars would be transferred from U.S. to Georgetown banks, and the money would be spent almost as soon as it arrived. Toil as hard as they might, the few dozen Temple Pioneers couldn't clear sufficient jungle on their own. Amerindians were hired on as crew, fifty or sixty at a time. Their pay was relatively low, about $35 monthly for each worker, and represented only a small portion of construction costs, which in some months reached six figures. Jones intended these alarming expenses to be temporary. It was always understood that, soon after enough jungle was cleared and some five hundred or so Temple members moved there, Jonestown would become self-sufficient. Until then, Jones accepted the financial outflow, although it grated.

With so many transactions taking place each month in multiple countries, keeping two sets of records — one official, one private — became staggeringly difficult. Over time, a code was developed to track the complicated finances. Though he publicly scorned the Bible in Temple services, a Bible became Jones's secret ledger, with coded account information scribbled along an inner seam on specific pages. This Bible was always kept in Jones's private quarters, limiting access to Carolyn, Maria, and Jones. Temple book-keeper Terri Buford estimated that the Temple's foreign accounts totaled about $8 million. In fact, the total was around $30 million.

Yet in several San Francisco services, Jones asked that everyone donate their wristwatches to the cause — these were in high demand for resale in Guyana, where, if an immediate amount of additional money wasn't received, the Jonestown project might very well fail. Every cent counts, Jones thundered at his followers, upbraiding them and sending collection plates around for an extra turn or two if the half dozen offerings regularly taken at each Temple meeting failed to produce satisfactory sums. They had no idea of the vast fortune their church had already amassed, or why, no matter how much they gave at Temple services, it was never enough to please their pastor.

CHAPTER FORTY-ONE:
DEFECTORS

From the moment he agreed to help George Moscone in the December 1975 runoff election, Jones expected the mayor to repay the favor by nominating him to a prestigious city board. But in March 1976, when Moscone came through, Jones was bitterly disappointed by his offer of a seat on San Francisco's Human Rights Commission. Years earlier in Indianapolis, Jones had eagerly accepted appointment to that city's toothless Human Rights Commission and, almost entirely on his own, made great strides in integrating the city. But on San Francisco's commission Jones would only be one of many working for greater progress in a progressive city. There would be no opportunity to stand out. So Jones refused the appointment, making it clear that he expected very soon to receive a more suitable nomination. Jones recommended Johnny Brown to serve in his place, but Brown wasn't appointed.

Two months later, Michael Prokes, identifying himself as a Temple "Associate Minister," wrote to Moscone informing the mayor that there was great disappointment among members that no one among them had yet been appointed to city commissions or given city jobs, despite the lengthy list of potential Temple candidates previously furnished to Moscone. The Temple members felt it was an "unfortunate fact" that others appointed or hired so far hadn't supported Moscone nearly as much as Jones and his followers had when the mayor was in danger of losing the December 1975 runoff. Accordingly, there was considerable "loss of morale" among the Temple congregation, along with "a general feeling that [Jim] is a little too idealistic about politics." On behalf of the Temple elders, Prokes suggested that the mayor "expedite the appointment [or assure the appointments at specific times] of those people on the [Temple] list that we have submitted to you . . . any immediate response . . . would be appreciated, sir, to either Jim or Timothy Stoen, one of his associate ministers who is now a principal attorney in the local D.A.'s office, a position which Jim certainly didn't ask for but which, nevertheless, boosted our people's esteem for the D.A."

Though Moscone continued attending occasional Temple services, he didn't respond to the letter. Jones was displeased, but chose to avoid making further demands for the time being. A recall election involving Moscone and the entire Board of Supervisors seemed probable, and even if Moscone was tempted to renege on his previous debt to Jones, a canny vote counter like Willie Brown would surely remind the mayor how much the support of Jones and Peoples Temple would be needed. Meanwhile, Jones was preoccupied with a sudden series of key defections, beginning in July with Grace Stoen.

By the summer of 1976, Grace Stoen had grown disenchanted with Peoples Temple and its leader. Jones now sometimes bragged that he would always be above everyone else: "You will never have my power. I was born with this power. Some people can sing. I was born to put the whammy on people. It is a great responsibility." Especially after forming a close relationship with Temple member Walter Jones (no relation to Jim), Grace could no longer stomach the Temple or its leader. She and Walter defected on July 4, sneaking away while Jones was preoccupied with the Temple's holiday celebration. Grace did not bring four-year-old John with her. The child was with his communal guardians; trying to take him away unexpectedly would have drawn too much attention. And there was no question that the child was well cared for. The day after leaving, Grace called Jones to explain why she'd left, and to arrange some plan of joint custody for their little boy. Jones said that the Temple upbringing was best for the child; Grace should come back. Her attempted defection would be forgiven.

Though she wouldn't tell Jones where she was, they talked more on the telephone and came to an initial agreement. Grace would tape a message for Temple members, explaining she was away on a church mission and hadn't defected. In return, she would be allowed to come to a September service in Los Angeles, see her son, and leave unmolested, though without the boy. That all happened as planned. Afterward, Grace met with Jones and Tim Stoen. What they said to each other is uncertain — in his memoir, Stoen writes only that "[Jones] tried to get her to come back to the Temple or at least tell him where she was living. She refused." But later in Jonestown, investigators found several undated documents, signed in flowing hand by Grace Stoen, granting permission for her son to be taken to Guyana, and releasing Jones and the Temple "of any and all liability, claims, causes and causes of action." The evident understanding was that if at some point the boy was sent to Guyana, the Temple would pay for his mother to periodically fly overseas to see him. Grace apparently accepted this as a possibility, and, to keep Jones open to more negotiation, signed the papers.

Tim Stoen's role was curious. He had earlier decided to separate from the Temple.

But whether he believed it possible that he might be John's biological father or not, Stoen considered the boy to be his son, too, and loved the child. In the wake of Grace's defection, which Stoen writes that he did not know about in advance and did not expect, the best way to ensure his continued contact with John was to stay with Jones and the Temple, doing his best to act as a go-between for his estranged wife and his pastor.

Jones was less concerned about Temple secrets Grace might reveal in depositions and testimony than in the possibility that he would lose control of his son. Jones took great personal delight in the child, who resembled him physically with black hair and dark, expressive eyes. By September, when the first few dozen settlers left the United States for Jonestown, Jones approached Tim Stoen and asked him to agree to send John, in the care of some of the same Temple women already raising him communally. Once the little boy was in Guyana, it would be difficult for Grace to get him back if American courts ever ruled in her favor.

Stoen wrote in his memoir that he agreed to let John go, "figuring it was Jones's way to get Grace to come back to the Temple, and that [John's stay in Jonestown] would be temporary because Jones, like me, would want access to John, and because he . . . was now riding high and would not soon, if ever, be leaving for Guyana." John Victor Stoen was whisked away to Guyana. His mother learned that the boy was gone only in November.

There were more defections that summer, significant enough that, in other times, they might have rocked the Temple as much as the loss of the Gang of Eight. Neva Sly fled, leaving behind her husband, Don, and their son. She had been disciplined for smoking and then, after a severe beating for continuing to smoke left her with injuries, she accepted the help of her co-workers and fled from Peoples Temple. Temple members tracked her down, and for months followed her everywhere, even confronting her at a restaurant and reminding her that Father knew where she was, she'd better not say or do anything against him and the Temple. She didn't — she just wanted to get away, even though it meant permanent estrangement from her husband and son, who remained loyal to the Temple.

Joyce Shaw left, too. She'd made herself practically irreplaceable as a foster parent for dozens of numerous waifs and teens taken in by the Temple. Shaw resented being questioned by the Temple Planning Commission. It felt especially offensive because, besides her constant responsibilities as a foster parent, she had a day job as well, contributing her entire salary to the Temple. In July 1976, less than two weeks after Grace Stoen and Walter Jones defected, Shaw did as well. Afterward she talked to her husband, Bob Houston, a few times, and also to Jones, but despite their pleas she chose not to return to Peoples Temple. Bob Houston worked two jobs and also served on the Planning Commission. He was seriously overworked, and then on October 4 Houston was found crushed to death in the Southern Pacific railroad yard, apparently having been lying on the track as a train passed. It was thought that he had fallen asleep or passed out there. The possibility that he'd fallen asleep and fallen onto the tracks at precisely the moment a train passed troubled some Temple members. In his sermons, Jones always warned anyone considering defection that something terrible would happen to those who left his protection, and he had always picked on Bob: Could he have used him in a final, terrible way, as an example of what might happen immediately to anyone leaving the Temple?

Bob Houston's father, Sam, worked as a photographer for the Associated Press. He was friendly with U.S. congressman Leo Ryan, whose 11th District encompassed a wide swath of the Bay Area above Oakland and Berkeley. Ryan, a Democrat, was highly popular among constituents but somewhat less so among colleagues in the House of Representatives. Most of the other members liked Ryan personally, but considered him a relentless seeker of publicity. To investigate prison corruption, Ryan had had himself anonymously incarcerated in Folsom Prison for a short time. He had also traveled to Newfoundland, where he placed himself dramatically in the path of hunters he claimed were about to kill baby seals. Each time, he reveled in the widespread media attention. Some fellow congressmen — "undoubtedly jealous of their peer's prowess in achieving positive headlines on a consistent basis," according to former speaker of the house Jim Wright — joked among themselves about what outrageous publicity stunt Ryan might pull next.

When Sam Houston poured out his concerns to Ryan, the congressman was intrigued. There were other pressing matters that needed Ryan's immediate attention, but he promised Houston that, when time permitted, he and his staff would look into the matter. Many members of Peoples Temple lived in or at least originally hailed from the 11th. Ryan felt this made it appropriate for him to investigate allegations about the church.

Jim Jones already felt certain that he and his church were under constant government surveillance, but he was simultaneously convinced of his invincibility. He was too smart, too *special,* to be brought down by enemies. Jones encouraged the planning of grandiose schemes that would allow the Temple either to strike back at powerful governmental foes or, if sufficiently threatened, make some grand revolutionary statement that might intimidate enemies or at least stand as a historic, defiant gesture. The concept of mass suicide, a Masada, had already been raised within the Planning Commission and in closed Temple meetings. Jones had additional ideas.

Terri Buford's Diversions operation was originally designed to spread false rumors about competing evangelists and their followers. Now she was given darker assignments. "Jim wanted me to go to Libya and make contact with [Muammar al-] Qaddafi there," she says. "He wanted us linked up with the right revolutionaries, that kind of connection. I never went, but that was just one thing that was talked about. There was talk about, if we had to retaliate after someone did something to us, poisoning some city's water supply. We did research about that."

Neva Sly adds that "we all thought he had that atomic bomb. It was supposed to be down in Mexico, right there if we needed it. [Jones] talked about it sometimes."

One plot was perhaps the most horrific of

all. "[Jones wanted] Maria Katsaris to go to flight school in San Francisco and learn to fly," Terri Buford says. "She'd get a plane and put a couple hundred Temple members on it and crash the plane, as a symbol we would rather die than corrupt ourselves by submitting to the American government. She said that she'd do it, she just didn't want to go to flight school. This was never going to be like 9/11, crashing into a building and killing innocent people. We were always going to be the only ones who died. [Jones] was always ready to kill us. That whole group suicide [idea] didn't start in Guyana."

Jones was indulging himself with fantasy. But he insisted that his followers, Planning Commission members in particular, fantasize right along with him. Just as so many of them had signed over personal property, they were required to put in writing, then sign, their intention to commit terrible acts (assassinating the president was perhaps the most popular), or else confess to having already committed them.

Jones's rambling sermons grew more bizarre. He challenged God ("I'm a liberator, he's a fucker-upper"), and claimed that, in another life, he personally witnessed a drugged, still living Jesus taken down off the cross by loyal followers ("He went to India and he did a lot of teaching over there. . . . I don't care whether you believe it or not"). A few times Jones even described himself as an extraterrestrial: "I was the greatest on [another] planet, [and] only I could get down here." His followers would endure endless earthly reincarnations until "you become sensitive, then you will be released from your earth-boundedness and you'll move on to an advanced field of teachers in another planet. . . . That's why I'm trying so hard."

Read decades later, such declarations seem nothing more than obvious, grandiose self-delusion. But many among Jones's followers didn't regard them that way. There were few brand-new members now. Jones already had sufficient numbers to impress politicians and plenty of people to send out on buses to march in support of freedom of the press or in protest of some bureaucratic act. Additional recruits, at least in San Francisco and Los Angeles, weren't worth the trouble of weeding through to find potential true believers. Among those who were already part of the Temple fellowship, only a handful remembered the days in Indianapolis, when Jim Jones wasn't declaring himself to be God. Followers who joined from the first Ukiah days onward had become conditioned to his claims as they gradually escalated. Tim Carter says, "It was like the frog in the pot of water. If you drop him in water that's already boiling, he'll try to hop right out. But put him first in a pot of lukewarm water and then turn up the heat little by little, and he'll stay in the pot even though he's finally being boiled to death." Some didn't believe any of it but followed Jones to help bring about the advancement of socialism.

And there were plenty somewhere in the middle, who believed in socialism and stopped short of considering Jones to be God, but still felt that he had some sort of power, whether to read minds or to see the future or to heal. To almost all Temple members, Jones was clearly special even if only in some undefinable way, and, thanks to him, great things were being accomplished. Despite occasional defections, the vast majority remained loyal.

Jones himself spent much of 1976 feeling more satisfied than concerned. In his mind, key defections had been dealt with. He controlled Grace Stoen because he had young John safely in Georgetown. Neva Sly and Joyce Shaw were sufficiently intimidated. By year's end, even with the defections and Mayor Moscone's tardiness with an appropriate city appointment, so many good things had happened for Jim Jones and Peoples Temple during the past months that it seemed impossible to regard 1976 so far as anything other than a magnificent success.

CHAPTER FORTY-TWO: "OUR YEAR OF ASCENDENCY"

Marceline Jones received an emotional blow during the first few weeks of 1976. Her husband informed her that sometime in the future he planned to move to Guyana, taking their children with him. Marceline would stay behind to oversee the Temple in California. Jones didn't offer her any opportunity to discuss it or the option of going to Guyana with her family while someone else took over Temple operations back in the States. She would do as she was told.

It crushed Marceline. She asked Jones if she could see a psychiatrist. He granted permission, but apparently the one chosen didn't adhere to any semblance of doctor-patient confidentiality, sharing with Jones what Marceline talked about in their sessions. This allowed Jones to put his own spin on the state of his wife's mental health. He told Charlotte Baldwin, his mother-in-law, that the psychiatrist had concluded that Marceline was so troubled it might be better to immediately separate her from the children. Jones said that out of compassion for his wife he'd let her remain with them, at least for the time being. But now he had an additional threat to hold over Marceline.

There was good news from Guyana. Things in Jonestown seemed to be going well. The Temple Pioneers were making steady, if slow, construction progress and, based on their letters and phone calls home, a strong camaraderie had developed among them. Jones still had concerns, mostly involving escalating costs. He dispatched Maria Katsaris to investigate, and she reported that "there is no way to follow where all the money goes once it comes from the U.S." More stringent accounting practices needed to be put in place. Jones was confident that all the kinks could be worked out. Perhaps the settlement wasn't yet the tropical paradise Jones described to followers in sermons, but it could become one. If — when — it did, and became a showcase of socialism, it would serve as an appropriate stage for Jones, a socialist kingdom of his personal design.

In February, at Jones's behest, the Temple board voted that the Guyana mission would be "fully and completely" independent from the U.S. office. Everything sent to Jonestown — equipment, supplies — would be at the mission's "total and unfettered control." So, eventually, would all the settlement's funds.

When Jones relocated there, he would be immune from potential interference by anyone back in the United States.

That accomplished, Jones reveled in his current stateside success. None was sweeter than the day in March when *San Francisco Chronicle* columnist Herb Caen wrote about Jones for the first time. Caen's column was widely accepted as the barometer of city celebrity. He never wasted ink on nonentities. Anyone he mentioned was understood to be among the San Francisco elite, and Caen's initial mention of Jones could not have been more glowing. He described the Temple leader relaxing at a prominent restaurant with two ex-mayors and Willie Brown, and lauded how Jones and the Temple supported many outstanding local causes. Those few who knew the real Jim Jones must have laughed at Caen's description of his personality, "soft-spoken, modest, publicity shy, and will not be pleased to see his name in the paper," but the vast majority of Caen's readers believed every word. With that, Jim Jones became not just a city leader, but a San Francisco celebrity.

Caen began mentioning Jones and the Temple on a regular basis. There was ample opportunity. Jones seemed to be everywhere at once, and not just in San Francisco. Though he had no real chance to become nearly as prominent in Los Angeles, he still did enough in that city to build, then maintain, a degree of political and civic influence. In May 1976, Peoples Temple and the Los Angeles Black Muslims co-hosted a "Spiritual Jubilee" at the city convention center. It was an epic event, and a who's who of California politics attended, including Lieutenant Governor Dymally, Carlton Goodlett, Angela Davis, and Los Angeles mayor Tom Bradley. Jones's relationship with Goodlett had grown especially warm. They became partners in an import-export company and co-investors in a Norfolk, Virginia, black newspaper.

In the summer, Jones led another cross-country bus tour. This one featured a stop in Lynn and had about it the air of a farewell visit. Six hundred followers piled out of the buses, and Jones made a special point of gathering them outside Myrtle Kennedy's home, introducing the gawky old lady as his "second mother." The Temple members were highly amused when Mrs. Kennedy described young Jim Jones as "a real active boy and a mischief-maker." Afterward, she and Jones talked privately. Mrs. Kennedy told her family that Jones asked her to move to Jonestown, where everything was perfect and she would be well cared for. She declined. The invitation was evidence that Jones had not forgotten an old friend who'd helped him along the way. To Jones, the opportunity to live in Jonestown was the most generous form of thanks possible. At least to some extent, he believed his own exaggerations.

After stops in Washington, D.C., Philadelphia, Cleveland, Detroit, and Chicago, the Temple's Greyhound caravan returned to California just in time for the July 4th Bicentennial celebrations. They were unaffected by Grace Stoen's defection, which Jones managed to keep quiet. Though their leader continued preaching about solemn subjects — Jones promised, "If you give yourself to socialism, you will not die by accident or in a sick bed, but you will determine your destiny and die where and when it can best serve socialism" — the congregation felt a growing sense of accomplishment. Praise in the newspapers for Jones was, followers believed, praise for the Temple and for them. The reverse would also be true. Any attack on him was taken personally by his followers. But in 1976 there was no negative media coverage. Most often, rank-and-file Temple members saw Jones at his best, charismatic in the most positive ways, joking, *caring.* They didn't experience the rantings in Planning Commission meetings or witness Jones's constant, almost casual, cruelty to his wife. For years, he'd done all he could to keep the Temple in a defensive, crisis mode, citing local rednecks or government agencies out to get them, a dangerous world where only Jim Jones's protection kept his followers safe.

Now, it was obvious that the Temple and its leader were gaining the influence that they'd always sought. This became increasingly evident in the fall.

Temple members were thrilled to learn that on Saturday, September 25, there would be a gala testimonial dinner honoring Jim Jones. The location was to be the San Francisco temple, and Jones's followers were assured that a glittering array of political notables would attend to pay tribute to the Temple leader. So that none of the luminaries would become upset or misunderstand, Jones explained, for that evening only his followers must address him as "Jim" and not "Father." Less pleasing was Jones's announcement that Temple members would be expected to each pay $20 admission, and also hit the streets to sell tickets to the general public. Jones expected a full house. Initially, advance sales were slow. Marceline, conducting a Sunday service in her husband's absence, chided the congregation for slipshod effort — it would be disrespectful to Father if there was even one vacant seat. The pep talk worked. By the evening of the dinner, all seats were spoken for.

Before that, Jones had another exciting announcement. The 1976 presidential campaign was well under way with Republican incumbent Gerald Ford challenged by Democrat Jimmy Carter. Carter's wife, Rosalynn, was coming to San Francisco for an event at the city's Carter campaign headquarters, and she had requested a private meeting with Jones. Although Jones warned his followers that "she wouldn't hesitate to place us all in concentration camps," he was going to take the meeting. In fact, Jones had been contacted by local Democratic leaders asking that he bring some Temple members to fill seats at the program. He agreed, so long as he was seated onstage near Mrs. Carter and allowed to make some remarks of his own. The Carter program organizers were happy to agree — in an era when many white Americans feared the Black Panthers and other slogan-shouting revolutionaries of color, it would be reassuring for the media covering Mrs. Carter's appearance to see seats filled with members of a prominent black church.

On September 14, Jones and several buses of Temple members arrived as planned. For a change, Jones was dressed in a well-tailored business suit. His son Jimmy had dragged him to the clothing store to make the purchase, and paid for it without letting Jones know that the suit cost $150. "He wouldn't have stood for it," Jim Jones Jr. remembers.

The event went well. Mrs. Carter was greeted with enthusiastic applause, which almost but not quite equaled the ovation Temple members gave their leader when he was introduced. Jones and Mrs. Carter had a few moments of private conversation, which, for her, was simply one more campaign courtesy rather than a discussion of any consequence. A few days later, Mrs. Carter made a follow-up phone call, intended as another gesture of thanks. Jones told her that he had considerable influence among Disciples of Christ churches, and would help the Carter campaign in any way she asked. Mrs. Carter said she hoped Jones would one day meet her sister-in-law, evangelist Ruth Carter Stapleton. The soon-to-be first lady would have been astonished to hear Jones, in one of his next sermons, announce that Jimmy Carter was considering appointing him U.S. ambassador to Guyana.

After Carter's election in November, Jones wrote to the first lady, telling her about a trip he'd just made to Cuba and suggesting possible new American policies toward that country. He received a brief, handwritten reply from Mrs. Carter. She thanked him for the letter, said she'd enjoyed meeting him during the campaign, and repeated that he and Ruth Carter Stapleton ought to meet. On the Carter end, that concluded business with Jones. For Jones, the short meeting and shorter note constituted a relationship that he bragged about to Guyanese officials on his next visit — surely they would want to cooperate fully with a personal friend and valued advisor of America's president and first lady. "We couldn't help but feel impressed," Kit Nascimento recalls.

Then came Jones's testimonial dinner. In front of a packed house, political heavyweights from Mayor Moscone to black militant Eldridge Cleaver paid Jones tribute by their presence. During his introduction of the guest of honor, Willie Brown described Jones as "a combination of Martin Luther King, Angela Davis, Albert Einstein, and chairman Mao." The highlight came when Jones was presented with "a certificate of honor," which read: "On the occasion of a dinner in his honor, in recognition of his guidance and inspiration in establishing the many humanitarian programs in Peoples Temple, and in deep appreciation for his tireless and invaluable contributions to all the people of the Bay Area."

After the program, when all the non-Temple guests were gone, Jones convened his followers. He said that the dinner had gone well — government agencies, especially the IRS, would never dare "call us in after this display of brotherhood." The media was under Temple control, too: "Newsmen will back us up if we're in trouble."

A few weeks later, Mayor Moscone offered Jones a place on the city Housing Authority, and he accepted. On the surface, this position had less potential for high-profile action

607

than the Human Rights slot Jones had scorned. But he understood what few others in San Francisco government yet had. The city had made great strides in diversity. Moscone kept his campaign pledge to involve minorities, gays, and lower-income citizens in leadership. But political influence so far had had little effect on where the newly empowered could live. From the first meeting Jones attended, the nature of the board changed dramatically. Previously, its members discussed and debated mostly in private because few citizens or members of the media bothered attending their meetings. Jones swooped in with an entourage of Temple members to cheer his every utterance and bodyguards to ward off potential assassins. The bodyguards never had to do anything, but their presence ratcheted up tension considerably. Temple press releases touted blatant mistreatment of the poor and minorities who could not afford decent places to live, and reporters began in-depth coverage of the Housing Authority, confident that Jones could always be counted on for colorful quotes. Within a few months, Moscone named Jones chairman, and the authority became Jones's personal fiefdom.

Right away, the Housing Authority voted to use over a $1 million in federal community development funds to acquire, through eminent domain, the decrepit International Hotel from a development group that wanted it razed and replaced with new, more profitable construction. In recent years the International had become a run-down, last-ditch home to elderly poor who could afford nothing better. Now they were in danger of being thrown into the street. Courts upheld the International's current ownership's right to dispose of the property as they wished. Thanks to publicity generated by Jones, thousands of marchers ringed the hotel, doing their best to thwart evictions. Temple members comprised a large percentage of the protesters. But it was all in vain. After numerous hearings, the authority's claim of eminent domain was finally denied. The International's ragged tenants were evicted, but Jones was once again acclaimed in the press as a spokesman for the downtrodden.

Only a month after Jones's gala testimonial dinner in San Francisco, the California State Senate in Sacramento also lauded Jones. Its Rules Committee passed a resolution citing him and Peoples Temple for "exemplary display of diligent and devoted service to, and concern for, their fellow man, not only in this state and nation, but throughout the world." When in October Democratic vice presidential candidate Walter Mondale made a quick campaign stop in San Francisco, Jones was one of several dignitaries invited to meet him. Jones later received a courtesy letter from Mondale avowing that "knowing of

[your] congregation's deep involvement in the major social and constitutional issues of our country . . . is a great inspiration to me." After the Carter-Mondale ticket was elected, Jones was quick to show the new vice president's letter to officials in Guyana.

It was no great leap for Jones to begin imagining a new role for himself. Showing more restraint than usual, he didn't immediately declare new ambitions, but set the stage with a few coy interviews. An article in the *Ukiah Daily Journal* noted, "Though many have asked him to do so, Rev. Jones has adamantly refused to consider running for public office" because Peoples Temple remained his priority. Jones didn't rule out a future run for office. For a man who already considered himself God or at least godlike, a campaign for the California State Assembly, mayor of San Francisco, lieutenant governor or governor of California, or something even higher, wasn't beyond consideration. If things kept going well for Peoples Temple, and for him personally, there need be no limit to Jones's political aspirations.

A certain new level of cockiness became evident in his sermons and Planning Commission machinations. When Steven Katsaris, the former Greek Orthodox priest, began complaining to friends in Mendocino County that his daughter, Maria, was being held virtually captive by Peoples Temple, Jones convened a Planning Commission meeting to discuss how to deflect the accusation. The consensus, orchestrated by Jones, was that if Katsaris approached government officials or the press for help, Maria would testify that her father had sexually molested her. It wasn't true, but since Jones wanted her to say it, Maria was agreeable. This stoked Jones's ego even more. His young lover was prepared to tell a ruinous lie about her own father just to protect Jones and the Temple.

In private Temple meetings, Jones was even disdainful of President-elect Jimmy Carter. There was no more mention of him supposedly offering Jones a government post. On November 12, Jones called Carter "a source for concern. He is not going to save our people. He is going to lead us to hell. Treachery and infamy are around us everywhere."

For the most part, Temple members responded positively to all that Jones said and did. They were caught up in the ongoing success. Jones even allowed his older sons and their friends to observe the tricks involved in his healings. Far from being disappointed, they enjoyed the entire process, especially when the healings were completed.

Jones's oldest sons were confident enough in the future of Peoples Temple to form their own plan for its future leadership, though they never explored it with their father. "After [Dad], we thought it could be Stephan in

Redwood Valley, Lew in Seattle, I'd get L.A., and Tim gets San Francisco," Jim Jones Jr. says. "You had someone extremely driven in Tim, Stephan who wanted to reach out and touch people, Lew just a good guy, and the one with the ability to get along with everybody, that was me. Agnes really wasn't with our family though she was in the Temple, and Suzanne was intelligent, but no girl was going to run something. [Dad] talked [gender] equality but for him, it was always his sons."

On November 1, the Temple board voted to move the Temple offices from Redwood Valley to San Francisco. Eight days later, it authorized spending $310,000 for major Jonestown-related purchases, including two diesel trucks and a cargo ship — it was confidently expected that soon Jonestown crops would result in food surpluses that could be shipped up and down the South American coast to communities in need.

For perhaps the only time in his life, Jones seemed almost content, even a little overwhelmed by his success. During the Temple Thanksgiving service in San Francisco, a choir soloist sang the ballad "A Place for Us" from the Broadway musical *West Side Story,* alluding to Jonestown as the Promised Land, and the whole chorus followed with a powerful rendition of a rewritten slavery-era spiritual, "Nobody Knows the Trouble I've Seen, Nobody Knows But Father." Jones dropped his head in his hands and sobbed. Many of his followers, greatly moved, cried, too.

Jones spent the last few days of December in Guyana. Besides Tim Stoen, who had a happy, if brief, reunion with John Victor, Jones brought with him Lieutenant Governor Dymally, who joined Jones in meetings with Prime Minister Burnham. Jones had the expectation of being treated as a fellow head of state; since all was going so well with building the Jonestown mission, and in light of Jones's apparent close relationship with the American president, Burnham obliged him. When Jones and his party arrived back at the San Francisco airport late on December 31, Jones blurted to Stoen, "This has been our year of ascendency."

In 1976, Peoples Temple and Jim Jones reached their apex. The following year would be different.

CHAPTER FORTY-THREE:
NEW WEST

For the children of Peoples Temple, 1977 began as usual with Christmas presents. Jones preached against the way well-to-do outsiders celebrated the holiday, buying their offspring dozens of expensive gifts while poor children had to do without. Each Temple kid got one gift worth $16 and received the present following New Year's so money could be saved by purchasing toys during after-Christmas sales. Their parents or guardians did not present the gifts. That pleasure was reserved for Jones, who would call the youngsters up during an early January service and hand each one a package wrapped with newspaper and string, since holiday wrapping paper and ribbon were expensive bourgeois affectations.

That annual ceremony brought Jones less pleasure than usual. He began the year beset by a personal family problem. His daughter Suzanne and son-in-law Mike Cartmell had separated. Both felt increasingly alienated from the Temple, but each considered the other a potential spy who might tattle to Jones if they talked about it. Jones had arranged their marriage. How dare they not enjoy a perfect union? Most of his fury was directed at Suzanne. As his daughter, she should always obey her father's wishes, and though he wished her to reconcile with her husband, Suzanne wouldn't.

There were numerous unhappy marriages within the Temple, often because of Jones's matchmaking. Even the happiest unions involved members whose first loyalty was to Jones rather than to each other. Marriages to outsiders were never approved. Jones had expected Suzanne and Mike to set a happy example. They were a disappointment to him.

So was his wife, in two significant ways. In early 1977, Marceline's health broke down. During a visit with her parents in Indiana, she had to be hospitalized for several weeks after suffering severe respiratory problems. Back home in San Francisco, she gave up her health agency job at the insistence of her doctors. So far as everyone but a few Temple insiders knew, the Jones family depended entirely on Marceline's income. The board met and voted an immediate $30,000 annual salary for Jones, who made a show of reluctantly accepting.

Marceline also infuriated Jones when she helped Stephan find an apartment separate from any Temple roommates. To Jones, Stephan was already too independent. His solution was to send Stephan to Jonestown. Jones may have meant it as a lesson, but instead it proved a blessing for Stephan. He loved it there, and at the same time escaped proximity to his demanding father.

Jones made a return trip to Cuba in January in the company of Dr. Carlton Goodlett and other dignitaries considered sympathetic by the Cuban government. The group was taken on tours of factories and schools, and Jones bragged that when he had last been in the country, he supported Castro in "the throes of revolution." But the Cuban leader declined a private meeting with the Temple leader, who was greatly offended.

February proved no better for Jones. Mike Cartmell defected on February 18, and about the same time Grace Stoen filed for divorce from Tim and requested custody of their son, John Victor. She'd warned Stoen that she was about to "take action," and Jones responded by sending Tim Stoen to Jonestown, where he could be with the child and also be effectively isolated from U.S. courts. Then Suzanne left the Temple, too, refusing further contact with her father and talking only intermittently to Marceline, who unsuccessfully begged her daughter to return.

The news was still good from Guyana. The Pioneers continued to clear jungle, plant crops, and build cabins in preparation for the first wave of settlers. There were only about fifty Temple members there. The cabins they built were ergonomic wonders, designed to house a family of four downstairs, and with small attics where one nonclaustrophobic person could sleep. There was no need for kitchens — meals would, of course, be communal — or bathrooms, since multi-hole outhouses and communal showers would also be utilized. Inspectors from the Guyanese government made occasional visits to ensure that all provisions of the lease agreement were being followed. They were impressed, as were officials from the American embassy in Georgetown, who also felt obligated to periodically check on the settlement. Embassy deputy chief Wade Matthews reported, "The people talked as though they were enthusiastic about their work, and, from outward appearances, seemed happy enough. There were a number of children who acted normally and who accompanied my own children down to a large and well-built cage to see their chimpanzee, which had been brought from California." Mr. Muggs was one of Jonestown's first residents.

Jonestown's original purpose was to serve as a self-sustaining agricultural mission, but as soon as it was habitable by a small number of settlers it became the Temple refuge for its most troublesome members, most of them teens, and a few older street toughs like Chris Lewis, who'd recently been cleared of murder charges in California. Tom Grubbs and Don Beck were dispatched to set up Jonestown classrooms. They did so without realizing that Guyana required all schools to conform to its own educational system — there would be grave repercussions later. Under the supervision of Gene Chaikin, now serving as Jones's lead Temple attorney in Tim Stoen's absence, the Temple had impoverished biological parents and legal guardians "sign permission for the kids to go to the PL [Promised Land] with whoever [in the Temple] was keeping them." Juvenile courts required annual reviews of custody matters. For minors now in Guyana, Chaikin explained, "If the court wants to see the child, [and] the [legal] guardian has no funds with which to [send the child] back to the U.S. at that time, does the court wish to send the money? [Of course not.] At this point, even if the parents object, what are their alternatives to effectively get their child back if [the child doesn't] want to come?" Chaikin assured Jones that "the possibility of child stealing charges at that point in time is remote."

Chaikin was wrong. Already, a San Francisco private investigator named Joseph Mazor had been contacted by parents who'd allowed their children to be temporarily brought into the Temple, only to find that the kids weren't coming back. It was, at first, a small thing to Mazor, but then he heard from a few other parents and sensed an opportunity for a big case. Mazor began poking around, and it was only a matter of time before he learned about the divorce/custody case initiated by Grace Stoen. Legal clocks had begun ticking.

Elmer and Deanna Mertle were active, too. They weren't the first disillusioned members to quit the Temple, convinced they'd been effectively robbed of their possessions by Jones and his church. But they were the first to attempt contacting authorities about it, additionally alleging that other crimes were being committed. They eventually spoke with a Treasury Department agent, claiming — correctly — that the Temple was smuggling guns into Jonestown, with the weapons hidden in secret compartments built into wooden supply crates. Jones had long promised followers that they would fight if outside forces attacked. It held true in Guyana as in America. They also accused Temple members of traveling on forged passports and other crimes. The Mertles' charges coincided with numerous Temple members applying for travel visas to Guyana — Jonestown was ready for its first few hundred settlers. That was enough for the U.S. Customs Service to covertly launch an investigation. A few Temple shipments to Jonestown were opened and inspected, but

Jones was apparently tipped off and no weapons were found. The gun smuggling resumed after the investigation was closed.

Defeated mayoral candidate John Barbagelata, still a member of the Board of Supervisors, continued to claim that invalid Temple votes had decided the 1975 election. Barbagelata didn't give up. He'd heard that foster kids taken in by the Temple were being shipped off to Jonestown and that public funds intended to support the children were being used on other expenses there. *San Francisco Chronicle* reporter Marshall Kilduff thought Barbagelata's new charge might be worth looking into, but Kilduff's editor turned down the request. That only made the reporter more determined. The *Chronicle* allowed its writers to accept outside freelance assignments, and in March 1977 *New West* magazine, a respected regional publication, accepted Kilduff's proposal to write an investigative piece on Jim Jones and Peoples Temple. Once again, Jones's sources alerted him. Temple members met with *New West*'s editor, and convinced him that a negative article would irreparably harm the church's reputation and outreach programs. Kilduff's deal was canceled. But then that *New West* editor was replaced, and the incoming editor thought Kilduff's idea was worth pursuing. The story assignment was reinstated, and, by April, Kilduff was hard at work.

Jones was concerned, but not panicky. *New West* was a monthly magazine, not a major daily newspaper. If Kilduff repeated a few claims by John Barbagelata, so what? While keeping an ear out for news of Kilduff's research progress, if any, Jones turned his attention to more immediate Temple business.

Peoples Temple purchased a residence in the Guyanese capital of Georgetown. Jones considered it vital that his people have constant access to government leaders. Forty-one Lamaha Gardens, two-story stucco and painted sunshine yellow, was located in one of Georgetown's few reasonably upscale neighborhoods. In addition to rooms suitable for offices and space for ham radio equipment, there were also a half dozen bedrooms, meaning some two dozen followers could live there. A spacious living area lent itself to entertaining; lots of male Guyanese officials, single or married, enjoyed chatting and dancing with pretty young Temple women — Jones made certain there were several of these ladies on hand at all hours. They limited themselves to flirting except for Paula Adams, who continued her affair with Guyanese ambassador to the United States Bonny Mann, doing her best not to let Jones or other Temple members realize that the affection Mann demonstrated toward her was mutual. As Jones hoped, Mann proved to be a constant source of inside information about

621

Prime Minister Burnham and his cabinet.

During the day, Temple members living at Lamaha Gardens either went about specific Jonestown business — finding and purchasing equipment, arranging medical and dental appointments in Georgetown for the jungle mission residents, or buying and shipping the food needed by Jonestown's growing population. The settlement was nowhere near self-sustaining. Experiments were in progress there to determine which crops could be grown. Meanwhile, Georgetown members bought sides of beef and bags of oranges, shipping them by boat from the capital to Port Kaituma, where they were picked up and trucked the rest of the way to the mission. They sent fish, too. Fishing boats working out of Georgetown allowed Temple members to gather up and keep the dregs of their daily catch. These fish were taken to a dock-side business where they were flash-frozen and shipped to Jonestown along with meat and fruit. The Temple also established a secondhand store in the capital to sell clothing and other possessions that newly arrived members didn't need in the jungle.

Others stationed at Lamaha Gardens went out each day "procuring," going door-to-door in Georgetown and its suburbs asking for donations to Peoples Temple. It was a difficult task in a city where poverty was rampant. But the Temple required its Georgetown procurers to average $100 a day each in donations, and anyone who consistently failed to do so risked being sent to Jonestown and the hard daily farm labor there. Those with a knack for soliciting money, Sharon Amos's daughter Liane among them, were never relieved of procurement duty. "The Guyanese people were so generous," Laura Johnston Kohl recalls. "They were always kind to us even if they didn't have any money to give." When Johnston Kohl made the mistake of getting romantically involved with a man in Georgetown, she learned that Jones wouldn't tolerate generosity of that nature. She was immediately transferred to Jonestown.

Those back in the settlement were in constant need of medical care. Sunstroke and dehydration were constant dangers, and there were always infected bug bites, joint sprains, and other assorted ailments brought on by constant heat and hard work. Jones found his mission doctor in Larry Schacht, a drug-addled dropout who found his way from Houston to the San Francisco temple and cleaned up thanks to its addiction program. Schacht wanted to be a doctor. Since his dubious background made admission to an American medical school unlikely, at Jones's behest Dr. Carlton Goodlett used his international connections to get Schacht a place in a Mexican medical school. After graduating,

Schacht pursued American certification at the University of California College of Medicine. All his tuition costs, there as in Mexico, were paid by Peoples Temple. Schacht understood what he owed to the church; his loyalty to Jim Jones was absolute. In 1977, fresh out of school, Schacht went to Jonestown, where even an experienced physician would have been hard-pressed to cope with the primitive conditions. Schacht had to learn everything on the job. Among the first textbooks he requested be sent to Jonestown from San Francisco were *Finger Acupuncture, The New Childbirth,* and *How to Stay Alive in the Woods.* Fortunately for the Jonestown settlers, their rookie doctor was assisted, and, sometimes, superseded, by several experienced nurses, including Joyce Beam and Annie Moore.

Tim Stoen was worrisome. Only a few weeks after he arrived in Guyana, Jones accused Stoen of being an undercover CIA agent. Jones probably just wanted to hear Stoen deny it and vow eternal allegiance; with Grace Stoen pursuing custody of John Victor, he wanted to be certain of Stoen's ongoing loyalty. But Stoen, already disenchanted enough with Jones and Peoples Temple to plan leaving, resented the accusation. In March, he disappeared briefly, spending a few unapproved days in London after a trip to Barbados and Port-of-Spain in Trinidad on Temple business. When Stoen returned to

Guyana on April 3, Jones was there on a visit. They talked about a non-Temple woman back in the Bay Area; Stoen loved her, and Jones said that he thought it might be possible for the two of them to marry and live together in Guyana. After Jones returned to San Francisco, Stoen felt frustrated, mostly because he'd spent so little time in Jonestown with John Victor.

On June 12, again without permission, Stoen flew to New York, and a few days later continued on to California. At an Oakland airport newsstand, Stoen noticed a headline in that day's *San Francisco Chronicle:* "Strange SF Break-in at Magazine." According to the story, an office of *New West* had been burglarized. A file containing material for an upcoming story to be cowritten by magazine staffer Phil Tracy and freelancer Marshall Kilduff seemed to have been moved, though nothing was taken. Tracy suspected that the file's contents "could have been taken out . . . and photographed." The material concerned Rev. Jim Jones and Peoples Temple.

The *New West* writers comprised an intimidating team. Kilduff was a smart, experienced journalist who'd previously reported on Jones as Housing Authority chairman, and Tracy had been an investigative reporter with New York City's *Village Voice.* They worked fast and covered their tracks well — try as he might, Jones couldn't ascertain whom they were talking to. Jones feared that his former personal attorney Tim Stoen might very well be a source.

It would have been typical of Jones to order a break-in of the *New West* offices, hoping to learn what Kilduff and Tracy were planning, but he and the Temple were innocent. The San Francisco police, called by the magazine to investigate, concluded there was no proof of any crime. It came out later that a *New West* staffer who'd left his keys at home climbed through an office window to let himself in, inadvertently displacing some files, including the one with material for the Peoples Temple story. But Tracy and Kilduff, increasingly familiar through their research with Temple subterfuge, assumed it was a break-in ordered by Jones. Afterward they were more determined to publish a hard-hitting exposé.

Jones wanted to be prepared for immediate legal retaliation when the story finally appeared. Stoen had left without permission, and Gene Chaikin was occupied with Jonestown issues, so the Temple hired perhaps the most controversial defense attorney in the Bay Area. Charles Garry, a white lawyer, had earned his reputation as chief counsel to the Black Panthers. He proudly proclaimed himself both a Christian and a communist, the perfect combination for Temple representation. Hiring Garry was a political risk for Jones — even liberal Democrats considered the lawyer part of a worrisome fringe element — but by summer 1977 Jones was no longer certain of full-spirited support from Mayor Moscone. The city recall election was scheduled for early August. Previously, Moscone would have desperately needed the support of Jones and Peoples Temple. But San Franciscans on the whole had decided they liked Moscone's open, all-inclusive administration. It seemed obvious that in the August balloting, the mayor was going to win by a landslide whether Peoples Temple was active on his behalf or not.

Jones knew very well that politicians can profess undying friendship one day and turn into enemies the next. How might Governor Brown, Lieutenant Governor Dymally, Mayor Moscone, and State Assemblyman Willie Brown react if the *New West* article laid bare unsavory Temple secrets? Charles Garry, at least, never wavered in public support of his clients, even if he believed that they'd committed whatever crimes they were charged with. Jones knew this because, after being retained by the Temple, Garry told Terri Buford, "I'm just like [television's] Perry Mason, except all of my clients are guilty." That was the kind of lawyer Jim Jones needed. Garry didn't come cheap. His initial monthly retainer was $5,000, and he billed many hours beyond that. In this, at least, Jones spared no expense.

In May, for a reason that became obvious a month later, Jones accelerated members' migration to Jonestown. He'd initially planned for a total population there of five hundred or six hundred. The process was expected to take as long as ten years. Now, he hustled that many out of the country within weeks. Tim Carter and Karen Layton were dispatched to New York, tasked with meeting Temple members flying in from California and getting them onto the one daily flight to Georgetown. Many Temple members, especially Jones's older followers, had never flown before and were confused. Other settlers flew from California to Florida and from there either flew or embarked by boat to Guyana. As much as possible, Jones didn't want outsiders to know how many of his followers were going overseas.

Back in San Francisco, Jones preached a lot about reincarnation, comparing the moment of death and then immediate additional life to a flame passed from one candle to the next. Suicide continued to be a constant topic. Jones was against individuals killing themselves for any selfish reason. He warned his followers that "anyone [doing so] will go back 500 generations [and] 10,000 years" in the quest to achieve enlightenment and move to a higher spiritual plane. On Memorial Day, he took part in a citywide anti-suicide rally on the Golden Gate Bridge, which was traditionally frequented by despairing jumpers. His remarks took a prophetic turn: "Suicide is a symptom of an uncaring society. . . . The suicide is a victim of conditions which we cannot tolerate." He added that, for the first time in his own life, he was in a suicidal mood.

Jones tried to discover what the *New West* story would include. Perhaps the writers might reveal federal investigations of Peoples Temple that Jones felt certain were under way. On Jones's instructions, loyal follower Richard Tropp wrote to the IRS, FBI, and the Treasury Department's Bureau of Alcohol, Tobacco and Firearms, demanding to know if any of these agencies were investigating the Temple. Spokesmen for each responded that there were none "at this time," which was true — the ATF investigation into possible Temple arms smuggling had closed down. But Tracy and Kilduff must have had *something.*

A few weeks before the August edition of *New West* was published, Jim Jones ran away, probably on the advice of Charles Garry, who didn't want his client on hand for questioning by the *New West* writers, or to face the media onslaught that was bound to follow after their article was published. Jones had already sent Stephan ahead to Guyana, and the other three boys — Lew, Jimmy, and Tim — soon followed. John Victor was already there. Kimo was coming with his mother, Carolyn. With the children he loved in Jonestown, under cover of night Jones made his way to the San Francisco airport and flew off to join them. Marceline was left in San Francisco to oversee the Temple in her husband's absence. She assumed, as Jones may have, that his trip to Jonestown would be temporary. But when the magazine finally reached newsstands, the story was worse than even the paranoid Jones could have imagined.

In bold lettering, the story's headline read "Inside Peoples Temple," and the subheadline ominously queried "Jim Jones is one of the state's most politically potent leaders. But who is he? And what's going on behind his church's locked doors?" Then came a half dozen devastating pages. In every line, Kilduff and Tracy got things right: Jones's maneuverings to ingratiate himself with Rosalyn Carter and California and San Francisco politicians; the Planning Commission and members being "called on the floor," that is, beaten; the real estate skulduggery; and how Temple members who left the church were tormented by Jones followers afterward. There was a great deal about Jones's personal background (he was credited with "courageous commitment" to Indianapolis integration) and the

Temple's locked-door policy when it wanted its services kept private. Early paragraphs detailed the Temple's seemingly endless supply of money, and Jones's appeal to a wide variety of followers. The writers asked how these things were possible — and then let disenchanted former Temple members provide the answers. Everyone was identified not only by name, but in accompanying photographs. That made them real to readers, rather than faceless, anonymous bellyachers, and immunized Tracy and Kilduff from potential charges by Jones and Charles Garry that they'd invented some or all of their sources.

Jones certainly must have expected the Mertles to be included, and Gang of Eight members Wayne Pietila, Mickey Touchette, and Jim and Terri Cobb could not have been a surprise. But Tracy and Kilduff had also found Ross Case, the former associate Temple minister who'd left the Temple in its early California iteration because he was uncomfortable with Jim Jones being worshipped as a god. There was old Birdie Marable, going into squirm-inducing detail about crammed Temple bus trips, and Laura Cornelious parroting Jones's description of imminent concentration camps in America. Walter Jones offered specific details about how state money sent to guardians for the care of foster children was turned over instead to the

Temple. Finally, crushingly, came the testimony of Grace Stoen, who didn't speak at all of the struggle with Jones over custody of their son, but did recount insider information with the kind of small, telling details — the makeup of the private compartment on Jones's Greyhound bus, how much money might be taken in at a single weekend service — that assured *New West* readers they were getting the real inside story.

On the last page, another headline in bold type led to the story's conclusion: "Why Jim Jones Should Be Investigated." The writers summarized their findings about Temple financial fraud, physical abuse of current members, and ongoing harassment of past ones. They noted that they'd wanted to give Jones an opportunity to respond: "[He] has been in Guyana for the last three weeks and was unavailable to us as this magazine article went to press . . . two spokesmen for the Temple, Mike Prokes and Gene Chaikin, denied all of the allegations made by the former Temple members we interviewed . . . [they] went on to deny that Jones's closest followers are planning to relocate in Guyana any time soon."

The article was the work of veteran investigative reporters who had confidence in their findings and certainty that there were more revelations to come: "The story of Jim Jones and his Peoples Temple is not over. In fact, it has only begun to be told. If there is any solace to be gained from the tale of exploitation and human foible told by the former Temple members in these pages, it is that even such a power as Jim Jones cannot always contain his followers."

Mayor Moscone issued a terse statement that if Jones and Peoples Temple had broken any laws, "appropriate law enforcement officials" should investigate and act. A few days after the *New West* article was published, Moscone overwhelmingly prevailed in the recall election by a two-to-one margin. Voters also opened up Board of Supervisors elections from at-large to specific city districts, breaking the remaining conservative stranglehold on politics in the city. The support of Jim Jones and Peoples Temple no longer mattered to George Moscone. A statement from the governor's office acknowledged that Jerry Brown had considered Jones for a position on the state prison board only because someone had suggested him as a candidate. Both San Francisco daily papers assigned reporters to begin their own investigations. It was embarrassing to be scooped on such a big story by a monthly magazine.

The former Temple members who cooperated with Tracy and Kilduff continued publicly opposing Jones and Peoples Temple. Potential retaliation no longer seemed inevitable. If Jones or any of his followers threatened them, the media would have material for perfect follow-up stories. The Mertles, the Gang of Eight members, and Grace Stoen were determined to keep doing something, although they weren't yet certain what.

Not everyone abandoned Jones. Willie Brown issued a strong statement of support, and on July 31 he spoke at a rally organized by the Temple on behalf of their absent leader. Back in Richmond, Indiana, Jones's mother-in-law, Charlotte Baldwin, told the local paper that "I'm sure Jim has made his mistakes, but nothing to warrant this. I feel he's been unjustly accused." Ten days after the *New West* article was published, Marceline Jones released a "To Whom It May Concern" letter through the Temple. She wrote, "If I were not married to Jim, I would still be a member of his congregation. His totally selfless life has been an inspiration to me."

Privately, Marceline told her friend Bonnie Burnham that "Jim's gone to Guyana until things blow over." But Jones never returned.

· · · ·

PART THREE:
GUYANA

· · · ·

CHAPTER FORTY-FOUR:
JONESTOWN

Until mid-June 1977, Jonestown was a relatively happy place. Only about five dozen people lived there, and they labored in the jungle from dawn until dark and sometimes through most of the night, when the flames of the fires they used to burn off undergrowth seemed to flicker as high as the stars. If the labor was exhausting, it was also rewarding — every day the settlement was a little more defined. The camaraderie among the Temple Pioneers was exceptional. Without being under constant supervision by others eager to spot some misdeed and report it to the Planning Commission, without enduring interminable services where Jim Jones ranted for hours, their lives were relatively relaxed and uncomplicated. And as they grew more familiar with the jungle, they were able to observe and appreciate its wonders as well as its dangers. Monkeys announced sunrise with their morning cries. Birds supplied unique music with their squawks and calls. Even snakes could be enjoyed for their serpentine grace and subtle markings, once the Pioneers sorted out which were poisonous. Amerindians wandered in and out of the camp. They were treated as guests, and many were astounded by wonders that the Pioneers took for granted — canned food, generator-powered lights, and, most of all, shoes. The Americans soon learned to keep their foot-gear out of sight. Otherwise, the shoes disappeared overnight.

A few additional settlers arrived every so often, usually teens from Peoples Temple who'd found too many ways to get in trouble back in California, but had no option in Jonestown other than obediently working in the jungle. Then, in May 1977, newcomers began arriving in much greater numbers, sometimes dozens at once, and housing became a problem. The cottages were constructed to comfortably fit perhaps a half dozen at most, and building these smallish residences hadn't been a priority since the Pioneers had expected a more gradual influx. Cottage construction had to be stepped up, which meant other crucial tasks, including clearing more jungle, were negatively affected. Previously, all newcomers pitched in. But now there were elderly arrivals and small children who needed constant supervision. That meant that the able-bodied had to work even harder. Food wasn't yet a problem. If the Jonestown fields weren't yielding bountiful daily harvests yet, sufficient supplies could still be shipped in from Georgetown on the *Cudjoe*. A hundred settlers, two hundred — adjustments were made. Unlike the Pioneers, some of the newcomers were unpleasantly surprised by their jungle surroundings. In his sermons, Jones had promised a tropical paradise, and instead they found a rough-and-tumble camp. But almost everyone accepted the conditions with good grace. At night, even with so many worn out from hours of physical labor, the Jonestown settlers gathered together and laughed and sang. Almost all of them were there because they wanted to be — the waiting list back in California was long enough so that there was competition for the privilege of being among the first to go. Those who came and didn't find jungle life to their liking felt little need to despair — at some point, surely they'd be allowed to return to the United States.

"I quickly came to love Jonestown," Laura Johnston Kohl recalls. "The spirit there was tremendous." Then Jim Jones arrived, and everything changed.

Jones could have adopted the patient attitude of those he had sent ahead to build Jonestown. It was a complex task requiring a long-term approach — it would take several harvest seasons just to test crops in the jungle soil, learning through trial and error which flourished and which couldn't be grown successfully. The lease agreement with the Guyanese government stipulated five years to get the mission up and running. Jones himself had agreed to that. But now circumstances were different. Jones had no intention of abandoning a position of power and importance in America to huddle impotently among a handful of followers making incremental progress toward building a jungle paradise. Despite the controversy back in San Francisco, in fact because of it, Jones arrived in Jonestown determined to demonstrate from the outset that he was undaunted, and in charge of something astonishing. That was why Jones wanted every possible follower crammed into the settlement immediately; he must lead a multitude, just as he had back in California. That they lacked proper housing, that feeding so many put an impossible strain on the still limited possibilities of Jonestown's fields, didn't concern him. Through his inspiration, they could quickly create a self-sustaining utopia, one that set a much more immediate socialist example for the world and simultaneously served as Jones's reminder to all of his enemies that, despite his retreat from San Francisco, they had failed to bring him down.

And so he took over control of everything. No task was assigned, no crop planted, no tool purchased, without Jones's approval.

Those wanting to begin romantic relationships had to apply for permission first, and
even if they received it had to endure a
probationary period before officially becoming a couple. Breakups had to be approved as
well.

All incoming mail was opened and read
before being passed on to the intended recipient. Outgoing mail was censored. Jones
insisted that letters from Jonestown contain
only glowing descriptions of bucolic life.
Unacceptable letters were returned to their
writers with scribbled margin notes instructing them about what changes must be made.
Jones's inner circle did the censoring, with
Carolyn Layton and Maria Katsaris forming
a two-woman buffer between even these
subordinates and Jones. Carolyn and Maria
were Jones's only real intimates, carrying out
his orders and guessing what he would want
done on those occasions when he was indis-
posed. There were plenty of drugs ordered
into Jonestown by camp physician Larry
Schacht, and a fair amount found their way
into Jones's possession.

For everyone else in Jonestown, privacy was
virtually nonexistent. Cottages were over-
crowded with as many as eight, then ten, then
a dozen or more occupants as newcomers
kept pouring in. Even with sixteen holes each,
the outhouses were constantly crowded. Real
toilet paper was a rare extravagance. Scrap

paper was most often used, and then leaves after paper became so scarce in Jonestown that every bit was needed for record keeping and letters. There was limited water available in primitive showers. Workers filthy from a day in the fields had only two minutes to rinse off, and they were warned to keep their mouths closed while washing, since the water was polluted. Jones had much nicer quarters and facilities. He lived with Carolyn, Maria, John Victor, and Kimo in a private cabin with soft beds, a private latrine, and a generator that powered a refrigerator filled with soft drinks and a floor fan. Jones's quarters were connected to the camp radio room. He didn't have to leave to make calls or broadcasts to the United States, and, if he chose, could even make camp announcements from the comfort of his home. During those times when he drugged himself into near-insensibility, which grew more frequent as the months passed, Jones wallowed in his bed out of sight of the rest of Jonestown's residents. The amenities didn't compare to what he'd left behind in San Francisco, but compared to everyone else in the settlement, Jones lived in luxury.

He surely felt he deserved to, considering all the demands made on him. Virtually every waking minute of Jones's day found him having to deal with some emergency or other. One constant was cash outlay. Tim Carter estimates that, at its population height of just over nine hundred, Jonestown's average monthly expenses were about $600,000. One-third of its residents were pensioners whose Social Security checks, totaling about $40,000 per month, were vital to the Jonestown budget. But at one point in 1977, at the behest of the Social Security office, the San Francisco post office stopped forwarding the checks to Guyana. It took time to untangle the bureaucratic red tape. At the same time, the FCC formally charged Temple ham radio operators in the United States and Guyana with breaking rules involving use of bandwidth. Fearing eavesdropping by the FBI and CIA, Jones wanted his radio operators to use varying signals and complicated, ever-changing code words and names to communicate. Other ham operators, hearing strange conversations, reported them to the FCC. Temple operators in the States had to respond to the charges and narrowly avoided prosecution. Jones couldn't risk any in-depth investigation. The Temple continued smuggling guns into Guyana, only a few at a time, and never enough to total a bristling arsenal. Jones constantly feared attack, from U.S. agencies or mercenaries hired by Temple enemies, and wanted enough arms to fight back. For a long while, Jonestown's radio code name for "guns" was "Bibles," on the theory that no outsider listening in would find anything unusual about a church mission asking its San Francisco office to send more Bibles to the jungle.

Jones had hoped Jonestown could raise most of the money it needed by selling surplus crops, but there weren't any. So pressure was put on the door-to-door procurers in Georgetown to step up their collection of donations. It was an impossible demand. They'd already covered much of the capital city, and there weren't any other major cities. Jonestown settlers began manufacturing toys, fine ones, cars and trains carved from wood and pretty little pigtailed dolls made from scraps of material. These were sent to Georgetown and sold there in open-air markets and a few department stores. The income derived was several thousand dollars a month — helpful, but by no means enough. Soon, fewer San Francisco communals were allowed to move to Jonestown. If they had full-time employment, their stateside paychecks were needed in Guyana far more than they were.

Newly arrived settlers were unnerved as Jonestown greeters rummaged through their personal baggage. All passports were confiscated, held under close guard by Jones and his lieutenants. Jewelry and knickknacks were appropriated for sale in Georgetown, and spare clothing was added to the inventory of the mission's communal warehouse. In California, everyone had very little. In Jonestown, they possessed only the clothes on their backs. Some items, particularly socks, deteriorated so quickly in the humid jungle that cartons of replacements had to be ordered from America every month, another unexpected expense.

Food proved most worrisome of all. Feeding a few dozen Pioneers was relatively inexpensive. Providing nine hundred settlers with three nourishing meals a day was prohibitive. Everyone wanted meat; Jones calculated that serving chicken or pork at a single Jonestown dinner cost $2,000. The old communal fallbacks of peanut butter sandwiches and oatmeal that worked back in the States weren't sufficient in the jungle, where so many adults and teens performed hard physical labor all day long. They needed lots of calories, protein in particular. Faced with crushing food costs, rice — which also had to be purchased rather than grown, but was at least inexpensive — became the primary Jonestown staple. Soaked in watery gravy, dotted sparingly with specks of meat, it was included in most meals. Cassava flour, raised in the fields and ground in Jonestown's own mill, was prepared in various ways. There were chicken coops and a piggery, but it was hard to keep the chickens alive long enough to produce eggs. Beverages were limited, too, usually water or a sweet, powdered drink called Flavor Aid, which was cheaper than the better-known Kool-Aid. Desserts were virtually unknown during weekday meals. Once each weekend, Jones made a point of rewarding each follower with a single cookie, dramatically handed out by him as settlers filed past.

With unexpected costs rising each month, Jones depended on donations at Temple services back in California to help make up the difference, but, in the wake of the *New West* article and Jones's absence, these were no longer robust. The Redwood Valley temple was up for sale, and the Los Angeles property, too. In San Francisco, attendance was down by half, and collections at Geary Boulevard temple services that once totaled $5,000 or more were now often only a few hundred dollars. Marceline, struggling to keep the San Francisco temple operating, passed along messages from remaining local followers: "I am really grateful to J.J. I have more than I deserve. I will do anything." "I miss J.J.'s presence and camaraderie, but I know he is opening doors for us in the P.L. [Promised Land]."

But Jones needed money more than uplifting missives. On its best months, Jonestown's combined income from its own operations and U.S. contributions reached perhaps $450,000, leaving a consistent monthly shortfall of about $150,000. The Temple had ample reserves in foreign banks to make up the difference for decades to come, but only Jones and a few others knew that. Subsidizing Jonestown indefinitely went against the whole purpose of the mission, which was to demonstrate that a purely socialist community could not only be egalitarian, but also self-sustaining in defiant contrast to the beliefs of capitalists. The settlers had to work harder, do better. But they kept falling short of Jones's expectations. Many left America owing back rent or taxes. The Temple's San Francisco office was deluged by calls from debt collectors. Jones established new guidelines for everyone working there. All members of the media were to be referred to Charles Garry. So were process servers. Above all, no one in the Temple office was to accept any type of legal papers.

Upon arrival in Guyana, most settlers stayed a few days at the Temple's Lamaha Gardens headquarters in Georgetown to become acclimated to the steamy climate and recover from jet lag. Many took advantage of their last contact with civilization by visiting bars and getting drunk. The *Cudjoe* often arrived in Port Kaituma with a load of hungover passengers. Jones reiterated the Temple's long-standing ban on alcohol, but it proved impossible for some Jonestown settlers to get through their grueling new lives without occasional relief from liquor. Some Amerindians living near the mission site were adept at concocting potent fermented beverages that the settlers called "jungle juice." Each week, at least a few Jonestown residents were discovered passed out on their beds or in the huts of the natives. And, periodically, even sober settlers were caught slacking off work assignments or sneaking a piece of fruit or a sandwich from the kitchen.

Back in San Francisco, anyone breaking Temple rules was called on the floor for whacks with a board or rubber hose. But after arriving in Guyana, Jones had been apprised by Marceline that post–*New West* media coverage continued to focus on the Temple's physical discipline. She suggested that a new method should be initiated in Jonestown, perhaps some form of peer pressure. Jones established the "Learning Crew." Rule breakers slept and ate separately from the rest of the settlers. They were required to run everywhere — to the fields, to the main camp pavilion for mission-wide meetings, even to the outhouse. No one was allowed to speak to or even look at them — they were pariahs. Learning Crew supervisors reported on their individual progress, or lack of it, to Jones. There was no set limit to the punishment. Jones would arbitrarily decide when someone was allowed to return to the main group.

Whether part of the Learning Crew or not, everyone in Jonestown was required to come to nightly meetings in the settlement's main pavilion, a large open-air structure built with wood beams and a corrugated tin roof. Settlers perched shoulder-to-shoulder on long picnic-style benches. For a time, there was room for everyone to sit down. As the Jonestown population grew to more than nine hundred, some settlers had to stand. Jones lounged onstage on a comfortable lawn chair. A sign slightly misquoting philosopher George Santayana hung behind him: "Those Who Do Not Remember The Past Are Condemned To Repeat It." Some nights, there was entertainment. Jones discouraged going to movies in the States, but the Temple regularly shipped film reels to Jonestown for the settlers, TV miniseries such as *Roots* or philosophically acceptable movies: *Little Big Man, The Candidate, The Diary of Anne Frank,* and *The Execution of Private Slovik. Executive Action,* a film about U.S. government subterfuge, was one of Jones's personal favorites. As a special treat for the children, Jones sometimes scheduled cartoons or tapes of *Sesame Street.*

Mostly, though, Jones spoke. Sometimes he still preached, but more often he gave his personalized accounts of recent U.S. and world news, much of it gleaned from Soviet sources and all of it embellished by his own imagination. In Washington, D.C., military leaders at the Pentagon had drawn up plans for killing blacks. Membership in the Ku Klux Klan had recently increased 100 percent, and even the children of Klan members openly wore white-sheet uniforms. Idi Amin of Uganda in Africa was proving himself to be a great leader — he intimidated antagonistic white leaders of other countries by "acting like a crazy nigger." Temple members should follow his example. Virtually every night, Jones described something shocking that just happened, some great evil that the Jonestown settlers escaped only because he had led them to the Promised Land. He went on for hours, either oblivious to or ignoring the fact that most of his audience, exhausted by their long days, struggled to stay awake. Officially, it was lights out in Jonestown at 11 p.m. But Jones often spoke until midnight or even later; settlers might only be dismissed at two or three in the morning, and Jonestown reveille came at 6 a.m.

Workdays lasted until six or six thirty. Sundays were half days; work was over at noon, but only two meals were served on Sundays instead of three, so everyone was even hungrier than usual. And while at work, no matter where on Jonestown's acres the settlers found themselves, it was impossible to escape Jones, or at least his voice. Sometimes they were pleased to see him. Jones would cheer up a hot, sweaty work brigade in the fields by initiating an impromptu water fight, or even work alongside them for a few minutes until urgent business called him away. Mostly, though, they listened to him, and involuntarily. Jonestown had a loud-speaker system that was audible in every part of the main settlement, and an eclectic collection of tapes featuring artists from the blues and jazz of B.B. King and Nat King Cole to the pop stylings of Percy Faith and the Ray Conniff Orchestra, with Earth, Wind and Fire and the O'Jays in between. But often, the tunes would be interrupted by Jones making an announcement, expanding on some topic he'd discussed the night before, or even playing a tape of one of his previous evening addresses.

Even before Jones himself arrived in Jonestown, Guyanese officials worried that too many settlers were arriving in a settlement that was clearly not yet ready to receive them. In April 1977, John Blacken, deputy chief of the American mission in Guyana, sent a message to the U.S. secretary of state: Peoples Temple had informed the Guyanese that they were bringing in 380 settlers. Guyana's leadership wanted to know why there was such a sudden influx. Was there hostility between the Temple and the American government? If not, and since, so far, the Guyanese considered Jonestown and the settlers living in it to be "an industrious, hardworking organization," Guyana would allow the

380 newcomers to enter the country. The secretary made no objection, and the first main wave of settlers came to Jonestown.

But Kit Nascimento, who'd worked in press capacities in America before joining Prime Minister Burnham's cabinet in Guyana, still had contacts among American journalists. When Jones came to Jonestown in June, this time apparently to stay for at least an extended period, Nascimento got in touch with U.S. reporter friends and was apprised of the controversy back in San Francisco.

"I went to see the prime minister and told him what I had learned," Nascimento says. "I think [Desmond Roberts] had already said something to him about the possibility of [Jonestown] getting smuggled guns. But the prime minister felt that we'd already contacted the U.S. [government through Blacken], and they had no complaints. [Burnham] wanted that place [Jonestown] between us and Venezuela. So long as Jones didn't break any of our laws, they could stay there. I said, 'We'd better start keeping a close eye on them,' but he didn't want to hear it. After that, among the prime minister and those closest to him, I assure you that Jones and his people were rarely, if ever, discussed."

When Jones arrived in Guyana in June, he expected that he would have constant, easy access to Burnham, on the order of one head of state meeting with another. He was surprised and alarmed to find that, though the Guyanese prime minister had met with Jones on occasional social circumstances like the Georgetown wedding of Jones's son Jimmy, Burnham now had no intention of dealing with Jones officially. Jones and Temple staff members in Georgetown were directed instead to Deputy Prime Minister Ptolemy Reid, a former veterinarian. Reid patiently discussed Jonestown concerns with Jones or his representatives, but never allowed them access to the prime minister. Jones couldn't understand why — was it possible that Burnham was somehow in league with the CIA and FBI? Had the Guyanese government joined in plots against him? Through his Temple mistress Paula Adams, Guyanese ambassador Bonny Mann was constantly badgered by Jones to find out. Mann found little to report, except that Kit Nascimento suspected Jones and his followers were always up to something illicit.

In Jonestown, frustrated by lack of progress there and lack of access to Burnham in Georgetown, Jones grew increasingly upset, and his unhappiness manifested itself in nightly diatribes at the pavilion and general snappishness. Given their hard lives of backbreaking labor, primitive surroundings, limited rations, strict rules, and constant haranguing by their leader, it was inevitable that some settlers grew dissatisfied with life in Jonestown, but those who did found it almost impossible to leave. Passports were locked away, and Jones made it clear that while the Temple paid all travel costs to Guyana, deserters would have to pay their own way back to the States. Given that no one was allowed to enter Jonestown without surrendering all they owned, and that most were either estranged from family outside the Temple or in only sporadic touch with them, very few could afford to go home.

In a few instances, they still tried. Less than a week after Jones arrived, Yolanda Crawford persuaded him to let her, her mother, and husband leave the settlement and return to the United States. They had to pay their own way, and Jones had requirements beyond that. In a deposition made a year later, Crawford described what was required of her before Jones granted permission:

> I was forced to promise [Jones] that I would never speak against the church, and that if I did I would lose his "protection" and be "stabbed in the back." Furthermore, Jim Jones ordered me to sign a number of self-incriminating papers, including that I was against the government of Guyana. . . . [Even] before leaving [the United States] for Guyana, I was ordered to fabricate a story and sign it stating that I killed someone and threw the body in the ocean. I was told that

if I ever caused Jim Jones trouble, he would give that statement to the police.

Chris Lewis and his wife left. Jones let him go — Lewis was a tough man who'd served him well as an enforcer and harasser of defectors back in California. Now he'd had enough of Jonestown, and Jones knew better than to threaten him. At least if Lewis retained some loyalty to Jones and the Temple, he might continue acting as an enforcer in San Francisco should the need arise.

A few months later, Leon Broussard sneaked away into the jungle, stumbling until a native encountered him and helped him to Port Kaituma. By coincidence, recently appointed U.S. consul Richard McCoy was there, preparing to make his first Jonestown visit. He spoke with Broussard, who described Jonestown as a virtual "slave colony" where anyone Jones wanted to punish was badly beaten or even buried alive. All he wanted, Broussard pleaded, was to return to America, but he had no money and Jones wouldn't even allow him to leave Jonestown, let alone go all the way home. McCoy promised to intercede. Jones called Broussard a liar, but agreed to give the man his passport and pay his airfare back to America. To McCoy, a precedent had been established. Whenever someone wanted to leave Jonestown, they would be allowed to do so, and, if they wanted to return to the United States, the Temple would pay for the trip. The new consul expected that there would be others wanting to go, perhaps asking his assistance in making such arrangements. But no one did. McCoy made occasional visits to Jonestown, where he interviewed individuals whose families or friends back in the United States had expressed concern about them. He explained that, if they wished to leave, he was there to help. But those he spoke to assured McCoy that they were happy where they were. No one appeared under pressure to say so. The diplomat was convinced that they meant what they said — and most of them did. For reasons as varied as the people themselves, leaving was not an option. Lack of access to passports and travel funds was the least of it.

Fully a third of Jonestown's population was pensioners, almost all of them black, who were attracted to the Temple by Jones's promises to care for them well in their old age. Their earlier lives had been a struggle. When Jones warned in the pavilion of sudden Klan expansion, or the U.S. government building concentration camps, they remembered well burning crosses and white sheriffs with fire hoses and snarling dogs. What Jones described was only a step or two beyond what they'd personally experienced, and so they believed what he told them. In Jonestown they had beds, albeit stacked bunks in cramped quarters, and regular meals, and immediate medical care when they needed it instead of endless hours in waiting rooms at public hospitals and impersonal, cursory treatment. They were asked to work, but not much, putting finishing touches on toys and dolls, tending small gardens. Sure, Jones wanted their Social Security checks and disability checks and any other money they had coming in, but look at all they got for it. The elderly people didn't want to leave.

There were almost three hundred children in Jonestown, most of them too young to do much work. They were there because they'd been brought by parents or guardians. As harsh as conditions were for adults, kids got the best of what was available. Newborns were tenderly cared for in a snug nursery, and toddlers warmly supervised and nurtured. Beginning at kindergarten age and continuing through high school, children participated in structured, competently taught classes that emphasized individual instruction, unlike the cattle pen public schools many of the youngsters had attended back home. They were expected to study hard and mind their teachers. Besides reading and writing and math, they had to study socialism. But there was plenty of time for skits and singing. None of the younger children were even yelled at. Discipline was tougher for the teens. When they messed up they were put on the Learning Crew, and a couple of constant screwups even got put down in that hole, though only after their parents said it was okay. The kids adjusted to their new surroundings, and were constantly reminded that Jonestown was *for* them. They were treasured, and knew it.

That left the middle third, the adults expected to do all the work without complaint and to respect and obey Jim Jones in all things. There were those among them who'd joined the Temple and stayed because of the healings, the miracles that this man could do. Jones didn't attempt many healings now — unlike the American temples with their private bathrooms and vast auditoriums, Jonestown's cramped quarters didn't lend themselves to smoke-and-mirror theatrics. But many settlers still believed in Jones as someone more than an ordinary man, maybe even a god, and, if he called them to live in the Guyanese jungle, then they would, and willingly.

There were others, and their number grew all the time, who were increasingly aware of his flaws and contradictions, who didn't automatically accept all he said and did and resented the sometimes bizarre demands that Jones made on them. But they'd come to Guyana with a purpose, to set the ultimate socialist example for a world that badly needed it. Just as older settlers bought into Jones's pavilion diatribes because they'd lived through atrocities in the past, Jonestown's other adults had seen plenty of terrible things themselves — Vietnam, riots in the streets of countless American cities, assassinations, the resignation of a president, confirmed acts by government agencies against principled citizens standing in opposition. It was easy to believe that the CIA and FBI were plotting against Peoples Temple and all that it stood for. All the hard work, all the sacrifices, was investment in a better world for the next generation. Beyond the dripping sweat and aching muscles, the skimpy meals and smelly outhouses, an even greater sacrifice might be ultimately required — death while fighting to defend the children, or else the end of one's life as the ultimate act of defiance. But there was little opportunity to dwell on that aspect of it. These people, ranging in age from late teens to mid- or even late sixties, worked so hard and long, then got so little sleep thanks to Jones and his nightly diatribes, that they were often too exhausted to think much, if at all. It was hard enough to get through a single day, let alone contemplate what might some-day be asked of them. Their focus was neces-sarily on the very basics: work hard, rest whenever possible, be prepared to fight the Temple's enemies. On his bad days, Jones's excesses were like the blistering sun or the biting insects, something to endure for the sake of the cause.

If there were still some among them — and Jones realized that there had to be — who at least occasionally thought about leaving with Jones's permission or escaping without it, there were other deterrents beyond passports and money. Relationships were involved. Many in Jonestown were part of extended family units, joined in the settlement by spouses, children, cousins, parents, or assorted in-laws. So, more than ever, Jones encouraged followers to spy on each other and report any hint of disloyalty. Someone unhappy in Jonestown and ready to run away ran a grave risk by discussing it in apparent confidence with family members or friends. No one completely trusted anyone else, and if Jones found out, punishment would result. Few wanted to be considered a traitor by loved ones or were ready to flee Jonestown while leaving those loved ones behind.

Then there was the ultimate barrier to escape, the jungle itself. A rough-cut road ran some two miles from the main Jonestown settlement to its guarded entrance, and from there another mile or so to a slightly wider road that led the rest of the way to Port Kaituma. On both sides along the way were great walls of towering trees, and snake-infested barbed brush. Any defector reaching Port Kaituma would have trouble going farther.

660

There were no boats between there and Georgetown on a regular basis, and few planes took off or landed from the narrow, potholed airstrip. Pursuers sent by Jones would have an easy time catching up.

Alternatively, escapees could make for Matthews Ridge, but that required struggling through the jungle itself for a dozen miles, then following a train track for twenty more. The strongest adults, let alone families with children or old people, would find it difficult to reach Matthews Ridge, if they didn't get lost forever in the jungle.

So they stayed, and at night listened to Jones recite his litany of outside forces conspiring against Jonestown — the media, the CIA, the FBI, even the Guyanese government. But a much different, lethal foe was emerging, comprised of previously individual enemies who understood Jim Jones and Peoples Temple very well, and who came together with the mutual goal of bringing him down for good.

CHAPTER FORTY-FIVE: CONCERNED RELATIVES AND THE FIRST WHITE NIGHT

It was inevitable that there would be former members who held grudges against Peoples Temple and Jim Jones, individuals and families who left out of disgust with Jones's paranoid preaching, staged healings, increasingly violent discipline, or resentment of surrendering property and possessions to the church. Many kept silent out of fear that the Temple would retaliate, others because they felt no one would believe the stories they had to tell. Sheer numbers were also intimidating — what good would a lone voice do when Jones had hundreds of followers ready to back him up against any accusation?

But the *New West* article in August 1977 had changed that. A number of former members came forward and defiantly testified. They not only survived unscathed, but, to at least some extent, *won* — though the Temple denied everything in a series of press releases, Jones fled the country. San Francisco's two daily newspapers began playing catch-up to *New West,* publishing their own stories about shady Temple real estate deals, seeking out more estranged followers to describe mistreatment by Jones and his minions. And, when doing so, many of the disaffected former members connected with others. They began meeting, often with Elmer and Deanna Mertle acting as hosts. Fellowship was comforting, and consensus was immediate: Jim Jones could not be allowed to bide his time in Guyana until the controversy in California passed. Pressure had to be maintained. The goal was obvious, but not the means. A shotgun approach — individually approaching reporters or elected officials — wouldn't work. The current anti-Temple story cycle could last only so long before the media and its audience grew tired of repetitive stories. *Jim Jones and Peoples Temple stole members' property. Followers were sometimes brutally beaten. The Temple had lots of money, some of it undoubtedly gained illicitly.* Something different was required, an angle for media coverage that would engage the public long-term and arouse such vigorous outrage that authorities would have to act, and Jones would finally be done for. There were plenty of highly vocal former members, but it was perhaps the quietest among them who became the necessary catalyst.

Grace Stoen was determined to regain

custody of her son through the courts. In the *New West* story, she never mentioned John Victor. But he was what she talked about when she met with the other former Temple members, and this mother's desperation to regain her child moved them all. In August 1977 the Mertles initiated a $1 million lawsuit against the Temple for houses they claimed were fraudulently taken from them, but that was property. From a public relations perspective, a five-year-old boy obviously had much wider appeal. Grace's struggle to wrest her little son from Jones's overseas clutches would clearly be a lengthy one — anyone even remotely familiar with Jones knew he'd never give up the boy easily — and perfect for ongoing media coverage. And Grace wasn't the only former follower desperate to regain a child from Guyana. Some had teenage children, or even younger ones, living apart from them in Jonestown, there because their parents, while still members of the Temple, signed over guardianship as part of the church's communal child rearing. A few of them had engaged seedy private eye Joe Mazor to try to get their youngsters back. At one point, uncertain of prevailing against Jones in court, even Grace met with Mazor. Still more disaffected, onetime Jones followers didn't have children in Guyana, but did have other family there — parents, siblings, cousins. The letters they sent back to the United States were suspiciously mechanical, full of praise for Jones and the jungle settlement, rarely answering directly any questions asked by their stateside loved ones about living conditions or a desire to come back or at least visit. The letters from Jonestown almost always asked for money, and in talking among themselves the former followers with grown daughters in Jonestown found that several of the young women reported the same thing: they were engaged to Larry Schacht, the settlement physician. This was clearly a ploy to reassure worried parents — who wouldn't want their daughter to marry a doctor?

Now the former members had a rallying theme — rescuing family members from Jonestown. Some, maybe all, might be held there against their will. Who could be certain? The group assumed a publicity-savvy name: Concerned Relatives. But it was one thing to have a name and message, quite another to wield it to maximum effect against Jones. A focused, step-by-step plan was required. Fortunately for the former members, someone with the necessary organizational skills and the knack for bold, calculating action was about to come among them. Grace and Tim Stoen were no longer estranged.

In July 1977, even before the *New West* article was published, Tim Stoen met with Grace in Denver. His hopes for reconciliation were dashed when she told him she was now with Walter Jones, but Stoen agreed with Grace that she should have at least joint custody of John Victor with Jim Jones. If it proved necessary, Stoen promised, he'd return to Guyana himself and initiate legal proceedings against Jones there. Stoen did not immediately align himself with the other former Temple members. But he knew about the others, and understood the potential of eventually joining forces. For the moment, Stoen's concern was helping Grace regain John Victor. Everything else was secondary.

On August 18, Grace Stoen went to court in San Francisco and formally requested custody of her son. Her petition noted that John Victor was in Jonestown, cited the various claims made against Jones in the *New West* article, and stated she feared for the little boy's safety in Guyana. The judge ordered Jones to appear in court on September 9 "to show cause" why Grace should not be awarded custody of the child.

Jones had prepared for such an action by Grace. In early August dozens of his followers testified for affidavits alleging mistreatment of John Victor by his mother. They also claimed that Grace had attempted to seduce underage boys in Temple foster care. Grace was even alleged to have behaved inappropriately with her son: "She would hug all over him in a sexual manner."

Jones's affidavit stated that in 1971 Tim Stoen personally requested him to do "anything of a sexual nature" that would keep a reluctant Grace in the Temple. Out of loyalty to Stoen, Jones agreed. Grace was supposed to utilize birth control, and to understand that the sex "wasn't a romantic thing." When Grace later told Jones that she was pregnant, he asked her to have an abortion, but she refused. She told Jones that "she had had no relationship with her husband Tim Stoen and the child was [his]." After John Victor's birth, Grace deteriorated emotionally and threatened suicide. She was clearly an unfit mother. Grace ran off with Walter Jones and deserted her son. Jones declared, "I am keeping John, not because I want to deprive her of him, but because I believe she is deeply injurious to him, because of her long history of mental imbalance. . . . I must say the whole situation with Grace was one of the gravest mistakes of my life."

The affidavits were prepared for future use in court if necessity arose, but Jones never intended for matters to go that far. He believed that so long as he stayed in Guyana, he was impervious to any orders from a U.S. court. The San Francisco order for him to appear on September 9 was just one more irritation, much like Marceline's apparent emotional deterioration as she stayed behind to defend him. About the same time the San

Francisco judge issued the order, Terri Buford wrote Jones that "Marcie is okay except between 8–10 in the morning and then it is tears and all the old tunes that you have heard before how she has to take a backseat in your life — only a wife in name for 12 years now — and how she had to sacrifice all for the cause. . . . She took estrogen the other day so hopefully her moods will improve."

Jones's American legal problems grew worse. Grace Stoen was divorcing Tim at the same time she was attempting to regain custody of John Victor from Jones. Donald King, the judge presiding over the divorce case, awarded custody of John Victor to Grace, and ordered Jones to produce the boy in his court on October 6. The order added, "Claimant Rev. Jim Jones is advised that a failure to appear at the time and place designated above may result in a decision adverse to himself. . . . Any previous declaration of statement signed by either Petitioner [Grace Stoen] or Respondent [Tim Stoen] authorizing Claimant Jones to act as guardian of said minor child is hereby declared null and void."

That crucial addendum changed everything. The Temple had considered its guardianship of Jonestown children legally protected by the permission forms signed by parents, sometimes as many as a half dozen forms for individual children. These were properly notarized (Temple membership included several notary publics), and copies were kept filed in both San Francisco and Jonestown. If Judge King's nullification of the papers Grace had signed granting custody of John Victor to Jones and the Temple held up, and Grace did get John Victor back, then legal precedent would be established for any future challenge of Temple guardianship. The new threat to Jones was twofold. He could lose John Victor, whom he loved, and also many or even most of the other Jonestown children. But these youngsters were a crucial element of Jones's hold over his adult followers in Guyana. He stressed repeatedly that, besides setting a socialist example for the rest of the world, the main reason they were there was to keep these children safe from a rapacious, capitalist society that would destroy them. If the children were gone, legally taken away, then many Jonestown adults would feel they had less reason to stay themselves. Grace Stoen's claim to her son had the potential to tear Jonestown apart, and with it Peoples Temple and Jim Jones. Then Grace, now with the support of Tim Stoen, ratcheted up the pressure, and Jones's ever-present paranoia turned to panic.

At the same time that Judge King made his ruling, Jeffrey Haas, the attorney representing Grace, wrote to Charles Garry, the Temple's lawyer in the United States: "In accordance with Judge King's directive, please find enclosed a copy of the order arising out of the hearing on August 19, 1977. . . . Demand is hereby made on you in your capacity as the legal representative of both the People's [sic] Temple and Mr. Jim Jones for return of the minor child, John Victor, to his mother in accordance with the court order. I trust that we can expect your co-operation and compliance."

That letter initially seemed no cause for additional concern. Jones's strategy remained the same. All U.S. court edicts would be ignored as he and five-year-old John Victor Stoen remained in Guyana, beyond American legal jurisdiction without the consent and co-operation of the Guyanese government. But then Haas and Grace Stoen carried the fight overseas. During the first week of September, Haas flew to Georgetown and appeared in a Guyanese court to request that the U.S. order for Jones to produce the boy be honored there. Justice Aubrey Bishop was sympathetic, and issued an order for Jones and John Victor to appear in his courtroom on September 8, when Jones would have to show cause why Justice Bishop should not award the child to his mother. Haas then flew to Port Kaituma with a copy of the order, and from there made his way to Jonestown with a Guyanese court officer to present the order to Jones.

Jones knew Haas was in Guyana almost

from the moment that he arrived in George-town — the Temple had informers every-where. To shore up the support of his follow-ers in Jonestown, and to reinforce his claims that enemies always lurked nearby, Jones staged an attack on himself on the night before Haas made his appearance in Justice Bishop's court. Jim Jones Jr. remembers, "Jim was telling me that people needed to believe we were going to be invaded, that there needed to be an act people could rally around. He told me to help him with it." Jimmy got his rifle and set up in a spot near Jones's cabin, and, when his father emerged, fired some shots that, as intended, missed by a wide margin: "My dad had told me, 'Don't worry, I'll make sure that anybody with me won't shoot back,' but that night he was be-ing guarded by Tim [Tupper Jones] and Johnny [Cobb], and when Jim came out and I shot, the next thing I know Tim and Johnny are shooting their shotguns right in my direc-tion and I had to run." In the uproar that fol-lowed, Jones announced that Temple enemies had come to assassinate him. Everyone must be on extra alert.

The atmosphere remained tense when Haas and the Guyanese court official arrived with Judge Bishop's order. They were met at the gate by Maria Katsaris, who demanded to know why they were there. The official told her they had come on Guyanese Supreme

Court business and asked to see Jones. Katsaris said the Jonestown leader was away; she didn't know when he'd be back. Haas and the court officer retreated to Port Kaituma, waiting to see how Justice Bishop would direct them to see that his order was delivered and obeyed.

Jones wondered, too. It was bad enough that Haas had come to Guyana, worse that Justice Bishop seemed sympathetic to him and Grace Stoen, worse still that Haas had been flown from Georgetown to Port Kaituma in a Guyanese military plane. Were Prime Minister Burnham and his government about to betray Jones and the Temple? Jones radioed his people at Lamaha Gardens in Georgetown, instructing them immediately to find Deputy Prime Minister Reid and demand to know what was going on. Jones soon received a report back that Reid was out of the country, in fact in America on official business.

An integral characteristic of paranoia is lack of perspective. To Jones, Reid's presence in America at exactly the same time as Justice Bishop made his ruling and Haas appeared at the Jonestown gate could mean only one thing — the U.S. and Guyanese governments, neither having any more pressing concerns than the destruction of Peoples Temple, were now in active collusion against him. Perhaps Burnham's government had even been overthrown in a military coup and replaced by more pro-American, anti-Temple leadership. These possibilities elicited Jones's most extreme reaction yet, and one that was, in retrospect, the beginning of the end.

About four thirty in the afternoon on September 7, one day before Justice Bishop had ordered Jones to produce John Victor in his Georgetown court, workers in the fields and brush around Jonestown were informed that they were to return to the settlement. It had been a long, exhausting day of labor, so everyone shouldered their hoes and shovels and began walking. But then they heard screams of "Get back as soon as you can," so they broke into weary jogs. As the field workers arrived in the main settlement, they saw old people and children stationed in a wobbly line brandishing pitchforks, shovels, and a few machetes. Jones got on the loudspeaker and announced that they were under attack. Everyone had to prepare for an immediate fight. Jones assumed the role of combat commander. He ordered Stephan and Tim Carter, who was temporarily in Jonestown rather than Georgetown, to gather all of Jonestown's security guards — there were perhaps two dozen, armed with rifles, handguns, and crossbows — in the mission kitchen so they would have clear shots down the road that led from the Jonestown gate. Carter, the former U.S. Marine who'd survived jungle fighting in Vietnam, told Jones, "You don't want to put all the weapons in one place, because then [the enemy] can just concentrate their fire there." Jones rearranged perimeter defenses, and, once those were in place, turned to a different logistic. Some of Jonestown's treasury was comprised of small gold bars. Jones had his son Jimmy and Johnny Cobb, another mission teen, load the gold into a bag and take it into the jungle. If Jonestown fell, the boys were to find some way to take the gold to the Soviet embassy in Georgetown — this would be a final, defiant demonstration of the Temple's socialist beliefs. Jimmy and Johnny lugged their heavy cargo off into the wild and, after going a short way from the mission, huddled with it. Jones had given them rifles, and they were ready to fight to defend the bullion. The teens learned only later that their weapons weren't loaded.

Back in Jonestown, Jones informed his makeshift troops that well-armed adversaries, a mix of mercenaries and Guyanese troops, were coming to take away not only John Victor Stoen, but all of Jonestown's children. Jones said that he knew who was behind it all — Tim Stoen, the Temple's foremost adversary. Everyone had to fight. Dig in. Get ready. The attack was coming.

Hours passed, and exhausted children and old people and some of the fighting-age adults who'd toiled in the fields since day-break began to totter. Jones refused to let any of them leave their posts. Food and water were passed around. Jones alternated between urging unblinking vigilance over the camp loudspeaker and communicating by radio to Lamaha Gardens in Georgetown and with the Temple office back in San Francisco. Marceline and the staff there were instructed to find Ptolemy Reid wherever he might be in the United States, and gain his promise that Jones did not have to comply with Justice Bishop's order.

All the next day, and the next, the alert remained in place — by now, Jones was calling it a siege and regularly describing vast forces arrayed just out of sight, poised for imminent attack. Reid had not been located. The date Justice Bishop demanded that Jones appear in court came and passed. Jones predicted that meant the attack surely was coming soon. On the second night of the siege, Jones changed tactics. He announced that everyone would be trucked to Port Kaituma in shifts under cover of dark; the *Cudjoe* was anchored there at the dock. Somehow, everyone in Jonestown would cram aboard, and they'd sail to Cuba, where they would ask for asylum. Surely they'd be taken in. Jones didn't explain why the enemies surrounding Jonestown would let the trucks pass, and everyone else was too exhausted to ask. At least, one way or another, it was going to be over. Seniors made up the first truckloads, and when they reached Port Kaituma, never sighting even a single adversary on the way or once they arrived, the old folks began stumbling up the gangplank. It was very dark. One elderly woman fell and broke her hip. Notified of this by radio back in Jonestown, Jones ordered the entire group back to the settlement. Nothing more was said about a sea exodus to Cuba.

Stephan Jones was sent out to keep watch by the Jonestown gate, and on the morning of September 9, Jeffrey Haas returned. Justice Bishop had ruled that if copies of his appearance edict were prominently posted near the settlement, Jones would be considered to have received the court order. Jones and John Victor retreated into the jungle, and Harriet Tropp and Joyce Touchette met with Haas. They told him that assassins had tried to shoot Jones, and refused to accept the order on Jones's behalf. The court official with Haas tacked up copies of the order on several settlement buildings. Settlers tore them down. Haas retreated to Georgetown, and the next day Justice Bishop issued a bench warrant for Jones's arrest. Temple members from Lamaha Gardens were in Bishop's courtroom; they rushed to radio the news to their leader in Jonestown. Previously, Jones had made up his warning about soldiers coming to take him and John Victor away. Now, it was a real possibility. The siege he'd instigated had extended for several days. His followers were on the verge of collapse. If Guyanese forces did come, Jonestown could no longer even briefly resist.

Jones got back on the radio to Marceline and told her that he and everyone else at Jonestown "are prepared to die." Marceline took it to mean that Jones was about to call for mass suicide, and her interpretation was reinforced when Jones let Jimmy, who'd been called back from guarding gold in the jungle, and then Stephan, tell her that they agreed with their father. Marceline begged for more time to locate Ptolemy Reid. Along with Debbie Layton and Terri Buford, who were with her at the San Francisco temple, she began a new series of frantic phone calls. As a tactic to delay any fatal orders by Jones, Marceline arranged for Angela Davis and Eldridge Cleaver to send radio messages of support for the Temple cause. Carlton Goodlett, speaking from San Francisco, advised Jones to calm down — the Guyanese government had invited him and the Temple into its country, and surely wouldn't abandon them so abruptly. Marceline finally reached Reid's traveling party — in Indiana, of all places — and received assurance that no Guyanese forces would attack Jonestown or come there to arrest Jones. After she told her husband, he promptly called everyone in Jonestown together and declared victory. Jeffrey Haas returned to the United States; Justice Bishop set a new hearing date for November. For the time being, Jones allowed his Jonestown followers to stand down and resume their normal schedules. He worried that Reid might have been sufficiently offended at being tracked down in the United States to withdraw his personal support, and in early October he wrote to the deputy minister that he had understood that the Guyanese government would handle "situations like that of my son, John Stoen, with a firm hand, by simply stating that there is no [American] jurisdiction. . . . We need to know where we stand. Personally, I am so weary of constant political harassment that I would gladly sacrifice myself if it would mean any assurance of peace for my people. But members of my organization will not accept that. They do not want to work and build without my presence." Reid promised Jones that no one would arrest him, in Jonestown, Georgetown, or anywhere else in Guyana. Jones didn't believe it; there was a new court date in Georgetown, so the matter of John Victor clearly wasn't resolved, and the custody of his little son and many more Jonestown children remained at risk. The September 1977 "White Night" — a settlement term for those occasions when Jones summoned everyone to deal with a sudden, life-threatening crisis — would prove to be only the first. In Jones's mind, his adversaries were wilier and more numerous than ever. The conspiracies against him had grown international in scope. He reacted accordingly.

CHAPTER FORTY-SIX:
DEATH WILL BE PAINLESS

Following what the settlers referred to as "the Six-Day Siege," Jones tightened Jonestown security. His personal guards were quick to react to even the slightest perceived danger. So many followers complained of feeling threatened by their own supposed protectors that Jones had to issue an order: guards must refrain from prowling settlement paths and fields with their weapons on full cock. "Sunday Open House" had been a Jonestown tradition — on those afternoons, Amerindians were welcome in the settlement, where they availed themselves of various medical treatments at the Jonestown clinic and enjoyed movies and snacks with Temple members. Now Jones discontinued the practice; enemies might plant spies among the natives. Amerindian admiration for what they considered Jonestown's modern wonders continued. Every now and then, native newborns would be deposited under cover of night by the Jonestown gate. Their mothers wanted the infants to grow up enjoying the same advantages as the American settlers, who always took the babies to raise. They joined a growing legion of Jonestown newborns, including Malcolm, the son of Tim Carter and Gloria Rodriguez; and Chaeoke, Jones's grandson, born to Lew Jones and Terry Carter, Tim Carter's sister.

Jones's own youngest offspring were thriving. Teachers who supervised John Victor Stoen and Kimo Prokes in Jonestown's preschool program remarked on both boys' precociousness. After the White Night in September, Jones openly acknowledged them as his children. John Victor's last name remained Stoen for a few months more — Jones had no desire to attract further legal fire. But "Kimo Prokes" was changed to "Kimo Jones" on the Jonestown school roster. The two half brothers lived with Jones, Carolyn Layton, and Maria Katsaris, who assumed the role of John Victor's mother and told him that his birth mother was dead. Everyone in camp loved Kimo, who was a jolly youngster. But some adults who still considered Jones to be at least in some way superhuman also detected divinity in John Victor. The boy had two Jonestown nicknames — "John-John" and "the Child God."

Jones accepted and even welcomed visits by Guyanese officials, seeing these as opportunities to demonstrate how everyone in Jonestown was fine, and how much progress the settlers were making in establishing their self-sustaining agricultural mission in the jungle. Each of these visits was painstakingly stage-managed. The Guyanese were led to specific buildings and fields, where, apparently by co-incidence, they would encounter settlers placed there in advance who would parrot memorized praise of their lives there and their leader. Then the government visitors would be invited to join the colonists in what they were told was a typically abundant Jonestown meal that included lots of meat and tasty desserts. All the settlers looked forward to these occasional feasts, which were their only opportunities to eat hearty portions of something other than rice and thin gravy. Usually, there would be entertainment, too — Jonestown boasted a snappy children's dance troupe, and, as had been the Temple tradition back in the United States, a professional-quality band and choir. The Guyanese inspectors always had a grand time, with Jones playing the role of genial host. For some, the only problem was overattentiveness by the settlers. Gerald Gouveia, a Guyanese military pilot who occasionally accompanied government officials to Jonestown, remembers, "Everywhere you went, one of them came right along with you. Why, if you went into the toilet, one of them would come and stand there beside you and talk to you while you did your business. But at least they were always friendly."

It was different for officials from the U.S. embassy. Jones considered them enemy agents and instructed his followers to treat them as such. Temple staffers living in Lamaha Gardens had to maintain cordial relations with American officials, if only for the opportunity to complain when Jones felt particularly harassed. But when members of the embassy staff traveled to Jonestown, it was assumed by the settlers that they were there for some nefarious purpose, most likely to try to take away some or all of the children — Jones hammered this belief home in his nightly diatribes. It made the settlers nervous enough when such visits were only occasional, perhaps once every three or four months, but beginning in the late fall of 1977 they became more frequent. Back in America, the Concerned Relatives had begun implementing their newly focused plan. Dozens of parents, grandparents, and siblings of Jonestown residents called on or wrote to members of the U.S. House and Senate, claiming that family members were either being held against their will in the Guyanese jungle or else were being brainwashed. The elected officials dutifully passed on the complaints to the State Department, which in turn instructed U.S. embassy staff in Georgetown to investigate. That required staffers to either fly or sail to Port Kaituma and then travel deep into the forbidding jungle to Jonestown, where the children or adults supposedly held against their will always said that they were fine and very happy. Jonestown had no fences surrounding it, and Jones was careful to keep his armed guards out of sight. When the embassy staffers returned to Georgetown, they invariably sent back reports that the settlers in question said they were fine, and indeed seemed to be. Afterward, top embassy officials could always expect visits from the Temple's Lamaha Gardens staff, who complained about harassment and emphasized that Peoples Temple was a church, with members exercising their constitutional right to worship — and live — as they pleased. There were veiled threats of lawsuits.

The embassy was well aware that controversial Charles Garry was the Temple's legal representative. Garry made a fall trip to Jonestown, returned to San Francisco, and in a press conference described it as "paradise." He clearly would relish a high-profile lawsuit alleging that the U.S. government was unlawfully persecuting an overseas Christian mission. So in January 1978, recently appointed U.S. ambassador to Guyana John Burke sent a confidential "Conditions at People's [*sic*] Temple Mission" memo to his superiors at the State Department:

Two visits to the People's [sic] Temple Agricultural Community [Jonestown] in northwest Guyana, conversations alone with a number of the persons living there, and inquiries of GOG [Government of Guyana] who visit Jonestown frequently, have convinced consul [Burke] that it is improbable that anyone is being held in bondage or against their will at the People's [sic] Temple Community. Consul has either met with or personally observed approximately 500–600 of the 800 people [Burke's estimate] residing there. They appear healthy, adequately fed and satisfied with their lives. . . .

Persons with whom [we have] talked in private — some of whom were allegedly held against their will — appeared spontaneous and free in their conversation and responses to [our] questions. . . . In short, there is no hard evidence available to support the numerous allegations which have been made.

Embassy believes that the Department [of State] should draw upon the above when responding to inquiries from Congress or other interested parties in the U.S. about conditions at Jonestown. We believe that to return continually to the community to "investigate allegations of Americans held against their will" could open the Embassy and the Department to charges of harassment. Accordingly, unless otherwise directed, we plan to have a consular officer visit [Jonestown] quarterly to perform routine consular services. At that time the consular officer can also follow up on any welfare/ whereabouts inquiries with members and relay family greetings, etc.

That message was forwarded by the State Department to appropriate members of the Senate and House, who in turn continued relaying family queries to the State Department, but more out of routine constituent service than any real expectation of immediate action. Leo Ryan was the exception. Former speaker of the house Jim Wright recalled, "[Ryan] continued mentioning to me that he was certain of nefarious activities by an alleged church group in Guyana. He intended to take action regarding them as soon as his own reelection efforts [in 1978] were concluded, and by that I assumed he would propose some form of formal congressional inquiry in the late fall or early winter of that year."

Jones knew nothing of that, or the secret memo by Ambassador Burke. What he understood for certain was that the enemy he perhaps feared most had made an open challenge. On November 17, 1977, Tim Stoen wrote directly to Jones, in care of the San Francisco temple: "I am asking your cooperation in delivering John Victor Stoen to

Grace Stoen and me." The timing of the letter was particularly apt. On November 18, the San Francisco Superior Court issued a new order for Jones to return John Victor to his mother. The November custody hearing in Justice Bishop's Guyanese court (which Jones did not attend) was inconclusive, with further consideration postponed. But Bishop did not dismiss the case, so Jones had to worry about Tim Stoen on two legal fronts.

Jones more than anyone understood Stoen's ability to construct, then carry out, plans of attack couched within legal limits. Stoen had utilized this talent on behalf of Jones and Peoples Temple for years. Now he was not only in position to use all his skill and insider knowledge against them, he had a burning, personal cause. He wanted John Victor back, and there was clearly antagonism even beyond that. Jim Jones Jr. says, "Tim for so long really believed in [Jones] and the Temple, I'd even say he loved my dad, and Dad went out and hurt him in the worst way, getting his wife pregnant." To a degree far beyond his fixation with any other enemy, Jones prepared for war. In consultation with Charles Garry, Jones laid out an attack plan focusing solely on Tim Stoen. The first step was "writing to the newspapers, or calling them, re TOS [Timothy O. Stoen]."

San Francisco Chronicle columnist Herb Caen, who continued championing Jones despite the *New West* article, began mentioning the legal battle for custody of John Victor, informing readers that Jones "care[s] so strongly" about keeping the child "because, according to well-informed sources, the true father of the child is — Jim Jones." Jones had followers write a new series of highly detrimental affidavits describing Stoen, particularly alleging that he mocked Prime Minister Burnham and the Guyanese government. If Stoen successfully rallied U.S. authorities against him, Jones wanted the protection of Guyana's leadership. Additionally, Temple members remaining in the San Francisco area were coached on possible ways to intimidate Stoen. One list suggested "send[ing] him literature from mortuaries," "[sending] floral wreath/hearse/ambulance etc. to his home," "sugar in [gas] tank," "write in his name to radical magazines/to gay magazines/ to right wing senators supporting them [so that record will be on file with them]," and "generally let him know that we know where he lives etc. . . . [have] people show up now and then." Even if most of these specific acts were never carried out, Stoen mentions several times in his memoir that he was followed and, on at least one occasion, specifically warned of a Temple plan to have him killed. During his Temple tenure, Stoen sat through Planning Commission meetings where the possible murder of traitors and enemies was discussed. Now he knew that there were similar conversations concerning him.

Jones drew on his followers' own dread of Stoen. During Stoen's time as Jones's chief legal strategist, he'd been feared by Temple members, who assumed that many of the harsher aspects of Temple life, especially the physical discipline, were instigated by him rather than Jones. In a sense, when Stoen went public with his support of Grace and, therefore, his opposition to Jones, it allowed Jones's followers to also fixate on a specific foe rather than generic enemies identified by social status or agency — racist whites, the capitalist elite, the CIA, the FBI. Jones took full advantage; once, during an evening gathering at the Jonestown pavilion, he asked everyone to write down their preferred means of killing Tim Stoen. The more they despised him, the more Jones believed that he could count on their loyalty.

Jones also dug in for extended courtroom battles for John Victor. It was expensive. Besides Charles Garry's hefty monthly retainer back in California, Jones engaged Guyanese attorney Lionel Luckhoo, perhaps the most famous trial lawyer in the country. Each consultation with Luckhoo routinely set Temple coffers back as much as $2,500. Plenty of other defense attorneys in Georgetown cost considerably less, but Jones was willing to spend whatever was necessary. Just as valuable as Luckhoo's courtroom skills were the veteran attorney's personal connections with Justice Bishop and the other members of Guyana's high court.

Jones was ready to spend even more. In September 1977, he ordered Debbie Layton to find Stoen in San Francisco and offer him a bribe to leave Jones and the Temple alone. Layton was to suggest $5,000 and go as high as $10,000 if necessary. Layton had trouble locating the former Temple attorney — Stoen had done a good job covering his tracks. When she finally confronted him in October outside San Francisco's Superior Court, Stoen firmly turned down the bribe, warning Layton that he was willing to sacrifice anything to return John Victor to Grace, because that was where the child belonged. When Layton reported back to Jones by radio, he was less dismayed by Stoen's refusal than by his apparent sincerity: "Dear God, he's become principled, too?"

Tim Stoen and the custody fight would have been sufficient stress for anyone, but for Jones they were only two critical concerns among many. Throughout the end of 1977 and into 1978, it seemed as though everything was going against him and Jonestown. The Stoens weren't the only parents among the Concerned Relatives making concerted efforts to regain their children. Howard and

Beverly Oliver took steps to legally revoke the power of attorney they had granted the Temple over their teenage sons Billy and Bruce. Bruce had turned nineteen in Jonestown, but Billy was seventeen and still a minor. The Olivers obtained a court injunction returning Billy's custody to them and flew to Guyana to collect him. Jones stalled, Billy stayed in Jonestown, and embassy officials in Georgetown told the Olivers it was a matter for the courts, rather than diplomats, to resolve. The Olivers ran out of money and returned to the United States, declaring they'd be back. That was the last thing Jones wanted at a time when he was trying to further delay any Guyanese court action involving John Victor. One contested Jonestown child was bad enough, but two?

And then there were three, though this child was an adult. Steven Katsaris was determined to rescue his daughter, Maria, from Jones and the Temple, or at least plead his case to her in person since her letters had grown increasingly impersonal and she refused his offers to pay her way back to California for a visit. Katsaris informed Maria he would arrive in Georgetown on September 26 and hoped she would meet him there. She didn't. Katsaris waited for a few days. Temple spokesmen told him that Maria was away on a trip to Venezuela with her boyfriend, whom she had identified in letters to her father as Jonestown doctor Larry Schacht. When Maria never appeared, Katsaris went home, but not before promising Temple members that he would return.

Maria was twenty-four, legally entitled to make her own decisions — unless she was being held under duress or chemically controlled through drugs. Based on his own observations of Jones and Peoples Temple in Redwood Valley, Steven Katsaris thought these things were possible. He was a naturally outspoken man and not one to be intimidated by Temple threats or soothed by a conciliatory letter like the one he received from Maria soon after his return to the United States She wrote that she was sorry to have missed him, that she'd heard he was concerned about her, but he wasn't to worry — she was fine. A month later, Maria wrote again, and her message was hostile. Temple leaders would allow Katsaris to see her if he returned to Guyana, but (referring to Concerned Relatives) "you have been cooperating with the worst kind of people, stirring up trouble. . . . [If] you do not stop this immediately, that's it. I will never see you anymore."

In Jonestown, Jones and Temple attorney Gene Chaikin prepared Maria for a possible confrontation with her father, or at least an interview with U.S. embassy officials investigating Katsaris's claims. She was provided with a list of nineteen possible talking points and allegations. A few were designed to turn Katsaris's wrath against a Temple enemy rather than the Temple itself: "Did Tim Stoen call your father an evil bastard? Did Tim Stoen often advise you against seeing your father?" Failing that, Maria was to make accusations that Katsaris could deny but also couldn't disprove: "Were you afraid of your father as a child? Did your father, Steven A. Katsaris, sexually molest you?"

At the end of October, Katsaris returned. As she'd promised, Maria met him, but she was accompanied by Carolyn Layton and two other Temple members. A U.S. embassy official was also present. The meeting went badly. Maria was standoffish. She assured her father again that she was fine and rebuffed his offer to bring her back to America. Katsaris finally told her that he would leave an airline ticket for her at the Georgetown embassy in case she ever wanted to come home. After his daughter left, he learned from the embassy officials that she had accused him of molesting her as a child. Jones had intended the allegation to make Katsaris back off, but it had the opposite effect. He was still determined to rescue his daughter, and now he began considering a lawsuit against the Temple for libel.

In October, a past Jones misstep came back to haunt him. Three years earlier, a Los Angeles judge ordered all records of Jones's lewd conduct arrest to be destroyed. But, although sealed from any public scrutiny, they still existed, and now California's attorney general requested that the judge's decision be overturned. The clear intention was to make them available to the press — Jones wasn't always unnecessarily paranoid. He ordered Garry to go to court and fight to keep the records private. Court maneuverings on both sides would certainly take months, and in Guyana Jones would have to fret through every minute. Media descriptions of him as a sexual deviate would lend even further credence to suits by parents to regain custody of Jonestown children — what judge, American or Guyanese, would allow little boys and girls to live in a remote jungle camp run by a pervert?

Another matter involving Jonestown kids also caused great concern. Jones and the Temple were proud of the school system they'd designed and implemented. Mission children were held to high standards of scholarship and class conduct. Their curriculum was designed by Temple adults who were educators, as were their teachers. But such home schooling did not comply with Guyana's strict educational rules — as part of the Burnham administration's effort to build a sense of national pride, the Ministry of Education required that all children study Guyanese history and culture. For a time it appeared that the ministry might require all Temple children to attend school in Georgetown. Jones, fearful that he would be arrested for defying Justice Bishop's court appearance order if he stepped outside Jonestown, let alone visited Guyana's capital city, had to rely on staff from Temple offices in Lamaha Gardens to meet with ministry officials and plead Jonestown's school case. A compromise was reached — the Jonestown curriculum would be adjusted to include the necessary Guyanese studies. Over the next few months, ministry observers would visit Jonestown classes to determine if the instruction provided was sufficient. If so, Jonestown's school would be officially certified. If not, all of the settlement's school-age children would have to attend Guyanese schools and, given the isolation of Jonestown, that meant boarding them away from the mission. Again, there would be no quick decision.

There was more. In early October, Marceline Jones had come to Jonestown. Hue Fortson had been dispatched to run the San Francisco temple in her place. Marceline was worn down, her physical ailments exacerbated by the pressure of constantly defending her husband and the Temple. Her arrival created a ticklish situation. Though Jones openly lived in Jonestown with Carolyn Layton and Maria Katsaris, most settlers still considered Marceline "Mother" to Jones's "Father." (In

Jonestown, he was referred to more informally as "Dad.") It was one more blow to the long-suffering woman, now fifty, when she learned that she would be quartered in a separate cottage, one nicer than most others but inferior to where Jones lived with his mistresses. Jones still used her as a buffer between himself and his U.S. critics. Marceline continued traveling back and forth, sometimes to Washington, D.C., where she pleaded the Temple's and Jonestown's case to members of Congress who had received complaints from Concerned Relatives. Thanksgiving 1977 found her in the United States, and she sent Jones a letter:

> I look forward to the time when I need never say goodbye again. I am grateful for the [word illegible] beauty there . . . there is none here.
> I'm willing to stay as long as necessary. Just hold me high in thought — I'm not the woman I used to be. Please give my love to our children. They were the light of my life, and I want them to know it.

But if Jones believed she was completely beaten down, he was wrong. Despite the humiliation of living apart from her husband in Jonestown, her time in the settlement proved at least temporarily a tonic for Marceline. She put her medical background to use in helping to overhaul Larry Schacht's disorganized management of the settlement clinic and devoted considerable time to helping supervise Jonestown's nursery — the babies and toddlers there included several of Marceline's grandchildren. Though she had little chance to spend time with her own children — Stephan and Tim were kept busy with security responsibilities, Lew was always busy with lower-profile tasks on his father's behalf, and Jones was about to send Jimmy to Georgetown as his newest representative there — Marceline began a quiet effort on their behalf, moving money in foreign banks to accounts in her children's names. That would provide them with at least some financial cushion if they ever chose to leave the Temple. Between November 3, 1977, and February 3, 1978, she shifted just over $31,000. Terri Buford, who in Jonestown became close to Marceline for the first time, refers to these accounts as her "out package." (Buford adds that at one point in Jonestown, Marceline slipped Stephan a bankbook indicating a substantial account in his name. Stephan hid the bankbook from his father, but someone discovered it and turned it over to Jones. Jones apparently took no action against his son or wife.)

November brought additional troubles — they seemed to come now in rapid succession. Two teenage boys, Tommy Bogue and

Brian Davis, tried to run away. They planned to make their way through the jungle to Venezuela and return to the United States from there. But their progress was slow, and they were overtaken by Jonestown security and returned to the mission. In front of all the other settlers, Jones said that the pair was lucky that they hadn't been killed by jungle beasts or government border guards. As punishment, they were placed in leg irons for several weeks. Jones wanted the punishment to be severe enough to discourage anyone with similar escape plans.

On November 13, the *San Francisco Examiner* published a story by reporter Tim Reiterman about the death of Bob Houston and Sam Houston's and Joyce Shaw's suspicions that Jones and the Temple were behind it. About 150 of the remaining San Francisco temple members staged a protest march, but to no avail.

Five days later, when Jones, as expected, failed to appear with John Victor Stoen, an order was issued by the California Superior Court to San Francisco district attorney Joseph Freitas, instructing him to "take all actions necessary" to locate Jones and "secure his compliance" in returning the child to his mother. Freitas, once among Jones's most public supporters, now wrote to the Guyanese minister of foreign affairs requesting help. He received none — Guyana's government wanted to stay out of the mess. Leo Ryan, not yet prepared to make an all-out effort but still concerned, asked Secretary of State Cyrus Vance to use his department's influence with the Guyanese. A State Department official informed Ryan that only U.S. courts could make formal extradition requests. When the *Examiner* wrote about Ryan's query to Vance, Jones, perhaps for the first time, became aware of the congressman as a dangerous adversary.

Lynetta Jones died in Jonestown on December 9. Larry Schacht concluded that the cause of death was cardiac arrest. Lynetta was buried near the settlement. Her son mourned, but not so much that he lost track of Jonestown's constant money concerns. Lynetta had an annuity that was arranged to make monthly payments over the course of her life, and Jones sent the U.S. bank involved a request for his mother's final check: $81.68.

The next day, former Temple enforcer Chris Lewis was shot to death in San Francisco. His demise, along with Lynetta's, meant Jones had death much on his mind. In an evening pavilion meeting on December 21, he asked how many of his followers had planned their deaths; anyone who wasn't prepared to die "may sell out." A bombshell announcement followed — because the U.S. government was so obviously determined to take John Victor, Jones planned "to ask Russia to take us." At that moment, Jones collapsed, sliding out of his chair onstage. Larry Schacht leaped to his side, crouching over the fallen Jonestown leader as many in the crowd wept. Then, dramatically, Jones got up and resumed talking. He said he'd just suffered "bleeding on the brain," a particularly painful affliction caused by low blood sugar, which in turn was caused by all the tremendous burdens he had to assume on behalf of his people. But he was recovered and had more to say about Russia. The weather would be harsh there. Some of the seniors might not survive. If the government came for the Jonestown children before everyone in the mission was ready to go, perhaps the adults would stand and fight while the kids escaped to Russia: "We built this land, and we won't give it up easy."

The immediate impact for all the settlers was one more daily assignment — in addition to all their daylong duties and nightly attendance in the pavilion, Jones now expected them to study Russian and attain at least conversational skills in preparation for the eventual move there. There was no debate, no vote of who was and wasn't in favor of leaving the jungle Promised Land, or, for that matter, a projected date of departure. It became a given that, at some point, they would go. Jones would tell them when. Meanwhile, it was one more secret to be kept from everyone in the outside world.

There was another new secret, this one between Jones and a very few trusted followers — Schacht, Carolyn Layton, Maria, and Gene Chaikin and his wife, Phyllis. With all that had been happening, Jones felt it was time to explore the most expedient means of committing the defiant act he'd alluded to for so long.

Jones had a question for Schacht. The young doctor, whom Jones had saved from drug addiction and sent to medical school, replied in a note, "There is a good chance I can develop germicidal means. . . . I am quite capable of organizing the suicidal aspect + will follow through + try to convey concern + warmth throughout the ordeal." In a separate note, Phyllis Chaikin suggested that everyone should be shot instead. Jones preferred poison.

In the months since the first White Night in September 1977, Jones occasionally proclaimed other such events, waking everyone up or calling them in from fields and classrooms to gather in the pavilion and hear more about the latest emergency — mercenaries arriving in Guyana to attack Jonestown, another attempt on his life — so around dawn on February 16, 1978, when orders blared that all must rush to the pavilion, everyone expected more of the same.

At first, it was. Jones announced that there

was apparently a restructuring of Guyana's government. The new leaders might be in CIA thrall. Guyanese soldiers had been spotted in Port Kaituma. An attack was imminent — what should be done? Someone suggested fleeing to Russia. Jones demurred. They weren't prepared for that yet. Old people or children might be lost in the confusion, and Jones refused to leave anyone behind. No, everyone would stay in Jonestown.

There was no work assigned that day. The settlers remained in the pavilion, growing progressively fearful. Jones periodically left to take radio reports, finally announcing that armed forces were on their way. They would attack in a matter of hours. Their intention was to kill all who lived in Jonestown, including the children. Rather than that, everyone present must take their own lives. That would rob their enemies of any triumph. There were some murmurs of disagreement, but no one openly argued. There was a sense that the time had finally come. Some of Jones's followers were pleased — this would be a true revolutionary gesture. Others, worn out from the months of tension, simply wanted to get it over with. Vats of dark liquid were produced. Everyone was told to line up, fill a cup, and drink. The poison in the drink would kill them in about forty-five minutes. Now some did protest. Guards pushed them forward and made them drink first. Jones promised that their deaths would be peaceful. As Edith Roller stood in line, she thought how ironic it was that she would not be able to record the event in her journal. Some, who'd been on the Planning Commission in San Francisco when their leader claimed to have poisoned their wine, suspected that Jones was conducting another test, and they were right. When everyone had swallowed their drinks, Jones declared, "You didn't take anything." It had been a test to see if they truly were willing to lay down their lives for the cause, and they had passed. As a reward, assignments were canceled for the rest of the day.

No one stood up and shouted at Jones for putting them through such a terrifying experience. True believers accepted that whatever Father did was right. Those increasingly disaffected with Jones but still loyal to the Temple's professed socialist cause shrugged the experience off as one more example of Jones's increasingly bizarre behavior. Many, sleep-deprived and emotionally exhausted, were just glad to get back to their beds.

Jones had wondered whether his followers would collectively obey an order for suicide, and now he knew. With that knowledge came certainty. In Jonestown or in Russia or wherever the uncertain future took him and his followers and hope was lost, there could be a grand gesture, one assuring Jim Jones's deserved place in human memory and history books. It had always been a possibility, but after this White Night it was no longer a matter of if, but when.

On Jones's instruction, Larry Schacht ordered one pound of sodium cyanide, enough for 1,800 lethal doses. It cost $8.85.

CHAPTER FORTY-SEVEN:
BETRAYALS

The next day, Jones reconvened everyone in the pavilion and instructed them to write essays on the topic "What I Would Do if This Were the Last White Night." The responses were chilling. Some suggested it would be better to die fighting, taking as many of the enemy with them as possible. One woman wrote that she was willing to take poison, but "only after putting the children to sleep. This would be hard for me because I don't like to face the fact of killing my own child." Another admitted, "I am scared of dying a long painful death. . . . I can't believe that after all this struggle and pain we all will die." Everyone wrote something, and though no one directly challenged the apparent certainty of future mass suicide, some now wondered if Jones actually intended to order such a precipitous act. It might be another of his ploys to gauge loyalty. Enough settlers thought so for Dick Tropp to send Jones a private memo: "People with a fair degree of savvy and intelligence [are beginning to believe that] White Nights are really a kind of elaborate ritual testing." Jones, satisfied that February 16 had served his purpose, did not respond.

He had other concerns. In January, Tim and Grace Stoen had come to Georgetown and met with Justice Bishop. They received no satisfaction. Bishop delayed consideration of John Victor's custody, and complained bitterly about badgering phone calls he'd received from "Americans" claiming to support the Stoens. They, in turn, believed the callers were actually Temple members — one more example of Jones's scheming. Other Guyanese officials were similarly uncooperative. The Stoens had three-week visas, but only a few days after their arrival were informed, without explanation, that they must immediately leave the country. They complained through the U.S. consulate and, at the last minute, were informed that they could stay after all. But the Stoens' money ran out; they returned to the United States, where Tim spent several days in Washington meeting with elected and State Department officials, pleading his case and asking for help. Though he received more assurances of concern and potential support than active assistance, Stoen's efforts were sufficiently worrisome to Jones that he dispatched Marceline to meet with the same officials and tell the Temple's side of the story. The result was, in effect, a draw.

Jones was also worried that his supporters in the Guyanese government might be wavering. Sharon Amos sent word to Prime Minister Burnham that Jones was ill; further stress from the Stoen custody case might kill him. Jones himself wrote a long letter to Deputy Prime Minister Reid, apologizing for Temple members in Georgetown contacting him so frequently: "[But] we need to know where we stand." So far as the Guyanese officials were concerned, Jones and Jonestown had become a constant irritant, but that aggravation was still outweighed by the settlement's useful presence near the Venezuela border. "We put up with them," Kit Nascimento says. "That is the best way to describe our feelings." Burnham and his ministers did not know Jones was exploring the possibility of leaving Guyana for Russia. Had they realized, Nascimento says, "Burnham would have thrown them right out of the country that very minute. We were keeping our bargain with Jones. He always wanted so much from us. All we asked was that he and his people stay where they were."

But in March, Sharon Amos and a few other Temple members based in Georgetown visited the embassies of socialist countries with diplomatic presence in the Guyanese capital — Russia, Cuba, and North Korea.

After removing all references to church or religion on Temple stationery, Jones also sent letters to the leaders of other socialist nations, enclosing pamphlets about Jonestown and inviting "any type of inquiry or communication." The letters elicited only polite, formal responses. Cuban and North Korean diplomats seemed interested in Jonestown, but not to the extent that they were willing to explore allowing the mission to move to their country. Russian ambassador Feodor Timofeyev was more forthcoming. He agreed to send along a letter from the Temple about potential relocation to his superiors in Moscow, and said he would personally visit Jonestown to see the settlement for himself. Jones took these gestures as a commitment rather than a first step, and informed everyone that they would definitely be moving to Russia. When a few settlers argued against it — they'd worked so hard to build a habitable home in the jungle — Jones snarled that if they didn't want to go to Russia, they could go back to America and the clutches of all the Temple's enemies there. And, if that's what they chose, "You can swim. We won't pay your fucking way."

Still, in case Russia didn't come through as he believed he'd been promised, Jones slightly hedged his bet. Around the same time she met with Timofeyev, Sharon Amos sent another letter to Prime Minister Burnham, this one asking for suggestions about "how we [at Jonestown] can do better. . . . We may make mistakes as people who are learning a new way of living, but we certainly want to improve." Amos also suggested to Ptolemy Reid that Jonestown might offer an additional benefit to the Guyanese national economy by becoming a tourist attraction: the settlers would create a man-made lake, stock it with fish, and also lead tourists on hunting expeditions.

Even while Amos was proposing substantial settlement improvements, Jones considered adopting more primitive means of reducing the constant costs for equipment repair. He radioed office workers in the San Francisco temple to ask that they find books on "manufacturing [methods] of the 18th and 19th century." In particular, he wondered whether horse-drawn plows might replace tractors.

Some days it seemed that Jones was everywhere in the settlement, wandering the fields and exhorting everyone to work harder, yammering for hours over the Jonestown sound system during the day and then lecturing in the pavilion far into the night, and presiding over endless meetings of the various settlement committees that convened after everyone else was finally allowed to go to bed. He bragged about his stamina, and, sometimes in the same breath, complained about how his health suffered because he had to do everything himself. He was as much a constant presence for the settlers as the jungle itself, and, like their surroundings, alternately inspiring and disconcerting.

There were times when Jones, at least in physical presence, disappeared for days, closed up in his cabin and attended only by Annie Moore, who became his personal nurse. Carolyn Layton, Maria Katsaris, and Jones's grown sons knew that he was incapacitated by drugs, tranquilizing himself into a stupor and eventually chemically coaxing himself back to pseudo-coherence with amphetamines. At least for the present, Jones managed to keep himself relatively drug-free and lucid during visits to Jonestown by Guyanese officials and American diplomats. In between, he indulged himself with drugs, treats like soft drinks and sugary snacks, and also, sporadically, sex. By this point, Jim Jones Jr. recalls, Carolyn Layton was his father's companion rather than bedmate. But Jones also expected other female followers to gratify him on demand. Like Marceline and Carolyn before her, Maria had to accept it.

In California, Jones was able to indulge himself without the knowledge of most followers. In Jonestown it wasn't possible. Jones had more privacy than anyone else, but the confines of the camp made it impossible for the settlers not to observe at least some of his carryings-on. The man who'd led them to believe he was a powerful god dripped with sweat, swelled from gluttony (Temple staff in San Francisco had to send new, larger shirts for Jones to disguise his bloated belly), and whined constantly about aches and pains — now the great healer apparently couldn't heal himself or anyone else. Soon after Debbie Layton and her mother, Lisa, arrived in Guyana, a Georgetown doctor diagnosed Lisa with inoperable cancer. For decades, Jones had showily removed tumors from the apparently afflicted. In Jonestown, Lisa was simply made as comfortable as possible while she awaited death.

Though most still believed in Jones as a leader, and as their spokesman against the racism, capitalism, and elitism that they all deplored, there was no longer, for most, any element of worship. "In Jonestown, after a while, Jim Jones lost his divinity," Laura Johnston Kohl says. "Everyone saw too much." Often, they heard too much. Jones's cabin was connected by phone to the camp radio and loudspeaker system. When lying on his bed, not completely blacked out in a drug stupor, he would harangue the settlement and workers in the fields with incoherent barks and mumbling. One day, overwhelmed by hours of gibberish, radio operators in the communications shack switched off Jones's phone, and everyone basked in the blessed silence.

711

Many sympathized with him: if Dad was breaking down from stress, it was undoubtedly caused, at least to some degree, by followers who either couldn't or wouldn't follow rules and live as perfect socialists. With Jones so often incapacitated, they began disciplining themselves and telling Jones about it so that he would know they were trying very hard to live right, and perhaps he would feel a little better. One teenage girl, just returned to Jonestown after working for a while in Georgetown, admitted that while in the city she'd succumbed to temptation and had a drink. She confessed to Jones in a note, "I let you down. I feel that [as punishment] I should fast and I am gonna fast for 1 week. Not eating will sure discipline me."

And there were moments when Jones fleetingly reminded others of what had attracted them to him in the first place — his unabashed playfulness in starting spontaneous water fights out in the fields, or those increasingly rare evenings when, instead of railing against enemies or whining about how much he sacrificed for others, Jones spoke movingly about the need for compassion and equality, and why Jonestown must set an example for the rest of the world. Some Jonestown settlers had followed him for so long that they had long since given up thinking for themselves; dozens of younger followers had never known anything other than life in Peoples

Temple and obedience to Jim Jones. Even those who otherwise had grave misgivings about their leader were in full agreement with his message that the outside world teemed with enemies.

In particular, they mistrusted the American government and all of its agencies. On March 14, 1978, Jonestown settler Pam Moton, certainly with the blessing of Jones, who had to personally approve any Temple missive, sent a blunt letter to all senators and members of Congress. It began, "We at Peoples Temple have been the subject of harassment by several agencies of the U.S. Government, and are rapidly reaching the point at which patience is exhausted." According to Moton, the false claims of Temple defectors had instigated unfair actions by the Social Security administration, the IRS, the Treasury Department, and the FCC. The persecution had to stop: "People cannot forever be continually harassed and beleaguered . . . without seeking alternatives that have been presented. I can say without hesitation that we are devoted to a decision that it is better even to die than to be constantly harassed from one continent to the next. I hope you can look into this matter and protect the right of over 1,000 people from the U.S. to live in peace."

Thanks to Concerned Relatives, many senators and members of Congress were already aware of Peoples Temple, and not in any positive way Moton's chastising letter didn't change any official opinions in Washington, but it did provide new impetus to Concerned Relatives' effort to turn public opinion against the Temple and its leader. Innocent children lived in Jonestown, and helpless old people, undoubtedly individuals of all ages who wanted to get away, and here, in writing, was the promise that they would die if Peoples Temple wasn't allowed to do whatever it wanted. Taken in that context, Moton's letter threatened not mass suicide but murder, and in California, Tim Stoen and Concerned Relatives took full advantage.

Stoen and Steven Katsaris served as primary drafters of a forty-eight-page document titled "Accusation of Human Rights Violations by Rev. James Warren Jones Against Our Children and Relatives at the Peoples Temple Jungle Encampment in Guyana, South America." Signed by twenty-five self-described "grief-stricken parents and relatives of thirty-seven persons in Jonestown," the document was a clever hybrid of testimony by members of Concerned Relatives and detailed descriptions of specific horrors supposedly taking place in Jonestown. The horrors were also conveniently listed in a series of bullet points for those who wanted the gist without too many details. A "decision to die" excerpt from Pam Moton's March 14 letter to Congress was the most damning material.

On April 11, with friends and media invited along, the Concerned Relatives marched to Peoples Temple in San Francisco, stopped outside the chain-link fence surrounding the property, and demanded to see whoever was in charge. Hue Fortson emerged, followed by a few other staffers. Fortson wouldn't let these visitors inside, but he did accept a copy of their accusation. Afterward, Concerned Relatives circulated flyers that summarized their accusations to the public and media and explained that those wanting to help could write to Guyanese prime minister Forbes Burnham and U.S. secretary of state Cyrus Vance, whose mailing addresses were included.

Besides attempting to attract attention and rally support, the manifesto and the flyers were intended as provocation, a means of goading Jones, increasing the pressure on him. It worked. Fortson immediately radioed Guyana, and within hours Jones proclaimed another White Night. Invective rather than faux poison was featured this time. Jones first railed against Fortson for accepting the Concerned Relatives' document, then turned his wrath on Tim and Grace Stoen who, he promised, would have "their brains blown out" if they ever dared come to Jonestown.

Within days, Prime Minister Burnham's office received a copy of the "Accusation" from

Concerned Relatives. Jones learned of this from his sources in the government, most likely Ambassador Bonny Mann. It was always Jones's way to immediately strike back. A week after Concerned Relatives made their visit to the San Francisco temple, Harriet Tropp in Jonestown read an official response to the media listening on a ham radio patch in Charles Garry's San Francisco office. Tropp had become an important figure in Jonestown, not only for her exceptional intellect and organizational skills but because she was one of the few who dared directly criticize Jones. At one point in early March 1978, wearied of Jones's constant complaints about disorganization in every aspect of settlement administration, Tropp fired off a blunt memo to her leader: "I think the essence of [our] problem, or at least one aspect of it, is that no one is willing to oppose your opinion in certain matters, and I frankly think that sometimes you are wrong, and no one is willing to say so." She was equally forthright at one evening gathering when Jones asked Jonestown women to explain — in writing — why they found him attractive. Tropp wrote that she didn't: "You are 47 and fat." But even then, she reiterated her devotion to the cause and willingness to lose her life for it, adding, "I don't have romantic illusions. They say the greatest orgasm is death, so I hope we have the great pleasure of dying together."

716

Now Jones wanted Tropp to explain Moton's March 14 letter in such a way that the press would not understand it as a vow of imminent mass suicide. In her radio transmission, she first impugned the motives of the Concerned Relatives, then described the Temple's successful efforts to provide "a constructive presence" overseas. Only then did she address Moton's letter:

If people cannot appreciate [our] willingness to die, if necessary, rather than to compromise the right to exist free from harassment and the kind of indignities that we have been subjected to, then they can never understand the integrity, honesty, and bravery of Peoples Temple, nor the type of commitment of Jim Jones and the principles he has struggled for all his life. It is not our purpose to die. We believe deeply in the celebration of life. It is the intention of Jim Jones, and has always been, to light candles rather than curse the darkness, to find and implement constructive solutions rather than merely complain about problems. But under these outrageous attacks, we have decided to defend the integrity of our community and our pledge to do this. We are confident that people of conscience and principle understand our position. We make no apologies for it.

717

The next day, the temple in San Francisco released a printed transcript of Tropp's broadcast. Though it had little real effect — negative stories about Jones and the Temple continued appearing in Bay Area newspapers with the exception of black community papers published by Carlton Goodlett — Jones felt that he and the Temple had at least responded. Back in Jonestown, he described a new potential action if Jonestown was invaded: surviving settlers could collaborate with Amerindians to escape to Peru. Meanwhile, from that moment forward no one was to leave "the bounds of the [settlement]" and go even a few steps into the jungle without Jones's permission.

Jones hoped to raise settlement spirits with progress reports about relocation to Russia, but there was no progress. At the Soviet embassy in Georgetown, Feodor Timofeyev responded to Sharon Amos's impatient inquiries by telling her that after passing along the Temple letter to Moscow there was nothing more he could do until he received a reply. Prospects looked brighter on April 16, when a reporter from the Soviet news agency TASS visited Jonestown and was given an elaborate guided tour. At the end of his day there, the reporter wrote, "It's very very impressive" in the settlement guest book, but afterward no story was published. Edith Roller noted in her journal that the only question the TASS reporter asked was, "Where are the TV sets?" Amos pressed Timofeyev to visit Jonestown, too, and, though he promised that he would, his duties in Georgetown always seemed to postpone the trip.

On May 10, U.S. consul Richard McCoy came from Georgetown on a Jonestown inspection trip. As usual, he was escorted around and allowed to meet with whomever he requested. Afterward McCoy noted in his official report that "in general, people appear healthy, adequately fed and housed, and satisfied with their lives on what is a large farm." But such government departmental memos were no effective counter to the active publicity efforts of Concerned Relatives. Jones decided that positive reports from relatives of Jonestown settlers were needed. Carolyn Layton wrote to her parents, urging them to come to Jonestown for a visit. Rev. John V. Moore remembers, "Barbara [Moore] and I were uncomfortable with some of the things [Jones] did, but we wanted to be affirming of the people of the Temple and our daughters. Also, we wanted to see our grandson [Kimo]." The Moores were met at the Georgetown airport by Debbie Layton, an especially poor choice to greet them. As a rebellious teen, Debbie had spent a portion of her high school years living with the Moores, who at the time were her brother Larry's in-laws through his marriage to their daughter Carolyn. While she was their guest, Reverend Moore recalls, Debbie caused so much trouble that they eventually sent her back to her parents. When she welcomed the Moores to Guyana, they felt uncomfortable. The Moores were taken to Jonestown, enjoyed time with Carolyn, Annie, and Kimo, and suffered through occasional short visits with Jones, who, Moore says, "seemed distressed, even to an extent disoriented."

Jones had good reason. Usually, he invented crises to create apprehension among settlers and test their loyalty to him, but this time the problem was real. Shortly after turning over the Moores to others for transport to Jonestown, Debbie Layton went to the U.S. embassy in Georgetown, where she requested protection and help returning to America. She signed a short statement claiming Jones planned a mass suicide in Jonestown and, after some false starts that included a brief return to the Temple house in Lamaha Gardens and phone conversations with Temple members who'd learned that she planned to defect, she eventually flew out to New York accompanied by Consul McCoy.

Besides Jones, only a few others — Carolyn Layton, Maria Katsaris, Terri Buford — knew as much about Temple finances as Debbie Layton. That alone made her defection dangerous, but there was also the strong suspicion that she would eagerly cooperate with Concerned Relatives and add to the damaging public charges they continued making against Jones and the Temple. Once again, Jones convened an emergency pavilion meeting, where he announced that someone he wouldn't name had defected, a person who might prove even more dangerous than Tim Stoen. Settlement security would be tightened. Because there were guests — the Moores, who were not at the pavilion — no other immediate action would be taken. Almost everyone guessed the defector was Debbie Layton. She had been unpopular with many settlers; Jones loyalists were not surprised by this betrayal of Dad. After dismissing his followers, Jones did make an additional order: Larry Layton, who had remained in California, must immediately be brought to Jonestown, hopefully before he learned what his sister had done: "If he knows, he might leave with her. Get him here by any means, including drugging." When Layton arrived in Jonestown, he learned for the first time that not only had his sister defected, his mother, Lisa, was dying of cancer.

The Moores stayed in Jonestown for a few days. At a meal they shared with Jones, Carolyn, Annie, and a few other Jonestown leaders, Jones ranted about conspiracies. Moore was struck by how quickly the others picked up on Jones's complaints and added their own: "They fed each other's fears. There seemed to be no objective voice questioning the reality of those fears. Jim went on and on, and they agreed with everything and encouraged him to say more." After returning to America, Reverend Moore wrote to his daughters, suggesting that "[you] keep in communication with people of different views than yours."

By this time, Marceline Jones rarely spoke in person to her husband. She had deliberately kept out of sight during the Jonestown visit by the Moores, fearing her presence would make Carolyn's parents uncomfortable. On May 15, after Debbie Layton's defection and the Moores' departure, she left a note for Jones, urging him to leave Guyana (apparently for Russia) while he could, with the settlement children "if some asylum could be arranged" and also "adults of your choosing." She, along with Larry Schacht, would remain with followers who were too old and weak to relocate: "I've lived long enough. . . . I promise — I [would] do all I can to relieve all here of their suffering." Confident that at least Stephan, Lew, Tim, and Jimmy were secure as part of their father's inner council, Marceline added, "I do not ask for the lives of my children if you think them unworthy." She was undoubtedly thinking of Agnes, who lived in Jonestown but was not part of Jones's immediate family circle. Marceline concluded, "I do implore you to allow me to do this. It would be my pleasure."

That same day, Tim Stoen and Steven Katsaris launched a new courtroom attack on Jones and the Temple in Mendocino County Superior Court, a $15 million libel suit against Jones "and his agents" for Maria Katsaris's allegations that her father had sexually molested her. Stoen didn't stop there. Over the next five weeks he filed two additional lawsuits; one for $18.5 million on behalf of elderly Wade and Mabel Medlock, who claimed the Temple had bilked them of all their property, and one for $22.9 million on behalf of Gang of Eight member Jim Cobb for libelous comments and "intentional infliction of emotional distress." Defending himself against the lawsuits would obligate Jones to return to America and appear in court, which in turn would make him liable to arrest for ignoring previous court orders to turn over John Victor Stoen — now called "John Jones" in Jonestown — to his mother. If Jones didn't contest the suits, the resulting adverse court decisions would trigger a new round of bad publicity. At the same time, Stoen sent a private message to Jones, telling Temple member Walter Duncan, who was about to go to Jonestown, that "if Jim Jones was smart, then he would return John Stoen to me and then I would get off his back."

Jones had no intention of doing that.

Besides the possibility that surrendering custody of John Victor would trigger the loss of many other Jonestown children, he remained adamant that the child was *his*. So long as the Guyanese courts failed to act, Jones felt that he and John Victor were safe in Jonestown. Charles Garry was ordered to initiate delaying actions on the three new lawsuits — these included a $150 million Temple lawsuit against Stoen. With luck, Jones, the child, and everyone else in Jonestown would relocate to Russia soon, and then Stoen, if he dared, could try his luck with the notoriously intransigent Soviet courts.

But for much of June, concerns about Tim Stoen were secondary to panic over Debbie Layton, who hadn't been heard from or of since her defection a month earlier. Now it became apparent that she'd been busy in the interim, meeting with State Department officials, the media, and Concerned Relatives. Supported by lawyer Jeffrey Haas — the same attorney who represented Grace Stoen in her fight to gain custody of John Victor — Debbie Layton supplied authorities and reporters with an eleven-page affidavit that revealed all she knew about unsavory aspects of Peoples Temple and Jones. She not only supplied specific numbers (over $65,000 in monthly Social Security checks received by Jonestown elderly) but also revealing details about work hours, poor nutrition, and the potential for "mass suicide," including the White Night of February 16, when Jones tricked everyone into thinking they were committing suicide by drinking poison.

The affidavit was provided to reporters, who pounced. The June 15 *San Francisco Chronicle* headline read "Grim Report from Jungle," and the lengthy article was accompanied by an equally large photograph of Debbie Layton. Many readers might not have paid much attention to the claims of a defector like Leon Broussard, who was overweight and black, but Debbie Layton was young, white, and extremely attractive. *Chronicle* reporter Marshall Kilduff, who'd cowritten the Temple exposé in *New West* that drove Jones from San Francisco to Guyana, was careful to provide a few balancing comments from Lisa and Larry Layton, who spoke to him by ham radio from Jonestown. Lisa Layton said her daughter's lies were "too ridiculous to refute." Larry Layton simply stated, "We are treated beautifully." Jones was not available for comment. Kilduff concluded the article with Debbie Layton's claims that Temple bank accounts in Europe, California, and Guyana totaled "at least $10 million."

Jones was determined that there would be no more defections by his most trusted confidants or anyone else. He told the other settlers that Debbie Layton left Jonestown only after stealing at least $15,000, and that she was "actively helping the conspiracy" against them. He used cancer-riddled Lisa Layton to try to lure her daughter back, with letters intended to elicit guilt ("I have been in intensive care . . . after I heard you left and how you left. Actually what you have done is worrying me into the grave") and offering forgiveness ("People have left before and been returned and were lovingly received by Jim and all the rest of us"). But along with Tim Stoen, Debbie Layton called other former Temple members, trying to rally them to the anti-Jones cause. John and Barbara Moore were contacted by both and urged to join the Concerned Relatives in an effort to rescue their daughters and grandson. Reverend Moore firmly declined: "Our previous encounters with Tim Stoen and Debbie Layton had not been in any way positive. We did not trust them."

Jones no longer trusted anyone with the exceptions of Carolyn, Maria, and, to a limited extent, his grown sons. Jimmy was about to marry his girlfriend, Yvette. The young couple planned to attend medical school together. But Jones had other ideas. Jimmy would move to Georgetown and serve as his primary ambassador there. Jimmy, who never liked life in the jungle, was glad to go until he learned that Yvette had to stay in Jonestown. "That began turning me against my dad. Then what really got me was, once after I went to Georgetown I had to come back with somebody [from the Guyanese government] who wanted to do an inspection, and also talk to Jim. We get there, and no Jim. I go to his [cottage], and he's lying there passed out from drugs. So here I am, dragging my father into the shower and standing in there with him, trying to get him in shape to go out and talk to the guest." As Jones's already heavy drug use increased, leaving him frequently incapacitated, Carolyn Layton and Maria Katsaris gradually assumed de facto leadership of Jonestown. While the two women issued orders in Jones's name, Annie Moore spent much of her time at Jones's side, administering drugs and monitoring his vital signs. While her older sister had long since related to Jones only as a human, and a flawed, if gifted, one at that, Annie still worshipped him and resented any demands on her time and nursing skills that took her away from his side. One afternoon when Annie was called away, she left a note by Jones's bedside: "I would rather be around you than anyone else in the world. . . . You have given everything to me so anything I can do for you is only right." Annie became extremely protective of Jones and suspected several others in camp of conspiring against him. "Before [mid-1978] Annie had been sweet, but then she turned into a bitch," Jim Jones Jr. remembers. "She became one of the

727

ones who would do anything [Jones] wanted just as soon as he said it."

Others did not. For the first time, some of Jones's followers began ignoring his more unreasonable commands. "One night I guess he'd been up imagining something bad, and he radioed me in Georgetown well past midnight," Tim Carter says. "He told me to call a [Guyanese] minister right away with some message. I said the man would still be asleep and [Jones] said he didn't care, just call him. I didn't. I thought the next day Jones would have forgotten all about it, and that's what happened. I wasn't the only one who did that."

Jones began relying on drugs not only for personal relief from stress, but to control certain followers. A hut was designated "the Extended Care Unit," where settlers demonstrating any worrisome behavior — complaining too much, acting especially tense — were confined and heavily sedated. Gene Chaikin left Jonestown without permission, hiding out temporarily in Trinidad with the intention of defecting permanently. But he left his wife, Phyllis, and their two children behind, and made the mistake of writing Jones a long letter explaining why he had left — general disenchantment, he said — and asking that his family be allowed to join him. Phyllis remained fiercely loyal to Jones. At her request, Gene came back to Jonestown to speak with her. He was held by members of Jones's security team, drugged, and placed for a time in the Extended Care Unit. Afterward, he resumed his previous place as a legal advisor, but was drugged and confined again any time there were visitors in the settlement, for fear he might approach them for help in a second escape attempt. Often, Chaikin had no idea that he was being drugged. Maria Katsaris would sometimes serve him cheese sandwiches laced with barbiturates. They were such a rare treat that Chaikin apparently never associated them with his stints in confinement.

July brought additional problems. Gordon Lindsay, a writer for the *National Enquirer* tabloid, arrived in Guyana to research what would certainly be a titillating feature on Jones and Jonestown. He received no co-operation from the Temple office in Georgetown and never made it to Jonestown before being expelled from the country by Guyanese officials. But he'd stayed long enough for Jones to feel certain that a story would still be written — in particular, Jones believed that Lindsay had chartered a plane to fly over the settlement and take photographs. He wanted the story quashed, but was uncertain how to proceed. A stern warning from Charles Garry wouldn't work — the *National Enquirer* thrived on publicity from lawsuits.

Bonny Mann forwarded to Jones "with

compliments" a letter he'd received from American Clare Bouquet, whose adult son Brian was a Jonestown settler. Mrs. Bouquet wrote to the Guyanese ambassador to the United States that everyone living in Jonestown was in danger. She enclosed a copy of the story about Debbie Layton from the *San Francisco Chronicle*. The letter was taken by Jones and Charles Garry to mean that Concerned Relatives must be widening their outreach to Guyanese and U.S. officials. It might be only a matter of time before Guyana's leaders succumbed to increasing American pressure. Relocation to Russia seemed the only viable option, but every time Sharon Amos met with Timofeyev in Georgetown, the Russian had a new excuse for the lack of progress. His latest claim was that more information was needed, an exact list of all Jonestown settlers proposing to immigrate to his country, and their ages. Also, he'd heard rumors that Jim Jones was extremely ill — could the Jonestown leader even travel, let alone survive a new, rugged pioneer experience in Russia? That concern could have been alleviated by Jones personally visiting Timofeyev at his embassy, but Jones still felt certain he'd be arrested the moment he set foot outside Jonestown. Deputy Prime Minister Reid assured Jones this would not be the case, but Jones insisted that Reid put the promise in writing. Reid wouldn't — he considered this a foolish request that reflected lack of trust on Jones's part, which was true.

A bit of good news — the Guyanese government agreed to approve the Jonestown school as meeting national requirements — was overshadowed by a new question of qualification. Guyanese officials notified Jones that Larry Schacht could not practice medicine in their country without first attending, and graduating from, a state-certified medical school. Beyond the necessity of Schacht's services in Jonestown on a daily basis, he was integral to Jim Jones's plans for an ultimate White Night, which might come anytime. Sending Schacht off to medical school was unthinkable. Jones and Schacht proposed to the Guyanese Ministry of Public Health that the settlement's doctor be allowed to take correspondence courses. The matter was taken under government advisement — one more source of uncertainty and stress for Jones.

Jones tried to ingratiate himself with the Burnham administration through the same tactic that had worked so well back in San Francisco. Burnham's People's National Congress (PNC), facing continued resistance from former prime minister Cheddi Jagan's People's Progressive Party (PPP), scheduled a July 10, 1978, national referendum that, if passed, would guarantee indefinitely the current PNC majority in Guyana's parliament.

731

Jones offered to make every Temple member in the country available as PNC campaign volunteers, and for several weeks before the election Temple members swarmed everywhere in Georgetown, passing out PNC leaflets and then, on election day, serving as poll watchers and vote counters. The PNC would have fixed the election even without Temple assistance, but the American volunteers still came in handy. The announced result was 97 percent for the PNC, ensuring that Burnham remained in control. One week later, Sharon Amos and Tim Carter met with Deputy Prime Minister Vibert Mingo. When they inquired about the Burnham administration's position on Jonestown-related matters, he responded that with the referendum decided, "the policy involving Peoples Temple would have to come up," a nebulous response that troubled Jones greatly. Amos tried to soothe her leader by explaining, "[Mingo] didn't say this in a negative way."

Back in Jonestown, there were occasional flare-ups against Jones's absolute control. One involved the continuing lack of meat. Jones expected everyone to accept the rations — good socialists ate what they were given. In some evening sessions he allowed settlers to offer comments on Jonestown life, and one night elderly Helen Snell complained that she wanted more meat, and refused to accept Jones's explanation that it was too expensive.

When Snell continued carping, Jones dramatically announced that from now on, whenever meat was served, he would give his own meager portion to her, although this sacrifice would undoubtedly cause additional damage to his already delicate health. As Jones hoped, there was a firestorm of protest from other settlers. For the sake of everyone, Dad needed his strength! Generous-hearted as he was, he could not risk his own life to gratify the greedy appetite of a selfish old woman. Peter Wotherspoon, whose genitals had once been pounded to near-pulp in San Francisco on Jones's orders, settled the matter with his own offer, asking Jones to "please allow" him to give Snell his portions of meat instead "for the greater good of the Collective." He asked Jones to forgive Snell for complaining: "her age" should excuse it. Jones grandly agreed.

Without Jones's permission, some of the young men in Jonestown began using a concrete slab as a basketball court; they hung makeshift baskets at both ends and played boisterous games after work and on the half days off Jones allowed on Sundays. Jones's own grown sons participated as well as their friends, many of whom served as camp security guards. Jones had always eschewed the concept of Temple sports teams, particularly the possibility of them playing outside squads. Such competition, in his mind, was anti-socialist. When he ordered the games discontinued, Marceline intervened, arguing that the young men needed to have some fun. In fact, they should get uniforms and, as an organized team, play Guyanese squads in friendly exhibition games that would promote goodwill and demonstrate to the government that it was the Temple's intent to integrate itself with the people of its host nation. Jones grudgingly agreed, and even allowed Sharon Amos to meet with Desmond Roberts, who oversaw many government-sponsored youth programs. Roberts decreed that Temple sports teams "could not participate in our national championships, but their basketball team could engage in exhibitions with our national team if they wished — that would be appropriate."

More meat with meals and a basketball team seemed like small concessions to the settlers, but loomed large with Jones. Any loss of control could eventually lead to total loss. The response when he offered to give up his meat portions to Helen Snell may have inspired his announcement on August 8 that he had terminal lung cancer. Jones said his goal was to live long enough "to give [new] leadership time to develop unselfishness, not to need recognition, and, least of all, to need appreciation." Meanwhile, he would suffer, and his already limited life span would be further reduced any time anyone in Jonestown did something hurtful. Jones added that despite all the healings he'd once accomplished, he'd now "forgotten how." He would try to remember, and then heal himself, but his concern for his people must take precedence.

Most were horrified by the news. Marceline asked Carlton Goodlett to come to Jonestown at once and examine her husband. Larry Schacht had made the diagnosis but Marceline wanted a second opinion. Goodlett examined Jones and afterward he told him and Marceline that he found no evidence of cancer, or any evidence of other serious diseases. His best guess, since Jones refused to leave Jonestown for examination in a better-equipped hospital setting, was that the problem was a fungus infection of the lung, which could be treated with rest and antibiotics. Goodlett's diagnosis was not shared with the rest of the settlers, or even with Jones's sons. The Jonestown-wide belief remained that Dad was dying of cancer, and everyone must obey him in all things, at peril of worsening his condition. The possibility was raised of easing Jones's burdens by establishing a triumvirate to run day-to-day activities: Harriet Tropp and Johnny Brown were obvious, along with Tish Leroy, who did some of the camp's bookkeeping. Carolyn Layton and Maria Katsaris would remain in their roles as Jones's chief aides. Nothing came of it —

Jones, even if actually terminally ill, would never have surrendered any control.

As one means of counteracting the Concerned Relatives' claims that no visitors were allowed in Jonestown to see for themselves that family members there were well, in August 1978 Jones invited one. When Juanell Smart's four children told her a year earlier that they wanted to go to Jonestown, her immediate reaction was to refuse permission: "But my mother was going to be there, and my uncle Jim McElvane. I thought, well, it'll be primitive there, it'll be too much for my kids and maybe if I let them live there for a while, they'll be ready to come back. But they seemed to love it, and when I was asked if I wanted to go over and see them, I took three weeks' leave from work and went to take a look. I was surprised, because when I got there, I didn't see anything wrong with it."

Smart stayed two weeks. She ate with the settlers, went wherever in camp she pleased, and joined everyone else for Jones's evening lectures in the pavilion: "He sometimes seemed a bit out of it, and I thought he might be on drugs. He didn't talk about religion, at least that I heard. He talked about stuff back in the U.S., in San Francisco, some politics. I saw and heard nothing about any group suicide plans. One night, they put on a musical where lots of people sang and danced — it was a talent show. Poncho, my daughter

Tanitra's boyfriend, sang a song with a line about finding a special place, and I thought to myself, 'Okay, that's what they did.' " After a few days, the settlers warmed enough to Smart that they gossiped with her a bit. Some of them, too, wondered if Jones was using drugs. Terri Buford, who'd privately wanted to defect for some time, sufficiently trusted Smart to ask if she'd join her for a sip of Johnnie Walker Red — Buford had some hidden in her cottage. Smart was happy to oblige.

"One night, they asked me what movie I'd like them to have, and my mother said to me, 'Jim would like to see one that was a favorite of his,' so I said, 'Let's see that.' As soon as I did, my kids walked right away, but not before Tanitra said to me, 'He always gets that one, we never get to see what we really want'. The last night I was there, Jim gave me a hug and said, 'Don't stay away too long.' I thought it had been nice of them to invite me to come like that, but not long after I got home, I got a call from Marceline. She wanted me to call these other parents and tell them I'd seen their kids in Jonestown and everything there was fine. So I knew why they'd let me come, and I didn't make any calls."

Jones's fascination with *Executive Action,* a film about right-wing conspirators, led him to invite an additional guest — Donald

Freed, one of the film's writers. Jones wanted a book that explained every plot against the Temple. He thought Freed should write it. The author enjoyed his visit enough to agree that he'd look into potential conspiracies. Back in America, Freed asked a friend, attorney Mark Lane, to help. Lane, a former New York State legislator and author as well as a lawyer, was one of America's most prominent conspiracy theorists. His book *Rush to Judgment,* a skeptical recounting of the official government investigation into the assassination of John F. Kennedy, had been a bestseller. Later, he served as an attorney for James Earl Ray, the accused assassin of Martin Luther King Jr. As with the murder of President Kennedy, Lane believed the U.S. government was in some way complicit in King's death, or at least covering up some aspects of the crime. That earned him the respect of Jones, who, over the strong protests of Charles Garry, hired Lane to investigate any U.S. government plots against Peoples Temple. Garry and Lane each thought that the other was not only an impediment to professional efforts, but a rival for the publicity that both men relished.

One of the first actions taken by Lane and Freed was to meet with private eye Joe Mazor. On September 5 in San Francisco, Mazor claimed Tim Stoen's harassment of Jones and the Temple was being financed by hostile agencies, which included the CIA. He also swore that he'd enlisted Ugandan dictator Idi Amin as an intermediary with Prime Minister Burnham as Mazor worked on behalf of clients to "rescue" children from Jonestown. Freed and Lane passed the information along to Jones by radio — that night in the settlement pavilion, Jones triumphantly announced that he finally had proof Tim Stoen was a CIA agent: "We have cracked the other side." Lane and Freed whisked Mazor to Jonestown so he could meet with Jones in person. Jones was staggered when Mazor claimed that he had led a band of armed mercenaries right up to the edge of the settlement with the plan of kidnapping Jonestown children and returning them to their families in the United States "Every word he said got [Jones] more worked up, and made a lot of [settlers] believe in a conspiracy," Tim Carter remembers. "After Mazor, the guards were all told to keep their eyes on the tree line, because that's where any attacks would come."

Although journalist Gordon Lindsay had been expelled from Guyana without ever seeing Jonestown, Lane said that the *National Enquirer* would soon publish a negative story. He offered to suppress it — Jones gladly agreed. Soon, Lane informed Jones that thanks to his intercession, the story would not run. "[Jones] had really gotten frustrated with Charles Garry," Terri Buford says. "He didn't think [Garry] had done enough about the lawsuits [against the Temple] and all the conspiracies [Jones] was sure were going on against him. Lane agreed with everything Jones said. That's how he became the one [Jones] trusted most."

The end of September brought a wave of new bills — a $44,000 note due on a new tractor, $22,000 for aluminum to patch roofs, $16,000 for livestock feed, $3,500 for one hundred cartons of soap. Jones turned his attention to financial matters. His own estimate was that only three hundred Temple members remained in America, almost all of them in San Francisco — income from collection plates was negligible. He formed one committee to investigate other ways of earning money, and another to determine whether Jonestown could realistically be expected to become totally self-sustaining. Timofeyev was still stalling on the question of Jonestown's relocation to Russia — Jones wanted that looked into, too, beginning with a list of preferable spots in the massive country.

Even as conspiracies, Russia, and money were foremost on Jones's mind, another ominous threat loomed. Though Jones didn't know it, back in America Congressman Leo Ryan was finally preparing to make his long-promised inspection of Jonestown.

CHAPTER FORTY-EIGHT: UNRAVELING

Early in September 1978, Leo Ryan discussed his investigative trip to Guyana with House Democratic majority leader Jim Wright. "It was his intention to bring more public scrutiny to Peoples Temple and Jim Jones," Wright recalled. "[Ryan] did not expect, if he went to Guyana and then to Jonestown, that Jones would cooperate with him. He said that he believed the San Francisco newspapers would send reporters with him so that Jones's intransigence would be documented, and he also hoped that the bigger newspapers like the *Washington Post* would do the same. Such coverage would increase the pressure on Jones to open Jonestown to visitors, and also to release anyone there who wanted to leave."

Ryan said that he would bring some members of Concerned Relatives with him, and also a few congressmen to demonstrate that concern about Jonestown wasn't confined to his own Bay Area district. Another plus would be if their area newspapers sent reporters, too. But when Ryan began informally checking with colleagues to see who was willing to join him on the trip, there were no takers.

"Leo's reputation as an avid seeker of publicity worked against him," Wright said. "The overall sense was that any other member [of Congress] going with him would play a supporting role so far as media coverage was concerned."

Still, the House of Representatives formally recognized Ryan's trip as a congressional investigation, so that it had the imprimatur of official U.S. government business. Ryan anticipated a November trip. Though he didn't immediately notify Peoples Temple of his plans, he did hold several meetings with Concerned Relatives, and asked the State Department to provide briefings. These briefings did not go well. Department staffers were still concerned about giving the impression that a religious organization was being harassed and were not encouraging about Ryan's trip. The congressman was displeased with what he considered a lack of cooperation and promised the Concerned Relatives that when he returned from Guyana he would "do something about it."

As Ryan fumed in Washington, Mark Lane made a triumphant return to Jonestown, where Jones's effusive greeting grew even warmer when the lawyer-author agreed to continue ferreting out proof that the U.S. government was engaged in a conspiracy against Peoples Temple. Some in Jonestown noticed Lane paying extra attention to Terri Buford. Tim Carter sent Jones a note suggesting that Lane's crush "could be used to our advantage, I feel." Buford, looking for a safer way to defect than fleeing through the jungle, felt it could work to *her* advantage. She suggested to Jones that everything Lane learned would be shared by the lawyer with his staff. To keep the Temple's secrets as closely held as possible, she should return to the United States with Lane and serve not only as his Temple liaison, but also as his personal secretary for whatever time it took for him to complete his investigation. Jones agreed, and when Lane went from Guyana to San Francisco, Buford was with him. She worked out of the Geary Boulevard temple offices, and plotted her eventual escape.

Lane worked fast. On September 27 he provided Jones with a memo titled "COUNTER OFFENSIVE," which laid out plans for Temple attacks on its enemies in the courts and through the press. From its opening line, "Even a cursory examination reveals that there has been a coordinated campaign to destroy the Peoples Temple and impugn the reputation of its leader Bishop Jim Jones," all ten pages stridently supported Jones's paranoia. Lane's final point particularly fueled

Jones's certainty that the U.S. Congress was particularly a den of enemies: "The efforts of the members of Congress have created a problem and should be met head on."

With Jones's blessing, Lane launched the "public relations counter offensive" described in the memo with a San Francisco press conference on October 3. Most Bay Area media sent reporters and camera crews. The lengthy event — a transcript required thirty-three pages — featured Lane at his flamboyant best. He announced that "I am now satisfied beyond any question" that all charges and allegations against Jones and Peoples Temple were supported by "American intelligence organizations. . . . It makes me almost weep." Lane invited questions from the press, using them as a basis for his own extrapolations. A query about shots being fired in Jonestown elicited a colorful, convoluted Lane response about potential attacks by mercenaries wielding rocket launchers and bazookas. When a reporter protested, "You're weaving a fabric of plausibility, and we're asking you for specifics," and Lane was subsequently pressed to offer any documentation that the CIA was involved, the lawyer neatly countered, "Where haven't [CIA agents] been before Jonestown?"

As Lane intended, coverage included his most inflammatory accusations. Jones was thrilled. Recently, Guyanese justice Bishop withdrew from the Stoen case, and Chief Justice Harold Bollers announced that court proceedings would have to begin from scratch. For the first time, there appeared to be cause for optimism. Even Charles Garry's petulant threat to "quit in ten days if [Lane] talks to the press anymore," didn't dismay him. Jones sent the San Francisco attorney word that Lane "gained us immense ground."

No ground was gained in the effort to move from Guyana to the USSR, however. Two days before Lane's press conference, Feodor Timofeyev made his long-delayed visit to Jonestown. During a lavish dinner, Jones hailed the Soviet Union as "Jonestown's spiritual mother." Timofeyev told Tim Carter, "[Jonestown is] more socialist than us. We should take lessons from you." But back in Georgetown, Timofeyev repeated that he'd received no response yet from his government regarding the Jonestown request. Sharon Amos asked if Jones and John Victor, at least, could emigrate. Timofeyev replied that a decision must be made about the Temple as a whole before there could be consideration of individual cases.

In mid-October, Marceline Jones visited her family in Indiana. While she was in Richmond, Marceline invited her parents to return with her to Jonestown for a brief visit. When they agreed, she contacted the San Francisco temple office and asked them to radio a personal request from her to Jones-town. Marceline wanted her parents told that she and Jones slept in separate cottages because she worked days and he was up working all night. Appearances remained important to her.

While Marceline was gone, Jones selected nineteen-year-old Shanda James as his latest lover, a departure for him because she was black. There was another difference: Shanda was honored by Dad's interest, but told him that she liked someone else. Jones responded by having Shanda drugged and confined to the Extended Care Unit. Occasionally, he had the groggy girl taken to his cottage, where, Tim Tupper Jones later told Lawrence Wright of *The New Yorker,* "He fucked her whenever he wanted to."

With Lane on the public relations offensive in the United States, Jones, in his coherent moments, focused most on finances and Russia. He appointed a Money Making Project Committee that included Harriet Tropp, Jack Beam, Michael Prokes, Johnny Brown, and Gene Chaikin, who wasn't confined in the Extended Care Unit since, for the moment, Jonestown had no visitors. Soon afterward, Chaikin, on behalf of the group, described Jonestown's financial dilemma so starkly in a memo that even Jones could not misinterpret the message: "We do not feel that as the community is now structured it can ever be financially self-sufficient . . . and we see that historically small, self-contained communities have always failed. . . . We will not be [self-sustaining] as long as we spend most of our time fighting rear guard actions . . . so long as we have to cover our ass, so long as p.r. has priority over production."

Jones and the committee considered new methods of raising money. Perhaps Peoples Temple, which eschewed alcohol for its members, could operate a chain of night-clubs. A meeting memo noted, "dance floor, juke box . . . live music. There is nothing like it here. Guyanese love to party and they have lots of money [here] and no facilities [to spend it]." Another group, the Jonestown Steering Committee, was included in further deliberations. Tim Carter remembers, "It was decided that Jonestown might start buying businesses. We also planned two restaurants in Georgetown, and Patty Cartmell and Rheaviana Beam opened a curio shop. It was ironic — the great socialists could only survive by becoming capitalists."

But the numbers still didn't add up. It was estimated that nightclubs and other new business ventures might bring in a net monthly income of $25,000 to $40,000. Jonestown would still run a minimum monthly deficit of $100,000. In his numerous foreign bank accounts, Jones had the financial wherewithal to make up the difference, but even those resources totaling an estimated $30 million or more couldn't stem the tide of red ink longer than twenty-five or thirty years. Jim Jones was forty-seven, and, despite his declarations of poor health, might well live long enough to see Jonestown, his grand statement of socialist convictions and proof of personal greatness, dwindle away in bankruptcy. If he was remembered at all, it would be as a failure. This was unthinkable. His committee predicted permanent insolvency for Jonestown "as [it] is now structured," but that was in the Guyanese economy. The USSR was different. State support there would make the difference. Chaikin, Richard Tropp, and Tom Grubbs were given a new assignment: finalize a list of potential sites for Russian relocation. As soon as the Soviet government agreed to take in Peoples Temple, negotiations could begin regarding not only when, but where. On October 25, they submitted their report, which suggested "the east coast of the Black Sea, south of the Caucasus Mountains" as the ideal area, and then listed several alternatives. As soon as relocation was approved, Jonestown should send an inspection team to evaluate any suggested site for "suitability for our people."

But during meetings in Georgetown, Timofeyev was no longer being cordial to Sharon Amos. In response to her latest request for a relocation update, he snapped

748

that the question of Temple emigration had become "a big headache." Perhaps the number of settlers allowed to relocate would be limited; the Soviet government feared that the CIA might sneak in a spy as part of the group. Amos, aghast, warned that the decision was taking so long that Jones might interpret it as a no. Timofeyev said that wasn't the case — his leaders simply needed more time. Meanwhile, Jones continued telling his followers that moving to Russia was a given.

On October 26, Marceline and the Baldwins arrived in Jonestown. Tim Carter left the same day, returning to San Francisco to deliver documents to be used by Charles Garry against Concerned Relatives. While he was in America, Carter received permission to visit his father in Idaho. During the side trip, he ate hamburgers, drank wine, and smoked. It was pleasant playing hooky, but after a few days he wanted to return to Jonestown. "Gloria and our son Malcolm were there, so I decided that's where my life was, no matter what." But instead of flying back to Guyana, Carter was instructed to return immediately to San Francisco, where Terri Buford had just defected.

When Mark Lane returned to his home in Memphis, Tennessee, after his San Francisco press conference, Buford stayed in the city, living and working in the Geary Boulevard temple, doing long-distance work for Lane and other Temple-assigned tasks as needed. She secretly made a flight reservation for New York on October 30, and informed other Temple staff that she had a dental appointment on the same day and time. After arriving in New York, she called Lane, who she suspected wasn't entirely loyal to Jones. Buford remembers, "[Lane] said he would hide me in Memphis if in exchange I'd help him write a book about the Temple. I wanted to get away where they couldn't find me, so I said that I would. Mark had a little apartment in Washington, D.C., and for a while before I went to Memphis he had me stay there."

After Debbie Layton's defection and subsequent blossoming into a prime source for negative media coverage, Jones was desperate not to let another young, well-informed female follower get away. Tim Carter was assigned to track Buford down. Earlier in the year, Jones had contemplated ordering Carter to pretend he had defected, then infiltrate Concerned Relatives as a spy. Now that seemed like an ideal means of locating Buford if, like Debbie Layton, she tried contacting the group immediately after defecting. Buford wasn't with Concerned Relatives, but Carter told its members anyway that he had defected. He also spoke with Suzanne Cartmell, Jones's estranged daughter. "That day's [*San*

Francisco] *Chronicle* had a story about Leo Ryan planning to go to Jonestown," Carter says. "Suzanne was freaked by that, because that information wasn't supposed to be public yet. They didn't want Jones to know." As soon as Jones did — someone from the Temple's San Francisco office contacted him immediately — Carter's assignment was changed again. Now he was charged with finding out all that he could about Ryan's intended visit.

"I went to see Elmer and Deanna Mertle in Berkeley," Carter recalls. "They were part of Concerned Relatives, but they both only seemed to want to destroy the Temple, not rescue anyone. Ryan's official plan was supposed to be, he would come alone with no Concerned Relatives or media, but it seemed clear that he would be coming with lots of them. He'd told [Concerned Relatives] that he expected to be turned away at the Jonestown gate, and then he would go back to the USA and schedule [congressional] hearings about Jonestown starting in February 1979. He told them that the only legal authority the U.S. government would have to act was if American citizens were being held there against their will. So if he didn't get in, Ryan could claim that, and if he did get in and even one person left with him, and then that person testified about nobody being allowed to leave, [Ryan] would have proof. So either way, he'd win."

Jones took Carter's report from California hard. Charlotte Baldwin, his mother-in-law, was still in Jonestown when he learned the details of Ryan's plan. She said later that Jones appeared "very near a mental collapse." The situation deteriorated rapidly. On November 1, Ryan formally wrote to Jones, notifying him of his intention to come. Ryan acknowledged that "my office has been visited by constituents who are members of your church, and who expressed anxiety about mothers and fathers, sons and daughters, brothers and sisters who have elected to assist you in the development of your church in Guyana. . . . It goes without saying that I am most interested in a visit to Jonestown." Ryan asked Jones to respond to Ambassador Burke at the embassy in Georgetown "since the details of our trip are still being arranged." Ryan added that he was acting as a member of the House Committee on International Relations.

Five days later, Mark Lane replied on behalf of Jones and the Temple, charging that "various agencies of the U.S. government" were actively persecuting the church, which currently had offers from two foreign nations for relocation of Jonestown, with the apparent implication that these were the USSR and Cuba: "You may judge, therefore, the important consequences which may result in the creation of a most embarrassing situation for the U.S. Government." Still, Lane did not entirely dismiss the possibility of Ryan visiting Jonestown. "A date which would be convenient for all of us should be arrived at through discussion."

Ryan's written reply was sharp: "No persecution, as you put it, is intended, Mr. Lane. But your vague reference to the creation of the most embarrassing situation for the American government does not impress me at all." He was coming in mid-month. Lane made clear that he wanted to meet with Ryan in advance of the trip, and if Ryan was admitted into Jonestown, Lane would accompany him.

The Guyanese government was almost as unhappy as Jones at the prospect of Ryan's arrival. "We considered Ryan coming here to be a damned nuisance," Kit Nascimento says. "It seemed to us that he was just some U.S. congressman looking for publicity. The American embassy contacted us on [Ryan's] behalf to seek protection for him while he was in Guyana. Our response was, 'Protect him from what?' Burnham's attitude toward Ryan's visit was, these people in Jonestown have broken no laws of Guyana. If you want to interview some of them, get their permission. You can't just show up here, demand that our government follow all of your instructions, and make them let you in. Burnham refused . . . to intervene in any way."

On November 7, Jones did admit an outside guest, U.S. consul Douglas Ellice. It was the fourth inspection visit of the year by American officials and followed routine. Ellice was treated to a sumptuous lunch, interviewed settlers whose families had expressed concern for their well-being — all of them assured Ellice that they were happy — and returned to Georgetown not certain what to believe. The accusations from back in the States were strident, but Jonestown seemed at least functional, if not in any way luxurious.

About the same time, the dozen or so members of the Jonestown basketball team left by boat from Port Kaituma for Georgetown, where they were scheduled to play a few exhibition games against the Guyanese national team over the next weeks. Jones initially refused them permission to go, but Stephan and Jimmy, who was back in the settlement for a while, had their mother intercede. Marceline told Jones that the games would be more proof to the Guyanese government that everything was fine in Jonestown. The players were thrilled at the chance to get away from settlement tension. "Any time we got out of there for Georgetown was like living a dream," Jim Jones Jr. says. "We could go to the movies and places to eat. We were going to have fun and play ball." Their departure caused a significant change in the makeup of Jones's bodyguards and settlement security. His sons and some of the other players comprised much of both groups' leadership. The remaining members of the gun-toting forces consisted of Jones's most fervid male followers. They felt honored to serve their leader and would follow his orders without hesitation.

Before the team left, Jones gave them a pep talk in front of the other settlers. He also mentioned, "I heard some congressman wants to come here. I think I'll tell him to stick it." In private, his wife and lawyers were frantically trying to convince him otherwise. A radio message from the attorneys advised, "Charles and Mark feel very strongly that Ryan should come in." Otherwise, "he'd have hearings and all of that stuff." Marceline's argument was simpler: Jonestown didn't have anything to hide. If a few settlers wanted to leave when Ryan came, let them.

Jones still dithered. He ordered staff at Lamaha Gardens to prepare a resolution declaring that Jonestown settlers "will not see or communicate" with "Ryan, any member of the so-called 'Concerned Relatives' organization, or persons associated with either of them." The resolution also noted that "the Jonestown community has requested police assistance from the Government of Guyana to protect their community from unwanted trespasses." Carolyn Layton sent additional instructions for staff there to meet with Deputy Minister Mingo, requesting that he deliver the resolution refusing Jonestown access to Ryan, and that he "refuse the assistance of the Guyanese government" to the congressman. Mingo wouldn't meet with Sharon Amos until November 14, and, when he did, he shouted at her that he had more to do than take care of Jim Jones and Jonestown.

The Jonestown settlers weren't sure if Ryan was coming in or not. Most were apprehensive. Jones's constant warnings about children being forcibly taken had their effect. But a few saw Ryan's visit, or at least Jones's preoccupation with it, as an opportunity. Some of the Parks and Bogue families were restless and wanted to leave. Monica Bagby and Vern Gosney, both young adults, felt that they'd had enough. If Ryan came and offered the opportunity to leave under his protection, they would probably take it. Two other families had been plotting a jungle escape for some time. If Ryan arrived in Jonestown and all eyes were on him, they would try to sneak away. One or two risked mentioning their plan to other disaffected settlers. Though remaining a minuscule percentage of all nine-hundred-plus Jonestown settlers, the number of potential defectors during a Leo Ryan visit grew.

Carolyn Layton combined love for Jim Jones with absolute devotion to the Temple cause. She could be calculating, even cold, and she felt that the time had arrived for ultimate pragmatism. Carolyn prepared and presented to Jones a neatly typed "Analysis of Future Prospects" that succinctly declared long-term hope for Jonestown in its present form was lost. Lawsuits and government agency investigations would drain the Temple's financial reserves. On a positive note, support from the Guyanese government might be grudging, but ought to be ongoing so long as Jonestown was useful as a border buffer against Venezuela. But the CIA apparently believed Jones was about to lead an armed revolution in Guyana: "The traitors may have convinced them of this . . . that is why they see us as such a terrible threat to be destroyed." One possibility was for Jones to flee to Cuba, taking "the children" (John Victor and Kimo) with him while Carolyn stayed behind "to hold the project together here. . . . I was just trying to think of a way the little boys could have a dad for a while."

There was a subsection titled "A FINAL STAND IF DECIDED ON." In it, Carolyn mused that, should Jones opt for the ultimate act, then the moment and method of group death was crucial. She wondered, "How will we have the knowledge to know now is the time to go ahead and do it? . . . Do you give everyone pills. . . . It would I presume have to be kind of a last minute thing." Her fear

was that a mass suicide would not be appreciated as a sincere and historic statement: "I
know we can't worry about how [what we
do] will be interpreted . . . maybe in some 50
years someone will understand and perhaps
be motivated. I don't have much illusion
about all that. I just hate to see it all go for
naught."

Jones called the Temple offices at Lamaha
Gardens and ordered the basketball team to
return to Jonestown. They didn't want to
leave — their games so far against the Guyanese national team had resulted in losses, and
they wanted at least one more try for a victory. Besides, they were having fun in the city.
Jones insisted, and Stephan finally refused on
behalf of the players. They were going to stay
in Georgetown awhile longer. Jones was
angry. He told Stephan that everyone on the
team was to avoid Leo Ryan and anyone else
who might be with him. Jones didn't want a
potential confrontation between Ryan and
the Jonestown basketball players turned into
scandalous headlines back in America.

On November 13, Jones claimed that concern about Ryan had caused him to suffer
through eight consecutive sleepless nights.
He was more likely wide awake from amphetamine use. No matter what the reason, Jones
was ill-tempered, uttering a constant series of
threats against the congressman, whom he
now considered almost as much an enemy as

Tim Stoen: "If Ryan enters this community illegally, he will not leave alive. . . . I'd like to shoot his ass." Jones was trailed everywhere by his bodyguards, all carrying their guns and becoming increasingly caught up in Jones's violent mood.

Richard Tropp thought it would be wise to prepare Jonestown for Ryan's arrival. Jones might not want him there, but if cooler heads prevailed and the congressman and his entourage were allowed in, they might as well try to make a good impression. Tropp sent a memo to the leaders of the Jonestown committees, ordering all trash to be picked up, children's art displayed that "reflect[ed] variety and creativity to counteract propaganda about our people being mind-programmed . . . our aim should not merely be to present a Clean and Neat Jonestown, and defend against the lies, but to EDUCATE this Congressman, to open his eyes to what we are doing here . . . no quiet, controlled set-up shit." As the cleanup began, Marceline's parents left Jonestown to begin their trip home to Indiana. Charlotte Baldwin signed the Jonestown guest book: "This is more than we could have imagined. So much has been accomplished in such a short time. The people so happy and well adjusted. Indeed, we hate to leave!"

In California, Leo Ryan had a final meeting with Concerned Relatives and Jonestown defectors. He went over their allegations, deciding which would be best to raise with Guyanese officials, and whom he would try to talk to if he was allowed to enter Jonestown. He still expected to be refused.

Tim Carter returned to Jonestown from California on Tuesday, November 14. That same day, Leo Ryan flew to Guyana. The congressman brought with him staff members Jackie Speier and James Schollaert. Nine members of the media came along: reporter Tim Reiterman and photographer Greg Robinson of the *San Francisco Examiner;* Ron Javers of the *San Francisco Chronicle;* producer Bob Flick, cameraman Bob Brown, sound technician Steve Sung, and reporter Don Harris of NBC; the *Washington Post*'s Charles Krause, and Gordon Lindsay of the *National Enquirer,* who hoped being part of Ryan's media entourage might help him gain access to Jonestown on his second try. Concerned Relatives had its own contingent, all of whom had family members in Jonestown: Tim and Grace Stoen; Howard and Beverly Oliver; Steven Katsaris and his son Anthony; Sherwin Harris, the former husband of Sharon Amos and the father of Liane Harris, the oldest of her children; Nadyne Houston and her daughter Carol Houston Boyd; former Gang of Eight members Jim Cobb, Mickey Touchette, and Wayne Pietila; and Clare Bouquet. Though she had no relatives in Jonestown, Bonnie Burnham was also along; it was believed that her close friendship with Marceline might help ease tensions and convince Jones to cooperate. The relatives hoped that at least some of them might be admitted into Jonestown. But none of them knew what was going to happen next, only that whatever did would be determined by Jim Jones.

CHAPTER FORTY-NINE: FINAL DAYS

On Wednesday evening, November 15, Temple staffers at Lamaha Gardens were startled to see a middle-aged man clambering over the cement block wall at the back of their yard. Congressman Leo Ryan arrived uninvited after enduring a long, frustrating day. Guyanese officials had made it clear they would not involve themselves in his visit. At the U.S. embassy in Georgetown, Ambassador John Burke told Ryan that he was on his own — on their trips to Jonestown, Burke and his people hadn't see any signs of settlers being held against their will. Jones and his church might very well claim unlawful harassment if Ryan tried to bully them into letting him visit. Temple lawyers Charles Garry and Mark Lane were also in Georgetown, and Ryan's initial meetings with them weren't productive, either. The attorneys, speaking on behalf of Jim Jones, informed him that he was currently denied permission to enter Jonestown. Even if that changed, media and members of Concerned Relatives certainly wouldn't be allowed access. Fed up with the hand-wringing and stonewalling, Ryan decided to spontaneously visit Lamaha Gardens and try his luck with the Temple members there.

He didn't have much. Sharon Amos told Ryan that he was trespassing on private property and asked him to leave. Ryan summoned his considerable personal charm, telling Amos that he was tired of negotiating through lawyers. He swore that he intended Jones and the Temple no harm. If everyone there was all right, and staying voluntarily, then their worried relatives could be assured of that, and the matter would finally be settled. He managed to speak to a few other Temple members in the house — Laura Johnston Kohl assured him that they, too, were "fine." Amos relented just enough to say that Jones was ill and couldn't see Ryan at the moment, leaving open the possibility that he eventually might. Ryan had to be content with that.

The others who'd arrived in Guyana with Ryan had their own reasons for discontent. When they'd landed around midnight, Ryan and his two staffers were whisked off to stay as guests at the U.S. embassy. A few members of the media were told there were problems with their visas and they might soon be expelled. Ron Javers of the *Chronicle* was even taken into custody. When everyone else reached the Pegasus Hotel, they were told that there had been a problem with their reservations and no rooms were available. It took hours to find other accommodations; Georgetown had only a few hotels. Then everyone had to wait around all day, hoping Ryan would notify them that arrangements had been made and they would soon be on their way to Jonestown. He didn't.

In Jonestown, Jones soon learned who had come to Guyana with Ryan. That he'd brought along media was bad enough. Though members of Concerned Relatives had officially come separately from the congressman, paying their own way, not as guests of or collaborators with the U.S. government, to Jones they were all part of the same force of invaders. He was especially furious that Tim and Grace Stoen had come. He certainly wasn't letting *them* into Jonestown. Ryan didn't know that Garry and Lane were spending as much time arguing with Jones as with him. An uncomfortable visit was better than another controversy in the media, the lawyers told Jones. The press was in Guyana with Ryan. They were going to print and broadcast *something* — it might as well be that Jim Jones let the congressman come to Jonestown and talk with whomever he wanted. Some settlers might ask to leave — so what? What could they tell the reporters that would be any worse than the details in Debbie Layton's affidavit?

Jones was adamant: no visitors. He closed himself off in his cottage, communicating by phone to the Jonestown radio shack, which in turn connected him to the lawyers in Georgetown.

The next day, as Ryan and the lawyers wrangled again, some of the Concerned Relatives contingent made their own visits to Lamaha Gardens. Bonnie Burnham and Clare Bouquet were both rebuffed. Sherwin Harris, whose twenty-one-year-old daughter, Liane, worked at Lamaha Gardens, was told that he might be able to see her sometime soon. Harris's visit particularly upset Sharon Amos. Any contact with her ex-husband "really made her paranoid," Tim Carter recalls. "If she'd been on edge before because of Ryan, having [Harris] there only made her worse."

That afternoon, Ambassador Burke agreed to meet with the Concerned Relatives, on the condition that the media was not included. It was an unsatisfactory session. Bonnie Burnham wrote later that, although the relatives poured out their hearts to the ambassador, "not a flicker of emotion showed in [Burke's] eyes." Before his guests left, Burke gave them copies of a press release stating, "The Embassy has no authority to require contacts between members of the People's [sic] Temple and persons whom they do not wish

765

to receive. The members of the Peoples Temple are protected by the Privacy Act of 1974, as are all American citizens."

Ryan and the Temple lawyers continued their negotiations all through Thursday and into Friday morning. The congressman took a harder line. During his visit to Lamaha Gardens, he said, "There was not a religious picture on the walls, there was no one saying prayers. I [did not hear] anyone mention God." Perhaps, when he returned to Washington he would look into whether Peoples Temple really deserved tax-exempt status as a church. The threat gave Garry and Lane a new argument to use privately on Jones — there was more than bad publicity and the potential loss of a few settlers at stake. Jones didn't entirely relent but did discuss possible parameters of a Ryan visit. If the congressman flew from Georgetown to Port Kaituma on Friday, stayed overnight to conduct interviews, and then left Saturday, Jones would be rid of him after perhaps twenty-four hours. Not even Ryan had suggested that the inspection visit last longer than that. Without consulting Lane and Garry, Jones decided that if Ryan did come, his stay must be even shorter. On Friday morning he sent Jim McElvane, Michael Prokes, and Johnny Brown to Port Kaituma with orders to use trees and brush to block the short, primitive runway. With Port Kaituma inaccessible by air, Ryan would have to fly instead to Matthews Ridge and take the train to Port Kaituma, a lengthy enough detour that would leave him only a few hours at best in Jonestown before returning to Georgetown on Saturday afternoon. The three men left to do Jones's bidding, but returned a few hours later to report that they hadn't been able to carry out his instructions. A Guyanese military plane had apparently broken down at the Port Kaituma airstrip, and a handful of soldiers were there guarding it. The Temple trio couldn't deliberately block the runway in front of military witnesses. If Ryan did come, he could fly into Port Kaituma after all.

Friday morning, Marceline involved herself in the negotiations. Jones was still closed up in his cottage. Marceline argued with him by phone from the Jonestown radio room, not caring that Tim and Mike Carter were also there and could hear everything. "She said that we should be proud of what we'd built, so let's show [Ryan] what we have," Tim Carter says. "Marceline really got mad at [Jones]. She said, 'I'm the one who's kept this together, not you.' I'd been around them for years and I'd never heard her argue with him before. Marcie challenging him in front of anyone else was very, very different." Marceline's aggressive attitude made the difference, though Jones never agreed outright that Ryan could come. For years, no one had argued so vehemently with him. Now, his wife and his lawyers simply refused to accept his decision to keep Ryan out.

Lane and Garry gave Ryan the go-ahead. They told him that he could bring along whomever he chose, but there was no guarantee that anyone other than the congressman would be allowed into Jonestown. Ryan took it as an indirect promise. He contacted Ambassador Burke and asked for help in acquiring the use of a plane to fly to Port Kaituma that afternoon, and to be on call to return Ryan and his party to Georgetown on Saturday afternoon. The plane needed to seat quite a few people — Ryan would bring staffer Jackie Speier, there were nine members of the media, and some of the Concerned Relatives wanted to go along on the chance that Jones might also admit them. The twin-engine Otter engaged by the embassy eventually held, along with its pilot, nineteen passengers — Ryan, Speier, the press, Lane and Garry, U.S. deputy chief of mission Richard Dwyer, Guyanese government information officer Neville Annibourne, and four of the Concerned Relatives: Beverly Oliver, Jim Cobb, Carol Boyd, and Anthony Katsaris. The plane took off from Georgetown about 2:30 p.m. Friday afternoon. During the hour-long flight, those who hadn't flown over the Guyanese jungle before were disconcerted by its dense vastness. When the Otter jounced to a stop on the Port Kaituma airstrip, its deplaning passengers were greeted by several grim-looking Jonestown settlers. After conferring with them, Lane informed the others that only he, Garry, Ryan, Speier, and Dwyer could go by truck to Jonestown. The press and Concerned Relatives would have to wait in Port Kaituma; Lane and Garry promised they would keep trying to gain Jones's permission for them to come.

Marceline Jones greeted the first arrivals. Ryan declined an immediate Jonestown tour. He wanted to talk with Jim Jones. After almost ninety minutes Jones appeared, wearing his usual dark glasses. Ryan explained again that the best way to stop controversy about Jonestown as a possible prison camp was to let everyone back at Port Kaituma in. Jones agreed, with one exception, Gordon Lindsay of the *National Enquirer.* Ryan agreed, and the truck was sent back to the airstrip. Lindsay returned to Georgetown on the Otter, which was scheduled to pick up Ryan and the others in Port Kaituma on Saturday afternoon. Everyone else went to Jonestown.

The settlers there had spent much of the day in frenzied preparation for the visit. The Jonestown kitchen worked extra shifts so the guests could enjoy fresh-baked bread and pastries. Paths were swept, bushes clipped, cottages cleaned — Jones intended making a positive impression. "Jonestown had never looked so good," Tim Carter recalls. When everything was ready, Marceline Jones addressed the settlers by loudspeaker, reminding them "to be in peace."

While the others were fetched from Port Kaituma, Ryan and Jackie Speier began interviewing Temple members whose families had expressed concern for them. None made any complaint. They acted content, and their responses seemed reasonably spontaneous. The congressman and his aide found no immediate evidence to support allegations that anyone was being held prisoner in Jonestown.

Jones met the second wave of arrivals at the pavilion. As night fell, dinner was served: pork, greens, potatoes, freshly baked biscuits. There was plenty of everything, which surprised some of the visitors and pleased all the settlers, many of whom remained uncomfortable with their guests but were grateful for full bellies. Afterward there was entertainment, with the Jonestown band performing at its best and some settlers singing solos. During part of the show, Jones sat to one side and allowed the reporters to ask questions. He seemed coherent but a little shaky. Jones mused that he might, someday, return to America, and called over John Victor. He pointed out how much the child resembled him. When Jones asked the little boy if he wanted to go back and live with Grace, John Victor simply said, "No."

Earlier in the day, Jack Beam suggested to Jones that Leo Ryan be asked to say a few words to the settlers after dinner. Jones had been noncommittal, but now when Beam asked again Jones agreed. Ryan was in fine fettle. He was in Jonestown, the NBC camera crew was filming everything, and at least so far the experience was reasonably pleasant. Ryan had been a politician for years and a schoolteacher before that. He knew how to gauge the mood of an audience — this one was hospitable but suspicious. He told them that he had come, "as all of you know," to conduct a congressional inquiry. "But I can tell you right now that from the conversations I've had with a few other folks here already this evening, that whatever the [allegations] are, there are some people here who believe that this is the best thing that's ever happened to them in their whole life." The crowd rose as one and roared in approval. Ryan joked, "Too bad you all can't vote in San Mateo County," his congressional district, and everyone laughed when Jack Beam bellowed, "By proxy!"

Jones had an announcement. That night in Georgetown, the Jonestown basketball team had played another game against the Guyanese national squad. They'd lost this game, too, but by only ten points, and proudly radioed the news to the settlement, where the information was passed along to Jones at the pavilion. Jones couldn't resist exaggerating. He reported that the Jonestown team had walloped the Guyanese by ten points, and the crowd cheered again.

There was more music, and the program concluded. The members of the media had assumed they would spend the night in Jonestown, and were unhappy when told that there was no room for them. Jim Cobb and Anthony Katsaris, the two male representatives of the Concerned Relatives, and Neville Annibourne, the Guyanese government official, were told the same thing. They would have to stay in Port Kaituma. A Temple truck drove them back to town, and the driver promised he would fetch them in the morning. Members of the NBC television crew seemed preoccupied with something. Sensing a scoop, Don Harris hadn't immediately told the other reporters that, during the evening's festivities, a man had passed him a note that read, "Vernon Gosney and Monica Bagby: Please help us get out of Jonestown." But one of the NBC crew gave the secret away, and the reporters passed much of the remaining night drinking in a Port Kaituma bar, wondering what would happen when Ryan tried acting on the request.

Ryan already had a plan. Besides passing the note to Harris, Gosney whispered to Deputy Chief of Mission Dwyer that he and Bagby wanted to get out of Jonestown that night; Gosney feared that if anyone reported to Jones that he'd talked to Dwyer, the deputy chief wrote later in his official report, they "would be in extreme danger." Dwyer told Gosney that he couldn't take him away immediately — he and Ryan were staying in Jonestown overnight. But Dwyer promised Gosney that he and Bagby could come with the Ryan delegation when they left the next afternoon.

After they were alone in the cottage that served as their overnight Jonestown quarters, Ryan and Dwyer decided that in the morning the congressman would add Gosney and Bagby to the list of settlers he wanted to interview. Ryan said he was saving his "best-documented cases" until then, and some of them might want to leave, too. It would be best to conceal the identities of those asking to leave Jonestown until the last possible minute, in case the Temple leader was tempted to break his promise that anyone who wanted to go with Ryan could do so.

But Jones almost certainly knew about Gosney and Bagby. Decades later, Gosney told playwright/author Leigh Fondakowski that he'd been seen passing his note to Don Harris. Caught by surprise, Harris dropped the scrap of paper; Gosney picked it up and handed it back to the NBC reporter. As he did, Gosney recalled, "a little kid sees me." From the moment they could walk and talk,

Temple youngsters were trained to report any rule breaking. Gosney remembered that the child began chanting, "He passed him a note, he passed him a note." A few Jonestown adults came over to Gosney "asking me questions," and the would-be defector felt unnerved enough to take the additional risk of speaking with Dwyer, asking that the diplomat get him out of Jonestown immediately.

It is virtually impossible that none of the settlers who asked Gosney questions failed to pass along suspicions to Jones or one of his advisors like Carolyn Layton or Maria Katsaris, particularly in the atmosphere of heightened suspicion caused by Ryan's visit. Once Jones was informed, it was equally uncharacteristic for him not to react immediately. That he didn't meant one of two things: either Jones began drugging himself into insensibility immediately upon retiring to his cottage after the evening program; or else he, Carolyn, and Maria were preoccupied with something that Jones considered even more important than a would-be defector.

Everyone at Lamaha Gardens had been anxiously awaiting word from Jonestown about how things had gone that night with Ryan. Around midnight, the radio crackled with a terse, three-word report: "Everything went okay."

Chapter Fifty:
"Some Place That Hope Runs Out"

Just before dawn on Saturday, November 18, nine settlers slipped out of Jonestown and into the jungle. The group included three children given fruit punch mixed with a little Valium to keep them quiet. The adults correctly guessed that with everyone else in Jonestown so preoccupied with Ryan's visit, it would take hours for their absence to be noticed. Their plan was to make their way through the jungle to the rail line, then follow the tracks into Matthews Ridge. From there, they would contact U.S. officials and ask for help. It was hard going through the thick brush, and they were surprised to encounter two other settlers who'd left the settlement that morning with the same plan. The eleven defectors walked until dark, when the engineer of a train heading in the same direction halted and offered them a ride the rest of the way.

Back in camp, everyone lined up for breakfast. Herbert Newell and Clifford Gieg never had a chance to eat. They were pulled out of line and told to sail the *Cudjoe* downriver to pick up some supplies. The driver who took them to Port Kaituma in one of the settlement trucks predicted that there would be trouble in Jonestown that day. Newell laughed and replied, "Nothing like that is going to happen."

Jones didn't appear for his scheduled breakfast with Leo Ryan. Tim Carter and a few others joined the congressman instead. Ryan ate fast and showed no interest in small talk. He wanted to begin his next round of interviews with settlers he guessed would be most likely to ask to leave. As Ryan and Speier began their meetings, settlers were instructed over the loudspeaker to return to their cottages unless they'd been assigned to specific functions. This was a gesture for Ryan, assuring him that anyone he asked to speak with would be available. Only the kitchen staff and security forces remained on the job. It was a hot day, typical of mid-November in Guyana. The rainy season usually began around the end of the month, though storms occasionally blew in early. The mugginess affected the visitors much more than the settlers, who were used to it. Everyone slapped at bugs.

In Port Kaituma, the media, Annibourne, and the male members of Concerned Relatives were up by 7 a.m. They'd been told the

776

night before that a Temple truck would pick them up at eight thirty for the trip of forty-five minutes or so to Jonestown, but no transportation arrived. The truck finally appeared a bit before 10 a.m. The reporters were annoyed. They were supposed to be back in Port Kaituma around 2 p.m. to meet the plane that would return them to Georgetown. Factoring in drive time to and from Jonestown, now they would only have about three hours in the settlement.

When the media arrived back at Jonestown, Marceline Jones greeted them and announced that she would take them on a tour, right after a breakfast of coffee and pancakes. Nobody wanted to eat. They could see Ryan and Speier off in a corner of the pavilion, talking earnestly to some settlers. Tim Reiterman of the *Examiner* saw Concerned Relative Carol Boyd, who'd spent the night in Jonestown. She told him that she'd been allowed to see Judy and Patricia Houston, her nieces, but some Temple adults had been right there with them, and everything the girls said seemed to be memorized praise of Jim Jones and Jonestown. There was no sign of Jones himself. The reporters were impatient, so Don Harris of NBC diplomatically suggested that they just have coffee. Cups were poured, and everyone took a few polite sips. At about 11 a.m., Marceline agreed to begin the tour. She took them first to the nursery, which was her special pride and joy. The *Washington Post*'s Charles Krause wrote later that all the reporters were impressed by "an incubator, a respirator, a bright playroom, a nurse's office, cribs, and other modern equipment." Perhaps Jonestown wasn't such a primitive camp after all.

Marceline took them to the school area next. She explained that one building was set aside as a classroom for special needs children. A settler who worked as the special needs teacher was there to answer the reporters' questions. Before they could ask any, the settler began telling them how different the Jonestown teaching system was, how much better for the children than the school she used to teach at back in California, where none of the children got the individual attention that they needed to overcome their disabilities and learn. The reporters and TV crew grew restless. Everything seemed almost too perfect, and certainly rehearsed. They asked to walk around by themselves, looking at whatever and speaking to whomever they wished. Marceline said that everyone must stay with her. The reporters saw that many of the Jonestown children were now gathered at the pavilion, watching *Willy Wonka and the Chocolate Factory*. Ryan and Speier were still conducting interviews. Most of the media wanted to stay reasonably close to the pavilion — if more defectors asked Ryan to help them leave, the reporters wanted to interview them on the spot. But Marceline kept the press moving away from the pavilion, and other minders had joined the group — Jack Beam, Johnny Brown, and Garry and Lane. Some adult settlers had left their cottages and milled near the pavilion. The reporters sensed tension — only later would they learn that news of the predawn defections was beginning to spread through Jonestown. Jim Jones had still not appeared. Someone came up and whispered in Marceline's ear. Reiterman wrote later, "Her expression tightened."

Marceline grimly led the group along. Krause and a few other reporters paused by a building that a sign identified as Jane Pittman Gardens. Its window shutters were closed tight, but they could hear people talking and coughing inside. The journalists' suspicions were aroused — perhaps would-be defectors were being held there. They asked to go inside, and were told that Jane Pittman was a dormitory for older female settlers who didn't want to be disturbed. When the reporters insisted, Johnny Brown knocked on the door. The elderly lady who stuck her head outside snapped, "We don't have our clothes on. Nobody wants to be interviewed." Garry briefly went inside, and returned to say that the women's refusal was "unequivocal." The journalists argued that if they weren't allowed inside, they would believe that Jonestown had something to hide. The argument grew sharp. Finally, the press was allowed in. They were shocked by the overcrowding — the women mostly lay on bunk beds stacked from floor to ceiling. But the building was clean. None of the ladies seemed in any way sick or neglected. Lane confided that the reporters had initially been refused admittance because of embarrassment about overcrowding, which was inevitable since Jonestown's population had grown faster than additional housing could be constructed. But now there was open antagonism between the reporters and some of Jones's more fervent followers.

With that, Marceline concluded her attempt at a guided tour, and the media returned to the pavilion area. Ryan was posing for a photograph there with Carol Boyd; Judy and Patricia Houston; and the girls' mother, Phyllis. Anthony Katsaris looked tense as he sat nearby with his sister Maria. Beverly Oliver seemed to be having better luck with her two sons. They appeared relaxed as they chatted. For the first time, the reporters mingled with settlers. But they hardly had time to ask more than a few questions — every answer they received consisted of rote praise for Jones and Jonestown, as well as denials that anyone was kept from leaving, or from communicating openly with outside family and friends. Then everything stopped. It was almost noon, and Jim Jones had finally appeared.

The Jonestown leader wore a red shirt outside khaki pants, and his favorite black shoes. Jones's dark glasses were in place; his hair was neatly combed. But his face was pale, and he worked his clenched jaw in a way that he often did when especially agitated. Aides whispered to Jones — this was probably the moment he learned about the eleven early-morning defectors — and then Ryan and Richard Dwyer came up to him and said that other settlers wanted to leave as well. Jones almost certainly knew about Gosney and Bagby, but the additional names were new to him and particularly upsetting. Edith Parks had joined Peoples Temple back in Indiana, but now she'd told Leo Ryan that she was being held prisoner in Jonestown and asked Ryan to help her get away. Her son Jerry wanted to leave, too, though his wife, Patricia, said she would stay. Jackie Speier asked Jerry's children, Dale, Brenda, and Tracy, if they wanted to go with their father or stay with their mother. They said they wanted to leave Jonestown with their father and grandmother. Then Patricia Parks said, "If my family's leaving, I've got to go with them." After that, twenty-year-old Chris O'Neal, nineteen-year-old Brenda Parks's boyfriend, said he would go, too.

Cheese sandwiches were set out for those

who felt hungry. While most people ate, Jones spoke with the would-be defectors, after first asking the newsmen to stay back and allow them some privacy. Jones summoned all the warmth he could, putting his arms around the shoulders of the Parks family members, reminding them that everyone else in Jonestown was part of their family, too. Marceline Jones promised Vern Gosney that if he stayed, things would be better because "we're going to have a lot of reforms." But no minds were changed. Ryan and Speier volunteered to go with the defectors while they returned to their cottages and gathered their few belongings. Gosney urged Ryan to hurry. The congressman assured him, "You have nothing to worry about. Nothing will happen."

The reporters and the NBC film crew cornered Jones, who turned and faced them like a great beast brought to bay by yowling hounds. He claimed that those who were leaving "were never really in it completely. . . . It's their choice. If they had expressed a desire to leave earlier, they could have."

It was then that the storm struck. Showers were common in the jungle, even before the official rainy season, but this was a maelstrom. Dark clouds boiled over the settlement, and a biting wind ripped through the camp. Raindrops hammered down. It was the worst storm anyone remembered since the first trees were cleared for the settlement.

Tim Carter recalls, "It felt like evil blowing into Jonestown." The red dirt, already damp from recent rain, turned to deep, sticky mud. Everyone caught out in the fury, defectors, settlers, and visitors alike, had no option other than to huddle miserably in the pavilion, packed in damp proximity that exacerbated already strained nerves. At some point, Carter says, "Some of the Bogues told [Ryan] that they wanted to leave. It was Edith, Jim, Teena, Juanita, and Tommy. Harold Cordell wanted to go, too. He and Edith had been a couple for a long time. But Harold had a twelve-year-old son who was living in Jonestown, that boy was named Tommy, too. The kid said he wouldn't go, so you've got this father and son, and the boy is screaming and crying for Harold not to go, and Harold is crying. Merilee Bogue starts screaming at her sisters, 'You're traitors!' All this is happening in a constricted area, and Jones and the congressman are right there. Jones's jaw got even tighter. The whole mood in Jonestown was bad before, but now it was even worse."

Ryan asked for and received all the defectors' passports. Garry produced money to pay their travel expenses. Ryan's mission of visiting Jonestown and bringing out any who wished to leave appeared to be almost accomplished. All that remained was taking them back to Georgetown, and then helping to facilitate their transportation back to the

United States. But there were fifteen of them now, plus Ryan and Speier, Dwyer, Annibourne, the nine newsmen, and the four members of Concerned Relatives. The plane that had flown Ryan and the other visitors into Port Kaituma the day before and was expected to return for them that afternoon had seating for only nineteen. A second plane would be needed. Ryan asked that someone radio the request in to Georgetown. They were going to be late getting to the airstrip in Port Kaituma, but surely the weather would delay the planes, too. For now, there was nothing for Ryan and the others to do but wait in the shelter of the pavilion until the storm passed and they could begin the six-mile trip from Jonestown to Port Kaituma. Though Jones and some of the settlers were obviously upset that anyone was leaving, Ryan and Jones's own lawyers agreed that since so few wanted to leave, Jonestown didn't look bad at all. Ryan thought the total was fifteen. The lawyers knew about the other eleven who were gone before the congressman got up that morning, but the total of twenty-six was still far fewer than they had anticipated — on the Friday afternoon flight from Georgetown to Port Kaituma, Lane told Krause of the *Washington Post* that he expected 90 percent of the settlers to remain, meaning at least ninety would ask to leave. If nothing else happened, it seemed entirely possible that Ryan would return to the United States and declare that he'd given everyone in Jonestown the opportunity to leave, and fewer than 2 percent — the fifteen that the congressman knew about — had asked to go. After that, it would be hard for Concerned Relatives to continue alleging that the settlement was a virtual prison camp.

But where the attorneys saw redemption, Jones saw the opposite. The Temple leader who considered one defection to be a staggering betrayal was deeply offended by twenty-six, and though that was an insignificant percentage of Jonestown's population, they would still serve as examples, and inspirations, to remaining settlers who might grow equally tired of jungle life or Jones's erratic rule. There inevitably would be more of them, and, after this, what was to prevent them from waiting until the next visit by embassy consuls to announce that they wanted to go, too?

And that was only part of the danger. The custody of John Victor remained an issue. Having humiliated Jones by taking more than two dozen of his followers away from him, Tim Stoen and his henchmen might turn their full attention to taking John Victor away next, and, after him, more and more Jonestown children. Jones had studied history, and knew that empires might crumble slowly at first, but once begun, disintegration escalated rapidly and total destruction was inevitable. To him, the twenty-six defectors represented the beginning of the end. Jones had frequently preached to his followers about Masada and how, after a lengthy siege, its outnumbered defenders made a final, grand gesture in defiance of their foes. Jonestown wasn't yet surrounded by an overwhelming number of enemies, but Jones expected that it eventually would be, and, as the afternoon storm subsided, he chose not to wait. Jones had been busy overnight and again in the morning, issuing instructions to his most trusted followers, not certain if he would give additional orders on Saturday afternoon, knowing only that he wanted everything ready if events forced his hand.

Now, as the afternoon storm finally passed and the sun came out again, Jones believed that they had.

A commotion triggered what would become hours of unfolding tragedy. The visitors and defectors were ready to leave. A Temple truck was driven over; they were to climb up into its bed and then embark on the bumpy ride to Port Kaituma. But as they began boarding, settler Al Simon hustled toward the truck, carrying a small child in each arm. He told Ryan that he wanted to leave and take his two children with him. But Simon's wife, Bonnie, ran up, tugging at the kids, screaming that they were hers, too, and her husband couldn't take them away. Ryan and the Temple lawyers tried to intercede, but the Simons clearly were not going to agree. Ryan said that he would stay behind in Jonestown while the other visitors and defectors went on to Port Kaituma and the flight back to Georgetown. A plane could return for him in the morning. Meanwhile, he'd try to work something out between Al and Bonnie Simon. Perhaps a few additional settlers might also decide to leave. If so, they could fly out with Ryan on Sunday.

Jones stood watching. He was flanked by several of his most trusted followers — Patty Cartmell, Jack Beam, Jim McElvane, Maria Katsaris. They whispered back and forth. Some of the remaining settlers shouted insults at the defectors boarding the truck. The bed was high off the ground and some had trouble getting up. Just as everyone was loaded and the driver prepared to pull out, a short, slight man wearing a poncho hauled himself aboard. Larry Layton told the others that he'd decided to defect, too. The departing settlers were immediately suspicious, and whispered to the newsmen that something was wrong; Larry Layton was devoted to Jones and would never leave him. But it was almost three o'clock, and if the pilots of the getaway planes were already at the Port Kaituma airstrip, how long would they wait for passengers before flying back to Georgetown

787

without them? Layton was allowed to stay. The driver started his engine and the heavy vehicle lurched forward, though not for long. A few hundred yards down the narrow road leading out of Jonestown, its wheels stuck fast in the thick mud. After a few minutes, a tractor rumbled up to push the truck free. As it did, more shouting erupted back in the settlement.

As Leo Ryan stood in the pavilion chatting with Lane and Garry, an assailant charged him from behind. Everyone in Jonestown was fond of Don Sly, who'd adapted so well to jungle life that he'd taken to calling himself Ujara in an attempt to leave his old American identity behind. Sly was a gentle man and not aggressive in any way. But now he held a knife to the congressman's throat and hissed, "Motherfucker, you're going to die." But he hesitated an instant, and that allowed Garry, Lane, and Tim Carter to pull him away before he could slash the blade across Ryan's windpipe. In the struggle, Sly was cut with the knife and blood splashed on Ryan, who crouched frozen in place. Security guards dragged Sly away. Jones came over, and instead of inquiring whether Ryan was all right, he asked, "Does this change everything?" The shaken congressman replied, "It doesn't change everything, but it changes [some] things." The lawyers were concerned about what Ryan would tell police. Ryan said that if Sly were turned over to the authorities to answer for the assault in court, that would be sufficient.

Tim Carter, watching and listening, thought that Don Sly would never have attacked Ryan without being ordered to by Jones: "The plan, obviously, was to kill Ryan right there, but it didn't happen." Jones was improvising. To ensure that all his followers would do what he soon would ask, it was necessary to convince them that a final line had been crossed, and that everyone in Jonestown was doomed anyway. Jones's original plan had Ryan dying at the Port Kaituma airstrip or aboard his flight back to Georgetown, but because of Al Simon's unfortunate timing, Ryan wasn't leaving Jonestown as Jones had anticipated. So Jones ordered loyal Don Sly to commit murder. But the lawyers and Carter intervened.

If Ryan had stayed in Jonestown after Sly's attack, Jones could have ordered someone else to try again, but now the congressman wanted to leave. He stumbled up the muddy road to where the truck was finally being pried free of the mud, and told the others what had happened. It was decided that Ryan should fly out immediately. Consul Richard Dwyer would go with the rest to Port Kaituma, see them safely off in the two planes that hopefully were awaiting them, then return to Jonestown to sort out the Simons mess and see if anyone else wanted to leave. On Sunday, Dwyer, whoever among the defectors and media couldn't get seats on the Saturday afternoon flights, and any other Jonestown defectors could fly back to Georgetown on another plane. Ryan was helped up onto the truck bed, and the vehicle rumbled off toward Port Kaituma. It was about three o'clock, and with the muddy roads, the six-mile trip would take at least an hour.

Jones watched as the truck drove away, standing with his arms folded, his mouth jerking with its nervous tic. Almost everyone had been instructed to return to their cottages. Jones muttered, "I've never seen Jonestown so peaceful." A few minutes later he said, "I think Larry Layton is going to do something. He's very loyal to me." One of the lawyers told Jones that, except for Sly's attack on Ryan, things had gone well. Very few people had asked to leave. Jones replied, "If they take 20 today, they'll take 60 tomorrow." He stalked back to his cabin.

A few dozen yards away, seven or eight armed men boarded a tractor-trailer and drove out of Jonestown.

The members of the Jonestown basketball squad knew they'd have to return to the jungle settlement soon, so they wanted to make the most of their remaining time in Georgetown. On Saturday afternoon, most of the team went to a movie. Jimmy Jones stayed behind at Lamaha Gardens, and he recalls that "about 3 or 4" that afternoon, Sharon Amos called him in to the radio room, saying that his father wanted to talk to him. "Dad said, 'You're going to meet Mr. Frazier,' which was code for everybody dies. I say, 'Can't we do something different?' and Dad says, 'Avenging angels are going to take care of things,' and then yells at me, 'You've got to step up and lead on this.' I wasn't going to do that. My brothers and the other guys on the [basketball] team were at the movies, so I sent someone to get them."

The players raced back to Lamaha Gardens. Sharon Amos was on the radio, taking a message from someone in Jonestown. It was a directive about how everyone was to die. Amos spelled the word out loud as code letters were transmitted to her: "K-N-I-V . . ."

Nineteen-year-old Stephan Jones knew that Sharon Amos would do anything that his father ordered. Unsure whether she had already transmitted instructions to the Temple office in San Francisco to also commit suicide, wanting to stall any immediate action in Lamaha Gardens, Stephan suggested that "Everyone wait a minute. . . . We need a plan or we won't accomplish anything. What are we going to use, butter knives?"

Aside from Amos and the basketball players, no one else at Lamaha Gardens knew what was going on, only that Amos and the Jones brothers had closed themselves in the radio room. After a few minutes, Stephan emerged, saying that he and a few others were going to the Pegasus Hotel to find the members of Concerned Relatives who were staying there. Before he left, Stephan told Lee Ingram, the basketball coach, to radio the San Francisco temple office and tell them not to do anything until Stephan spoke to them. Stephan also asked Ingram not to let Sharon Amos out of his sight. Despite the messages received by his brother Jimmy and Sharon Amos, Stephan believed all was not yet lost. In an essay written decades later he recalled, "I thought I had time to stop Dad."

The truck carrying Ryan and all the rest reached the Port Kaituma airstrip around four fifteen. To their consternation, there was no sign of any airplanes other than the damaged Guyanese military craft guarded by several soldiers. While the others waited by the airstrip, Dwyer and Annibourne asked the Temple truck driver to take them to the government district office in town so they could use the radio to ask what had happened to their planes. As they met the North West District officer, whom Dwyer afterward identified as Mr. Thomas, two planes buzzed overhead toward the airstrip. The Temple driver hustled back to the truck and drove in the same direction. Dwyer and Annibourne had to ask Mr. Thomas for a lift. He complied. When they reached the airstrip, they saw that the planes — the nineteen-passenger Otter and a five-seat Cessna — had landed. Their prospective passengers were lined up between them, and a discussion was taking place. Ryan and Speier assumed responsibility for deciding who would go immediately and who must stay in Port Kaituma overnight. With thirty-three people and only twenty-four seats, nine people would have to wait. Dwyer, who intended to return to Jonestown, would be one, and Ryan and Speier felt that the rest should come from among the Concerned Relatives and the newsmen. But the NBC crew wanted to leave immediately and as a unit — they had film to edit and a broadcast to make. The print journalists argued that they had stories to file, too. The defectors wanted to get out of Port Kaituma as soon as possible. They warned that Jones might change his mind anytime, and continued complaining that Larry Layton couldn't be trusted.

As the bickering continued, the Temple truck driver parked his vehicle about two hundred yards away, just to the side of the runway. He was joined there by the men on the newly arrived tractor-trailer, who watched as the discussion on the runway concluded. After the defectors, Ryan and Speier decided that the media with the most urgent deadlines would have next claim on available seats. The smaller Cessna was farther up the airstrip, not far from the disabled Guyanese military aircraft and about thirty yards from the Otter. The NBC crew asked to film a quick interview with Ryan before he boarded, and the congressman agreed. Meanwhile, Larry Layton began arguing with Jackie Speier as she indicated to five people that they should board the Cessna. Layton insisted that he be placed on that plane, which apparently would take off first. When Speier refused, Layton appealed to Ryan, who told his aide to go ahead and let Layton on the Cessna. Then, before he participated in the NBC interview, Ryan said that he would frisk all passengers for weapons before they boarded — a gesture to the defectors, who were still insisting that Layton was up to something. A few of the men who'd arrived on the tractor-trailer wandered over, and one shook Layton's hand. Then they returned to their parked vehicle. Ryan frisked Layton, said that he hadn't found anything, and allowed Layton to board the Cessna behind Vern Gosney, Monica Bagby, and Dale and Tracy Parks. Most of the other defectors shuffled into line by the Otter. At the side of the plane, Ryan began taping his interview with the NBC crew. Then Don Harris looked past the congressman. The tractor-trailer was moving down the runway toward them. "I think we've got trouble," Harris said.

Jones's original plan was simple. He would have a loyal follower join the other defectors, who with them would board an airplane along with Leo Ryan in Port Kaituma and fly off to Georgetown. After the plane was aloft, Layton would take the pistol hidden under his poncho, shoot the pilot, and die with everyone else as the aircraft crashed in the near-impenetrable jungle. Layton was the obvious choice for assassin. He worshipped Jones, and was always eager to demonstrate his devotion. Layton must have felt honored when his beloved leader called him in late Friday night or sometime Saturday to give him such a critical assignment. That he would die completing it would mean less than the thrill of knowing Jones placed so much trust in him.

But then, during the storm that struck Jonestown, there were more defectors and now there would be two planes leaving Port Kaituma. Layton couldn't bring down both. Jones's solution was to send additional assassins to kill Ryan and the others at the airstrip. In frisking Layton, Ryan missed the pistol, but it would have made no difference if he'd found and tried to take it away from him. From the moment the tractor-trailer reached the airstrip while the congressman and Speier were still sorting passengers for the Otter and

Cessna, Leo Ryan was a dead man.

Almost immediately after Harris blurted his warning, someone else shouted, "Hit the dirt," but it was too late for that. Aboard the Cessna, Layton yanked out his pistol and began shooting, wounding Vern Gosney and Monica Bagby before Dale Parks wrestled the gun away from him. Parks tried to shoot Layton, but the gun misfired. On the runway, the Jonestown assassins fired volleys of shots from their mixed armaments of rifles and shotguns. Patricia Parks, on the steps of the portable gangplank rigged up to the door of the Otter, was struck in the back of the head, died instantly, and tumbled down onto the cracked tarmac. Ryan, Speier, Harris, *Examiner* photographer Greg Robinson, Anthony Katsaris, and NBC cameraman Bob Brown and soundman Steve Sung all fell, either dead or grievously wounded. Krause, slightly wounded, played dead beside them. Reiterman, Dwyer, and Beverly Oliver of Concerned Relatives were also hit; they managed to scramble into the brush beside the airstrip. Some of the defectors who'd already boarded the Otter yanked the door shut.

The gunmen moved forward and fired more shots into their fallen victims. There was nothing to prevent them from storming the Otter and Cessna and killing everyone left alive there, or charging into the brush to hunt down those who'd run. Instead, they returned to the truck and tractor-trailer and drove away. The four Guyanese soldiers who'd been standing guard by the disabled army plane watched from a distance. They said later that they'd been prepared to intervene, but decided against it because it was Americans shooting Americans, and they might somehow be blamed if they became involved.

Cautiously, the survivors emerged from the brush and the Otter. They examined the fallen on the tarmac and determined that Ryan, Bob Brown, Harris, Greg Robinson, and Patricia Parks were dead. Anthony Katsaris, Steve Sung, and Jackie Speier were still alive, but badly hurt, perhaps mortally. At that moment there was movement away from the runway, and when someone shouted, "They're coming back," Jim Bogue told his son, Tommy, and daughter Teena to run into the jungle. They did, along with Tracy and Brenda Parks and Chris O'Neal, Brenda's boyfriend. The five of them ran so far and so long that they became lost. But the assassins hadn't returned — it was assumed later that, having killed Ryan and, for good measure, some of the media, they felt they'd accomplished their purpose. The shooting of Patricia Parks was accidental.

The landing gear and fuselage of the Otter had been torn apart by the gunfire; the craft was clearly inoperable. But the Cessna was fine, and, as some of the survivors couched on the runway with their dead and badly wounded and others cautiously emerged from the brush, its pilot proved it by flying off, taking the Otter's pilot with him, leaving all their passengers but Monica Bagby behind as they fled back to Georgetown, frantically radioing ahead near-incoherent reports of bloody carnage.

Some residents of Port Kaituma appeared at the edge of the airstrip. Dwyer and Dale Parks had Larry Layton between them. Dwyer had Layton's gun. Some of the locals offered to take Layton to the town jail and led him off. Layton didn't resist. Eventually Mr. Thomas, the same North West District officer who'd earlier given Dwyer and Neville Annibourne a lift from his office to the airstrip, emerged from the brush where he'd been hiding. He promised that a plane would be summoned from Georgetown to evacuate the wounded, but it was already dusk. Landing in Port Kaituma was tricky enough in full daylight. Mr. Thomas said he would light oil pots set along the runway, but Dwyer guessed from his tone that there would be no aircraft arriving until morning. There was nothing to do but cover the five corpses, then get the badly wounded into shelter and hope that they could survive until help arrived.

About 4 p.m. in Jonestown, the camp loud-speaker system clicked on, and Jim Jones's son Lew announced a meeting in the pavilion. Nothing in his tone indicated any sense of emergency — it was just friendly Lew, same as always — and no one was surprised by the summons. It had been a tense, hectic day. Of course Dad wanted to get everyone together and talk about what had occurred. The chief concern among the settlers was that he'd ramble on well into the night. No one hurried to the pavilion. Gloria Rodriguez sent Tim Carter on ahead with their fifteen-month-old son, Malcolm, saying it was probably going to be a long meeting, so she needed to fetch extra diapers.

Carter didn't immediately take a seat in the pavilion. Instead, carrying Malcolm in his arms, he walked around the side and saw Jones talking with Marceline, Lane, Garry, Johnny Brown, and Jim McElvane. Richard Tropp was standing nearby. Jones glanced at Tropp and Carter and snarled, "What is this, a fucking convention?" Gloria Rodriguez, diapers in hand, found Carter and took their baby into the pavilion. Carter watched as Jones finished his conversation with the others. Moments later Jones turned to Tropp and the two men began arguing. Harriet Tropp joined them. Tropp, raising his voice, said to Jones, "There must be another way," and Jones replied, "Tell me what it is." Harriet Tropp snapped at her brother, "Oh, Dick, stop being such a pain in the ass. You're just afraid to die."

Off to the side of the pavilion, Lane and Garry were being led by armed guards to a cabin. Jones had issued orders for the two lawyers to be held there. Other guards, all of them carrying rifles or shotguns, began prowling all four sides of the pavilion and the perimeters of camp. That was different. Many in the pavilion noticed, and expected Jones to momentarily take the stage and explain. But their leader was now in hushed conversation with Maria Katsaris, who whispered in Jones's ear. Carter eavesdropped as Jones winced and asked her, "Is there a way to make it taste less bitter?" and Katsaris shook her head. Somewhere in Jonestown, human guinea pigs had sampled the deadly potion. Jones asked Katsaris, "Is it quick?" She replied, "Yeah, it's really quick, and it's not supposed to be painful at all." Jones nodded and told her, "Okay, do what you can to make it taste better." Larry Schacht had spent months perfecting the perfect blend of Flavor Aid, tranquilizers, and potassium cyanide. Even at this last moment, Jones expected his faithful physician-chemist to tinker with the mix just a little more.

The delay in Jones's appearance onstage worried the crowd. First the guards, and then this — what was going on? The mounting tension got to settler Shirley Smith, who leaped on stage and began yowling, "Whooo,

800

I'm gonna be a freedom fighter," bounding about and endlessly repeating the phrase at high volume. Occasionally, during meetings when Jones whipped the crowd into a frenzy, someone would be overcome with emotion, jump up, and begin screaming. He or she would always immediately be led away and calmed down. Not this time.

Carter understood what was about to happen. Thinking only of rescuing his wife and child, he approached Jones offstage and said, "Let me take Gloria and Malcolm, and then I'll go out and get [kill] Tim Stoen. That'll be revenge for what we're doing now." Jones glanced at Carter, then asked, "Will you take care of [kill] Malcolm first? Let me think about it." With that, he turned and finally went out onstage. Carter, stunned, began walking into the pavilion, looking for his family, but he'd taken just a step or two when Maria Katsaris tapped him on the shoulder and said, "Come with me, I have something for you to do." Carter's brother, Mike, came to the pavilion from the radio shack, and Katsaris told him to come along, too. As she led the Carters away from the pavilion, Jones walked to the center of the stage and began speaking.

Peoples Temple tape-recorded almost all of Jones's sermons and addresses at meetings, including this one, his last. He began, "How very much I've tried to give you the good life." Jones's voice was clear, his tone resigned. There was about to be a catastrophe involving Congressman Leo Ryan's plane, he explained. "One of those people on the plane" was "gonna shoot the pilot, and down comes that plane into the jungle." It wouldn't be the fault of anyone in Jonestown, Jones said — "I didn't plan it, but I know it's gonna happen." But they still would be blamed. Soon, their enemies would "parachute in here on us."

Jones proposed a solution that would spare the Jonestown children from enslavement and the settlement seniors from slaughter: "My opinion is that we be kind to children and kind to seniors and take the potion like they used to take in ancient Greece, and step over quietly, because we are not committing suicide. It's a revolutionary act. We can't go back. They won't leave us alone. They're now going back to tell more lies, which means more congressmen. And there's no way, no way we can survive."

Some of his audience felt certain that this was just Dad testing them again, leading them right up to the brink. Surely he'd back off at the last second, as he so often had before. But others weren't certain. Don Sly, who'd been turned loose the moment that Ryan left the settlement, stood and asked, "Is there any way that if I go, that it'll help us?" Many in the pavilion cried, "No," and Jones

802

said it, too: "You're not going. I cannot live that way. I've lived for all, and I'll die for all."

Christine Miller, a successful real estate broker back in California, called out, "Is it too late for Russia?" When Jones said that it was, Miller challenged him. Had he asked the Russians? How did it make sense to kill "1,200 people" in response to the defection of so few? Jones reminded her of the plane that was about to crash, and Miller said that the plane she was talking about was one taking everyone in Jonestown to Russia. Jones asked if Miller really thought "Russia's gonna want us with all this stigma" from Ryan's imminent murder. She replied, "Well, I don't see it like that. I mean, I feel like as long as there's life, there's hope. That's my faith."

Jones had always held his followers close by stressing hope, that no one was so lowly that a better life was impossible. Now, wanting their acquiescence in their own deaths, and even in these last minutes still able to read not only the mood, but the potential, of an audience, he neatly used Miller's own words to make his case: "Well, someday everybody dies, some place that hope runs out, because everybody dies. I haven't seen anybody yet [who] didn't die. And I'd like to choose my own kind of death for a change. I'm tired of being tormented to hell, that's what I'm tired of."

Most of the crowd shouted in approval.

■ ■ ■

The Carter brothers could hear Jones's amplified voice as Maria Katsaris led them to a room near the radio shack. There were two cots. The Carters sat on one, and Katsaris on the other. She told them, "Mike Prokes is going to take money to the Soviet embassy in Georgetown. It fills three suitcases, and they're heavy. Are you willing to help?" When they said that they were, she said they should wait there while she went to clear it with Jones. While she was gone, they heard the lengthy exchange between Jones and Miller. There was a brief pause — Katsaris had probably called Jones to the side of the stage to get his approval for the Carters to help carry the suitcases of money. Then the brothers heard Jones say, apparently to quiet Miller so he could continue, "Someone get in touch with the Soviets and see if they'll take us."

Then Katsaris returned. She said that Jones agreed. The Carters were taken to their cottages to change clothes, and then over to the West House, Jones's personal cabin, where Mike Prokes and Carolyn Layton were busy typing letters. Their sister, Terry Carter, was also there. The Carter brothers saw three plastic suitcases, two larger than the other, all stuffed with cash. Some gold bullion had been crammed in, too, but then removed. The gold was so heavy that it would have torn through the bottom of the suitcases. Now it was piled beside them. Merilee Bogue was entertaining John Victor and Kimo, trying to keep the little boys distracted. Annie Moore shuffled papers, evidently looking for some specific documents. The adults all seemed calm for people who knew they were about to die. Someone brought Prokes and Mike Carter their passports. Tim Carter, who'd just returned to Jonestown from California a few days before, still had his. Katsaris gave pistols to Prokes and the Carters, and told them to deliver the suitcases to the Soviet embassy in Georgetown. She didn't explain how they would get there. They assumed they were to walk from Jonestown to Port Kaituma and then find transportation. Katsaris told them that if they made it and turned the suitcases over, then they could go wherever they wanted: "Have a nice life. Don't be taken alive. If you're caught, kill yourselves. Is that understood?" They said it was. Katsaris told them, "Security will leave you alone," and wished them good luck.

Tim Carter was trying hard to think clearly. What he wanted was to get back to Gloria and Malcolm. It was still possible that Jones was testing everyone again. When Prokes suggested to Carolyn Layton that perhaps a Temple truck should take him, the Carters, and the suitcases down the road from Jonestown to the main road leading to Port Kaituma to save some time, Carter volunteered to go and ask Jones. As he left the cottage, he heard Kimo and John Victor begin crying, and his sister, Terry, and Katsaris attempting to soothe them.

While instructions were being given to the three couriers in West House, Jones moved on from verbal sparring with Christine Miller. Someone in the crowd asked if he wouldn't at least spare John Victor, and Jones refused: "He's no different to me than any of these children here." Of course, the six-year-old *was* different to Jones — retaining custody of John Victor, and the subsequent court battles with Tim and Grace Stoen, had helped precipitate this final crisis. But Jones preferred that the child die rather than be returned to his birth mother because then Grace and Tim Stoen would, in some sense, have *won*.

Carter was hurrying to the pavilion when more cheering erupted. The tractor-trailer was back from Port Kaituma, and the men leaped off and ran into the pavilion shouting, "We got the congressman!" Bob Kice, one of the gunmen, told Carter, "We got the congressman and some others. They're all dead."

Jones made the formal announcement: "It's all over. The congressman has been murdered." Schacht and the Jonestown nurses appeared at the side of the stage. They brought with them bundles of filled syringes. It was time. Jones wanted the infants, toddlers, and older children to be first. "It's simple, it's simple," he promised their parents. "Just, please get it, before it's too late. The GDF [Guyana Defence Force] will be here, I tell you. Get movin'."

Some parents didn't move fast enough to suit Jones. He warned them, "They'll torture some of our children here." Some of the guards stepped up. No one was given the choice of whether to participate. Jones told the armed men to allow parents who wanted to die with their children to join them in the line: "Who wants to go with their child has a right. . . . I think it's humane."

There is nothing humane about death by cyanide. As a means of suicide, its only advantage is absolute lethality if taken in sufficient dosage. Cyanide robs the body's cells of the ability to absorb oxygen in the blood. Suffocation is sure — and slow. In *The Poisoner's Handbook,* Deborah Blum writes, "The last minutes of a cyanide death are brutal, marked by convulsions, a desperate gasping for air, a rising bloody froth of vomit and saliva, and finally a blessed release into unconsciousness." As the nurses used syringes to squirt poison into the mouths of the first few infants, many parents herding their children forward hesitated, particularly when the babies began foaming at the mouth and convulsing.

Jim McElvane took over the stage microphone, allowing Jones a few moments to catch his breath and observe the poisoning process. As McElvane began cheerily describing the pleasures of death — "It feels good. . . . You've never felt so good as how that feels" — Tim Carter was about to reach Jones's side. Just before he did, he saw nurse Sharon Cobb squirting poison into his fifteen-month-old son's mouth. "Gloria was standing right there next to him, she was going to go next, I saw that and I felt guilty that I wasn't saving them. On that last day, it felt like walking through mental quicksand. I believe all of us were a little bit drugged ahead of time, maybe at that last meal. They used to tranquilize Gene Chaikin by putting drugs in cheese sandwiches, and that's what we all had for lunch in Jonestown that day, cheese sandwiches." When Carter was asked later why he didn't charge off the stage and simply knock over the poison vat, he replied, "There was no vat out there yet, only the syringes."

Carter approached Jones and asked about a truck to take the money couriers to the main road. Jones said, "That's not a good idea." He reached out, took Carter by the arm and added, "Son, I'm sorry it had to end this way.

I love you." Carter pulled free. He found Gloria and Malcolm about ten yards away. A dozen other mothers and babies lay around them. All were foaming at the mouth. Some were jerking spasmodically. Gloria held Malcolm. The little boy was already dead; Gloria had froth on her lips, tears streamed down her face and she couldn't speak. Carter knelt beside Gloria, cradling her and the baby in his arms, and repeated, "I love you so much," until she was gone, too. The guards began urging the remaining children and some of their parents toward the nurses and syringes. Many of the children were screaming in fright, and some of the adults screamed, too, but the stage microphone was pointed away from them and none of the screams would be audible on the tape. Those who refused to move forward were pushed ahead by the guards. Carter says, "By that point all the people in the pavilion were realizing that they were surrounded by these people with guns, and that they had only two choices — fight and be held down and injected, I know that happened to some of them, or else think, 'My time is up,' and go ahead and take the poison."

Maria Katsaris, back from West House, took the microphone from McElvane and tried to soothe the crowd: "There's nothing to worry about. Everybody keep calm and try and keep your children calm." A moment later, listening to the wails of the dying children, she said, "They're not crying from pain. It's just a little bitter tasting."

Jones returned to the front of the stage and said, "You got to move." One who wasn't moving was his wife. Marceline stood far to the side; if Jones had expected her to help, she wasn't. Instead, she screamed, "You can't do this!" Even those settlers most devoted to Jones loved Marceline, too. He was Father and she was Mother. Alone among everyone left in Jonestown, her resistance might inspire enough opposition to ruin Jones's last defiant gesture. He had to stop or at least quiet her, and knew exactly how. Marceline had spoken with Jones before he took the pavilion stage, and he'd surely told her then that besides the mass suicide about to take place in Jonestown, he'd also radioed Lamaha Gardens in Georgetown and ordered everyone there, including their three sons on the basketball team, to take their own lives, too. Marceline Jones once wrote to her husband that she lived for her children. Now he expected her to obediently die with them, and, as a reminder, said sharply, "Marceline? You got forty minutes," or about the time it might take everyone at Lamaha Gardens to line up and kill themselves. Jim Jones Jr. says, "My mother was all by herself there. We [Tim, Stephan, and Jimmy] were in Georgetown, so she didn't have her team that could have tried to stop it with her. She got told right then by [Jones] that her children had died or were going to die, so why would she want to keep on living? [Jones] understood her. He understood her so well."

Marceline knew her loss was not limited to three sons in Georgetown. Lew was there in Jonestown, and Agnes, as well as Lew's little son, Chaeoke, and Agnes's four children. They would die, too. Anguished, she watched as the last of more than two hundred children were administered poison from syringes. By half past five, no later than 6 p.m., almost all of the little ones were gone, and it was the turn of the adults.

Tim Carter left Gloria and Malcolm where they lay, and made his way back toward West House. "I did not give a fuck about anything," he remembers. "I kept thinking, 'They murdered my son.' But there was also a voice in my head saying, 'You cannot die,' and I made a choice that day. I wanted to kill myself on the spot, but maybe I could tell what had really happened.' " Carter's brother and Mike Prokes were waiting with the suitcases. On his way back to them, Carter passed Carolyn Layton. She reflexively asked, "What's wrong?" He said, "They've murdered my son," and she replied, "Oh, Tim, we had no other choice."

The three men each picked up a suitcase and walked through the settlement toward the road that led to the front gate. It was hard going, especially carrying the heavy suitcases, which Carter remembers "weighed forty or fifty pounds each." A layer of mud as much as six or eight inches deep covered every bit of ground. They left two of the suitcases behind even before they were out of Jonestown, burying one in a cleared field and the other in the settlement piggery, making certain to note the exact spots so the cases could be retrieved later — by whom, they had no idea. The three men didn't talk much — what was there to say? — and took turns carrying the remaining, smallest suitcase as they trudged toward Port Kaituma. The last thing they heard behind them in Jonestown was Jones's voice over the loudspeaker. He was saying something that sounded like, "Mother, Mother, Mother."

The Carter brothers and Prokes weren't the only ones on their way out of Jonestown. During the confusion at the pavilion, Odell Rhodes and Stanley Clayton individually managed to sneak off into the jungle. Grover Davis didn't sneak at all. As soon as the poisoning began, he walked up to a perimeter guard — it was Ray Jones, husband of Jim Jones's daughter Agnes. Ray asked, "Where do you think you're going?" Davis said simply, "I don't want to die." Ray said, "Have a good life," and stood aside while Davis walked out to the edge of Jonestown, where he hid in a ditch. Garry and Lane also talked their way past the armed men holding them in a cabin, and circled through the brush until they found the road to Port Kaituma.

One more person escaped death, though not immediately from Jonestown. Some of the oldest settlers never came to the pavilion. They lay on cots in their dormitories; guards and settlement nurses took syringes and cups of poison and dosed the elderly men and women there. Hyacinth Thrash was asleep; they mistakenly believed that she was already dead and left her alone.

As the couriers departed West House with their cash-crammed suitcases, the adults in the pavilion began shuffling into line. Some went proudly; they worshipped Jim Jones, believed that they were making a grand revolutionary statement, and looked forward to a new consciousness on some higher plane. Others accepted poison as a preferable alternative to slaughter by the enemy forces they believed must be converging on Jonestown. Whether death was dreamless sleep or reincarnation or spiritual relocation to someplace better, they were ready. Most of the rest were too tired or disgusted to spend their last moments fighting armed guards. Asked decades later what he thinks he would have done, Jim Jones Jr. said there's no question:

"My wife and my mother were going to be gone, they drank what they were told to. If I'd been there with the rest of the real security team, then no, we would never have gone out to shoot Leo Ryan. But back there [at the pavilion]? I can see myself saying, 'I'm tired of this shit. Fine, all right, I'll drink your goddamn poison.'"

But there were holdouts. They refused to move or shouted defiance or cried as they begged to be spared. Jones urged, "Lay down your life with dignity. . . . Stop these hysterics. This is not the way for people who are socialists or communists to die."

Marceline must have started screaming again, because on the tape recovered later, Jones, using the name she was called by most Temple members, commanded, "Mother, Mother, Mother, Mother, please. Mother, please, please, please. Don't do this. Don't do this. Lay down your life with your child[ren], but don't do this."

A few people in the poison line thanked Jones for all that he'd done for them. His response was to call for more of the poison that would kill them: "Where's the vat, the vat, the vat? Where's the vat with the green 'C' on it? Bring the vat with the green 'C' in, please, bring it here so the adults can begin."

The vat was fetched, and as a woman who was about to die shouted "Go on to Zion, and thank you, Dad," Jones began a rambling monologue: "We used to think this world was not our home. Well, it sure isn't. . . . We said, one thousand people who said, 'We don't like the way the world is.' " He interrupted himself to tell someone in line, "Take some," and then continued. "Take our life from us. We laid it down. We got tired. . . . We didn't commit suicide. We committed an act of revolutionary suicide protesting the conditions of an inhumane world."

Then the tape ran out.

Concerned Relative Sherwin Harris spent much of Saturday afternoon and early evening at Lamaha Gardens. When he returned to the Pegasus Hotel, he happily reported that he'd had a fine time visiting with his daughter, Liane, who'd even agreed to see her father again on Sunday. Most of the other Concerned Relatives passed Saturday in the Pegasus lobby or swimming pool. They expected Leo Ryan and his traveling party to return from their Jonestown trip by 3 p.m. Ryan would immediately go into a meeting with Prime Minister Burnham, while Jim Cobb, Beverly Oliver, Carol Boyd, and Anthony Katsaris, the four Concerned Relatives who'd accompanied the congressman, would return to the Pegasus and brief everyone about who they'd seen and what they'd learned. But about the time Ryan and the others were supposed to arrive, someone

phoned the Pegasus to tell those waiting there
that the flight from Port Kaituma was delayed
and now would reach Georgetown about 5
p.m. No reason was given, or any cause for
alarm. Then came a second call. The anticipated arrival time would be 7 p.m., and
Congressman Ryan was bringing nine extra
people back to Georgetown with him. The
Concerned Relatives at the Pegasus were
thrilled — who was coming? Which of their
family members might be included?

Shortly after 7 p.m., newcomers burst into
the hotel lobby — but they were Stephan,
Tim, and Jimmy Jones, plus one or two other
members of the Jonestown basketball team.
The wild-eyed young men demanded that the
Concerned Relatives tell them what was going on in Jonestown. No one had any information to offer. Some of the Concerned
Relatives thought that the Temple members
had come to kill them as part of some plot
and were relieved when they abruptly left.
But they had a new concern — what *had*
happened in Jonestown? Stephan Jones had
said something to Tim Stoen about his father
wanting everyone to die. Why was the plane
delayed so long in Port Kaituma? As they
talked among themselves, someone from
hotel management told them to go upstairs
to their rooms — *now.*

The Jones brothers' next stop was the U.S.
embassy. "We still thought we might have

some time, that if we could just get to Jonestown we could stop whatever my dad was doing," Jim Jones Jr. says. "The embassy could fly us there, we figured. But when we got to the embassy, it was closed up for the night. We got somebody on the intercom and tried to tell him what was going on, but they still wouldn't let us in. So we got in the car and went back [to Lamaha Gardens]."

Except for Sharon Amos and Lee Ingram, who'd been ordered by Stephan Jones to keep an eye on her, no one else at Lamaha Gardens — about four dozen Temple members not including the other members of the Jonestown basketball team — had any idea what was going on. Sometime after 7 p.m., several Georgetown policemen appeared at the door and asked if everything was all right. A few of the Temple members assured them that things were fine. Lee Ingram went to ask them who had been at the door, and that was all the opening that Sharon Amos needed. She gathered her three children — Liane, twenty-one; Christa, eleven; and Martin, ten; plus nine-year-old Stephanie Morgan — and took them into a bathroom along with adult Temple member Chuck Beikman, a relatively simple-minded, mostly illiterate former Marine who always did as he was told. Amos shut the door behind them. Odd sounds emanated from the bathroom, and then blood began leaking out under the door.

Stephan, Tim, and Jimmy Jones jumped from their car and ran to the front gate of Lamaha Gardens. Someone told them, "Sharon killed herself and her children." The Jones brothers and Ingram hurried to the bathroom. It was hard to get the door open. Amos's lifeless body was blocking it from the inside. They shoved their way in. Liane, Christa, and Martin lay sprawled on the gory floor. Chuck Beikman, knife in hand, stood holding Stephanie, whose neck bled from several cuts. Ingram wrenched the injured Stephanie free. Martin and Christa were dead. Liane was in her death throes and quickly expired. All four had had their throats slit. The wounds of Amos and Liane Harris were self-inflicted. As her leader had ordered, Amos's death tools were knives.

The Georgetown police were called. The dead were taken away in body bags, and Chuck Beikman was arrested. Some of the dazed Temple members tried to clean up the blood in the bathroom and adjacent hallway, with limited success. They were unable to reach anyone in Jonestown. As soon as he'd sent his final messages to Lamaha Gardens, Jones shut down the radio line between the settlement and Georgetown. Exhausted and frightened, not knowing what had happened in Jonestown, only that it was bad, everyone at Lamaha Gardens tried to sleep. Jim Jones Jr. remembers, "I woke up a few hours later when a soldier stuck a gun in my mouth. We were all paraded outside, and they told us that more people were dead."

In Port Kaituma, the survivors of the airstrip attack passed a long, nervous night. Just after midnight a radio message from Georgetown finally reached the government's North West District office there, promising that help was on the way. But the troops would not arrive for hours yet, since they were flying into Matthews Ridge, taking the train some of the way to Port Kaituma, and then hiking the last few miles. Until then, everyone must stay where they were. Some of those sheltering in the river town's primitive houses were badly hurt and barely conscious, but the others, wounded and unharmed alike, feared that every night noise signaled the return of the Temple assassins. Tommy and Teena Bogue, Tracy and Brenda Parks, and Chris O'Neal were still missing and presumed to be somewhere in the jungle.

It was quiet in Jonestown, except for the rustle of night creatures emerging from the jungle, the small animals who hid from larger predators by day, then crept out under cover of darkness to scavenge whatever edible scraps they might find. On this night, they feasted.

CHAPTER FIFTY-ONE: WHAT HAPPENED?

The first word that something terrible had happened in Guyana reached the U.S. State Department on Saturday around 9 p.m., a flash message from "African" Georgetown that Congressman Leo Ryan and eight to ten people were attacked "by a truck-load of whites" as they attempted to board a small plane. There was no confirmation that anyone had died. Reporters routinely covering the State Department soon learned of the message, and from there national and international news agencies clamored for more information. By the next day, when Ryan's death was announced, the first murder of a U.S. congressman engaged on official business in American history and apparently at the hands of some jungle church cult comprised of U.S. citizens, journalists and broadcast crews began swarming into Georgetown. They demanded facts from spokesmen for the Guyanese government, who had very few to offer. Yes, five people had died on Saturday afternoon at Port Kaituma: Congressman Leo Ryan, NBC crew members Don Harris and Bob Brown, *San Francisco Examiner* photographer Greg Robinson, and Jonestown defector Patricia Parks. Several others who were badly wounded had been brought out of Port Kaituma by plane on Sunday morning, then medevaced to a U.S. naval station in Puerto Rico. It was hoped that they would recover. [All of the Port Kaituma wounded did survive.] Five people who'd been lost in the jungle after the shooting had been located. Otherwise, there was nothing specific yet to tell. "The news was all over the world, but nothing substantial was known by us," Kit Nascimento recalls. "We really had no idea of what might be going on."

There were two immediate questions: What had happened in Jonestown, and how many were dead?

The Guyana Defence Force troops led into Jonestown on Sunday morning by Desmond Roberts sent back only vague reports. There were bodies everywhere. Amerindians darted through the settlement, grabbing what they could, and despite Roberts's efforts to control his men some of the GDF soldiers were also looting rather than investigating. Skip Roberts, the Georgetown police commissioner, was dispatched to take over. When he arrived in Port Kaituma, he recruited reluctant assistants. After discarding their last suitcase of cash and their guns by the railroad tracks outside town, Mike Prokes and Tim and Mike Carter were arrested by Port Kaituma police. They were held in a cassava mill because the Port Kaituma jail had only one cell, which was occupied by Larry Layton. Skip Roberts asked them to help identify the dead in Jonestown. The lawyers also arrived. When he saw the Carters and Prokes there, Charles Garry exclaimed, "I can think of better ways to fire your attorneys than this."

The scene at Jonestown was horrific. Soldiers and investigators were shocked when elderly Hyacinth Thrash tottered out of her cabin and asked what was going on. The old lady was dehydrated and confused, but otherwise all right. Everyone else was dead, including settlement dogs and Mr. Muggs, the pet chimpanzee. The animals had been shot. The GDF gingerly poked around the human remains. Because of the heat, humidity, vermin, and maggots, advanced decay had already set in. Many corpses had burst open. Tim Carter and a few of the other Jonestown escapees who had also reached Port Kaituma identified some of the bodies. They found Jones, who lay sprawled onstage in the pavilion. "His abdomen was all swollen and bulging up from under his shirt," Carter recalls. Even in death, Jones stood out from the rest because he appeared dead from a gunshot wound to the head rather than poison. Soon afterward, Annie Moore, also dead by gunshot, was discovered in Jones's cabin. No bullet wounds were found on other bodies, but some had odd abscesses that a Guyanese pathologist later testified were caused by injection; they had apparently refused to drink poison, and were held down and forcibly injected. Tim Carter also noted abscesses on numerous bodies. Everyone had to die for Jones's final statement to have the impact that he wanted. Because of the corpses' continuing deterioration, no firm count of those forcibly injected could be made. Estimates ranged from as few as twenty to as many as a third of the Jonestown dead.

The total announced deceased fluctuated for several days. The first report, based mostly on a haphazard count by the first arriving soldiers, was 383. The information was released by the Guyanese government and reported on air and in print. The Concerned Relatives in Georgetown, Temple members held under house arrest in Lamaha Gardens, and family members of Jonestown settlers back in the United States all felt hopeful — maybe their loved ones were still alive. If there had been more than nine hundred people in Jonestown on Saturday, and only 383 bodies, then perhaps everyone else was still alive — but where? The Guyanese government also wondered, though for a different reason. If five or six hundred people were loose somewhere in the jungle, perhaps they still comprised a rebel army. The first formal Jonestown body count, completed on Monday, increased the number of dead to 408, still not even half of the settlement population.

On Tuesday the GDF was replaced by American troops, who discovered that the name tags placed on bodies identified earlier were illegible because rain had washed away most of the ink. They started over, and to their astonishment, the bodies they inspected proved to be only a top layer. There was another underneath, and another beneath that. The bottom layer was mostly comprised of infants and children, who apparently had been the first to die. The lower layers of dead were even more badly decomposed than the top layer. The U.S. commander contacted Washington to request snow shovels to scrape up some of the remains. Immediate identification of most bodies was impossible. Remains were shipped by air to Dover Air Force Base in Delaware, where a mixed team of military and civilian pathologists would try to figure out names from fingerprints on file in the United States and Guyana and from dental records.

The announced number of dead grew to 700 on Thursday, 780 on Friday, and finally, a week after the tragic event, 909. Counting Sharon Amos and her three children, plus

Ryan and the other four killed in Port Kaituma, the final death count of November 18, 1978, was 918.

The sheer magnitude of the number, and the manner of death, made Jonestown/ Peoples Temple a story that simultaneously horrified and fascinated the public. There was demand to know more, to know *everything,* and the media did its best to oblige. Every available Georgetown hotel room was occupied by press, who congregated at the U.S. embassy and Guyanese government offices demanding information that no one had, and haunted the lobbies of the Pegasus and Park hotels where the Concerned Relatives and the various Jonestown survivors remained. The Guyanese were still trying to sort out who might be blamed. Almost four dozen Temple members remained under house arrest at Lamaha Gardens. Larry Layton was transferred to a Georgetown jail where Chuck Beikman was incarcerated. Mike Prokes and the Carter brothers were also held for a time, then allowed to move to the Park Hotel, where some of the Concerned Relatives begged to be protected from them. Stories had appeared about supposed armed bands of Temple members bent on wreaking revenge for Jim Jones, not only in Guyana, but in San Francisco. That fear became even more widespread on November 27, when an embittered former Board of Supervisors member named Dan White gunned down Mayor George Moscone and Supervisor Harvey Milk. Though it was soon determined that White had acted alone, there was initial widespread suspicion that Peoples Temple was somehow involved. If more than nine hundred of its unbalanced members had been willing to kill themselves on the command of the Temple's very weird leaders, why wouldn't some of its surviving members in San Francisco murder the mayor and a supervisor?

In the weeks immediately following November 18, media outlets vied to describe Jim Jones and Peoples Temple in the most provocative terms possible. In that pre-Internet age when facts — and unsubstantiated innuendo — were not immediately available in a few computer keystrokes, TV, radio, and print reporters had to actively seek out sources, whose frequently florid testimony was reported immediately because of the competition between stations and newspapers to break the latest story first. Fact-checking suffered; any connection with Jones or the Temple was considered a sufficient credential to warrant someone's appearance on a program or quotes in an article, and the more inflammatory the better. Jim Jones had wanted his grand gesture to make an impression on the entire world, and, to that extent, he succeeded. But the Jonestown deaths quickly became renowned not as a grandly defiant revolutionary gesture, but as the ultimate example of human gullibility.

Previously, any investigative reporting on Jim Jones and Peoples Temple was almost entirely confined to reporters in Indianapolis and San Francisco. Even with the bus trips and services around the United States, Jones and the Temple had only a regional reputation. Now all the biggest news outlets scrambled for information, some wanting the scandalous even more than the significant, and plenty of both was discovered. In Lynn, in Richmond, in Indianapolis, and Mendocino County and Los Angeles and San Francisco, Jones and the Temple had made enough impact that there were many people eager to add to the growing opinion that everything about the group and its leader was warped from the start. The political figures who'd eagerly sought Temple support mostly declared that they'd hardly interacted with Jones or his followers at all. Only Willie Brown and Carlton Goodlett spoke at all of the Temple's many positive programs. In Georgetown, Jonestown survivors were encouraged to add salacious insights. Tim Carter, reeling from the loss of his wife and son, was asked by one famous TV journalist to describe his Jonestown sex life — some reporters assumed that Jonestown was a commune and free love was the predominant pastime.

But one misconception evolved into part of the cultural lexicon. Initially, most news outlets correctly reported that the Jonestown settlers died by ingesting cyanide that was stirred into a vat of Flavor Aid, an inexpensive powdered drink. But some reports mentioned Kool-Aid. As a familiar brand, "Kool-Aid" proved more memorable to the public than "Flavor Aid." "Don't drink the Kool-Aid" became a jokey catchphrase for not foolishly following deranged leaders. "It . . . still hurts every time I hear it," says Juanell Smart, who lost four children, her mother, and her uncle in Jonestown. "I hated that people laughed when they said it, like what happened was somehow funny."

There was nothing funny about what investigators found at Jonestown. Besides the mounting body count, they discovered that some of the Jonestown dead left messages explaining what they'd done. These provided convincing evidence that many went willingly to their deaths. In a stenographer's notebook found by her side, Annie Moore defended Jones: "His love for humans was unsurmountable and it was many whom he put his love and trust in and they left him and spit in his face." Annie expected some "mentally fascist person" to find the notebook and throw it away, but she wanted the world to know that "we died because you would not let us live in peace! From Annie Moore." An unsigned document, usually attributed to Richard Tropp, began "Collect all the tapes, all the writing, all the history. The story of this movement, this action, must be examined over and over. . . . I am sorry there is no eloquence as I write these final words. We are resolved, but grieved that we cannot make the truth of our witness clear." Teenage Candace Cordell scribbled a succinct message in ink on her forearm as she waited in line to die: "Why couldn't you leave us alone?"

Guns were found in Jonestown — ten handguns, fourteen rifles, and eight shotguns, enough to arm the Port Kaituma airstrip assassins and a squad of Jonestown security guards, but far fewer than had been expected. Even with the possibility that additional firearms were stolen by the GDF or natives, it was still too meager an arsenal to arm a substantial band of insurrectionists. The Guyanese government could stop worrying about a large-scale revolt.

Filed documents far exceeded what investigators anticipated. In Jones's cottage, in various Jonestown buildings, there were stacks of letters, invoices, index cards, and other records, so many that after the FBI declassified most of them, they totaled almost sixty thousand printed pages plus several hundred tapes of Jones's sermons and radio broadcasts that, if transcribed, would potentially add another twenty to thirty thousand pages to the total. Each document had to be scrutinized, every tape listened to — it took the FBI uncountable man-hours, the mass of trivial information making it hard to ferret out anything substantial.

There was an astonishing amount of money found in Jonestown, too. Even before the U.S. forces arrived, Guyanese police and the GDF, led to the locations by the Carters and Prokes, took possession of the three cash-filled suitcases Jones had intended for the Soviet embassy in Georgetown. It took some time for Guyana to return the estimated $300,000 to the United States. Another $635,000 was found in Jones's cabin, along with Guyanese currency worth an additional $22,000 in American dollars. No one seems to know what happened to the gold bullion. There were bundles of uncashed Social Security checks. Additional investigation by the U.S. government turned up about $7 million in foreign banks. Back in the United States, Terri Buford tried to cooperate with the FBI, but there were many foreign accounts she did not know about. The Bible listing these accounts in secret code was never recovered from Jones's cabin. Its pages may have ended up plugging gaps in the walls of Amerindian huts, or else providing spiritual comfort to some soldier of the GDF who never realized the significance of the pencil scribblings along its spine.

The greatest mystery, though, involved the bodies. For the next four and a half months, military and civilian staff struggled to identify as many as possible. The number of bodies involved, and the demand by loved ones, relatives, and friends of all the deceased for something to mourn and bury, made it a tense, frustrating task. Photographs were useless. Faces were decomposed. Clothing didn't help. Jonestown settlers routinely traded garments so name tags sewn into shirts and pants were no help. Dental records were spotty. Lots of settlers hadn't been to a dentist in years, if ever. Some identities were determined from fingerprint records, but in hundreds of instances the skin on all ten fingers was destroyed. Because the infants and children had decomposed the most, more than two-thirds of them were never identified. The total count of unidentified bodies was 409. After a considerable search for a burial site that would accept these remains, Evergreen Cemetery in Oakland offered ground for a mass grave, where they were interred on May 11, 1979.

The remains of Jim and Marceline Jones caused special concern. It was November 30 before Marceline's remains were identified in Dover, but once they were, Walter and Charlotte Baldwin wanted their daughter, along with the rest of her immediate family, buried in Richmond's Earlham Cemetery. None of the Baldwins' great-grandchildren had been identified, but there was still Marceline, Jim, Lew, and Agnes. The Baldwins contacted a local funeral parlor to coordinate with Dover Air Force Base. But when word got out journalists and newscasters from around the country wanted to cover the services, and demanded to know the date and time. Of greater concern was the FBI, which warned of possible violence in the cemetery commited by Peoples Temple followers. Local residents complained that their town would be desecrated by Jim Jones's remains. The undertaker and the Baldwins decided to have Jones's body cremated and his ashes deposited in the Atlantic Ocean. Marceline, Lew, and Agnes were buried in Earlham Cemetery without incident.

None of Marceline's surviving children were present. Suzanne had been estranged from her parents, and Stephan, Jimmy, and Tim were still trying to extricate themselves from the authorities in Guyana. The Guyanese wanted badly to prosecute someone for the tragedies, if only to demonstrate to the world that theirs was a law-abiding nation, not a haven for religious zealots and murderers. Larry Layton was locked up, though there was some doubt whether he could be tried for murder, let alone convicted. He'd shot people at the airstrip, but none of his victims had died. Chuck Beikman was a more obvious possibility. He'd been closed in the bathroom where four people died and had been prevented from cutting the throat of a nine-year-old girl. Hearings to determine the charges to be brought against Beikman commenced shortly after his arrest, and when Stephan Jones was required to testify, he came perilously close to being charged with murder himself.

Nineteen-year-old Stephan had been under crushing pressure since the afternoon of November 18, when he tried desperately to avert the suicides in Jonestown and Georgetown that were ordered by his father. Stephan was more successful convincing Temple members in San Francisco not to kill themselves. Laura Johnston Kohl remembers that, through much of the awful night, "Stephan called [the San Francisco temple] every half hour, telling them they shouldn't commit suicide. They would have, if it hadn't been for him. He was a real hero."

In the days that followed, Stephan assumed leadership of the Temple survivors in Georgetown. His increasing sense of guilt for his father's action boiled over during the Beikman hearings. Furious at hearing the slow-witted ex-Marine described as a cruel, cunning killer, and hoping to save him, Stephan blurted that he was the one who killed the children in the Lamaha Gardens bathroom. He was promptly remanded to a dank cell.

Stephan remained there for weeks, until the Guyanese reluctantly concluded that he was innocent. They retained Layton and Beikman in custody, and in December began allowing surviving Temple members to return to America. Most, exhausted and sickened by all they'd endured, were glad to go — only to learn that their troubles were far from over.

Based on what they'd read in magazines and newspapers and seen on television, many Americans considered surviving Temple members pariahs, apparently capable of any deranged act. One Pan American pilot refused to take off from the Georgetown airport because some of the Temple men were supposed to be onboard. Upon landing in the United States, everyone was questioned by FBI agents, who could not be shaken in their belief that Temple hit squads roamed the country, ready to strike. Before being permitted to go on their way, they were relieved of their passports, and told these would only be returned upon repayment to the government of their travel and living costs. All of the survivors had been penniless, so the United States covered airfare as well as their meal and lodging expenses incurred in Georgetown while the Guyanese government required their presence during its investigations.

The government also wanted reimbursement for every cent spent on airlifting bodies from Guyana to Dover Air Force Base, and all costs incurred during the lengthy identification process. In all, the estimated bill was $4.3 million. The approximately eighty survivors could hardly be expected to come up with even a modest fraction of that amount, so U.S. investigators and attorneys turned to what remained of Peoples Temple in San Francisco. It was known by now that there had been a lot of money in Temple domestic and foreign accounts, along with property and capital investments that undoubtedly had substantial value. One story in the *San Francisco Examiner* estimated Temple assets at $26 million — enough to pay back the government if the FBI located the money, but not enough to satisfy the suits brought against the church by relatives of the Jonestown dead and former members now in full cry that they had been defrauded. By October 1979, there were 695 claims totaling $1.78 billion.

About $7.3 million in foreign accounts was located, and the government claimed that. All Temple properties, from land to printing presses, were impounded and put up for public auction. Remaining members in San Francisco offered up $295,000 from domestic Temple bank accounts. In all, about $13 million in assets were eventually recovered. Creditors felt certain there was more, and would have pressed Peoples Temple for it, but were unable to do so, because Peoples Temple no longer existed.

In the immediate aftermath of November 18, the San Francisco temple was besieged by picketers, and by friends and family members of Jonestown settlers who couldn't be certain whether their loved ones were among the four hundred initially reported dead. They were sure that someone in the barricaded temple must know who still lived, but the few dozen members inside didn't know. Then, as the death total rose until finally it was announced that all in Jonestown were certainly deceased, the picketers' anxiety turned to fury. Many threats were made before they finally dispersed. The murder of George Moscone and Harvey Milk added to a citywide sense of bewilderment and despair, but nowhere did it match the sense of loss and helplessness inside the fenced property on Geary Boulevard. In those dark days, there was one act of kindness. Dianne Feinstein, now acting mayor of San Francisco, came calling, not to badger the Temple members for money or to threaten them, but to ask if they were all right and to take some of them to breakfast. Through Charles Garry (who had made his way safely back along with Mark Lane), a few members declared for a short time that Peoples Temple would go on, that its mission to feed the hungry and clothe the naked remained, despite what happened in Guyana. But common sense prevailed over hubris. On December 3, only thirty people attended the Temple's Sunday services, and three days later papers were filed requesting that the organization known as Peoples Temple be formally dissolved.

Jim Jones was gone, and so was his church.

CHAPTER FIFTY-TWO:
AFTERMATH

In the aftermath of Jonestown and the dissolution of Peoples Temple, the U.S. Congress launched an official investigation. More than nine hundred people were dead, including Congressman Ryan. Almost three hundred of them were children. Based on initial media coverage, the potential for tragedy involving Jim Jones and Peoples Temple was evident long before November 18. Who had missed, or, worse, ignored the obvious? Responsibility had to be established, and blame assigned.

"The Guyanese government was determined not to be the villain of this piece," Kit Nascimento recalls. "The American government, the American public and press, took us for easy targets, and this was clearly unfair. We had a public information officer who was overwhelmed, so [Prime Minister] Burnham asked me to take over."

As orchestrated by Nascimento, Guyana's defense was simple. They'd been tricked into accepting an American religious colony that was endorsed by high U.S. officials, including First Lady Rosalynn Carter and Vice President Walter Mondale. Whatever happened at Jonestown, the Port Kaituma airstrip, and Lamaha Gardens in Georgetown was no fault of the Guyanese. An official statement bluntly claimed, "Guyana's involvement was not much greater than if a Hollywood movie team had come here to shoot a picture on some aspect of American life. The actors were American, the plot was American. Guyana was the stage, and the world was the audience." Nascimento was dispatched to the United States, where he appeared on several major television news broadcasts, always declaring that his country was victimized by Jones and Peoples Temple, too. "We suffered a devastating setback in world opinion," he says. "We weren't to know what was going on in the jungle. If Jones was so bad, why didn't his own government do something to stop him before he even got here?"

That was a question that both the U.S. State Department and the FBI wished to deflect. State launched an internal investigation that concluded its embassy personnel had done all that was legally possible. Staff had made regular trips to Jonestown and met with settlers whose families back in America claimed were being held there against their will. None of them indicated they were prisoners or asked to leave. By law, there was nothing else the State Department could do. It had no authority to interfere with an "American religious establishment." U.S. citizens had the right to worship as they pleased, even if that included following a lunatic and living in the jungle. If Jones or any of his followers were committing crimes, that fell under the jurisdiction of the FBI.

The FBI was equally adamant that it was blameless. The agency claimed that its only alert involving the Temple came in June 1978, when the office of U.S. senator S. I. Hayakawa of California passed on a letter from a constituent claiming Americans were held prisoner in Jonestown. After dutifully investigating and determining that "the people involved were adults who allegedly went to Guyana on their own," the FBI turned the information over to the State Department for further action, if any was required.

On May 21, 1979, investigators made their official report to the U.S. House of Representatives Committee on Foreign Affairs. The report found that the U.S. embassy staff in Guyana had been careless and demonstrated lack of common sense. There was considerable misinterpretation of laws regarding religious rights and freedoms, and the State Department in Washington and embassy staff in Guyana did not communicate efficiently about it. State Department personnel were reluctant to challenge Peoples Temple because of the church's "tendency to litigate" and because the Temple was able to muster "massive public pressure" whenever it felt threatened. State was also intimidated by Jones's influence with San Francisco city government. The Guyanese had "looked the other way"; the Temple may have bribed some of its leaders, and there was "probably" an affair between an unidentified Temple representative and a high Guyanese official. But no individual culpability was cited, only collective bad judgment.

The Guyanese issued their own "Confidential: Inventory Analysis of the People's [sic] Temple Agricultural Settlement, Jonestown, North West District," which in a few short paragraphs absolved the Burnham administration of any responsibility, went on for several hundred pages listing everything found in Jonestown, and concluded that Jonestown might still offer benefits to Guyana by becoming a tourist attraction or eventually being turned into a shopping mall.

Both governments agreed that someone had to legally answer for all the deaths, and the most obvious options were Larry Layton and Chuck Beikman; both remained in Guyanese custody. Even here there was disagreement. Guyanese leaders wanted to wash their hands of the entire Jonestown affair by shipping the men back to American courts. But by U.S. law, America had no jurisdiction over any kill-ings committed in Guyana with the exception of the murder of a U.S. congressman. Leo Ryan was dead, but neither Layton nor Beikman killed him on November 18. The assassins who did had all died that same day in Jonestown.

Beikman was present in the bathroom when Sharon Amos killed her children; a Guyanese court sentenced him to five years in prison for his involvement in those deaths. Beikman served his entire sentence and returned to his old home in Indiana, where he died in 2001. But Layton appeared likely to escape punishment altogether. The Guyanese obligingly tried him for murder, and he was acquitted. He'd shot Jonestown defectors at the Port Kaituma airstrip on November 18, but none of them died, and no one claimed that Larry Layton killed Leo Ryan.

But the United States was determined that Layton should pay for some crime. He was extradited to America at the government's request, and charged with conspiring to murder a congressman. Layton swore that he couldn't remember much, and his first trial ended with a hung jury. But he was convicted in a second trial, and though Layton was a cooperative, even model, prisoner eligible for release after five years, he served eighteen before finally being paroled in 2002. Afterward, he moved to Northern California, where he lives in virtual anonymity, avoiding the media. He has only the most occasional, fleeting contact with former Temple members who had known him in Mendocino County, San Francisco, and Jonestown.

There was no smooth reassimilation for anyone who had been part of Peoples Temple. Even those who left prior to Jonestown were considered suspect. Something had to be wrong with anyone who'd even briefly followed Jim Jones. Violent events heightened the perception that Peoples Temple and death were synonymous. On March 13, 1979, Michael Prokes called a press conference at a motel in Modesto, California. He promised reporters that if they attended, they'd get a front-page story, and they did. After handing out a statement defending Jones and Peoples Temple, Prokes retreated to a bathroom and shot himself, leaving behind more pages urging that his death encourage further investigation into Jonestown — then the world would finally learn about the conspiracies that undermined an admirable organization and cause. In February 1980, Temple defectors and co-organizers of Concerned Relatives Elmer and Deanna Mertle, who had changed their names to Al and Jeannie Mills to avoid Temple retaliation, were found murdered in their home. The crime was never solved, but police investigators assured the FBI that there was no indication that any former Temple members or a Temple hit squad were involved.

There were books, too — by *Examiner* reporter Tim Reiterman (written with fellow journalist John Jacobs), the *Washington Post*'s Charles Krause, Debbie Layton, Mark Lane, Jeannie Mills (published before her death), Bonnie Burnham Thielmann, and many more. A few were objective, others sincere but one-sided, and some overtly self-serving. None were blockbuster bestsellers, but collectively they kept the subject of Jim Jones and Peoples Temple before the public, as did several sensationalistic movies. In Indiana, members of the Jones family assiduously avoided the press. Even though they greatly resented print, television, and film depictions of themselves as uneducated and racist, they tried to remain anonymous out of fear that relatives of those who died in Jonestown might retaliate against Jones's kin. In Richmond, the Baldwins did their best to meet with the media and politely explain that Marceline Baldwin Jones was a wonderful person, and that they were as surprised as anyone by what happened in Jonestown.

The survivors straggled back to America and tried to rebuild their lives. Tragic ends awaited some. In Georgetown, Paula Adams had been torn between her loyalty to Jones and her love for Laurence "Bonny" Mann. Immediately following November 18, Adams, along with Stephan Jones, served as primary spokespersons in Georgetown for Peoples Temple. Mann divorced his wife and married Adams. They moved to Washington, D.C. But Mann and Adams separated, and in October 1983 he murdered her and their child, then killed himself.

Suzanne Jones reunited with her brothers after they were finally allowed to leave Guyana and return to California. But she remained resolutely opposed to any further acknowledgment of family ties to Jim Jones or Peoples Temple — after Suzanne remarried and had children, she did not tell them about their family history, and, on the few occasions when Stephan, Jimmy, and Tim cooperated with print or television interviews, she threatened never to speak to them again. Suzanne died of breast cancer in 2006.

Stephan, Jimmy, and Tim Jones did their best to put what had happened in Guyana behind them. It wasn't easy — each had more than his share of personal struggles. But all three eventually built decent lives and remain close. Though Tim Jones now avoids all public comment, Stephan and Jimmy occasionally speak to interviewers. Stephan also contributes occasional essays to the Jonestown Institute website, which has become an almost therapeutic forum for former Temple members, family, and friends to share opinions and memories among themselves and with the public. Formally called "Alternative Considerations of Jonestown and Peoples Temple," the website is maintained by Rebecca Moore, sister of Carolyn Layton and Annie Moore, and her husband, Fielding McGehee. Besides essays, it includes access to information about all aspects of Peoples Temple in the United States and Guyana, detailed timelines, and transcriptions of most of Jim Jones's recorded sermons and addresses as well as Edith Roller's minutely detailed journals of life as a Peoples Temple member.

For years, Moore and McGehee have also served as conduits for out-of-touch or even estranged Temple members to reconnect. Separate from Jonestown Institute gatherings, the remaining Temple "family" — it can be properly described as nothing else — also gathers annually on November 18 for memorial services at Evergreen Cemetery in Oakland. Monuments there mark the mass grave, engraved with the names of all who perished that day in Guyana, including Jim Jones. His inclusion sparked controversy in the press and hard feelings among some survivors and relatives of the deceased, but majority opinion held that all the dead were, in some sense, victims, including Jones, whose delusions, compulsions, or criminality — there's considerable debate which — cost him his life.

These survivors represent the same diversity

of race, background, personality, education, and professional achievement that characterized Peoples Temple at its zenith. Every year there are fewer of them. But the pain and frustration persist. The only ones who understand are themselves, a rainbow family brought together by Jim Jones and bound eternally by shared loss and suffering.

One major source of contention remains, and they debate it among themselves, or with interviewers who they hope might offer some fresh perspective: Was Jim Jones always bad, or was he gradually corrupted by a combination of ambition, drugs, and hubris? There is no definitive answer: Jones was a complicated man who rarely revealed all of his often contradictory dimensions to anyone.

It seems certain that, at some level, Jones truly hated racial and economic inequality. As a teenager he preached against such evils in rough Richmond neighborhoods where he stood to gain nothing by it other than insults and beatings. In Indianapolis, Jones fought, often single-handedly, to bring about integration in a highly segregated city, and to a great extent succeeded. Under Jones's leadership, Peoples Temple acted on the biblical precepts of feeding the hungry and clothing the naked. Temple addiction programs saved lives. Temple scholarship programs educated young men and women whose schooling would otherwise have been limited to the corrupting influence of the streets. In one of the deepest, most dangerous jungles in the world, one thousand Americans, many of them recent big-city ghetto dwellers who had never so much as mowed a lawn, for almost four years built and maintained a farm settlement that came very close to being self-sustaining. Had the events of November 18, 1978, not occurred, Jonestown might have lasted indefinitely. In all the years since, the Guyanese government has made frequent attempts to establish similar farm communities in its forbidding North West District. None have succeeded. Jim Jones was undeniably a man of great gifts, and one who, for much of his life and ministry, achieved admirable results on behalf of the downtrodden.

Yet he was also a demagogue who ultimately betrayed his followers whether he always intended to or not. In every society there are inequities, and in America the most obvious of these affect people of color and the poor. Demagogues recruit by uniting a disenchanted element against an enemy, then promising to use religion or politics or a combination of the two to bring about rightful change. Those as gifted as Jones use actual rather than imagined injustices as their initial lure — the racism and economic disparity in America that Jones cited were, and still are, real — then exaggerate the threat until followers lose any sense of perspective. In

848

Indiana, Jones and Peoples Temple opposed poverty, prejudice, and segregation. In San Francisco, he began warning of American concentration camps for blacks and a coming police state. By the time he and some nine hundred Temple members were in isolated Jonestown, where there were no opposing views to be heard, his warnings escalated to imminent slaughter by U.S. government agents, Guyanese soldiers, and mercenaries — and because they'd been led along in gradual progression, many of his followers believed enough to voluntarily lay down their lives at his command.

Typical, too, was the gradual shifting of Jones's attitude toward his followers. In Indiana, and in the early years in Mendocino County, he retained a protective sense about them: perhaps most were gullible sheep, but he was their shepherd, responsible for their well-being. As the reputation of Peoples Temple and Jones's own influence and ambition grew, that perspective changed. In Jones's mind, the members of Peoples Temple became soldiers, and he was their general. All generals accept that, in war, at least some troops are expendable. Jones believed himself locked in a life-and-death struggle with the U.S. government, the American and Guyanese courts, and the Concerned Relatives members. Rather than submit in any way — by giving up custody of John Victor Stoen, by allowing even a couple dozen out of more than nine hundred settlers to leave Jonestown and his personal control — Jones was willing to die in a final defiant gesture that would have significant impact only if everyone else died with him: soldiers sacrificed for Jim Jones's final victory. On that afternoon in Jonestown, when he told his followers that there was no other way, he believed it. As far as Jones was concerned, if he had come to some place that hope ran out, then so had they.

But there was something unique about Jones and those who chose to follow him. Traditionally, demagogues succeed by appealing to the worst traits in others: Follow me and you'll have more, or, follow me and I'll protect what you already have against those who want to take it away from you.

Jim Jones attracted followers by appealing to the best in their nature, a desire for everyone to share equally. Beyond the very poorest members of society, who were clothed and fed and treated with respect, no one materially benefited from joining and belonging to Peoples Temple. Most members sacrificed personal possessions, from clothing and checking accounts to cars and houses for the privilege of helping others. They gave rather than got. It was never the Temple's agenda to overthrow a government or in any sense force others to live as its members believed they should. Juanell Smart writes, "I do not want people to think we thought we were better than anyone else. Far from it, for all of us had our shortcomings. We just wanted to set an example of how people could live together in real equality and harmony." Then, they hoped, everyone else would be moved to emulate them.

Jack Beam, one of Jones's oldest and most devoted followers, who died with his leader in Jonestown, effectively described Peoples Temple in a poorly spelled but heartfelt affidavit written sometime in 1978: "[Members] believe that service to the Diety can best be expressed by service to ones fellow man, that they must — on a religious-philosophical imperitave — demonstrate goodness rather than just talking about it, and that this demonstration must be an ongoing part of their everyday lives."

These intentions weren't enough. Peoples Temple is considered an example, but not in any positive sense. Kool-Aid rather than equality is what the rest of the world remembers. The survivors are left to console themselves, and even find some pride in the sincerity of their effort. Jim Jones Jr. sighs, smiles, and concludes, "What I'd say about Peoples Temple is, we failed, but damn, we tried."

It's hard to recognize the old Jonestown site now. Once again, it bristles with thick, barbed brush. Within months of the tragedy, Amerindians had carried off almost every useful scrap of material for their own dwellings. In the decades since, the jungle has reasserted itself. All that's left are some bits of the cassava mill; a mounted, rudimentary map of what the settlement looked like; a small white monument honoring the Jonestown dead; and several metal skeletons of trucks and tractors, all of them impaled by the trunks of towering trees that have split apart the vehicles' rusted metal ribs. The road into Jonestown has become overgrown, too, and vehicles can't complete the six-mile trip from Port Kaituma. Those determined to reach the site have to cut the last part of their way in with machetes.

Just as demagogues lead their well-intentioned followers into tragedy, so the jungle inevitably reclaims its own.

ACKNOWLEDGMENTS

I sincerely thank Jim Donovan, my agent, for his patience and support. At Simon & Schuster, I'm grateful to Jon Karp, Leah Johanson, Cary Goldstein, Julia Prosser, Dana Trocker, and Stephen Bedford (and I'll miss Maureen Cole). My researchers were all invaluable; in alphabetical order they are Diana Andro, Anne E. Collier, Jim Fuquay, Andrea Ahles Koos, Marcia Melton, and Sara Tirrito. Carlton Stowers, James Ward Lee, and Doug Swanson read the book in progress; their suggestions made it better. I received tremendous support from Rebecca Moore and Fielding McGehee, founders and operators of the Jonestown Institute website, and from Marie Silva at the California Historical Society in San Francisco. I'm indebted to everyone who was in some way associated with Jim Jones, Peoples Temple, and/or Jonestown and agreed to be interviewed for this book, as well as to those who declined interviews but were helpful in other ways.

Everything I write is always for Nora, Adam, Grant, and Harrison.

Special thanks to Cash.

LIST OF INTERVIEWS

Baldwin, Ronnie
Beach, Janice L.
Black, Linda
Bowman, Joyce Overman
Carter, Tim
Chilcoate, Avelyn
Cox, Bill
Domanick, Joe
Fortson, Hue
Gouveia, Gerald
Grubbs, Richard
Haldeman, Ron
Hargrave, Neva Sly
Hayes, Bob
Hinshaw, Gregory
Horne, Roberta
Jackson, Janet L.
Jackson, Bill
Jones Jr., Jim
Knight, Max
Kohl, Laura Johnston
Lambrev, Garrett

Luther, Jeanne Jones
Madison, James H.
Manning, Bill
McGehee, Fielding
McKee, Dan
McKissick, Larry
Mills, Ernie
Moore, Rebecca
Moore, Rev. John V.
Mutchner, John
Nascimento, Kit
O'Shea, Terri Buford
Rickabaugh, Colleen
Roberts, Desmond
Seay, Scott
Sheeley, Rachel
Smart, Juanell
Stadelmann, Richard
Straley, Kay
Swanson, Alan
Townshend, Bill
Townshend, Ruth
Willmore Zimmerman, Phyllis
Willmore, Chuck
Wise, Lester
Wisener, Monesa
Wright, Jim

NOTES

FBI files regarding the tragic events at Jonestown and Port Kaituma and the history of Peoples Temple begin with the designation RYMUR (for Ryan Murder) followed by the numerals 89-4286. Additional identification numbers and letters for each document, and sometimes for each page of each document, follow. These were recorded by hand. Legibility varies greatly — at least dozens and probably hundreds of different individuals made these notations.

Additionally, many of the files supplied by the FBI in response to Freedom of Information Act requests were faded with age, marred by wide, erratic mark-outs redacting some material, or otherwise damaged to the point where some of their identifying codes could not be read or else were missing in part or altogether. Every RYMUR file cited includes as much of its identification code as possible. I hope this doesn't frustrate readers too much; it certainly frustrated me and my researchers.

One former Peoples Temple member would agree to be interviewed only if his/her identity was protected. Because this individual had crucial information to offer, I agreed.

Prologue

Most of the material comes from interviews with Desmond Roberts, Gerald Gouveia (the army pilot who flew the first rescue plane into Port Kaituma on the morning of November 19, 1978), and Kit Nascimento, then serving as a minister under Prime Minister Forbes Burnham. Details of Burnham's November 18 evening meeting with U.S. ambassador John Burke were found in a telex report sent by the ambassador to the State Department in Washington, D.C., immediately afterward. The report was declassified by the U.S. government in 2014.

The Cessna airplane at Port Kaituma has been variously described as seating five or six. On the afternoon of November 18, it didn't matter — only three people were onboard during its flight from Port Kaituma to Georgetown. According to Tim Reiterman in *Raven,* the third person was Jonestown defector Monica Bagby, who was wounded in the attack at the Port Kaituma airstrip. (Tim Reiterman, *Raven: The Untold Story of the Rev. Jim Jones and His People* [New York: Tarcher Perigee, 2008; originally published by Dutton Adult, 1982], p. 535).

One: Lynetta and Jim

In most cases it's impossible to be certain what someone was feeling — frustration, jealousy, resentment. But Lynetta often wrote and spoke about her childhood and life in Crete and Lynn. She exaggerated her accomplishments and very much enjoyed describing tribulation at the hands of supposed enemies, but in describing her own day-to-day emotions she could be and usually was quite explicit.

Copies of records regarding James Thurman Jones's breakdown and subsequent hospitalization were provided to me by Indiana historian Joyce Overman Bowman. She found these records through the Ohio Historical Society, recently renamed the Ohio History Connection.

In several instances, information from FBI RYMUR investigation files has been transcribed by Fielding McGehee III and posted on the Jonestown Institute's "Alternative Considerations of Jonestown & Peoples Temple" website, http://jonestown.sdsu.edu/. It will be easier for most readers to refer to the Jonestown Institute site than to request files from the FBI through the Freedom of Information Act, so in these cases I'll cite the Jonestown Institute source.

Lynetta described her childhood self: "Lynetta Jones Interviews 1 & 2," Jonestown Institute.

Lynetta was sustained in these hard times: Rebecca Moore, Anthony B. Pinn, Mary R. Sawyer, eds., *Peoples Temple and Black Religion in America* (Bloomington: Indiana University Press, 2004), pp. 123–24.

Typically, Lynetta later bragged: "Lynetta Jones Interviews 1 & 2," Jonestown Institute.

Lynetta was treated, probably for tuberculosis: Joyce Overman Bowman interview.

Sometime in 1926, Lynetta believed that she'd found him: In her Jonestown reminiscences, Lynetta claimed she'd "known [Jim] for a long time," and that she called off engagements to him "about eight times" before they finally married. Given her two marriages in the preceding six years, it seems more likely they married soon after meeting. ("Lynetta Jones Interviews 1 & 2," Jonestown Institute.)

John Henry Jones was prominent: Jeanne Jones Luther interview.

Their father expected them: Ibid.

As a disabled veteran: On July 12, 1973, a fire destroyed much of the military's National Personnel Records Center in St. Louis where most World War I military records were stored. These records were not kept in duplicate and were not copied on microfilm. An estimated 80 percent were lost in the fire, apparently including the files on James Thurman Jones. This makes it impossible to learn details of where and when he was caught in a German gas attack, the treatment he received immediately after that, and the specific amount of the disability pension he was awarded. The $30 suggested here is an estimate based on information provided by the army.

There were corn and soybeans to plant and tend: Roberta Horne interview.

Four times a day, trains passed through: Ibid.

this made Crete not a village but a "stop place": Monesa Wisener interview.

They called it "living smart": Linda Black interview.

Lynetta, who defied local custom for women by smoking in public: Larry McKissick interview.

"much more lucrative ways": RYMUR 89-4286-FF-1-71 and 72.

She would have been glad to escape: Ibid.

most of her in-laws admired her spunk: Jeanne Jones Luther interview.

she would weave a tale of becoming ill: RYMUR 89-4286-EE-1-L-100.

Jim snapped from the stress: Joyce Overman Bowman interview.

In her tale, she refused to leave: RYMUR 89-4286-FF-1-72.

His father and brothers would assume: Jeanne Jones Luther interview.

But once the child started school: Ibid.

Two: Lynn

Lynn existed to serve the needs: Bob Hayes, Joyce Overman Bowman, and Bill Townshend interviews.

There was a comforting sense of shared schedules: Roberta Horne and Bill Cox interviews.

There were no rivalries between preachers: Bill Townshend and Richard Grubbs interviews.

Men in Lynn had social clubs: Bill Townshend interview.

The power base of the Klan had drifted north: James H. Madison, *A Lynching in the Heartland: Race and Memory in America* (New York: Palgrave Macmillan, 2001), pp. 38–39; Leonard J. Moore, *Citizen Klansmen: The Ku Klux Klan in Indiana, 1921–1928* (Chapel Hill: University of North Carolina Press, 1997), pp. 17, 27, 58, 81; James H. Madison, Gregory Hinshaw, and Kay Straley interviews.

Lynn's public school stood out: Gregory Hinshaw, Monesa Wisener, Jeanne Jones Luther, Bill Cox, and Richard Grubbs interviews.

The Depression brought about one major change: Bill Townshend interview.

Some part-time work was found for him: Bob

Hayes interview.

The Grant Street house was minimally furnished: Bill Townshend interview.

It was particularly galling: Jeanne Jones Luther interview.

Jim's health continued to fail: Jeanne Jones Luther and Joyce Overman Bowman interviews.

his respiratory problems weren't helped: Bill Cox and Bill Manning interviews.

Town children liked Jim: Bob Hayes interview.

Up close, his appearance was startling: Chuck Willmore interview.

she made a spectacle of herself by smoking: Linda Black and Monesa Wisener interviews.

But there was one thing about Jim and Lynetta Jones: Bill Townshend, James H. Madison, and Jeanne Jones Luther interviews.

"[My husband's family felt]": RYMUR 89-4286-FF-7-e-1 and 2.

Old Jim mostly filled his time: Roberta Horne, Rachel Sheeley, Chuck Willmore, and Bill Manning interviews.

Three: Jimmy

One weekend morning, twelve-year-old Max Knight: Max Knight interview.

There was nothing unusual about this: Joyce Overman Bowman interview.

Jimmy still had plenty of adults: Jeanne Jones

Luther interview.

Lynetta had a rule: Chuck Willmore interview.

The little waif's plight seemed obvious: Joyce Overman Bowman interview.

Myrtle was a scarecrow of a woman: Bill Manning interview.

Over the next few years, he joined them all: Bill Townshend interview.

Jimmy somehow managed to retain: Bill Manning interview.

Jim Jones sat down and scribbled a note to Myrtle Kennedy: Ibid.

In September 1977, Jim Jones would claim: RYMUR 89-4286-O-1-B-1.

by Jones's own later admission: RYMUR 89-4286-O-1-B-7.

Once he knocked on the door: Max Knight interview.

Four: Growing Up

This was typical throughout Indiana: James H. Madison, *The Indiana Way* (Bloomington: Indiana University Press, 2000), pg. xiii; James H. Madison interview.

He ran the streets like everybody else: Jeanne Jones Luther interview.

Jimmy sneaked them into the house: Chuck Willmore interview.

The only time anyone ever saw them interacting: Ibid.

candy bars, rare and prized treats: Bob Hayes

864

and Jeanne Luther Jones interviews.

One day he and the Willmore brothers: Chuck Willmore interview.

Jimmy led a contingent of kids: Jeanne Jones Luther interview.

Instead of flying, he hit the ground hard: Chuck Willmore interview.

Around the same time: Bill Townshend, Bill Cox, Bob Hayes, and Jeanne Jones Luther interviews.

he was fascinated with the Nazis: Jeanne Jones Luther interview. As an adult, Jones claimed he most admired the Russians during World War II, and that admiration in part led to his belief in socialism. But his cousin Jeanne remembers him whipping her across the calves when she didn't goose-step properly.

Jimmy and Lester became summer pals: Lester Wise interview.

He offered explicit facts-of-life lectures: John Mutchner interview.

there was a new rumor: Kay Straley, Max Knight, and Chuck Willmore interviews.

It was better for Old Jim to be thought of: Linda Black interview.

Jimmy started dressing differently: Bill Manning, Joyce Overman Bowman, and Richard Grubbs interviews.

Jimmy developed the odd habit: Monesa Wisener interview.

he was not considered an exceptional student: Bill Townshend and Bob Hayes interviews.

fourteen-year-old Jimmy Jones not only formed: John Mutchner and Bill Cox interviews.

she took another Lynn man as her lover: Jeanne Jones Luther interview. I asked several other older Lynn residents about Lynetta's affair. Two reluctantly admitted that they might have heard about it, but would not share specifics or allow themselves to be quoted. Even Jeanne Luther told me, "I know the man's name but I'm not going to tell it to you, because I think he still has family around here and I don't want to hurt them." In *Raven,* Tim Reiterman identifies Lynetta's lover as Shorty Beverly.

One day Jimmy attached himself to Sara Lou: Richard Grubbs interview. I would have very much liked to ask Sara Lou herself about Jim Jones, but she long ago died in childbirth.

a new faith came to Lynn: Joyce Overman Bowman, Bill Townshend, Linda Black, Roberta Horne, and Bob Hayes interviews.

She later described a dramatic scene: RY-MUR 89-4286-BB-1B-Z-12.

there were three black enclaves: Monesa Wisener and Gregory Hinshaw interviews.

Jimmy would find someplace to stand: Rachel Sheeley interview. While many people in Lynn are willing to talk openly and in great detail about Jim Jones, there's considerable reluctance to acknowledge him among those who knew (or, at least, knew of) Jones in Richmond. A few older Richmond residents cautiously acknowledged that, as children, they heard something about teenage Jim preaching to indigent African Americans, but no one would say much more.

He took to ostentatiously carrying a Bible: Bill Cox interview.

Jimmy was asked to conduct a mock funeral: Phyllis Willmore Zimmerman interview.

Five: Richmond

when he moved away: Lynetta's boyfriend supposedly moved to Richmond before she and Jimmy did, so it's possible, even likely, that in the summer of 1948 she chose to follow him there in an attempt to keep the relationship going. If that was her intention, she apparently failed. Reiterman, *Raven,* p. 26.

Recently, he'd started hinting: Max Knight interview.

Lynn had a hotel: Joyce Overman Bowman interview.

His enduring love for Lynetta: James T. Jones's grave can be visited in Mount Zion Cemetery just outside Winchester in Randolph County. Although both of their names are on the headstone, Lynetta is not buried there with him.

One girl was greatly offended: Janice L. Beach interview.

But Jimmy made a few friends: Richard Stadelmann interview.

Though she would later claim to be a senior employee: Space does not permit listing and contradicting every one of Lynetta's exaggerated claims about her life. After this, I will only mention the most critical ones.

Reid management noticed: Max Knight's late wife was a Reid Hospital supervisor, and gave Max glowing reports about his young friend's fine performance as an orderly there.

discussed it with a former girlfriend: Phyllis Willmore Zimmerman interview.

Six: Marceline

For general information about the history of Richmond, readers are referred to *Richmond: A Pictorial History* by Gertrude Luckhardt Ward (St. Louis: G. Bradley Publishing, 1994). It's a nice town with friendly people. Unlike in Lynn, however, very few residents acknowledge Jim Jones ever lived there. They consider him a blight on their town.

Walter was a fine Christian man: Janet L. Jackson interview.

neighbors remember its front yard: Ruth Townshend interview.

and believed that the Lord sometimes sent her

messages: Bill Jackson interview. Bill, who married Charlotte's granddaughter Janet, eventually gave up a successful career in banking to embark on his own ministry. Charlotte Baldwin told him that she dreamed he would do this.

One of Charlotte's edicts: Janet L. Jackson interview.

Marceline once shocked them: RYMUR 89-4286-FF-1-95-c.

She had a sweet singing voice: Janice L. Beach interview.

Marceline's faith was never negative: Avelyn Chilcoate interview.

Marceline showed little interest: Janice L. Beach and Avelyn Chilcoate interviews.

Even as a little girl: Avelyn Chilcoate interview.

"[Marceline] wanted a bigger adventure": Ibid.

"She said she'd met a boy": Ibid.

Seven: Jim and Marceline

Much of the information comes from a lengthy interview with Ronnie Baldwin, the cousin of Marceline Jones who as a boy lived with her and Jim in Indianapolis for fifteen months.

Richmond Arquette, a member of the famous show business family, is developing a documentary film focusing mostly on surviving former members of Peoples Temple. After we learned how to contact Ronnie from sources in Indiana, Richmond and I agreed it might be intimidating for him to talk at the same time to people pursuing complementary but separate projects. Accordingly, I provided Richmond with a set of questions and he interviewed Ronnie. Afterward, with Ronnie's consent, Richmond shared the interview transcript with me.

One night in late 1948: RYMUR 89-4286-BB-1B-Z-63.

"Marceline was always very smart": Janice L. Beach interview.

He'd once been a highly touted basketball star: RYMUR 89-4286-BB-1B-Z-63.

Astonished to discover that he expected them: Reiterman, *Raven,* p. 33.

His first semester grades: California Historical Society, MS 4126, Box 3, Folder 12.

As he recalled it: RYMUR 89-4286-O-I-B-4.

Marceline's version was less vulgar: RYMUR 89-4286-FF-1-95b.

Another time, Jim and Marceline argued: RYMUR 89-4286-O-I-B-4.

"He took an awful lot of the starch out of me": RYMUR 89-4286-FF-I-95a.

Avelyn thought Charlotte's advice was selfish: Avelyn Chilcoate interview.

Years later when Marceline's youngest sister, Sharon, divorced: Janet L. Jackson interview.

Another of Marceline's relations also appealed to Jim: Ronnie Baldwin interview.

Jim began attending these meetings: Ibid.

The faith's governing body adopted a new, formal social creed: Rebecca Moore, *Understanding Jonestown and Peoples Temple* (Westport, CT: Praeger, 2009), p. 12.

Methodist leaders had always encouraged social activism: Scott Seay interview.

he took Marceline and Ronnie to black churches: Ronnie Baldwin interview.

In the summer of 1952: Moore, *Understanding Jonestown and Peoples Temple,* p. 12; Reiterman, *Raven,* p. 41.

Eight: Beginnings

Reporter William B. Treml gushed: "Mom's Help for Ragged Tramp Leads Son to Dedicate His Life to Others," *Richmond Palladium-Item,* March 15, 1953.

Ronnie Baldwin had lived: Ronnie Baldwin interview.

He recalled thinking: RYMUR 89-4286-O-1-B-8. All of Jones's reminiscences included in Chapter 8 are drawn from this document and RYMUR 89-4286-O-1-B-9.

So was Marceline, who said: RYMUR 89-4286-BB-18-Z-64.

A quarter century later: RYMUR 89-4286-1304-67c.

Nine: A Church Where You Get Something Now

Much of the information in this chapter comes from my interview with Ron Haldeman, who now lives in a retirement home in Indianapolis.

Jones exclaimed at the coincidence: Right up to the time of our interview, Ron Haldeman believed what Jim Jones told him about being a devout Quaker for his entire life. It says a lot about Jim Jones's personal charm that when I told Haldeman this wasn't true, he laughed and said, "Well, I guess I'm not surprised. That's like him, to let me think what I wanted, help me get the wrong idea, to make me want to help him. Jimmy, well, that was him. He sure convinced me."

Eventually, blacks comprised more than 10 percent: Richard B. Pierce, *Polite Protest: The Political Economy of Race in Indianapolis, 1920–1970* (Bloomington: Indiana University Press, 2005), p. 11.

The school district sent black teenagers to Crispus Attucks: Randy Roberts, *But They Can't Beat Us: Oscar Robertson and the Crispus Attucks Tigers* (Indianapolis: Indiana Historical Society/Champaign, IL: Sports Publishing, 1999), p. 39.

who in 1943 were instrumental in forming the Indianapolis Citizens Council: Emma Lou

Thornbrough, *Indiana Blacks in the Twenti-eth Century,* ed. Lana Ruegamar (Blooming-ton: Indiana University Press, 2000), pp. 112–13.

he decided to visit Community Unity: Ron Haldeman interview. After so many years, Reverend Haldeman could not recall the specific complaint and resulting letter at this first Community Unity service he at-tended. He offered the example of the old black woman and the electric company as one such incident, though it might have oc-curred during one of his later visits.

Marceline was pleased with Community Unity's early success: Ibid. Haldeman and his first wife became close friends with Jim and Marceline Jones.

So Jones worked, too: Reiterman, *Raven,* p. 46; Avelyn Chilcoate and John Mutchner interviews.

But Jones wanted much more: Ron Haldeman interview.

Ten: Peoples Temple

he was careful not to ask too much: Ron Haldeman interview.

Marceline described the scene: Denise Ste-phenson, *Dear People: Remembering Jones-town* (Berkeley: Heyday Books, 2005), pp. 10–11.

Jones was frustrated: RYMUR 89-4286-O-1-B-9.

Jones asked Haldeman for a favor: Ron Haldeman interview.

There were tax considerations, too: Scott Seay interview.

He told Marceline that real social change: RYMUR 89-4286-FF-1-95d.

She stopped mentioning: Avelyn Chilcoate interview.

He was an instant success: Moore, *Understanding Jonestown and Peoples Temple,* pp. 12–15; Rebecca Moore interview.

Joe and Clara Phillips, a white husband and wife: Garrett Lambrev, "Joe Phillips: A Reflection," *Jonestown Report* 15 (November 2013), last modified March 20, 2014. Garrett was known as Garry to Peoples Temple members so that is the name I used in the book.

A strict protocol was observed: Juanell Smart and Jim Jones Jr. interviews. I discussed Jones's healings with dozens of people, most of them former members of Peoples Temple who'd witnessed them in person. Juanell Smart was married to David Wise, who for some time served Jones as an assistant pastor and one of his chief accomplices in using chicken guts for faked cancer healings. Wise explained the whole process to Juanell, who many years later described it to me. Jim Jones Jr. confirmed

the use of chicken guts and added an amusing story, which appears in a later chapter.
But a few surviving eyewitnesses: Garrett Lambrev interview.
Jones promised he would raise the money: RYMUR 89-4286-O-1-B-9.
the word "Temple" was carved in stone outside the building: Ron Haldeman interview.

Eleven: Gaining Influence

she had the critical background and skills: Ron Haldeman interview.
Jim Jones of Peoples Temple received much of the credit: Ibid.
the Joneses' own home was renovated: Moore, *Understanding Jonestown and Peoples Temple,* p. 17.
Inspectors from the Marion County Welfare Department made regular visits: Scott Seay interview.
One who came away impressed after hearing Jones: Reiterman, *Raven,* pp. 50–53.
He noticed some weaknesses, too: Jim Jones Jr. interview.
the church opened a café: Moore, *Understanding Jonestown and Peoples Temple,* p. 17.
On its first day of operation: RYMUR 89-4286-BB-1B-Z-77.
When they screamed for "Here Comes Peter Cottontail": RYMUR 89-4286-FF-I-95d.
For some parents: Juanell Smart interview.

"God is here on earth today": Jill Watts, *God, Harlem U.S.A.: The Father Divine Story* (Berkeley: University of California Press, 1992), p. 48.

Twelve: Father Divine
Though I studied dozens of articles and books and conducted several interviews about Father Divine, as I wrote this chapter I kept coming back to two sources. *Peoples Temple and Black Religion in America,* edited by Rebecca Moore, Anthony B. Pinn, and Mary R. Sawyer (Bloomington: Indiana University Press, 2004), was essential not only in helping me understand the parallels between Father Divine's Peace Movement and Peoples Temple, but also certain elements of African American religion that informed Jim Jones's ministry far beyond what he cherry-picked from Father Divine.

Information gleaned from *God, Harlem U.S.A.: The Father Divine Story* by Jill Watts (Berkeley: University of California Press, 1992) can be found in virtually every paragraph of this chapter. Specific references include pp. 1–5, 30, 31, 86, 105, 107–12, 113, 119, 125, 137, 153–59, 160–66, and 167–71. If, as I did, you find Father Divine fascinating, then I urge you to read Jill Watts's book.

Jones's visit extended for an entire day: Ron

Haldeman interview.

It was the first of many: Ibid.

Max Knight, who'd become a reporter for Richmond's daily newspaper: Max Knight interview.

The key, Jones believed: Ron Haldeman interview.

Jones published and distributed: California Historical Society, MS 4124, Box 1, Folder 10. This pamphlet was thirty-two pages long. The last time Father Divine is mentioned is on page 27. Jones never wanted his followers to forget who their actual leader was.

Thirteen: "All Races Together"

Brown v. Board of Education *was understood:* David Halberstam, *The Fifties* (New York: Ballantine, 1994), pp. 428–41. This book is a masterful example of telling the essential stories of a decade in immensely readable form.

Black folks around the city took notice: Reiterman, *Raven,* p. 54.

It was a unique combination: Moore, Pinn, and Sawyer, eds., *Peoples Temple and Black Religion in America,* p. 152.

"His message was always very stark": RYMUR 89-4286-HH-6-A-2.

Their furniture was a hodgepodge: Ron Haldeman interview.

A slumber party for the Temple kids: RYMUR 89-4286-FF-1-95-e.

Agnes had not proven to be the ideal child: Jim Jones Jr. interview.

It was Marceline who first proposed: Ron Haldeman interview.

in May 1959 there was a weekend outing to the zoo: Jim Jones Jr. interview.

it happened on the night that little Stephanie died: Ibid.

Case heard about Jim Jones: Reiterman, *Raven,* pp. 66–68.

To leadership in the Disciples denomination: Scott Seay interview. Historically, there are several branches of the Disciples of Christ; of these, the "Christian Church" is the most liberal, and the most attractive to and attracted by Jim Jones. I simply use "Disciples" or "Disciples of Christ."

Best of all, from Jones's perspective: Ibid.

The position was considered so nonprestigious: Moore, *Understanding Jonestown and Peoples Temple,* p. 17; Reiterman, *Raven,* pp. 68–69.

Fourteen: A Man to Be Reckoned With

blue-collar whites in Indianapolis enjoyed relative comforts: David Halberstam, *War in a Time of Peace: Bush, Clinton, and the Generals* (New York: Scribner, 2002), p. 105.

Many believed that communists orchestrated:

878

In Los Angeles, police officers attended mandatory seminars where lecturers insisted that this was true. Jeff Guinn, *Manson: The Life and Times of Charles Manson* (New York: Simon & Schuster, 2014), p. 114.

When Robert Welch founded the ultraconservative: Rick Perlstein, *Before the Storm: Barry Goldwater and the Unmaking of the American Consensus* (New York: Nation Books, 2009), pp. 114–19.

the Indiana General Assembly passed legislation: Madison, *A Lynching in the Heartland,* p. 245.

Jones thought it was more important: Ron Haldeman interview.

Jones was offered a job at $25,000 a year: RYMUR 89-4286-BB-1B-Z-68; FBI Tape Q 775.

Jones received 55 percent of all collections taken: RYMUR 89-4286-A-36-c-12.

Through Peoples Temple he formed an employment service: Ron Haldeman interview.

Jones called on them there: Reiterman, *Raven,* p. 66. Reiterman writes that Jones failed to impress the Muslims when he explained he had adopted a black child.

Jones wrote to the party leadership: California Historical Society, MS 4126, Box 3, Folder 12.

Marceline used chewing gum as bribes: Jim

Jones Jr. interview.

Jones even used personal illness: RYMUR 89-4286-EE-1-I&J-73.

Fifteen: Breakdown

Jim Jones met his childhood friend: Max Knight interview.

Sometimes he'd ask Ron Haldeman: Ron Haldeman interview.

When Jones absolutely had to be away on a Sunday: Ibid.

Jones held regular "corrective fellowship" sessions: Moore, *Understanding Jonestown and Peoples Temple,* p. 32.

In an undated, handwritten letter to Earl Jackson: RYMUR 89-4286-1099.

For Jones, the Disciples of Christ had two specific attractions: Scott Seay interview.

Observers from the Disciples regional office attended some Sunday services: Ron Haldeman interview.

Peoples Temple routinely misrepresented: I was allowed to study copies of the Disciples annual reports at the denomination's seminary in Indianapolis. The falsifications are blatant.

he began incrementally revealing the considerable divide: Lambrev, "Joe Phillips: A Reflection."

In 1961, many Americans lived in fear: Before his death in 2015, I conducted several interviews for this book with former U.S. speaker of the house Jim Wright. Speaker Wright spoke at length about "bomb paranoia" in America during the 1950s and 1960s.

After his election in November 1960: Richard Norton Smith, *On His Own Terms: A Life of Nelson Rockefeller* (New York: Random House, 2014), p. 363.

Kennedy said Americans should be prepared: Perlstein, *Before the Storm,* pp. 142–43.

Jones offered details: Garrett Lambrev interview; Lambrev, "Joe Phillips."

His only previous foreign trip had been to Cuba: Moore, *Understanding Jonestown and Peoples Temple,* p. 18.

Now he visited British Guiana: Reiterman, *Raven,* p. 77.

Jones applied for an unspecified job: California Historical Society, MS 4126, Box 3, Folder 12.

"Now a shift has come about": Caroline Bird, "9 Places in the World to Hide," *Esquire,* January 1962.

Sixteen: Brazil

Jones's journey began inauspiciously: Garrett Lambrev interview; Reiterman, *Raven,* p. 78.

Sensing her dejection: Stephenson, *Dear People,* p. 59.

the Joneses rented a sparsely furnished: Bonnie Thielmann with Dean Merrill, *The Broken God* (Colorado Springs: David C. Cook, 1979), p. 23. Thielmann's memoir provides the best record of Jim Jones's sojourn in Brazil.

It was in a Belo Horizonte post office: Ibid., pp. 19–22, 24–25, 27.

People were leaving: Moore, *Understanding Jonestown and Peoples Temple,* p. 19; Rebecca Moore interview.

Their family dinners were spare: Thielmann, *The Broken God,* p. 25.

For a while, Jack and Rheaviana Beam: Moore, *Understanding Jonestown and Peoples Temple,* p. 19; Reiterman, *Raven,* pp. 82–83.

In May 1963 Ed Malmin wrote: RYMUR 89-4286-FF-1-66.

As Jones told the story to his followers: RYMUR 89-4286-O-1-B-12 through 18.

Ed Malmin provided a solution: Thielmann, *The Broken God,* pp. 34–35.

he suspected Ijames and Case: Ron Haldeman interview.

Seventeen: Looking West

Malmin found himself reduced: Reiterman, *Raven,* pp. 86–87.

state and local government had taken huge strides: James H. Madison interview;

Thornbrough, *Indiana Blacks in the Twentieth Century,* pp. 169–70.

But such things would never happen there: Scott Seay and Juanell Smart interviews.

Jones had to move the Temple: Moore, *Understanding Jonestown and Peoples Temple,* p. 19.

WIBC removed him from the airwaves: RYMUR 89-4286-FF-I-95a.

"The mind that was in Christ Jesus": Edith Roller Journal, 7/7/75, Jonestown Institute.

Ross Case and Archie Ijames especially: Reiterman, *Raven,* p. 93.

Jones sent scouts ahead: Ibid., p. 92.

a Disciples vetting process followed: Scott Seay interview.

the Disciples wanted Jones confirmed as a candidate: Ibid.

Temple congregants were offered coffee and donuts: Ron Haldeman interview.

Everyone loved San Francisco: Jim Jones Jr. interview.

A propitious meeting in the restaurant: Lambrev, "Joe Phillips"; RYMUR 89-4286-FF-I-96a through c.

Ross Case was deeply troubled: Reiterman, *Raven,* pp. 98–99.

Jones's overriding means of persuasion: Ibid., pp. 94–95.

Jones preached a final Peoples Temple service: Ron Haldeman interview.

It was a jolly journey: Jim Jones Jr. interview.

A place that didn't want them: Alan Swanson and Garrett Lambrev interviews.

Eighteen: Redneck Valley

Marceline Jones stunned a local banker: "Messiah from the Midwest," *Time,* December 4, 1978.

Jones filed articles of incorporation: RYMUR 89-4286-A-31-a-5b, 5c, and 5d; RYMUR 89-4286-A-32-A.

Within days of his staff's first inquiries: Dan McKee interview via email.

Temple members soon nicknamed their new home: Alan Swanson interview.

Later, some former Temple members decided: Teri Buford O'Shea interview. Later in life, she changed the spelling of her name from "Terri" to "Teri." When I had several conversations with her in 2015, she was "Teri." This accounts for the difference in spelling between the text and chapter notes.

"a level of planning and forethought": Stephan Jones, Griot Institute, Bucknell University, April 10, 2013.

Temple members were assigned writing duties: Alan Swanson interview.

"for the gracious letter to my husband": California Historical Society, MS 3800, Box 2, Folder 38.

"It's hard to admit, but my father": Colleen Rickabaugh interview.

Nineteen: Dead End

Lambrev also had a wide spiritual streak: Garry Lambrev interview.

The Jones family, out for a weekend drive: Jim Jones Jr. interview.

Jones also recruited: Stephenson, *Dear People,* p. 21; Garry Lambrev, "A Peoples Temple Survivor Remembers," *Jonestown Report* 8 (November 2006), last modified March 6, 2014, Jonestown Institute; and Garry Lambrev, "Questions That Remain," *Jonestown Report* 5 (August 2003), last modified March 14, 2014, Jonestown Institute.

Jones announced that the church would stage: Garry Lambrev interview.

In August 1966, he announced: Ibid.

In October, Jones interrupted: RYMUR 89-4286-1-I&J-2; Lambrev, "Joe Phillips"; Garry Lambrev interview.

Another disagreement in 1968: RYMUR 89-4286-1-96a.

Members became accustomed: Alan Swanson and Jim Jones Jr. interviews.

Judge Robert Winslow finished last: Robert L. Winslow went on to a distinguished career in private legal practice. In his most famous case, he successfully represented Doris Day in a fraud and malpractice suit that won the actress a $22.8 million settlement. Winslow died in 1996.

Twenty: Resurrection

A colorful car caravan made the one-hundred-mile trip south: Garry Lambrev interview.

Jones instructed these followers: Alan Swanson interview.

A bus chugged into the fairgrounds parking lot: Garry Lambrev interview.

For those in the city's black churches: David Talbot, *Season of the Witch: Enchantment, Terror, and Deliverance in the City of Love* (New York: Free Press, 2012), p. 277.

congregants included county social service employees: Laura Johnston Kohl and Teri Buford O'Shea interviews.

This was the egalitarian, interracial culture that they'd yearned for: Garry Lambrev interview.

One day Jimmy Jr. came home looking puzzled: Jim Jones Jr. interview.

" 'Niggardly' means to be treated cheatedly": Tape Q 612, Jonestown Institute.

Now in California, he went to all that he could: Scott Seay interview.

Those that came enjoyed a carefully orchestrated reception: There are many descriptions of how Temple members welcomed visitors in Redwood Valley. I found the best

886

to be pp. 114–29 in *Six Years with God: Life Inside Rev. Jim Jones's Peoples Temple* (New York: A&W Publishers, 1979) by Jeanne Mills, whose name when she joined the Temple was Deanna Mertle.

Few realized that the chatty Temple members visiting with them: Laura Johnston Kohl and Tim Carter interviews. Both joined Peoples Temple after 1969, but the methods of gleaning information from visitors for use by Jones remained essentially the same.

Garry Lambrev had joined Peoples Temple: Garry Lambrev interview.

Twenty-One: Carolyn

"One time when she and Stephan were visiting": Janet L. Jackson interview.

"All of Marceline's family felt like": Avelyn Chilcoate interview.

There was one hiccup: Janice L. Beach interview. Marceline confided this only to her mother, but Charlotte Baldwin mentioned it to a few others, including Marceline's longtime friend Janice.

Her new, crucial Temple role: Garry Lambrev and Alan Swanson interviews.

Jones decreed in a handwritten document: RY-MUR 89-4286-1099.

Agnes wanted to please her parents: Laura Johnston Kohl and Jim Jones Jr. interviews.

Suzanne, who in 1969 was seventeen: Jim

Jones Jr. interview.

Stephan was crown prince: Juanell Smart and Fielding McGehee interviews.

Carolyn announced to her parents: John V. Moore interview.

The Laytons attended several different services: Fielding McGehee and Rebecca Moore interviews.

Then, to her parents' horror: John V. Moore and Rebecca Moore interviews.

The Moores decided not to criticize: John V. Moore interview.

Patty Cartmell took Carolyn aside: This was told to me by a former Temple member who witnessed the Patty Cartmell–Carolyn Layton conversation, and who insisted on not being identified.

Jones, always open with youngsters: Jim Jones Jr. interview; Stephan Jones, "Like Father, Like Son," *Jonestown Report 5* (August 2003), last modified March 14, 2014, Jonestown Institute.

Marceline wrote a note to Jones: Stephenson, *Dear People,* pp. 59–60.

Twenty-Two: A Socialist Example

Peoples Temple socialism was intended: Neva Sly Hargrave and Laura Johnston Kohl interviews.

For many blacks and whites, attending Temple services: Garry Lambrev interview.

When Elmer and Deanna Mertle joined the Temple: Mills, *Six Years with God,* pp. 131–33.

everyone was addressed in some personal way: Laura Johnston Kohl and Hue Fortson interviews; Neva Sly Hargrave, "A Story of Deprogramming," *Jonestown Report 6* (October 2010), last modified March 8, 2014, Jonestown Institute.

After Jones fetched some strays out of a busy Ukiah street: Ukiah Daily Journal, October 27, 1975.

The Temple process for breaking addiction: Neva Sly Hargrave interview.

But in a handwritten document: RYMUR 89-4286-QQ-2-H-1 through 4.

He found him: When I contacted Tim Stoen to request an interview for this book, he politely but firmly declined, citing a personal policy of not commenting on Peoples Temple that had been in effect for ten years. There are ample public documents and FBI files that describe many of Stoen's actions, and other surviving Temple members offered me their memories and opinions of him. Several previous books about Jim Jones and Peoples Temple, especially Tim Reiterman's *Raven* and *Awake in a Nightmare: Jonestown, the Only Eyewitness Account* (New York: W. W. Norton, 1981) by Ethan Feinsod, devote considerable space to Stoen. But I always prefer an individual's own words. In 2003 Stoen had granted a lengthy interview to Hank Sims of the *North Coast Journal,* and I gleaned considerable information from Sims's "Standing in the Shadows of Jonestown," which was published in *North Coast*'s September 2003 issue.

Then in December 2015, Stoen self-published *Marked for Death: My War with Jim Jones the Devil of Jonestown* (Charleston: CreateSpace, 2015). Though all memoirs are to some extent self-serving (we inevitably remember some critical things in ways that present us in the best light), *Marked for Death* is of great value to anyone who wants to understand the intricacies of Peoples Temple. I still wish Tim Stoen had talked to me, but I'm grateful that in *Marked for Death* he tells his story from his own perspective, frequently supplying specific dates that have been missing in previous Temple chronicles and church records. In particular, Stoen's description of his first contact with Peoples Temple is invaluable.

One Sunday in September: Stoen, *Marked for Death,* pp. 62–68.

But it was different between Jones and Stoen: Jim Jones Jr., Garry Lambrev, Laura Johnston Kohl, and Tim Carter interviews.

what other Temple members didn't realize:

Stoen, *Marked for Death,* pp. 24, 117.

Stoen had concluded that God was too slow: Ibid., p. 59.

Grace Grech was much younger: Reiterman, *Raven,* pp. 106–13.

Soon afterward, she shocked her husband: Stoen, *Marked for Death,* p. 81.

Grace felt overwhelmed: Rebecca Moore and Laura Johnston Kohl interviews.

Seven years later, when they had become enemies: RYMUR 89-4286-FF-2-17-A and B.

Twenty-Three: Money

Ten percent of personal income: Laura Johnston Kohl, Tim Carter, Garry Lambrev, and Alan Swanson interviews.

A running joke among the members: Laura Johnston Kohl interview.

a document was eventually circulated: RYMUR 89-4286-X-3-f-38.

The resulting inventory of donated property: Garry Lambrev and Alan Swanson interviews.

$15,000 was a typical sum: RYMUR 89-4286-B-4-a-54 through 61.

One of these, besides touting Jones's appearance: San Francisco Chronicle, September 21, 1968.

For the first time, Jones regularly attracted: John V. Moore interview.

Jones and his close advisors quickly became expert: Teri Buford O'Shea, Laura Johnston Kohl, Rebecca Moore, and Fielding McGehee interviews.

Soon, besides nursing homes, these included: Moore, *Understanding Jonestown and Peoples Temple,* pp. 24–26.

he began scheduling the programs on a regular basis: Laura Johnston Kohl interview.

Temple ladies offered snacks for sale: Laura Johnston Kohl, *Jonestown Survivor: An Insider's Look* (Bloomington: iUniverse, 2010), p. 51.

each photo was good for protection: Hue Fortson interview.

Often, photo sales at a single service: Kohl, *Jonestown Survivor,* pp. 52–53.

letters began offering additional personal protections: California Historical Society, MS 4124, Box 1, Folder 3.

Jones's new travel schedule kept him away: Alan Swanson interview.

Others, loyal to the mission: Juanell Smart and Tim Carter interviews.

By 1973, Peoples Temple of Redwood Valley claimed: Scott Seay interview. Reverend Seay also granted me access to Disciples of Christ denominational records, which allowed me to be exact in the membership and income reported by Peoples Temple from its Indianapolis inception.

Twenty-Four: Worker Bees

Sometimes a dozen people slept in space: Teri Buford O'Shea and Laura Johnston Kohl interviews.

Experienced members like the Mertles didn't consider it wrong: Mills, *Six Years with God*, p. 147.

The approach to potential full-time Temple workers: Hue Fortson interview.

Even car payments and automotive insurance: Ibid.

whose operator followed rigid guidelines: California Historical Society, MS 3800, Box 4, Folder 57.

This meant many communals dressed: Alan Swanson interview.

sneaking naps in the church hallways whenever they could: Ibid.

Stephan Jones would recall decades later: Stephan Jones, Bucknell University presentation.

Going to a movie or to dinner: Alan Swanson interview.

There was also the example of Jim Jones himself: Laura Johnston Kohl, Garry Lambrev, and Hue Fortson interviews.

Anyone idle was sharply informed: Hue Fortson interview.

Jones took particular pride in his knack: Garry Lambrev interview.

Members often competed: Hue Fortson interview.

Predictably, the atmosphere of mandatory humility: Laura Johnston Kohl interview.

Twenty-Five: On the Road

These buses were purchased from Greyhound: RYMUR 89-4286-B-4-a-33.

The Temple acquired a dozen: Neva Sly Hargrave interview. Some former members remember there being thirteen Greyhounds. Others recall ten or eleven. Neva Sly Hargrave, who trained and served as a driver, remembers twelve, plus the smaller yellow bus used to haul equipment.

The Temple built an extensive garage: Alan Swanson interview.

Seats were removed to make room for a private area: Neva Sly Hargrave interview.

Temple members were trained to drive them: Ibid.

The trips were planned with the precision: Tim Carter and Laura Johnston Kohl interviews; Kohl, *Jonestown Survivor,* pp. 54–56.

Jack Beam and Patty Cartmell were nearly always present: Neva Sly Hargrave interview.

sometimes there would be $10,000 or more in bills and change: Tim Carter and Hue Fortson interviews.

Several weeks before the event: Laura John-

894

ston Kohl interview.

These touted Jones and the scheduled programs: California Historical Society, MS 4214, Box 1, Folder 9.

When the venue opened: Alan Swanson, Neva Sly Hargrave, Tim Carter, and Laura Johnston Kohl interviews.

By now they were presented in particularly compelling fashion: Neva Sly Hargrave interview.

Jones could, if he wished, quote Maine senator Edmund Muskie: Perlstein, *Before the Storm,* pp. 590–92.

Veteran political reporter Jules Witcover described it: Jules Witcover, *Very Strange Bedfellows,* p. xvi.

an advance crew was already hundreds of miles away: Laura Johnston Kohl interview.

Twenty-Six: Failures

the vetting process was extensive: Tim Carter, Laura Johnston Kohl, Rebecca Moore, and Garry Lambrev interviews.

Who brought with her: Deborah Layton, *Seductive Poison: A Jonestown Survivor's Story of Life and Death in the Peoples Temple* (New York: Anchor, 1999), p. 51.

Moore and his wife, Barbara, were greatly put off: John V. Moore interview.

He received an invitation: Neva Sly Hargrave interview.

Jones personally passed out rolls of toilet paper: Joyce Overman Bowman interview.

Jones couldn't resist bragging: Reiterman, *Raven* pp. 209–10. Reiterman's description in *Raven* of Jones's disputed cancer healing is classic: "[He] ordered [the alleged cancer] paraded around like a saint's relic." Also Julia Scheeres, *A Thousand Lives: The Untold Story of Jonestown* (New York: Free Press, 2012), p. 52.

Father Divine retired from public appearances: Watts, *God, Harlem U.S.A.,* p. 173.

Jones contacted Mother Divine and asked to visit: My description of the trip and its immediate aftermath draws on four sources: Leslie Wagner-Wilson, *Slavery of Faith* (Bloomington: iUniverse, 2009), pp. 27–28; also Reiterman, *Raven,* pp. 139–41; Mills, *Six Years with God,* pp. 176–79; and Watts, *God, Harlem U.S.A.,* pp. 174–75.

Simon Peter, one of the former Peace Mission members: In January 2014 I learned to my great astonishment that Mother Divine was not only still alive, but at least nominally in charge of what remains of the Peace Mission ministry. I contacted the Peace Mission office to request an interview. Though this was not allowed, Mission spokesman Roger Klaus did respond to my emailed questions with copies of documents from Mission files. I cite the material he provided regarding the letter from Simon Peter to Mother Divine and her reply to it. Klaus also quoted Mother Divine's post-Jonestown comment about Jones, his charisma, and the perils of spiritual illusions. It's hard to disagree with her about that.

Jones sent them a new, lengthy letter: California Historical Society, MS 4124, Box 1, Folder 9.

About a half dozen long-term members: RY-MUR 89-4286-1776 and 1777.

Jones occasionally mentioned Father Divine: Juanell Smart interview.

Twenty-Seven: Drugs

she gloried in her self-assumed role: Jim Jones Jr., Rebecca Moore, and Laura Johnston Kohl interviews.

He sometimes appointed committees and advisory boards: Ron Haldeman interview.

Survivors agree he led on a "need to know" basis: Tim Carter, Teri Buford O'Shea, and Garry Lambrev interviews.

Once, just before the Temple's Greyhound convoy left: Hue Fortson interview.

He loved mysteries and action films: Jim Jones Jr. interview.

he took vacations with his family: Ibid.

On at least two occasions he withdrew: RY-MUR 89-4286-A-2-A-31. One withdrawal was for $2,000, the other for $4,000.

They knew him well and harbored no belief: Garry Lambrev interview.

he began abusing drugs on a regular basis: Lawrence Wright, "The Orphans of Jonestown," *The New Yorker,* November 22, 1993; Stephan Jones, "Like Father, Like Son"; Jim Jones Jr. interview.

Access to these drugs wasn't a problem: Garry Lambrev interview.

A more obvious side effect: Laura Johnston Kohl interview.

He claimed this was because: Hue Fortson interview.

Everyone was to be on the lookout for questionable behavior: Laura Johnston Kohl, Teri Buford O'Shea, and Tim Carter interviews.

Some of Jones's bodyguards were armed: Reiterman, *Raven,* pp. 202–3.

sentries posted outside his closed office door heard: Hue Fortson interview.

Twenty-Eight: Sex

Carolyn initially found some solace: California Historical Society, MS 3802, Box 1, Folder 3.

Ijames tried tactfully warning Jones: Reiterman, *Raven,* p. 172.

Terri Buford was working in an adjacent office: Teri Buford O'Shea interview.

Debbie Layton's account in her memoir: Layton, *Seductive Poison,* pp. 73–83.

he included Cartmell by putting her in charge: Tim Carter interview.

Most, though not all, of the time Jones confined himself to adults: Fielding McGehee and Laura Johnston Kohl interviews.

A young man recently recruited to the Temple: Tim Carter interview.

the younger male leaders were warned: Hue Fortson interview.

"I have to be all things to all people": Ibid.

Survivors remember Grace complaining: Rebecca Moore interview.

she mentioned that she and Tim had not been intimate: Ibid.

Tim Stoen was a passionate believer: Jim Jones Jr. interview.

he adopted an "open marriage" policy with Grace: Stoen, *Marked for Death,* p. 85.

Twenty-Nine: Family

Tim Tupper, the child of a Temple member: Jim Jones Jr. interview.

There were perks that all of them enjoyed: Ibid.

Other Temple youngsters learned: Alan Swanson interview.

trays of white liquid in the refrigerator: Talbot, *Season of the Witch,* p. 297.

Once they found him facedown: Wright, "The Orphans of Jonestown."

"[It] looked like we were a family again": Stephan Jones, "Like Father, Like Son."

Stephan Jones was twelve when he swallowed: Ibid.

after hearing her brother-in-law preach: Janet L. Jackson interview.

But on February 6, 1972, Tim Stoen signed a statement: RYMUR 89-4286-FF-4-A-175.

Stoen said that as a lawyer: Stoen, Marked for Death, p. 86.

If he had any doubt — or any hope — it wasn't true: In his memoir, Stoen does not state whether he directly asked Grace if Jim Jones was John Victor's biological father. Grace Grech Stoen has never made a definitive public statement on the subject. She did not respond to my request for an interview. Several former Temple members have told me that in 1972 and afterward, Grace said that Jim Jones was the father of her son.

She told someone that if she could be any animal: Thielmann, The Broken God, p. 89.

she rented an apartment in Santa Rosa: Jim Jones Jr. interview.

new members felt Marceline was hard to get to know: Juanell Smart interview.

She had fallen in love with a psychologist: This and my description of the Jones family meeting are based on an interview with Jim Jones Jr.

Stephan said decades later: Stephan Jones, Bucknell University presentation.

It was different for Suzanne: Jim Jones Jr.

interview. Much of my description of Mike Cartmell's courtship of and subsequent marriage to Suzanne Jones is based on articles contributed by Cartmell on the Jonestown Institute website.

Thirty: The Planning Commission

Jones always maintained the illusion: Ron Haldeman interview.

its Board of Elders consisted of loyalists: Garry Lambrev, "The Board (of Elders)," *Jonestown Report 9* (November 2007), last modified March 4, 2014, Jonestown Institute.

she would feed her three children only birdseed: Ibid.; Garry Lambrev interview.

Membership on the formal Board of Directors of the Peoples Temple: Moore, *Understanding Jonestown and Peoples Temple,* pp. 35–36.

No one other than Jones understood: Laura Johnston Kohl and Hue Fortson interviews.

Marceline occasionally attended: Reiterman, *Raven,* p. 162.

He viewed the P.C. as his best means: Juanell Smart interview.

No matter how long the meetings dragged: Ibid.

Marceline asked if she could respond: Mills, *Six Years with God,* p. 244.

So Jones instituted a rule: Edith Roller Journal, 10/27/76, Jonestown Institute. As will be described in a later chapter, Jones assigned Temple member Edith Roller to keep a daily journal, which would eventually be used in a book about Peoples Temple. Until her death in Jonestown, Roller compiled notes about virtually every day of her Temple life, sometimes in excruciating detail, including what she ate at every meal and the occasional irregularity of her bowel movements. But there is also a great deal of fascinating information, including details about communal life in San Francisco and descriptions of Temple services. While transcripts of her journal are included in files provided by the FBI, the best transcript can be found on the Jonestown Institute website, and I urge readers who want to read Roller's journal to look there.

These often involved beatings: Alan Swanson, Neva Sly Hargrave, and Garry Lambrev interviews.

The belief was that it was better for the Temple to deal: Tim Carter interview.

Consequences weren't as severe: Garry Lambrev interview.

Thirty-One: Los Angeles

Sometimes, seating in rented school auditoriums: Hue Fortson interview.

1336 South Alvarado Street: For those interested, the church still stands. In 1978 it was sold by Peoples Temple to the Seventh

Day Adventists for $378,000. Though it is currently not open to the public, you can park outside.

Jones bragged that "if race wars and concentration camps don't come": Tape Q 612, Jonestown Institute.

Just by its attractive appearance: Juanell Smart interview.

Jack Beam would inform the latest soon-to-be corpse: Tim Carter interview. Carter tells a fascinating story of his experience as a temporary corpse. After he was "revived," he came under considerable criticism for his performance.

At the back of the main room: Rebecca Moore, Laura Johnston Kohl, and Teri Buford O'Shea interviews.

At first, Smart was reluctant to attend: Most of Juanell Smart's reminiscences about her time in Peoples Temple are derived from two interviews I conducted with her. A few of her quotes are taken from "My Life in — and After — Peoples Temple," *Jonestown Report* 6 (October 2004), last modified March 13, 2014, an essay she wrote for the Jonestown Institute. It can be found on the Institute website.

Thirty-Two: San Francisco

For information about San Francisco history and politics I frequently relied on *Season of the Witch,* David Talbot's 2012 bestseller about the city. It's an excellent book, and I recommend it to anyone interested in San Francisco or just looking for a rousing story about colorful people doing interesting, outrageous, and sometimes appalling things.

But San Francisco's considerable visual charms: Talbot, *Season of the Witch,* pp. xv–xvii.

J. Alfred Smith, pastor of a politically active black church in Oakland: Moore, Pinn, and Sawyer, eds., *Peoples Temple and Black Religion in America,* p. 139.

Jones had his followers inundate the district: Moore, *Understanding Jonestown and Peoples Temple,* p. 27; California Historical Society, MS 4124, Box 1, Folder 9.

The Temple paid $122,500: Moore, *Understanding Jonestown and Peoples Temple,* p. 26.

The black pastors banded together and called on: Reiterman, *Raven,* p. 264. In *Marked for Death,* Tim Stoen attributes this anecdote to "writer Kenneth Wooden."

Lynetta Jones had become one of Goodlett's patients: Carlton B. Goodlett, "Notes on Peoples Temple," last modified November 21, 2013, Jonestown Institute.

Peoples Temple members sent him gifts of homemade candy: Talbot, *Season of the Witch,* p. 276.

Once, Planning Commission members were left

waiting: Jim Jones Jr. interview.

Thirty-Three: Narrow Escapes

Only in closed meetings did he rant for hours:
Teri Buford O'Shea interview.

Jones once urged followers not to use Crest toothpaste: Mills, *Six Years with God,* p. 136.

On a pleasant day when Jones was present:
For my description of this event, I referred
to Reiterman, *Raven,* pp. 201–2; Scheeres,
A Thousand Lives, p. 27; RYMUR 89-4286-
FF-1-106-d (Stephan Jones's account); and
my own interviews with Alan Swanson and
Jim Jones Jr., who were both present in the
Redwood Valley temple parking lot when
Jones was "shot."

In the early 1970s, San Francisco's two major daily newspapers: Talbot, *Season of the Witch,* pp. 76–83.

*dozens of letters praising Jones and the Temple
began arriving:* This detail and almost every
other one cited about Kinsolving and his
investigative series come from the *Examiner*
stories themselves: "The Prophet Who
Raises the Dead," " 'Healing' Prophet
Hailed as God at S.F. Revival," "D.A. Aide
Officiates for Minor Bride," and "Probe
Asked of People's [*sic*] Temple," published
by the *Examiner* on consecutive days,
September 17–20, 1972, and also "The
People's [*sic*] Temple and Maxine Harpe,"

"The Reincarnation of Jesus Christ — in Ukiah," "Jim Jones Defames a Black Pastor," and "Sex, Socialism, and Child Torture with Rev. Jim Jones," which were withheld by the *Examiner* after the first four installments were printed. All eight articles can be viewed on the Jonestown Institute website.

they were summoned into action for this: Reiterman, *Raven,* pp. 212–13; Mills, *Six Years with God,* pp. 181–82; Thielmann, *The Broken God,* pp. 82–83.

Stoen suggested ominously: In 2005, Lester Kinsolving suffered a heart attack. Tim Stoen, now decades removed from his involvement with Peoples Temple, heard about Kinsolving's illness and wrote his former adversary to apologize for his opposition to Kinsolving's Temple series, to acknowledge that Kinsolving was right and "I was totally wrong," and to ask forgiveness. According to the *Santa Rosa Press Democrat,* where Kinsolving forwarded a copy of the letter, the former journalist said, "I was deeply moved and very grateful that [Stoen] wrote me. . . . Heavens, I'm a Christian. We have no choice but to forgive." In his 2015 memoir, *Marked for Death,* Stoen does not refer at all to Kinsolving or the *Examiner* investigative series.

Jones turned to one of the newest Temple

members: Thielmann, *The Broken God,* pp. 82–83.

Moore learned about it only: John V. Moore interview.

Thirty-Four: Reaching Out

Kinsolving's stories helped with Temple recruitment, too: Mills, *Six Years with God,* p. 183.

One of the prospective members who'd read the Examiner *stories:* Tim Carter interview.

About the same time Tim Carter first visited: I met Merrill Collett at a book festival in 2013. Afterward he sent me an email about his unpleasant experience at Peoples Temple. He subsequently supplied more details, again via email, at my request.

Johnny Moss Brown, a native of the Fillmore District: Laura Johnston Kohl and Tim Carter interviews.

Maria Katsaris loved children and animals: Rebecca Moore and Fielding McGehee interviews; Reiterman, *Raven,* pp. 188–98.

Her first church assignment was in the letters office: Tim Carter interview.

When four reporters from the Fresno Bee *were briefly incarcerated:* Edith Roller Journal, 9/12 and 9/19/76, Jonestown Institute.

At one Geary Boulevard service, Jones launched into: Tim Carter interview.

Jones taught his followers: Hue Fortson interview.

But outside the Los Angeles temple on January 7, 1973: Mills, *Six Years with God,* pp. 203–4; Reiterman, *Raven,* pp. 230–31. It is possible that the fainting spell suffered by the elderly woman was staged by Jones so he could demonstrate his healing powers. According to Jeannie Mills in *Six Years with God,* before the old lady collapsed Jones told the congregation that "I have had a revelation that something strange might happen tonight. No matter what happens, I don't want anybody to call an ambulance." But after examining the fallen woman, that is what Marceline Jones, a trained nurse, did. It is highly unlikely she would have deliberately sabotaged her husband's plan, since she was cooperating with him in public during this time. Perhaps he failed to inform her in advance. My opinion is that whether or not Jones intended to stage a "raising up" that night, Marceline genuinely believed the woman needed medical assistance, and, acting on her best professional judgment, sent for an ambulance. It was a genuine medical emergency, with long-term, cataclysmic results for Jim Jones.

he bragged in subsequent sermons: Tape Q 612, Jonestown Institute.

Los Angeles police had long memories: Joe Domanick interview. Domanick, who won a prestigious Edgar Award for his investigation of the LAPD, discussed the department's long history of vendettas. The opinion that they eventually acted on a departmental grudge against Jim Jones is my own. I would add that I agree with Domanick's view that recent LAPD administration has effectively initiated a more progressive atmosphere and positive attitude among city police.

Thirty-Five: The Gang of Eight

in fact, it was better, more righteous, *to be black:* Moore, Pinn, and Sawyer, eds., *Peoples Temple and Black Religion in America,* p. 174.

Archie Ijames's position became more ceremonial: Tim Carter interview.

The Temple purchased three apartments: Mills, *Six Years with God,* pp. 210–14.

One young woman fled: Ibid., pp. 214–15.

Jim Cobb was a different matter: Reiterman, *Raven,* pp. 219–25.

They left behind a letter: Copies are available to peruse at the California Historical Society in San Francisco and on the Jonestown Institute website. It's a lengthy document. At the CHS, its official location is CHS MS 3802, Box 11, Folder 70.

Jones walked purposefully onto the stage: Tape Q 1057-3, Jonestown Institute. The date of this Temple service is unknown, but clearly it takes place soon after the Gang of Eight defections and is the first time Jones has publicly addressed the subject. Don't just read the transcript. Set aside time and listen to the whole thing. Jones had to be at his best that day, and he was.

Thirty-Six: Consequences

They must be more observant: Alan Swanson and Teri Buford O'Shea interviews.

Blank pieces of paper were distributed: Juanell Smart, Hue Fortson, Teri Buford O'Shea, and Tim Carter interviews.

or else boasted about his sexual prowess: Tim Carter interview.

Sandy Bradshaw wrote, "The only person": RYMUR 89-4286-BB-6-JJJJJJJ.

The changes were more incremental: Laura Johnston Kohl and Rebecca Moore interviews.

a small item with the headline: RYMUR 89-4286-I-1-a-6-g.

Jones orchestrated the whole thing: Stoen, *Marked for Death,* p. 98.

Peter Wotherspoon was a pedophile: Neva Sly Hargrave and Tim Carter interviews.

more troubling to several P.C. members: Fielding McGehee and Juanell Smart interviews.

Efrein complied — disobeying could have been interpreted: Laurie Efrein Kahalas, *Snake Dance: Unravelling the Mysteries of Jonestown* (Toronto: Red Robin Press, 1998), pp. 150–57.

"Nothing is to be said in public or private": Edith Roller Journal, 1/4/77, Jonestown Institute.

Most dissatisfied members were destitute: Alan Swanson interview.

"I had no idea of how I was supposed to look": Teri Buford O'Shea interview.

Bonnie Burnham, frustrated by contradictions: Thielmann, *The Broken God,* pp. 93–95.

Afterward, Marceline stayed overnight with Burnham: Ibid., pp. 100–101.

He announced that anyone leaving the Temple must move: Garry Lambrev interview; Edith Roller Journal, 8/17/75, Jonestown Institute.

at one point he spoke on the telephone: Tape Q 775, Jonestown Institute.

That April, Jones reminded everyone: Tape Q 1057-4, Jonestown Institute.

In a subsequent sermon, he described: Tape Q 958, Jonestown Institute.

Thirty-Seven: The Promised Land

sometime, somehow, true believers would throw off their shackles: Moore, Pinn, and Sawyer, eds., *Peoples Temple and Black Religion in America,* pp. 19, 76.

Elderly African Americans, mostly recruited in San Francisco: Fielding McGehee interview.

Tim Stoen presented them: Mills, *Six Years with God,* p. 227.

The Mertles were one of the few couples in the Temple: Ibid., pp. 224–30.

On September 10, 1973, the seven-member Temple board: RYMUR 89-4286-A-32-A (rest indecipherable).

At the next meeting: RYMUR 89-4286-A-32 (rest indecipherable).

In early December 1973, Tim Stoen led: Stoen, *Marked for Death,* pp. 5–7.

Guyana was in economic distress: Kit Nascimento interview.

The National Service was Burnham's brainchild: Desmond Roberts and Kit Nascimento interviews.

While Port Kaituma itself wasn't much: Gerald Gouveia interview.

They reached an agreement for an initial lease: RYMUR 89-4286-C-4-a-7; Reiterman, *Raven,* pp. 275–76.

The Guyanese jungle is triple canopy: Tim Carter interview. Much of my additional description comes from personal experience. In November 2014, photographer Ralph Lauer and I flew to Port Kaituma and were guided from there to the old Jonestown site. The jungle has almost completely reclaimed the area, so much of what we saw — and had to work our way through — was similar to the first experience of the Jonestown Pioneers and their Amerindian guides.

when they tried, the chainsaw blades shattered: Tim Carter interview.

Jones demanded detailed records of all daily expenditures: RYMUR 89-4286-A-3-B-13 and QQ-8-d-1.

Worm larvae permeated the jungle soil: RYMUR 89-4286-EE-1-S-178.

lighting deliberate "burns" to rid partially cleared land: Jim Jones Jr. interview.

Yet the Pioneers persevered: Leigh Fondakowski, *Stories from Jonestown* (Minneapolis: University of Minnesota Press, 2012), pp. 197–98, 202–3.

he first teased followers by announcing: Tape Q 1057-4, Jonestown Institute.

Jones demanded that all those with life insurance policies cash them in: Mills, *Six Years with God,* pp. 217–18.

members were expected to hand Jones: Ibid., pp. 216–18.

The church printing operation turned out a snappy "Operation Breadbasket" pamphlet: California Historical Society, MS 4124, Box 1, Folder 3.

at least once committing statutory rape: Tape Q 775, Jonestown Institute.

Jones expected the women to get abortions: I was told this by one of the former Temple members who aborted a child by Jones. She

asked that her name not be published.
Los Angeles police had received numerous complaints: Reiterman, *Raven,* pp. 231–33. *Raven*'s is by far the best, most complete description to be found of Jones's arrest and its immediate aftermath.

Thirty-Eight: Kimo

Stephan Jones thought that his father: Stephan Jones, Bucknell University presentation.
Tim Stoen was the exception: Stoen, *Marked for Death,* p. 114.
After the little boy's second birthday: Ibid., p. 90.
In sermons during private Temple meetings: Reiterman, *Raven,* pp. 235–36.
he first offered to exchange himself: RYMUR 89-4286-l-1-a-6c.
Adams and the first few Temple women in Georgetown: Laura Johnston Kohl interview.
Adams was allowed to continue the affair: Teri Buford O'Shea and Laura Johnston Kohl interviews.
Jones made a major misstep: Stoen, *Marked for Death,* p. 109; Reiterman, *Raven,* pp. 247–50; Eileen Cox, "A Guyanese Perspective of Jonestown, 1979," *Jonestown Report* 15 (November 2013), last modified December 13, 2013, Jonestown Institute.
Jones and Mertle purchased fruit in Port Kai-

tuma: Mills, *Six Years with God,* p. 282.

Almost overnight, her shyness morphed: Tim Carter interview.

in the event of his death he wanted Marceline: RYMUR 89-4286-1099.

In February 1974, she sent: RYMUR 89-4286-EE-4-AAC.

Jones made it known that he'd sent her away: Tim Carter interview.

Jones embellished the story: Mills, *Six Years with God,* pp. 275–78.

Stephan warmed to her a little more: Stephan Jones, "My Brother's Mother," *Jonestown Report* 11 (November 2009), last modified March 14, 2014, Jonestown Institute.

they signed last will and testaments: RYMUR 89-4286-B-1-i-1a through 1i; RYMUR 89-4286-B-1-k-1a through 1i.

Sandy Ingram gushed that the ragged patch: Edith Roller Journal, 9/9/75, Jonestown Institute.

Jones, Carolyn, Maria, and a few others began making: RYMUR 89-4286-A-40-a-42b.

she soon bragged that meals for each communal: Garry Lambrev, "My Friend Teresa King: From the Avenue of Fleas to Jonestown," *Jonestown Report* 12 (October 2010), last modified December 28, 2013, Jonestown Institute.

"If you come for one of us": Fielding McGehee interview.

a few weeks later Jones sternly noted: Edith Roller Journal, 9/6/75, Jonestown Institute; Scheeres, *A Thousand Lives,* p. 47.

That same September, Jones reemphasized that point: Surviving participants from this Planning Commission meeting have different recollections of the approximate date. Based on my own research, late September 1975 seems most likely. Tim Carter, Teri Buford O'Shea, and Laura Johnston Kohl interviews.

in one service, he demanded: Edith Roller Journal, 8/9/75, Jonestown Institute.

In October there was a startling defection: Mills, *Six Years with God,* pp. 12–16.

November 5, state assemblyman Willie Brown called on: Stoen, *Marked for Death,* p. 117.

Thirty-Nine: City Politics

George Moscone's background was classic poor-boy-makes-good: Much of the history cited in this chapter is based on Talbot's *Season of the Witch.* To save endless "Ibid." citations, I refer the reader to Talbot, pp. 143–54, 233–34, 248–54, and 278–80. I think it's impossible to understand the experiences of Jim Jones and his followers in San Francisco without understanding the city itself, and for that, it's necessary to read Talbot's book cover to cover. The opinions expressed in this chapter, though, are my own.

On November 4, 1975: All voting totals in the November 4, 1975, mayoral election and December 11 runoff were supplied to me by the city of San Francisco.

A spokesman for the Moscone campaign later told: San Francisco Examiner, November 19, 1978.

Jones bragged that his followers produced: Fondakowski, *Stories from Jonestown,* p. 166.

Jones had an additional asset: Jim Jones Jr. interview.

When Moscone called Jones: RYMUR 89-4286-X-3-i-22.

The Temple also produced a list of members: California Historical Society, MS4126, Box 2, Folder 9.

beyond Michael Prokes being named: Reiterman, *Raven,* p. 268.

Once, when Brown missed speaking: Edith Roller Journal, 6/6/76, Jonestown Institute.

Forty: More Money

Marceline had personal accounts of as much as $200,000: RYMUR 89-4286-A-37-a-31.

his mother, Lynetta, had accounts totaling $89,584: RYMUR 89-4286-RR-1-F-3.

Throughout his life, Jones was never able to accept: Jeanne Jones Luther and Ron

Haldeman interviews.

in 1975 he assigned Tim Stoen to research: Stoen, *Marked for Death,* p. 118.

dressing his female couriers in I. Magnin suits: Layton, *Seductive Poison,* pp. 83–84.

at least one authorized her, along with Stephan and Marceline: RYMUR 89-4286-RR-1-A.

Amerindians were hired on as crew: RYMUR 89-4286-A-26-d-16dd, A-26-e-1b.

Jonestown would become self-sufficient: Laura Johnston Kohl and Teri Buford O'Shea interviews.

In fact, the total was around $30 million: Tim Carter and Teri Buford O'Shea interviews. This figure was also quoted to me by another former Temple member involved in these overseas transactions who asked not to be identified.

Jones asked that everyone donate their wristwatches: Edith Roller Journal, 4/13/76, Jonestown Institute.

Forty-One: Defectors

"I was born to put the whammy": Edith Roller Journal, 5/22/76, Jonestown Institute.

She and Walter defected on July 4: Reiterman, *Raven,* pp. 286–93; Stoen, *Marked for Death,* pp. 125–26.

investigators found several undated documents: RYMUR 89-4286-B-3-h-3, 4, and 6.

Neva Sly fled, leaving behind: Neva Sly Hargrave interview.

Joyce Shaw left, too: Ibid.; Reiterman, *Raven,* pp. 298–300.

The possibility that he'd fallen asleep: A continuing point of contention between Peoples Temple survivors is whether Bob Houston was killed on Jim Jones's orders. Clearly, with Jones, anything was possible. Yet for all his threats to anyone who left the Temple, and for all the verbal roughing up these defectors frequently endured from Temple thugs like Chris Lewis, there is no other instance where physical violence, let alone a fatal attack, was carried out. Even if Bob Houston actually typed and signed a letter of resignation on the morning of the day he died, Jones had no immediate reason to kill him. Though I can understand why others who were personally familiar with Jones believe otherwise, my own opinion is that on learning of Houston's death, Jones thought he might as well make some use of it. So he had a letter of resignation typed above Houston's signature on a blank sheet of paper and made it known that Houston had died only hours after quitting the Temple — an example of what might happen to anyone else who gave up Jones's protection by leaving.

Bob Houston's father, Sam, worked as a photographer: Reiterman, *Raven,* pp. 1–3.

somewhat less so among colleagues: Jim

Wright interview. At the time, Wright was the majority leader of Congress. As such, he regularly heard complaints from some members about others. Wright repeatedly emphasized that although he liked Leo Ryan, he also believed that the California congressman was "more interested than most" in personal publicity.

Now she was given darker assignments: Teri Buford O'Shea interview.

Jones's rambling sermons grew more bizarre: Edith Roller Journal, 5/22/76, 11/3/76, 11/14/76, Jonestown Institute; Tapes Q 962, Q 353, Q 1018, Jonestown Institute.

There were few brand-new members now: Garry Lambrev interview.

Forty-Two: "Our Year of Ascendency"

Her husband informed her that sometime in the future: RYMUR 89-4286-615 (further designation illegible).

He dispatched Maria Katsaris to investigate: RYMUR 89-4286-QQ-2-A-1.

the Temple board voted that the Guyana mission: RYMUR 89-4286-A-32-a-147 through 149.

Herb Caen wrote about Jones for the first time: Stoen, *Marked for Death,* p. 122.

Peoples Temple and the Los Angeles Black Muslims co-hosted: Ibid., p. 125.

They became partners in an import-export com-

pany: Reiterman, *Raven,* p. 265.

Jones made a special point of gathering them: Richmond Palladium-Item, June 29, 1976.

Mrs. Kennedy told her family: Bill Manning interview.

"If you give yourself to socialism": Edith Roller Journal, 5/26/76, Jonestown Institute.

for that evening only: Ibid., 9/3/76.

Less pleasing was Jones's announcement: Ibid.

Jones had another exciting announcement: Ibid., 9/11/76.

The event went well: Ibid., 9/15/76.

Mrs. Carter made a follow-up phone call: Reiterman, *Raven,* pp. 303–5.

Jimmy Carter was considering appointing him: Edith Roller Journal, 10/19/76, Jonestown Institute.

He received a brief, handwritten reply: California Historical Society, MS 3800, Box 2, Folder 36.

Willie Brown described Jones: Layton, *Seductive Poison,* p. 65; Reiterman, *Raven,* pp. 306–8.

But it was all in vain: Reiterman, *Raven,* pp. 268–70.

"Though many have asked him to do so": Ukiah Daily Journal, February 25, 1977.

Maria would testify that her father: RYMUR 89-4286-S-1-F-1a.

Jones was even disdainful of President-elect

Jimmy Carter: Edith Roller Journal, 11/12/76, 11/26/76, Jonestown Institute.

Eight days later, it authorized spending: RYMUR 89-4286-A-33-a-201.

During the Temple Thanksgiving service: Edith Roller Journal, 11/25/76, Jonestown Institute.

Jones blurted to Stoen: Stoen, *Marked for Death,* p. 2.

Forty-Three: *New West*

Each Temple kid got one gift: Hue Fortson interview; Edith Roller Journal, 1/1/77, Jonestown Institute; Mills, *Six Years with God,* pp. 168–69.

Marceline's health broke down: RYMUR 89-4286-615 (only designation legible).

The board met and voted an immediate $30,000 annual salary: RYMUR 89-4286-A-32-a-175 through 178.

she helped Stephan find an apartment: Jim Jones Jr. interview; Wright, "The Orphans of Jonestown."

Jones made a return trip to Cuba: RYMUR 89-4286-bb-b-7c; Goodlett, "Notes on Peoples Temple"; Reiterman, *Raven,* p. 284.

Grace Stoen filed for divorce: RYMUR 89-4286-B-1-c-1e; Stoen, *Marked for Death,* pp. 2, 135.

talking only intermittently to Marceline: Fielding McGehee interview.

Embassy deputy chief Wade Matthews reported: Moore, *Understanding Jonestown and Peoples Temple,* p. 44.

Mr. Muggs was one of Jonestown's first residents: Laura Johnston Kohl, "Oral History Interview: Don Beck," *Jonestown Report* 17 (November 2015), Jonestown Institute.

Tom Grubbs and Don Beck were dispatched: Ibid.

Under the supervision of Gene Chaikin: RYMUR 89-4286-B-2-c-1.

a San Francisco private investigator named Joseph Mazor: RYMUR 89-4286-S-1-F-1a.

Elmer and Deanna Mertle were active, too: Mills, *Six Years with God,* pp. 57–63.

That was enough for the U.S. Customs Service: RYMUR 89-4286-2180 (no further designation legible).

Temple members met with New West*'s editor:* Reiterman, *Raven,* p. 325.

Peoples Temple purchased a residence: Stoen, *Marked for Death,* p. 32; Laura Johnston Kohl interview.

They sent fish, too: Laura Johnston Kohl interview.

Jones found his mission doctor: RYMUR 89-4286-X-6-a-2; Goodlett, "Notes on Peoples Temple."

Among the first textbooks he requested: RYMUR 89-4286-QQ-5-A-13.

Jones accused Stoen: Stoen, *Marked for*

Death, p. 1.

In March, he disappeared briefly: Ibid., pp. 18–19.

Stoen flew to New York: Ibid., pp. 36–37.

The New West *writers comprised:* Fondakowski, *Stories from Jonestown,* pp. 111–13.

It came out later: Ibid., pp. 112–13.

the Temple hired perhaps the most controversial defense attorney: Reiterman, *Raven,* pp. 372–73.

His initial monthly retainer was $5,000: RYMUR 89-4286-1681 (only legible designation).

Tim Carter and Karen Layton were dispatched: Tim Carter interview.

Other settlers flew from California to Florida: Laura Johnston Kohl interview.

He warned his followers: Edith Roller Journal, 4/21/76, Jonestown Institute.

On Memorial Day, he took part: Reiterman, *Raven,* p. 321.

On Jones's instructions, loyal follower Richard Tropp wrote: RYMUR 89-4286-MM-5-20 and 21, MM-6-4 and 5.

Jim Jones ran away: In Debbie Layton's book, *Seductive Poison,* she describes Jones receiving a call from the *New West* editor, who read the article to him in mid-July, weeks prior to its publication. But in the article, Kilduff and Tracy write that they were unable to reach Jones for comment

924

before the article went to press and were told that he was in Guyana, and had been for three weeks. After brief, initial contact, Layton did not respond to my emails requesting an interview, so I was unable to ask her about this apparent contradiction.

Jones's mother-in-law, Charlotte Baldwin, told the local paper: Richmond Palladium-Item, October 23, 1977.

Marceline told her friend Bonnie Burnham: Thielmann, *The Broken God,* pp. 109–11.

Forty-Four: Jonestown

The Americans soon learned: Teri Buford O'Shea interview.

he took over control of everything: Laura Johnston Kohl interview.

All incoming mail was opened: RYMUR 89-4286-EE-5-A and B; EE-1-H-48; C-7-e-1a; Tim Carter interview.

the FCC formally charged: RYMUR 89-4286-E-5-A-28 through 41.

Jonestown's radio code name for "guns" was "Bibles": Teri Buford O'Shea interview.

their stateside paychecks were needed in Guyana: Edith Roller Journal, 8/15/77, Jonestown Institute.

Newly arrived settlers were unnerved: Ibid., 1/28/78; Fondakowski, *Stories from Jonestown,* pp. 89–92, 201; Wagner-Wilson, *Slavery of Faith,* pp. 68–76; Laura Johnston

Kohl interview.

Jones calculated that serving chicken or pork: Edith Roller Journal, 2/5/78, Jonestown Institute.

Jones made a point of rewarding: Layton, *Seductive Poison,* p. 5.

Marceline, struggling to keep: RYMUR 89-4286-x-7-a-5a.

Jonestown's combined income from its own operations: Tim Carter interview.

The Temple's San Francisco office: California Historical Society, MS 3800, Box 4, Folder 57.

Many took advantage: Feinsod, *Awake in a Nightmare,* pp. 110–13.

fermented beverages that the settlers called "jungle juice": Ibid., pp. 116–17.

Jones had been apprised by Marceline: Stephenson, *Dear People,* pp. 79–80.

Jones established the "Learning Crew": Moore, *Understanding Jonestown and Peoples Temple,* pp. 48–49; Wagner-Wilson, *Slavery of Faith,* pp. 84–85; Stephenson, *Dear People,* p. 82; Scheeres, *A Thousand Lives,* p. 123.

more often he gave his personalized accounts: Tim Carter, Teri Buford O'Shea, and Laura Johnston Kohl interviews; Moore, Pinn, and Sawyer, eds., *Peoples Temple and Black Religion in America,* p. 117; Edith Roller Journal, 7/28/78, Jonestown Institute; RY-

MUR 89-4286-EE-1-H-58; Scheeres, *A Thousand Lives,* pp. 128–29.

Jonestown had a loudspeaker system: Jim Jones Jr. and Tim Carter interviews.

John Blacken, deputy chief of the American mission: Stephenson, *Dear People,* pp. 72–73.

Burnham now had no intention of dealing with Jones: Kit Nascimento interview.

Yolanda Crawford persuaded him to let her: RYMUR 89-4286-FF-I-107 a-d.

Leon Broussard sneaked away into the jungle: Reiterman, *Raven,* pp. 355–60; Scheeres, *A Thousand Lives,* pp. 89–90.

recently appointed U.S. consul Richard McCoy: In the U.S. Foreign Service, consuls are diplomats who report to the U.S. ambassador.

Forty-Five: Concerned Relatives and the First White Night

There is some disagreement among Temple survivors about the term "White Night." A few insist that it was never used in Jonestown and was invented as a useful descriptive term afterward. Others recall it in regular use — "night" because Jones usually summoned emergency gatherings after the workday concluded, and "white" as the opposite of "black," since traditional usage of "black" indicated something bad and thus, in the minds of Temple members, smacked of racism.

In August 1977 the Mertles initiated: Mills, *Six Years with God,* p. 71.

even Grace met with Mazor: RYMUR 89-4286-S-1-b-1a, B-2-d-5.

it was one thing to have a name and message: Fielding McGehee interview.

Tim Stoen met with Grace in Denver: Stoen, *Marked for Death,* pp. 137–39.

Stoen did not immediately align himself: Jeanne Mills (Deanna Mertle) wrote in *Six Years with God* that Stoen eventually moved next door to her and her husband.

Grace Stoen went to court in San Francisco: RYMUR 89-4286-B-1-c-1r.

"She would hug all over him": RYMUR 89-4286-FF-1-30.

Jones's affidavit stated that: RYMUR FF-I-111-b.

The affidavits were prepared for future use in court: Since Jones never appeared in court to contest Grace Stoen's charges, the documents were never made public by the Temple. They were found among Jonestown records recovered in the aftermath of November 18, 1978.

"Marcie is okay except": RYMUR 89-4286-BB-7-d-7.

The order added: RYMUR 89-4286-B-1-c-1k.

That crucial addendum changed everything: Rebecca Moore interview.

Jeffrey Haas, the attorney representing Grace: RYMUR 89-4286-B-1-c-1n.

Haas flew to Georgetown and appeared: Reiterman, *Raven,* p. 361.

They were met at the gate by Maria Katsaris: Ibid., p. 362.

About four thirty in the afternoon on September 7: Much of my description of this first White Night is derived from interviews with Tim Carter and Jim Jones Jr., who were both present. I also drew on material from Wright, "The Orphans of Jonestown"; Fondakowski, *Stories from Jonestown,* pp. 211–12; Moore, *Understanding Jonestown and Peoples Temple,* pp. 75–80; Scheeres, *A Thousand Lives,* pp. 92–99; and Wagner-Wilson, *Slavery of Faith,* pp. 88–91.

Carlton Goodlett, speaking from San Francisco: Goodlett, "Notes on Peoples Temple."

in early October he wrote to the deputy minister: RYMUR 89-4286-BB-3-a-5.

Forty-Six: Death Will Be Painless

So many followers complained of feeling threatened: RYMUR 89-4286-C-7-c-12a.

The boy had two Jonestown nicknames: Rebecca Moore interview.

John Burke sent a confidential: All other government documents were obtained from

929

the FBI through Freedom of Information Act requests. But I got this one from WikiLeaks, which conveniently made the document available online as I was writing this book.

Tim Stoen wrote directly to Jones: Stoen, *Marked for Death,* p. 146.

Jones laid out an attack plan: RYMUR 89-4286-B-3-g-3.

Jones engaged Guyanese attorney Lionel Luckhoo: RYMUR 89-4286-A-25-c-3.

he ordered Debbie Layton to find Stoen: Layton, *Seductive Poison,* pp. 131–32.

Howard and Beverly Oliver took steps: RYMUR 89-4286-B-i-i-14a.

Steven Katsaris was determined: Reiterman, *Raven,* pp. 384–89.

She was provided with a list: RYMUR 89-4286-B-3-j-1.

a past Jones misstep came back to haunt him: RYMUR 89-4286-EE-1-I and J-143.

Another matter involving Jonestown kids: RYMUR 89-4286-EE-1-K-17, BB-17-jjj-1.

Hue Fortson had been dispatched: Hue Fortson interview.

she sent Jones a letter: RYMUR 89-4286-EE-1-I&J-164.

Marceline began a quiet effort: RYMUR 89-4286-A-14-a-3 through 12.

Two teenage boys, Tommy Bogue and Brian Davis: Scheeres, *A Thousand Lives,* pp. 106–13.

the San Francisco Examiner *published a story:* Edith Roller Journal, 11/15–16/77, Jonestown Institute; Reiterman, *Raven,* pp. 377–78.

an order was issued by the California Superior Court: RYMUR 89-4286-L-1-a-1; Scheeres, *A Thousand Lives,* p. 125; Reiterman, *Raven,* p. 378.

Larry Schacht concluded that the cause: RYMUR 89-4286-B-2-d-1.

A bombshell announcement followed: RYMUR 89-4286-C-11-d-11c.

Jones collapsed, sliding out of his chair: RYMUR 89-4286-C-11-d-14c.

"There is a good chance I can develop": Houston Press, January 30, 2013.

Phyllis Chaikin suggested that everyone: Ibid.

around dawn on February 16, 1978: Edith Roller Journal, 11/16–17/77, Jonestown Institute; Scheeres, *A Thousand Lives,* pp. 148–51; RYMUR 89-4286-1206 (rest illegible); RYMUR 89-4286-1576 (rest illegible); RYMUR 4286-C-5-a-33; Layton, *Seductive Poison,* pp. 178–81.

On Jones's instruction, Larry Schacht ordered: RYMUR 89-4286-2233-00-3-E2.

Forty-Seven: Betrayals

The responses were chilling: RYMUR 89-4286-C-5-a-33.

Tim and Grace Stoen had come to Georgetown:

Stoen, *Marked for Death,* pp. 153–82.

Jones himself wrote a long letter: RYMUR 89-4286-BB-17-ee.

"We won't pay your fucking way": Edith Roller Journal, 3/18/78, Jonestown Institute.

this one asking for suggestions: RYMUR 89-4286-BB-2-44.

Jonestown might offer an additional benefit: RYMUR 89-4286-BB-17-xx-2 and 3.

tranquilizing himself into a stupor: Jim Jones Jr. and Teri Buford O'Shea interviews.

radio operators in the communications shack: Tim Carter interview.

they began disciplining themselves: RYMUR 89-4286-1-O-15-a.

It began, "We at Peoples Temple": The complete text can be found on the Jonestown Institute website.

Stoen and Steven Katsaris served: Stoen, *Marked for Death,* pp. 195–200.

the Concerned Relatives marched: Ibid. Hue Fortson interview.

she reiterated her devotion: Stephenson, *Dear People,* pp. 89–90.

In her radio transmission: The complete text can be found on the Jonestown Institute website.

At the Soviet embassy in Georgetown: RYMUR 89-4286-GG-1-E-1.

a reporter from the Soviet news agency TASS: Edith Roller Journal, 4/16/78, Jonestown Institute; RYMUR 89-4286-c-6-1-m.

Richard McCoy came from Georgetown: Scheeres, *A Thousand Lives,* p. 168.

The Moores were met: John V. Moore interview.

Debbie Layton went to the U.S. embassy: Layton, *Seductive Poison,* pp. 213–68. Layton's memoir goes into considerable detail about her defection. I've reduced it to the basics here.

She had been unpopular: Tim Carter, Laura Johnston Kohl, and Teri Buford O'Shea interviews.

Jones did make an additional order: Teri Buford O'Shea interview.

she left a note for Jones: Stephenson, *Dear People,* p. 103.

Tim Stoen and Steven Katsaris launched: Stoen, *Marked for Death,* pp. 205–6.

Stoen sent a private message to Jones: Ibid., pp. 212–13.

Debbie Layton supplied authorities and reporters: The complete text of the affidavit can be found on the Jonestown Institute website.

He told the other settlers that Debbie Layton: RYMUR 89-4286-FF-11-A-1 through 55.

Carolyn Layton and Maria Katsaris gradually assumed: Tim Carter, Jim Jones Jr., Laura Johnston Kohl, Fielding McGehee, and Teri Buford O'Shea interviews.

One afternoon when Annie was called away:

California Historical Society, MS 3802, Box 1, Folder 1.

A hut was designated "the Extended Care Unit": Reiterman, *Raven,* pp. 449–50; RYMUR 89-4286-1722 (rest illegible).

cheese sandwiches laced with barbiturates: Tim Carter interview.

Gordon Lindsay, a writer for the National Enquirer: Scheeres, *A Thousand Lives,* p. 172.

Bonny Mann forwarded to Jones "with compliments": RYMUR 89-4286-D-3-A-3b.

more information was needed: RYMUR 89-4286-G-1-a-8c.

Larry Schacht could not practice medicine: RYMUR 89-4286-D-a-A-1 through 5.

the same tactic that had worked so well: Kit Nascimento interview; *Guyana Journal,* April 2006; RYMUR 89-4286-D-2-a-11a, D-a-A-1 through 5.

Helen Snell complained that she wanted more meat: RYMUR 89-4286-EE-2-uv-12A.

some of the young men in Jonestown: Wright, "The Orphans of Jonestown"; Fondakowski, *Stories from Jonestown,* pp. 219–20; Desmond Roberts interview.

Snell may have inspired his announcement: Edith Roller Journal, 8/8/78, Jonestown Institute.

afterward he told him and Marceline: Carlton Goodlett, "Notes on Peoples Temple."

One of the first actions taken: RYMUR 89-

4286-S-1-G-2-1 through 77.

a wave of new bills: RYMUR 89-4286-A-26-
a-3 through 13.

Forty-Eight: Unraveling

The congressman was displeased: San Francisco Examiner, November 20, 1978.

Tim Carter sent Jones a note: RYMUR 89-
4286-C-7-g-4a.

She suggested to Jones: Teri Buford O'Shea
interview.

he provided Jones with a memo: RYMUR 89-
4286-NN-6-A-1 through 9.

*Lane launched the "public relations counter of-
fensive":* RYMUR 89-4286-X-3-m-3a
through 32; X-4-m-3u and 3v.

Justice Bishop withdrew from the Stoen case:
Washington Star-News, December 6, 1978.

Even Charles Garry's petulant threat: RYMUR
89-4286-PP-9-1.

Feodor Timofeyev made his long-delayed visit:
Reiterman, *Raven,* pp. 446–47; RYMUR
89-4286-Q-352 (rest illegible).

she contacted the San Francisco temple office:
RYMUR 89-4286-BB-7-A-37.

*Jones selected nineteen-year-old Shanda
James:* Wright, "The Orphans of Jonestown"; Jim Jones Jr. interview.

*He appointed a Money Making Project Commit-
tee:* RYMUR 89-4286-C-7-h-10; C-7-h-7.

Chaikin, on behalf of the group: RYMUR 89-

4286-GG-1-C-1 and 2.

he snapped that the question: RYMUR 89-4286-G-1-f-3 and 6e.

Tim Carter left the same day: Tim Carter interview.

She secretly made a flight reservation: Teri Buford O'Shea interview.

On November 1, Ryan formally wrote to Jones: Stephenson, *Dear People,* pp. 107–8; RYMUR 89-4286-AA-1-f-6; AA-1-f-1.

Jones did admit an outside guest: Reiterman, *Raven,* pp. 470–71.

Jones initially refused them permission to go: Jim Jones Jr. interview.

Their departure caused a significant change: Ibid.

"I heard some congressman wants to come here": RYMUR 89-4286-Q-161 (rest illegible).

He ordered staff at Lamaha Gardens: RYMUR 89-4286-AA-1-Q-1 and 2.

Mingo wouldn't meet with Sharon Amos: RYMUR 89-4286-E-3-A-2.

a few saw Ryan's visit: Reiterman, *Raven,* pp. 472–73.

Carolyn prepared and presented: RYMUR 89-4286-X-3-a-32a.

Stephan finally refused on behalf of the players: Jim Jones Jr. interview.

Tropp sent a memo to the leaders: RYMUR 89-4286-AA-1-k-1.

Charlotte Baldwin signed the Jonestown guest

book: RYMUR 89-4286-c-6-a-2-i.

Leo Ryan had a final meeting: Moore, *Understanding Jonestown and Peoples Temple,* p. 91.

Bonnie Burnham was also along: Thielmann, *The Broken God,* pp. 113–22.

Forty-Nine: Final Days

Temple staffers at Lamaha Gardens were startled to see: Laura Johnston Kohl interview.

Sharon Amos told Ryan that he was trespassing: RYMUR 89-4286-E-3-A-2-13; E-3-A-2-11.

The others who'd arrived in Guyana with Ryan: Thielmann, *The Broken God,* pp. 123–35; Reiterman, *Raven,* pp. 481–84; Charles Krause, *Guyana Massacre: The Eyewitness Account* (New York: Berkley, 1978), pp. 13–20.

Jones soon learned who had come: Feinsod, *Awake in a Nightmare,* p. 171.

Bonnie Burnham and Clare Bouquet were both rebuffed: RYMUR 89-4286-E-3-A-2-4.

Ambassador Burke agreed to meet: San Francisco Chronicle, San Francisco Examiner, November 17, 1978; Thielmann, *The Broken God,* pp. 125–27.

The congressman took a harder line: San Francisco Examiner, November 24, 1978.

On Friday morning he sent Jim McElvane: Tim

Carter interview.

The Jonestown kitchen worked extra shifts: Ibid.

Marceline Jones addressed the settlers by loud-speaker: Ibid.

As night fell, dinner was served: Reiterman, *Raven,* pp. 492–94.

Jack Beam suggested to Jones that Leo Ryan be asked: Tim Carter interview.

Jones had an announcement: Stephan Jones, "Death's Night," *Jonestown Report* 12 (October 2010), last modified March 29, 2016, Jonestown Institute.

Don Harris hadn't immediately told the other reporters: Reiterman, *Raven,* p. 503.

a man had passed him a note that read: Fondakowski, *Stories from Jonestown,* p. xiii.

Ryan already had a plan: Stephenson, *Dear People,* pp. 118–19.

"He passed him a note": Fondakowski, *Stories from Jonestown,* pp. 224–25.

the radio crackled with a terse, three-word report: RYMUR 89-4286-1304 (rest illegible).

Fifty: "Some Place That Hope Runs Out"

This chapter contains material from my interviews with Tim Carter, Jim Jones Jr., Laura Johnston Kohl, Kit Nascimento, Desmond Roberts, Gerald Gouveia, and one email exchange with Tracy Parks.

Authors whose books provided critical information include Tim Reiterman (*Raven,* pp. 503–70); Denise Stephenson (*Dear People* pp. 110–42); Charles Krause (*Guyana Massacre,* pp. 65–107); Laura Johnston Kohl (*Jonestown Survivor,* pp. 74–78); Leigh Fondakowski (*Stories from Jonestown,* pp. 221–34); Bonnie Thielmann (*The Broken God,* pp. 131–36); Tim Stoen (*Marked for Death,* pp. 233–35); Mark Lane (*The Strongest Poison* [Charlottesville, VA: The Lane Group, 1980], pp. 142–69); Rebecca Moore (*Understanding Jonestown and Peoples Temple,* pp. 92–102); Leslie Wagner-Wilson (*Slavery of Faith,* pp. 96–102); and Julia Scheeres (*A Thousand Lives,* pp. 212–34).

Various descriptions of the attack at the Port Kaituma airstrip come from articles in the San *Francisco Examiner* (November 20, 1978, November 24, 1978) and *Newsweek* (December 4, 1978).

Herbert Newell and Clifford Gieg never had a chance: Herbert Newell, "The Coldest Day of My Life," *Jonestown Report* 12 (October 2010), last modified December 18, 2013, Jonestown Institute; RYMUR 89-4286-1842.

Jones spoke with the would-be defectors: Los Angeles Times, November 27, 1978.

he asked, "Does this change everything?": *Washington Post,* November 26, 1978.

Amos spelled the word out: Here and in much of my additional description of events in Georgetown on 11/18/78, I use information from "Death's Night," a gripping essay by Stephan Jones provided courtesy of the Jonestown Institute.

the Jonestown assassins fired volleys of shots: There is some doubt about the identities of the Port Kaituma shooters. RYMUR 89-4286-1681-C-1 and 2 list those posthumously indicted for the attack as Wesley Karl Breidenbach, Ronnie Dennis, Stanley Gieg, Eddie James Hallmon, Ronald De Val James, Earnest Jones, Robert Kice, Thomas Kice, Anthony Simon, Ron Tally, Albert Touchette, and Joe Wilson. Certainly some, probably most of them, were involved. In any event, all the men named by the FBI died in Jonestown later that day after taking poison.

He began, "How very much I've tried": Tape Q 042, Jonestown Institute.

the adults in the pavilion began shuffling into line: I base part of the description here on remarks made by Stephan Jones during his lecture at Bucknell University.

Fifty-One: What Happened?

The first word that something terrible had happened: RYMUR 89-4286-1.

After discarding their last suitcase of cash: Tim

Carter interview.

Charles Garry exclaimed: Ibid.

one misconception evolved into part: Omaha World-Herald, August 7, 2015.

These provided convincing evidence: RYMUR 89-4286-1894 x-1-a-50 through 54; Stephenson, *Dear People,* pp. vx–xvii; Fondakowski, *Stories from Jonestown,* p. 251; Tim Carter interview.

Guns were found in Jonestown: RYMUR 89-4286-2334.

There was an astonishing amount of money: Teri Buford O'Shea, Fielding McGehee, and Tim Carter interviews; *Washington Post,* November 29, 1978; "How Much Did Peoples Temples Have in Assets?," edited by Fielding McGehee, last modified May 24, 2014, Jonestown Institute.

For the next four and a half months: Rebecca Moore, "Last Rights," last modified August 31, 2014, Jonestown Institute.

The Baldwins contacted a local funeral parlor: Ernie Mills interview.

Stephan blurted that he was the one: Jim Jones Jr. interview; Stephan Jones, "Chuck," *Jonestown Report* 12 (October 2010), last modified December 18, 2013, Jonestown Institute.

Before being permitted to go on their way: Laura Johnston Kohl and Tim Carter interviews.

The government also wanted reimbursement:

RYMUR 89-4286-915; 1780, 2164, and 2195; *New York Times,* October 11, 1979; Stephenson, *Dear People,* pp. 142–43; Fondakowski, *Stories from Jonestown,* p. 301; Teri Buford O'Shea and Laura Johnston Kohl interviews.

Dianne Feinstein, now acting mayor: Tim Carter interview.

On December 3, only thirty people: New York Times, December 4, 1978.

three days later papers were filed: RYMUR 89-4286-2164.

Fifty-Two: Aftermath

State launched an internal investigation: RYMUR 89-4286-1961.

The FBI was equally adamant: RYMUR 89-4286-2124.

On May 21, 1979, investigators made their official report: RYMUR 89-4286-2180.

Both governments agreed that someone had to legally answer: New York Times, November 27, 1978; RYMUR, 89-4286-1936, 2164.

Michael Prokes called a press conference: RYMUR 89-4286-1992, 2006, 2035.

they tried to remain anonymous: Jeanne Jones Luther interview.

Suzanne Jones reunited with her brothers: Jim Jones Jr. interview.

"I do not want people to think": Smart, "My Life in — And After — Peoples Temple."

"[Members] believe that service to the Diety":
RYMUR 89-4286-FF-2-15c.

All other opinions expressed in this chapter are my own, and are based on extensive interviews including at a Jonestown Institute Labor Day Reunion in San Diego in 2014.

BIBLIOGRAPHY

BOOKS

Atwood, Craig; Hill, Samuel S.; Mead, Frank S. *Handbook of Denominations in the United States, 13th Edition.* Nashville: Abingdon Press, 2010.

Blum, Deborah. *The Poisoner's Handbook.* New York: Penguin Press, 2010.

Brailey, Jeff. *The Ghosts of November.* Self-published, 1998.

Brown, Willie. *Basic Brown: My Life and Our Times.* New York: Simon & Schuster, 2008.

Burrough, Bryan. *Days of Rage: America's Radical Underground, the FBI, and the Forgotten Age of Revolutionary Violence.* New York: Penguin Press, 2015.

Cox, Bill. *Snippets.* Self-published.

Dalton, David. *James Dean: The Mutant King.* Atlanta: A Cappella Books, 2001.

Didion, Joan. *Slouching Towards Bethlehem: Essays.* New York: Farrar, Straus & Giroux, 1968. (Paperback reprint, 2008.)

————. *The White Album: Essays.* New York: Farrar, Straus & Giroux, 1979. (Paperback reprint, 2009.)

Domanick, Joe. *To Protect and Serve: The LAPD's Century of War in the City of Dreams.* New York: Pocket Books, 1994.

Eliade, Mircea (editor-in-chief). *The Encyclopedia of Religion, Vol. 4.* New York: Macmillan, 1987.

Feinsod, Ethan. *Awake in a Nightmare: Jonestown, the Only Eyewitness Account.* New York: W. W. Norton, 1981.

Ferm, Vergilius. *An Encyclopedia of Religion.* Westport, CT: Greenwood Press, 1976.

Fondakowski, Leigh. *Stories from Jonestown.* Minneapolis: University of Minnesota Press, 2012.

Guinn, Jeff. *The Life and Times of Charles Manson.* New York: Simon & Schuster, 2014.

Halberstam, David. *The Fifties.* New York: Ballantine, 1994.

————. *War in a Time of Peace: Bush, Clinton, and the Generals.* New York: Scribner, 2002.

Kahalas, Laurie Efrein. *Snake Dance: Unravelling the Mysteries of Jonestown.* Toronto: Red Robin Press, 1998.

Kohl, Laura Johnston. *Jonestown Survivor: An Insider's Look.* Bloomington: iUniverse, 2010.

Krause, Charles. *Guyana Massacre: The*

Eyewitness Account. New York: Berkley, 1978.

Lane, Mark. *The Strongest Poison.* Charlottesville, VA: The Lane Group, 1980.

Layton, Deborah. *Seductive Poison: A Jonestown Survivor's Story of Life and Death in the Peoples Temple.* New York: Anchor, 1999.

Madison, James H. *A Lynching in the Heartland: Race and Memory in America.* New York: Palgrave Macmillan, 2001.

————. *The Indiana Way.* Bloomington: Indiana University Press, 2000.

Mills, Jeanne. *Six Years with God: Life Inside Rev. Jim Jones's Peoples Temple.* New York: A&W Publishers, 1979.

Moore, Leonard J. *Citizen Klansmen: The Ku Klux Klan in Indiana, 1921–1928.* Chapel Hill: University of North Carolina Press, 1997.

Moore, Rebecca. *Understanding Jonestown and Peoples Temple.* Westport, CT: Praeger, 2009.

Moore, Rebecca, Anthony B. Pinn, and Mary R. Sawyer, eds. *Peoples Temple and Black Religion in America.* Bloomington: Indiana University Press, 2004.

Perlstein, Rick. *Before the Storm: Barry Goldwater and the Unmaking of the American Consensus.* New York: Nation Books, 2009.

Pierce, Richard B. *Polite Protest: The Political Economy of Race in Indianapolis, 1920–1970.*

Bloomington: Indiana University Press, 2005.

Reiterman, Tim. *Raven: The Untold Story of the Rev. Jim Jones and His People.* New York: Tarcher Perigee, 2008. Originally published by Dutton Adult, 1982.

Roberts, Randy. *But They Can't Beat Us: Oscar Robertson and the Crispus Attucks Tigers.* Indianapolis: Indiana Historical Society/Champaign, IL: Sports Publishing, 1999.

Scheeres, Julia. *A Thousand Lives: The Untold Story of Jonestown.* New York: Free Press, 2012.

Smith, Richard Norton. *On His Own Terms: A Life of Nelson Rockefeller.* New York: Random House, 2014.

Stephenson, Denise. *Dear People: Remembering Jonestown.* Berkeley: Heyday Books, 2005.

Stoen, Timothy Oliver. *Marked for Death: My War with Jim Jones the Devil of Jonestown.* Charleston: CreateSpace, 2015.

Talbot, David. *Season of the Witch: Enchantment, Terror, and Deliverance in the City of Love.* New York: Free Press, 2012.

Thielmann, Bonnie, with Dean Merrill. *The Broken God.* Colorado Springs: David C. Cook, 1979.

Thornbrough, Emma Lou. *Indiana Blacks in the Twentieth Century.* Edited by Lana Rue-

gamar. Bloomington: Indiana University Press, 2000.

Wagner-Wilson, Leslie. *Slavery of Faith.* Bloomington: iUniverse, 2009.

Ward, Gertrude Luckhardt. *Richmond: A Pictorial History.* St. Louis: G. Bradley Publishing, 1994.

Watts, Jill. *God, Harlem U.S.A.: The Father Divine Story.* Berkeley: University of California Press, 1992.

Articles

Bird, Caroline. "9 Places in the World to Hide." *Esquire,* January 1962.

Cox, Eileen. "A Guyanese Perspective of Jonestown, 1979." *Jonestown Report* 15 (November 2013). Last modified December 13, 2013. Jonestown Institute.

Goodlett, Carlton B. "Notes on Peoples Temple." Last modified November 21, 2013. Jonestown Institute.

Hargrave, Neva Sly. "A Story of Deprogramming." *Jonestown Report* 6 (October 2004). Last modified March 8, 2014. Jonestown Institute.

"How Much Did Peoples Temple Have in Assets?" Last modified May 24, 2014. Jonestown Institute.

Jones, Stephan. "Chuck." *Jonestown Report* 12 (October 2010). Last modified December 18, 2013. Jonestown Institute.

————. "Death's Night." *Jonestown Report* 12 (October 2010). Last modified March 29, 2016. Jonestown Institute.

————. "Like Father, Like Son," *Jonestown Report* 5 (August 2003). Last modified March 14, 2014. Jonestown Institute.

————. "My Brother's Mother." *Jonestown Report* 11 (November 2009). Last modified November 21, 2013. Jonestown Institute.

Kinsolving, Lester. "D.A. Aide Officiates for Minor Bride." *San Francisco Examiner*, September 19, 1972.

————. " 'Healing' Prophet Hailed as God at S.F. Revival." *San Francisco Examiner*, September 18, 1972.

————. "Jim Jones Defames a Black Pastor." *San Francisco Examiner*, September 1972. Not published.

————. "Probe Asked of People's [*sic*] Temple." *San Francisco Examiner*, September 20, 1972.

————. "The People's [*sic*] Temple and Maxine Harpe." *San Francisco Examiner*, September 1972. Not published.

————. "The Prophet Who Raises the Dead." *San Francisco Examiner*, September 17, 1972.

————. "The Reincarnation of Jesus Christ — in Ukiah." *San Francisco Examiner*, September 1972. Not Published.

————. "Sex, Socialism, and Child Torture

with Rev. Jim Jones." *San Francisco Examiner,* September 1972. Not published.

Kohl, Laura Johnston. "Oral History Interview: Don Beck." *Jonestown Report* 17 (November 2015). Jonestown Institute.

Lambrev, Garret [Garry]. "A Peoples Temple Survivor Remembers." *Jonestown Report* 8 (November 2006). Last modified March 6, 2014. Jonestown Institute.

———. "The Board (of Elders)." *Jonestown Report* 9 (November 2007). Last modified March 4, 2014. Jonestown Institute.

———. "Joe Phillips: A Reflection." *Jonestown Report* 15 (November 2013). Last modified March 20, 2014. Jonestown Institute.

———. "My Friend Teresa King: From the Avenue of the Fleas to Jonestown." *Jonestown Report* 12 (October 2010). Last modified December 28, 2013. Jonestown Institute.

———. "Questions That Remain." *Jonestown Report* 5 (August 2003). Last modified March 14, 2014. Jonestown Institute.

"Messiah from the Midwest." *Time,* December 4, 1978.

Moore, Rebecca. "Last Rights." Last modified August 31, 2014. Jonestown Institute.

Newell, Herbert. "The Coldest Day of My Life." *Jonestown Report* 12 (October 2010). Last modified December 18, 2013. Jonestown Institute.

Sims, Hank. "Standing in the Shadows of Jonestown." *North Coast Journal,* September 2003.

Smart, Juanell. "My Life in — And After — Peoples Temple." *Jonestown Report* 6 (October 2004). Last modified March 13, 2014. Jonestown Institute.

Treml, William B. "Mom's Help for Ragged Tramp Leads Son to Dedicate His Life to Others," *Richmond Palladium-Item,* March 15, 1953.

Wright, Lawrence. "The Orphans of Jonestown." *The New Yorker,* November 22, 1993.

ABOUT THE AUTHOR

Jeff Guinn is the author of *Manson: The Life and Times of Charles Manson*, *The Last Gunfight: The Real Story of the Shootout at the O.K. Corral and How It Changed the American West*, and *Go Down Together: The True, Untold Story of Bonnie & Clyde*, which was a finalist for an Edgar Award in 2010. He was a longtime journalist who has won national, regional and state awards for investigative reporting, feature writing and literary criticism. He has written sixteen books including *New York Times* bestsellers. One of only 32 members of the Texas Literary Hall of Fame, he lives in Fort Worth, Texas.

The employees of Thorndike Press hope you have enjoyed this Large Print book. All our Thorndike, Wheeler, and Kennebec Large Print titles are designed for easy reading, and all our books are made to last. Other Thorndike Press Large Print books are available at your library, through selected bookstores, or directly from us.

For information about titles, please call:
  (800) 223-1244

or visit our website at:
  gale.com/thorndike

To share your comments, please write:
  Publisher
  Thorndike Press
  10 Water St., Suite 310
  Waterville, ME 04901